MEMOIRS BY HARRY S. TRUMAN

MEMOIRS BY

Harry S. Truman

1945: YEAR OF DECISIONS

This edition published in 1995 by SMITHMARK Publishers,
a division of U.S. Media Holdings, Inc., 16 East 32nd Street,
New York, NY 10016.

SMITHMARK books are available for bulk purchase for sales
promotion and premium use. For details write or call the
manager of special sales, SMITHMARK Publishers Inc.,
16 East 32nd Street, New York, NY 10016; (212) 532-6600.

This edition published by arrangement with Doubleday,
a division of Bantam Doubleday Dell Publishing Group, Inc.
and W.S. Konecky Associates, Inc.

ISBN: 0-8317-1578-2

Printed in the United States of America

10 9 8 7 6 5 4 3 2 1

TO THE PEOPLE OF ALL NATIONS

ACKNOWLEDGMENTS

In the writing of my memoirs and the story of a very trying period of history, I have received invaluable aid and suggestions from many people. A vast amount of research of my personal papers and documents was necessary in my efforts to achieve a true and accurate picture.

I owe a great debt of gratitude to Mrs. Truman, on whose counsel and judgment I frequently called.

I wish to express my special thanks to many members of my administration who took time to go over with me various phases of the past in which they had a part: Dean Acheson, General of the Army George C. Marshall, Samuel I. Rosenman, John W. Snyder, Rear Admiral Sidney Souers, Rear Admiral Robert L. Dennison, W. Averell Harriman, General of the Army Omar Bradley, Charles F. Brannan, Charles Sawyer, Philip B. Perlman, Thomas E. Murray, Stanley Woodward, John Steelman, Charles Murphy, Major General Robert B. Landry; as well as Oscar Chapman, Gordon Dean, J. Howard McGrath, Clark Clifford, Edwin W. Pauley, and Judge Caskie Collet.

To Dean Acheson and Samuel I. Rosenman, who painstakingly read and criticized my manuscript, I wish to convey my special gratitude.

During the past two years David M. Noyes and William Hillman were constantly at my side, helping me to assemble and edit this work. With their collaboration this book has been made possible. To Dave and to Bill I can only say a thousand times, thank you.

To Professor Francis E. Heller of Kansas University I wish to express my sincere appreciation for the invaluable service he rendered. Among those who also helped with historical research during some periods was Professor Morton Royse.

A very heavy burden fell on my personal staff during the writing and rewriting of these memoirs, and I wish to acknowledge with thanks the devoted work of Mr. Eugene Bailey, Miss Rose Conway, and Miss Frances Myers.

I have used some passages from *Mr. President* by William Hillman (Farrar, Straus & Young) for inclusion in my memoirs as part of the historical record.

H. S. T.

PREFACE

I have often thought in reading the history of our country how much is lost to us because so few of our Presidents have told their own stories. It would have been helpful for us to know more of what was in their minds and what impelled them to do what they did.

The presidency of the United States carries with it a responsibility so personal as to be without parallel.

Very few are ever authorized to speak for the President. No one can make decisions for him. No one can know all the processes and stages of his thinking in making important decisions. Even those closest to him, even members of his immediate family, never know all the reasons why he does certain things and why he comes to certain conclusions. To be President of the United States is to be lonely, very lonely at times of great decisions.

Unfortunately some of our Presidents were prevented from telling all the facts of their administrations because they died in office. Some were physically spent on leaving the White House and could not have undertaken to write even if they had wanted to. Some were embittered by the experience and did not care about living it again in telling about it.

As for myself, I should like to record, before it is too late, as much of the story of my occupancy of the White House as I am able to tell. The events, as I saw them and as I put them down here, I hope may prove helpful in informing some people and in setting others straight on the facts.

No one who has lived through more than seven and a half years as

President of the United States in the midst of one world crisis after another can possibly remember every detail of all that happened. For the last two and a half years I have checked my memory against my personal papers, memoranda, and letters and with some of the persons who were present when certain decisions were made, seeking to recapture and record accurately the significant events of my administration.

I have tried to refrain from hindsight and afterthoughts. Any schoolboy's afterthought is worth more than the forethought of the greatest statesman. What I have written here is based upon the circumstances and the facts and my thinking at the time I made the decisions, and not what they might have been as a result of later developments.

That part of the manuscript which could not be physically included in the two volumes of the memoirs, I shall turn over to the Library in Independence, Missouri, where it will be made available to scholars and students of history.

For reasons of national security and out of consideration for some people still alive, I have omitted certain material. Some of this material cannot be made available for many years, perhaps for many generations.

In spite of the turmoil and pressure of critical events during the years I was President, the one purpose that dominated me in everything I thought and did was to prevent a third world war. One of the events that has cast a shadow over our lives and the lives of peoples everywhere has been termed, inaccurately, the "cold war."

What we have been living through is, in fact, a period of nationalistic, social, and economic tensions. These tensions were in part brought about by shattered nations trying to recover from the war and by peoples in many places awakening to their right to freedom. More than half of the world's population was subject for centuries to foreign domination and economic slavery. The repercussions of the American and French revolutions are just now being felt all around the world.

This was a natural development of events, and the United States did all it could to help and encourage nations and peoples to recovery and to independence.

Unhappily, one imperialistic nation, Soviet Russia, sought to take advantage of this world situation. It was for this reason, only, that we had to make sure of our military strength. We are not a militaristic nation, but we had to meet the world situation with which we were faced.

We knew that there could be no lasting peace so long as there were large populations in the world living under primitive conditions and suffering from starvation, disease, and denial of the advantages of modern science and industry.

There is enough in the world for everyone to have plenty to live on happily and to be at peace with his neighbors.

I believe, as I said on January 15, 1953, in my last address to the American people before leaving the White House: "We have averted World War III up to now, and we may have already succeeded in establishing conditions which can keep that war from happening as far ahead as man can see."

H. S. T.

Independence, Missouri
August 5, 1955

CHAPTER 1

During the first few weeks of Franklin Delano Roosevelt's fourth administration, I saw what the long years in the presidency had done to him. He had occupied the White House during twelve fateful years—years of awful responsibility. He had borne the burdens of the reconstruction from the great depression of the 'thirties. He shouldered the heavier burdens of his wartime leadership. It is no wonder that the years had left their mark.

The very thought that something was happening to him left me troubled and worried. This was all the more difficult for me because I could not share such feelings with anyone, not even with the members of my family. I kept saying to myself that this man had often demonstrated amazing recuperative powers. Only a few months earlier, during the closing days of the 1944 presidential campaign, he had ridden for four hours in an open car through a driving rain in New York City and had seemed none the worse for it.

Knowing something of the great responsibilities he was forced to carry, I did not want to think about the possibility of his death as President. The rumors were widespread but not publicly discussed. But there had always been baseless rumors about Franklin D. Roosevelt.

We all hoped that victory against our enemies was near. Under Roosevelt's inspiring leadership the war was approaching its climax. The things he stood for and labored for were about to be realized. The world needed his guiding hand for the coming transition to peace.

On February 20, 1945, while I was presiding over the Senate, a rumor that the President was dead swept through the corridors and across the floor. I left my place at once and headed for the office of Les Biffle, Secretary of the Senate. As I entered, I said to Biffle, "I hear the President is dead. What will we do? Let's find out what happened."

Biffle called the White House and was informed that it was Major General Edwin M. Watson—"Pa" Watson, the appointment secretary to the President—who was dead. He had died at sea aboard the U.S.S. *Quincy* while returning with President Roosevelt from the Yalta conference. And later that same day I received a wireless message from the *Quincy*. In it President Roosevelt asked me for my opinion and advice about his appearing before a joint session of Congress to make a personal report on the results of his just completed conference with Churchill and Stalin.

I met with the President a week later and was shocked by his appearance. His eyes were sunken. His magnificent smile was missing from his careworn face. He seemed a spent man. I had a hollow feeling within me, for I saw that the journey to Yalta must have been a terrible ordeal.

I tried to think how I could help him conserve his strength. With Mrs. Roosevelt and their daughter Anna, who was the President's close confidante, I had already discussed the problem of the strain of appearing before Congress. I recalled the expressions of pain I had seen on the President's face as he delivered his inauguration speech on January 20 on the south portico of the White House. Apparently he could no longer endure with his usual fortitude the physical pain of the heavy braces pressing against him.

With that in mind, and in order to spare him any unnecessary pain, I urged that he address Congress seated in the well of the House, and I explained that I had already cleared this unusual arrangement with the congressional leaders. He had asked for no such consideration, but he appeared relieved and pleased to be accorded this courtesy.

I shall never forget that day. The President's appearance before a joint meeting of the Senate and the House was a momentous occasion both for him and for the country. He was to report directly to Congress on the outcome of the deliberations at Yalta—deliberations that were bound to have a profound effect on the future peace of the world. He was anxious for bi-partisan support and wanted the full and sympathetic backing of Congress on foreign policy.

The speech was arranged for Thursday, March 1, 1945, and Mrs. Roosevelt, as well as Anna and her husband, Colonel Boettiger, were with him as he drove from the White House. Princess Martha and Crown Prince Olaf of Norway were also in the presidential party, which reached the Capitol just a little after noon.

The President was met in the same way he had always been met. Formerly, however, he had spoken from the rostrum of the House of Representatives, with the stenographers for the Congressional Record in their usual places before him, and with the presiding officers of the Senate and the House side by side behind. This time, however, the microphone-laden table that had been set up for his use stood in the well of the House chamber within little more than arm's length of the first curved row of seats.

The chamber was filled as he entered, and Speaker Rayburn and I, together with the others who had met him, followed him in and took our places on the rostrum. The justices of the Supreme Court were in the places they always occupy on such occasions. The rows of seats were solidly filled with senators and representatives. I vaguely caught a glimpse of the many members of the diplomatic corps. Here and there a uniform was visible, and I remember looking up into the gallery for Mrs. Roosevelt and daughter, and for Mrs. Truman and our daughter, while the audience, which had risen in honor of the President as he entered, resumed their seats. The President looked about him and at the papers that lay before him.

Even before Speaker Rayburn let the gavel fall and introduced "the President of the United States," it was plain that this appearance of the nation's leader before Congress was to have about it an unusual atmosphere.

"Mr. Vice-President, Mr. Speaker, and members of the Congress," he began. "I hope that you will pardon me for the unusual posture of sitting down during the presentation of what I want to say, but I know that you will realize it makes it a lot easier for me in not having to carry about ten pounds of steel around on the bottom of my legs, and also because of the fact that I have just completed a 14,000-mile trip."

Everyone present was intent on his words, but unhappily the famous Roosevelt manner and delivery were not there. And he knew it. He frequently departed from his prepared script. At one point he brought in a mention of "a great many prima donnas in the world who want to be heard," and he interrupted his text at another point to warn his listeners that "we haven't won the war." But these attempts to get away from his excellent script with lighthearted references and more thoughtful asides were not of much help.

Congress was stirred. Many members of both Houses were awed by his dramatic display of sheer will power and courage, and there were very few who were critical of what he said.

I saw the President immediately after his speech had been concluded. Plainly, he was a very weary man.

"As soon as I can," he said to me, "I will go to Warm Springs for a rest. I can be in trim again if I can stay there for two or three weeks."

He left Washington for the South on March 30, 1945.

I never saw or spoke with him again.

Shortly before five o'clock in the afternoon of Thursday, April 12, 1945, after the Senate adjourned, I went to the office of House Speaker Sam Rayburn. I went there to get an agreement between the Speaker and the Vice-President on certain legislation and to discuss the domestic and world situation generally. As I entered, the Speaker told me that Steve Early, the President's press secretary, had just telephoned, requesting me to call the White House.

I returned the call and was immediately connected with Early.

"Please come right over," he told me in a strained voice, "and come in through the main Pennsylvania Avenue entrance."

I turned to Rayburn, explaining that I had been summoned to the White House and would be back shortly. I did not know why I had been called, but I asked that no mention be made of the matter. The President, I thought, must have returned to Washington for the funeral of his friend, Bishop Atwood, the former Episcopal Bishop of Arizona, and I imagined that he wanted me to go over some matters with him before his return to Warm Springs.

On previous occasions when the President had called me to the White House for private talks he had asked me to keep the visits confidential. At such times I had used the east entrance to the White House, and in this way the meetings were kept off the official caller list. Now, however, I told Tom Harty, my government chauffeur, to drive me to the main entrance.

We rode alone, without the usual guards. The Secret Service had assigned three men to work in shifts when I became Vice-President. However, this guard was reinforced, as a routine practice, during the time President Roosevelt was away on his trip to Yalta and again when he went to Warm Springs. A guard had been placed on duty at my Connecticut Avenue apartment, where I had lived as Senator and continued to live as Vice-President, and another accompanied me wherever I went. These men were capable, efficient, self-effacing, and usually the guard who was on duty met me at my office after the Senate had adjourned. But on this one occasion I slipped away from all of them. Instead of returning from Speaker Rayburn's office to my own before going to the car that was waiting for me, I ran through the basement of the Capitol Building and lost them. This was the only time in eight years that I enjoyed the luxury of privacy by escaping from the ever-present vigil of official protection.

I reached the White House about 5:25 P.M. and was immediately taken in the elevator to the second floor and ushered into Mrs. Roosevelt's study. Mrs. Roosevelt herself, together with Colonel John and Mrs. Anna Roosevelt Boettiger and Mr. Early, were in the room as I entered, and I knew at once that something unusual had taken place. Mrs. Roosevelt seemed calm in her characteristic, graceful dignity. She stepped forward and placed her arm gently about my shoulder.

"Harry," she said quietly, "the President is dead."

For a moment I could not bring myself to speak.

The last news we had had from Warm Springs was that Mr. Roosevelt was recuperating nicely. In fact, he was apparently doing so well that no member of his immediate family, and not even his personal physician, was with him. All this flashed through my mind before I found my voice.

"Is there anything I can do for you?" I asked at last.

I shall never forget her deeply understanding reply.

"Is there anything *we* can do for *you?*" she asked. "For you are the one in trouble now."

The greatness and the goodness of this remarkable lady showed even in that moment of sorrow. I was fighting off tears. The overwhelming fact that faced me was hard to grasp. I had been afraid for many weeks that something might happen to this great leader, but now that the worst had happened I was unprepared for it. I did not allow myself to think about it after I became Vice-President. But I had done a lot of thinking about it at the Chicago convention. I recall wondering whether President Roosevelt himself had had any inkling of his own condition. The only indication I had ever had that he knew he was none too well was when he talked to me just before I set out on my campaign trip for the vice-presidency in the fall of 1944. He asked me how I was going to travel, and I told him I intended to cover the country by airplane.

"Don't do that, please," he told me. "Go by train. It is necessary that you take care of yourself."

Sometime later, too, Mrs. Roosevelt had seemed uneasy about the President's loss of appetite. She remarked to me at a dinner shortly after the elections, "I can't get him to eat. He just won't eat."

She was very devoted to the President, as he was to her. Mrs. Roosevelt was also close to the President in his work. In a way, she was his eyes and ears. Her famous trips were taken at his direction and with his approval, and she went on these long, arduous journeys mainly in order to be able to inform and advise him.

But now, as I stood there with her, I was thinking of a letter I had written to my mother and my sister a few hours earlier. They had not received it yet—would not receive it until this terrible news of the President's death had reached them. But once my letter had arrived, they would know how little I had anticipated this overwhelming hour.

Dear Mamma & Mary [I had written]: I am trying to write you a letter today from the desk of the President of the Senate while a windy Senator . . . is making a speech on a subject with which he is in no way familiar. The Jr. Sen. from Arizona made a speech on the subject, and he knew what he was talking about. . . .

We are considering the Mexican Treaty on water in the Colorado River and the Rio Grande. It is of vital importance to Southwestern U.S. and northern Mexico. Hope we get it over some day soon.

The Senators from California and one from Utah and a very disagreeable one from Nevada (McCarran) are fighting the ratification. I have to sit up here and make parliamentary rulings—some of which are common sense and some of which are not.

Hope you are having a nice spell of weather. We've had a week of beautiful weather but it is raining and misting today. I don't think it's going to last long. Hope not for I must fly to Providence, R.I., Sunday morning.

Turn on your radio tomorrow night at 9:30 your time, and you'll hear Harry make a Jefferson Day address to the nation. I think I'll be on all the networks, so it ought not to be hard to get me. It will be followed by the President, whom I'll introduce.

Hope you are both well and stay that way.

Love to you both.

Write when you can.

Harry

That is what I had written only a few hours earlier, but now the lightning had struck, and events beyond anyone's control had taken command. America had lost a great leader, and I was faced with a terrible responsibility.

It seems to me that for a few minutes we stood silent, and then there was a knock on the study door. Secretary of State Stettinius entered. He was in tears, his handsome face sad and drawn. He had been among the first to be notified, for as Secretary of State, who is the keeper of the Great Seal of the United States and all official state papers, it was his official duty to ascertain and to proclaim the passing of the President.

I asked Steve Early, Secretary Stettinius, and Les Biffle, who now had also joined us, to call all the members of the Cabinet to a meeting as quickly as possible. Then I turned to Mrs. Roosevelt and asked if there was anything she needed to have done. She replied that she would like to go to Warm Springs at once, and asked whether it would be proper for her to make use of a government plane. I assured her that the use of such a plane was right and proper, and I made certain that one would be placed at her disposal, knowing that a grateful nation would insist on it.

But now a whole series of arrangements had to be made. I went to the President's office at the west end of the White House. I asked Les Biffle to arrange to have a car sent for Mrs. Truman and Margaret, and I called them on the phone myself, telling them what had happened—telling them, too, to come to the White House. I also called Chief Justice Harlan Fiske Stone, and having given him the news, I asked him to come as soon as possible so that he might swear me in. He said that he would come at once. And that is what he did, for he arrived within hardly more than fifteen or twenty minutes.

Others were arriving by now. Speaker Rayburn, House Majority Leader John W. McCormack, and House Minority Leader Joseph W. Martin were among them. I tried personally to reach Senator Alben W. Barkley, Senate majority leader, but I could not locate him. I learned later that word of the President's death had reached him promptly and that he had gone at once to see Mrs. Roosevelt. In fact, he was with her in the White House while the group about me was gathering in the Cabinet Room.

There was no time for formalities and protocol. Among the people there were a score or so of officials and members of Congress. Only three women were present—Mrs. Truman and Margaret and Secretary Frances Perkins.

The Cabinet Room in the White House is not extensive. It is dominated by the huge and odd-shaped table, presented to the President by Jesse Jones, at which the President and the members of the Cabinet sit, and by the leather-upholstered armchairs that are arranged around it.

Steve Early, Jonathan Daniels, and others of the President's secretarial staff were searching for a Bible for me to hold when Chief Justice Stone administered the oath of office.

We were in the final days of the greatest war in history—a war so vast that few corners of the world had been able to escape being engulfed by it. There were none who did not feel its effects. In that war the United States had created military forces so enormous as to defy description, yet now, when the nation's greatest leader in that war lay dead, and a simple ceremony was about to acknowledge the presence of his successor in the nation's greatest office, only two uniforms were present. These were worn by Fleet Admiral Leahy and General Fleming, who, as Public Works Administrator, had been given duties that were much more civilian in character than military.

So far as I know, this passed unnoticed at the time, and the very fact that no thought was given to it demonstrates convincingly how firmly the concept of the supremacy of the civil authority is accepted in our land.

By now a Bible had been found. It was placed near where I stood at the end of the great table. Mrs. Truman and Margaret had not joined me for over an hour after I had called them, having gone first to see Mrs.

Roosevelt. They were standing side by side now, at my left, while Chief Justice Stone had taken his place before me at the end of the table. Clustered about me and behind were nine members of the Cabinet, while Speaker Rayburn and a few other members of Congress took positions behind Chief Justice Stone. There were others present, but not many.

I picked up the Bible and held it in my left hand. Chief Justice Stone raised his right hand and gave the oath as it is written in the Constitution.

With my right hand raised, I repeated it after him:

"I, Harry S. Truman, do solemnly swear that I will faithfully execute the office of President of the United States, and will to the best of my ability, preserve, protect and defend the Constitution of the United States."

I dropped my hand.

The clock beneath Woodrow Wilson's portrait marked the time at 7:09.

Less than two hours before, I had come to see the President of the United States, and now, having repeated that simply worded oath, I myself was President.

S

CHAPTER 2

The ceremony at which I had taken the oath of office had lasted hardly more than a minute, but a delay followed while the inevitable official photographs were taken. Then, after most of those present had gripped my hand—often without a word, so great were their pent-up emotions—and after Mrs. Truman and Margaret had left, everyone else withdrew except the members of the Cabinet.

We took our places around the table, though Postmaster General Walker's chair was vacant, for he was ill, and as we did so, Secretary Early entered. The press, he explained, wanted to know if the San Francisco conference on the United Nations would meet, as had been planned, on April 25.

I did not hesitate a second. I told Early that the conference would be held as President Roosevelt had directed. There was no question in my mind that the conference had to take place. It was of supreme importance that we build an organization to help keep the future peace of the world. It was the first decision I made as President.

When Early had left, I spoke to the Cabinet. I told them briefly, as I had already told some of them individually, that I would be pleased if all of them would remain in their posts. It was my intention, I said, to continue both the foreign and the domestic policies of the Roosevelt administration. I made it clear, however, that I would be President in my own right and that I would assume full responsibility for such decisions as had to be made. I told them that I hoped they would not hesitate to give me their advice—that I would be glad to listen to them. I left them in no doubt that they could differ with me if they felt it necessary, but that all final policy decisions would be mine. I added that once such decisions had been made I expected them to support me. When there is a change in administration, there are bound to be some changes in the Cabinet, but I knew how necessary it was for me to keep an open mind on all the members of the Cabinet until we had had an opportunity to work together. Their experience with President Roosevelt and their knowledge were necessary to me in this crisis.

I intended, also, to maintain a similar attitude toward the heads of all the federal agencies. But I had some mental reservations about the heads of certain temporary war agencies.

That first meeting of the Cabinet was short, and when it adjourned, the members rose and silently made their way from the room—except for Secretary Stimson.

He asked to speak to me about a most urgent matter. Stimson told me that he wanted me to know about an immense project that was under way—a project looking to the development of a new explosive of almost unbelievable destructive power. That was all he felt free to say at the time, and his statement left me puzzled. It was the first bit of information that had come to me about the atomic bomb, but he gave me no details. It was not until the next day that I was told enough to give me some understanding of the almost incredible developments that were under way and the awful power that might soon be placed in our hands.

That so vast an enterprise had been successfully kept secret even from the members of Congress was a miracle. I had known, and probably others had, that something that was unusually important was brewing in our war plants. Many months before, as part of the work of the Committee to Investigate the National Defense Program, of which I was chairman, I had had investigators going into war plants all over the country. I had even sent investigators into Tennessee and the state of Washington with instructions to find out what certain enormous constructions were and what their purpose was.

At that time, when these investigators were sent out, Secretary Stimson had phoned me to say that he wanted to have a private talk with me. I told him that I would come to his office at once, but he said he would rather come to see me.

As soon as he arrived, I learned that the subject he had in mind was connected with the immense installations I had sent the committee representatives to investigate in Tennessee and the state of Washington.

"Senator," the Secretary told me as he sat beside my desk, "I can't tell you what it is, but it is the greatest project in the history of the world. It is most top secret. Many of the people who are actually engaged in the work have no idea what it is, and we who do would appreciate your not going into those plants."

I had long known Henry L. Stimson to be a great American patriot and statesman.

"I'll take you at your word," I told him. "I'll order the investigations into those plants called off."

I did so at once, and I was not to learn anything whatever as to what that secret was until the Secretary spoke to me after that first Cabinet meeting. The next day Jimmy Byrnes, who until shortly before had been Director of War Mobilization for President Roosevelt, came to see me, and even he told me few details, though with great solemnity he said that we were perfecting an explosive great enough to destroy the whole world. It was later, when Vannevar Bush, head of the Office of Scientific Research and Development, came to the White House, that I was given a scientist's version of the atomic bomb.

Admiral Leahy was with me when Dr. Bush told me this astonishing fact.

"That is the biggest fool thing we have ever done," he observed in his sturdy, salty manner. "The bomb will never go off, and I speak as an expert in explosives."

But on my first evening as President my principal concern was about the San Francisco conference. After the Cabinet meeting Stettinius, Early, and Daniels suggested that something needed to be done further to reassure our allies and the world that the San Francisco conference would be held as planned. We went to the Oval Room of the executive office to discuss the matter.

I felt strongly about the idea on which the United Nations organization was based and had been supporting it in every way I could on the Hill. I wanted to scotch any rumors or fears in the United States and abroad that there would be any changes in the plans that had been made. It was with that in mind that I decided to issue a statement at once, reassuring our allies of my support of the coming conference.

Meanwhile the White House correspondents were asking for a press conference, since they were not present when I took the oath of office.

"For the time being," I told Steve Early to inform them, "I prefer not to hold a press conference. It will be my effort to carry on as I believe the President would have done, and to that end I have asked the Cabinet to stay on with me."

During those first few hours, painful as they were because of our tragic loss, my mind kept turning to the task I had inherited and to the grave responsibilities that confronted our nation at that critical moment in history. From my reading of American history I knew there was no cut-and-dried answer to the question of what obligations a President by inheritance had in regard to the program of his predecessor—especially a program on which a great President had recently been re-elected for the fourth time.

Fortunately that program was no problem for me. I had not only been elected on the platform in which it had been outlined and which I had helped to write at the Chicago convention, but also I believed in it firmly and without reservation. Its principal objectives were to win the war through co-ordinated military and economic action with our allies; to win an organized peace, along lines already laid down during the war years, in close co-operation with our allies and other peace-loving nations; and at home to operate the government in the interest of all the people.

Neither as a member of the Senate nor as Vice-President had I undergone any conscious change in my basic philosophy of government or in my beliefs in the relationship of government to the people. I classify myself as a Jefferson Democrat living in modern times. I apply his principles to the situation as it is today. We often hear about Jefferson's attitude toward the power of the federal government and the power of the state governments. We hear much talk of what he would have done. It seems to me that he would probably have met conditions as he found them and that he would not have departed from his fundamental beliefs. Had he lived in our day, I believe he would have adjusted himself to this industrial age without abandoning his principles.

I had made my campaign for the Senate on the basis of a policy I have pursued all my life—that the country should be operated for the benefit of all the people. In Jackson County, Missouri, when I came to the point of expending great amounts of public money for contracts, it was openly done with all the figures shown, and the lowest bidder got the contract. I upset the specially favored contractor policy of my predecessors and awarded the contracts in the interest of the people and taxpayers. The simple truth as I see it, and as I saw it then, was that the country should be run for the benefit of all the people and not for just the special crew who has the inside track. No one will question, I believe, that that was the basic thought and practice of Jefferson, Jackson, and Lincoln.

I always fully supported the Roosevelt program—both international and domestic—but I knew that certain major administrative weaknesses existed. President Roosevelt often said he was no administrator. He was a man of vision and ideas, and he preferred to delegate administration to others—sometimes to others who were not ideally suited to carry out what he had in mind. I was well aware of this, and even on that first day

I knew that I would eventually have to make changes, both in the Cabinet and in administrative policy.

Many problems confronted me, and I was tired. Within half an hour of the time the Cabinet meeting adjourned, I left for our apartment at 4701 Connecticut Avenue.

When I arrived, I found Mrs. Truman, Margaret, and Mrs. Truman's mother, Mrs. Wallace, at the apartment of General Jeff Davis, our next-door neighbor. The Davises had had a ham and turkey dinner that evening, and they gave us something to eat. I do not know when Mrs. Truman and Margaret had eaten last, but I had had nothing since noon. Shortly, we returned to our apartment, where I went to bed and to sleep.

On April 13 I began my first full day in office. I was up at six-thirty, and at nine o'clock, after a walk and breakfast, I left for the White House with Hugh Fulton, who had served as my counsel on the Truman Committee and who had been waiting with the Secret Service men until I was ready to leave.

As I entered the White House car, I noticed Tony Vaccaro, Capitol Hill correspondent for the Associated Press, as he stood on the curb. I told him to hop in, and the three of us drove to the White House together. In our conversation I remember saying that few men in history equaled the one into whose shoes I was stepping and that I silently prayed to God that I could measure up to the task.

When we reached the White House, I went at once to the oval executive office. President Roosevelt's belongings were numerous in the room. Ship models and ship prints were especially obvious, and the desk was laden with mementos. Everywhere were signs of the man who had labored there so long. I had no wish to change the room as yet, but I was forced to use the desk, and so I asked an aide to put away the former President's belongings. Except for the objects on the desk, I carefully avoided disturbing the late President's possessions. I even attempted, as much as possible, to keep from interfering with his personal staff, who were already overwhelmed with duties in connection with the plans for the coming funeral.

As yet, of course, I had no adequate staff of my own. Matthew J. Connelly, my vice-presidential secretary, was already with me, but he was as new to the executive offices as I. He needed help, and I found it necessary at once to call in William D. Simmons, who had been the executive office receptionist for several years. His familiarity with the surroundings simplified many problems that arose, and he answered many of my phone calls, received many of my callers, and otherwise took on the duties of a secretary during those early, unplanned hours.

My first official business was with Secretary of State Edward R. Stettinius, Jr., who reported to me on current diplomatic matters and discussed some of the plans for the coming United Nations Conference at San Francisco.

Stettinius informed me that at President Roosevelt's request the State Department prepared for the President each day a two-page summary of the important diplomatic developments, and he handed me the current report.[1] He asked whether I wished to have this daily summary continued, and he informed me that an up-to-date reference book on the major points of the foreign policies of the United States was being prepared for me.

I told Stettinius that I would welcome both the daily summary and the reference book, but I requested him to let me have that same day an outline of the background and the present status of the principal problems confronting this government in its relations with other countries. These written reports, along with material from other departments and from the Joint Chiefs of Staff, came to me regularly from then on and were immensely helpful in filling gaps in my information. In fact, they were indispensable as aids in dealing with many issues, and from the first I studied them with the greatest care. Night after night I went over them in detail and never went to bed until I had thoroughly digested the information they contained.

The report I requested from Stettinius reached me that afternoon. I found no time to read it until that evening at home, when I could do so without interruption. This was the report:

FROM THE STATE DEPARTMENT:

April 13, 1945

SPECIAL INFORMATION FOR THE PRESIDENT

UNITED KINGDOM. Mr. Churchill's policy is based fundamentally upon cooperation with the United States. It is based secondarily on maintaining the unity of the three great powers but the British Government has been showing increasing apprehension of Russia and her intentions. Churchill fully shares this Government's interpretation of the Yalta Agreements on Eastern Europe and liberated areas. He is inclined however to press this position with the Russians with what we consider unnecessary rigidity as to detail. The British long for security but are deeply conscious of their decline from a leading position to that of the junior partner of the Big Three and are anxious to buttress their position vis-a-vis United States and Russia both through exerting leadership over the countries of Western Europe and through knitting the Commonwealth more closely together.

FRANCE. The best interests of the United States require that every effort

---

[1] This supplemented the verbal report of the Secretary to the President.

be made by this Government to assist France, morally as well as physically, to regain her strength and her influence.

It is recognized that the French Provisional Government and the French people are at present unduly preoccupied, as a result of the military defeat of 1940 and the subsequent occupation of their country by the enemy, with questions of national prestige. They have consequently from time to time put forward requests which are out of all proportion to their present strength and have in certain cases, notably in connection with Indochina, showed unreasonable suspicions of American aims and motives. It is believed that it is in the interest of the United States to take full account of this psychological factor in the French mind and to treat France in all respects on the basis of her potential power and influence rather than on the basis of her present strength. Positive American contributions toward the rebuilding of France include: present and future rearming of the French Army; support of French participation in the European Advisory Commission, the control and occupation of Germany, the Reparations Commission and other organizations; and the conclusion of a Lend-Lease Agreement. De Gaulle has recently stated his appreciation of the necessity for the closest possible cooperation between France and the United States.

SOVIET UNION. Since the Yalta Conference the Soviet Government has taken a firm and uncompromising position on nearly every major question that has arisen in our relations. The more important of these are the Polish question, the application of the Crimea agreement on liberated areas, the agreement on the exchange of liberated prisoners of war and civilians, and the San Francisco Conference. In the liberated areas under Soviet control, the Soviet Government is proceeding largely on a unilateral basis and does not agree that the developments which have taken place justify application of the Crimea agreement. Permission for our contact teams to go into Poland to assist in the evacuation of liberated prisoners of war has been refused although in general our prisoners have been reasonably well treated by Soviet standards. The Soviet Government appears to desire to proceed with the San Francisco Conference but was unwilling to send their Foreign Minister. They have asked for a large postwar credit and pending a decision on this matter have so far been unwilling to conclude an agreement providing for the orderly liquidation of lend-lease aid. In the politico-military field, similar difficulties have been encountered in collaboration with the Soviet authorities.

POLAND. The present situation relating to Poland is highly unsatisfactory with the Soviet authorities consistently sabotaging Ambassador Harriman's efforts in the Moscow Commission to hasten the implementation of the decisions at the Crimea Conference. Direct appeals to Marshal Stalin have not yet produced any worthwhile results. The Soviet Government likewise seeks to complicate the problem by initiating and supporting claims of the Warsaw Provisional Polish Government to represent and speak for Poland in international matters such as the San Francisco Conference, reparations and territorial questions. Because of its effect on our relations with the Soviet Union and other United Nations and upon public opinion in this country, the question of the future status of Poland and its government remains one of our most complex and urgent problems both in the international and the domestic field.

THE BALKAN AREA. The chief problem facing this Government in Rumania, Bulgaria and Hungary concerns the operation of the Allied Control

Commissions which were set up for the execution of the respective armistices. The essence is in the relations with the Soviet Government which, as the power in military control and as the predominant element in the ACC's, uses its position for unilateral political interference in the respective countries. This conflicts with the definite responsibilities of this Government under the Yalta Declaration on Liberated Europe. We have invoked this declaration for Rumania (a minority Government imposed by intimidation) and Bulgaria (in anticipation of unfair elections). The Soviet Government rejected the first, but we are renewing the request, and has not yet replied to the second.

There are no immediate problems in Yugoslavia though here too we may be obliged to invoke the Yalta Declaration unless the government shows more moderation toward democratic elements in the country which are not yet represented in the administration.

GERMANY. The policy of the United States toward Germany was outlined in a memorandum approved by President Roosevelt on March 23, 1945. The principal features of that policy are: destruction of National Socialist organizations and influence, punishment of war criminals, disbandment of the German military establishment, military government administered with a view to political decentralization, reparation from existing wealth and future production, prevention of the manufacture of arms and destruction of all specialized facilities for their production, and controls over the German economy to secure these objectives.

Agreements have been reached with the United Kingdom and the Soviet Union on the text of the instrument of unconditional surrender on control machinery for Germany, and on zones of occupation. France has approved the first two agreements. The War Department is now studying the zone originally allocated to the United States with a view to transferring a portion of it to France in conformity with the Crimea undertaking.

No tripartite or quadripartite agreement on the treatment of Germany during the period of military government has been reached. This Government, however, has submitted the memorandum of March 23 for negotiations in the European Advisory Commission meeting in London. This Government has prepared a program of reparation for presentation to the forthcoming conference in Moscow on that subject.

AUSTRIA. The four principal Allies have declared their intention to liberate Austria from German domination and reestablish it as a free and independent country. The European Advisory Commission is this week actively discussing plans for the zoning of Austria for occupation by forces of these countries, and for an inter-Allied military government of Austria pending the reestablishment of a democratic Austrian state.

ITALY. Although a cobelligerent since October 1943, Italy is still subject to an armistice regime and considerable control by the Allied Commission. Chiefly through our efforts, Italy's status has improved, but less than we desire in view of the British policy of keeping Italy dependent. We have been unable to end the anomaly of Italy's dual status as active cobelligerent and as a defeated enemy. Great pressure is being brought to bear by groups in this country to make Italy one of the United Nations—a step essentially in accordance with our policy but not with that of certain other allied governments.

Our gravest problem at present, aside from the country's economic distress, is to forestall Yugoslav occupation of an important part of northeastern Italy, prejudicing by unilateral action a final equitable settlement of this territorial dispute and precipitating serious trouble within Italy. Difficulties may be encountered in maintaining Allied (Anglo-American) military government in this area.

SUPPLIES FOR LIBERATED AREAS. A problem of urgent importance to the U.S. is that of supplies for areas liberated from enemy occupation. The chaos and collapse which may result in these countries from starvation, unemployment and inflation can be averted principally by making available essential civilian supplies. Political stability and the maintenance of democratic governments which can withstand the pressures of extremist groups depend on the restoration of a minimum of economic stability. To do our part we must carefully analyze the needs and reserves of all claimants, military and civilian, domestic and foreign, and insist that they be reduced to absolute essentials. This will involve a reexamination both of U.S. military requirements and supply procedures and of U.S. civilian consumption. The British Cabinet Members are here to discuss critical food and other supply problems with the U.S. and Canada and have authority to reach decisions. It is essential that we organize ourselves at once to meet this problem. The Department is prepared to play its full role in this matter.

During the day friends and acquaintances arrived from time to time, and, as I could, I saw them. The day was not organized, of course. Official tasks were numerous, but as yet no schedule had been arranged, and there were many interruptions.

Only a little while after Secretary Stettinius left, I met with the military leaders for the first time. It was eleven o'clock when Secretary of War Stimson and Secretary of the Navy Forrestal came in with General George C. Marshall, Army Chief of Staff, Admiral Ernest J. King, Chief of Naval Operations, Lieutenant General Barney M. Giles of the Air Force, and Admiral William D. Leahy, Chief of Staff to the President. I knew and respected all these men, and it was comforting to know that I would be advised by leaders of such ability and distinction.

In their report to me they were brief and to the point. Germany, they told me, would not be finally overcome for another six months at least. Japan would not be conquered for another year and a half. Their summary covered our far-flung military operations, but there was little detailed examination of our various positions. Everywhere, it appeared, our forces and those of our allies were doing well.

It did not take them long to give me the latest war developments and prospects, and when they had finished, I told them that I considered it urgent to send some word to our armed forces as to what they could expect from me. I added, however, that before doing so I thought I should first address Congress. As the new Chief Executive, I wanted the support of the legislative arm of the government, as I wished to assure our people, our armed forces, and our allies that we would continue our efforts unabated.

The military leaders agreed, and as they were leaving I asked Admiral Leahy to remain with me.

Leahy had occupied a unique position in the White House under President Roosevelt. He was a man of wide experience and was well known for his directness of expression and independence of judgment. Direct in manner and blunt in expression, he typified the Navy at its best, and Roosevelt had appointed him to act in a highly confidential role as chief of staff to the Commander in Chief. Prior to World War II there had been no such position in our government, but in Leahy's hands it soon proved to be immensely useful.

When the others had left, I told him that I would like to have him continue in a similar capacity under me.

"Are you sure you want me, Mr. President?" he asked. "I always say what's on my mind."

"I want the truth," I told him, "and I want the facts at all times. I want you to stay with me and always to tell me what's on your mind. You may not always agree with my decisions, but I know you will carry them out faithfully."

With Admiral Leahy in the White House, I felt that, whether they were good or bad, all the information and communications bearing on the war would reach me promptly. Furthermore, I felt convinced that he would see that I got the facts without suppression or censorship from any source.

The admiral looked at me with a warm twinkle in his eyes.

"You have my pledge," he told me. "You can count on me."

When Leahy left, I reached for the telephone and called Les Biffle again. During my years as senator I had worked closely with Biffle. He was always unusually well informed on legislative matters and was a parliamentarian who intimately understood the shadings and opinions of the dominant figures on the Hill. When I had called him earlier, I had asked him to arrange a luncheon in his office that noon with the leaders of Congress. I was anxious to meet the policy-making heads of both parties so that I might tell them of my earnest desire and need for the fullest co-operation between the legislative and the executive branches of the government.

I drove to the Capitol, surrounded and followed, as I was to be from that time on, by my ever-present Secret Service guards, and shortly after noon we sat down to lunch in Biffle's office—thirteen senators, four members of the House of Representatives, Les Biffle, and the very new President of the United States.

I was glad to see these congressional leaders—Senators Barkley, Vandenberg, Connally, George, O'Mahoney, Hill, Magnuson, Pepper, White, Austin, La Follette, Hatch, and Wheeler, together with Speaker Rayburn,

House Majority Leader McCormack, House Minority Leader Martin, and House Democratic Whip Ramspeck. I was deeply touched by the cordial reception they gave me.

I had come, I told them, in order to ask that a joint session of the Senate and the House be arranged so that I might address them in person. It would not be fitting, of course, to call such a meeting until the funeral of Franklin Roosevelt had been held, but I suggested that they make the necessary arrangements as soon as possible thereafter—Monday, April 16, three days hence.

Some of the group were opposed, and others were doubtful. Most, however, were in agreement. I asked each one for his opinion and listened carefully to what they had to say. I then outlined my reasons for considering it imperative to let the nation know through Congress that I proposed to continue the policies of the late President. I felt that it was important, too, to ask for continued bi-partisan support of the conduct of the war.

The points I made appeared convincing, for those who had been doubtful now expressed their agreement.

"Harry," remarked one senator with whom I had long worked closely, "you were planning to come whether we liked it or not."

"You know I would have," I replied, "but I would rather do it with your full and understanding support and welcome."

As I was leaving the Senate office, a long line of white-shirted page boys gathered outside to greet me. Reporters crowded in and joined the line as well, and I shook hands with every one of them.

"Boys," I said, "if you ever pray, pray for me now. I don't know whether you fellows ever had a load of hay fall on you, but when they told me yesterday what had happened, I felt like the moon, the stars, and all the planets had fallen on me. I've got the most terribly responsible job a man ever had."

"Good luck, Mr. President," said one of the reporters.

"I wish you didn't have to call me that," I told him.

I turned away from that long line of serious faces and entered the Senate cloakroom. I looked into the empty Senate Chamber and entered the silent vice-presidential office. These were the surroundings in which I had spent ten active, happy years. In a way, this had been my political home, and here I had experienced the most exciting adventure I had ever expected to have. Less than twenty-four hours before, I had been here presiding over the Senate. But now I was President of the United States and had to return to the White House, there to take over the job in which my great predecessor had only yesterday been stricken.

It was later that day when I signed the first official document to which

I added my name as President. The proclamation as I wrote it read, in part, as follows:

TO THE PEOPLE OF THE UNITED STATES:

It has pleased God in His infinite wisdom to take from us the immortal spirit of Franklin Delano Roosevelt, the 32nd President of the United States.

The leader of his people in a great war, he lived to see the assurance of the victory but not to share it. He lived to see the first foundations of the free and peaceful world to which his life was dedicated, but not to enter on that world himself.

His fellow countrymen will sorely miss his fortitude and faith and courage in the time to come. The peoples of the earth who love the ways of freedom and of hope will mourn for him.

But though his voice is silent, his courage is not spent, his faith is not extinguished. The courage of great men outlives them to become the courage of their people and the peoples of the world. It lives beyond them and upholds their purposes and brings their hopes to pass.

The proclamation, I believe, well expressed the feeling of the country, as it surely expressed what was in my mind and heart.

Messages were coming in throughout the day, of course, and one from Prime Minister Churchill was handed to me.

"Pray accept from me," it read, "the expression of my personal sympathy in the loss which you and the American nation have sustained in the death of our illustrious friend. I hope that I may be privileged to renew with you the intimate comradeship in the great cause we all served that I enjoyed through these terrible years with him. I offer you my respectful good wishes as you step into the breach in the victorious lines of the United Nations."

In cabling the Prime Minister in reply, I assured him that there would be no change in our close relations. "I am grateful for your message of sympathy to me and to this nation," I told him, and I concluded my message by saying, "You can count on me to continue the loyal and close collaboration which to the benefit of the entire world existed between you and our great President."

Other messages of sympathy and support arrived in great numbers. They came from sovereign heads of nations. They came from men and women in all walks of life. They came from many parts of the world. One was a special message from His Holiness Pope Pius XII. Ambassador Harriman cabled from Moscow, saying that Foreign Secretary Molotov had called on him at three o'clock in the morning to express his sympathy on Roosevelt's death and to extend his respects and good wishes. Later in the day, too, a message came from Stalin.

"In the name of the Soviet Government and in my personal behalf," it read, "I express deep condolences to the Government of the United States of America on the untimely death of President Roosevelt. The American people and the United Nations have lost in the person of Franklin Roosevelt a great world statesman and the herald of world organization and security after the war. The Government of the Soviet Union expresses its deep sympathy to the American people in this heavy loss and its confidence that the policy of collaboration between the great powers engaged right now in the war against the common foe will continue to grow strong in the future."

My reply to Stalin was as follows:

"My countrymen join with me in sincerely thanking you for your message of sympathy, which is a source of great comfort in our loss. It is my conviction that President Roosevelt's sacrifice for the cause of freedom will serve to strengthen the determination of all peoples that the goal for which he so faithfully strove shall not have been in vain."

From the leaders and citizens at home there was an unprecedented expression of deep mourning, and there were many tenders of support. As one that suggested how united America was, the message I received from Senator Arthur Vandenberg stands out in my mind. Arthur Vandenberg was a great American and a highly respected Republican leader. I especially appreciated the message he sent.

"Good luck," it read, "and God bless you. Let me help you whenever I can. America marches on."

As was to be expected, the press had a banner day. The country's newspapers largely forgot their customary partisanship. There was a good deal of speculation, and there were some doubts as to the course I would follow, especially in regard to President Roosevelt's program. Some papers carried vague reports that the troops at the fronts feared the effect that the President's death would have on the consummation of peace, and some foreign dispatches suggested that the same question was being asked by peoples and their leaders all over the world.

Some congressmen were in doubt as to whether I would continue Roosevelt's foreign policy. A few senators wanted to know whether I intended to give strong support to the proposed international organization, and at the same time some of the old isolationists even imagined that I would go further than the late President had. This latter point of view, I suppose, was based on the fact that I had taken the lead, along with Senators Ball, Burton, Hatch, and Hill, in trying to get a resolution passed to encourage the administration in its efforts to set up a new international organization.

My real concern at the moment, however, was divided between the war situation on the one hand and the problems of the coming peace on the other. We were close to victory, but the situation that would follow was not so clear. Already I was coming to be more fully informed on the most important and pressing problems in this complicated field, for I had been reading many documents and diplomatic messages that were being brought to me. I could see that there were more difficulties ahead. Already we were at odds with the Soviet government over the question of setting up a truly representative Polish government, and there were troubles in other areas. Many of these seemed to indicate an ominous trend. The next few months, I knew, could well be decisive in our effort to achieve an orderly world, reasonably secure in peace.

James F. Byrnes was at his home in Spartanburg, South Carolina, when he heard the radio announcement of Roosevelt's death. Later that evening Secretary Forrestal had called him on the phone to say that a plane was being sent for him. He came at once, and when I was told he was in Washington I invited him to the White House. His appointment was for 2:30 P.M.

I had known Byrnes well for years, and I wanted to get his firsthand account of what had gone on at Yalta, and all the information he had of the meetings between Roosevelt, Churchill, and Stalin. I had heard that he had personally made shorthand notes of all the secret meetings he had attended. I greeted him as an old friend when he entered, and we talked for half an hour about everything he could recall without referring to his notes. Then I asked him to transcribe his notes for me, especially since he had indicated that there were no available stenographic or official transcripts of the Yalta meetings. It was not until some ten days later that I received from him a typed and leather-bound transcript of his notes, which bore as a title, "The Crimean Conference, Minutes of Meetings, prepared by James F. Byrnes."

During our discussion I had told Byrnes that I was considering asking him to become Secretary of State after the San Francisco conference. In considering Byrnes for this most important Cabinet post, a number of factors influenced me. The first of these was the question of succession to the presidency. Under the law, as matters now stood, the next man in line after me was the Secretary of State, Edward R. Stettinius, Jr. Stettinius, however, had never been a candidate for any elective office, and it was my feeling that any man who stepped into the presidency should have held at least some office to which he had been elected by a vote of the people. I already had in mind the idea of recommending to Congress a change in the order of succession in case the Vice-President, as well as the President, were to die in office.

I felt that the Speaker of the House, as an elected representative of the people of his district as well as the chosen representative of the majority of the elected representatives of the people, was the proper man under our form of government to be the next in line after the Vice-President to assume the presidency. This would necessitate legislation, of course, and that would take time. Pending a change in the law, I felt it my duty to choose without too much delay a Secretary of State with proper qualifications to succeed, if necessary, to the presidency. At this time I regarded Byrnes as the man best qualified. He had served many terms in the House and in the Senate, where he had acted as chairman of important committees. His record was so conspicuous that President Roosevelt had named him an associate justice of the Supreme Court of the United States. Later Roosevelt called on him for very special service by asking him to move into the White House to become assistant to the President, in charge of war mobilization. Byrnes agreed, but to do this he sacrificed a lifetime post of great prestige and resigned from the Supreme Court.

With this impressive record, I felt that Byrnes could make a further major contribution if he were to be appointed Secretary of State. But this was not all. There was still another consideration, though it was mostly personal.

Byrnes had felt that by virtue of his record of service to the party and the country he had been the logical choice to be the running mate of Franklin Roosevelt in the 1944 election. In fact, he had asked me to nominate him and give him my support before that convention.

As it turned out, Roosevelt and the convention willed otherwise, and Byrnes, undoubtedly, was deeply disappointed and hurt. I thought that my calling on him at this time might help balance things up.

At three-thirty that afternoon, not long after Byrnes had left, Secretary of State Stettinius made his second call of the day. He was accompanied by Charles Bohlen, the State Department's expert on Russia, who had acted as interpreter at all the Roosevelt meetings with Stalin. The three of us plunged into the harassing question of Poland and the difficulties we were having with the Soviet leaders because of it.

As Vice-President, I had been familiar only with the basic elements of the Polish problem. Now, however, the full picture was becoming clearer to me since I had read the secret documents, including the messages between Roosevelt, Churchill, and Stalin. The plain story is this: We and the British wanted to see the establishment in Poland of a government truly representative of all the people. The tragic fact was that, though we were allies of Russia, we had not been permitted to send our observers into Poland. Russia was in full military occupation of the country at the time and had given her full support to the so-called Lublin government— a puppet regime of Russia's own making.

Both Great Britain and the United States had made their viewpoints clear, but Russia refused to budge no matter what we proposed in our efforts to compose the matter. She persisted in this attitude even in disregard of the agreement into which she had entered at Yalta. As a result of this, it had become apparent, because of the activities of the anti-Communist Poles, both in Poland and abroad, that what we actually faced in Poland was not merely a political situation but one that seriously threatened civil war. This had been clear, I now learned, even at the time Roosevelt, Churchill, and Stalin met at Yalta. In fact, at that meeting the question of a provisional or interim government for Poland had taken up more time than any other subject.

The reports now being made to me by Byrnes, Stettinius, and Bohlen, and my study of secret messages and cables, revealed the three alternatives that faced the negotiators at Yalta. First, there was the Polish government-in-exile, which had been established in London early in the war. This was made up of real Polish patriots, but its relations with the British had cooled. On the other hand, it was in close touch with the very active underground resistance movement in Poland which was determined in its opposition to the Russian-sponsored Lublin government and which had also opposed the Red Army which had moved through Poland.

Though the government-in-exile had long since been recognized by both Great Britain and the United States, it was obvious that those who composed it could not be forced on the Russians as a group, and no attempt had been made by Roosevelt or Churchill to do that.

A second alternative had been the one sponsored by Stalin. He had insisted—and he still maintained this view—that the Lublin group or, as it was being called by this time, the Warsaw government, was a fully functioning de facto government and should continue. He claimed, though we had information to the contrary, that it was purely Polish in origin and policy and that it had the support of the overwhelming majority of the population. His real reason for favoring this group, of course, was that it was subservient to the Soviet government.

After much discussion it became apparent at Yalta that neither the Polish government-in-exile nor the Warsaw provisional government, as such, would be accepted by all three powers. Consequently, the discussion turned to the third alternative. This was that the Warsaw provisional government then functioning in Poland should be broadened by the inclusion of certain democratic leaders who were still in Poland and by others who were living abroad at the time. This new government would then be pledged to hold free and unfettered elections as soon as possible on the basis of universal suffrage and the secret ballot. In this proposed election, furthermore, there were to be candidates representing all the democratic and anti-Nazi political parties of Poland.

This was the compromise solution to which Roosevelt, Churchill, and Stalin had finally agreed. Properly carried out, it might very well have solved the problem. We were now faced, however, with the failure of the Russians to live up to this agreement.

This was the matter on which I felt impelled to act so promptly now. In fact, when I had cabled Churchill my reply to his message of sympathy, I told him that I was also about to cable my views and suggestions on this Polish matter, and late on the afternoon of April 13 this second message was sent.

Churchill had already proposed a joint public statement by the American and British governments concerning our difficulties with the Russians and had let me know that he was under some compulsion to speak on this subject in the House of Commons. I felt that military and political collaboration with Russia was still so important that the time was not ripe for a public statement on this difficult and still unsettled Polish situation. Some positive steps, however, were certainly called for, and I now suggested to Churchill that a joint British-American message be sent to Stalin, putting definite proposals to him and setting them forth in direct language. I even included a sample text and asked for his comments and suggestions, in case he approved the plan.

The situation, as Churchill saw it—and as I now saw it too—was that the Russians had no intention, if they could prevent it, of seeing a new provisional government of national unity organized on the lines to which they had agreed at Yalta. The reason for this attitude was that they were in no doubt that such a government would mean the end of the Lublin group's Communist control in Poland.

If there were any genuine fears by the Russians that we were attempting to impose a new and unfriendly Polish government on them, it seemed to me that the proposals set forth in my message to Churchill would dispel them, or at least would give a definite basis for further discussions.

"Stalin's reply to you and to President Roosevelt," my message began, "makes our next step of the greatest importance. Although with a few exceptions he does not leave much ground for optimism, I feel very strongly that we should have another go at him."

I then agreed with several arguments Churchill had offered, but contended that any public announcement of a breakdown in the negotiations would dash the hopes of the Polish people and might also adversely affect our political and military collaboration with the Soviet Union. And finally I added the suggested text of the note I had in mind. This pointed out that the British and United States governments had tried to be constructive and fair in their approach to the problem. It also attempted to correct certain erroneous impressions the Russians pretended to have of certain earlier communications. And finally it outlined four points.

The first of these suggested the names of three Poles from London and four from Warsaw who were to be invited to come to Moscow for consultation, leaving a place for one more Warsaw Pole who was to be selected by Russia. The second suggestion was that the group from Warsaw be permitted to arrive in Moscow first "if desired." Third, the Polish leaders who were to be called for consultation were to be permitted to suggest other names, so that all major Polish groups might be represented at the discussions. Fourth, we would make it clear that Great Britain and the United States had no wish to commit themselves in advance to any formula for determining the new Government of National Unity.

This Polish problem was not the only difficulty that had arisen in connection with Russia. One of the serious obstacles to the launching of the imminent United Nations Conference in San Francisco centered around Stalin's reluctance to send his Foreign Minister Molotov instead of a lesser envoy. In fact, Secretary Stettinius now brought me a message from Ambassador Harriman stating that he and Stalin had discussed this subject at a meeting that very day. Stalin, the message said, had voiced his deep sorrow over the death of President Roosevelt and had expressed his desire to work with me as he had with Roosevelt. Harriman, seizing this opening, had suggested that the most effective method of assuring the United States and the world of the Soviet desire to continue collaboration would be for Molotov to go to the United States, first to see me, and second to attend the conference at San Francisco. Harriman added that he was expressing his personal opinion but that he felt sure I would concur.

Stalin replied that if, with the approval of the President, Harriman could be authorized to renew the hope he had just expressed, arrangements would be made for Molotov to visit both Washington and San Francisco.

Stettinius and I felt that here was a little progress, and I instructed him to draft a reply. Then, with the message to Churchill about Poland also approved, I turned to a long memorandum from the Secretary of State requesting instructions for the American delegation to the forthcoming conference in San Francisco.

My desk was piled with papers, and all through the day I had been alternately reading and conferring. I have always been a heavy reader, and it is easy for me to concentrate. Fortunately, too, my memory is retentive, and this helped me greatly as I conferred with advisers and experts or found it necessary to make decisions. Nevertheless, on that first full day as President I did more reading than I ever thought I could. I even selected some papers to take home so that I might study them before retiring and upon waking. This was the first step in a routine of nightly work that I found to be one of the most trying but also one of the necessary duties of a President.

It was now evening, and I was weary. I picked up the papers I had decided to take with me, and as I left my desk I heard a loud buzzing. It was the signal to the Secret Service, who now came through the corridors to escort me home. An automobile was waiting for me at the Executive Avenue entrance—a closed car that was followed by a long, open one which carried the Secret Service men, some of whom rode standing on the running board.

Kind and considerate as the Secret Service men were in the performance of their duty, I couldn't help feeling uncomfortable. There was no escaping the fact that my privacy and personal freedom were to be greatly restricted from now on. I even began to realize, as I rode toward my apartment that evening, that our neighbors were beginning to be imposed upon. They were no longer able to come and go as they pleased. To enter their own homes it was now necessary for them to be properly identified and cleared by the Secret Service men.

They were all very nice about it, but Mrs. Truman and I felt that the sooner we could move to an official residence the easier it would be on neighbors and friends, from many of whom we hated to part. Furthermore, it was now necessary for me to be available at all times for messages and official callers, and such business could not be adequately conducted in an apartment house on Connecticut Avenue.

I had told Mrs. Roosevelt that Mrs. Truman and I had no intention of moving into the White House until she had had all the time necessary in which to make other arrangements. In the meantime, Blair House, which stands across Pennsylvania Avenue from the White House and which serves as an official guest house for foreign dignitaries visiting Washington, was being made ready for us as our temporary official residence.

CHAPTER 3

On Saturday morning, April 14, I arose at dawn. I have
always been an early riser, but this was earlier than usual.
The body of Franklin Roosevelt was to arrive that morning from Warm
Springs, Georgia, and I was going to the Union Station to meet the
funeral train.

Before breakfast I added some additional notes to the outline of the
speech I was preparing for my appearance before Congress on Monday.
With the help of Steve Early and Judge Rosenman, Roosevelt's personal
counsel, I had already begun this outline. I then studied the memorandum
from the Secretary of State in which he dealt with the coming United
Nations Conference at San Francisco. Our delegates were waiting for
final instructions, and I had agreed to meet the full delegation early Tuesday morning. It was necessary that we decide what our attitude was to be
on problems having to do with such matters as the presidency of the conference, as well as on the very complex question of trusteeships and the
number of votes the Russians were to have.

At Yalta, Roosevelt and Churchill had agreed to support at San Francisco Stalin's proposal that two Soviet republics, White Russia and the
Ukraine, be admitted to initial membership. Now, however, the Russians
were taking the position that the commitment at Yalta extended to giving
these two Soviet republics the right to be represented at the San Francisco
conference itself.

I got to the White House at 8:30 A.M. and was met by Steve Early and
Bill Simmons. When I reached my desk I found many telegrams and

communications already there, and I read as many as I could before nine o'clock, when my first appointment was scheduled.

My first visitor that morning was John W. Snyder of St. Louis. He was one of my closest personal friends, and I already knew that I wanted him in my administration in a trusted capacity. There was an important post vacant—that of Federal Loan Administrator, from which, not long before, Fred Vinson had resigned to become Director of War Mobilization and Reconversion—and Snyder was ideally fitted for it. He was an experienced banker who had been executive assistant to RFC Administrator Jesse Jones and the director of the Defense Plants Corporation.

"I don't think you ought to appoint me to that job," he told me when I had explained what I had in mind. "I'm not sure I am the right man."

"I think you are the right man for the place," I replied. "I'm sending your name to the Senate."

Later I telephoned Jesse Jones and said "the President" had appointed Snyder as Federal Loan Administrator.

"Did he make that appointment before he died?" asked Jones.

"No," I answered. "He made it just now."

Everyone, including myself, still continued to think of Roosevelt as "the President."

When Snyder left, Secretary of the Treasury Morgenthau came in for a brief conference. He was with me only a few minutes, and I asked him to submit to me as soon as possible a comprehensive report on the state of the nation's finances. Secretary of Commerce Wallace and Justice Byrnes then joined me, and presently the three of us left for the Union Station. Mrs. Truman and Margaret were making arrangements to leave with me that evening for Hyde Park in order to be present at the interment of President Roosevelt. For that reason they were unable to go with me to the station.

The train bearing the body of Franklin Roosevelt arrived at the Union Station at ten o'clock. I went aboard at once, accompanied by Wallace and Byrnes, and we paid our respects to Mrs. Roosevelt, who had accompanied the body from Warm Springs. Brigadier General Elliott Roosevelt and Anna Roosevelt Boettiger were with their mother, and present also were Colonel John Boettiger and some of the younger members of the Roosevelt family.

The body of the late President was to lie in state during the day in the East Room of the White House, and as the funeral procession was formed I took the place that had been assigned to me. Slowly we moved through the streets that were massed with mourners all the way to the White House.

I shall never forget the sight of so many grief-stricken people. Some wept without restraint. Some shed their tears in silence. Others were grim and stoic, but all were genuine in their mourning. It was impossible now to tell who had been for him and who had not. Throughout that enormous throng all of them were expressing their sense of loss and sadness at the passing of a remarkable man.

I saw an old Negro woman with her apron to her eyes as she sat on the curb. She was crying as if she had lost her son, and when the cortege passed along Constitution Avenue, most of those who lined the street were in tears.

The procession reached the White House at eleven o'clock, and the flag-draped casket was borne into the East Room. It was placed before a french door, banked high with lilies, roses, and other flowers. Five members of the armed forces stood guard, with an American flag on a standard at one side of the coffin and the blue presidential banner at the other. Chairs were placed before the bier for members of the immediate family, members of the Cabinet, and other state dignitaries.

Again I paid my respects to Mrs. Roosevelt, and then returned to the executive offices of the White House.

I had received word that Harry Hopkins had left a sickbed in the Mayo Clinic at Rochester, Minnesota, in order to attend the funeral of his chief and friend. He had already arrived in Washington, and I had sent word that I wanted very much to see him. An appointment had been set for eleven-thirty that morning.

Hopkins had been close to Roosevelt throughout his administration. He had performed many confidential tasks and, as the President's personal representative, had carried out a number of secret missions. He was a man whom Roosevelt trusted implicitly and leaned upon heavily. He was a dedicated man who never sought credit or the limelight, yet willingly bore the brunt of criticism, just or unjust. He was a rare figure in Washington officialdom and was one of my old friends. I, too, trusted him implicitly, and unless his health had been seriously impaired I hoped that he would continue with me in the same role he had played with my predecessor.

Before I went to the Senate, and while I was still presiding judge in Jackson County and Hopkins was WPA Administrator, I had worked with him in the WPA setup in Missouri. When I was junior senator, I had his ear in getting action from the White House on matters that concerned the state I represented. He proved helpful to me again in 1944, shortly after I was nominated for the vice-presidency. At that time I wanted to know from him the more intimate side of the President's approach to public matters and his estimate of certain people, and so the two of us had a long personal conversation just before my luncheon with the President on the White House lawn late in July 1944. In great detail he described to me President Roosevelt's attitude on domestic questions and his opinions of leading legislative and executive personalities. He also gave me the President's judgment on certain international problems and his appraisal of the leading personalities and heads of foreign states. Many times since then the information he gave me proved invaluable.

He spoke of Roosevelt's special fondness for Churchill and of Churchill's for Roosevelt too. He told me how they dealt with each other. "Roosevelt and Churchill," he said, "have had a strong influence on each other in world affairs."

What I now wanted from Hopkins was more firsthand information about the heads of state with whom I would have to deal, particularly Stalin. But I also wanted to go over the whole situation with Hopkins in regard to Russia and Poland and the United Nations.

Harry Hopkins had always looked pale and cadaverous, but when he entered my office this time, he looked worse than ever before. He was ill, of course, and the death of Roosevelt had affected him profoundly. If I had not known his great patriotism and his spirit of self-sacrifice, I would have hesitated to tax his strength.

"How do you feel, Harry?" I asked as we shook hands.

"Terrible," he replied, and I knew what he meant.

"I hope you don't mind my calling you in at this time," I went on, "but I need to know everything you can tell me about our relations with Russia—all that you know about Stalin and Churchill and the conferences at Cairo, Casablanca, Teheran, and Yalta."

"One reason I'm glad to be here," he replied, "and am glad to offer all the assistance I can is because I'm confident that you will continue to carry out the policies of Franklin Roosevelt. And I know that you know how to carry them out."

We talked for over two hours. We did not even take time out for luncheon. Instead, I ordered a tray for each of us from the White House kitchen, and with our minds on other things we ate a bite or two there at my desk.

Hopkins was a storehouse of information and was rarely at a loss for a word or a fact. Furthermore, he was usually able to describe and characterize the many important figures he had met. Certainly he understood the leaders of the Soviet Union.

"Stalin," he told me, "is a forthright, rough, tough Russian. He is a Russian partisan through and through, thinking always first of Russia. But he can be talked to frankly."

He assured me that he would be glad to do all he could, but as he was about to leave he suddenly asked, "Did you know that I had planned to retire from the government on May 12?"

I told him that I knew nothing of his plans to retire and, if his health permitted, I wanted him to stay. He left without giving me any positive reply, but he promised to give the matter serious thought.

Ed Flynn, the New York Democratic leader, was my next caller. He had been a close political associate of President Roosevelt and had come to pay his respects to me. Nevertheless, he hesitatingly brought up some of the political consequences that might result from Mr. Roosevelt's death. These were matters that I felt to be inappropriate at the moment, and when I suggested as much he understood.

At 2:15 P.M. Admiral Leahy, accompanied by Justice Byrnes, came in with two messages from Churchill. Our armies and the Russian armies were rapidly approaching each other from the east and west, and it now seemed only a matter of days before forward units would meet in Eastern Germany or Czechoslovakia. With this in mind, Churchill's first cable suggested that we anticipate this historic event by an announcement by the heads of the Big Three powers.

"A link up of Soviet and Anglo American forces in Germany is rapidly approaching," his message read. He thought it would be heartening for all our peoples if the occasion could be marked by short messages broadcast by me, Marshal Stalin, and himself. He asked me to let him know if I agreed to his proposal, saying he was sending a similar message to Marshal Stalin.

"I thoroughly approve of the suggestion made in your cable," I replied. "If Stalin agrees, I would be pleased to receive from you for consideration your draft of the message."

The Prime Minister's second cable dealt with the question of a final all-out air attack against Germany. The blow he had in mind would have for its objective the smashing of the German war industries that had so far managed to survive all our bombing efforts.

There was good reason for this, for the Germans were reported to be ready for a suicidal last-ditch stand, and our Chiefs of Staff were of the opinion that such an effort might prolong the fighting for another six months.

On March 29 Roosevelt had sent Churchill the details of a project prepared by the Chiefs of Staff for launching pilotless old bombers against large industrial targets in Germany. These bombers, carrying huge loads of explosives, were to be guided by remote control and set off by timing devices. Churchill had been disturbed by this proposal and probably partly on that account had delayed his answer for two weeks.

What naturally troubled him was that the Germans might retaliate on London.

In his cable to me, which actually was a reply to Roosevelt's message, Churchill understandably stressed the point that the British people had suffered greatly from German bombings and might have to suffer more if this project was put into practice. Nevertheless, he left the decision to us and ended his message in characteristic terms.

The Prime Minister's message said that he had received a telegram from President Roosevelt on March 29. He regretted that there had been a delay in replying to this communication, but he felt it was his duty to refer it to the British Chiefs of Staff. Churchill said that if the United States military authorities really considered this practice necessary to bring about the end of the German war, the British would not dissent.

However, he said first that the war situation had turned so much in our favor that large-scale bombing of German cities was no longer of its former importance. He added that if the Germans had a number of war-weary bombers that could make the distance, London was the obvious and indeed the only target, and even a few very big explosions in London would be demoralizing to the people at a time when they had hoped that their prolonged ordeal was over.

Churchill added in this connection that a calculation had been made showing that in the greater London area one person in 131 had been killed by enemy action, including London citizens in the armed forces and 30,000 civilians killed by the air onslaught. This figure of one in 131, Churchill said, represented far the highest losses sustained by any similar locality on the Allied side in the second great war.

He concluded: "Having put the facts before you I leave the decisions entirely in the hands of your military advisers, and we shall make no complaint if misfortune comes to us in consequence."

I reviewed with the Chiefs of Staff the project to which Churchill had referred, and having done so, I cabled a reply.

"Taking into account all the considerations involved," my message said, "it seems to me this project concerning war-weary, explosive ladened aircraft should not be pressed further in Europe at this time. I am instructing my Chiefs of Staff accordingly."

A little later, when Byrnes had returned to my office in order to go over with me my notes for the speech to Congress on Monday, another message from Churchill arrived. Anthony Eden, the British Foreign Minister, was on his way from London to San Francisco for the conference, and I had agreed to see him. It was with that in mind that I now read this latest Churchill message, which bore upon the Polish issue.

Churchill cabled that he had just read the draft of the joint message which I proposed we should send to Stalin. In principle Churchill said he was in complete agreement with its terms, "but there is one important point which Eden will put before you, and as you and he will be able to discuss the text together, any points of detail can I am sure be adjusted." He said he would consult the Cabinet on Monday if the final draft had reached him by then, and he hoped we might dispatch the message with our joint authority on that very day, as he strongly agreed with me that our reply was of high urgency.

Churchill went on to say: "Meanwhile Eden will no doubt discuss with you our impressions of what is actually happening in Moscow and Warsaw. As I see it, the Lublin Government are feeling the strong sentiment of the Polish nation, which though not unfriendly to Russia, is fiercely resolved on independence, and views with increasing disfavour a Polish Provisional Government which is, in the main, a Soviet puppet. They are, therefore, endeavouring, in accord with the Soviet Government, to form a government more broad-based than the present one, by the addition of Polish personalities (including perhaps Witos) whom they have in their power but whose aid they seek and need. This is a step in the right direction but would not satisfy our requirements or decisions of Crimea Conference."

The war situation in the Pacific was as pressing as the war in Europe, and it, too, demanded my immediate attention. The Japanese had shortly before taken over Indo-China, and Churchill and Roosevelt had exchanged messages on the whole question of Southeast Asia. Admiral Mountbatten, commander of the Southeast Asia Command (SEAC), was preparing to carry out counter military operations. Plans had already been made for such "pre-occupational" activities as would be required before the regular forces could advance. What were known as "pre-occupational" activities were actually clandestine operations, including guerrilla warfare, in territory which was technically, if not actually, occupied by the enemy Japanese.

Some of our own units under the command of Admiral Mountbatten had been engaged for some time in such operations in Burma. A French resistance movement was already active in Indo-China. The situation was further complicated by the fact that forces of the China Command would also soon be operating in the same theater.

Churchill had reported the situation to Roosevelt on April 11, saying that Mountbatten had been in conference with General Wedemeyer, then chief of staff and military adviser to Generalissimo Chiang Kai-shek, commander of the China Theater. He reported also that the two had come to a satisfactory agreement on the procedure to be followed, thus settling difficulties which had arisen over theater commands. Churchill, however, had proposed to Roosevelt that directives be sent to Admiral Mountbatten and General Wedemeyer to keep one another completely informed on all operations, plans, and intelligence. But Mountbatten was to be left free to conduct whatever pre-occupational activities he decided were needed for the advance of his regular forces.

When the matter came to my attention, I found that General Wedemeyer had reported a somewhat different agreement between himself and Admiral Mountbatten. Wedemeyer understood that Mountbatten would notify him before undertaking any operation in Indo-China and that the operation would not be undertaken until approval was given by the generalissimo. He further understood that if the proposed SEAC operation could not be integrated with China Theater plans, then Mountbatten would not undertake it. According to our Chiefs of Staff, the arrangement as reported by General Wedemeyer conformed to accepted practice and was the proper way of handling operations that overlapped adjoining theaters. Theater commanders were almost always sensitive on such matters, and the generalissimo was no exception.

The procedure, as Wedemeyer had reported it, seemed to me a satisfactory method of solving the problem of SEAC forces operating in the generalissimo's theater, and I so informed Churchill on April 14.

I had been constantly busy since returning to the executive offices. And now, shortly before four o'clock, I was joined by Mrs. Truman and Margaret, who were to go with me to the Executive Mansion for the service that was to be conducted by the Right Reverend Angus Dun, Bishop of the Episcopal Diocese of Washington, before the flag-draped coffin in the East Room.

At Mrs. Roosevelt's request, there were no eulogies. The late President's favorite hymns were sung by all of us, the first being "Eternal Father, Strong to Save." Mrs. Roosevelt asked Bishop Dun to repeat, as part of the service, the expression of faith which President Roosevelt used in his first inaugural address in 1933—"The only thing we have to fear is fear itself."

At the conclusion of the service, Mrs. Truman, Margaret, and I returned to our apartment, where I rested for a time before resuming the reading of documents and reports.

The body of President Roosevelt was removed from the White House shortly after 9:30 P.M. and, accompanied by Mrs. Roosevelt and her family, was borne to the Union Station and placed again aboard the funeral train.

Mrs. Truman, Margaret, and I boarded the train a little later for the night trip to Hyde Park. Cabinet officers, members of the Supreme Court, military leaders, high government officials, friends of the Roosevelts, and representatives of the press and radio also occupied many of the cars of the long special train that carried the body of Franklin Roosevelt on his last trip home.

We arrived at Hyde Park about nine-thirty on Sunday morning and soon thereafter went to the Roosevelt garden, where the final ceremony took place. There Franklin Delano Roosevelt was buried.

We left for Washington at noon. With us were Mrs. Roosevelt, Anna, Elliott, and other members of the Roosevelt family. Mrs. Roosevelt, wonderfully in command of herself, broke the tension by talking about some of the household problems of the White House which we would have to face. Elliott complained about having been starved by the menus of Mrs. Nesbitt, the White House housekeeper. To which Mrs. Roosevelt replied that Mrs. Nesbitt had been properly trying to keep within the food budget.

The schedule that lay ahead for me was so pressing that I spent a good part of the return journey working on the speech I was to make at the joint session of Congress on the following day. I went over some of the points in the speech with the legislative leaders who were on the train. I discussed others with members of the Roosevelt administration.

Almost every presidential message is a complicated business. Many individuals and departments of the government are called on to take some part in it in order to maintain full co-ordination of policy. Experts and researchers are assigned to check and compile data, because no President can or should rely entirely on his own memory. Careful consideration must be given to every element of a presidential speech because of the impact it may have on the nation or the world.

A speech by the President is one of the principal means of informing the public what the policy of the administration is. Because of this, presidential messages have to be written and rewritten many times.

All presidential messages must begin with the President himself. He must decide what he wants to say and how he wants to say it. Many drafts are usually drawn up, and this fact leads to the assumption that presidential speeches are "ghosted." The final version, however, is the final word of the President himself, expressing his own convictions and his policy. These he cannot delegate to any man if he would be President in his own right.

Back in Washington that evening, I felt that an epoch had come to an end. A great President, whose deeds and words had profoundly affected our times, was gone. Chance had chosen me to carry on his work, and in these three days I had already experienced some of the weight of its unbelievable burdens.

As I went to bed that night I prayed I would be equal to the task.

I rose early. On this day, Monday, April 16, 1945, I was to make my first address to Congress as President. I hoped it would go well. I looked over my speech and penciled in some changes. Next I read some papers and dispatches on the latest developments in the Polish situation, for at ten o'clock that morning I was to receive Anthony Eden, British Foreign Secretary, and Lord Halifax, the British Ambassador. There was much for me to do, and even before I sat down to breakfast I had covered a good deal of ground. I got to the White House executive office at eight o'clock, and the Secretary of State was my first visitor, followed by Admiral Leahy. Both of them brought me more dispatches. One was from Churchill, quoting a telegram he had received from Stalin.

"I agree with you," the Stalin message read, "that it would be a good thing to give short messages to troops from you, the President and myself in connection with the expected meeting of our troops, if in fact President Truman has no objection to it. We should of couse come to an agreement about the day on which statements should be made."

The Secretary of State next handed me a memorandum summarizing a report from Harriman on Stalin's previous reply to Roosevelt and Churchill on the Polish question. This summary read in part:

Harriman considers that Stalin's replies to President Roosevelt and Churchill in regard to the Polish question contribute little of a concrete nature toward a solution of the impasse now existing. It is possible that Stalin's only concession regarding Mikolajczyk[1] may lead to others which will make it possible to find a common ground for a satisfactory solution. Harriman refutes a number of Stalin's assertions regarding the work of the Polish Commission.

He recommends that we should adhere to our interpretation of the Crimea decisions under which the Provisional Government now functioning in Poland should be reorganized on a broad Democratic Basis and that members of this government should play a prominent role in the new government. Harriman points out that Stalin essentially is asking us to agree to the establishment of a thinly disguised version of the present Warsaw regime and recommends that we continue to insist that we cannot accept a whitewash of the Warsaw regime. Regarding the question of observers, Harriman believes that the real reason for Soviet reluctance to permit them is a fear that observers might discover the small support actually possessed by the Warsaw government. . . .

Other reports and messages followed until, at ten o'clock, Secretary Stettinius escorted Mr. Eden and Lord Halifax into my office.

---

[1] A Polish leader who had been suggested by Great Britain and the U.S. for participation in the hoped-for Moscow talks.

Eden brought me greetings and messages from Churchill as well as the Prime Minister's version of the joint communication we were to send to Stalin on the Polish issue. Together, the British Foreign Secretary and I went over our respective drafts and agreed upon a final text.

We discussed the importance of having Molotov present at the San Francisco conference, and I informed the British Foreign Secretary that Stalin had just sent word through Harriman that Molotov would attend. And finally, we agreed to meet again before his departure for the conference.

When Eden and Halifax left, I sent the following message to Ambassador Harriman in Moscow:

You are instructed, together with the British Ambassador who will receive similar instructions, to arrange immediately for an interview with Marshal Stalin and hand to him the following text of a joint message from the Prime Minister and myself. If you are unable to see Marshal Stalin before your departure, you and the British Ambassador should transmit the message to Marshal Stalin through the appropriate channels.

(In the event that Ambassadors Harriman and Clark Kerr have departed the Chargé d'Affaires with his British colleague should address a joint communication to Marshal Stalin transmitting the message from the President and the Prime Minister.)

FROM THE PRESIDENT AND THE PRIME MINISTER FOR MARSHAL STALIN

We are sending this joint reply to your messages of April 7 in regard to Polish negotiations for the sake of greater clarity and in order that there will be no misunderstanding as to our position on this matter. The British and United States Governments have tried most earnestly to be constructive and fair in their approach and will continue to do so.

Before putting before you the concrete and constructive suggestion which is the purpose of this message we feel it necessary, however, to correct the completely erroneous impression which you have apparently received in regard to the position of the British and United States Governments as set forth by our Ambassadors under direct instructions during the negotiations.

It is most surprising to have you state that the present Government functioning in Warsaw has been in any way ignored during these negotiations. Such has never been our intention nor our position. You must be cognizant of the fact that our Ambassadors in Moscow have agreed without question that the three leaders of the Warsaw Government should be included in the list of Poles to be invited to come to Moscow for consultation with the Commission.

We have never denied that among the three elements from which the new Provisional Government of National Unity is to be formed the representatives of the present Warsaw Government will play, unquestionably, a prominent part.

Nor can it be said with any justification that our Ambassadors are demanding the right to invite an unlimited number of Poles. The right to put forward and have accepted by the Commission individual representative Poles from abroad and from within Poland to be invited to Moscow for consultation cannot be interpreted in that sense.

Indeed in his message of April 1 President Roosevelt specifically said QUOTE in order to facilitate the agreement, the Commission might first of all select a small but representative group of Polish leaders who could suggest other names for consideration by the Commission. END QUOTE.

The real issue between us is whether or not the Warsaw Government has the right to veto individual candidates for consultation. No such interpretation in our considered opinion can be found in the Crimea decision. It appears to us that you are reverting to the original position taken by the Soviet delegation at the Crimea which was subsequently modified in the agreement. Let us keep clearly in mind that we are now speaking only of the group of Poles who are to be invited to Moscow for consultation. With reference to the statement which you attribute to Ambassador Harriman it would appear that real misunderstanding has occurred since from his reports to his Government the remark in question would appear to refer to the Polish Government in London and not, as you maintain, to the Provisional Government in Warsaw.

You mention the desirability of inviting eight Poles—five from within Poland and three from London—to take part in these first consultations and in your message to the Prime Minister you indicate that Mikolajczyk would be acceptable if he issued a statement in support of the Crimean decision. We, therefore, submit the following proposals for your consideration in order to prevent a breakdown, with all its incalculable consequences, of our endeavors to settle the Polish question. We hope that you will give them your most careful and earnest consideration.

1. That we instruct our representatives on the Commission to extend immediately invitations to the following Polish leaders to come to Moscow to consult: Bierut, Osubka-Morawaski, Rola-Zymierski, Bishop Sapieha; one representative Polish political party leader not connected with the present Warsaw Government (if any of the following were agreeable to you they would be agreeable to us: Witos, Zulawski, Chacinski, Jasiukowicz); and from London, Mikolajczyk, Grabski and Stanczyk.

2. That once the invitations to come for consultation have been issued by the Commission the representatives of Warsaw could arrive first, if desired.

3. That it be agreed that these Polish leaders called for consultation could suggest to the Commission the names of a certain number of other Polish leaders from within Poland or abroad who might be brought in for consultation in order that all major Polish groups be represented in the discussions.

4. We do not feel that we could commit ourselves to any formula for determining the composition of the New Government of National Unity in advance of consultation with the Polish leaders and we do not in any case consider the Yugoslav precedent to be applicable to Poland.

We ask you to read again carefully the American and British message of April 1 since they set forth the larger considerations which we still have very much in mind and to which we must adhere.

By now the morning was gone, and I had had no time since reaching the executive offices to give more thought to the speech I had prepared. I went over it again but made no further changes.

I rose from my desk and heard the buzzing signal that called my Secret Service guard. I had not yet grown accustomed to that—was never really to grow accustomed to it, though I ultimately learned to take it in stride. Now, however, my mind was elsewhere.

It was shortly after noon and time for me to leave for the Hill, where I was to give my first address to Congress.

CHAPTER 4

The day was clear, and the temperature had moderated somewhat since morning, though the warmth of summer had not yet come to Washington. Tulips were blooming in the White House garden.

My car was waiting, and when I entered it I was driven from the White House grounds, with the Secret Service car following behind.

A little more than forty-eight hours before, the streets had been filled with silent mourners as Franklin Roosevelt's body had been slowly carried to the White House. Now the traffic was normal.

The route by which I was taken led up Pennsylvania Avenue and around the Capitol to its eastern front. There the car was driven into the narrow passage beneath the broad stairway that leads up to the formal entrance to the Capitol's southern wing. Guards were waiting at the archway before which the car stopped, and I was led inside and directly to the elevator. It, too, was waiting, and in another moment I stepped out on the floor above, where I was met and taken to the Speaker's office. Less than four days before I had entered Sam Rayburn's private office with no such formality.

I was greeted by a delegation appointed by Speaker Rayburn and President Pro-Tempore McKellar of the Senate, and I conferred for half an hour or so with those who were gathered in the room. Then at one o'clock the delegation that had met me escorted me to the House floor and to the rostrum.

I entered the House chamber at 1:02 P.M. and was greeted by a standing ovation which I knew to be a tribute to the office of the President.

Senators, representatives, and justices of the Supreme Court were there before me. Members of the Cabinet, high government officials, and many members of the diplomatic corps had risen to their feet. Those who filled the galleries had also risen. I looked up and caught a glimpse of Mrs. Truman and Margaret.

For me it was a very stirring moment. I was so affected that I completely forgot an important bit of protocol.

"Mr. Speaker," I began.

Rayburn, who was with Senator McKellar on the rostrum just behind me, interrupted me at once.

"Just a minute, Harry," he whispered as he leaned toward me. "Let me introduce you."

He spoke softly, but the microphones that stood before me had been turned on, and he was heard all over the chamber and all over the country over the radio networks. Then he straightened up:

"The President of the United States," he said in his full voice.

I had now been introduced, and so I went ahead.

I pledged myself to carry out the war and peace policies of Franklin Roosevelt, and I made it clear that I would work for the peace and security of the world. I asked for public support for a strong and lasting United Nations organization. I called upon all Americans to help me keep our nation united in defense of those ideals which had been so eloquently proclaimed by Roosevelt.

I reaffirmed our demand for unconditional surrender and expressed my full confidence in the grand strategy of the United States and our allies. I expressed, as well, my confidence in the ability of Admirals Leahy, King, and Nimitz, and Generals Marshall, Arnold, Eisenhower, and MacArthur to carry out the tasks assigned to them, and left no doubt that this direction would remain unchanged and unhampered.

There were many indications of approval of what I said. I was applauded frequently, and when I reaffirmed the policy of unconditional surrender the chamber rose to its feet.

"At this moment," I concluded, "I have in my heart a prayer. As I have assumed my heavy duties, I humbly pray to Almighty God in the words of King Solomon, 'Give therefore Thy servant an understanding heart to judge Thy people, that I may discern between good and bad: for who is able to judge this Thy so great a people?'

"I ask only to be a good and faithful servant of my Lord and my people."

I returned to the White House, and with Steve Early and Bill Hassett, two of my able secretaries, I tackled another batch of accumulated work. Also, I was advised that Blair House had been readied for us and that we could move in that evening. Mrs. Truman, her mother, Mrs. David W. Wallace, and Margaret were already moving out of the Connecticut Avenue apartment. Since Blair House is directly opposite the old State Department Building and little more than diagonally across Pennsylvania Avenue from the White House, I decided I would go and come on foot, little realizing what security precautions would be required on that short walk.

It was a little after five when, flanked by Secret Service men, I started for our new home. I had given no thought to the problem of getting there and was somewhat surprised when, as we reached the corner of Pennsylvania Avenue at the cross street of Executive West, the traffic lights turned red in all directions. They remained red, too, until I had reached the front entrance to Blair House.

This was about the time of the heavy traffic hour, and I had no knowledge at first that the lights had changed because of a request of the Secret Service. But when I did find out, I asked that the normal traffic signals be restored, for I felt that I could wait and observe the traffic regulations along with the other pedestrians. However, this didn't work well either, for the Secret Service began to worry about the crowds that waited to watch me go by. To allay the anxiety of the security people I eventually had to arrange to make four trips daily from the rear of the White House all the way around to the rear of Blair House and back. It became monotonous, and I didn't like it, but there was little else that I could do.

It was that evening, I remember, that I wrote my mother and my sister my first letter to them as President.

Dear Mamma & Mary [it began]: Well, I have had the most momentous, and the most trying time anyone could possibly have, since Thursday, April 12th.

Maybe you'd like to know just what happened. We'd had a long, drawn out debate in the Senate and finally came to an agreement for a recess at 5 P.M. until Friday, Apr. 13th.

When I went back to my office, a call from Sam Rayburn, Speaker of the House, was awaiting me. Sam wanted me to come over to the House side of the Capitol and talk to him about policy and procedure and, as Alice in Wonderland would say, "shoes and ships and sealing wax and things." . . .

But—as soon as I came into the room Sam told me that Steve Early, the President's confidential press secretary wanted to talk to me. I called the White House, and Steve told me to come to the White House "as quickly and as *quietly*" as I could. Well I told Sam I had to go to the White House on a special call and that he should say nothing about it.

I ran all the way to my office in the Senate by way of the unfrequented corridors in the Capitol, told my office force that I'd been summoned to the White House and to say nothing about it. . . .

When I arrived at the Pennsylvania entrance to the most famous house in

America, a couple of ushers met me . . . and then took me up to Mrs. Roosevelt's study on the second floor.

She and Mrs. Boettiger, her daughter and her husband the Lt. Col., and Steve Early were there. Mrs. Roosevelt put her arm on my shoulder and said, "Harry, the President is dead."

It was the only time in my life, I think, that I ever felt as if I'd had a real shock. I had hurried to the White House to see the President, and when I arrived, I found I was the President. No one in the history of our country ever had it happen to him just that way.

. . . We waited for Bess and Margaret to arrive. We then had to scurry around and find a Bible for me to put my hand upon to take the oath. They finally found one. If I'd known what was afoot, I'd have used Grandpa Truman's Bible, which was in my office bookcase.

You of course know from the papers what happened and what has happened since.

Saturday afternoon, the White House funeral; Sunday morning the burial at Hyde Park, today my speech to Congress.

This afternoon we moved to this house, diagonally across the street (Penn. Ave.) from the White House, until the Roosevelts have had time to move out of the White House. We tried staying at the apartment, but it wouldn't work. I can't move without at least ten Secret Service men and twenty policemen. People who lived in our apartment couldn't get in and out without a pass. So—we moved out with suitcases. Our furniture is still there and will be for some time. . . . But I've paid the rent for this month and will pay for another month if they don't get the old White House redecorated by that time.

My greatest trial was today when I addressed the Congress. It seemed to go over all right, from the ovation I received. Things have gone so well that I'm almost as scared as I was Thursday when Mrs. R. told me what had happened. Maybe it will come out all right.

Soon as we get settled in the White House you'll both be here to visit us. Lots of love from your very much worried son and bro.

Harry

I wrote Mamma often, and regularly each weekend would telephone her and sister Mary, who lived with her. I was deeply devoted to her, and we were very close. She was a wonderful mother. At ninety-two she was still keen and alert and saw things in their true perspective, even at a time like this. When asked by a press representative at her home in Grandview, Missouri, to comment on how she felt about her son being President, she said, "I can't really be glad he is President, because I'm sorry that President Roosevelt is dead. If he had been voted in, I'd be out waving a flag, but it doesn't seem right to be very happy or wave a flag now."

We were settled in Blair House now, at least for a time—a mansion with a long history as a social center of Washington where important members of the government, from Jackson's time on, were entertained by succeeding heirs of the Blair family. At various times six Cabinet members had lived in it, and four Presidents—Jackson, Van Buren,

Lincoln, and Taft—often visited there as friends. On many other occasions, too, other presidents and leading figures visited the house, which became the property of the United States Government in 1942.

We took up residence there with some trepidation. This had nothing to do with politics. I suppose that the demands of protocol and the many things that had to do with officialdom made us uneasy about our prospects for a reasonable family life.

Mrs. Truman had been happy as the wife of a senator and had fallen in love with Washington. She had many friends among congressional wives and others in official and private life. She knew, however, that these relationships would probably change now that she was the First Lady of the Land. She was entirely conscious of the importance and dignity of White House life. She was not especially interested, however, in the formalities and pomp or the artificiality which, as we had learned from our years in Washington, inevitably surround the family of a President. In this connection, we had our daughter Margaret to think of, a schoolgirl who wanted and needed friends. Would she now be isolated from all the normal relationships that are so important in the lives of youngsters?

That night in Blair House I studied a report which had been handed me by the Secretary of State. It dealt with the world's critical food situation. There existed at that time a most serious shortage, not only of certain basic foods but also of cotton, wool, and coal. The situation was especially grave in certain liberated areas which had suffered from a disastrous winter the year before. "The end of hostilities," the report I read explained, "would aggravate an already critical situation. The success of any plan agreed upon at San Francisco can be seriously jeopardized, if not defeated, by internal chaos in the liberated countries."

With this situation in mind the Secretary of State recommended that I instruct the military authorities to review and revise their food and material requirements downward so as to make available additional supplies to these areas.

"On the side of U.S. domestic requirements," his report continued, "certain of the civilian agencies seem reluctant to carry out the 'tightening of the belt' anticipated by President Roosevelt without further instructions from you. . . . I also recommend that you instruct the appropriate civilian agencies particularly the War Food Administration to explore all possible reductions in U.S. consumption."

I was familiar with these difficulties from my experience on the Hill and felt that the Secretary of State was rightly alarmed. I regarded this as one of the most urgent crises I had to resolve.

I met with the American delegates to the San Francisco conference for the first time on Tuesday morning, April 17. They were presented to me by Secretary of State Stettinius. The delegation was made up of the Secretary himself, who was chairman, Senators Connally and Vandenberg, Congressman Bloom and Eaton, Governor Stassen, who, as a commander in the Navy, had just reached Washington from the Pacific, and Dr. Virginia Gildersleeve. Cordell Hull, who was a member of the delegation, was ill and could not attend. This delegation had been appointed by President Roosevelt and was an excellent and representative one.

The members knew what the people and the government expected them to strive for at San Francisco. I told them that what we wanted to accomplish was to set up an international organization to prevent another world war. I emphasized that I wanted them to write a document that would pass the U. S. Senate and that would not arouse such opposition as confronted Woodrow Wilson.

Following this meeting I signed an amended Lend-Lease bill which extended this most useful law for another year. Lend-Lease was part of our arsenal of war. I was on old ground here, for through my work on the Truman Committee I had gained much knowledge of the impact of war mobilization on the civilian economy. I also knew, quite apart from any thought of the isolationist group that was ready to turn its back on the world as soon as it thought our immediate war interests had been served, what had been bothering the Senate about the use of Lend-Lease funds. Hardly more than a month before, as Vice-President, I had cast the deciding vote in the Senate in order to get the bill passed.

Here at home we had been untouched by the ravages of war. Even here, of course, we were faced with the sizable problem of reconversion to peacetime production as soon as facilities became available. But for our allies who had suffered so greatly from war devastation the need was desperate. Something would have to be done to cushion the shock of reconstruction, but I did not consider this to be a proper continuing function for Lend-Lease. I knew that if we undertook to use any Lend-Lease money for rehabilitation purposes we would open ourselves to congressional criticism. However, the critical problem of rehabilitation that our allies were facing was still with us, and we had to find a way to meet it. The reconstruction of Europe was a matter that directly concerned us, and we could not turn our back on it without jeopardizing our own national interests. It seemed to me that the proper way to accomplish this was through the Export-Import Bank and, so far as possible, through the International Bank.

The approaching end of the war in Europe meant that decisions would have to be made soon in our own war production program. There was no reason why this should interfere with stepping up supplies for the Pacific.

By this time we had developed such an enormous industrial capacity that the country was already confronted with surplus war production facilities. Supplies to the Pacific, once the war in Europe had been ended, could be increased even while we began to reduce our total output.

The President's relations with the press are of the utmost importance. By way of the press he maintains a direct contact with the people. I was especially interested, therefore, when at 10:30 A.M. on April 17, 1945, I held my first press and radio conference.

It is often helpful for a President to judge, from questions put to him by the reporters, what is going on in the minds of the people. Good reporters are always in close touch with developments and with what the people want to know. I have always made a sharp distinction between the working reporter and the editor or publisher. I always got along well with the reporters. They try to do an honest job of reporting the facts. But many of their bosses—the editors and publishers—have their own special interests, and the news is often slanted to serve those interests, which unfortunately are not always for the benefit of the public as a whole.

Important as I knew the White House press conferences to be, I felt compelled to announce that I would cut them to one a week. I did this so as to be able to devote more of my time to the heavy load of business my office had to handle. I needed time to keep up with the mounting developments on the home front and elsewhere in the world. I decided also to continue the practice established by my predecessor of barring direct quotation of my replies and comments while permitting indirect quotation. The idea of a press conference is to find out what the President thinks about pending matters, but it must be obvious that he should not be quoted directly on every question. That could often change an answer from an expression of opinion to a final commitment. This would serve no useful purpose, for in order to avoid commitment on matters still pending, the President would be reluctant to answer or even to suggest a clue that might reveal his line of thought.

At the time my first press conference was held I had been President less than five days. It was the first opportunity the reporters and White House correspondents had to question me.

"The first thing I want to do," I told them, "is to read the rules.

" 'News emanating from the President's conferences with the press will continue to be divided in categories already known to you, and in keeping with the practice of President Roosevelt's news meetings with the press.

" 'These categories are: first, off the record, confidential announcements which are to be kept secret by the newspapermen attending the conference and not passed on by them to outsiders.

" 'Background—or not for attribution—information which may be given to the press for its guidance and use, the source of which cannot be published nor disclosed. In other words, it cannot be attributed to the President.

" 'News information which may be attributed to the President, when it is given to the press by the President at his conference, but which cannot be directly quoted.

" 'Statements by the President cannot be directly quoted, unless he gives special permission.' "

I then told them that Steve Early and Bill Hassett, Jonathan Daniels and Judge Samuel I. Rosenman, all of whom had served under President Roosevelt, had offered to stay and help me get things organized. I added that Matthew J. Connelly was to be my confidential secretary.

I then read a letter from Mrs. Roosevelt to me.

"My dear Mr. President:
"There have been many thousands of letters, telegrams and cards sent to me and my children, which have brought great comfort and consolation to all of us. This outpouring of affectionate thought has touched us all deeply, and we wish it were possible to thank each and every one individually.
"My children and I feel, in view of the fact that we are faced with the paper shortage and are asked not to use paper when it can be avoided, that all we can do is to express our appreciation collectively. We would therefore consider it a great favor if you would be kind enough to express our gratitude for us.
"Sincerely,
"Eleanor Roosevelt"

I was now open to questions.

I told them I favored the international monetary program that had been sent to Congress by President Roosevelt, and that I favored the Reciprocal Trade Agreements program as well.

A question was asked about an appointment, and I replied that I was not prepared to discuss appointments as yet.

I was asked what I thought of the proposed Missouri Valley Authority, and I referred my questioner to a speech I had given on the subject. I was asked how I stood on the Fair Employment Practices Act, the right to vote without being hampered by poll taxes, and other matters that were of especial interest to Negroes, and I referred my questioner to my Senate record.

"Mr. President," I was asked, "is there any possibility that you will go to the United Nations Conference at San Francisco near the end?"

"There is not," I answered.

"Will you send a message, Mr. President, to the San Francisco conference?" To which I replied, "I shall probably welcome the delegates by an opening statement when they arrive for their first meeting."

"Over the radio?"

"Yes."

"Could you tell us, Mr. President, some of the considerations that led to your decision not to go to San Francisco?"

I answered, "I have a competent delegation going to San Francisco to negotiate and represent the interests of the United States. I shall back them up from this desk right here—where I belong."

"Do you expect to see Mr. Molotov," I was asked, "before he goes to San Francisco?"

"Yes," I replied. "He is going to stop by and pay his respects to the President of the United States. He should."

"Mr. President, do you have a desire, as soon as possible, to meet the other Allied leaders—Marshal Stalin and Prime Minister Churchill?"

"I should be very happy to meet them," I said, "and General Chiang Kai-shek also. And General de Gaulle; if he wants to see me I will be glad to see him. I would like to meet all of the Allied heads of governments."

Other questions followed, usually unrelated questions that forced my mind to leap in many directions.

Would Mrs. Truman have a press conference?

Did I intend to lift the ban on horse racing?

What were my views on the disposal of synthetic-rubber plants?

What about my Cabinet?

What about a rumor that Stalin had reached an agreement "with the new Polish government approved by the United States and Great Britain"?

Some of these I refused to discuss. Some I answered. Some I merely put off to a more appropriate time. And finally I heard the signal that always ends these conferences: "Thank you, Mr. President."

I kept my calendar of appointments clear that afternoon so as to devote my time to handling many administrative matters that had been accumulating.

Russian Foreign Minister Molotov, French Foreign Minister Bidault, Sergio Osmeña, President of the Philippines, and T. V. Soong, Foreign Minister of China—all were due for special talks at the White House in the next few days.

A cable from Ambassador Harriman had just informed me that Molotov was leaving Moscow that very day, going by a Soviet route across the Pacific. He would therefore take two days longer to get to Washington than if he had flown across the Atlantic. Harriman himself, coming by the shorter route, was due the next day with a report on his last talk with Stalin and a report on his talks with Molotov's deputy, Vishinsky.

His cable informed me that Vishinsky had told him that there was "a great public demand" for the conclusion of a Soviet-Polish treaty of mutual assistance and that one was now being prepared. Harriman, in reply, had properly cautioned Vishinsky that the world might interpret the signing of such a treaty, before the formation of a new Polish government, as an indication that Russia did not intend to carry out the Yalta agreements. Vishinsky, in what was typical Russian fashion, argued the necessity of such a treaty and maintained that the Crimea decisions did not preclude its negotiation.

I was disturbed. This was another Russian maneuver aimed at getting their own way in Poland, and I made up my mind that I would lay it on the line with Molotov. At the same time I directed the State Department to register a protest in Moscow.

The department advised me later that our Embassy at Moscow was instructed to inform Vishinsky that the American government was much disturbed over the indications that the Soviet government was considering the conclusion of a treaty of mutual assistance with the governmental authorities then functioning in Poland. It was also instructed to request Vishinsky to defer action in this matter until the subject could be discussed with Molotov during his coming visit to me. I was advised later by the State Department that the British government was sending similar instructions to the British Embassy in Moscow.

Russia was being arbitrary about Poland and was arbitrary about Bulgaria as well. The Secretary of State informed me that the American suggestion for tripartite supervision of Bulgarian elections, in order to ensure that they would be democratically conducted in accordance with the Yalta decision, had been rejected by Russia. The Soviet government declared that "foreign interference" in the holding of these elections was not needed. The Russians argued that there was no such "interference" in the recent Finnish elections and that Bulgaria deserved no greater mistrust than Finland.

A few hours after my first press conference was held, I went for the first time to the super-secret Map Room in the White House. Very few of the White House staff had access to this carefully guarded room, and very little was ever said about it. I had first learned that it existed after I became Vice-President, when President Roosevelt sent me the following memorandum as he was getting ready to leave for Yalta:

January 28, 1945

HIGHLY CONFIDENTIAL
Memorandum for the Vice President:
   If you have any urgent messages which you wish to get to me, I suggest you send them through the White House Map Room. However, only *absolutely urgent* messages should be sent via the Map Room. May I ask that you make them as brief as possible in order not to tie up communications. If you have very lengthy messages the Map Room officer will have to exercise his discretion as to whether it is physically possible to send them by radio or whether they will have to be sent by pouch.

F. D. R.

The Map Room was planned by President Roosevelt and was located on the ground floor of the White House, directly across the hallway from the elevator. Every morning Roosevelt would come down in the elevator from his living quarters and go to this closely guarded room.

It was lined with a map of the world and maps on larger scales of Europe and Asia, on which were outlined the locations of all major military forces in the world. Detailed maps showed the battle lines everywhere, and from the center of the room it was possible to see at a glance the whole military situation. It was an immensely important intelligence center. There had been nothing like it in the First World War. This was the first global war that had ever been fought with fronts on every ocean and every continent.

Changes in the battle situation were immediately marked on the Map Room maps as messages came in from commanders in the field. Messages came constantly throughout the day and night, so that our military picture was always accurate up to the moment. I frequently met our top military leaders in this room and went over in detail the situation on each front.

So accurate and complete was the information that was gathered together here that the Map Room became the very heart of all the military information necessary to conduct this global war. It played an important part in co-ordinating the decisions of the Allied forces. And certainly it helped me quickly to visualize the world situation and to grasp the basic military strategy.

By a special communications system and by means of special devices set up in this room Churchill and I were able to telephone each other in complete security. These conversations were transcribed and kept as part of the diplomatic record for future reference.

It was at ten o'clock that night—the sixth evening since I had become President—that I addressed our armed forces throughout the world.

"All of us have lost a great leader, a farsighted statesman, and a real friend of democracy," I told them over the radio. "Our hearts are heavy. However, the cause which claimed Roosevelt also claims us. He never faltered . . . nor will we. . . . I have done as you do in the field, when the commander falls. My duties and responsibilities are clear. I have assumed them. Those duties will be carried on in keeping with our American tradition. . . . As a veteran of the First World War I have seen death on the battlefield. . . . I know the strain, the mud, the misery, the utter weariness of the soldier in the field. And I know, too, his courage, his stamina, and his faith in his comrades, his country, and himself. We are depending upon each and every one of you."

I closed with a quotation from Lincoln, now engraved in all our hearts: "With malice toward none; with charity for all; with firmness in the right, as God gives us to see the right, let us strive on to finish the work we are in. . . ."

CHAPTER 5

I felt as if I had lived five lifetimes in my first five days as President. I was beginning to realize how little the Founding Fathers had been able to anticipate the preparations necessary for a man to become President so suddenly. It is a mighty leap from the vice-presidency to the presidency when one is forced to make it without warning.

Under the present system a Vice-President cannot equip himself to become President merely by virtue of being second in rank. Ideally, he should be equipped for the presidency at the time he is elected as Vice-President. The voters, instead of considering a vice-presidential candidate as a sort of appendage to the presidency, should select him as a spare Chief Executive. As such he should be kept fully informed of all the major business transacted by the President.

I had spent a great deal of time reading the history of past administrations, and because of this, when I became Vice-President, I was familiar with the incongruities and inadequacies of that office.

John Tyler was the first Vice-President to succeed to the presidency as the result of the death of the Chief Executive. Tyler's brother was the father of my great-grandmother, and the whole Tyler family is mixed up with both sides of my father's family. I never held a high opinion of John Tyler, although he did bring Texas into the Union. It was he who established the precedent that when a Vice-President succeeds as Chief Executive he becomes President in fact and not merely an acting President.

I could now appreciate how Tyler had felt on finding himself suddenly catapulted into the nation's highest office. It takes some time for a man to adjust himself to such an overwhelming responsibility. In my own case it was not until nearly five months later, when I delivered my first policy message to Congress on September 6—a message in which I outlined a twenty-one-point program for postwar recovery and readjustment—that I realized to what extent I had assumed the full responsibility of the presidency in my own right.

No Vice-President is every properly prepared to take over the presidency because of the nature of our presidential, or executive, office. The President is the man who decides every major domestic policy, and he is the man who makes foreign policy and negotiates treaties. In doing these things it would be very difficult for him to take the second man in the government—the Vice-President—completely into his confidence. The President, by necessity, builds his own staff, and the Vice-President remains an outsider, no matter how friendly the two may be. There are many reasons for this, but an important one is the fact that both the President and Vice-President are, or should be, astute politicians, and neither can take the other completely into his confidence.

The Vice-President, as President of the Senate, associates continually with the shrewdest politicians in the country, and this is also true of the Speaker of the House. Members of the House and Senate have to be politicians in order to be elected. The President cannot afford to have his confidential matters discussed in Senate cloakrooms. A leak from the White House to the senators and representatives is always worth a headline, and that compels a President always to be on guard when he is being interviewed by members of Congress. That is also one of the reasons why it is very difficult for a President to take the Vice-President completely into his confidence.

Such a possible leak, every President realizes, need not be the result of an intentional act on the part of the Vice-President. But an unintentional leak can be as harmful as an intentional one and, conceivably, might upset the whole program on which a President is working. Matters such as this may be of great importance, and they should be weighed in any analysis of the relationship between the President and the Vice-President.

This relationship is not, and was not designed to be, similar to that which surrounded the consuls in ancient Rome. There were two equally powerful consuls, and they were hardly ever in agreement. Hannibal was successful against Rome very largely because of the rivalry between the consuls. Under our system there is no rivalry between the President and the Vice-President.

But very few Vice-Presidents have been in complete agreement with the policies of the presidents with whom they have served. The fact that both the President and the Vice-President are nominated and elected makes for a formal relationship despite appearances between the two. Woodrow Wilson fell out with Vice-President Marshall in 1917–18. In Harding's administration Coolidge was Vice-President, and I believe there was little warm feeling between them. When Coolidge was elected President, he had Charles G. Dawes as Vice-President, and the two were not close. After Hoover was elected President, he and Vice-President Curtis were not very congenial.

Franklin D. Roosevelt renewed the practice of arranging for a Vice-President to sit with him in the Cabinet. John Nance Garner attended all Cabinet meetings, but Garner's philosophy of government was not in line with Mr. Roosevelt's program to deal with the depression. After two terms the President decided he wanted a different vice-presidential candidate as his running mate, and he chose Henry Wallace. From the time he was inaugurated, Wallace sat with the President in Cabinet meetings, but the President was not very happy over the result, and many of his political friends helped persuade him that Wallace should not be considered for another term.

The presence of the Vice-President at Cabinet meetings is necessarily an informal arrangement. Actually he attends such meetings only by invitation of the President. In my eighty-two days as Vice-President only a few Cabinet meetings were held, for the President was abroad the greater part of the time or at Warm Springs. I attended when meetings were called, but I soon learned that little of real importance was discussed, for Franklin Roosevelt usually had conferences with individual members of the Cabinet before and after the meetings, and it was then that detailed discussions usually took place.

My approach was different. I had each member of the Cabinet lay important matters before the Cabinet as a whole, and each person present was given an opportunity to discuss the subjects that were under consideration and to give his views. Under Roosevelt the Cabinet meetings were rather formal affairs. At the few I attended there was no exchange of views in round-table fashion, and there was no "on-the-table" discussion of matters that were pending. I rarely said anything, and when I spoke at all it was only in answer to questions put to me by the President in relation to legislative matters on which he wanted help. It was customary for Cabinet members to see the President before these meetings or to sit around afterward and talk with him. At these times there were usually three or four waiting their turn. The President's physical handicap, of course, kept him in his chair until they left, and it seemed to me they took advantage of it.

I believe Roosevelt took a great deal of pleasure in getting one member of the Cabinet to argue against another and in then hearing what they had to say. I watched him do it. He would beam when Ickes jumped on Hopkins, or Hopkins on Ickes. He sometimes seemed amused when Morgenthau raised mischief with the Secretary of State on how he was handling things. Roosevelt often made a game of it, but he never lost sight of the objective he had in view, which was to win the war and then make a peace program that would work.

Roosevelt had a lot of fun while he was President. He could not get around very well, and it would stimulate him to watch others match wits.

As Vice-President I also went to the White House for the President's meetings with the so-called "Big Four." These were usually arranged for Monday mornings, but there were only a few such meetings. The "Big Four" is the term we applied to a group made up of the Vice-President, the Speaker of the House, the majority leader of the House, and the majority leader of the Senate, and at these meetings with the President we discussed a wide assortment of subjects. Domestic and foreign problems of many kinds came up for discussion, and the President would tell us what sort of legislation he was interested in. I felt these meetings to be of value, and I continued them in somewhat enlarged form during my administration.

Roosevelt preferred to go to the Map Room alone to be "briefed." I usually had the Chiefs of Staff outline the ever-changing military situation for the Cabinet members and the Big Four. In this way I kept every Cabinet member informed as to what was going on at all times. The Big Four, each time we met, gave me an outline of what was pending and suggested the proper approach in order to get things done in Congress.

When I had been in the Senate and was serving as chairman of the Committee to Investigate the Defense Program, I had been in the habit of seeing the President at least once a week, and more often if he thought it necessary, about matters that came before the committee. Many of these visits were off the record, and that was also true when I had meetings with General Marshall, Secretary of War Stimson, and other leaders. In this way I came to know all these remarkable men very well. My relations with Roosevelt were such that I considered myself his friend.

My association with him was close and cordial and interesting, and there was no change when I became Vice-President. I had been elected to the Senate in 1934 on a platform that called for support of the President and his policies, and I never failed to live up to that promise. That, I believe, is one of the reasons he decided to make his 1944 statement to the Democratic leaders in Chicago's Blackstone Hotel which resulted in my becoming Vice-President.

Henry Wallace in 1940 and I in 1944 were nominated as vice-presidential candidates because President Roosevelt wanted it that way. It is also true that Garner had been nominated because Roosevelt wanted him. I know that Barkley was nominated in 1948 because he was one of the two men I favored.

The relationship between the President and the Vice-President is complicated, and it is complicated further by the fact that the Vice-President is in between the legislative and the executive branches of the government without, in the last analysis, being responsible to either. The Vice-President cannot become completely acquainted with the policies of the President, while the senators, for their part, look on him as a presiding officer only, who is outside the pale as far as the senatorial club is concerned.

The Vice-President is hardly ever seriously consulted by the Senate in legislative matters, except perhaps in cases where he has technical or special knowledge. He is almost certain to find that the majority and the minority leaders are always kind and friendly, but he is a sort of fifth wheel in the eyes of the Senate. He can push the President's policies if he is well liked by the Senate, for its members will listen to him. And when it comes to a tie vote, he has his say, but that does not happen often—once in a term, perhaps, but rarely oftener than that.

The Vice-President, on the other hand, may have considerable status as a party member. He is considered as the No. 2 man in the party setup, and this may—or may not—give him influence in the Senate. It depends upon the man. If the senators find him likable, he has considerable influence, and this was true of Garner and Barkley, both of whom were outstanding vice-presidents. If he is not liked or is not familiar with politics or with the Senate approach to things, he is left on the outside. Wallace, as an example, and for these reasons, among others, had very little influence with the Senate. Barkley, as Vice-President, was in a class by himself. He had the complete confidence of both the President and the Senate. He had been majority leader longer than any other senator in the history of the Senate. He and I were personally very close, and he was in complete agreement with the policies and platform of the 1948 convention.

On the sixth morning of my presidency—that is, on April 18—a group of leading Republican senators, headed by Senator Robert A. Taft of Ohio, called on me. After I had delivered my message to Congress, I had invited them to come and talk to me about the general situation. They were cordial and kind at this meeting, and we talked about the manner in which we were carrying on the war.

"Speaking for the Republicans," Senator Taft remarked, "we would be glad to be called in from time to time, and we think it would be useful to you if we were briefed."

I replied that I would be glad to do as he suggested. I always found Senator Taft to be a highly ethical, straightforward, and honorable man. I held him in the highest respect. He was a man of his word, and whenever he told me that he was satisfied to go along with me, I always knew he would. From my point of view, of course, he was a violent partisan, and I disagreed with him strongly on what the role of government was in relation to the people. Nevertheless, he was an important member of the Senate who represented and spoke for his side vigorously and ably.

He was the son of a Republican president and was shrewdly able to use this fact to advantage in exploiting the Republican viewpoint. He had a sense of dynasty. Like John Quincy Adams and Benjamin Harrison, he wanted to keep the presidency in the family.

When this group of Republican senators had left, I sent for Harold Smith, Director of the Budget. The federal budget is a most intricate and complicated matter, and I had to learn how the federal income was keeping up with expenditures and what the size of the deficit was going to be.

I felt that it was important for me to get into the business side of the government quickly, because many problems touching on our commitments at home and abroad were coming up for review. I had served on the military appropriations subcommittee of the Senate and thus had had an opportunity to study the present budget—a fact which was very helpful to me now.

I had a high opinion of Harold Smith, as most of the members of Congress did. He was an efficient and honest public servant. There was some feeling—and this was also true of all other heads of important government agencies—that Smith was inclined to get into policy-making, but if that was the case, I certainly had no difficulty with him on that score.

As soon as Director Smith came in I touched on some of the problems of the Executive.

"You probably know these problems," I remarked, "better than anyone else around."

My remark seemed to reassure him. Nevertheless, he appeared to have something on his mind that he wanted to resolve before getting down to business. I sensed what it was.

"I know what is on your mind," I told him, "and I am going to beat you to it. I want you to stay. You have done a good job as Director of the Budget, and we have always thought well of you on the Hill. I have a tremendous responsibility, and I want you to help me."

His response was characteristic of the man.

"You can count on me, Mr. President. I will stay for the duration. But may I point out that the Office of the Budget Director has become an arm of the President, and it calls for frequent contact and confidential relations with the President. I believe you ought to have a man who would act as your personal right arm."

"I know how important to the Chief Executive the Director of the Budget is," I replied. "There is not a single problem that arises that does not involve some question of appropriation or personnel. If I ever want another director of the budget, you will be the first to know about it. That is the way I do business."

Smith appeared to have something else he wanted to get off his mind. It seemed to him, he told me, that, as Budget Director, he was always bringing troubles and bad news to the attention of the President. For the last budget, he said, President Roosevelt had given him a complete delegation of authority because he needed every moment he could spare to deal with international affairs and the conduct of the war. Smith supposed that this delegation of authority might now be withdrawn.

I argeed. I pointed out that, since the budget involved matters of the highest policy, authority should properly be exercised by the President.

He pointed out that the work on the budget would involve a good deal of time with me, probably two sessions a week, and I agreed to such an arrangement. In fact, I made it clear that I would like it, for I had long been accustomed to dealing with facts and figures. I fully intended to plunge deeply into the business of government, and the budget meetings he had suggested would provide a good opportunity.

We then got down to specific matters.

In view of the close approach of V-E Day, we discussed a number of changes in the 1946 budget, and I asked that the Bureau prepare revised estimates for early submission to congressional committees. I also suggested that he discuss these revisions with the Secretaries of War and Navy and with General Marshall.

My morning had been well filled by the time Smith left, but now, at 11:15 A.M., I met with Secretary of State Stettinius, Secretary of War Stimson, and Secretary of the Navy Forrestal.

First I instructed them to confer on all matters affecting political and military problems in war areas, and next they submitted to me a memorandum on the subject of trusteeships of liberated territories, recommending that I issue a directive on the subject to the chairman of the American delegation at San Francisco. Already the terms of this directive had been discussed with the members of the delegation and had their approval. It only remained for me to issue the necessary instructions in connection with it. Since its terms were in keeping with American policy to foster the advancement of social, economic, and political welfare of the civilian populations in the territories affected, I approved the directive, which read as follows:

Statement of *Recommended Policy on Trusteeship*
It is not proposed at San Francisco to determine the placing of any particular territory under a trusteeship system. All that will be discussed there will be the possible machinery of such a system.

The United States Government considers that it would be entirely practicable to devise a trusteeship system which would apply only to such territories in the following categories as may, by trusteeship arrangements, be placed thereunder, namely: (a) territories now held under mandate; (b) territories which may be detached from enemy states as a result of this war; and (c) territories voluntarily placed under the system by states responsible for their administration. It shall be a matter for subsequent agreement as to which of the specific territories within the foregoing categories shall be brought under the trusteeship system and upon what terms.

This system would provide, by agreements, for (1) the maintenance of United States military and strategic rights, (2) such control as will be necessary to assure general peace and security in the Pacific Ocean area as well as elsewhere in the world, and (3) the advancement of the social, economic, and political welfare of the inhabitants of the dependent territories.

With this matter off my hands, and with the secretaries gone, I signed the Mexican Water Treaty. By way of this treaty the United States and Mexico joined hands in a constructive, businesslike program to apportion between them and develop to their mutual advantage the waters of our common rivers.

I had presided over the Senate at the time this bill was debated. As a matter of fact, it was the very last business in the Senate in which I took part as Vice-President, and I was glad to sign it as evidence of our continued good-neighbor policy.

I had been pleased and relieved to have Steve Early, Bill Hassett, Jonathan Daniels, and Judge Rosenman offer to stay on and help me get things organized. I needed their experience in tackling the never-ending flow of paper work. I had also sent for Charles Ross, a former classmate, who was now head of the Washington Bureau of the St. Louis *Post-Dispatch*. It was he who now was ushered in, and I offered him the post of press secretary, a position for which both his personality and his experience well fitted him. He was interested, I knew, but he asked for a little time in which to consider it and said he would talk it over with his publishers.

Difficulties within China and in her relations with the United States, Britain, and Russia were growing daily, and that afternoon I received the following memorandum from the Secretary of State:

April 18, 1945

MEMORANDUM FOR THE PRESIDENT
Subject: *Messages from Ambassador Hurley*

I am transmitting to you herewith copies of two messages from Ambassador Hurley, one from Teheran and one from Moscow, reporting on his conversations with Churchill and Eden and with Stalin and Molotov pursuant to his instructions from President Roosevelt to discuss with the Chiefs of the British and Soviet Governments our policy toward China.

Churchill and Eden agreed to support American efforts for the unification of all military forces in China in the prosecution of the war against Japan and for the establishment of free united democratic government in China. Churchill, however, branded the American long range policy toward China as "the great American illusion," disapproved the withdrawal of U.S. resources in Burma and India for the stabilization of our military position in China, declared in reference to Hong Kong that the British Empire would give up nothing and took the view that Britain is not bound by the principles of the Atlantic Charter.

Stalin and Molotov stated that they wish closer and more harmonious relations with China, that they do not desire civil war in China and that they are not supporting the Chinese Communist Party. They spoke favorably of Chiang Kai-shek and said that they would support the U.S. policy in regard to the unification of the armed forces of China and to the establishment of a free unified democratic government in China.

E. R. Stettinius, Jr.

The two messages from Hurley, who was our Ambassador to China, were attached. The mission on which he was now reporting had been a personal one for President Roosevelt, and in view of the President's death I instructed Hurley to carry it out before resuming his post in Chungking.

With the war progressing at an ever-accelerated pace, we were now up against the question of zones to be occupied by the principal allies. In this connection Prime Minister Churchill raised several issues in a message that now reached my desk.

"Your armies soon, and presently ours, may come into contact with Soviet forces," Churchill's cable read. "Supreme Commander should be given instruction by Combined Chiefs of Staff as soon as possible how to act."

In his view, Churchill said, there were two zones:

(1) A tactical zone in which our troops should stand on the lines they had reached unless there was agreement for a better tactical deployment against continuing resistance of the enemy. This should be arranged by the supreme commander through the military missions in Moscow or, if convenient, across the line in the field. The Combined Chiefs of Staff had already taken up the issue of instructions to cover this phase.

(2) An occupational zone on which Churchill said he had agreed with President Roosevelt on the advice of the Combined General Staffs. In his view, this zone should be occupied within a certain time from V-E Day, "whenever this is declared, and we should retire with dignity from the much greater gains which the Allied troops have acquired by their audacity and vigour.

"I am quite prepared to adhere to Occupational Zones. But I do not wish our Allied troops or your American troops to be hustled back at any point by some crude assertion of a local Russian general." This, Churchill said, had to be provided against by an agreement between the governments so as to give Eisenhower a fair chance to settle on the spot "in his own admirable way."

The occupational zones, Churchill declared, were outlined "rather hastily at Quebec in September, 1944, when it was not foreseen that General Eisenhower's armies would make such a mighty inroad into Germany." The zones, he added, could not be altered except by agreement with the Russians. But he suggested we should try to set up an Allied Control Commission in Berlin the moment V-E Day occurred, and should insist upon a fair distribution of food produced in Germany between East and West Germany. As it stood, Churchill said, the Russian occupational zone had the smallest proportion of people and grew by far the largest proportion of food, adding: "The Americans have a not very satisfactory proportion of food to feed conquered populations. And we poor British are to take over all the ruined Ruhr and large manufacturing districts, which are, like ours, in normal times large importers of food. I suggest that this tiresome question should be settled in Berlin by A.C.C. before we move from tactical position we have at present achieved. The Russian idea of taking these immense food supplies out of food producing areas of Germany to feed themselves is very natural. But I contend that feeding the German population must be treated as a whole and that available supplies must be divided *pro rata* between the occupational troops.

"I should be most grateful if you would let me have your views on these points, which from information I receive from many sources are of highest consequence and urgency."

I did not wish to reply without further study and the advice of the Chiefs of Staff.

Another full day was coming to a close, and I gathered together the papers I needed to take with me. The signal to the Secret Service guards sounded as I left the office, and with them following along I once more walked to Blair House. This time, however, the regular traffic signals operated undisturbed, and I waited my turn to cross.

I worked that evening, as usual, but before I went to bed I wrote another letter to my mother and sister.

Dear Mama & Mary, Well, the Washington Post had your pictures yesterday morning and the finest kind of statements from both you and Vivian. My Press Staff said that the smartest press agent in the world could not have written any better ones. I told them that my family all told the truth all the time and that they did not need a press agent.

I have had a most strenuous time for the last six days. I was sworn in at 7:09 P.M. Eastern War Time Apr. 12, and it is now 9 P.M. April 18th. Six days President of the United States! It is hardly believable.

Before I was sworn in, I had to make two decisions of world-wide import—to carry on the war and to let the Peace Conference go ahead at San Francisco. Saturday and Sunday were spent on the last rites for the departed President. Monday, the Congress had to be told what I would do. It took all Sunday afternoon, half the night and until 11 A.M. Monday to get the job done on the speech. But I guess there was inspiration in it for it took Congress and the country by storm, apparently. Spent Monday afternoon seeing people and making all sorts of decisions, everyone of which would touch millions of people. Tuesday morning all the reporters in town and a lot more came to cross question me. They gave me a pretty hefty fifteen minutes, but even that ordeal seemed to click.

Had to spend all afternoon and evening preparing a five minute speech for the radio for the fighting men and women. It was after one o'clock when I turned in. This day has been a dinger too. I'm about to go to bed, but I thought I'd better write you a note. Hope you are both well.

Lots of love,

Harry

CHAPTER 6

My appointment calendar for Thursday, April 19, was crowded. Senator Taft was my first visitor. He called for a personal chat during which he renewed his pledge of co-operation. Then followed a number of unofficial visitors whom a President has to see, because part of his duties are to receive citizens, leaders and spokesmen of representative organizations. These visits are valuable to the President, for they help him keep in touch with the cross section of American interests and opinion.

I like people. I like to see them and hear what they have to say. But seeing people takes time and effort. It is more than a mere ceremonial duty, and although it is a heavy burden on the President, he cannot share it with anyone, for in the White House he is the only directly elected representative of all the people.

On this particular morning, when these visits had been completed, I met with the Big Four for the first time in my new capacity. Senator McKellar, as President pro tempore of the Senate, occupied the place in this group that had formerly been mine, but otherwise its members remained the same and included Senate Majority Leader Barkley, Speaker Sam Rayburn, and House Majority Leader John W. McCormack.

At this first meeting I gave them the latest information on the war and diplomatic fronts and outlined the need for revisions in the federal budget now that we were approaching the end of the European war.

At eleven-thirty I met for half an hour with General George Marshall, Chief of Staff of the Army, in order to review the rapid developments that were taking place on the European front. I discussed with him the draft of a message I proposed to issue following the meeting of the British, American, and Russian armies in Germany, and when we had gone over it I cabled it to the British Prime Minister, from whom a related message had just arrived.

The following quoted message [my cable to Churchill read] is a preliminary draft of the message which I propose to issue following the meeting of the Anglo American and Soviet Armies in Germany at a date and time that will be agreed upon by the three of us.

I will be very pleased to receive any comments and suggestions that you may wish to make.

QUOTE. The Anglo American armies under the command of General Eisenhower have met the Soviet forces where they intended to meet—in the heart of Nazi Germany. The enemy has been cut in two.

This is not the hour of final victory in Europe, but the hour draws near, the hour for which all the American people, all the British people and all the Soviet people have toiled and prayed so long.

The union of our arms in the heart of Germany has a meaning for the world which the world will not miss. It means, *first,* that the last faint, desperate hope of Hitler and his gangster government has been extinguished. The common front and the common cause of the powers allied in this war against tyranny and inhumanity have been demonstrated in fact as they have long been demonstrated in determination. Nothing can divide or weaken the common purpose of our veteran armies to pursue their victorious purpose to its final allied triumph in Germany.

Second, the junction of our forces at this moment signalizes to ourselves and to the world that the collaboration of our nations in the cause of peace and freedom is an effective collaboration which can surmount the greatest difficulties of the most extensive campaign in military history and succeed. Nations which can plan and fight together shoulder to shoulder in the face of such obstacles of distance and of language and of communications as we have overcome, can live together and can work together in the common labor of the organization of the world for peace.

Finally, this great triumph of Allied arms and Allied strategy is such a tribute to the courage and determination of Franklin Roosevelt as no words could ever speak, and that could be accomplished only by the persistence and the courage of the fighting soldiers and sailors of the Allied nations.

But, until our enemies are finally subdued in Europe and in the Pacific, there must be no relaxation of effort on the home front in support of our heroic soldiers and sailors as we all know there will be no pause on the battle fronts. UNQUOTE.

With these matters attended to, General Marshall left, and next I saw His Excellency Huseyin Ragip Baydur, the Turkish Ambassador, and Dr. Charles Malik, the Minister of Lebanon, both of whom came in to pay their respects.

It was now noon and time to receive Sergio Osmeña, President of the Philippines. It was a pleasure for me to greet President Osmeña, as I am sure it was for Secretaries Stettinius, Stimson, Forrestal, and Ickes, who joined us. The war in the Pacific was going well, and though the Philippines had suffered terribly as a result of the Japanese invasion, our forces had now returned to the islands, which had been very largely freed. Osmeña, however, was concerned about the postwar period. He brought up the urgent need that the people of the Philippines would have to rebuild their war-devastated land, and he wanted to know what American assistance they might expect. I told him that America would not fail them. We had promised freedom and independence to the Philippines. I assured President Osmeña that I would ask Congress for generous aid to help reconstruction in the Philippines.

The Secretaries of State, War, and Navy remained with me when President Osmeña departed, and I next received T. V. Soong, Foreign Minister of China, who informed me that after he attended the San Francisco conference he would be on his way to Moscow to conclude a treaty of trade and mutual assistance with Russia.

I expressed the hope that China and Russia could reach an agreement satisfactory to both countries. I told the Chinese Foreign Minister that the United States wanted to see China emerge strong and prosperous from this war and to become a leading power in Asia. I therefore urged him to go to Moscow as soon as he could so that relations between China and Russia could be established on a firmer basis in the interest of organizing the peace of the world.

Soong said he had something else on his mind. He said China wanted more help from us. We already were giving Chiang Kai-shek substantial help, but Soong now pleaded for increased shipments of gold. Inflation, I knew, had been added to China's other problems. I told Soong I would do all I could.

There was one more visitor. Foreign Minister Georges Bidault of France, who, with Henri Bonnet, the French Ambassador, was now brought in. Bidault was on his way to the San Francisco conference and had come in for a brief visit to pay his respects, bringing greetings from General de Gaulle and expressing the sorrow of the French people over the news of President Roosevelt's death.

I told Mr. Bidault how much I appreciated the word he brought and in what high esteem the American people and I myself held the French Republic. Having made their courtesy call, they left, and it was now time to go to lunch.

As a relief from official duties I had asked my brother Vivian, as well as Fred Canfil and Ted Sanders, to join me at lunch. Canfil was United States Marshal for the Western District of Missouri, and Sanders was a Democratic leader in that state. I spent as much time as I could with them after lunch, listening to the news from home. This gave me a break and a change, and I went back to work refreshed.

There were many others whom I saw that day. Robert E. Hannegan, chairman of the Democratic National Committee, was one, and the Reverend Dr. Frederick Brown Harris, chaplain of the Senate, was another. Now and again I was photographed with some of my callers on the terrace behind the presidential offices—once with twenty-two military legal officers from thirteen South and Central American countries, all of whom had been attending law conferences in the United States.

At the end of appointments for the day I turned to the accumulated papers that demanded my attention. There were many documents to sign, a bill to veto, reports and messages and diplomatic cables to be read. When I was ready to make my way across Pennsylvania Avenue to Blair House, I again found it necessary—as I did from then on—to take with me another accumulation of papers.

On the morning of April 20 I found that I was faced with what I was told was the longest list of scheduled callers in the memory of any member of the executive office staff. As yet the Secret Service had not succeeded in convincing me that I should permit myself to be driven in one of the big White House cars from Blair House to the executive offices, and, with my usual Secret Service guards, I had walked across the street that morning. I had made only a little dent in the work that faced me when the time for my first appointment arrived.

Not many weeks before, during the battle for Iwo Jima, Joe Rosenthal, an Associated Press photographer, had taken his inspired photograph of the American flag being raised on Mount Suribachi. Never before, perhaps, had any photograph been so enthusiastically received, and now, with the Seventh War Loan campaign about to begin, Secretary Morgenthau was to bring, as a gift to me, a painting made from that photograph for use as a War Loan campaign poster. In addition, he was to bring with him, for presentation to me, three of the surviving marines portrayed in that picture—Pfc. Rene A. Gagnon of Manchester, New Hampshire, Pharmacist's Mate John H. Bradley of Appleton, Wisconsin, and Pfc. Ira Hayes of the Pima Indian Reservation in Arizona.

The ceremony was a simple one and took but little time. I gladly accepted the painting and commended the three survivors. I told them the spirit they had displayed had been caught by the photographer and typified the greatness of those who wore their country's uniform.

When it was over I asked Secretary Morgenthau to stay. He reported to me on the current situation with regard to the financing of the war, as well as on the many other operations conducted by the Treasury. Our expenditures for the current fiscal year, he told me, were estimated at ninety-nine billion dollars, of which eighty-eight billion had been set aside for war activities. Our receipts, on the other hand, had been estimated at only forty-six billion, or less than half of the total that was being spent.

The Secretary also reported on the plans of the Treasury to wage an extensive nationwide campaign against tax evaders and black-market operations. He described for me in detail how vigilant the Treasury Department had been in this respect.

I knew that the resources of the United States were under enormous pressure, not only because of the direct costs of the war, but also because of the many requests other nations were making on us. The Secretary reported on the most important of these.

China, Morgenthau said, wanted "greatly enlarged gold shipments" because of severe inflation.

Great Britain wanted to dispatch a financial mission to the United States immediately after V-E Day to discuss the whole question of financial assistance to the United Kingdom. They were more worried about their postwar international position, the Secretary told me, than about almost any other subject.

France was sending its Finance Minister to discuss the financial side of their reconstruction problem.

The Mexican Finance Minister was asking for assurances that we would continue the stabilization agreement under which they were operating.

Cuba wanted to know whether we wished to extend our gold-sale agreement for another four years.

The Indian government had requested that we lend-lease them an additional 210,000,000 ounces of silver, although the Secretary pointed out that there was some question as to whether they needed so large a quantity for anti-inflation purposes.

The Secretary concluded his report with a summary of enemy assets in the United States and in neutral countries, and of the future of Lend-Lease.

Edward Scheiberling, national commander of the American Legion, followed Morgenthau to discuss veterans' problems.

Shortly before noon, Dr. Stephen S. Wise, chairman of the American Zionist Emergency Council, came in to talk to me about the Jewish victims of Nazi persecution and the serious problem of the resettlement of the refugees, which led naturally to a discussion of a proposed Jewish state and homeland in Palestine.

I had before me President Roosevelt's records and statements regarding Palestine. And the Secretary of State had sent me a special communication two days before, expressing the attitude and the thinking of the State Department on Palestine.

"It is very likely," this communication read, "that efforts will be made by some of the Zionist leaders to obtain from you at an early date some commitments in favor of the Zionist program which is pressing for unlimited Jewish immigration into Palestine and the establishment there of a Jewish state. As you are aware, the Government and people of the United States have every sympathy for the persecuted Jews of Europe and are doing all in their power to relieve their suffering. The question of Palestine is, however, a highly complex one and involves questions which go far beyond the plight of the Jews in Europe.

"There is continual tenseness in the situation in the Near East," the communication concluded, "largely as a result of the Palestine question, and as we have interests in that area which are vital to the United States, we feel that this whole subject is one that should be handled with the greatest care and with a view to the long-range interests of the country."

Since I was in agreement with the expressed policy of the Roosevelt administration on Palestine, I told Rabbi Wise that I would do everything possible to carry out that policy. I had carefully read the Balfour Declaration, in which Great Britain was committed to a homeland in Palestine for the Jews. I had familiarized myself with the history of the question of a Jewish homeland and the position of the British and the Arabs. I was skeptical, as I read over the whole record up to date, about some of the views and attitudes assumed by the "striped-pants boys" in the State Department. It seemed to me that they didn't care enough about what happened to the thousands of displaced persons who were involved. It was my feeling that it would be possible for us to watch out for the long-range interests of our country while at the same time helping these unfortunate victims of persecution to find a home. And before Rabbi Wise left, I believe I made this clear to him.

From time to time throughout that morning, and also after lunch, I received individual senators and congressmen who came to pay their respects and to renew their personal friendship. I welcomed each one who came and hoped I would be able to find time soon to visit with every one of my former colleagues of both parties. But in the midst of this I found it necessary to cable Prime Minister Churchill, informing him that it would be impracticable for me to broadcast the joint "linking-up message" we had planned. "I therefore propose to issue it," I told him, "as a statement from me to the press and radio for release on the date and hour that is agreed upon. Since I have had no communication on this subject with Marshal Stalin will you be kind enough to transmit this information to him."

The impossibility, because of mechanical complications, of putting Moscow, London, and Washington on a radio hookup at the same time had ruled out simultaneous broadcasts, and I took this method of suggesting that each of us should issue a statement instead.

Sometime during that busy morning I received a message from Prime Minister Churchill in response to my message of six days before in which I had suggested closer co-operation by Admiral Mountbatten, supreme commander of Allied forces in Southeast Asia, with Generalissimo Chiang Kai-shek, commander of the China Theater.

"We are willing," Churchill's message read, "to give full and fair trial to the arrangements you have been good enough to propose. If difficulties arise I am sure you would wish me to present them to you. Orders have been given in accordance with this message to Admiral Mountbatten."

At the same time another message from the Prime Minister approved the text of the proposed three-power message to be issued when the British, Russian, and American troops met in Germany.

"Thank you," he cabled, "for your draft message on link up. I can think of no improvement. It will do good to the troops to hear it."

At noon I held an important policy meeting on our relations with Soviet Russia. Ambassador Harriman had just returned from his post in Moscow, and with Secretary of State Stettinius, Under Secretary of State Joseph C. Grew, and Charles E. Bohlen, the department's Russian expert, he attended the conference in my office.

I thanked Harriman for the vital service he had performed in connection with inducing Molotov to attend the San Francisco conference. I expressed the hope that he would return to Moscow and continue his excellent work there when the San Francisco conference was over. Then I asked him to tell us what the most urgent problems were in relation to the Soviet Union.

The Soviet Union, Harriman replied, had two policies which they thought they could successfully pursue at the same time. One was the policy of co-operation with the United States and Great Britain, and the second was the extension of Soviet control over neighboring states by independent action. He said that certain elements around Stalin misinterpreted our generosity and our desire to co-operate as an indication of softness, so that the Soviet government could do as it pleased without risking challenge from the United States.

In Harriman's opinion the Soviet government had no wish to break with the United States, because they needed our help in their reconstruction program. He felt, for this reason, we could stand firm on important issues without running serious risks. Harriman outlined a number of specific difficulties which he encountered at his post at Moscow, pointing out the deterioration of the Soviet attitude since the Yalta conference.

At this point I stopped Harriman to say that I was not afraid of the

Russians and that I intended to be firm. I would be fair, of course, and anyway the Russians needed us more than we needed them.

Harriman replied that there were some quarters in Moscow that believed it was a matter of life and death to American business to increase our exports to Russia. He made it clear that he knew this to be untrue but that a number of Russian officials nevertheless believed it. I declared that it was ridiculous for the Russians to think this, and I repeated that we intended to be firm with the Russians and make no concessions from American principles or traditions in order to win their favor. I said that the only way to establish sound relations between Russia and ourselves was on a give-and-take basis.

Ambassador Harriman continued that, in his judgment, we were faced with a "barbarian invasion of Europe." He was convinced that Soviet control over any foreign country meant not only that their influence would be paramount in that country's foreign relations but also that the Soviet system with its secret police and its extinction of freedom of speech would prevail. In his opinion we had to decide what our attitude should be in the face of these unpleasant facts.

He added that he was not pessimistic, for he felt that it was possible for us to arrive at a workable basis with the Russians. He believed that this would require a reconsideration of our policy and the abandonment of any illusion that the Soviet government was likely soon to act in accordance with the principles to which the rest of the world held in international affairs. Harriman observed that obviously in any international negotiations there is give-and-take, and both sides make concessions.

I agreed, saying I understood this and that I would not expect one hundred per cent of what we proposed. But I felt we should be able to get eighty-five per cent.

Harriman then outlined the issues involved in the Polish question. It was his belief that Stalin had discovered that an honest execution of the Crimea decision would mean the end of the Soviet-backed Lublin control over Poland. With this in mind he felt that it was important for us to consider what we should do in the event that Stalin rejected the proposals contained in the joint message Churchill and I had sent, and if Molotov proved adamant in the negotiations here in Washington.

Harriman then asked how important I felt the Polish question to be in relation to the San Francisco conference and our participation in the proposed United Nations Organization.

I replied emphatically that it was my considered opinion that, unless settlement of the Polish question was achieved along the lines of the Crimea decision, the treaty of American adherence to a world organization would not get through the Senate. I said I intended to tell Molotov just that in words of one syllable.

Secretary Stettinius asked if I would want the conversation on Poland to continue in San Francisco if Molotov arrived late in Washington and there was not sufficient time for a full discussion among the British, Russian, and American foreign ministers. I said I hoped it would not interfere with the work of the conference, but he had my approval to proceed that way.

Harriman then asked whether or not we would be disposed to go ahead with the world organization plans even if Russia dropped out.

I replied that the truth of the matter was that without Russia there would not be a world organization.

Before concluding the meeting I said that I was trying to catch all the intricacies of our foreign affairs and that I would look, of course, to the State Department and our ambassadors for information and help.

I ended the meeting by saying, "I intend to be firm in my dealings with the Soviet government," and asked Harriman and Stettinius to see me again before my meeting with Molotov.

Before leaving, Harriman took me aside and said, "Frankly, one of the reasons that made me rush back to Washington was the fear that you did not understand, as I had seen Roosevelt understand, that Stalin is breaking his agreements. My fear was inspired by the fact that you could not have had time to catch up with all the recent cables. But I must say that I am greatly relieved to discover that you have read them all and that we see eye to eye on the situation."

"I am glad," I said, "that you are going to be available to our delegation in San Francisco. And keep on sending me long messages."

I then called a special press conference to announce that I was appointing Charles G. Ross as my press and radio secretary effective May 15.

Charlie was a native of Independence, Missouri, and had been a classmate of mine in the Independence High School in the class of 1901. I informed the White House correspondents that Mr. Joseph Pulitzer, publisher of the St. Louis *Post-Dispatch,* had granted Ross a two-year leave of absence.

Charlie then telephoned from my desk to our former schoolteacher, Miss Tillie Brown, at Independence to tell her about his appointment. Although frail, she became quite excited and in a high voice said, "You and Harry have made good, and I am very proud of you." I got on the phone to say I was reporting to my teacher. She was flustered and had too many kind things to say.

Many foreign missions on their way to attend the San Francisco conference had already arrived in the United States, and most of them were now in Washington. All were busy in the capital preparing for the conference. I had arranged for a reception at Blair House to welcome the heads of the missions. The reception was at four o'clock in the afternoon, and as I greeted them I expressed my pleasure at meeting them. I said that it was my hope that our relationship would continue "on the same cordial plane, nationally and with the world, as it is between you and me."

On the following morning, April 21, I went directly to the Map Room for my daily briefing on the war situation. German resistance was collapsing on all fronts. There was a rumor from Switzerland that Hitler had left Berlin. There could be no doubt that the end of the war in Europe was in sight.

During the morning I met with Secretary Stettinius and handed him a letter of instructions to take with him to San Francisco. We had discussed this matter previously and had decided that it would be helpful if he had such a written directive from me which he could use publicly if necessary.

"My dear Mr. Secretary," these instructions began. "As you are aware, at the Crimean Conference President Roosevelt on behalf of the Government of the United States agreed that at the San Francisco Conference the United States would support a Soviet proposal to admit the Ukrainian Soviet Socialist Republic and the White Russian Soviet Socialist Republic to initial membership in the proposed International Organization.

"You have explained to me that in agreeing to support the proposal of the Soviet Government on this question President Roosevelt felt that the importance of the Ukraine and White Russia among the Soviet Republics and their contribution to the prosecution of the war and the untold devastation and sacrifices which their people have undergone in the cause of the United Nations entitled them to special consideration.

"The decision as to the admission of these two Republics as initial members in the proposed International Organization is of course a matter for the Conference itself to decide. In the loyal execution at the Conference of the obligation assumed on this question by President Roosevelt on behalf of the United States Government, I direct you to cast the vote of the United States in favor of the Ukrainian and White Russian Republics as initial members of the International Organization."

After Secretary Stettinius left, I met with Senator Carl Hatch and then with Ambassador Harriman, who was followed by Fred M. Vinson, the War Mobilization Director. The next appointments were with the heads and assistants of the offices of the White House.

Although it was Saturday and I had already seen him once, Secretary Stettinius personally brought me a memorandum that afternoon.

"Mr. Molotov will arrive this evening and sleep at Great Falls, Montana," it read. "The take-off time tomorrow morning is uncertain but it is now rather definite, weather permitting, that he will reach Washington Sunday evening. I shall notify Mr. Connelly by telephone immediately after Mr. Molotov arrives in order that he may receive your instructions as to when you desire to receive him."

I then handed Stettinius a message to be transmitted to Stalin:

"Referring to arrangements for making an announcement of the linking up of our armies in Germany, I will see that General Eisenhower is given instructions to inform the Soviet, British and United States Governments at earliest possible date when an announcement may be made by the three Chiefs of Government of the Soviet-Anglo-American Armies meeting in Germany.

"In order that the announcement may be made simultaneously in the three capitals, I would like to have your agreement that the hour of the day recommended by Eisenhower be twelve o'clock noon Washington time."

Returning to Blair House, I wrote to my mother and sister.

Dear Mamma & Mary, Well I've been the President for nine days. And such nine days no one ever went through before, I really believe. The job started at 5:30 on the afternoon of the 12th. It was necessary for me to begin making decisions an hour and a half before I was sworn in, and I've been making them ever since.

The two high points in the whole nine days were the appearance before Congress on Monday and the press conference on Tuesday. Evidently from the comments in all the papers and magazines both appearances were successful.

But it is only a start and we'll see what develops. It has been necessary to talk to all the people you read about—Byrnes, Hopkins, Baruch, Marshall, King, Leahy, and all the Cabinet collectively and one at a time. I've seen a lot of Senators and Representatives too. . . .

Tomorrow we are going to church at the Chapel at Walter Reed Hospital, and I'm going to call on Gen. Pershing. He's bedfast now, and I thought I ought to go say hello to my first World War commander.

Surely appreciated your letter. You both have done fine under this terrible blow. Just keep yourselves well and don't worry. When we get into the White House, we'll send for you, and you can pay us a visit. They are painting and cleaning house now, and it will be some time before we get moved in.

Love to you both,

Harry

On Sunday, April 22, I attended church at the Walter Reed Hospital and visited General Pershing. I wanted to pay my respects to him.

I invited Secretary Stettinius, Ambassador Harriman, Mr. James Dunn, Assistant Secretary of State, and Mr. Bohlen to Blair House in preparation for my meeting with Molotov that evening. The Secretary of State told me of the arrangements that had been made for Molotov's reception at the airport. There would be no military honors, but after dinner I was to receive Mr. Molotov with Ambassador Harriman present and with Mr. Bohlen acting as interpreter.

Despite our suggestion that the Soviet-Polish treaty negotiations be postponed, Moscow and the Lublin government had concluded the pact. Secretary Stettinius therefore asked whether I intended to make any reference to the matter when Molotov arrived. I replied that I preferred not to raise that question myself, but that if Molotov chose to mention it I would tell him quite frankly that it had not been helpful in furthering a solution of the Polish question.

At this point in our discussion Mr. Eden, the British Foreign Minister, arrived, and when he too raised the question of the Soviet-Polish treaty I repeated what I had just told the Secretary of State. Mr. Eden then inquired whether it would be possible for me to visit England any time during the coming summer for a meeting with Prime Minister Churchill. I said I hoped to be able to do so but that I could not give a definite answer now because of the pressure of problems in the domestic field. I assured him that I wished to meet Mr. Churchill soon, and was told that if I found it impossible to visit Europe in the months ahead, the Prime Minister, if he could get away, would be prepared to come to Washington. I said that if the San Francisco conference got off to a good start it might be a good time for the Prime Minister to come here.

Stettinius and Eden both said that the relations between Great Britain and the United States had never been better or closer, and were on the basis of complete frankness. I declared that I would do everything in my power to maintain them on that plane.

It was at eight-thirty that evening that I received Molotov at Blair House. With me were Secretary Stettinius, Ambassador Harriman, and Mr. Bohlen, while Mr. Molotov was accompanied by his official interpreter, Mr. Pavlov.

I welcomed the Soviet Foreign Minister to the United States and inquired about his long trip by air. I assured him of my admiration for the war deeds of Marshal Stalin and the Soviet Union and expressed the hope that it would be possible to maintain the relationship which President Roosevelt had established between our two countries.

Molotov said he brought greetings to me from Stalin and expressed his pleasure in hearing personally from me that I intended to continue the policy of friendship.

This afforded me the opportunity to tell Molotov that I stood squarely behind all commitments and agreements entered into by our late great

President and that I would do everything I could to follow along that path.

In response Molotov declared that the government and the people of the Soviet Union shared that hope, and he was sure they could work out successfully any difficulty which lay in the path. I agreed that we must work out these difficulties.

The Russian Foreign Minister expressed the belief that a good basis for agreement existed in the Dumbarton Oaks and the Crimea decisions, and I replied that I stood firmly by those decisions and intended to carry them out. I said that I wanted to bring up at this point that the most difficult question relating to the Crimea decision was the Polish matter. The proper solution was of great importance because of the effect on American public opinion.

Molotov expressed his understanding of that point but contended that the matter was even more important for the Soviet Union. Poland, he said, was far from the United States but bordered on the Soviet Union. The Polish question was therefore vital to them. And here again he added that he thought the Crimea decisions provided a suitable basis for a solution.

I agreed, but I pointed out that in its larger aspects the Polish question had become for our people the symbol of the future development of our international relations. I said that there were a number of minor matters which I hoped that he, together with Mr. Eden and Mr. Stettinius, would settle here in Washington. Molotov replied that he thought an agreement could be easily reached on these points, provided the views of the Soviet Union were taken into consideration. He said the Soviet government attached the greatest importance to the San Francisco conference and that, with the military developments of recent weeks, political questions had taken on greater importance. I agreed, pointing out that this was one of the reasons I wanted to talk to him.

Molotov asserted that the discussions between the three heads of state had always been fruitful and had led to good agreements. He inquired whether the agreements in regard to the Far Eastern situation made at Yalta still stood. They did, I replied, and again I repeated that I intended to carry out all the agreements made by President Roosevelt. I expressed the hope that I would meet with Marshal Stalin before too long, and Molotov replied that he knew the marshal was eager to meet with me.

Molotov then left with Stettinius to join Eden in talks at the State Department.

I spent most of Monday morning, April 23, meeting with different congressmen, including the Missouri delegation from the House. I also met with a group of forty Democratic senators, former colleagues of mine, who renewed their pledge of support. Then J. Edgar Hoover of the Federal Bureau of Investigation called at eleven-thirty and was followed by the Postmaster General, Frank Walker. After Walker came the District of Columbia commissioners and, finally, Brigadier General Frank T. Hines, head of the Veterans Administration.

In connection with Molotov's visit I held an important conference at two o'clock with my chief diplomatic and military advisers. Those present were Secretary of State Stettinius, Secretary of War Stimson, Secretary of the Navy Forrestal, Admiral Leahy, General Marshall, Admiral King, Assistant Secretary of State Dunn, Ambassador Harriman, General Deane, and Mr. Bohlen.

We discussed Russia and the Polish problem, and Stettinius reported that though Molotov had arrived Sunday in apparent good spirits, which he had maintained even after his Blair House talk with me, overnight the atmosphere had changed. At the evening meeting with Eden in the State Department great difficulties had developed over the Polish question. Moreover, a continuance of the foreign ministers' meeting this morning had produced no improvement. In fact, a complete deadlock had been reached on the subject of carrying out the Yalta agreement on Poland.

The Secretary pointed out once more that the Lublin, or Warsaw, government was not representative of the Polish people and that it was now clear that the Russians intended to try to force this puppet government upon the United States and England. He added that it had been made plain to Molotov how seriously the United States regarded this matter and how much public confidence would be shaken by failure to carry out the Crimea decision.

It was now obvious, I said, that our agreements with the Soviet Union had so far been a one-way street and that this could not continue. I told my advisers that we intended to go on with the plans for San Francisco, and if the Russians did not wish to join us, that would be too bad. Then, one by one, I asked each of those present to state his views.

Secretary Stimson said that this whole difficulty with the Russians over Poland was new to him, and he felt it was important to find out what the Russians were driving at. In the big military matters, he told us, the Soviet government had kept its word and the military authorities of the United States had come to count on it. In fact, he said they had often done better than they had promised. On that account he felt that it was important to find out what motives they had in connection with these border countries and what their ideas of independence and democracy were in areas they regarded as vital to the Soviet Union.

Mr. Stimson remarked that the Russians had made a good deal of trouble on minor military matters and it had sometimes been necessary in these cases to teach them manners. In this greater matter, however, it was his belief that without fully understanding how seriously the Russians took this Polish question we might be heading into very dangerous waters, and that their viewpoint was undoubtedly influenced by the fact that before World War I most of Poland had been controlled by Russia.

Secretary Forrestal expressed the view that this difficulty over Poland could not be treated as an isolated incident—that there had been many evidences of the Soviet desire to dominate adjacent countries and to disregard the wishes of her allies. It was his belief that for some time the Russians had been under the impression that we would not object if they took over all of Eastern Europe, and he said it was his profound conviction that if the Russians were to be rigid in their attitude we had better have a showdown with them now rather than later.

Ambassador Harriman, in replying to Mr. Stimson's question about issues and motives, said he felt that when Stalin and Molotov had returned to Moscow after Yalta they had learned more of the situation in Poland and had realized how shaky the provisional government was. On that account they had come to realize that the introduction of any genuine Polish leader such as Mikolajczyk would probably mean the elimination of the Soviet hand-picked crop of leaders. It was his belief, therefore, that the real issue was whether we were to be a party to a program of Soviet domination of Poland. He said obviously we were faced with the possibility of a break with the Russians, but he felt that, properly handled, it might still be avoided.

At this point I explained that I had no intention of delivering an ultimatum to Mr. Molotov—that my purpose was merely to make clear the position of this government.

Mr. Stimson then said he would like to know how far the Russian reaction to a strong position on Poland would go. He said he thought that the Russians perhaps were being more realistic than we were in regard to their own security.

Admiral Leahy, in response to a question from me, observed that he had left Yalta with the impression that the Soviet government had no intention of permitting a free government to operate in Poland and that he would have been surprised had the Russians behaved any differently. In his opinion, the Yalta agreement was susceptible of two interpretations. He added that he felt it was a serious matter to break with the Russians but that he believed we should tell them that we stood for a free and independent Poland.

Stettinius then read the part of the Yalta decision relating to the formation of the new government and the holding of free elections and said he felt that this was susceptible of only one interpretation.

General Marshall said he was not familiar with the political aspects of the Polish issues. He said from the military point of view the situation in Europe was secure but that we hoped for Soviet participation in the war against Japan at a time when it would be useful to us. The Russians had it within their power to delay their entry into the Far Eastern war until we had done all the dirty work. He was inclined to agree with Mr. Stimson that the possibility of a break with Russia was very serious.

Mr. Stimson observed that he agreed with General Marshall and that he felt the Russians would not yield on the Polish question. He said we had to understand that outside the United States, with the exception of Great Britain, there were few countries that understood free elections; that the party in power always ran the elections, as he well knew from his experience in Nicaragua.

Admiral King inquired whether the issue was the invitation to the Lublin government to San Francisco.

I answered that that was a settled matter and not the issue. The issue was the execution of agreements entered into between this government and the Soviet Union. I said that I intended to tell Mr. Molotov that we expected Russia to carry out the Yalta decision as we were prepared to do for our part.

Ambassador Harriman then remarked that while it was true that the Soviet Union had kept its big agreements on military matters, those were decisions it had already reached by itself, but on other military matters it was impossible to say they had lived up to their commitments. For example, over a year ago they had agreed to start on preparations for collaboration in the Far Eastern war, but none of these had been carried out.

General Deane said he felt that the Soviet Union would enter the Pacific war as soon as it was able, regardless of what happened in other fields. He felt that the Russians had to do this because they could not afford too long a period of letdown for their people, who were tired. He said he was convinced after his experience in Moscow that if we were afraid of the Russians we would get nowhere, and he felt that we should be firm when we were right.

I thanked the military leaders and said I had their points of view well in mind. Then I asked Stettinius, Harriman, Dunn, and Bohlen to stay behind to work out subjects for my next talk with Molotov, which was scheduled for five-thirty.

When Molotov arrived, Secretary Stettinius, Ambassador Harriman, Mr. Bohlen, and Admiral Leahy were with me in my office. Molotov was accompanied by Ambassador Gromyko and interpreter Pavlov.

Unlike the evening before, there was little protocol, and after greeting the Russian Foreign Minister and his associates, I went straight to the point. I was sorry to learn, I said, that no progress had been made in solving the Polish problem.

Mr. Molotov responded that he also regretted that fact.

I told him that the proposals which were contained in the joint message from Churchill and me and which had been transmitted to Moscow on April 16 were eminently fair and reasonable. We had gone as far as we could to meet the proposals of the Soviet government as expressed in the message from Marshal Stalin on April 7. The United States Government, I pointed out, could not agree to be a party to the formation of a Polish government which was not representative of all Polish democratic elements. I said bluntly that I was deeply disappointed that the Soviet government had not held consultations with representatives of the Polish government other than the officials of the Warsaw regime.

I told Molotov that the United States was determined, together with other members of the United Nations, to go ahead with plans for the world organization, no matter what difficulties or differences might arise with regard to other matters. I pointed out that the failure of the three principal allies who had borne the brunt of the war to carry out the Crimea decision with regard to Poland would cast serious doubt upon their unity of purpose in postwar collaboration.

I explained to Molotov that in Roosevelt's last message to Marshal Stalin on April 1 the late President had made it plain that no policy in the United States, whether foreign or domestic, could succeed unless it had public confidence and support. This, I pointed out, applied in the field of economic as well as political collaboration. In this country, I said, legislative appropriations were required for any economic measures in the foreign field, and I had no hope of getting such measures through Congress unless there was public support for them. I expressed the hope that the Soviet government would keep these factors in mind in considering the request that joint British and American proposals be accepted, and that Mr. Molotov would be authorized to continue the discussions in San Francisco on that basis.

I then handed him a message which I asked him to transmit to Marshal Stalin immediately.

"There was an agreement at Yalta," this communication read, "in which President Roosevelt participated for the United States Government, to reorganize the Provisional Government now functioning in Warsaw in order to establish a new government of National Unity in Poland by means of previous consultation between representatives of the Provisional Polish Government of Warsaw and other Polish democratic leaders from Poland and from abroad.

"In the opinion of the United States Government the Crimean decision on Poland can only be carried out if a group of genuinely representative democratic Polish leaders are invited to Moscow for consultation. The United States Government cannot be party to any method of consultation with Polish leaders which would not result in the establishment of a new Provisional Government of National Unity genuinely representative of the democratic elements of the Polish people. The United States and British Governments have gone as far as they can to meet the situation and carry out the intent of the Crimean decisions in their joint message delivered to Marshal Stalin on April 18th.

"The United States Government earnestly requests that the Soviet Government accept the proposals set forth in the joint message of the President and Prime Minister to Marshal Stalin, and that Mr. Molotov continue the conversations with the Secretary of State and Mr. Eden in San Francisco on that basis.

"The Soviet Government must realize that the failure to go forward at this time with the implementation of the Crimean decision on Poland would seriously shake confidence in the unity of the three governments and their determination to continue the collaboration in the future as they have in the past."

Molotov asked if he could make a few observations. It was his hope, he said, that he expressed the views of the Soviet government in stating that they wished to co-operate with the United States and Great Britain as before.

I answered that I agreed, otherwise there would be no sense in the talk we then were having.

Molotov went on to say that he had been authorized to set forth the following point of view of the Soviet government:

1. The basis of collaboration had been established, and although inevitable difficulties had arisen, the three governments had been able to find a common language and that on this basis they had been settling these differences.

2. The three governments had dealt as equal parties, and there had been no case where one or two of the three had attempted to impose their will on another and that as a basis of co-operation this was the only one acceptable to the Soviet government.

I told him that all we were asking was that the Soviet government carry out the Crimea decision on Poland.

Mr. Molotov answered that as an advocate of the Crimea decisions his government stood by them and that it was a matter of honor for them. His government felt that the good basis which existed was the result of former work and that it offered even brighter prospects for the future.

The Soviet government, he added, was convinced that all difficulties could be overcome.

I replied sharply that an agreement had been reached on Poland and that there was only one thing to do, and that was for Marshal Stalin to carry out that agreement in accordance with his word.

Molotov said that Marshal Stalin, in his message of April 7, had given his views on the agreement, and added that he personally could not understand why, if the three governments could reach an agreement on the question of the composition of the Yugoslav government, the same formula could not be applied in the case of Poland.

Replying sharply again, I said that an agreement had been reached on Poland and that it only required to be carried out by the Soviet government.

Mr. Molotov repeated that his government supported the Crimea decisions but that he could not agree that an abrogation of those decisions by others could be considered a violation by the Soviet government. He added that surely the Polish question, involving as it did a neighboring country, was of very great interest to the Soviet government.

Since Molotov insisted on avoiding the main issue, I said what I had said before—that the United States Government was prepared to carry out loyally all the agreements reached at Yalta and asked only that the Soviet government do the same. I expressed once more the desire of the United States for friendship with Russia, but I wanted it clearly understood that this could be only on a basis of the mutual observation of agreements and not on the basis of a one-way street.

"I have never been talked to like that in my life," Molotov said.

I told him, "Carry out your agreements and you won't get talked to like that."

CHAPTER 7

In the final rush of our armies into Germany a problem arose which required the exchange of views among Great Britain, Russia, and the United States. This involved the zones of occupation in Germany which had been agreed upon by the three powers at London in the European Advisory Commission in January 1945.

As our armies poured into Germany, it was impossible to have them meet at precisely the lines earlier designated, and many of our troops had overrun those lines. It was therefore necessary to get agreement among Great Britain, Russia, and ourselves on new directives to the military so that our forces could be rearranged in accordance with the plan of occupation.

This was the problem Churchill had in mind when he sent me his message of April 18. After consultation with my military advisers I cabled Churchill a suggested message that the two of us might send to Stalin. "The approaching end of German resistance makes it necessary that the United States, Great Britain and the Soviet Union decide upon an orderly procedure for the occupation by their forces of the zones which they will occupy in Germany and Austria." I therefore proposed, first, that our troops in both Germany and Austria should retire to their respective zones "as soon as the Military situation permits." Secondly, I suggested that in order to avoid confusion, each commander, when he felt himself prepared to occupy any portion of his proper zone that was held by other Allied troops, should inform his own government of the sector he was prepared to occupy. And thirdly, I proposed that the government concerned should then consult the other two in order that the necessary instructions might be issued for the immediate evacuation of the area involved and its occupation by the troops of the country to which it was assigned. "It is of course essential," I said, "that we promptly reach an agreement on the zones which we are to occupy in Austria."

Because of the great importance of the Polish problem, I had also sent Churchill a copy of the message I had handed Molotov for delivery to Stalin. And now, on April 24, the day after my second talk with Molotov, I received this reply from the Prime Minister:

I have carefully considered the message you had handed to Molotov for Marshal Stalin and have brought it before the War Cabinet, who have authorized me to inform you of their entire agreement with the course you have adopted. I shall now therefore send to Marshal Stalin the message contained in my immediately following telegram.

"I have seen the message about Poland which the President handed to M. Molotov for transmission to you and I have consulted the War Cabinet on account of its special importance. It is my duty now to inform you that we are all agreed in associating ourselves with the President in the aforesaid message. I earnestly hope that means will be found to compose these serious difficulties which, if they continue, will darken the hour of victory."

Representative Robert T. Doughton, chairman of the powerful House Ways and Means Committee, came to see me about the budget and taxes. Mr. Byron Price came in about the role of the press in handling the war news. Leo Crowley came to talk about Lend-Lease and its future.

The Secretary of State sent me a report in which he referred to the observations of George F. Kennan concerning Ambassador Hurley's interview with Stalin. These observations had been contained in a personal message to Ambassador Harriman, and the Secretary's report, summarizing Kennan's message, contained the following passage:

Kennan comments upon the statements attributed to Stalin by Ambassador Hurley to the effect that Stalin agreed unqualifiedly to our Chinese policy, stated that this policy would be supported by Russia and said that he would support immediately action looking toward the unification of Chinese armed forces under Chiang Kai-shek. Kennan does not question that Stalin was correctly cited but calls attention to the fact that words have a different meaning to the Russians. Stalin is prepared to accept the principle of unification of Chinese armed forces and the principle of a united China since he knows that these conditions are feasible only on terms acceptable to the Chinese Communists. Stalin is also prepared to accept the idea of a free and democratic China since a free China means to him a China in which there is a minimum of foreign influence other than Russian. Kennan is convinced that Soviet policy will remain a policy aimed at the achievement of maximum power with minimum responsibility and will involve the exertion of pressure in various areas. He recommends that we study with clinical objectivity the real character and implications of Russian Far Eastern aims, and comments that it would be tragic if our anxiety for Russian support in the Far East were to lead us into an undue reliance on Russian aid.

I realized only too well the implications in this message—and in other related messages as well. The attitude Russia had assumed had been troubling me right along. During the day I received from Secretary of War Stimson the following communication:

Dear Mr. President, I think it is very important that I should have a talk with you as soon as possible on a highly secret matter. I mentioned it to you shortly after you took office but have not urged it since on account of the pressure you have been under. It, however, has such a bearing on our present foreign relations and has such an important effect upon all my thinking in this field that I think you ought to know about it without much further delay.

I knew he was referring to our secret atomic project, and I instructed Matt Connelly, my appointment secretary, to arrange for the Secretary to come in the next day, Wednesday, April 25.

One of the most revealing and disquieting messages to reach me during my first days in the White House was one that arrived from Marshal Stalin on the night of April 24. It showed plainly that Churchill and I were going to have persistent, calculated resistance from Stalin in our dealings with the Russians.

This was the message from Stalin:

I have received your joint message with Prime Minister Churchill of April 18, and have also received on April 24 the message transmitted to me through V. M. Molotov.

1. From these messages it is clear that you continue to consider the Provisional Polish Government not as a kernel for the future government of national unity, but just like one of the groups equal to any other group of Poles.

Such an understanding of the position of the Polish government and such an attitude toward it is very difficult to reconcile with the decisions of the Crimea Conference on Poland. At the Crimea Conference all three of us, including also President Roosevelt, proceeded from the fact that the Provisional Polish Government, as the one now operating in Poland and enjoying the confidence and support of the majority of the Polish people, should be the kernel, i.e., the main part of the new reorganized government of national unity. You, evidently, do not agree to such an understanding of the matter. Declining the Yugoslav example as a pattern for Poland, you thereby confirm that the Provisional Polish Government cannot be considered as a basis and kernel for the future government of national unity.

2. It is also necessary to take into account the fact that Poland borders on the Soviet Union, which cannot be said of Great Britain and the United States.

The question on Poland has the same meaning for the security of the Soviet Union as the question on Belgium and Greece for the security of Great Britain.

You, apparently, do not agree that the Soviet Union has a right to make efforts that there should exist in Poland a government friendly toward the Soviet Union, and that the Soviet government cannot agree to existence in Poland of a government hostile toward it. Besides everything else, this is demanded by the blood of the Soviet people abundantly shed on the fields of Poland in the name of liberation of Poland. I do not know whether there has been established in Greece a really representative government, and whether the government in Belgium is really democratic. The Soviet Union was not consulted when these governments were being established there. The Soviet Government did not lay claim to interference in these affairs as it understands the whole importance of Belgium and Greece for the security of Great Britain.

It is not clear why, while the question of Poland is discussed it is not wanted to take into consideration the interests of the Soviet Union from the point of view of its security.

3. Such conditions must be recognized unusual when two governments— those of the United States and Great Britain—beforehand settle with the Polish question in which the Soviet Union is first of all and most of all interested and put the government of the USSR in an unbearable position trying to dictate to it their demands.

I have to state that such a situation cannot favor a harmonious solution of the question of Poland.

4. I am ready to fulfill your request and do everything possible to reach a harmonious solution. But you demand too much of me. In other words, you demand that I renounce the interests of security of the Soviet Union, but I cannot turn against my country.

In my opinion there is one way out of this situation; to adopt the Yugoslav example as a pattern for Poland. I believe this would allow to come to a harmonious solution.

Without any attempt to hide his role in diplomatic niceties, Stalin for the first time in addressing Churchill and me used the "Big I Am."

After the arrival of Stalin's disturbing message, the morning was taken up mostly in meetings with senators and congressmen who continued to offer their good will and co-operation. I was greatly encouraged by this evidence of their desire to work more closely with the President. As senator and as Vice-President I had observed the gradually widening breach between Congress and the Chief Executive. This is natural and even inescapable under our systems of checks and balances, but party lines were too often crossed in the contest between the two branches of government, and important legislation was compromised and sometimes lost because Congress felt a need to assert its authority.

With the war and its consequent effect on the home front reaching a climax, I wanted to do everything I could to encourage the fullest co-operation and exchange of information between Congress and all branches of the Executive Department. I therefore welcomed these visits from members of both Houses and arranged to see as many of them as I could, no matter how crowded my day was. That day I saw Senators Mc-Kellar, Bankhead, Scott Lucas, Hugh B. Mitchell, James M. Tunnell, Lister Hill, and Congressmen J. Buell Snyder, Hatton W. Sumners, and Emanuel Celler.

At noon I saw Secretary of War Stimson in connection with the urgent letter he had written.

Stimson was one of the very few men responsible for the setting up of the atomic bomb project. He had taken a keen and active interest in every stage of its development. He said he wanted specifically to talk to me today about the effect the atomic bomb might likely have on our future foreign relations.

He explained that he thought it necessary for him to share his thoughts with me about the revolutionary changes in warfare that might result from the atomic bomb and the possible effects of such a weapon on our civilization.

I listened with absorbed interest, for Stimson was a man of great wisdom and foresight. He went into considerable detail in describing the nature and the power of the projected weapon. If expectations were to be realized, he told me, the atomic bomb would be certain to have a decisive influence on our relations with other countries. And if it worked, the bomb, in all probability, would shorten the war.

Byrnes had already told me that the weapon might be so powerful as to be potentially capable of wiping out entire cities and killing people on an unprecedented scale. And he had added that in his belief the bomb might well put us in a position to dictate our own terms at the end of the war. Stimson, on the other hand, seemed at least as much concerned with the role of the atomic bomb in the shaping of history as in its capacity to shorten this war. As yet, of course, no one could positively know that the gigantic effort that was being made would be successful. Nevertheless, the Secretary appeared confident of the outcome and told me that in all probability success would be attained within the next few months. He also suggested that I designate a committee to study and advise me of the implications of this new force.

I thanked him for his enlightening presentation of this awesome subject, and as I saw him to the door I felt how fortunate the country was to have so able and so wise a man in its service.

From the time I first sat down in the President's chair I found myself part of an immense administrative operation. There had been a change of executives, but the machinery kept going on in its customary routine manner, and properly so. It would have been sheer nonsense to expect anything else.

There is a story of the great, but not good, queen, Catherine of Russia, who in her way was as dictatorial as any of her modern successors. It seems that a river with a rapid current flows through the Baltic city of Riga, and in Catherine's time a bridge was built across it. This bridge, I am told, still stands and carries a bronze tablet which reads, in Russian: "Oh current, stop thy flow. The Queen demands it."

From my experience in the Senate, I knew how difficult it was to make much of a dent in routine administrative methods. In fact, from my committee's experience, I knew this was also true of private industry and even of emergency activities connected with the war. But I had some ideas of my own on certain details of war administration, and I hoped to make some changes in procedures that involved the Executive.

From the time I became President I made it plain, in my relations with the military, that I was interested in the details of actual administration as much as in the larger objectives. I had implicit faith and trust in Marshall, but I took the position that the President, as the Commander in Chief, had to know everything that was going on. I had had just enough experience to know that if you are not careful the military will hedge you in.

It had long been customary for the "high brass" in the Army and Navy to "take over" the Secretary of War and the Secretary of the Navy as well as the military committees of the two Houses. I knew this, for I had been on the military committee in the Senate. And more than that, I had understood perfectly that they had tried to surround me even as chairman of my special committee.

I should make it clear that these very capable officers did not try to get around the President on major policies. The Chiefs of Staff were always most co-operative. But on the administrative level the military usually tried to take over, especially in the management of purchases where vast sums of money were being spent.

I knew, for example, that Army and Navy professionals seldom had any idea of the value of money. They did not seem to care what the cost was, and one of my first moves was to request a complete survey of their whole spending policy. As a result, adjustments began to come about automatically in the Army and Navy.

The pressure of appointments continued, and I had to find time to read the urgent messages in between visitors. Ambassador Winant in London then notified me that Churchill wished to talk to me over the transatlantic telephone. Heinrich Himmler, the German Gestapo chief, had approached the Swedish government with an offer to surrender the German forces on the Western Front.

This was my first telephone conversation with Churchill. It was recorded in the presence of Admiral Leahy, General Marshall, Admiral King, General Hull, and Colonel Park, and I am able to give it here, without editing, exactly as it was recorded:

"Churchill: Is that you, Mr. President?

"Truman: This is the President, Mr. Prime Minister.

"Churchill: How glad I am to hear your voice.

"Truman: Thank you very much, I am glad to hear yours.

"Churchill: I have several times talked to Franklin, but . . . **Have** you received the report from Stockholm by your Ambassador?

"Truman: Yes, I have.

"Churchill: On that proposal?

"Truman: Yes. I have just a short message saying that there was such a proposal in existence.

"Churchill: Yes, it's of course . . . we thought it looked very good.

"Truman: Has he anything to surrender?

"Churchill: I called the War Cabinet together and they proposed my telegraphing to tell Stalin and also repeating our news through the usual channels to you.

"Truman: What has he to surrender: Does that mean everything, Norway, Denmark, Italy, and Holland?

"Churchill: They mentioned Italy, and Yugoslavia. We mentioned everything and have included that to take in Denmark and Norway. Everything on the Western Front, but he hasn't proposed to surrender on the Eastern Front. So we thought perhaps it would be necessary to report it to Stalin; that is, of course, to say that in our view the surrender must be simultaneous to agree to our terms.

"Truman: I think he should be forced to surrender to all three governments, Russia, you and the United States. I don't think we ought to even consider a piecemeal surrender.

"Churchill: No, no, no. Not a piecemeal surrender to a man like Himmler. Himmler will be speaking for the German state as much as anybody can. And therefore we thought that his negotiations must be carried on with the three governments.

"Truman: That's right, that's the way I feel exactly.

"Churchill: I see, of course, that's local surrender on the front, Himmler's allied front. And then Eisenhower is still authorized to make the surrender, well, then he will wish to surrender.

"Truman: Yes, of course.

"Churchill: You understand that?

"Truman: I understand that. If he is speaking for the German government as a whole, that ought to include the surrender of everything, and it ought to be to all three governments.

"Churchill: Certainly, what we actually sent was that there could be no question as far as His Majesty's Government is concerned of anything less than unconditional surrender simultaneously to the three major powers.

"Truman: All right. I agree to that.

"Churchill: Have you said anything to the Russians yet?

"Truman: No, I haven't. I was waiting to hear from you. I haven't received the message from Stockholm. This information that you are giving me now is the only information that I have on the subject, except that I was informed that your conversation was based on a message that you had from Stockholm.

"Churchill: Yes.

"Truman: I have no other information except what I am receiving now from you.

"Churchill: I see. I can give you the message which our Ambassador in Stockholm sent me. Would you like me to read it to you?

"Truman: I would appreciate it very much if you will.

"Churchill: Yes. It is a little long. Tell me if you don't hear it as it comes.

" 'The Swedish Minister for Foreign Affairs wants me and my United States colleague to call upon him at 23 hours, April 25 . . . and Bernadotte of the Swedish Red Cross were also present. Bernadotte had just returned from Germany via Denmark tonight. Himmler was on the Eastern Front and asked him to come from Prensburg to meet him at the . . . and Bernadotte requested . . . where the meeting took place at ten o'clock this morning, April 24. Himmler, though tired, and admitting Germany was finished, was still strong and coherent. Himmler said that Hitler was so desperately ill, he might be dead already, and in any case would be so in two days' time.'

"Could you hear that all right?

"Truman: Yes, I could hear.

"Churchill: 'And General Finisberg of Himmler's staff told Bernadotte that it was hemorrhage of the brain.

" 'In that statement, that while Hitler was still active he would not have been able to take the steps he now proposed but that as Herr Hitler was finished he was now in a position of full authority to act. He then asked Bernadotte to forward to the Swedish Government his desire that they would make arrangements in order to arrange for him to meet General Eisenhower in order to capitulate on the whole Western Front. Bernadotte remarked that such a meeting' (Bernadotte is a Swede, a

Swedish Red Cross man) 'was not necessary in that Himmler could simply order his troops to surrender. That announcement asked him to forward Himmler's request to the Swedish Government, and that Norway and Denmark were included in this capitulation. If this were the case, there might be some point in a meeting because special technical arrangements might have to be made with Eisenhower and de Gaulle if the Germans were to lay down their arms in those two countries. He then replied that he was prepared to order the troops in Denmark and Norway to surrender to either British, American, or Swedish troops. He in there hopes to continue resistance on the Eastern Front at least for a time, which Bernadotte told him was hardly possible, in fact, that it would not be acceptable to the Allies. Himmler mentioned, for instance, that he hoped that the Western Allies rather than the Russians would be first to make this step in order to save the civilian populations.

" 'Then he said that Himmler's staff officer, Herr Stinsberg, was eagerly awaiting to hear something and was putting through immediate delivery to Himmler any message which it might be desired to convey. Bernadotte remarked to . . . that if no reaction at all was forthcoming from the Allies that may mean a lot of unnecessary suffering and loss of human life, but the Minister of Foreign Affairs at . . . explained that he thought this was such an important piece of news that he ought to communicate it to my United States colleague and me (that's the British Ambassador) immediately. Is it okay with you?

" 'I wrote that my United States colleague and I remarked that in reference to the Axis' unwillingness to surrender on the Eastern Front looks like a last attempt to sow discord between the Western Allies and Russia. Obviously the Nazis would have to surrender to all the Allies simultaneously.'

"Truman: That is right. That is exactly the way I feel. He ought to surrender to all the Allies at once.

"Churchill: 'The Minister for Foreign Affairs and Government, while admitting that this motive could not be excluded, pointed out that the fact that the Nazi chiefs would order capitulation of all troops on the whole Western Front, and in Norway, and Denmark might be of great advantage for all the Allies, including Russia, and would in fact lead to early total capitulation,' (these are all the Swedes talking) 'and they say in any case, the Minister for Foreign Affairs hoped to clear this up, this provision. He said pass it on to the British and United States governments who were, as far as the Swedish Government were concerned, at complete liberty to transmit it to the Soviet Government. That the Swedish Government would in no way be, or propose to be, an instrument in promoting any attempt to sow discord between the Allies. The only reason for not informing the Soviet Government directly was because Himmler had stipulated that this information was exclusively for the Western Allies.' (He said that if the United States colleague is sending a telegram to say so.) Of course we are not bound by that, and it's our duty to tell Stalin, in my opinion.

"Truman: I think so, too. Have you notified Stalin?

"Churchill: I held it up for about two hours, hoping to get an answer to the telegram I sent you, but I have now released the telegram. This is the telegram I have sent.

"Truman: All right, then you notify Stalin, and I shall do the same immediately of this conversation between us.

"Churchill: Exactly. Here is what I have said to Stalin and I have telegraphed it over to you. The telegram immediately following is one I have just received exactly from the British Ambassador in Sweden.

" 'The President of the United States has the news also.' I thought you had gotten it. Your telegram has not gotten through.

"Truman: No, I haven't received my telegram as yet.

"Churchill: 'There can be no question as far as His Majesty's Government is concerned, arranging thus an unconditional surrender simultaneously to the three major powers.'

"Truman: I agree to that fully.

"Churchill: 'We consider Himmler should be told that German folk either as individuals or in units should everywhere surrender themselves to the Allied troops or representatives on the spot. Until this happens, the attack of the Allies upon them on all sides and in all theaters where resistance continues will be prosecuted with the utmost vigor!

" 'Nothing in the above telegram should affect the release of our oration [?].' I sent it off a few minutes ago and I was sending it to you with the following telegram from me, you see. That which I read you. I called the War Cabinet together at once and they approved of this telegram I've just read you.

"Truman: I approve of it too.

"Churchill: The one I sent to Stalin?

"Truman: I approve of that telegram you sent to Stalin, and I shall immediately wire Stalin on exactly the same line.

"Churchill: Thank you so much. That is exactly what I wanted. We hoped you would find it possible to telegraph to Marshal Stalin and to us in the same sense.

"Truman: Mr. Prime Minister, would you please repeat your message to Stalin and repeat it slowly so I can take it down here?

"Churchill: I have already done so through the American Embassy over an hour and a half ago, and it should be with you almost immediately. Would you like me to send you also the telegram I got from Stockholm today?

"Truman: I would very much.

"Churchill: I will. You will get it very soon. You will get the one from me, the one I just sent out.

"Truman: I would like for you to repeat the one which you sent to Stalin so I can send one substantially like it to him.

"Churchill: Good. I hope I may . . .

"Truman: Would you do it slowly, please, Mr. Prime Minister?

"Churchill: The telegram immediately follows. It is a long one.

"Truman: I thank you very much.

"Churchill: 'I have just received from the British Ambassador in Sweden . . . The President of the United States has the news also.' (That is what I thought.) 'There can be no question as far as state history is concerned about anything else but unconditional surrender simultaneously to the three major powers. We consider Himmler should be told that German folk, either as individuals or in units, should everywhere surrender themselves to the Allied troops or representatives on the spot. Until this happens, the attack of the Allies upon them on all sides and in all theaters where resistance continues will be prosecuted with the utmost vigor. Nothing in the above telegram should affect the release of our oration [?].' (That is intact.) That is what I sent, I think, about half an hour ago.

"Truman: Thank you very much. I shall get one off immediately to him, and I certainly do appreciate your talking to me on it.

"Churchill: I'm delighted. I am sure we would be pretty well in agreement, and I hope that Stalin will wire back and say, 'I agree too.' In which case we could authorize our representatives, in Stockholm, to tell Bernadotte that you will pass on the message to Himmler. Because nothing can be done about that until we are all three agreed on it.

"Truman: All right.

"Churchill: You have my text and your own, and let's see what Stalin says.

"Truman: All right.

"Churchill: Thank you very much, indeed.

"Truman: Thank you.

"Churchill: You remember those speeches we were going to make about the link up in Europe?

"Truman: I didn't understand that last statement, Mr. Prime Minister.

"Churchill: You know what I am talking about, the speech, the statements that are written. Well, I think they should be let out just as they would be anyhow as soon as the link up occurs.

"Truman: I think you're right on that. I agree on that.

"Churchill: Anything helps to beat the enemy.

"Truman: I agree with that.

"Churchill: Good. I rejoice that our first conversation will be about the first of June. It's very good news.

"Truman: I hope to see you someday soon.

"Churchill: I am planning to. I'll be sending you some telegrams about that quite soon. I entirely agree with all that you've done on the Polish situation. We are walking hand in hand together.

"Truman: Well, I want to continue just that.

"Churchill: In fact, I am following your lead, backing up whatever you do on the matter.

"Truman: Thank you. Good night."

Without further delay I cabled Marshal Stalin.

"I am informed by the American Minister to Sweden," my message to Stalin read, "that Himmler, speaking for the German government in the absence of Hitler due to incapacity, approached the Swedish government with an offer to surrender all the German forces on the western front including Holland, Denmark and Norway.

"In keeping with our agreement with the British and Soviet governments it is the view of the United States government that the only acceptable terms of surrender are unconditional surrender at all fronts to the Soviet, Great Britain and the United States.

"If the Germans accept the terms of paragraph 2 above, they should surrender on all fronts at once to the local commanders in the field.

"If you are in agreement with paragraphs 2 and 3 above, I will direct my minister in Sweden to so inform Himmler's agent.

"An identical message is sent to Churchill."

It was that same evening, at eight o'clock, that I spoke over the radio from the White House to the delegates who had assembled in San Francisco for the opening of the United Nations Conference.

"At no time in history," I began, "has there been a more important conference, or a more necessary meeting, than this one in San Francisco which you are opening today.

"On behalf of the American people, I extend to you a most hearty welcome."

I then referred to the delegation President Roosevelt had appointed to represent the United States and expressed my complete confidence in them. I referred to Roosevelt himself and to his high ideals, his foresight, and his determination. I referred as well to the great sacrifice he and so many others had made in the cause of liberty.

"You members of the conference," I went on to say, "are to be the architects of the better world. In your hands rests our future. By your labors at this conference we shall know if suffering humanity is to achieve a just and lasting peace."

I warned them of the ever-increasing brutality and destructiveness of modern warfare and of the danger that it might ultimately crush all civilization.

"It is not the purpose of this conference," I told them, "to draft a treaty of peace in the old sense of that term. It is not our assignment to settle specific questions of territories, boundaries, citizenship and reparations.

"This conference will devote its energies and its labors exclusively to the single problem of setting up the essential organization to keep the peace. You are to write the fundamental charter.

"The essence of our problem here, is to provide sensible machinery for the settlement of disputes among nations.

"We must build a new world," I concluded, "a far better world—one in which the eternal dignity of man is respected.

"As we are about to undertake our heavy duties, we beseech Almighty God to guide us in building a permanent monument to those who gave their lives that this moment might come.

"May He lead our steps in His own righteous path of peace."

On Thursday, April 26, I had my second conference with the Director of the Budget, Harold D. Smith. Developments on the war front were compelling a swift restudy and reappraisal of policies and commitments, both foreign and domestic. I had previously instructed Smith to prepare new estimates for various war agencies such as the War Manpower Commission, the Office of War Information, the War Production Board, the Office of Civilian Defense, and the Maritime Commission. We would be safe, I thought, if we were to reduce some of these agencies and drastically cut, or even eliminate, others. During the war so many agencies had been set up that the government had grown to unwieldy proportions. As an example of this, I cited to Smith the condition in the field of manpower.

So many organizations were functioning in this area that our permanent department in the government, the Department of Labor, had been virtually dormant. In view of this fact, I asked Smith to prepare a presidential order directing that the scattered labor functions now administered by the wartime agencies be placed within the Department of Labor and under the direction of the Secretary of Labor.

I told Smith in confidence that in view of this fundamental reorganization of the Labor Department it would probably be necessary to appoint a new secretary of the department. Labor-management relations had grown tense and explosive because of the wage and price controls of the war years, and the Department of Labor in the period ahead would require a secretary who, in addition to having the full support of labor, would have the experience and reputation necessary for dealing successfully with Congress. I suggested to Smith that he defer his conference with the Department of Labor until I had found a successor to Miss Perkins.

Miss Perkins had already expressed her desire to be relieved of the post, saying, "I have survived my usefulness." I held her in very high regard and believed she had done a good job despite the fact that many of her responsibilities had been taken from the department by the emergency agencies. She understood the problems of labor and had played an important role in the development of relations between labor and management. She was convinced that a new head of the department during the postwar period would have the advantage of a fresh start and better support from the Congress.

I first met Miss Perkins in 1933, when the New Deal administration had come into power. At that time she had appointed me employment director for the state of Missouri in connection with the federal government's activities to meet the economic crisis. From June 1933 until I went to the Senate, I combined these federal duties with the job of running Jackson County and first came to understand and appreciate Miss Perkins' ability and stature. As the years went by I learned what a fine human being she was. When I came to Washington as a senator, I saw her from time to time, and on occasion we were members of a group which lunched at the Allies Inn, a cafeteria where, with other government employees, we carried our own trays and talked over common problems.

From labor I turned to the housing problem and asked Smith to make a comprehensive survey of housing and what the government was doing about it. Frankly, I thought the housing situation was a mess. What government participation there was had not been adequately managed during the war. And housing would play an important role in the planning of our peace economy.

I cautioned Smith that in planning for peace we should not lose sight of the fact that, even with victory in Europe, we still had a major war to win in the Pacific. Any premature letdown of morale in the departments and war agencies would be harmful. Therefore, in making cuts in the budget for the war agencies, we had to keep in mind that we might create a wholesale exodus of personnel, thus crippling the usefulness of the agencies that still had work to do.

Our methods, I said, should be guided by orderly liquidation and by the proper briefing of the department heads who would be affected. Smith agreed and promised that before recommending any cuts to me he would consult with the heads of all departments and agencies.

I was particularly anxious that such agencies as the Office of Price Administration, the Petroleum Administration for War, and the Foreign Economic Administration should not be touched because of their importance to economic stabilization. Smith recommended a reduction in the budget of the Maritime Commission of four billion dollars in contract authorization and three billion dollars in cash. This was what I wanted, and I approved the slash. And I added that this was a good time to liquidate the Office of Civilian Defense and to reduce the budgets of the Office of Censorship and the Office of Defense Transportation.

Unemployment compensation and old-age assistance, on the other hand, formed a very different problem. They would increase when our war production changed over to peacetime industry. In fact, many of the older men and women had already been withdrawn from the labor market, and we had to keep an eye on the human and economic consequences of this trend.

Smith submitted a memorandum proposing to appropriate a sum of money for the Red Cross. He told me that President Roosevelt had twice before rejected this proposal but had recently reversed himself and asked that the item be included. Smith, however, declared that he himself was still opposed to the proposal, and I agreed. It was my belief that if we undertook to appropriate money for the Red Cross we would find ourselves obliged to appropriate money for many other private groups as well. There was also the possibility that appropriations of this nature would tend to undercut the UNRRA program. I intended to discuss the whole subject of foreign relief with Governor Lehman, head of UNRRA. I asked Smith for all available data on the relief situation in the countries where UNRRA was now functioning.

We next took up the proposed Lend-Lease appropriations concerning which I had already had a talk with Leo Crowley, Administrator of the Foreign Economic Administration. The amount suggested by Smith was slightly below that of the previous year, one reason being that resistance to Lend-Lease was growing in Congress. This was fostered by the isolationist bloc, which grew bolder as victory in Europe approached. The country was being flooded with isolationist propaganda under various guises, and many of us were apprehensive lest the isolationist spirit again become an important political factor.

Lend-Lease was intended to provide our allies with the weapons of war and the matériel necessary to supplement their own war production.

Under broad interpretations of what constituted matériel, however, some supplies were diverted to civilian use and industrial rehabilitation, and this became one of the targets at which the critics aimed.

The original Lend-Lease Act was introduced in the House of Representatives and Senate on January 10, 1941. After hearings and debate, it was passed by both branches and signed by President Roosevelt on March 11, 1941. Thereafter it was extended twice, and on April 17, five days after I had become President, I signed the third extension, approving an act which had come before the Senate when I was presiding as Vice-President.

Smith recalled that a Republican-sponsored amendment which would have prohibited the President from contracting for use of the Lend-Lease program for postwar relief, rehabilitation, or reconstruction had resulted in a 39–39 vote, and that I, as Vice-President, had cast the deciding vote which defeated the amendment. The act had then passed the Senate on April 10 by unanimous voice vote.

I understood that if we were to use Lend-Lease funds for rehabilitation purposes we would open ourselves to a lot of trouble with the Senate. However, Leo Crowley also recognized this fact and had suggested that a better way to handle rehabilitation would be to enlarge the Export-Import Bank so as to make funds available for that purpose and also to encourage more use of the International Bank. I explained Crowley's suggestion to Smith, with whom I then discussed the problem of making unilateral loans to foreign countries. Such loans, of course, would lead to repercussions at home and might cause Allied suspicion of our moves. They might even provide Russia with an excuse, if she needed one, to undertake unilateral arrangements of her own. For these reasons I was opposed to unilateral action in any field. Loans to some countries, however, were so essential to their survival that I felt it necessary to make them even at some risk that they would not be fully repaid.

Smith had previously sent President Roosevelt a Bureau of the Budget memorandum concerning the organization of intelligence in the government, and I had read it. In it he had pointed out that a tug of war was going on among the FBI, the Office of Strategic Services, the Army and Navy Intelligence, and the State Department. He added that recently the Bureau of the Budget had worked closely with the General Staff of the Army, which had reorganized the intelligence operations in the Army, and I was now told that the Budget Bureau itself had some experienced and competent people who had become specialists in the problems of intelligence organization.

I considered it very important to this country to have a sound, well-organized intelligence system, both in the present and in the future.

Properly developed, such a service would require new concepts as well as better-trained and more competent personnel. Smith suggested, and I agreed, that studies should be undertaken at once by his specially trained experts in this field. Plans needed to be made, but it was imperative that we refrain from rushing into something that would produce harmful and unnecessary rivalries among the various intelligence agencies. I told Smith that one thing was certain—this country wanted no Gestapo under any guise or for any reason.

At the conclusion of my long session with the Director of the Budget, I again called his attention to Lend-Lease, emphasizing the importance of refining the estimates still further. This was to be my first budget as President, and I hoped to be able to justify every detail it contained.

Early that morning I had received a group of Pennsylvanians headed by Senators Joseph F. Guffey and Francis J. Myers. Mrs. Emma Guffey Miller, Senator Guffey's sister and Democratic national committeewoman from Pennsylvania, was in the group, which also included David L. Lawrence, chairman of the Democratic State Committee, and James P. Clark, chairman of the Democratic City Committee of Philadelphia. The delegation assured me of the solid support of their state's Democratic organizations, and I heard Mayor Lawrence say something about supporting me in 1948. I could say nothing, of course, because any comment would have been improper. In the position I occupied a day seemed like an eternity, and I had no right or mind to look ahead in that direction. This was hardly a time for political speculation. War was still raging, and a shattered world needed restoration. I could give no serious thought to anything else.

It was the next day that I received the following cable from Marshal Stalin:

I have received your message of April 26. Thank you for your information of the intention of Himmler to capitulate on the Western Front. I consider your proposed reply to Himmler along the lines of unconditional surrender on all fronts, including the Soviet front, absolutely correct. I ask you to act in the spirit of your proposal, and we Russians pledge to continue our attacks against the Germans.

For your information I wish you to know that I have given a similar reply to Premier Churchill, who communicated with me on the same question.

I replied immediately.

I have today sent the following message to Minister Johnson, Stockholm:
QUOTE. Replying to your message of April 25, 3 A.M., inform Himmler's agent that the only acceptable terms of surrender by Germany are uncondi-

tional surrender on all fronts to the Soviet Government, Great Britain and the United States.

If the above stated terms of surrender are accepted the German forces should surrender on all fronts at once to the local commanders in the field.

In all theaters where resistance continues the attack of the Allies upon them will be vigorously prosecuted until complete victory is attached. UNQUOTE.

CHAPTER 8

On the evening of April 26, among the reports and messages I had taken with me to Blair House, I was especially interested in a memorandum dealing with the occupation of Germany when the fighting ended.

Some three weeks before his death, on March 23, President Roosevelt had issued a general directive for the treatment of Germany after our forces had established themselves in the designated zones. Roosevelt had also issued instructions that more detailed directives be prepared. And for this purpose a committee had been formed. It was made up of representatives of the State, War, and Navy departments and of the Foreign Economic Administration, and it had begun its work under the chairmanship of Assistant Secretary of State Will Clayton. As yet, the work of this committee had not been completed, and I asked Assistant Secretary of War John J. McCloy to prepare a memorandum for me on this whole subject. This memorandum was now in my hands, and I studied it in preparation for a conference with the committee the next morning.

McCloy's memorandum advised me that the committee's work would shortly be completed. He went on to say that President Roosevelt had in mind the appointment of a civilian as High Commissioner for Germany but had agreed to permit General Eisenhower to operate as military governor of that part of Germany we were to control and as a representative on the Control Council for Germany. No civilian commissioner would be appointed for at least the initial period. During its first phase the occupation would be primarily a military operation anyway. Pacification operations would necessarily be in military hands. It was thought better that the initial impact on the German people should be exclusively military. The Germans would understand it better.

General Eisenhower, the memorandum said, had often shown such marked political acumen as to justify this arrangement, and General Lucius D. Clay, who had been selected to assist Eisenhower as deputy, was already in Europe recruiting men for the staff he would require.

McCloy's report pointed out the imperative need in Germany for food, fuel, and transportation. The destruction of cities, towns, and facilities had been immense, the vast number of displaced persons formed an enormous problem, and the dissolution of society and its facilities was shocking. "There is complete economic, social and political collapse going on in Central Europe, the extent of which is unparalleled in history unless one goes back to the collapse of the Roman Empire, and even that may not have been as great an economic upheaval.

"In this atmosphere of disturbance and collapse, atrocities and disarrangement," the memorandum added, "we are going to have to work out a practical relationship with the Russians. It will require the highest talents, tolerance and wisdom in order to accomplish our aims.

"The need for topnotch men is painfully apparent. It may require assistance from the President in order to shake loose from the agencies and civilian life men of the quality, character and strength needed."

McCloy reported a talk with General de Gaulle, who said he did not favor a scorched-earth policy for Germany, but believed there should be some economic controls, especially an international control of the Ruhr. De Gaulle wanted the left bank of the Rhine from Cologne to the Swiss border under French political control.

I then turned to a report on China from the State Department. It summarized the basic lines of policy toward China which this country had been following to date:

Our major objectives with respect to China are: effective joint prosecution of the war against Japan; and from a long-range standpoint, the establishment of a strong and united China as a necessary principal stabilizing factor in the Far East.

POLITICAL. Toward both the immediate objective of defeating Japan and the long-term objective of peace and security, we seek to promote establishment of broadly representative Chinese government which will bring about internal unity, including reconcilement of Kuomintang-Communist differences and will effectively discharge its internal and international responsibilities.

While favoring no political faction, we continue to support the existing government of China, headed by Chiang Kai-shek, as the still generally recognized central authority which thus far offers the best hope for unification and for avoidance of chaos in China's war effort. However, with regard to our long-term objective and against the possible disintegration of the authority of the existing government, it is our purpose to maintain a degree of flexibility to permit cooperation with any other leadership in China which may give greater promise of achievement of unity and contributing to peace and security in east Asia. We are, meanwhile, assisting China, as a nation, to attain a position of recognized equality among the major powers.

We seek the cooperation of the Soviet Union and Great Britain as essential to the success of such policies. Toward that end we aim to promote friendship and mutual trust in Sino-Soviet and Sino-British relations. Where specific territorial or other issues exist, we would welcome, and assist when appropriate, amicable remedial arrangements, including, for example: facilitation of the passage of Soviet trade through Manchuria, with the possible designation by China of a free port; restoration of Hong Kong to China and the perpetuation by China of its status of a free port; and adjustment of China's claims to outlying territories, such as Tibet and Outer Mongolia, with the concerned Soviet or British interests, as well as with aspirations of the native peoples of such territories for local autonomy.

As a further basis for peace and stability, we favor the establishment by China of close and friendly relations with Korea, Burma, Thailand, Indochina and other neighboring areas, without Chinese domination over such areas.

ECONOMIC. Our short-term policy is directed toward the strengthening of the economic basis of China's war effort through: expansion of supply routes and services into China; lend-lease supplies to the limit of transport facilities; and joint Sino-American measures to strengthen China's war production, increase its supply of consumer goods, improve its internal transport systems, and combat its serious inflation.

Our long-range policy centers on the development of an integrated and well-balanced Chinese economy and a fuller flow of trade between China and other countries. Toward these objectives we seek full economic collaboration among China, the United States, Britain, the Soviet Union and other peace-loving nations on a basis of equality of opportunity, respect for national sovereignty, and liberal trade policies. We hope that China, for its part, will contribute to such collaboration, so necessary to China's agricultural and economic development, through the institution of reasonable policies calculated to encourage legitimate trade and enterprise.

We ourselves would expect—taking due account of the policies which may be followed by the Chinese Government and of actual conditions affecting American trade with and in China—to extend to China all practicable economic, financial and technical assistance which she may require in connection with her efforts to plan an integrated and well-balanced economy. We look forward to promoting mutually profitable Sino-American trade by all practicable means and to negotiating soon with China a comprehensive, modern commercial treaty.

MILITARY. Our established military policy relating to China is thus far confined to the immediate objective of effective joint prosecution of the war through direct military assistance to China, promotion of Sino-American military cooperation, and assistance in mobilizing all of China's human and material resources against Japan. Parallel with our efforts to strengthen the political and economic bases of China's war effort, already outlined, we are undertaking to reorganize, train and equip part of the Chinese National Army as a compact striking force capable of playing a major part in driving the Japanese from China. We are also seeking to bring about vitally needed

Chinese military unity through integration of the Communist forces with those of the National Government.

From the standpoint of our long-range political objective of a strong China able to contribute to peace and security, we would logically expect to assist China to develop a modern and effective postwar military organization. In view, however, of the uncertain present political situation in China and its potentialities for civil war and complications with Soviet Russia, we are not prepared to commit ourselves with the present Chinese Government for the rendering of such assistance until we are convinced that that government is making progress toward achieving unity and toward gaining the solid support of the Chinese people.

This memorandum expressed to a large degree my preliminary thinking about China.

The San Francisco conference, which convened on April 25, was now in the early stage of discussion. The first progress report from our delegation reached my desk the morning of April 27. It dealt with organizational details and the statements of Stettinius, Soong, Molotov, and Eden.

Stettinius stressed two points: first, that we considered it essential that the United Nations Charter should be subject to amendment later in accordance with experience and changing circumstances; and, second, the United Nations Organization must be based on the unity of the major powers, who would bear the chief responsibility, as well as the sovereign equality of all states, large and small.

Soong, speaking for China, said that all nations must be ready to make sacrifices of sovereignty in order to achieve collective security.

Molotov declared that the U.S.S.R. was a firm supporter of a strong and effective international organization, that it would co-operate fully in creating and maintaining such an organization, and that he was confident of success in this task.

Eden laid emphasis on the fact that the great powers, because of their preponderance in armed force and resources, must exercise self-restraint.

During that same morning I saw Senator Owen Brewster of Maine and Senator Robert M. La Follette of Wisconsin. The Speaker of the House, Sam Rayburn, came to talk about pending legislation.

Rayburn was followed by the committee, headed by Assistant Secretary Clayton, dealing with the problems of Germany's occupation. He came with Acting Secretary of State Grew, Foreign Economic Administration Director Crowley, Assistant Secretary of War John J. McCloy, and Under Secretary of the Navy Ralph Bard. Secretary of the Treasury Henry Morgenthau joined the meeting. McCloy, who had recently returned from a special mission to Germany, presented a detailed report.

McCloy pointed out that General Eisenhower, as Supreme Allied Commander, was, for the present, in command of the whole Western Front, where the Allied armies occupied forty-three per cent of Germany, but he would lose that position very soon after V-E Day. He would then become just one of the four members of the Allied Control Council and military governor of only that portion of Germany that was to be occupied by American troops.

McCloy made it clear that the chaotic conditions which existed in Germany and the limited stores of food that were available there might, unless rapid steps were taken to correct the situation, result in actual starvation on a widespread scale. "One of the chief elements of disorder is the immense number of previously enslaved people who will be running around loose, as well as Germans who have been made homeless by the devastation of victory."

McCloy said his visit to Germany had been taken in order to convey to General Eisenhower the last thoughts of President Roosevelt on the administration of Germany, particularly in the light of the President's March 23 directive. In addition, he had gone in order to see that the minds of the American authorities on both sides of the Atlantic were in accord.

General Clay, he explained, was to be Eisenhower's deputy as military governor and Eisenhower's representative on the Allied Control Council when Eisenhower was not present.

These appointments had been made prior to President Roosevelt's death, and I informed the committee that I heartily approved them. I then asked the committee to complete its work on the directive to be issued and to present it to me for final study and approval. Rapid developments were under way in Germany, and I urged them to complete their task as quickly as possible.

With this meeting completed, I received Oliver Lyttelton, British Minister of Production, who told me in some detail how serious the food and supply situation was in Great Britain. The only good supply of food in Britain at the moment was wheat. There were serious shortages of fats, oils, sugar, meat, and most dairy products, as well as of coal, transportation, and textiles. It was imperative that supplies arrive very soon, and I suggested that Lyttelton confer with the various United States government agencies charged with the responsibility for aiding our allies. I assured him that I would intervene personally. In fact, shortly after he left, I saw Secretary of Agriculture Wickard and Secretary of Commerce Wallace and told them of my conversation with Lyttelton, instructing them to do what was possible to help our British allies.

I had luncheon with Federal Judge Lewis B. Schwellenbach, a former colleague in the United States Senate from the state of Washington. I told Judge Schwellenbach I wanted him to join my Cabinet as Secretary of Labor, and I outlined my plans for a reorganization of the Labor Department. I needed someone who not only understood the problems of labor but who could also deal with Congress on a co-operative basis. The reconversion of American industry from war production to peacetime output would raise many labor and industrial questions, and I was glad when Schwellenbach accepted.

News was flashed to me that the expected linking up of American, British, and Russian military forces had just taken place in Germany. Anglo-American forces under the command of General Courtney Hodges had finally met Marshal Ivan S. Konev's First Ukrainian Army on the Elbe River. Germany was cut in two.

Events were now moving swiftly, and I issued my long-prepared statement on behalf of the United States simultaneously with the release of statements by Churchill and Stalin. Agreement on the texts of what we three now gave to the press and radio had been reached earlier by cable. But despite careful preparation there was a last-minute mix-up in the timing of these statements, and it actually necessitated a pre-dawn telephone call from London by Prime Minister Churchill to me.

At two o'clock I met with General Marshall, Admiral Leahy, and a group of top military men to discuss the latest military situation and Himmler's attempt to get Sweden to intervene in arranging for a surrender of Germany to the Western powers. We had stood firm against any separate action, as I had already informed Stalin. General Marshall handed me a message from General Eisenhower.

"I hope it is fitting for me to register my extreme satisfaction," Eisenhower had cabled, "with the message sent to Mister Johnson at Stockholm. Two nights ago when the Prime Minister called me up upon his first receipt of the message from Sweden, I advised him strongly to take the attitude expressed in your [the President's] message. He agreed completely that the offer looked like a last desperate attempt to create a schism between ourselves and the Russians. In every move we make these days we are trying to be meticulously careful in this regard."

When the military left, I turned for a time to some paper work, and at four-thirty Edwin W. Pauley and Dr. Isador Lubin arrived. I told Pauley that I was appointing him Ambassador and personal representative of the President in matters relating to reparations. Lubin, I added, was to be his deputy and was to have the rank of Minister. Both were to be American representatives on the Allied Reparations Commission, and they were to negotiate an agreement with the British and the Russians concerning reparations from Germany.

When they left, I picked up my usual stack of papers and went to Blair House.

I set aside part of Saturday morning, April 28, to see a number of senators and congressmen.

For the past two days there had been rumors that Germany had surrendered unconditionally—rumors that were based largely on Himmler's eleventh-hour communication with Sweden attempting to avoid a surrender to the Russians by offering to give up to the Western Allies. We paid no attention to these rumors, but they gained momentum as a result of a statement by Senator Connally, a member of our delegation at San Francisco. Senator Connally told the Associated Press that the United States was momentarily expecting Germany's unconditional surrender. Secretary of State Stettinius telephoned me asking for confirmation. I instructed Admiral Leahy to check by telephoning General Eisenhower, who informed Leahy that there was no foundation for the report. Shortly after nine-thirty that evening I called the White House correspondents into my office and informed them that I had just checked with Supreme Headquarters in Europe and that there was no truth to the report of unconditional surrender.

I was up before six on the morning of Sunday, April 29, and before breakfast I wrote Mama and Mary. It had been more than a week since my last letter, but I had found a little spare time now.

Dear Mamma & Mary:—Received your letter with the one from Dr. Graham in it and was glad to get it. Hope you and Mary have not been bothered too much. It is terrible—and I mean terrible—nuisance to be kin to the President of the United States. Reporters have been haunting every relative and purported relative I ever heard of, and they've probably made life miserable for my mother, brother and sister. I am sorry for it, but it can't be helped.

A guard has to go with Bess and Margaret everywhere they go—and they don't like it. They both spend a lot of time figuring how to beat the game, but it just can't be done. In a country as big as this one there are necessarily a lot of nuts and people with peculiar ideas. They seem to focus on the White House and the President's kin. Hope you won't get too badly upset about it.

Between the papers and the nuts they surely made life miserable for the Roosevelt family. Maybe they can have some peace now. I hope so.

I must caution both of you to take good care of your health. Don't let the pests get you down. I'm writing this before breakfast—before anyone is up.

Love to you both.

Harry

Several dispatches were delivered to me at Blair House that morning. One of them was a long cable from Prime Minister Churchill transmitting his message of the same day to Stalin on the subject of Poland.

We were making very little headway with Stalin over the explosive

Polish question. Stalin's cable to me of a few days before had left me greatly concerned, and though in my meetings with Molotov I had urged him to try to work out a solution with the British and American delegations at San Francisco, Stalin's response, which had been sent to Churchill as well as to me, had dimmed any hope of an early solution.

Churchill was now addressing a fervent personal appeal to the Russian Premier. His message to Stalin, which lay before me, expressed distress at the misunderstanding that had grown over the Crimea agreement about Poland. Churchill said he had certainly gone to Yalta with the hope that both the London and Lublin Polish governments would be swept away and that a new government would be formed from Poles of good will, among whom the members of Bierut's (Lublin) government would be prominent. But Stalin had not liked this plan, Churchill reminded him, and the British and the Americans had agreed that there would be no sweeping away of the Bierut government and that instead it should become a "new" government, reorganized on a broader democratic basis, with the inclusion of democratic leaders from Poland itself and from Poles abroad. The British Prime Minister pointed out that the Yugoslav example which the Russians now insisted should be followed in Poland was not satisfactory.

Tito, he said, had become a complete dictator and had proclaimed his first loyalty was to Soviet Russia, and the concessions made in Belgrade to the members of the government-in-exile were to the extent of six only, against twenty-five of Tito's own nominees.

Churchill declared that the pledge given for a sovereign free and independent Poland, with a government adequately representing all the democratic elements among Poles, was a matter of honor and duty for us. "After all," he went on, "we have joined with you, largely on my original initiative, early in 1944, in proclaiming the Polish-Russian frontier which you desired, namely, the Curzon Line, including Lwow for Russia. We think you ought to meet us with regard to the other half of the policy which you equally with us have proclaimed, namely, the sovereignty, independence, and freedom of Poland, provided it is a Poland friendly to Russia."

Churchill climaxed this appeal to Stalin by painting a picture of what the world might be like if divided into two camps. "There is not much comfort in looking into a future where you and the countries you dominate, plus the Communist parties in many other states, are all drawn up on one side, and those who rally to the English-speaking nations and their associates or dominions are on the other," he said. "It is quite obvious that their quarrel would tear the world to pieces and that all of us leading men on either side who had anything to do with that would be shamed before history. Even embarking on a long period of suspicions, of abuse and counter-abuse, and of opposing policies would be a disaster hampering the great developments of world prosperity for the masses which are attainable only by our trinity. I hope there is no word or phrase in this outpouring of my heart to you which unwittingly gives offence. If so, let me know. But do not, I beg you, my friend Stalin, underrate the divergencies which are opening about matters which you may think are small to us but which are symbolic of the way the English-speaking democracies look at life."

I heartily backed the British Prime Minister's plea to establish a free Poland and prevent a divided world. But I was afraid it would do little to change Stalin's attitude. The following morning a message from our delegation in San Francisco reported that discussions on Poland had reached an impasse.

Stettinius, Eden, and Molotov had gone to San Francisco with the idea of discussing the Polish matter further during the course of the conference. The message I now received informed me that Molotov's insistence on using for Poland the formula that had been applied in the case of the Yugoslav government had deadlocked the discussions. I now felt that it would be necessary for me to address Stalin directly once again.

I went to church at 11:00 A.M. at the Foundry Methodist Church. I had been invited by the preacher, who was also chaplain of the Senate. My experience that morning showed that it would be difficult for me to appear at any church without being on exhibition. I preferred to worship without distracting the congregation.

Among my early callers on the morning of Monday, April 30, were Congresswoman Edith Nourse Rogers of Massachusetts, Congressman John H. Tolan, and Senator Guy M. Gillette. Next, Judge Samuel I. Rosenman arrived, and I asked him to continue in his assignment to negotiate with our allies on dealing with war criminals. He was with me only a few minutes, and I gave him the following letter designating him as my personal representative in these negotiations:

April 30, 1945

Dear Judge Rosenman:
I wish you to act as my personal representative in continuing your negotiations with the representatives of the United Kingdom, the Soviet Union and the Provisional Government of France for the purpose of obtaining agreement as to the method, procedures and tribunals for trying the war criminals of this war.
I understand that in your preliminary talks in London in these negotiations—to which you had been originally assigned by the late President—the British representatives had stated that the policy of their government was to

dispose politically of the top-ranking Nazis and Fascists—without any trial. The Government of the United States is opposed to such policy.

Therefore you will please insist upon a fair method of trial, but one which will be as short and expeditious as possible. Those guilty of the atrocities which have shocked the world since 1933 down to date must be brought to speedy justice and swift punishment—but their guilt must be found judicially under rules of procedure adopted by the four great powers which will admit of no delay or evasion of any kind.

Very sincerely yours,
Harry S. Truman

At 10:30 A.M. I saw Joseph E. Davies, former Ambassador to Russia, whom I had asked to come in as I had previously asked Hopkins. I explained that I wanted him to go to London to see Churchill. Hopkins, I added, was to see Stalin in Moscow, and I considered both assignments to be of primary importance because it was imperative for me to know whether the death of Roosevelt had brought any important changes in the attitudes of Stalin and Churchill.

I wanted personal, on-the-spot reports from men with judgment and experience, for it was necessary for me to know more than I was able to get from messages and cables or even from telephone conversations. I told Davies that one of the principal reasons for sending him to London was that he had been Ambassador to Moscow and was personally familiar with the Russian situation. Because of that he could discuss effectively with Churchill our mounting difficulties with Russia. Furthermore, Churchill had already suggested that he and I meet with Stalin, and I wanted to find out what I would have to face if I were to agree to such a meeting. I especially needed in more detail the personal attitudes of Churchill and Stalin and felt that both Davies and Hopkins would report fully and frankly to me. There were many other questions I wanted answered, of course, and I wished to learn how far these two leaders were prepared to go in their attempts to solve the problems that confronted us.

Davies was not well. In fact, when I saw how drawn he looked, I was hesitant to make such great demands upon him. But he waived any consideration of his health and agreed to go.

Davies left, and I saw William Green, president of the American Federation of Labor. I told him about my intention to appoint Judge Schwellenbach as Secretary of Labor and to reorganize the Department of Labor more along the lines of the Department of Commerce.

I said I thought the Department of Commerce had become a channel to the White House for business and industry and that such organizations as the United States Chamber of Commerce and the National Association of Manufacturers co-operated closely and in full harmony in their relations with government through the Department of Commerce. Their rivalries as organizations ceased when they came to Washington.

I regretted that this was not the case with labor, which was divided into a number of powerful organizations and did not utilize the facilities of the Department of Labor as a basis for co-operative effort. I expressed the hope that, with the reorganization, labor could be induced to use the new Department of Labor as effectively as business was using the Department of Commerce. I added that it was not enough for labor to use its political strength every four years and divide into rival groups, with each group negotiating for itself alone. Neither the interests of labor nor the country were advanced by these divisions. I told Green I intended also to see Phil Murray of the CIO and George Harrison of the railroad brotherhoods and urge them to make more use of the Department of Labor. Green said that labor was well aware of the handicaps of so many divisions and had been hoping for more unity from the days of Gompers. He was glad to hear of the plans for the Department of Labor and the selection of Schwellenbach for the post of Secretary.

After Green, other callers followed at fifteen-minute intervals: Governors Herbert R. O'Conor of Maryland, J. Howard McGrath of Rhode Island, and Robert Kerr of Oklahoma; Elmer Davis, Director of the Office of War Information.

I had no guest for lunch, but in my office at two-thirty my first three major appointees were sworn in: John W. Snyder as Federal Loan Administrator, Edwin W. Pauley as U.S. representative on the Allied Reparations Commission, and Edward D. McKim as chief administrative assistant to the President.

This was the last day of April 1945. Only eighteen days had passed since I had become President. It is astonishing how much had happened and was crowded into those few days. I felt as if I had lived through several lifetimes. Among the many burdensome duties and responsibilities of a President, I soon experienced the constant pressure and necessity of making immediate decisions.

CHAPTER 9

One of the difficulties I encountered in connection with being President was the intrusion of journalistic curiosity about my personal affairs and my family. Stories were being written about my early life, associations, and education, intended, perhaps, to shed some light on the reasons for my actions and what course I would be likely to take. Would I continue the New Deal or would I modify it? Would I retain or dismiss the liberals in the government? Would I be more partisan politically than my predecessor? These speculations about what I would do led to many baseless conclusions. Far too often they grew out of inaccuracies or even untruths about my life.

Ultimately, when books came to be written about me, many questionable or untrue statements began to appear as if they were actual parts of "the record." One such book—it was a book for children—contained, it seemed to me, more inaccuracies than facts and more false quotations than true ones from individuals who purportedly had been interviewed about me.

I believe it fair to say that a great deal of misinformation about me has gained a foothold in this way, and I suppose that some of these "facts" will not be dislodged easily. Still, I hope to prevent the spread of further misinformation, and for that reason I digress at this point to write about myself. I do so without any introspective trimmings.

My parents were married on December 28, 1881. I was born in Lamar, Missouri, at four o'clock in the afternoon on May 8, 1884. When I was about a year old, the family moved to Cass County, Missouri, south of Harrisonville, where my father ran a farm and where my brother Vivian was born on April 25, 1886. In 1887 we moved to the Sol Young farm in Jackson County, two miles south of Hickman's Mill and six miles north of Belton in Cass County. Later on, a railroad promoter by the name of Blair built a rail line from Kansas City to Springfield, Missouri, and established a station a mile south of the Young farm. It was named Grandview because it was on a high point of land, the highest point in the vicinity, in fact. Lawrence, Kansas, is visible forty miles west, Kansas City eighteen miles north, Lee's Summit eight miles east, and Belton six miles south. The site would have made a wonderful observatory from which to study the heavens.

My sister Mary Jane was born there on August 12, 1889.

My grandfather Truman lived with my father wherever he went, and I remember him very well. He was a dignified, pleasant man, particularly with Vivian and me. I fear he spoiled us. My grandfather Young and our lovely grandmother, who had beautiful red hair and who made wonderful cookies, also gave us free rein. My grandmother Truman had died before my parents were married.

We had the whole 440 acres to play over and 160 acres west across the road for the same purpose. Some of my happiest and most pleasant recollections are of the years we spent on the Young farm when I was between the ages of three and six.

I had a bobtailed Maltese gray cat and a little black-and-tan dog not much bigger than the cat. The old cat was named Bob, because one day when he was asleep in front of the big fireplace in the dining room a coal of fire popped out, lit on the end of his tail, and burned off about an inch of it. I can well remember his yowls, and I can see him yet as he ran up the corner of the room all the way to the ceiling. The little dog was called Tandy because of his black-and-tan color.

These two animals followed Vivian and me everywhere we went, and me alone when Vivian was asleep or too tired to wander over the farm. I was missed on one occasion and was discovered in a cornfield a half mile from the house, enjoying the antics of the cat and dog catching field mice.

On another occasion we were playing south of the house in a beautiful pasture with a lovely maple grove in front of it. We had a new little wagon all painted red. I would pull Vivian and a neighbor boy our age named Chandler, and then the Chandler boy, with Vivian's help, would pull me. We discovered a mud hole at the end of the grove, and I pulled the wagon with the two boys in it into the hole and upset it. It seemed a good thing to do, and it was repeated several times, taking turn about. When my mother found us, we were plastered with mud and dirty water from head to foot. What a grand spanking I got as the ringleader!

Then there was a long porch on the north side of the house which made a great race track, a swing in the front hallway for rainy days, and a big one in the yard for sunny ones.

My grandfather Young would take me to the Belton Fair, when it was running, in a big two-wheeled cart with high wheels like the one that used to be shown hitched to Nancy Hanks, the great trotter. I would sit in the judges' stand with Grandpa and watch the races, eat striped candy and peanuts, and have the best time a kid ever had.

We had an old bachelor uncle named Harrison Young who visited us once in a while. He lived in Kansas City, which seemed a long way off, and he would bring Vivian and me the most wonderful things to play with and all kinds of candy, nuts, and fruit. When he came it was just like Christmas.

My grandfather Young had a half sister in St. Louis who would visit us about once a year. When she came she would take us over to the back pasture, which seemed miles away but wasn't more than a half mile. We would hunt birds' nests in the tall prairie grass and gather daisies, prairie wild flowers, and wild strawberries. When we returned to the house we'd require a good scrubbing and a long nap.

In the fall, when the apples and peaches were ripe, they were picked, the peaches dried and the apples buried in the ground with straw and boards above them. In midwinter the apples would be dug up, and were they good! My mother and grandmother dried a lot of peaches and apples, and what fine pies they would make in the winter. There were peach butter, apple butter, grape butter, jellies and preserves, all made in the kitchen by Mama, Grandma, and the German hired girl. All were good cooks.

Later, after the fall freeze, came hog-killing time, with sausages, souse, pickled pigs' feet, and the rendering of lard in a big iron kettle in the smokehouse. Vivian still has that kettle. Mama used to tell me that the only reason it was there was because it had been too heavy for the Kansas Red Legs to carry when they robbed the house during the Civil War, burned it, and killed all the four hundred fat hogs, taking only the hams.

We had a cousin, Sol Chiles, who lived with us at the time. He was about eighteen years old, and he really made life pleasant for us. About the time we moved to Independence, he went to live with his mother, my mother's older sister, Aunt Sally. She was a lovely person, as were all my many aunts.

There was Aunt Sue, who lived in Arizona. She was my mother's oldest sister and the best talker of them all. Later on she taught me how to play cribbage.

Aunt Ada, Mama's youngest sister, lived in Illinois. She taught me how to play euchre. Aunt Laura, Mama's other sister, lived in Kansas City, and we always enjoyed visiting her.

My father had three sisters and a brother. The youngest was Aunt Matt, who was a schoolteacher. She'd come to see us, and it was an event, sure enough. She taught us all sorts of outdoor games. Aunt Ella lived in Independence. She was my father's oldest sister, and we saw a lot of her and her three daughters after we moved to Independence. We grew up and went to school with cousins Nellie and Ethel Noland, Aunt Ella's daughters. Nellie would translate my Latin lesson for me when I was in high school, and I would escort Ethel to parties and learn how to be polite from her. I was always afraid of the girls my age and older.

Aunt Emma, Papa's other sister, lived on a farm about four miles northeast of the Young farm. There were four children in her family, and we really had a grand time when we spent the day with them.

Those were wonderful days and great adventures. My father bought me a beautiful black Shetland pony and the grandest saddle to ride him with I ever saw. Vivian has just had that lovely saddle rehabilitated for his three-year-old granddaughter, sixty-five years later.

My father would let me ride over the farm with him beside his big horse. He and Grandpa Young were partners in the operation of the farm and the handling of herds of cattle and mules as well as hogs and sheep. I became familiar with every sort of animal on the farm and watched the wheat harvest, the threshing and the corn shucking, mowing and stacking hay, and every evening at suppertime heard my father tell a dozen farm hands what to do and how to do it. In addition to the six hundred acres where we lived, there was another farm of nine hundred or a thousand acres four miles away, which had to be operated too.

When we moved to Independence in December 1890, my father bought a big house on South Chrisler Street with several acres of land, a wonderful strawberry bed, and a fine garden. At the same time, he was operating a farm southeast of town and went into buying and selling cattle, hogs, and sheep.

We began making acquaintances with neighbor boys as soon as we were settled. We had an old Negro woman who washed for us every week and sometimes cooked for us. She had three boys and two girls, and what a grand time we had. There was also another family of Negroes who were friends of our cook. There were a boy and a girl in that family.

With our barns, chicken house, and a grand yard in which to play, all the boys and girls in the neighborhood for blocks around congregated at our house. We always had ponies and horses to ride, goats to hitch to our little wagon, which was made like a big one. An old harness maker in Independence made Vivian a set of double harness just like the big set.

We would harness two red goats to the little wagon and drive it everywhere around the place. Years later this good old harness man defeated me for eastern judge of the Jackson County Court.

About this time my parents decided that we should start attending Sunday school. My mother took us to the nearest Protestant church, which happened to be the First Presbyterian at Lexington and Pleasant streets, and we attended regularly every Sunday for as long as we lived in Independence.

We made a number of new acquaintances, and I became interested in one in particular. She had golden curls and has, to this day, the most beautiful blue eyes. We went to Sunday school, public school from the fifth grade through high school, graduated in the same class, and marched down life's road together. For me she still has the blue eyes and golden hair of yesteryear.

My mother had taught me my letters and how to read before I was five years old, and because I had a hard time reading newspaper print I was taken to an oculist for an eye examination. I was fitted with glasses and started to school in the fall of 1892, when I was eight years old. The glasses were a great help in seeing but a great handicap in playing. I was so carefully cautioned by the eye doctor about breaking my glasses and injuring my eyes that I was afraid to join in the rough-and-tumble games in the schoolyard and the back lot. My time was spent in reading, and by the time I was thirteen or fourteen years old I had read all the books in the Independence Public Library and our big old Bible three times through.

In 1896 my father sold the house on Chrisler Street and bought one at 909 West Waldo Avenue at North River Boulevard. North River was the road to Wayne City Landing, which was the river port for Independence before the railroad came.

I have one or two vivid recollections of the Chrisler Street place that deserve mention. In the fall of 1892 Grover Cleveland was re-elected over Benjamin Harrison, who had defeated him in 1888. My father was very much elated by Cleveland's victory. He rode a beautiful gray horse in the torchlight parade and decorated the weather vane on the tower at the northwest corner of the house with a flag and bunting. The weather vane was a beautifully gilded rooster.

My first year in school was a happy one. My teacher was Miss Myra Ewing, with whom I became a favorite, as I eventually did with all my teachers. When I started the second grade, my teacher was Miss Minnie Ward.

In January of 1894, my second year at Noland School, Vivian and I had severe cases of diphtheria from which I had difficulty recovering.

My legs, arms, and throat were paralyzed for some months after the diphtheria left me, but Vivian made a rapid and complete recovery. My father and mother had sent Mary Jane back to the farm, and she did not have the disease. She also missed the measles and the mumps when we had them later.

The school board had decided to build a new school on South River, just back of the present auditorium of the Latter-Day Saints, and I never returned to the Noland School. The new school was the Columbian, and I went to summer school to Miss Jennie Clements the summer after my sickness to catch up. I skipped the third grade and went directly into the fourth, where Miss Mamie Dunn was my teacher.

We found West Waldo Street to be a most pleasant neighborhood, and there were boys and girls our age all around us with whom we became acquainted at once.

Next door, to the east, lived the Burrus family. There were three boys and five girls, three of the girls the ages of Vivian, Mary, and me. Next door east of the Burrus family lived the Wrights. Miss Emma and Miss Florence were lovely ladies. Miss Florence was a schoolteacher at the Ott School, and Miss Emma taught music. Arthur Wright was the oldest boy and was a partner with his father in a tailor shop in Kansas City. Lofton Wright was the second boy in the family and died after an operation for appendicitis. The youngest boy was named James, who became a very good friend of mine and who died of a heart attack at the age of thirty-five.

West on Waldo lived the Pittman family. There were Miss Maud, a schoolteacher, and Miss Ethel, then an older boy, and Bernard, who was Vivian's age and his pal. South and west of us on Blue Avenue lived the Smith boys, and at the other end of the block, just back of us on White Oak Street, lived the Chiles family with two boys, Henry and Morton, just the ages of Vivian and me. At the corner of Delaware and Waldo, east of us, were the Sawyers, the Wallaces, and the Thomases. Lock Sawyer was older than we were, and the Wallaces were a year or two younger. Bess, Frank, and George Wallace all belonged to the Waldo Avenue gang. Across the street at Woodland College were Paul and Helen Bryant. Paul and Vivian were great friends and raised pigeons and game chickens in partnership.

We had wonderful times in that neighborhood from 1896 to 1902. Our house soon became headquarters for all the boys and girls around. We had a large front yard, and our back yard was surrounded by a high board fence to keep the stock safely off the street. Uusually there were goats, calves, two or three cows, my pony, and my father's horses to be taken care of. The cows had to be milked and the horses curried, watered, and fed every morning and evening. In the summertime the cows had to be taken to pasture a mile or so away after morning milking and returned the same evening. The goats and calves had to be taken to the big public spring at Blue Avenue and River, two blocks south of our house, for water.

There was a wonderful barn with stalls for horses and cows, a corn-crib and a hayloft in which all the kids met and cooked up plans for all sorts of adventures, such as trips to Idlewild, a sort of wilderness two blocks north, and pigtail baseball games which I umpired because I couldn't see well enough to bat.

It was a very happy time, not fully appreciated until a long time afterward. There was a woodpile on which my brother and I had to work after old Rube, a good old colored man with a limp, had sawed the cord wood into the proper length for the cooking stove. The wood had to be split and carried to the wood box in the kitchen for "Aunt" Caroline's use in making cookies, corn bread, and all sorts of good things to eat.

Like us, Jim Wright and the McCarrolls were interested in raising pigeons. We had fantails, pouters, and many kinds of common everyday pigeons. We carried on quite a trading business in pigeons, chickens, cats, and pups. My mother was very patient with us and our pals and always came to our defense when we went a little too far and the various fathers decided to take a hand.

We also had a garden, which had to be weeded in season and a yard to be mowed and raked too. Somehow we managed to get most of the chores done which had been laid out by my father and still have time to play and enjoy the company of our pals too.

After a while we began to grow up. The gang scattered here and there, and shortly the serious business of education, jobs, and girls began to take all our time.

Education progressed, and we learned geometry, music, rhetoric, logic, and a smattering of astronomy. History and biography were my favorites. The lives of great men and famous women intrigued me, and I read all I could find about them.

We had an excellent history teacher, Miss Maggie Phelps, and an English teacher, Miss Tillie Brown, who was a genius at making us appreciate good literature. She also made us want to read it.

Our science teacher was Professor W. L. C. Palmer, who became principal of the high school and afterward superintendent of all the schools. He married our mathematics and Latin teacher, Miss Adelia Hardin.

I do not remember a bad teacher in all my experience. They were all different, of course, but they were the salt of the earth. They gave us our high ideals, and they hardly ever received more than forty dollars a month for it.

My debt to history is one which cannot be calculated. I know of no other motivation which so accounts for my awakening interest as a young lad in the principles of leadership and government.

Whether that early interest stemmed partly from some hereditary trait in my natural make-up is something for the psychologists to decide. But I know that the one great external influence which, more than anything else, nourished and sustained that interest in government and public service was the endless reading of history which I began as a boy and which I have kept up ever since.

In school, history was taught by paragraphs. Each great event in history was written up in one paragraph. I made it my business to look up the background of these events and to find out who brought them about. In the process I became very interested in the men who made world history. The lives of the great administrators of past ages intrigued me, and I soon learned that the really successful ones were few and far between. I wanted to know what caused the successes or the failures of all the famous leaders of history.

The only way to find the answers was to read. I pored over Plutarch's *Lives* time and time again and spent as much time reading Abbott's biographies of famous men. I read the standard histories of ancient Egypt, the Mesopotamian cultures, Greece and Rome, the exploits of Genghis Khan and the stories of oriental civilizations, the accounts of the development of every modern country, and particularly the history of America.

Reading history, to me, was far more than a romantic adventure. It was solid instruction and wise teaching which I somehow felt that I wanted and needed. Even as a youth I felt that I ought to know the facts about the system of government under which I was living, and how it came to be.

It seemed to me that if I could understand the true facts about the growth and development of the United States Government and could know the details of the lives of its presidents and political leaders I would be getting for myself a valuable part of the total education which I hoped to have someday. I know of no surer way to get a solid foundation in political science and public administration than to study the histories of past administrations of the world's most successful system of government.

While still a boy I could see that history had some extremely valuable lessons to teach. I learned from it that a leader is a man who has the ability to get other people to do what they don't want to do, and like it. It takes a leader to put economic, military, and government forces to work so they will operate. I learned that in those periods of history when there was no leadership, society usually groped through dark ages of one degree or another. I saw that it takes men to make history, or there would be no history. History does not make the man.

History showed me that Greece, which was not as big as the state of Missouri, left us ideas of government that are imperishable and fundamental to any society of people living together and governing themselves. It revealed to me that what came about in Philadelphia in 1776 really had its beginning in Hebrew times. In other words, I began to see that the history of the world has moved in cycles and that very often we find ourselves in the midst of political circumstances which appear to be new but which might have existed in almost identical form at various times during the past six thousand years.

Especially in reading the history of American Presidents did I become aware of the value of knowing what has gone before. I learned that the idea of universal military training, which was being hotly debated when I was in my teens, had first been recommended by President Washington in 1790. I learned of General McClellan, who traded his leadership for demagoguery and eventually defied his commander in chief, and was interested to learn how President Lincoln dealt with an insubordinate general.

These lessons were to stand me in good stead years later, when I was to be confronted with similar problems. There were countless other lessons which history taught that would prove valuable to me. There was the miserable performance of the Committee on the Conduct of the War in the 1860s, which did such a poor job for the federal government that Douglas Freeman, talking about his biography of Robert E. Lee, told me the committee was worth several divisions to the Confederacy. I was thoroughly familiar with the antics of that committee, and as chairman of the Senate special committee to investigate the defense effort in the 1940s, I avoided every pitfall into which my predecessors had fallen.

I learned of the unique problems of Andrew Johnson, whose destiny it was to be thrust suddenly into the presidency to fill the shoes of one of history's great leaders. When the same thing happened to me, I knew just how Johnson had coped with his problems, and I did not make the mistakes he made.

History taught me about the periodic waves of hysteria which started with the witch craze during colonial days, produced the abominable Alien and Sedition Acts of the 1790s, flourished again in the Know-Nothing movement, the anti-Masonic hysteria, anti-Catholicism, the Ku Klux Klan, the Red scare of 1919. When the cycle repeated itself during my administration in the form of anti-Communist hysteria and indiscriminate branding of innocent persons as subversives, I could deal with the situation calmly because I knew something about its background that students of history would know but perhaps not appreciate. When we are faced with a situation, we must know how to apply the lessons of history in a practical way.

I was beginning to realize—forty years before I had any thought of becoming President of the United States—that almost all current events in the affairs of governments and nations have their parallels and precedents in the past. It was obvious to me even then that a clear understanding of administrative problems presupposes a knowledge of similar ones as recorded in history and of their disposition. Long before I ever considered going into public life I had arrived at the conclusion that no decisions affecting the people should be made impulsively, but on the basis of historical background and careful consideration of the facts as they exist at the time.

History taught me that the leader of any country, in order to assume his responsibilities as a leader, must know the history of not only his own country but of all the other great countries, and that he must make the effort to apply this knowledge to the decisions that have to be made for the welfare of all the people.

My first paying job was opening up a drugstore in Independence for Mr. Jim Clinton at six-thirty in the morning, mopping the floors, sweeping the sidewalk, and having everything shipshape when Mr. Clinton came in. When everything was in order, there were bottles to wipe off and shelves to dust. There must have been a thousand bottles to dust and yards and yards of patent-medicine cases and shelves to clean. At least it seemed that way, because I never finished the bottles and shelves by schooltime and had to start the next morning where I'd left off the day before. By the time I got around them all, it was time to start over. How I hated Latin-covered prescription bottles and patent-medicine shelves!

The drugstore had plate-glass windows in front with a big glass jar shaped like an enlarged Greek vase in each window. Each vase was filled with colored water and oil in layers. How they kept those colors from mixing I don't know. Then the vases were surrounded by displays of patent medicine that had to be cleaned and dusted, and once a week the windows had to be washed and redecorated.

You walked through a front door onto a tile floor with showcases on each side and a soda fountain on one side in front. Behind the cases on one side were interminable rows and rows of bottles with those Latin abbreviations on them. One in particular I remember, because Mr. Clinton told me to be careful not to break it. He said no more Icy Toed Feet were to be obtained. The mark on the bottle was *Ici. Toed. Foet.* I never found out what it was.

After the bottles and the patent-medicine cases had been cleaned, then the prescription case had to be dusted very, very carefully.

In a little closet under the prescription case, which faced the front and shut off the view of the back end of the store, was an assortment of whiskey bottles. Early in the morning, sometimes before Mr. Clinton arrived, the good church members and Anti-Saloon Leaguers would come in for their early-morning drink behind the prescription case at ten cents an ounce. They would wipe their mouths, peep through the observation hole in the front of the case, and depart. This procedure gave a fourteen-year-old boy quite a viewpoint on the public front of leading citizens and "amen-corner-praying" churchmen.

There were saloons aplenty around the square in Independence, and many leading men in town made no bones about going into them and buying a drink. I learned to think more highly of them than I did of the prescription-counter drinkers.

I'll never forget my first week's wages—three big silver dollars. It was the biggest thing that had happened to me, and my father told me to save it for myself when I tried to give it to him on coming home that Saturday night.

After a few months at this morning and night work, my high school studies became rather heavy, and my father suggested that I quit my job and study harder, which I did.

I began going to my aunt Ella Noland's house to study Latin and algebra with Cousin Nellie and Cousin Ethel and, incidentally, my beautiful young lady with the blue eyes and golden hair. This happened about twice a week, and on two other nights Fielding Houchens and I would go out to Miss Maggie Phelps's house and take special courses in history and geography. We were hoping to obtain appointments either to West Point or to Annapolis. I was anxious for a higher education, and because my father was having financial troubles about this time, I knew he would not be able to send me to college two years hence when I finished high school. Unfortunately my poor eyesight kept me from getting an appointment.

My high school experience is one that I will never forget. In my last year we organized a magazine for publication by the senior class and called it the *Gleam,* after Tennyson's poem, *Merlin and the Gleam.* It has been published ever since by each senior class. The editors were Charlie Ross, Tasker Taylor, Howard Morrison, and myself, and I really think we got out a good magazine.

I was graduated in 1901, a short time after my seventeenth birthday.

Bess Wallace, who afterward became Mrs. Truman, was graduated in the same class, as was Charlie Ross, who was to be my press secretary in the White House.

I spent part of the summer on the farm, and during that summer I paid a visit to my aunt Ada in Murphysboro, Illinois. She was my mother's youngest sister and a favorite of all of us. I spent a month there and had a grand time with my cousins, whom I had never seen before. Aunt Ada had no children, but Aunt Sally's older married daughter lived with Aunt Ada and had four children. Two of them were about my age. Aunt Sally's daughter, Cousin Sudie Wells, and her two daughters sat on the platform in Murphysboro, in the campaign of 1948.

On the way home I stopped in St. Louis to see my mother's aunt, Hettie Powell. She used to visit us on the farm when I was very small, and I liked her very much. I saw my first professional horse races in St. Louis at that time. My cousin, Aunt Hettie's son, took me to the races, and I had a fine time.

In the fall of 1901 I got a job as timekeeper on the Santa Fe Railroad, working for a contractor named L. J. Smith. I kept that job until the contract was finished, living in hobo camps along the Missouri River where the Santa Fe Railroad ran. I became very familiar with hobos and their viewpoints. I learned what it meant to work ten hours a day for $1.50, or fifteen cents an hour. The contractor paid thirty cents an hour for a wagon, team of horses, and a driver.

These old hobos were characters in their own right. It was my duty to pay them off on Saturday nights if they wanted to be paid. The pay-off took place in a saloon either in Sheffield or Independence. The object in paying the men in a saloon was to give them a chance to spend all their money right there and guarantee their being back to work on Monday morning. The checks were time checks and were signed by me as timekeeper. If I made a mistake in favor of the hobos, I lost the money; but if the mistake favored the contractor, he kept it. If a man drew his time under two weeks, he was discounted ten per cent of his pay. The contractor got this ten per cent instead of the saloonkeeper. My salary was thirty-five dollars a month and board, but I received a very down-to-earth education in the handling of men.

The contract was finished along in May or June of 1902, and my father and I took a trip to southern Missouri. He had forty acres of land in Oregon County, of which Alton is the county seat. We went to Thayer and hired a buggy and a team of horses and drove up the Eleven Point River for quite a distance to Thomasville. In making this drive we crossed the river thirteen times in eight miles. It was at flood stage, and the water came up to the bed of the buggy each time we crossed it. We visited the forty acres that my father owned and found it more perpendicular than horizontal. It ran straight up the side of a mountain and certainly was not worth much. We had a grand trip, however, and returned home very much more familiar with southern Missouri land than when we left.

When we came back I took a job in the mailing room of the Kansas City *Star* at seven dollars a week.

My father sold the house on Waldo Avenue and bought another at 903 North Liberty Street, where we stayed a few months, and then bought a house in Kansas City at 2108 Park Avenue.

Vivian and I went to work at the National Bank of Commerce at thirty-five dollars a month. We worked in that part of the bank called the "zoo," which handled the transit checks that came through the bank as through a clearinghouse. The bank had more than twelve hundred correspondents in Kansas, Missouri, and Oklahoma, and it was our duty to list these checks, charge them against the account of the bank on which they were drawn, and give credit to the bank from which they came.

A short time after we started, Vivian left to go to work for the First National Bank, and I was promoted to personal filing clerk for the president and cashier of the bank. My salary was increased from thirty-five to forty dollars a month.

My father traded the house at 2108 Park Avenue for eighty acres of land in Henry County and moved to Clinton. I changed jobs and went to work at the Union National Bank, where I was paid sixty dollars a month as a bookkeeper. Vivian and I stayed on in Kansas City and boarded with a good old lady at 1314 Troost Avenue, where we paid five dollars a week for room and board, which included breakfast and dinner. We usually bought a ten-cent box lunch and spent the noon hour eating it in a five-cent picture show. We would go home weekends to be with the family in Clinton. I remember that my father had put in a big crop of corn that year, and when the Grand River flooded, it washed the whole crop away.

In 1904 we moved back to the farm at Grandview. My old bachelor uncle, Harrison Young, had been living with my grandmother on the farm, and he decided he wanted to quit. So we moved in with my grandmother and ran the farm for the next ten or twelve years.

When I was growing up it occurred to me to watch the people around me to find out what they thought and what pleased them most. My father and mother were sentimentalists. My father had been raised by a religious man, Grandfather Truman, who set the women of his family on a pedestal and kept them there. No one could make remarks about my aunts or my mother in my father's presence without getting into serious trouble.

My sister Mary Jane, named for his mother, was my father's favorite, and he made my brother and me look after her to see that she was properly protected in play and at school. We were a closely knit family and exceedingly fond of each other.

My mother was partial to the boys, both in the family and in the neighborhood. I used to watch my father and mother closely to learn what I could do to please them, just as I did with my schoolteachers and playmates. Because of my efforts to get along with my associates I usually was able to get what I wanted. It was successful on the farm, in school, in the Army, and particularly in the Senate.

Whenever I entered a new schoolroom I would watch the teacher and her attitude toward the pupils, study hard, and try to know my lesson better than anyone else. I followed a similar program in my bank jobs. In this way I gained a reputation in the bank of always finishing the task that was set before me and of helping the others get theirs done as well. Once in a while I would take the chief clerk of the Union National Bank, the head bookkeeper, and the paying teller to the farm for a chicken dinner. My mother was great on fried chicken, baked ham, hot biscuits, and custard pie. We would have a grand time, walk over the farm, look at the livestock, take horseback rides, and then go back to town for more work at the bank.

In 1905 Battery B of the National Guard of Kansas City was organized by George R. Collins, who became captain of the organization. Fred Boxley, who became first lieutenant, afterward was county counselor of Jackson County when I was presiding judge of the county court. There were about sixty men in the organization, and most of them were very fine fellows who worked in banks and stores around town and who would go out to a rented armory once a week and pay a quarter for the privilege of drilling.

I joined the battery the year it was organized. And when I attended my first National Guard camp at Cape Girardeau, Missouri, I was a private in the rear ranks and acted as the No. 2 man on the old three-inch gun, which was the U. S. Army's light artillery equipment. I learned many things, including how to handle Army horses.

In 1906 I quit the bank and went back to the farm, where I stayed until the war of 1917 came along.

One day in late 1908 a cousin of my mother came to the farm to look at some stock. I noticed a Masonic pin on his coat and told him I had always wanted to be a member. A few days later he brought me an application for membership in Belton Lodge No. 450 at Belton, Missouri. On February 9, 1909, I received my first degree.

Frank Blair was cashier of the Bank of Belton, where we did our banking, and W. B. Garrison was the assistant cashier. Both were enthusiastic Masons. Frank was deputy grand master and district lecturer for the 34th Masonic District of Missouri, and Billy Garrison was master of Belton Lodge. These two men very patiently taught me the lectures and the ritual for the various degrees. I received my third degree on March 9, 1909. Shortly after that the grand lecturer of Missouri, James R. Mc-Lachlan of Kahoka, came to Belton for a three-day stay. I attended every meeting for the three days and then followed the grand lecturer to Holden and to St. Joseph. I became letter-perfect in all three degrees and accompanied Frank Blair on his official visits in the 34th District. There were nine or ten lodges in the district, and during the winter months all of them were visited.

At the next lodge election I was elected junior warden and served during 1910. In 1911 I organized a lodge at Grandview, No. 618, and was made master U.D. along in May or June. I went to the Grand Lodge meeting in St. Louis, obtained a charter for Grandview, and became a regular attendant at the yearly meetings of the Grand Lodge.

Grandma Young, who lived to be ninety-one, died in 1909, leaving the six-hundred-acre Blue Ridge farm to my mother and Uncle Harrison. Other members of the family contested the will, but the matter was settled out of court, and in 1916, when Uncle Harrison died, he left his share of the farm to my mother, my brother, my sister, and me.

The great mid-continental oil fields were being opened at about this time, and test drilling was extensive in Missouri and adjoining states. Interest was very widespread, and I decided to try my fortune in this mushrooming new industry. The resulting experience was one which taught me a good deal about finance and human nature as well.

It all started when Jerry C. Culbertson, a Kansas City attorney who had known our family for years and who had once handled an investment for us in a zinc mine near Joplin, called me into his office one day. He introduced me to a man named David H. Morgan, who had just moved to town from Tulsa, Oklahoma. Morgan, I soon learned, was a businessman with a degree in law and with extensive experience in the oil industry. He was also a fine gentleman who was to become a lifelong friend of mine.

Culbertson had just completed an agreement with Morgan for the organization and promotion of an oil company, and he invited me to come in as a one-third partner.

I decided to make the suggested investment, and after I had executed five thousand-dollar notes endorsed by my mother, the contract was drawn up on September 25, 1916, making Morgan president of the new firm, Culbertson secretary, and myself treasurer.

The financial structure which Culbertson had worked out was typical of thousands that appeared during the first quarter of the twentieth century. He called the oil concern the Atlas-Okla Oil Lands Syndicate to signify the fifteen hundred acres of land in eastern Oklahoma which Morgan had turned over to the corporation in exchange for his share of interest. There was also formed a brokerage firm known as the Morgan & Company Oil Investments Corporation to handle sales of shares, purchases and management of oil properties, leases, etc., on a regular commission basis.

I was enthusiastic about the possibilities of Morgan & Company, and it soon became widely known through Culbertson's promotion techniques.

Culbertson soon decided, however, that the original syndicate formed on the fifteen hundred acres of land which Morgan had owned was not suited to the type of promotion he planned, and he therefore proceeded to revamp it. In March 1917 the reorganization was completed in the form of a common-law trust with sixty thousand shares, and the Atlas-Okla Oil Lands Syndicate became the Morgan Oil & Refining Company. All assets, lands, and other property belonging to the original syndicate were transferred to this new company.

In the meantime, Morgan, who was the practical oil man of the organization, was in the field, inspecting and leasing thousands of acres of oil properties for the company in Kansas, Oklahoma, Texas, and Louisiana. On some of these properties, test wells were drilled to completion, but these, unfortunately, proved to be dry holes. On others, drilling was in progress when the entry of the United States into World War I suddenly put an end to the company's activities.

I have always wondered how things would have turned out in my life if the war had not come along just when it did. Morgan & Company had just begun drilling on a huge block of leases we owned in the northwest corner of Greenwood County, Kansas, when the war-created manpower shortage forced us to dispose of all our leases. In fact, I was already in France when drilling stopped at a depth of fifteen hundred feet in that particular well. Other companies and operators who bought our interests in Greenwood County continued drilling, and later in the year 1917 they struck Teeter Oil Pool, one of the largest ever opened up in the state of Kansas.

When the United States entered World War I in the spring of 1917, the Missouri National Guard decided to expand Battery B in Kansas City and Battery C in Independence into a regiment. I helped in that expansion, and we raised six batteries as well as a supply and headquarters company in Kansas City and Independence, and also a battery for the 1st Missouri Field Artillery in St. Louis.

The regiment was organized, and all the officers were elected by the members of the organization. The batteries elected their officers, and the officers elected the staff. I was elected first lieutenant in Battery F when it was organized on May 22, 1917.

I had hoped that I might be a section sergeant, a post for which I was well qualified. I had not hoped for a commission, and when I found myself a lieutenant, I had a tremendous amount of work to do in order to become familiar with my job. At that time light artillery batteries had two first lieutenants, a senior and a junior, and I was the junior lieutenant of Battery F in the 2nd Missouri Field Artillery.

We trained and drilled in Kansas City at Convention Hall and on the streets, and on August 5, 1917, we were sworn in as part of the federal service and became the 129th Field Artillery of the 35th Division. On September 26, 1917, we entrained for Camp Doniphan at Fort Sill, Oklahoma.

The colonel appointed me regimental canteen officer, and I asked Eddie Jacobson, a member of Battery F and a man with merchandising experience to help me. We collected two dollars per man from each battery and from each headquarters and supply company. This gave us twenty-two hundred dollars, whereupon Eddie and I set up a store, a barbershop, and a tailor shop. We went to Oklahoma City and stocked up our store with things that would not ordinarily be issued by the government—cigarettes, paper, pens, ink, and other items the men would want to buy.

Each battery and company was ordered to furnish a clerk for the store. Eddie and I sewed up their pockets, and I deposited our sales intake every day. After operating the canteen for six months, we paid the twenty-two hundred dollars back, plus fifteen thousand dollars in dividends. Many other canteens of the 35th Division were failures, and some of the men who ran them were sent home, but after our arrival in France I was promoted, largely because of the work Eddie Jacobson and I had done.

In addition to my duties as canteen officer, I performed all the regular duties of a battery officer. I took my turn as officer of the day, equitation officer, and firing-instruction officer for the battery. I attended the Fort Sill School of Fire and did foot drill as well as whatever else needed to be done. When it came time for my captain to make an efficiency report on his lieutenants, he made such a good one on me that the C.O. sent it back with the comment, "No man can be that good."

I was examined for promotion in February 1918 and was picked for the Overseas School Detail. I left Camp Doniphan by train on March 20, 1918, and arrived about four o'clock the next morning at Rosedale, Kansas (now part of Kansas City, Kansas). I asked a switchman if I could call my fiancée in Independence.

"Call her," he said. "The phone's yours. But if she doesn't break the engagement at four o'clock in the morning, she really loves you."

I called her at once, and she didn't scold me. I also called my mother and sister. They all wept a little, but all of them, I think, were glad to know an overseas lieutenant.

I went on to New York and spent a few days at Camp Merritt at Tenafly, New Jersey. It was my first opportunity to see New York City, and my first visit there came when I was given a twenty-four-hour leave, which also gave me a chance to purchase some extra spectacles. I was very nearly blind without glasses and felt that I had better get three extra pairs. The man who gave me the examination and made the glasses for me would not allow me to pay for them. He said I was paying him by going overseas in the service of the country.

On March 30, 1918, we sailed for France on the *George Washington*, and we arrived at Brest on the morning of April 13. Ashore, we were put up at the Continental Hotel, where we stayed for a week or two before being sent to the 2nd Corps Field Artillery School at Montigny-sur-Aube. The school was in charge of Dick "By God" Burleson, a brother-in-law of Governor Vardaman of Mississippi and a nephew of the Postmaster General. He and Colonel Robert M. Danford (afterward major general, chief of field artillery) taught me how to fire a French 75. I spent five weeks at this school and then rejoined the regiment. I was made battalion adjutant of the 2nd Battalion under Major Melvin Gates, and then we were sent down to Angers for more training at one of Napoleon's old artillery camps, Coëtquidan. We arrived there on July 4, and on July 11 I was put in command of Battery D of the 129th Field Artillery. Then, after a stay at Angers, we were moved up to the Vosges Mountains, where we went into position.

We fired our first barrage on the night of September 6. We were occupying an old French position which probably was fairly well known to the Germans, and as soon as we had finished the barrage they returned the compliment. My battery became panic-stricken, and all except five or six scattered like partridges. Finally I got them back together without losing any men, although we had six horses killed.

We moved from the Vosges to the St. Mihiel drive, then from September 12 to 16 we occupied positions on the 35th Division's front for the Meuse-Argonne drive, which started on September 26. My battery fired three thousand rounds of 75 ammunition from 4 A.M. to 8 A.M. on the morning the drive began. I had slept in the edge of a wood to the right of my battery position the night before, and if I had not awakened and got up early that morning, I would not be here, for the Germans fired a barrage right on the spot where I had been sleeping.

At eight o'clock we finished firing and pulled out for the front. As we marched on the road under an embankment, a French 155 battery fired over our heads. As a result of that, I still have trouble hearing what goes on when there is a noise. I went back and told the French captain what I thought of him, but he could not understand me, so it made no difference.

We came to the front line at a little town, or what was left of it, called Bourevilles. I stopped the battery and went forward with my executive officer and the battalion commander, Major Gates. We located a battery of the enemy and sat in a ditch while they fired machine guns over us. We finally went back, and I spent the rest of the night getting my battery across no man's land.

At 5 A.M. on September 27 the operations officer of the regiment, Major Patterson, came to my sleeping place under a bush and told me to fire a barrage in ten minutes. I told him to go to hell, that I could not figure a barrage in ten minutes but I'd try! We moved on up behind the infantry and went into position on a road between Varennes and Chepy about 10 P.M. on September 28. In going into position I rode my horse under a tree, and a low-hanging branch scraped my glasses off. In desperation I turned around, hoping to see where they could have fallen, and there they were, on the horse's back, right behind the saddle.

I put the battery in position and the next day we moved into an orchard a half mile ahead. We fired on three German batteries, destroying one and putting the other two out of action. Then the regimental colonel threatened me with court-martial for firing out of the 35th Division sector! But I had saved some men in the 28th Division to our left, and I believe some of them showed their gratitude in 1948.

One of my lieutenants was acting as communications officer that afternoon and was wearing a headphone. He looked up, saw a German plane, and remarked to the battery executive that the "so-and-so" German was dropping something. The bomb exploded, cut the phone from his head but left him unhurt. A little later I was up in front of the infantry without a weapon of any kind, observing the enemy fire from every direction. An infantry sergeant came up and told me that my support had moved back two hundred yards and that I'd do well to come back too. I did.

In October notice caught up with me that I was a captain. I had been in command of Battery D since July 11, and as far back as May

I had seen in the New York *Times* that I was a captain. During all that time I wore the bars and did a captain's duty, but I was never paid for it because the official notice did not reach me until October. My claim for back pay was turned down because I had not "accepted" the commission earlier.

We supported the 35th Division and the 1st Division until October 3, when we were moved in front of Verdun in the Sommedieu sector. On October 27, 1918, we were moving along from one front-line zone to another when a French newspaper was distributed along the line. Headlines in block letters informed us that an armistice was on. Just then a German 150-mm. shell burst to the right of the road and another to the left.

"Captain," one of the sergeants remarked, "those blankety-blank Germans haven't seen this paper."

Some ten days later Roy Howard, of the Scripps-McCrae papers, also sent a message to the United States proclaiming an armistice. Such false newspaper reports are terrible things, and the people responsible for them are no better than criminals.

We went into new positions on November 6 and prepared barrages for the next day's drive on Metz. The 129th Field Artillery was then supporting the 81st (Wild Cat) Division, and five days later, at five o'clock in the morning, Major Patterson, the regimental operations officer, called me and told me that there would be a cease-fire order at eleven o'clock. I fired the battery on orders until 10:45 A.M., when I fired my last shot at a little village northeast of Verdun.

Firing stopped all along the line at eleven o'clock on November 11, 1918, and the silence that followed almost made one's head ache. We stayed at our positions all day and then crawled into our pup tents to sleep. That night, however, the men of the French battery just behind our position got their hands on a load of wine which had come up on the ammunition narrow gauge, and every single one of them had to march by my bed saluting and yelling, *"Vive President Wilson! Vive le capitaine d'artillerie américaine!"* No sleep that night. The infantry sent up all the flares they could lay their hands on, fired Very pistols and rifles and whatever else would make a noise all night long.

The next day we were ordered to leave our guns in line and fall back to the echelon. After that we spent our evenings playing poker and wishing we were home.

On December 7 a number of officers were given a leave, and I was one. We went to Paris, where we spent three happy days. I attended a performance of *Manon* at the Paris Opéra, went to the Opéra-Comique to hear *Carmen,* and then to the Folies-Bergère, which turned out to be a disgusting performance.

We went on to Nice, stayed at the Hotel Méditerranée, and saw the American Bar in the Hotel Negresco. We visited the Casino in Monte Carlo but could not play because we were in uniform. They did give us each a five-franc chip, and that was all we had from the famous gambling hell. We had lunch one day in the Casino de Paris, about seven or eight of us sitting at a big round table in the rear of the place, when all of a sudden every waiter there rushed to the front and began bowing and scraping. We were informed that Madame la Princesse de Monaco had come in. Our lieutenant colonel was facing the front and could see the performance. He watched very closely and pretty soon he reported, "Oh hell, she's taking beer! Can you imagine a princess drinking beer?" It was quite a disappointment for all us common folk.

We went back to the regiment, which was moved a couple of times and finally sent to Brest. On April 9, 1919, we embarked on the German passenger ship *Zeppelin* and arrived in New York City on April 20, a beautiful Easter Sunday morning. I had been gone from that city just a year and twenty days.

We were sent to Camp Mills and then ordered to Camp Funsten, Kansas, where we were discharged on May 6, 1919. It was from there that I went home to the Blue Ridge farm.

CHAPTER 10

I returned to civilian life on May 6, 1919. I was thirty-five years old.

Bess Wallace and I decided to go ahead with our plans for marriage, and we set the day, June 28, 1919, less than eight weeks after I was discharged from the Army. We were married in the Trinity Episcopal Church in Independence. After a wedding trip to Chicago and Port Huron, Michigan, we returned to live at 219 North Delaware Stree' in Independence.

In the meantime Eddie Jacobson and I made plans to open a men's furnishing goods store in Kansas City. Eddie Jacobson is as fine a man as ever walked. He had worked with me in the successful operation of the canteen at Camp Doniphan, and because that had been such a profitable experience on limited capital, we felt that we might do well in a business partnership. The idea of a haberdashery was Eddie's, and it was agreed that he would be the buyer and that I would act as salesman.

We pooled our savings and raised the additional capital required to lease a building on Twelfth Street near the Muehlebach Hotel and lay in a complete stock of merchandise. I had a sale of equipment and stock on the farm that netted me over fifteen thousand dollars, which I immediately invested in the store. We bought thirty-five thousand dollars' worth of merchandise, and by fall we were open for business.

This was a period of general prosperity. During the first year of operation we sold over seventy thousand dollars' worth of merchandise and had a good return on our investment. Our second year began well too. In 1921, however, after the Republicans took over the U. S. Government under the presidency of Warren G. Harding, Andrew Mellon was made Secretary of the Treasury. He immediately started a "wringing-out" process which put farm prices down to an all-time low, raised interest rates, and "put labor in its place."

On January 1, 1921, Jacobson and I had a thirty-five-thousand-dollar inventory at cost. And this figure was sound. We actually had a chance to sell out at inventory price about this time, but we refused. Before the year was out, values had fallen so greatly that on January 1, 1922, the value of that inventory had shrunk to less than ten thousand dollars. Our creditors and the banks we owed began to press us, and when we closed out later in 1922 we were hopelessly in debt.

Much of our stock of goods had been purchased from Kansas City concerns, and both Eddie and I wanted every creditor to receive every possible dollar. In fact, we intended to pay every creditor in full as soon as we were able, notwithstanding any settlement that might be made with them. We consulted an attorney, Phineas Rosenberg of Kansas City, who after investigating the condition of the business advised settlement with our creditors.

Rosenberg then wrote to each merchandise creditor, stating the financial condition of the partnership and explaining that existing economic conditions were causing our business to suffer losses. He also notified them, at our direction, that both Jacobson and I wished to avoid further losses to creditors and wished also to avoid all expense incident to liquidation so as to give our creditors all that remained in the business without deductions of any kind. Without exception, the merchants in whose debt we were agreed to this settlement. The stock of the store was closed out, and payments were made on the various accounts in accordance with the agreement. Jacobson and I, however, continued thereafter to make payments on the various accounts from time to time until all of them were settled in full.

There were other debts too. We were committed at the time for bank loans which we had negotiated in the operation of our business. We were committed also for the balance of the rental for the store, which we had originally leased for five years. The bank loans were not included in the settlement with the merchandise creditors because it was agreed that these loans should be repaid dollar for dollar, whereas the merchandise creditors had already made profits from previous sales to our firm.

The Security State Bank and the Twelfth Street Bank (now the Baltimore Bank) had made the loans, and they held notes signed by both Jacobson and me. We owed the Twelfth Street Bank twenty-five hundred dollars, but the indebtedness to the Security State Bank amounted to more than five thousand at the time. This latter was secured by a deed to a 160-acre farm in Johnson County, Kansas. I had purchased this farm sometime before for the equivalent of $13,800, but I valued it at considerably more than that figure. I had paid five thousand dollars for it in the form of property which I had owned in Kansas City and had assumed a mortgage of eighty-eight hundred dollars which was on the farm at the time of my purchase. After our store closed in 1922, I, along with Jacobson, gave a note to the Security State Bank for sixty-eight hundred dollars, with the farm listed as security to cover the principal and interest then due.

Neither Jacobson nor I wished to go into bankruptcy, as so many were doing during that period. We both wanted to pay all the indebtedness in full. Still, we did not find that easy, for our incomes were not large. Mine, in fact, was very limited, for it was in the fall of that year that I entered local politics, and Jacobson's was not large, although he had been able to obtain employment as a salesman. From time to time we made such payments as we could on these accounts. It was a struggle for both of us during the next several years, and in February 1925 Jacobson finally found himself unable to withstand the pressure. He was forced to file a petition in bankruptcy. Among his debts he listed the note, which at that time stood at fifty-six hundred dollars. As a result of this development there were those who tried to force me into bankruptcy at the same time. I resisted, however, and continued to make such payments as I could.

In the meantime the whole affair became complicated by the fact that the Security State Bank, which had made the loan originally, had itself run into financial difficulties. Its assets were taken over by the Continental National Bank, and our note was included among these transferred assets. In December 1923 a suit was filed on behalf of the bank to recover on the note, although it was not until April 30, 1929, that judgment for $8,944.78 in principal and interest was recorded in favor of the Security State Bank against both Jacobson and myself.

Matters became more involved when the Continental National Bank got itself into trouble financially, and its liquidation was in progress for several years. During this period certain of the assets, including notes, securities, and other property, were sold by the receiver for various small sums at the order of the court. Among these was our note, which by court order was sold for one thousand dollars. My brother Vivian purchased it at that price. Meanwhile the 160-acre farm which I had deeded to the bank as security had been taken over.

Our other lender, the Twelfth Street or Baltimore Bank, had made us a twenty-five-hundred-dollar loan in January 1922. Complete records of this loan and of the subsequent payments and renewals have been preserved in the bank's files, and they show that during 1922, 1923, and 1924, long after the close of the haberdashery store, we reduced the indebtedness by numerous payments, some as small as twenty-five dollars, until, with a final payment of two hundred dollars in December 1924, we discharged that obligation in full.

One of the obligations not included in the settlement with the merchandise creditors when we closed out our business was for store rental under the lease which we had originally signed with Louis Oppenstein, owner of the property at 104 West Twelfth Street. This lease was for a five-year period, and it had some time to run after the store closed. Settlement of the account was made later, and the property then became available to the owner for other purposes. Oppenstein has since died.

This was a hard experience for me, at the age of thirty-eight, to fail in a business venture in which I had invested a considerable amount of money and time. I have since come to realize that thousands of others went through similar experiences during those postwar years, although my difficulties came to be more widely publicized and distorted because I later became President of the United States.

There has been quite a bit of talk about my start in politics in Jackson County. It was in 1921, while the store was still doing very well, that I was asked if I would consider the nomination for judge of the county court for the Eastern District. In the store Eddie Jacobson and I used to meet many of the men with whom we served in France. One of our customers was Jim Pendergast, who had been a lieutenant in the 129th and who had later gone into the 130th Field Artillery, where he commanded a battery on the front.

When the time came for the Pendergast organization to endorse someone as candidate for eastern judge in 1922, a meeting was held at Twenty-sixth and Prospect streets, with representatives from every township in the county. Jim's father, Mike Pendergast, informed the gentlemen there that he thought it would be a good thing for them to support me as that candidate. He said I was a returned soldier, a captain "whose men didn't want to shoot him"!

The judges of these Missouri county courts are not judges in the usual sense, since the court is an administrative, not a judicial, body. It levies taxes. Expenditures for roads, for homes for the aged, and for schools for delinquent children are supported by orders of this court on the county treasurer, and the court also orders such payments as are necessary to state institutions for the support of the insane. The only really judicial act the court performs is to make a finding of insanity when that has been recommended by two reputable physicians. Each county in the state has a county court made up of three judges, two of whom represent districts, while the third is elected at large for the whole county.

For years my father and other members of our family had been interested in county affairs. My father had been road overseer in Washington Township, where the farm is located, from 1910 until the time of his death in 1914, and I had succeeded him. I had also been postmaster of Grandview before World War I, and at every election from 1906 on I had been Democratic clerk. I was familiar with local politics, and Mike Pendergast's suggestion appealed to me. I told him that I would like to run.

The failure of our business followed, and when the time came in 1922, I filed for eastern judge. Even with Mike Pendergast's backing it was far from certain that I could win the nomination. The primary campaign was a very bitter fight. There were five candidates: a banker named Emmett Montgomery from Blue Springs who had the support of the Shannon faction, known as the "Rabbits"; a road overseer by the name of Tom Parent, who had the support of the Bulger faction; James Compton, who had been eastern judge by appointment once and who had been trying to be elected ever since; George Shaw, a road contractor, who was honest (very unusual for a contractor of county business in Jackson County at that time) and who had been broken by the Bulger court; and myself, who had the support of the "Goats," or Pendergast faction.

I did not know any of the factional leaders at the time except Bulger, who was presiding judge and who was not so well thought of by the people generally.

I had an old Dodge roadster which was a very rough rider. I kept two bags of cement in the back of it so it would not throw me through the windshield while driving on our terrible county roads. I went into every township—there were seven of them—and into every precinct in the county in the Eastern District. Luckily I had relatives all over the county, and through my wife I was related to many more.

When the votes were counted, I had a plurality of nearly three hundred. Mr. Shannon said the voters preferred a busted merchant to a prosperous banker. Most people were broke, and they sympathized with a man in politics who admitted his financial condition.

The election that followed was a walkaway. All the Democrats on the ticket won in the county, although we three judges of the county court promptly began a factional fight among ourselves. The presiding judge was a member of the Shannon faction—the "Rabbits." The other district judge and I were "Goats," and we promptly took all the jobs. We ran the county, but we ran it carefully and on an economy basis.

Counties in Missouri are a part of the state government and are also a part of the sovereign power of the state. A county cannot be sued, and damages against the county can be allowed only by legislative act, unless the county itself passes a resolution authorizing it. I spent a great amount of time with the county counselor learning county procedure under state laws.

I also became completely familiar with every road and bridge in the county. About that time the State Highway Commission had begun the construction of a Missouri road system by getting right of ways across the county for the state, and I soon became acquainted with the state system and what the Commission had in view for the western end of the state.

I visited every state institution in which the county had patients. This included the state asylums in St. Joseph, Nevada, Fulton, and Farmington, where the insane patients were sent. Jackson County had an institution of its own at Little Blue to take care of the indigent aged. This institution had usually five or six hundred patients, both men and women, in the winter and about four hundred in the summer. The county had no hospital, but it maintained a county physician whose business it was to visit the county home at Little Blue once or twice a week and who cared for those indigent people who could not pay doctors' bills.

In 1924 I ran for re-election as eastern judge. The Democratic party in the county split over the fact that the Shannon faction thought it had not obtained a fair division of the jobs, and I was defeated by 867 votes. I was defeated by the old harness maker, Henry Rummel, who had made the beautiful set of harnesses for my brother and me when we were children. This was the only defeat I ever suffered in an election. Rummel is still alive, by the way, a fine old gentleman.

Our daughter Margaret had been born on February 17, 1924. And now, only a little over two years since Eddie Jacobson and I had lost our business, I was out of a job again. But I had many friends, and in January 1925 I was able to make a connection with the Automobile Club of Kansas City, where I spent about a year and a half adding to its membership. It gave me a substantial income.

In 1926, when the election machinery was being oiled up by the party leaders, I was slated to run for presiding judge of the county court.

I was always interested in civic, fraternal, and public affairs, and because these widened my acquaintance and kept me in contact with many people, they no doubt played some part in my political fortunes.

When I was discharged from the Army I continued in the reserve. In 1921, after I had attended camp at Fort Leavenworth as a major of the Field Artillery Reserve, I decided to try to get all the local Army, Navy, and Marine Corps reserve officers in the greater Kansas City area together in the interest of national defense. A meeting was called in 1921, and I was made president of Reserve Officers Association Chapter No. 1. When the organization was expanded on a state-wide basis, I became president of the state association. I never held any of these offices, however, except during the organization period. I always trained a successor in every organization in which I had a leading part.

I was active in the 22nd Masonic District. This covered Jackson County as a whole, but as it grew it was split into two districts, and in 1924, on the death of the deputy grand master for the new 59th District, I was appointed district deputy grand master and lecturer.

Because of these and other activities, as well as the fact that I had been a very active district judge from 1922 to 1924, I entered the 1926 campaign with reasonably good prospects of success. Mike Pendergast had suggested that I run for county collector of Jackson County, and I was in a willing frame of mind to do this because it was a good public office with a substantial income. Mike and I went to see his brother Tom and discussed the matter with him. He said he had already promised to support someone else for that job, but he thought, because of my experience as eastern judge, I ought to be a candidate for presiding judge. That was my first meeting with Tom Pendergast.

I was elected that fall with a majority of sixteen thousand votes. I immediately went to work to set up a system of roads, to construct new public buildings, and to try to get the county on a sound financial basis.

The county court previous to the one to which I had been elected in 1922 had run the county into debt. It is customary in the state of Missouri for counties to borrow money on tentative tax levies made in January and February. There were some $2,400,000 in outstanding warrants which were protested and which drew six per cent interest from the date of their issue. The borrowings are made monthly on tax anticipation notes, which are as good as gold because they are a first lien on tax collections, and only ninety per cent of the anticipated revenue can be borrowed.

The roads were in terrible shape in the county, and the public buildings were all run down. Some were on the verge of falling down.

I made it my business to go to Chicago and St. Louis in order to discuss the matter of county borrowing with some of the bankers in those cities, and as a result I finally succeeded in getting the interest rate on tax anticipation notes cut to four per cent and, eventually, to two and a half. The local bankers had had a bonanza at six per cent.

At this time Kansas City itself was calling a bond issue for a great many improvements, and I got the political bosses to agree to let the county propose an issue of road bonds for six and a half million dollars.

The political bosses and the Kansas City *Star* did not think the county bonds would be approved by the voters, but they were, and a second issue was later approved for three and a half million dollars more in road bonds and five million for a new courthouse in Kansas City, for the rehabilitation of the courthouse in Independence, and for the construction of a hospital at the county home in Little Blue. I had told the taxpayers just how I would handle the bond money, and they believed me.

All these projects were successfully carried out, and without one breath of scandal, while I was presiding judge. I was responsible for the spending of sixty million dollars in tax funds and bond issues. I succeeded in getting thirty-five or forty more miles of roads built from the ten-million-dollar bond issue than the engineers had anticipated, and the public buildings were constructed without any difficulty whatever. In fact, when this work was completed, there was money left in the bond fund which was turned into the sinking fund, with the exception of thirty-six thousand dollars, which was used for the Andrew Jackson statues at the courthouses in Independence and Kansas City.

After visiting Chicago, St. Louis, Minneapolis, St. Paul, and Cincinnati, I organized the Greater Kansas City Regional Planning Association. This organization was expanded eventually into a state organization and made many contributions to the improvement of the county and the state.

In 1930 I was re-elected presiding judge by a majority of fifty-eight thousand votes, and I continued my policies and my program. I succeeded in having the protested warrants refinanced on an income basis, and when I left the county its finances were in first-rate shape. By that time, too, it had one of the best road systems in the United States and had a fine new set of public buildings as well. All the bonds that were connected with my program have been paid off on their due dates, and the county is one of the few financially solvent counties in the state.

Although I was to become very well acquainted with Tom Pendergast, I barely knew him when I was first elected presiding judge of the Jackson County Court. He was a power in local politics, of course, and when the bond issues for Kansas City were up for consideration I went to see him. I told him I would like very much to issue bonds for the rehabilitation of our roads in the county and for some new public buildings. A new courthouse was needed for Kansas City, and the courthouse in Independence required remodeling. A hospital was badly needed at the county home. Pendergast replied by saying that there was no possibility of the county supporting such a bond issue—that the same idea had been turned down on two previous occasions in the last ten years. I argued, however, that if I could tell the taxpayers just how I would handle their money I felt sure it would carry. My confidence was justified, too. The bonds for the county were carried with a three-fourths majority, which was much better than the city bonds did, some of which had not been carried at all.

When the first contracts were to be let, I got a telephone call from Tom Pendergast saying that he and some of his friends were very anxious to see me about those contracts. I knew very well what was in the wind, but I went to their meeting. I told them that I expected to let the contracts to the lowest bidders, just as I had promised the taxpayers I would do, and that I was setting up a bi-partisan board of engineers to see that specifications were carried out according to contract, or else the public would not pay for them.

Pendergast turned to the contractors and said, "I told you he's the contrariest man in the state of Missouri." When the contractors had left, he said, "You carry out the agreement you made with the people of Jackson County." And I never heard anything from him again.

In 1934, when I had been presiding judge of Jackson County for eight years, I expected to run for Congress. Two years earlier new congressional districts had been set up for the state of Missouri, with the Fourth District in eastern Jackson County, with two or three eastern wards of Kansas City added. This was the district I hoped to represent in Congress, and if I had been permitted to run, I feel confident that I could have been its representative. I was maneuvered out of this and finally ended up by running for the U. S. Senate.

Two fine and very experienced congressmen opposed me for the nomination for senator. They were John J. Cochran of St. Louis and Jacob L. Milligan of Richmond, Missouri. Each of them had already been in Congress for many years and they had wonderful reputations. Fortunately for my prospects, however, I had become acquainted with all the county judges and county clerks in the state of Missouri and was very familiar with the operations of the so-called "courthouse gangs" in all the country counties. I had their support when I went into sixty of Missouri's 114 counties, where I made from six to sixteen speeches a day. I made my campaign on the basis of support for President Franklin D. Roosevelt, and when the votes were counted, I came out with a plurality of 44,000 in the primary. I carried Jackson County by 130,000 votes. In the fall elections, when I opposed Senator Roscoe C. Patterson of Springfield, the Republican incumbent, I won with a majority of over a quarter of a million votes.

CHAPTER 11

It was a great day for me on January 3, 1935, when I
entered the chamber of the United States Senate to take
my seat for the first time. I had always thought of the Senate as one of
the world's greatest deliberative bodies, and I was aware of the honor
and responsibility that had been given to me by the people of my state.

Although I was nearly fifty-one years old at the time, I was as timid
as a country boy arriving on the campus of a great university for his first
year. There was much to learn about the traditions of the Senate, and
I can honestly say that I went there to learn all I could about my new
role in the federal government. I realized that the more I knew about it
the better I could perform my duties as a senator. Even before I had
left Kansas City for Washington I had read the biographies of every
member of the Senate and had studied every piece of information I could
find on our chief lawmaking body. I was to learn later that the estimates
of the various members which I formed in advance were not always accurate. I soon found that, among my ninety-five colleagues, the real
business of the Senate was carried on by unassuming and conscientious
men, not by those who managed to get the most publicity.

I very distinctly remember taking the oath as a senator. As an officer
in the Army and as a county official, I had probably taken the same
oath a dozen times, but now it seemed far more impressive than at any
other time until I took the oath of office as President in 1945. My colleague, Senator Bennett Clark, escorted me to the Vice-President and in
turn escorted me back to my seat.

As I walked back to my seat from the desk of the Vice-President I had a prayer in my heart for wisdom to serve the people acceptably. And it was not only the people of Missouri I had in mind, but the people of every part of the United States, for I felt myself to be a representative of all Americans.

The first meeting of the Senate, which had convened at noon, was over in a very short time. At two o'clock it was called back into session for an announcement. The House of Representatives, we were told, had a quorum present, had elected its officers, and was prepared to meet jointly with the Senate on the following day to hear the annual message to the Congress by the President of the United States. With that announcement made, the Senate adjourned. My first day as senator was officially over, and I looked forward with eager anticipation to the next.

It was after the Senate had adjourned the following day that I began to have the conviction that I was now where I really belonged. I had been pleased by President Roosevelt's address calling for basic reforms to replace the emergency relief measures of his administration. I knew that the program he was enunciating for the welfare and security of all classes of Americans was a program that I could support wholeheartedly. In fact, it was one which I had already put into effect on a local level.

From the long list of bills and resolutions introduced in the Senate during the afternoon session which followed the joint meeting with the House I could see that I was going to be busier than I had ever been in Jackson County if I expected to keep up with all that was going on. The desk in my office, which was at first in Suite 248 in the Senate Office Building, was already piled high with documents and correspondence calling for my attention. That night I returned to my new residence at Tilden Gardens, just west of Connecticut Avenue in the northwest section of Washington, with an armload of papers to read and study. I did not realize it then, but that was a practice I was going to keep up for the next eighteen years.

When I first moved my family to Washington I rented a furnished apartment at Tilden Gardens, 3016 Tilden Street. In the years that followed we occupied several different apartments at the same address and one in Sedgwick Gardens on Connecticut Avenue. Later we moved to a new apartment building called the Warwick on Cathedral Avenue, and from there to 4701 Connecticut Avenue, where we stayed until we moved to Blair House.

My ten years in the Senate had now begun—years which were to be filled with hard work but which were also to be the happiest ten years of my life.

I will always remember the cordial reception which Burton K. Wheeler, J. Hamilton Lewis, and Carl Hayden gave me at the beginning of my experience in the Senate. They did not have the attitude of some of the liberals in that august body—like George Norris of Nebraska, for example, and Bronson Cutting of New Mexico—who looked upon me as a sort of hick politician who did not know what he was supposed to do. This attitude did not bother me, however. I knew it would change in time.

Ham Lewis, on the other hand, came over and sat down by me during one of the first sessions. He was from Illinois and was the whip in the Senate at that time.

"Don't start out," he told me, "with an inferiority complex. For the first six months you'll wonder how you got here, and after that you'll wonder how the rest of us got here."

Carl Hayden of Arizona was extremely helpful to me in matters of Senate procedure. He took the trouble to explain some of the technicalities and customs of the Senate which appear pretty confusing to the newcomer. More than most of the men I was to know in Washington, Hayden knew how to get the necessary action on any job that needed to be done. In every contact I had with him I came to respect him as one of the hardest-working and ablest men in the Senate.

Burton Wheeler was chairman of the Interstate Commerce Committee, and he welcomed me when I later asked him if it would be permissible for me to sit with him when the committee began holding its railroad finance hearings. As a result of this I eventually became a member of one of the subcommittees and finally vice-chairman. I wouldn't have been able to obtain this valuable experience if it had not been for Wheeler. There were others, too, who were always considerate and helpful. Vice-President Garner was very kind to me and became one of the best friends I had in the Senate.

On the day on which I was sworn in there were twelve other freshman senators from the Democratic side. The thirteen of us were always close together, and we came to be known as the "Young Turks." The group included Lew Schwellenbach of Washington, who was later to become my Secretary of Labor, and Sherman Minton of Indiana, an able senator who is now an efficient and intelligent justice of the Supreme Court.

I was closely associated also with some Republican senators, and Charles McNary of Oregon was one of whom I became very fond. He and I used to discuss at great length the matters that were pending in the Appropriations Committee. I became well acquainted with William Borah of Idaho as well. He was very able in committee and thoroughly understood legal language. He could analyze a bill as well as any man in the Senate.

Arthur Vandenberg of Michigan was another Republican for whom I soon came to have the greatest respect, and I believe it was mutual. One time I happened to enter the chamber when a heated argument was going on. Vandenberg saw me come in and called on me to speak. I happened to have the information that was needed to settle the argument completely.

"When the senator from Missouri makes a statement like that," Vandenberg said when I had finished, "we can take it for the truth."

That was a remark I never forgot.

Two of the Senate's most expert storytellers sat on either side of me. Nate Bachman, the junior senator from Tennessee, was one of them, and Joe Guffey of Pennsylvania was the other. My association with both these men was most enjoyable. Bachman could get any controversy on the Senate floor settled by stepping out of the chamber and asking someone to say to the troublemaking senator, "Nate Bachman wants to see you in the secretary's office." Nate would then call in another senator or two, tell a few stories, and harmony would be restored.

When I later became chairman of the Committee to Investigate the National Defense Program, many of its members became my very good personal friends—Mon Wallgren, Harley Kilgore, Owen Brewster, Homer Ferguson, Tom Connally, and Harold Burton. Senator Warren Austin of Vermont also became a very close friend of mine. He and I later held the hearings and wrote the Civil Aeronautics Act based on a bill introduced by Pat McCarran, the senator from Nevada.

I have named a few, but it would not be possible for me to single out all the members of the Senate whose acquaintance I cherished. Among them were some of the finest men I have ever known. The percentage of "no-goods" was small. In the make-up of society in general the "no-goods" form a small percentage, but it was smaller still in the Senate. I recall only two senators with whom I would rather not associate and whose word I did not trust.

It was fascinating to study these men and to observe their public performances. One of the most sensational performers of that time, of course, was Huey Long of Louisiana. He had been elected to the Senate in 1930 but was not sworn in until 1932 because he wanted to finish out his term as governor. When he arrived, however, he soon began to establish new records for filibustering, reading from the Batlimore *Sun* and the New York *Times,* then from the Bible. Nobody else could talk while the filibuster was running.

I was in the chair the last time Senator Long spoke. All the senators had left the chamber, for that was the usual procedure whenever Long took the floor, and afterward I walked across the street with him.

"What did you think of my speech?" he asked.

"I had to listen to you," I told him, "because I was in the chair and couldn't walk out." He never spoke to me after that.

It was customary for Long to attack some connection of a senator. He once attacked Pendergast long before Pendergast ever got into trouble. Then he came around to me afterward and said he didn't mean anything personal—it was just for the effect in Louisiana. He did the same thing to Senator Carter Glass.

"You're the orneriest man in this Senate," Glass told him, "and I'd just as soon get my knife and cut your heart out."

He actually started after Long, but Senator Joe Robinson stopped him.

"Carter," Robinson remarked, "you can't catch him. You'd better sit down."

"All right," Glass replied, "but Long had better leave me alone."

Glass later referred on the Senate floor to the horse the ancient Romans had elected to the Senate, and remarked that they had done better than the state of Louisiana—at least the Romans had sent the whole horse.

There were some of the keenest minds in the country in the Senate, and it was a mistake to tangle with them. I never did unless I had all my facts before I spoke.

There was a lot of fun to be had in the Senate, but there was more work to do than ninety-six men could ever keep up with. I was not a good attendant at social affairs in Washington. I usually got to my office at seven o'clock in the morning and got home for dinner at 7 P.M. Out of the entire enrollment of the Senate, when I was there, there were thirty or forty who worked like Trojans; there were fifteen or twenty who worked pretty well, and the rest did comparatively little.

Ever since my experience as a member of that body I have wanted to write a monograph on "The Working Senator" and his contributions in the public interest. Most of the senators who really apply themselves never get much attention in the headlines. They have a hard grind and have no time to make personal attacks on other senators or people outside the Senate. On that account they do not always make good news copy.

It was customary in my day to put each freshman senator on two major committees and also on a number of minor ones, and four days after becoming a member of the Senate I was assigned to the committees which were to keep me occupied throughout my first term. It was my good fortune to be made a member of two of the Senate's most important committees, each of which was in a field of legislation of particular interest to me. One was the Appropriations Committee, and the other was the Interstate Commerce Committee.

The Appropriations Committee, composed of twenty-four members, was the largest of all the Senate committees and was under the chairmanship of Carter Glass of Virginia. I never missed a meeting, for this committee examined in detail every federal expenditure and worked out the budget. By way of these meetings I became thoroughly acquainted with the fiscal aspects of the national administration and gained an insight into the workings of federal finance that was of inestimable value to me in later years.

Senator Burton Wheeler of Montana was chairman of the twenty-man Interstate Commerce Committee, and when I became a member in 1935 I brought with me a special interest in transportation and communication systems that dated back to my youth. One of my early hobbies had been investigating the part which open avenues of communication had played in the shaping of history.

I had learned from my reading that Alexander's empire fell apart at his death primarily because there was no easy access from one section of the empire to another. Rome's supremacy over such a long period of time was in large part due to her wonderful roads, some of which are still in use as arterial highways in various parts of Europe. The British built their empire by maintaining unprecedented sea lanes for their merchant and military shipping. The history of America can be read in the study of such trails as the Boston Post Road, the Braddock Road, the Cumberland Road, the National Pike, Boone's Lick Trail, the Santa Fe Trail, and Padre's Trail, and the construction of the transcontinental railroads. Also, the famous clipper ships had much to do with keeping the Pacific coast in the Union.

Back in 1924 my interest in the subject had resulted in my being made president of the National Old Trails Road Association. In that capacity I made a number of talks on the historical importance of roadways and channels of communication, including an address before the Congress of the Daughters of the American Revolution in Washington. But my interest had by no means been confined to the history of the subject. As presiding judge in Jackson County I had worked hard and long for a Kansas City regional plan which, among other things, would make a complete study of transportation and communication needs for the entire six-county area, and I had supervised the road-building program of Jackson County as well.

Nor was my interest confined to local areas. I was concerned about the plight of the great Missouri Pacific Railroad, a transcontinental public carrier system which had been driven into bankruptcy before I went to the Senate. I was aware of the increasing highway needs of the country in 1935 and was conscious of the urgency of co-ordination of regulations concerning the expanding air transport industry. I looked on my assignment to the Interstate Commerce Committee as a possible opportunity to help do something about these pressing needs.

Of the two smaller committees to which I was assigned, I most enjoyed my work on the Public Buildings and Grounds Committee. This committee of fourteen had Senator Tom Connally of Texas as its chairman and was responsible for recommendations concerning the architectural requirements of the national capital. Before my first term was over I had come to be closely acquainted with Senator Connally, and the two of us put in a great amount of work together on this committee.

I was one of seven senators serving on the Printing Committee, a joint committee of the Senate and the House, of which Carl Hayden of Arizona was chairman. The function of the Printing Committee is to supervise the work of the Public Printer. It makes rules on the contents of the Congressional Record and the pamphlets printed for the Congress.

A minor committee to which I was temporarily assigned was the District of Columbia Committee. I soon got off, however, for I did not wish to become a part of local Washington politics. I was of the opinion, and still am, that the District should have self-government. It should be made a territorial government or incorporated like any other city, perhaps under a city-manager form of government. It had its own government at one time, but this became so corrupt that it had to be abolished. Most senators and congressmen seem to feel that a municipal government might exercise some influence or control over the national government, as has been the case in a number of foreign capitals. At any rate, I did not stay on the District of Columbia Committee because I had no interest in becoming a local alderman.

These assignments meant that my work was cut out for me for the next six years. I felt that I couldn't have been put on committees more suited to my interests, with the exception of not having been assigned to the Military Affairs Committee. Ever since World War I, I had maintained an active interest in the Army and its administration, and I would have welcomed an assignment to the Military Affairs Committee. Even this, however, was to come to me in my second term.

There were actually only two other committees in the Senate of equal or superior rank to the two major committees on which I served. These were the Finance Committee, which passes on all tax matters, and the Foreign Relations Committee. Long service in the Senate is generally a prerequisite for membership on either of them. I believe, however, that the committees to which I had been appointed were the ones most useful to my own training and development.

During my early days in the Senate I seldom participated in the speech-making and arguments on the floor. I was content most of the time to have my vote recorded on the issues that came up and was almost never absent during my first term. I introduced my first public bill on May 15, 1935. It was entitled "A bill to provide for insurance by the Farm Credit Administration of mortgages on farm property, and for other purposes." It was referred by Vice-President Garner to the Committee on Banking and Currency, where it died.

I introduced and succeeded in having the Senate pass a bill on safety on the highways in interstate commerce. It required drivers to pass an examination on rules laid down by the Interstate Commerce Commission based on the experience of states where highways were safest. At that time Massachusetts, New York, and California had the best highway drivers' laws. This bill was twice passed by the Senate and killed each time in the House.

The real work of a senator is done in committee rather than on the floor of the Senate. Some committee projects require years of study, research, correspondence, and hearings, and these activities are never published in the Congressional Record. I made it my business to master all of the details of any project confronting a committee of which I was a member.

Most of my early career as a senator was devoted almost exclusively to committee work. The work itself was useful, but I was more concerned about equipping myself with facts and schooling myself in those disciplines which would enable me to get the business of the Senate done efficiently than I was in making myself heard in debate. My time for speaking was to come later.

Though I was engrossed in the work of the various committees during my first term in the Senate, I was also an active participant when legislation was dealt with on the floor. My votes were cast in support of all those important measures of the Roosevelt program which were written into the statute books at so rapid a pace between 1935 and 1940. I was a New Dealer from the start. In fact, I had been a New Dealer back in Jackson County, and there was no need for me to change. I believed in the program from the time it was first proposed.

In my first year as a senator it was my privilege to vote for several history-making bills which helped to rebuild the social structure of American life. One of these was the Wagner Labor Relations Act of 1935.

The NRA was having hard sledding in many places, and a law to give the working people equality at the bargaining table was a necessity.

Injunction and the "yellow dog" contract had been outlawed, but that was not enough. I had set up the employment service in Missouri in 1933 and 1934 and therefore had come into close contact with the great army of the unemployed, and the attitude of a large number of the big employers had become clear to me. I had seen some terrible riots in Missouri over decent wages and hours.

As the executive officer of the largest and richest county in Missouri (largest in population—St. Louis is an independent city and has no county government) I had co-operated with the cities and towns in the county to help make jobs so that people could work for bread and butter —very little butter—without being charity patients.

The Wagner Act was a great step forward, even though experience later showed that it needed amendment—but I wanted it *properly* amended.

Another measure which I supported by my vote was the Social Security Act of 1935. This was an attempt to place an anchor to windward for old age and for periods of unemployment. I thought it was a move in the right direction, although it lacked health insurance for hospitals and doctor bills. I tried to remedy this lack when I became President.

I also voted for support of Roosevelt's request for American adherence to the World Court. I had been a supporter of President Wilson and the League of Nations and knew that this was a great thing and another step in the right direction. The resolution failed by a few votes to reach the required two-thirds majority.

Legislation to strengthen the Tennessee Valley Authority, which was still a new experiment in 1935, received my wholehearted support. I saw the tremendous potentialities of the experiment and wished to see it applied to other great waterways of the United States—particularly the Missouri Valley. I remembered the effort to sell Wilson Dam to Henry Ford. I had always felt that this project, and others like it, should belong to the people.

The Guffey-Snyder Coal Act was a measure with which I became thoroughly familiar, because the bill was handled by the Interstate Commerce Committee. At the suggestion of Jasper Bell of the Fifth Missouri District, Senator Carter Glass of Virginia, and Joe Guffey, the author of the bill, I recommended Walter Maloney as commissioner for the Coal Commission which was set up by the act. This law saved the coal industry from ruin.

During the first few months of the first session of the Seventy-fourth Congress, a fierce battle was raging in Washington over the Wheeler-

Rayburn bill, sponsored jointly by the chairman of the Interstate Commerce Committee in the Senate and Sam Rayburn, chairman of the corresponding committee in the House. This was the bill that later became the Public Utility Holding Company Act of 1935, and its purpose was to destroy the cartels through which the power trusts were able to maintain exorbitant rates and which permitted them to juggle securities involving the welfare of millions of people without any control by either the public or the government.

Naturally the public utilities organized a giant lobby, with unlimited financial backing, to fight this legislation. Wendell Willkie, president of Commonwealth and Southern's public utility empire, was one of the leaders of the opposition. The lobby maintained expensive headquarters in the Mayflower Hotel, from which they proceeded to bring pressure on senators and representatives. Stockholders all across the country, as well as newspapers and various pressure groups, were used to the fullest extent to try to influence members of Congress.

As a member of the Interstate Commerce Committee which was sponsoring the bill, I found myself a target of the opposition within three months of the time I had taken my seat in the Senate. Representatives of the public utilities lobby came to see me and asked me to vote against the bill. I told them that I was personally opposed to the monopolistic practices which were squeezing the consumer to death and that I would vote in favor of the bill.

Next the lobby sent people out to Missouri to get the Democratic organization there to exert pressure on me. That failed also. And finally a propaganda campaign financed by the utility magnates was launched in the state of Missouri among my constituents, many of whom held securities. I was swamped with letters and telegrams urging me to vote against the bill. I did not let these messages alter my own convictions because I knew that the "wrecking crew" of Wall Street was at work behind the scenes and that it was responsible for the thirty thousand requests which eventually piled up on my desk. I burned them all, and an investigation of this uncalled-for propaganda barrage, which was aimed at many besides myself, was later undertaken by Senators Hugo Black, Sherman Minton, and Lew Schwellenbach.

The hearings on the bill were the most remarkable that I ever had anything to do with. Included among the financiers who came down to Washington to testify—in addition to Willkie—were John W. Davis, John Foster Dulles, the Whitneys of the New York Stock Exchange, Hopson, and numerous other Wall Street glamor personalities.

As the time for a vote on the hotly disputed bill drew closer, the pressure increased. The only metropolitan newspaper in Missouri that had never been politically unfriendly toward me—the Kansas City *Journal-Post*—was opposed to the legislation which I was supporting. On June 11, when the roll was called for the yeas and nays, fifty-six senators voted for the bill and thirty-two voted against it. Unfortunately I was detained on important business elsewhere and did not get to vote, although I had made advance arrangements to do so in case the margin in its favor gave evidence of being slender. Nevertheless, after the bill was passed, a two-column editorial on page one of the Kansas City *Journal-Post* proceeded to "skin me alive" for the stand I had taken. I paid no attention to the incident, knowing that I would be the target for many more similar attacks by special interests if I continued to ignore their demands and did what I knew to be right for the majority of the people. I never considered any other course.

Less dramatic measures for which I voted in 1936, but nevertheless important ones, were bills extending federal loans to tenants to purchase farms, and repealing publication of income tax returns. I voted against a proposal to reduce relief appropriations by two billion dollars and against a measure to restore anti-trust laws to full force and end NRA exemptions.

In 1936 the administration of President Roosevelt was busy erecting new legislation to take the place of the Agricultural Adjustment Administration which a hostile Supreme Court had declared unconstitutional the year before. The result was the Soil Conservation Act of 1936, which passed with the aid of my vote. I gave this bill a lot of study. I was well informed on AAA and had made a national broadcast concerning it from the General Electric station at Schenectady in 1935.

My first vote against the Roosevelt program came in 1936, when I voted for a bill to advance the payment date for the soldier bonus. The President had opposed the idea, and when the legislation passed both Houses, he vetoed it. I voted to override the veto, and the measure was passed without Roosevelt's approval. I thought the bill was right. I was not in favor of the bonus in the first place, but since it had been passed I believed it should be paid.

Another important measure for which I cast my vote in 1936 was one that provided for returning control of relief programs to the individual states. I always acted on the theory that whatever could be adequately handled on the local, or state, levels should not be under the control of the federal government unless emergency conditions prevailed, as had been the case during the early 1930s.

I supported a bill advocating flood-control financing entirely by the federal government and another creating the Commodity Exchange Commission.

The year 1937 was another busy one for the Senate so far as New Deal legislation was concerned. One of the most important bills for which I voted, when it first came up, was the Fair Labor Standards Act. President Roosevelt's request for a "floor under wages and a ceiling on hours" appeared to be not only sensible but imperative. This bill and the Walsh-Healy Act were fundamental New Deal measures and were intended to help the little people in labor who had no lobby and no influence.

I always strongly supported the rank and file of labor, but I was not blind to labor's faults. In the same year that I voted for the Fair Labor Standards Act I also supported a measure sponsored by Senator Byrnes condemning the sit-down strike as an unfair tactic.

I voted in favor of the much-disputed Neutrality Act of 1937, because I thought it would help to keep us out of involvement in the civil war then going on in Spain. However, I saw the need for its revision in 1939 and again in 1941 as global warfare made the original measure unworkable. I believe it was a mistake for me to support the Neutrality Act in the first place. I was misled by the report of the munitions investigation, which was headed by Gerald Nye, a demagogue senator from North Dakota. He was an "America Firster," although I did not know it at the time.

An outstanding accomplishment of the New Deal administration had been the Trade Agreements Act of 1934. I voted for its extension in 1937 and again in 1940. The policy of reciprocal trade, which gives the President power to lower tariff rates without consulting Congress, freed the tariff issue to a large extent from its traditional entanglement in politics. Later, as President, I myself was to call for still another extension of this important legislation.

I had a particular interest in that subject which dated back to high school days, when I had headed a debate team supporting the idea of "Tariff for Revenue Only." I remained a convert to the idea from that time on. President Grover Cleveland had been one of the leading advocates of the theory.

A bill to make the Civilian Conservation Corps a permanent organization received my full support and my vote. I thought it might lead to a universal training program, which I advocated throughout my political career.

In 1937 I supported President Roosevelt's Supreme Court reform proposal. Roosevelt grew impatient with the blocking of the New Deal program by the Court's interpretation of the Constitution. He felt that the Court was predominantly conservative because of the advanced age of a number of the justices who would not retire. He therefore proposed to add a justice for each member of the Court over seventy who did not elect retirement. I knew from my study of history that there was nothing sacrosanct about the number nine, that the membership of the Supreme Court had fluctuated during our history from five to ten. President Lincoln wanted to enlarge the Supreme Court to eleven. I saw no reason why the number of the justices could not be increased so that the nation would have, within constitutional bounds, a more forward-looking approach to changing times and conditions.

I was opposed to the move, which was also made in 1937, to increase individual income taxes on incomes of six thousand dollars or more. Later I voted against increasing the normal surtax of corporations from forty per cent to sixty per cent. I was always against measures calling for an overtax to reduce profits on contracts with the government; I supported instead the idea of renegotiation.

There was mixed with such measures the principle of double taxation. I thought the best solution was to make those who had gouged the government return their ill-gotten gains directly rather than to penalize the decent corporations.

Finally, in 1937 I voted for the Bituminous Coal Act, which increased government supervision of the soft-coal industry. As a member of the Interstate Commerce Committee I had an opportunity to see the need for protection of three groups who were dependent upon the industry— the public, the government, and labor—from mismanagement of something in which they had common economic interests.

Other issues before the Senate that year included the $112,000,000 Gilbertsville Dam project, continued subsidy of farm interest rates, low-cost housing, and the confirmation of Hugo Black for membership in the Supreme Court against the opposition of minority groups who resorted to a smear campaign. I voted in favor of all these bills and resolutions.

One of the President's plans in 1938 with which I was in hearty accord was his program for reorganization of the executive branch of the government. The proposal, based on a painstaking study of the government machinery by a committee headed by Louis Brownlow, contained some of the same principles as my own reorganization plans ten years later.

Those who understand the position of the Chief Executive, as Roosevelt did and as I came to later, have known for years of the need for reorganizing the executive branch in the interest of greater efficiency and economy. Such plans, however, are usually looked on with suspicion and fears which are quickly exploited by administration opponents.

Basically, the 1938 measure called for the delegation of power to the President to reorganize federal agencies, to terminate or create them as changing needs require, to establish a new Department of Welfare, and to exercise greater freedom in emergencies to allocate appropriations without recourse to the Congress but subject to review by an auditor general. The proposal passed the Senate, with the aid of my vote, by a margin of 49 to 42. It was defeated in the House. It was difficult then, and is now, for lawmakers to see that government—local, state, and national—necessitates a continuing organization which becomes obsolete, moth-eaten, and cumbersome if it is not constantly adjusted to current needs. Reorganization should be an unending process—with reasonable checks on it, of course.

Also in 1938 I voted for the new Agricultural Adjustment Act, for an amendment to the Housing Act to stimulate construction by private capital, for a resolution limiting debate on the anti-lynching bill (in an unsuccessful effort to break the filibuster against it), and for a proposal to tax federal tax-exempt securities. During that same year I voted against a measure prohibiting certain political activities by relief officials. I also voted nay on a bill denying aid to public projects competing with privately owned public utilities. This, I felt, was a vital measure on public policy.

As my first term drew to a close, the attention of the Congress was being diverted somewhat from domestic reform legislation by the outbreak of war in Europe and the increasing threat to our national security. Ever since my arrival in Washington I had agitated for legislation that would strengthen national defense, but such measures were slow in maturing. It was not until the very eve of our entry into the war that the Senate turned its full attention to mobilization and defense proposals, and by that time my second term was well under way. Before my first term ended, however, I cast my vote for such defense legislation as came before the Senate. During 1939 I also voted for increased appropriations to investigate violations of civil liberties; to raise the federal contribution to old-age pensions; to carry out a proposed $1,615,000,000 public-works program; and to provide $225,000,000 in parity payments on wheat, corn, rice, and tobacco.

Measures which I opposed included one to increase the Treasury price for newly mined domestic silver to 77.57 cents. This was a "sheep, silver, sugar" bill! I was not against a plan to allow the TVA to issue $110,-000,000 in bonds to acquire private power facilities, but I voted against the bill because it was not in the right form. Believing that water carriers should be regulated the same as buses, trucks, air lines, and railroads, I voted against a bill exempting water carriers from Interstate Commerce Commission jurisdiction. I also voted against continuing the mandatory arms embargo, because there never should have been one in the first place. Republican Spain was lost on account of the embargo.

In the final year of my first term I voted to abolish the Hatch Act restriction on federal officeholders. I had never been sold on the Hatch Act. I voted, however, in favor of extending its restrictions to the states, because if it applied to federal people the state personnel should also be included. I supported a move to limit campaign gifts to five thousand dollars—a rule which should be strictly enforced. I was also in favor of a bill prohibiting the use of strikebreakers and spies in labor disputes, and voted for an additional $212,000,000 for farm parity payments in 1940.

I cast my vote against a proposal to give the Senate veto power over reciprocal trade pacts. The Senate should not have such power. I fought the proposed reduction of non-defense appropriations by $500,000,000.

The chief domestic issue with which I was occupied during the last few years of my first term was the regulation of the major modes of transportation. The hearings in which I participated and the work which I did in this area resulted in three major pieces of legislation—the Civil Aeronautics Act, the Transportation Act of 1940, and the Bus and Truck Act.

Senator Warren Austin of Vermont and I wrote the bill setting up an administrative director for the Civil Aeronautics Board who was under the appointive power of the President. For the first time this made the Board a quasi-judicial body with an administrator authorized to conduct independently all the business of the agency, with his own counsel, thus removing it from the possibility of undue pressure from members of the Congress in connection with appointments or policies.

When I reported the bill out of committee, it was placed on the Senate calendar. Senator McCarran then took the reported bill off the calendar and had it reintroduced as a new bill, which he succeeded in having referred to the Commerce Committee instead of the Interstate Commerce Committee, where it had originated. By this maneuver, when the conference committee was named to work out the bill with the House Interstate and Foreign Commerce Committee representatives, the name of Harry S. Truman was not listed.

When Senator Bennett Clark saw what had happened, he went to Vice-President Garner, who made the appointments to the conference committee, and told him that if I was not placed on the committee Garner could accept his resignation. This put me on the conference committee, where I was able to keep McCarran from deleting the provision for setting up an independent administrator in the CAB and keeping the Board under the control of the Congress instead of subject to the appointive power of the President. The bill was finally passed the way Austin and I had written it.

In 1939 I introduced the Wheeler-Truman bill, proposing changes in the interstate commerce laws regulating the financing of the railroads. This became the Transportation Act of 1940. I had worked on the problem since February 4, 1935—a problem which occupied more of my attention during my first term in the Senate than any other undertaking. On that date Burton K. Wheeler, as chairman of the Interstate Commerce Committee, had introduced in the Senate a resolution calling for an inquiry into the financial difficulties which were crippling the major railroad systems of the country. The basis of the resolution was the need for public knowledge concerning the management and disposition of billions of dollars invested by individuals and by the government in the rail carriers, and for adequate protective legislation based upon such knowledge. With the railroad industry in a state of near collapse following the early years of the depression, Wheeler's resolution called for government investigation into the causes of this condition in order that remedial legislation could be enacted to rehabilitate this vital segment of the national economy.

As soon as the Senate authorized the Interstate Commerce Committee to proceed with the inquiry within a stipulated budget of ten thousand dollars, Wheeler named a subcommittee to do the work. He selected Alben Barkley of Kentucky, Vic Donahey of Ohio, Wallace White of Maine, and Henrik Shipstead of Minnesota. Wheeler was the chairman of the subcommittee. Max Lowenthal and Sidney J. Kaplan were named as counsel and assistant counsel to the subcommittee. I was not a member to begin with, but I asked Wheeler if I could attend the meetings. He said he would be delighted to have me, and when some of the members lost interest he put me on the subcommittee.

This was the group that was supposed to diagnose the ills of the prostrate railroad systems of the nation and to come up with a workable remedy. The task was to require five long years of research. Testimony and depositions were taken. Hearings were conducted. Much accumulated data was analyzed and evaluated, and finally, to rectify the situation, a bill was hammered out in such shape as to be acceptable to both Houses of Congress.

Although the ultimate result of all this work was to be the Transportation Act of 1940, it was impossible to visualize it in its eventual form when I first started the undertaking in 1935. Neither could I foresee that this was to be a law which I would invoke as President of the United States to avert a nationwide rail crisis in 1947.

I tackled my end of this assignment in the way I had long before learned to be the only sound approach to any problem. I began at once to read all of the records I could locate of earlier testimony concerning the railroads. I read past newspaper accounts of the industry's financial tangles. I ransacked the Library of Congress for every book on the subject of railroad management and history, and at one time had fifty volumes sent by the Library to my office in the Senate Office Building. Even before the subcommittee met for the first session, I had completed a good deal of background reading. In the discussion which took place at that first meeting, Wheeler saw that I had equipped myself with a considerable store of information on the subject and eventually he made me vice-chairman of the subcommittee.

Within a short time the subcommittee to investigate railroad finances was in operation. It was a fascinating and helpful experience to help organize the committee and get it into action, but the task was not as simple as some may suppose who have never been close to the workaday routine of the Congress. Stenographic and clerical help had to be lined up. Suitable office space and equipment had to be provided. Documents had to be impounded, witnesses subpoenaed, and all legal technicalities carefully checked in advance. All this was required before the real work of gathering testimony and holding hearings could begin. Nevertheless, they were under way by late 1936, and the subcommittee's eyes were being opened wide by the increasing volume of undeniable evidence of graft and corruption which lay at the root of the railroad situation. I saw in my assignment as vice-chairman of this subcommittee a genuine opportunity to get to the bottom of the dishonest practices which had wrecked some of our greatest carrier systems, and I dedicated myself to pushing the inquiry until the whole truth was revealed. As a result of my interest and application to the job, Wheeler virtually turned the work of the subcommittee over to me and allowed me to conduct the investigation with a free hand.

It should be understood, of course, that in addition to his committee tasks a senator's work on the floor of the Senate consumes much time. He must inform himself and cast his vote on hundreds of measures, which may range all the way from amendments to the Constitution to bills awarding relief to individuals.

In addition to voicing my vote on practically all the business that came before the Senate during my first term, I introduced many bills and resolutions. I offered amendments to numerous proposals. Now and then I presented committee reports. I made a few speeches and remarks concerning pending legislation and submitted for publication in the Congressional Record pertinent information with respect to the work of committees on which I served. All of these activities, of course, are permanently recorded in the Record, although I never paid much attention to getting space in its pages.

Almost before I knew it my first term in the Senate was coming to a close. The years since 1935 had been the busiest and the happiest of my life, and I decided early in 1940 that I would make a fight for renomination in the August primary and for re-election in the November general elections.

My desire to retain my seat in the Senate for another six years was based on some specific reasoning. I had worked hard. I had worked very hard. I felt that I had made a good record in the Senate, and I believe that I had won the respect of that body. I had been attacked and vilified by the metropolitan press in the state of Missouri, and this put me in a fighting mood.

The President had offered, in a roundabout way, to put me on the Interstate Commerce Commission. I sent him word, however, that if I received only one vote I intended to make the fight for vindication and re-election to the Senate. The President really was encouraging Stark, my opponent.

At a meeting I called in St. Louis, my friends were unanimous in advising me not to run. Politically, the situation that confronted me in my home state was not an inviting one. In the first place, Tom Pendergast had been sent to prison in connection with an income-tax-fraud investigation, and the Jackson County organization which had supported me in the 1934 campaign had fallen into discredit as a result. Secondly, I was faced with the united opposition of the metropolitan newspapers in Missouri. Most of them had objected to my stand on New Deal measures designed to achieve a higher standard of living for the people. Republican for the most part, these newspapers naturally disapproved of the investigations in which I had participated and which shed so much light on the wrongdoings of special interest groups. The St. Louis *Post-Dispatch* was the one great metropolitan daily which approved the investigations and their results, but even it disapproved of me because of my Democratic background in western Missouri.

I realized that attempts would be made to link my name with the misdeeds and misfortunes of Pendergast and to make it appear that I was the product of a corrupt political machine. This did not bother me personally, because I had an unblemished record to point to. But I did not discount the influence that such propaganda might have.

In addition to all this, I lacked an organization and I had no money to put into an expensive state-wide campaign. I had made many loyal friends in Washington who would have gladly offered their support, but most of them had campaigns of their own to worry about. While I felt that I could count on the endorsement of the New Deal leaders, I knew that I would be entirely on my own in getting my campaign under way out in Missouri.

When I made this trip to St. Louis in the spring to discuss plans for my renomination with a group of friends and party leaders, I saw that my opposition was formidable indeed. Two men had already announced their intentions to unseat me in the fall—Governor Lloyd C. Stark and District Attorney Maurice Milligan.

I had known Lloyd Stark for many years and had helped him obtain the office of governor four years before. He was the head of a large nursery at Louisiana, Missouri, and had been very active in American Legion politics in the state. He had also had his lightning rod up for governor for some time. He was elected in 1936. Late in 1939 he came to my Washington office to tell me he did not intend to run against me for the Senate in 1940. I told my secretary, however, that Stark would be my main opposition in the 1940 primary. And he was.

Stark had made an able governor and was well liked by many Missourians. I thought he had the backing of the powerful St. Louis machine of which Mayor Dickmann was head and of which Bob Hannegan was an active member. (When the votes were counted, however, I carried St. Louis.)

Maurice Milligan was the other candidate for the nomination. He was United States district attorney at Kansas City and had been the chief prosecutor in the investigation which had sent many Pendergast workers to jail. I had opposed his confirmation because I thought that more qualified lawyers were available for the job—but with the Jackson County organization in disrepute, Milligan was riding a wave of popularity and was saying that he would take my job away from me in November.

These were unencouraging prospects; nevertheless, I was determined to run for re-election. I sent my secretary out to set up an organization of supporters, to collect funds, and to run the campaign in Missouri until I could come out in late summer after the adjournment of the third session of the Seventy-sixth Congress. We rented a building in Sedalia for our state headquarters and by mail and by telephone began recruiting volunteers and donors for work and money to help in the campaign.

A campaign committee was made up of long-time friends from various sections of the state. Harry Vaughan, a lieutenant colonel in the Army Reserve Corps in St. Louis and a friend of many years' standing, was treasurer of the committee.

This was the nucleus of the state-wide organization that I began to build through the summer of 1940. The response to our call for assistance was heart-warming. Money began to come into the headquarters, and workers for counties and towns were signing up by the score.

I knew that I could not count on a big vote in the cities, where I was opposed almost without exception by the political organizations and the press. The Kansas City *Journal* was the only large newspaper which openly supported me. The rural papers showed less bias against me and more appreciation for the facts of my political record, and I went after the farm vote. My record of support for every New Deal measure offering relief to the oppressed farm population assured me of voting strength in Missouri's rural areas.

Organized labor saw in me an advocate of their rights, too, because of my voting record in the Senate. As the time for the primary election drew near in August, the railroad labor unions pledged their support and distributed literature in my behalf among the laboring elements of the state.

I also had divisions set up inside the committee to go after the veteran vote—on the basis of my service, both in and out of uniform, in behalf of the armed forces. I appealed to the minority votes on the grounds of the civil-rights legislation which I had supported in the Senate. But I did not restrict my campaign to classes of society. I was running for re-nomination by all Missourians who were interested in honesty and efficiency in government.

I was aware that the only way to win the renomination was to go to the people with my record and my platform. I went into seventy-five counties during the hot months of July and August, speaking day and night and meeting hundreds of thousands of voters in the cities, towns, and villages.

I always made it my business to speak plainly and directly to the people without indulging in high-powered oratory. The truth, I felt, is what voters need more than anything else, and when they have that, they can vote intelligently. When they cannot get the facts from other sources, an honest candidate is obligated to go out and give it to them in person.

As the weeks of campaigning rolled by, it was obvious that the race for junior senator from Missouri had narrowed down to Governor Stark and myself. Milligan remained in the race, but his following was small. Stark had started with a comfortable lead, but more and more of the people rallied to me. We were running about even when the time for voting came around.

In the final days of the campaign my chances were given an impetus when Senator Bennett Clark announced his support and made some speeches in my behalf. And the biggest break was when Bob Hannegan, who had been working for Stark, sensed that he was backing the wrong man and switched his support to me. He was a tremendous political influence in St. Louis, and I was able to carry that part of the state in the primary election.

Right up to the day of the election it was a close fight between Stark and me, and a hard one. Both Stark and Milligan repeatedly attempted to employ "guilt by association" tactics in linking me with the Pendergast machine, which no longer existed.

One of my favorite stories, which I would tell with respect to the criticism and attacks leveled against me by my opponents, had to do with two old bachelors who had once lived on the farm next to ours out in the country. They were always borrowing money, handling cattle, and carrying on all sorts of transactions, and their farm property was involved in most of the deals, although it had never left their possession. One day they came into the office of the Bank of Belton with the abstract. Rolled up, it was six inches in diameter. Frank Blair, the cashier of the bank, asked one of the old fellows, "Is this the abstract to your place?"

"Yes," he drawled, "but you don't need to look at it. It's been through hell three times with its hat off."

I sometimes felt that way about myself, and consequently I was not bothered by the 1940 political fight. I had learned in advance what it would be like.

The whirlwind finish resulted in a narrow victory for me. I won the nomination with a plurality of only about eighty-three hundred votes. Still, that was enough, and I felt great satisfaction in the knowledge that my victory had been won by hard work and by the loyal support of those who believed in what I was trying to do.

The cost of my campaign was a little more than $21,000. Of this, $17,887.87 was donated to the campaign, and I had to bear the balance of $3,685.89 myself. There had been 1,026 contributors in all.

My Republican opponent in the general election was Manvelle Davis, but my victory in the primary had virtually guaranteed re-election in November. When the votes were counted on November 5, I had received 930,775 to 886,376 for Davis.

I was still the United States senator from Missouri.

In St. Louis only a few weeks before that election I had been elevated to the post of grand master of Masons in Missouri, and Forrest C. Donnell, who was the Republican candidate that year for governor, was a couple of stations behind me in the Grand Lodge line. He was afterward grand master himself.

During the political campaign that followed, Donnell and Manvelle Davis appeared together at a Republican meeting in Wellsville, and Davis, who had been vilifying me consistently, continued to do so there.

He quoted lies published in the St. Louis *Post-Dispatch* and the Kansas City *Star* and apparently had a grand time doing it.

A very good Catholic friend of mine, however—Jim Wade by name—was present at the Wellsville meeting and, having heard what Davis said, approached Forrest Donnell to ask if I had not been elected grand master of Masons in St. Louis.

Donnell said that I had been.

"Then is it possible," Jim asked, "that he could have been elected to that office and be the low sort of person Manvelle Davis has been saying he is?"

Donnell, to his credit, replied, "Of course not."

That statement was promptly broadcast by Jim Wade, and it cost Davis thousands of votes.

CHAPTER 12

When I was sworn in for the second time as senator on January 3, 1941, this country was preparing for war. We had suddenly realized that we were unprepared to face the dangers that confronted us and had begun a frantic attempt to remedy that situation. We had decided to build a two-ocean navy and to train and arm a million men a year for a period of five years. We had begun to spend money by the billion to accomplish those two purposes. We proposed to give all-out aid to Great Britain, Greece, and China and were getting ready to spend more billions to do it.

Our national defense machinery, which had never been quite adequate, suddenly had to be expanded to enormous proportions. Contracts for construction, for supplies, and for munitions were negotiated in desperate haste. Washington was full of people seeking contracts, most of them sincerely desiring to be of help to the government, some seeking only their own selfish interests.

It had become necessary to let enormous contracts for the expansion of airplane plants and for the construction of new ones. Munitions plants were being constructed throughout the nation. Clothing, supplies, munitions, battleships, airplanes, and everything necessary for the defense program were being purchased at a rate never before dreamed of. Some sixteen and a half billions in appropriations were authorized and appropriated for defense. This did not include the appropriation of seven billions for aid to Britain or the four billions for the Army, both of which were pending at the time in the House of Representatives. When these appropriations were completed and authorized, defense expenditures during the first few months of 1941 would exceed twenty-five billions of dollars.

I was concerned about charges that the huge contracts and the immense purchases that resulted from these appropriations were being handled through favoritism. There were rumors that some of the plants had been located on a basis of friendship. I feared that many of the safeguards usually observed in government transactions were being thrown aside and overlooked, although these safeguards would in no way have slowed up the program. I knew, too, that certain lobbyists were seeking the inside track on purchases, contracts, and plant locations. There were rumors of enormous fees being paid to these gentlemen and of purchases having been concentrated among a few manufacturers of supplies.

I saw cliques in labor and in capital, each greedy for gain, while small production plants by the hundreds were being pushed aside and kept inactive by big business. The big fellows, in the name of the government, were putting thousands of small concerns out of business that should have been producing for the total war effort.

I was concerned about these small shops and factories and I tried to figure out how they could be used more effectively in the nation's over-all defense program. Because of the shortage of machine tools, big companies were sometimes attempting to buy, and even to requisition, machines belonging to small businesses. When these machines were moved, workmen had to follow, which added to the concentration of population and created more housing problems. On the other hand, the problem of vacant housing developed in the communities they had left.

I gave a lot of thought to this situation, and when I realized that it was growing increasingly worse, I decided to take a closer look at it. I got into my automobile and started out from Washington to make a little investigation on my own. I drove thirty thousand miles in a great circle through Maryland and from there down to Florida, across to Texas, north through Oklahoma to Nebraska, and back through Wisconsin and Michigan. I visited war camps, defense plants, and other establishments and projects which had some connection with the total war effort of the country, and did not let any of them know who I was.

The trip was an eye-opener, and I came back to Washington convinced that something needed to be done fast. I had seen at first hand that grounds existed for a good many of the rumors that were prevalent in Washington concerning the letting of contracts and the concentration of defense industries in big cities.

I had decided to make a speech on the subject before the Senate in order to emphasize the need for action and call on the Senate for a committee to investigate the situation. Such a committee would have the power of the United States Senate to bring action where it was needed.

I talked over the prospects of a committee with my close friends—with John Snyder, in particular, and Senate leaders whose advice I respected—and they were interested. I explained that I was not going to do any witch-hunting. I was not after publicity. I had already been re-elected. Conditions were going from bad to worse so far as national defense was concerned, and my aim was to correct them.

I drafted a resolution calling for a special committee to investigate the national defense effort. On February 10, 1941, I submitted the resolution. In my speech on the resolution I cited many instances of irregularities in the awarding of contracts and pointed out the great danger of concentrating the manufacturing in limited areas. From seventy to ninety per cent of the contracts let so far had been concentrated in an area smaller than Missouri. The big manufacturers were getting bigger all the time, and the very small producers were being threatened with the necessity of going out of business or starving to death. As a result, the national defense program was suffering.

My resolution called for a committee of five senators to investigate the conduct of the defense program and requested twenty-five thousand dollars for expenses. The resolution was referred by Vice-President Wallace to the Senate Committeee on Audit and Control of Contingent Expense, of which James F. Byrnes was chairman. He immediately whittled down the amount of the appropriation and recommended ten thousand dollars. After a week of haggling a grant of fifteen thousand dollars was agreed upon, and the special committee was authorized.

Byrnes's committee had expanded the membership of the new committee from five to seven, including two Republicans, and I exercised great care in their selection. As author of the resolution, I became chairman of the committee. Technically the selection of committee members is made by the Vice-President. Actually, however, they are chosen in conferences, and I consulted not only Wallace but also Barkley and Minority Leader McNary and, on occasion, President Roosevelt himself. Eventually the following senators were named to the special committee: Tom Connally of Texas, Carl Hatch of New Mexico, James Mead of New York, Mon Wallgren of Washington, Joseph Ball of Minnesota, and Owen Brewster of Maine. Ball and Brewster were the two Republican members.

My committee was now formed and ready to go to work. First of all, what we needed was a good lawyer to act as the committee counsel. I went to see Attorney General Robert H. Jackson and asked him to find a lawyer who had common sense, who would be loyal to the objectives of the committee, and who would make a hard-hitting investigator. I felt that a counsel for a legislative inquiry committee should be a person of tact as well as ability. It would not be easy to find the right man.

Jackson recommended to me one of his assistants, who had recently been the successful prosecutor in the Judge Manton case in Philadelphia and the Hopson case in New York. His name was Hugh Fulton. He was an excellent lawyer and a first-rate investigator. His salary was set at nine thousand dollars, which was more than half of my total appropriation.

I made sure at the outset that every member of the special committee had the same attitude toward the objective for which the committee existed. Although there was such a mass of information and misinformation confronting us that we hardly knew where to begin, our purpose was clear-cut and specific. The committee had been authorized and directed by the United States Senate to investigate the operation of the program for the procurement and construction of all supplies, materials, munitions, vehicles, aircraft, vessels, plants, camps, and other articles and facilities connected with the war program. It had also been directed to examine the types and terms of all contracts awarded; the methods by which they were awarded; the contractors selected; the utilization of small business concerns through subcontracts or otherwise; geographical distribution of contracts and locations of plants and facilities; the effects of such a program with respect to labor and the migration of labor; the practices of management or labor; and the benefits accruing to contractors with respect to amortization for purposes of taxation or otherwise.

In other words, the committee was directed to examine every phase of the entire war program.

It was not organized to tell the war agencies what to do or how to do it. It was not to substitute its judgment for their judgment. Its function was to assure that intelligent consideration would be given to the important and difficult problems presented by the war program and that the victory would be won with the least cost in lives and property.

The membership of the committee was both non-sectional and bipartisan. Its members had no preconceived notions, no partisan views to promote, no beliefs to prove. I was determined that the committee was not going to be used for either a whitewash or a smear in any matter before it but was to be used to obtain facts and suggest remedies where necessary.

The idea of the committee was to conduct the investigation of the defense effort simultaneously with the war program in order that mistakes could be remedied before irretrievable damage was done. We were interested in doing a surgeon's job to cure, not in performing an autopsy to find out why the patient died.

The members of the committee agreed at the beginning that the committee's investigations were to be thorough and complete and that it was to find the facts and to make conclusions only when they were clearly compelled by the facts. Our motto was, "There is no substitute for a fact. When the facts are known, reasonable men do not disagree with respect to them." This policy meant that the committee's work was going to be more arduous and difficult, but less sensational. We were not seeking headlines. We did not want publicity. We wanted only results. Anything we had to say we would say on the floor of the Senate only and in our formal reports.

The power to investigate is necessary to the intelligent exercise of the powers of Congress. This is especially true in wartime, when the Congress must delegate many of its powers. Only by investigation can it review the exercise of them and ascertain how and to what extent they should be modified—by legislation if necessary, by executive action if possible.

The nature of the congressional investigating committee has suffered violence at the hands of some who have not understood or appreciated the scope and function of such a committee. Too often, in recent times, the committees have been used for publicity rather than for the original purposes intended. As chairman of the Special Committee to Investigate the National Defense Program, I made up my mind that it was going to fulfill without fanfare the purpose for which it was created. That was the understanding I had with the members of the committee, and without exception they lived up to it.

While the committee had been taking shape, I had been reading the records of the Joint Committee on the Conduct of the War between the States. These historic records constitute a most interesting set of documents. That committee of the Union Congress was said by Douglas Southall Freeman, the biographer of Robert E. Lee, to have been of material assistance to the Confederacy. I became familiar with its mistakes and was determined to avoid the same errors in the conduct of my special committee. Here, as in many other instances, I found the teachings of history to be valuable in my own approach to current problems.

The first hearing of the committee took place on April 15, 1941. Secretary of War Henry L. Stimson was the first witness, and he presented a lengthy statement setting forth the difficulties of mobilization, procurement, and expansion which confronted the Army as a result of the unexpectedly successful military tactics of Germany in the new European war. He called attention to the magnitude of the task of making preparations for modern war and recited the obstacles encountered. He was followed by Under Secretary of War Robert P. Patterson, who revealed that of the government's ordnance requirements, less than ten per cent was manufactured in government arsenals, the remainder being supplied under contract by private industry.

During the first week of the investigation the committee devoted its time to accumulating the background information necessary for intelligent consideration of the defense problem. Secretary of the Navy Frank Knox, for example, described the problems that had arisen when the Navy affected a seventy per cent expansion within a period of months, and expressed concern over the possible shortage of aluminum and steel forgings. William S. Knudsen, Director of the Office of Production Management, described the organization of his agency and the procedure for assigning contract priorities. Sidney Hillman, Associate Director of the OPM, was questioned on the relation of labor disturbances and strikes to the over-all war-production program. During the first week the committee established confidence and a working relationship with the executive branch of the government.

We interviewed General George Marshall, Chief of Staff, and Brigadier General Harry L. Twaddle of the Operations and Training Division of the War Department on the mobilization program and cantonment needs. We took testimony from approximately a dozen generals and civilian experts connected with the camp-construction program.

On April 23 the committee made a trip to Fort Meade, Maryland, to inspect that camp. This was only the first of several camps the committee inspected in order to learn whether or not the War Department had been on its toes during the last twenty years and had made any worth-while emergency plans.

This was especially important, for approximately a billion dollars had already been expended on camp construction—an enormous amount even in those days of astronomical figures. Furthermore, the War Department had plans for constructing still more camps, and I felt that it should not make the same mistakes in the proposed new camp construction that it had made in the program now being completed.

This phase of the investigation was interrupted by a situation that arose in the coal industry. A strike resulting from the inability of operators in the North and the South to come to an agreement with labor constituted the most urgent national defense bottleneck during the latter part of April. I announced that if coal was not being taken from the ground by April 25 the committee would summon the representative of all the operators, and John L. Lewis, the representative of the miners, and proceed to find out why we could not have the coal in the emergency. If it was necessary to "take them for a bus ride to get them together," I said, we would do it in order to get coal.

Lewis was demanding for the miners a wage increase of approximately seventeen per cent in the northern mines and twenty-five per cent in the southern ones, and because the miners' annual wage contract with the operators had expired, work had been halted. To complicate the matter, a bitter fight was going on over the wage differentials between northern and southern groups of coal operators.

As none of those involved showed any intention of yielding, the committee summoned Lewis and representatives of the operators to testify on April 28. As a result of this hearing it became clear that the southern operators were the ones who were holding up a settlement. I had the committee notify them, therefore, that unless coal was being mined within twenty-four hours the owners of the mines would be called to testify before the committee and to show why their wage dispute should come ahead of the national safety. That night the deadlock was broken, and the miners, with no further delay, returned to their work.

Meanwhile the investigation into the new camp-construction program continued. Additional testimony was taken from Army officials and contractors. Architects and renters of equipment were questioned. Careful inspections were made of various camps in an effort to ascertain the good and bad points of the construction program.

As the facts began to pile up under the committee's relentless searching and inquiry, evidence of an appalling amount of waste in camp construction began to accumulate. We learned that there had been a lack of foresight in planning and a large amount of inefficiency in operation, as a result of which several hundreds of millions of dollars had been lost.

As an Army officer myself, I had always assumed that the War Department had paid some attention to the bitter lessons we learned with respect to camp construction during World War I. I had assumed that, when the time came, carefully drawn up plans would be taken from the files and put into operation with a minimum of delay. I was utterly astounded to find that, although a postwar study had been made of camp-construction problems encountered in the first war, all of the copies of it had been lost by the War Department and that the general in charge of the construction division of the Quartermaster Corps had actually been proceeding under the assumption that there never would be another war!

I wanted to know why the Army was not better prepared in such matters as these when the United States, as a part of its relief program, had been spending billions of dollars for the WPA—the Works Progress Administration—and might just as well have used some of it, at least, to make a few plans. I found that the answer was not that the Congress had been tightfisted with the Army or that the WPA would not make the funds available. It was because the armchair generals in charge of such matters, although they knew that public planning projects were worth while, did not think it permissible for the Army to use such funds.

The investigation was turning up other disquieting evidence also. The Army apparently had not realized that there was not enough secondhand construction equipment available in the country to provide for a billion-dollar camp-construction program in addition to the large amount of construction necessary for other defense purposes. As a result, it went through the farce of pretending to rent equipment on bids. The demand was unlimited, the supply very definitely limited, and with contractors bidding against each other at government expense, rentals went sky-high.

The only limit to this equipment renters' paradise was a provision that the government could take possession of the equipment when the rentals exceeded the fancy evaluations which the equipment dealers quoted. During the time my committee was investigating this situation the Army finally began to exercise this right to acquire equipment. However, the so-called recapture valuations were sometimes as much as sixty-four per cent above the cost of new equipment, and it was common practice to set the recapture values at thirty to thirty-five per cent above cost. The chief of the Quartermaster's Equipment Unit estimated that, had the government purchased the equipment new instead of through the device that was used, it could have done so at a saving of from twelve to thirteen million dollars on that item alone.

I learned that most of the work the government was having done was being let on cost-plus-fixed-fee contracts. There was no attempt to ask contractors what they had been in the habit of making in peace time or even what they were willing to take. Huge fixed fees were offered by the government in much the same way that Santa Claus passes out gifts at a church Christmas party. I asked the contractors to submit their own estimates on every expense they had which came out of their fees and for which they did not obtain reimbursement, and I compared these estimates with their average annual profits as reported by them for the years 1936 through 1939.

After careful investigation I found that the fees allowed to contractors by the government sometimes made it possible for them to earn, on a three-month job at government risk, three or four times as much as they had formerly been able to make at their own risk in an entire year of work. In one case it was nearly fifteen times as great. The same thing was also true of architectural engineers. I believed that the contractors and architectural engineers of the United States were just as patriotic as anybody else and that it was not necessary to pay them such fees.

Long before the committee had completed its investigation of the camp-construction program it became clear to me that part of the blame for the waste and confusion lay at the door of some labor unions. For example, investigation at Fort Meade, Maryland, showed that nobody was hired unless okayed by the unions and that both common laborers and skilled mechanics were being charged fees for work permits, and on that one job alone approximately two hundred thousand dollars was taken in by the unions through such fees. At other camps we found similar conditions to exist. In one instance a price of three hundred dollars was set on the work permit.

During that period of preparation we paid a terrific price for lack of planning and inefficiency. I hoped, however, that the War Department had learned some real lessons and that in the camp-construction program to follow it would not make the same mistakes. As a matter of fact, it soon began taking steps to remedy many of the defects to which my committee had drawn attention. The press, too, was beginning to take notice of the committee and its work. Congress had often authorized special committees to investigate financiers, banks, railroads, and public utilities, but never before in recent decades had there been an investigation of an administration with the full co-operation of the administration itself. The denunciation of unnecessary waste and inefficiency by the committee made it clear that we were not pulling any punches. We did not wish to make it appear that the Army alone was responsible. The investigation of the camp-construction program was merely the beginning. The spotlight of inquiry was to be turned elsewhere, as well—on other agencies of the government, on big business, on labor, and on other segments of the economy involved in the total defense effort.

By this time the procedure of the special committee had become well established. With the help of Hugh Fulton, the chief counsel, and an increased appropriation, I had assembled a staff of some fifteen investigators in addition to the original members of the committee. One of these young investigators was Matthew Connelly, who later became my appointment secretary in the White House.

Every morning I would meet early with Fulton, and together we would go through the dozens of letters which had been screened by the investigating staff. We would go through big stacks of reports and letters and notes which constituted leads, some of which developed into major investigations, such as shipbuilding or housing. Fulton and I would decide tentatively at these early-morning sessions whether the investigation should be ordered on a certain subject or whether the project should be pushed aside for the time being.

Once or twice a week the full committee met in private session in the small room behind my office which came to be known as the "doghouse."

We often had agency heads confer with us at these private sessions, and when in 1942 Manpower Chief Paul V. McNutt and War Production Board Chairman Donald Nelson were appointed we continued this practice. In this way we could get much accomplished without a great deal of publicity. Perhaps half of the committee's work was done in these unpublicized meetings.

After these informal conferences with other members of the committee I would draw up a schedule of hearings and send each member a memorandum of the next investigation coming before the group, a list of witnesses, and so forth. I also made many trips with the investigators to inspect particular situations on the spot before coming to a decision about calling a hearing.

As nearly as I could, I distributed the work so that every member of the committee found his special abilities challenged to the utmost. By giving specific assignments to each one, there were no overlapping jobs, and in this way each member was left alone to do his work without interference from me or any of the others.

As soon as the work of the committee became known, we had a steady list of callers at Room 449 in the Senate Office Building, which was committee headquarters, and also at Room 248, which was my office. Every day there was an assortment of government officials, labor representatives, lobbyists, and occasionally plain citizens, all of whom had ideas about improving the war effort.

There were manufacturers who felt that their products had been discriminated against. There were producers who complained that they could not get priorities for their products. There were industrialists who accused competitors of using their official positions as dollar-a-year men for private gain. And there were small businessmen who complained that they could not get government contracts for their services and products which would be helpful in winning the war.

I made a point of listening to all of them, and whenever complaints or suggestions deserved it, I sent messages to the governmental agencies involved and got immediate action wherever possible.

There was the usual number of crackpots with ideas for ending the war quickly. I remember one man who had an idea for building an airplane for every soldier in the Army and filling each plane with a few yards of dirt. His idea was that at a given signal thousands of individually manned planes would fly over enemy capitals and completely cover them with United States soil, thus ending the war without further ado.

The hearings themselves were conducted in Washington and in dozens of other cities around the country. Members of the committee usually sat on one side of a long table, and witnesses were seated across from us.

I always tried to stay in the background and to allow the questioning by the counsel and the members to elicit all of the information needed on any subject. I spoke up, however, whenever I felt that it was necessary to keep the investigation within its proper channels. I never permitted irrelevant questioning or any browbeating of witnesses. I had to call one of the senators to order at one hearing when he called John L. Lewis a "charlatan" to his face.

All of the hearings were public, and all of the proceedings were made public in a series of reports. These reports were written by Fulton and myself and were delivered to the Senate from time to time. Copies were made available for the press, and as the committee's position became more widely recognized, the hearings were covered by large numbers of reporters and photographers.

The reports did more than simply summarize our findings. Many of them contained definite recommendations for legislation to correct abuses that had been brought to light. A number of the suggestions made in the committee reports were enacted into legislation by the Congress, but the influence of the committee was beginning to make itself felt through other than legislative channels. In many cases the mere knowledge that we were interested in a particular subject was enough to cause everyone concerned, whether manufacturers, government officials, or labor, to clear up the problems themselves before the committee could get to them.

Wrongdoers were learning to respect the "Truman Committee," and consequently many of them began to clean house hurriedly because of a fear that they might be next to come before the committee to explain their role in the national defense effort. And this was exactly what I was trying to bring about. Those whose operations were aboveboard had, of course, nothing to fear.

The net result was more concerted effort toward winning the war, a tightening of efficiency between civilian and military programs, and the reduction of losses in materials, time, and manpower.

On January 15, 1942, I delivered to the Senate the first annual report of the Special Committee Investigating the National Defense Program. During 1941 the committee had held about seventy hearings and had interviewed 252 witnesses. More than three thousand pages of testimony had been gathered on such subjects as aluminum, copper, lead, zinc, steel, the automobile industry, small business, labor, the aviation program, plant financing, lobbying, shipbuilding, defense housing, the ordnance plants, and government administration of the war production program, in addition to information gathered at the first hearings on camp construction.

With respect to aluminum, it had been discovered that the country would be short more than six hundred million pounds of aluminum per year and that this shortage existed despite drastic civilian curtailment. On May 12, 1941, William L. Batt, Deputy Director of the Division of Production, had described to the committee the processes involved in the manufacture of airplanes. The amount of aluminum required for that year alone, he said, would be 1,400,000,000 pounds. This metal alone constituted fifty-four to eighty per cent of the weight of airplanes, including the motors, and although maximum aluminum production amounted to about thirty million pounds a month, total military needs called for approximately fifty-two million pounds a month. These figures were only guesses, because the airplane industry was new, organizations were expanding, and planning was difficult, but a jump of twenty million pounds a month could be regarded as a reasonable estimate.

Two days after this information had been given to the committee we heard the testimony of a civilian who had correctly anticipated an aluminum shortage more than a year before the production officials of the War Department finally decided to enforce priorities on the use of the metal. He was Richard S. Reynolds, president of the Reynolds Metal Company of Richmond, Virginia. Reynolds was not himself a producer of the metal. Instead, he was a manufacturing consumer. Nevertheless, he had mortgaged his eighteen establishments to the RFC for twenty million dollars and had proceeded to erect new aluminum plants, one in Alabama and another in Washington, which within twelve months were expected to begin the production of sixty million pounds of aluminum a year.

In addition to these Reynolds plants there were four major producers of aluminum in the United States—the Aluminum Company of America, the Dow Chemical Company, the American Magnesium Corporation, and I. G. Farben, a German corporation. The representatives of these four industries were interrogated by the committee in order to determine what had to be done to get more aluminum for the defense effort. In the course of these hearings it became apparent that undue control was being exercised over the sources of magnesium and of bauxite—the claylike ore used in the production of aluminum—and that preferences were being given in the allocation of aluminum priorities by the committee set up by the Office of Production Management for that purpose.

"It looks very much to me," I said at one of the hearings, "as if the members of the priority committee represent du Pont, General Motors, and people who are most interested in these priorities. I can't see that that is for the welfare and benefit of the country. I don't believe that is good public policy. The fellow who is most vitally interested makes the decision for his own welfare and benefit. They have their own business at heart."

As a result of the revelations of the committee, recommendations were made for the use of government funds in building mammoth new aluminum plants, and the output of this vital metal was consequently stepped up to meet war needs. The committee also criticized as taking undue advantage of the government the contract made between the Defense Plants Corporation and the Aluminum Company of America, and as a result of this criticism these two organizations negotiated a supplemental agreement dated December 12, 1941, which corrected many, but not all, of the defects in the original contract.

In looking further into the problem of metal supplies, the committee found that the Office of Production Management had failed to realize the necessity of increasing the production of copper, lead, and zinc until long after the probability of shortage was apparent. Production of these three metals proved so disappointing as to be a definite deterrent to the preparedness program.

In the critical year of 1941 automobile companies had scarcely even begun to produce defense articles. Automobile manufacturers were not required to utilize their plants for the defense program. They were permitted not only to continue but to increase their civilian output. Before the declaration of war the automobile industry had contended that only about ten per cent of their equipment could be used for defense. After the adoption of wartime priorities, however, when the production of automobiles was stopped, they reversed themselves and found they could convert their plants in a relatively short time.

One of the problems that gave the committee the most concern was the fate of the small businessmen. They had been almost completely ignored in the awarding of defense contracts, and their existing facilities were hardly being utilized at all. Because of priority restrictions they were often unable to obtain the necessary materials to continue in their regular business. In addition, they found themselves competing for labor with large contractors who were operating under huge government orders.

The committee found that leadership in both labor and industry had been too much concerned with its own interests and too little concerned with the national welfare. The defense program was very seriously handicapped by strikes and threatened strikes. I felt that many demands for wage increases were inspired by the reports of tremendous profits being made by companies with defense contracts.

Also during the first year of hearings the committee was engaged in an inquiry into the adequacy of the aviation program and its administration. At the outbreak of the war our aircraft production was so limited that the armed services had planes enough only for skeleton forces, and much of this equipment was of inferior quality. The armed services had merely purchased what the manufacturers had to offer instead of planning to use available facilities to produce what they needed at maximum capacity. Many manufacturers and experienced groups who had available facilities for manufacture were, because of priorities or official indifference to their possibilities, entirely idle or were merely operating as technical schools, repair stations, experimental plants.

One method of financing new plant construction for the defense program was through the Defense Plants Corporation, a subsidiary of the Reconstruction Finance Corporation. This organization had an enormous task before it but had been placed in a bad bargaining position. It had the duty to make certain that money was provided as quickly as possible for urgently needed plant expansion. On the other hand, orders for plant expansion did not originate with the Defense Plants Corporation but came from the Office of Production Management. The committee soon learned to appreciate the difficulties that were involved.

In my first report to the Senate I condemned the action of lobbyists, whose attempts to buy and sell influence were weakening the public confidence in the integrity of government officials. A direct result of their activities was the widespread belief that government officials could be influenced. This made businessmen the dupes of peddlers of influence who approached them with stories of their close connections in Washington and with promises of contracts if they were paid a commission, usually five or ten per cent of the contract price. In most instances the Washington connections were nonexistent, and the peddlers of influence were simply acting on the supposition that the businessmen in question could obtain their contracts merely by making a serious and determined effort. The practice was difficult to expose and eliminate, however, because the businessmen who were duped by it hated to admit that their greed had led them to attempt what they thought was bribery of government procurement officers. In cases where they obtained no contracts they seldom had a way of proving the extortion. I suggested legislation to alleviate the evils inherent in this kind of lobbying.

Continuing with my report, I pointed out that as of September 1, 1940, the Navy had made arrangements for about four billion dollars of shipbuilding at a ratio of seventy per cent in private yards and thirty per cent in naval yards. The scope of the program had since been increased. Before the emergency the ratio had been about fifty-fifty, but Admiral Samuel Murray Robinson had testified that it had not been possible to increase naval-yard capacity as much as that of the private shipyards.

One of the principal reasons given was that the naval yards were located many generations ago in congested areas where it was impossible, except at very high cost, to acquire more land.

At the hearing Admiral Robinson had stated that it was almost impossible to compare the costs of private with naval-yard shipbuilding because of the Navy's method of keeping its books. I felt that in a matter of this importance the Navy should take steps to ascertain the actual facts. I stated to the Senate that the Navy should be able to build ships as efficiently as private enterprise, and if there was a wide disparity between the cost of building ships in naval yards and the prices charged for similar ships in private yards the Navy should require reduction of profit to a reasonable amount.

We found that the Navy was extremely liberal with the private shipbuilders. Nine of the thirteen companies which had cost-plus-fixed-fee contracts were entitled to receive fees, plus possible bonuses, which exceeded the amount of their net worth on December 31, 1939, as estimated by them. The fees, plus possible bonuses, bore no relation whatever to the average net profits of the companies during the period from 1936 to 1940. In one case it exceeded by nearly eight hundred times the average annual net profits; in other cases by twenty, thirty, and forty times the average annual net profits. I believed that these fees and bonuses were excessive and that it should not have been necessary to give so large a reward to the private shipbuilding companies.

The profits for repairs and ship-conversion work were found to be even more staggering. The Navy had permitted the shipyards to charge their regular hourly rates for repairs despite the fact that such rates had been fixed at a time when there was very little business and when the entire overhead of the organization had to be charged to a comparatively small volume of work. At one of the hearings the representatives of the Todd Shipbuilding Corporation had testified that Navy ship-conversion contracts "gave us a profit of $1.80 a day on every man we had, and I think we had around thirty-five thousand. If it hadn't been for taxes, we couldn't have handled our profits with a steam shovel."

Also, during the year the committee had investigated the defense housing program. There it found many mistakes, gross waste, extravagances, inefficiency, and petty jealousies on the part of the administrative heads of the program. The cause of some mistakes could be corrected only by legislation. The committee had recommended amendments to the Lanham Act, the basic defense housing statute, before a subcommittee of the Senate Committee on Education and Labor and before the United States Senate in December.

The committee had also begun a nationwide investigation of Army ordnance-plant construction. Hearings had been held on the cost of construction of the Wolf Creek Ordnance Plant and the Milan Ordnance Depot. It had been found that the cost was far in excess of a reasonable value for the facilities turned over to the government. No plans had been available at the outset inasmuch as the design for a modern ordnance plant had to be developed as it was built, and the best the War Department could supply was a cost estimate based on 1917 experiences. Careless construction of a vast amount of roads at an exorbitant cost, improper practices in purchasing and in the handling of payrolls by placing relatives and friends in sinecure positions, and the improper establishment of accounting records were the principal causes of the excessive cost.

The War Department had failed to conduct an adequate investigation of these projects. Even after the committee had instituted its investigation the department did not make a thorough check of the matters to which their attention had been called.

The committee had received similar complaints with respect to a number of the other ordnance projects, and I announced that we would continue our investigation of ordnance-plant construction until practices such as found at Wolf Creek and the Milan Ordnance Depot had been eliminated from the construction program.

The most spectacular portion of the first annual report to the Senate was on the bungling of the Office of Production Management and its unwillingness to use the facilities at its disposal. I pointed out that the OPM's record had not been impressive and that it had made mistakes of commission and omission which were inexcusable. Too often it did nothing, seeking to avoid problems by refusing to admit that they existed.

The committee had found that some of the so-called dollar-a-year men and those working WOC (without compensation), who had flocked to Washington from industry and business to offer their services in the defense effort, were continuing to receive pay from their companies. This was not wrong in itself. But we had discovered that between June 1, 1940, and April 30, 1941, the Army and Navy had given contracts totaling almost three billion dollars to sixty-six firms whose officials had served the government at a dollar a year.

There had also been too much dissension within the Office of Production Management. This had caused uncertainty to business and had been a hindrance to increased production. In almost every case the OPM had either failed to foresee the nature and extent of problems or had tended to minimize the difficulties and to take halfhearted measures in the vain hope that the problems would solve themselves.

The committee had already recommended ending the dual control by Knudsen and Hillman at OPM and the setting up of a War Production

Board under the direction of one chairman. By the time of my first report to the Senate the President had already announced his intention to create such an agency. Thus President Roosevelt received public credit for establishing the War Production Board because of his advance knowledge of the committee's report. That was all right with me. I wanted action more than credit.

I had already determined that Hillman would have to go as Associate Director of OPM along with Knudsen. I had told the Senate on October 29, 1941, of an attempt by Hillman to have a construction contract withheld from the low bidder because he feared that an award to that firm would be followed by labor troubles.

"A responsible company has made a low bid," I told the Senate at that time, "which it is prepared to perform and is capable of performing if not illegally interfered with. Mr. Sidney Hillman advises that it be denied the contract and that the taxpayers pay several hundred thousands of dollars more because Mr. Hillman fears trouble from what he calls irresponsible elements in the American Federation of Labor.

"I cannot condemn Mr. Hillman's position too strongly. First, the United States does not fear trouble from any source; and if trouble is threatened, the United States is able to protect itself. If Mr. Hillman cannot, or will not, protect the interests of the United States, I am in favor of replacing him with someone who can and will."

Donald M. Nelson had been an official in the Office of Production Management, and his appointment as head of the War Production Board signified for the first time the creation of a one-man supervision responsible to the President and to the Congress for the immediate co-ordination of the national war effort. The purpose of the War Production Board was to exercise general direction over the war procurement and production program.

Nelson's management of War Production was a vast improvement over the two-headed monster it succeeded. He was surrounded by good men who were honestly anxious to win the war as quickly and efficiently as possible—many of them, to be sure, dollar-a-year men.

By continued lessons of experience and a fear of exposure, a creditable job was finally accomplished. The war was won with equipment from our industrial plants.

The real work of the special committee was only beginning, because now the nation was at war. Its record in 1941 had already proved that it could perform a very valuable function by assuring that the necessary implements of war were produced speedily and efficiently and that each dollar expended for war purposes would produce a dollar's worth of the necessary war supplies. To that end I devoted most of my time and energy during the early years of the war.

As the committee's investigation proceeded into 1942, the evidence of waste and confusion became more shocking than ever. I saw that the war effort was bogging down because of red tape and bureaucratic waste, because of overlapping jurisdictions and the failure to delegate authority, and because of conflicts between military and civilian agencies. I was so disturbed by our findings that I wrote an article late in 1942 for *American Magazine* which revealed to the public just how chaotic the conditions really were in our war production program.

For example, when our committee tried to find out what was being done to solve the rubber shortage, we had to go to no less than seven separate government agencies—the War Production Board, the Reconstruction Finance Corporation, the Office of the Petroleum Co-ordinator, the Office of Defense Transportation, the Price Administrator, the Board of Economic Warfare, and the Department of Agriculture.

We found thousands of pounds of virgin copper piled to the rafters inside certain naval warehouses awaiting future use in ships, while a nearby factory was threatened with an imminent shutdown on a vital Army contract for want of the selfsame metal. Yet the Navy refused to loosen up with any of its hoard.

A motor-truck producer notified the Army that year that he would be unable to obtain engines until October. Nevertheless, the War Department told him to keep on stockpiling parts and building motorless chassis, thereby tying up materials and equipment which the Navy urgently required to complete its small-boat construction program.

Vanadium is a rare metal that is very important in the manufacture of alloy steel, and early in 1942 the Army-Navy Munitions Board estimated that in the year ahead we would require between fifty and sixty million pounds. However, fifty million pounds was just about ten times the entire annual output of vanadium for all the countries of the world.

While the new War Production Board was operating more efficiently, it nevertheless did not avoid all the mistakes of the old OPM. In March, for instance, WPB issued an order for conserving steel, which would have limited safety-razor manufacturers to an output equivalent to one blade per week for each adult male in the United States. However, it was quickly discovered that America's razor-blade consumption had never exceeded that amount. When this fact was called to their attention, the WPB officials hastily amended their order, stating that lawn mowers, not razor blades, were what they really had in mind.

When the Republic Thunderbolt pursuit plane first came out the Air Force was committed to liquid-cooled motors in pursuit ships and looked with disfavor on the new plane, which utilized the air-cooled engine. After the Japanese Zero fighter and the German Focke-Wulf 190 had proved conclusively the case for the latter type of power plant, the Air Force commanders ceremoniously disinterred the Thunderbolt, rechristened it the P-47, and hailed it as the wonder plane. As a result of five years' delay we had far too few of these fighters with which to challenge the enemy.

With the country's steel furnaces pleading for more scrap, the War Production Board, early in the summer of 1942, launched a publicity campaign to persuade the public to turn in its old metal. The results were disappointing. One reason was that the scrap dealers had been subjected to a welter of confusing and often contradictory orders issued by the Iron and Steel Branch, Scrap Section of the War Production Board, by the Bureau of Industrial Conservation, by the Office of Price Administration, by the Office of Defense Transportation, and by the local scrap-collection agencies. There were fifteen million tons of steel lying around the countryside in abandoned bridges, mines, and railroad tracks which could not be collected for the sole reason that the price ceilings set by OPA made salvage operations unprofitable. Then again, the junk peddler with his rickety old wagon and a single horse used to form the first and vital link in the scrap-collection chain, but price ceilings, plus unfamiliar paper work, were rapidly driving the junk man from the field.

With the peddler disappearing, the dealer was forced by necessity to go out and collect the scrap himself, but here he ran up against the regulations of the Office of Defense Transportation, which had ruled that driving must be cut by twenty-five per cent and that only full truckloads could be carried. In one instance a farmer had eight tons of metal in the form of old farm machinery he wanted to dispose of. However, the dealer could not go and get it because eight tons would not constitute a full load for his ten-ton truck!

The committee was alarmed to discover that for the first six months of the war year 1942 factories were permitted to continue consuming quantities of steel, copper, tin, and lead in the manufacture of toy electric trains, go-carts, mechanical games, and other non-defense products. The need for complete conversion of industry to war production was growing more and more urgent, and the committee recommended an over-all order affecting every industrial firm equally and at the same time. Such an order, however, was slow in coming from the War Production Board.

The disclosure of these and similar shortcomings of our war production program and the constant probing of the committee into other avenues of possible waste and duplication of effort resulted in the review and renegotiation of several war contracts at a saving to the government of more than a hundred fifty million dollars within the first nine months of the war. The indirect economies which the committee had achieved were conservatively reckoned at between two and three billion dollars.

But we were still uncovering new problems more rapidly than solutions were being provided for old ones. The record showed that from the outset the nation's steel requirements were badly underestimated and its ability to meet these requirements was greatly overcalculated. Top officers of the iron and steel industry, possibly fearful that their postwar profits would be menaced by an increase in ingot capacity, insisted that they could and would fulfill every demand of the defense program. The steel men buttressed their position by pointing to the smallness of the orders which the War and Navy Departments then estimated their war orders would consume. Consequently a considerable portion of the blame for the current shortage in steel could be traced to the military planners who had failed to anticipate the vast quantities of all raw materials required for waging total war.

I had learned that because of the want of strong leadership at the top certain dollar-a-year men had delayed the construction of new furnaces. While these men were serving the government without compensation, they had *not* been able to divorce their viewpoint completely from that of their former companies, to which they still looked for payment of their salaries. I was not opposed to the dollar-a-year men because they were businessmen; I wanted more businessmen in government, especially in the war effort. However, I knew it was human that a steel man, for example, who had been loaned to the war administration would hesitate to order any action which might injure the postwar standing of the company or the industry to which he hoped eventually to return.

By June 1943 the special committee had issued twenty-one reports covering an increasing variety of subjects. These included gasoline rationing and fuel oil, lumber, barges, farm machinery, food shipping losses, and many others. In its investigation into shipping losses the committee discovered that twelve million tons of American shipping had been destroyed by German U-boats during 1942. This was one million tons more than all of our shipyards were producing. The policy of the Navy had been a hush-hush attitude toward these losses, and Secretary Knox denied the figures which were published by the committee. He was invited to an executive session of the committee to determine what the true figures were. He reversed his original stand and admitted that the committee's figures were accurate. The result was a stepped-up offensive which wiped out the submarine domination of the shipping lanes.

Also in 1942 the committee pointed out that manpower as well as basic commodities would become scarce. It warned against the assumption that the complicated manpower problem could be dealt with by such unwieldy means as a universal manpower draft. The committee stressed that the chief way to alleviate manpower shortages would be to use efficiently the manpower we had. It made eighteen practical suggestions on how government, labor, and industry could co-operate to achieve more efficient utilization of manpower. Many of these suggestions were adopted.

The committee was responsible for savings not only in dollars and precious time but in actual lives. We found that the Wright Aeronautical Corporation, located at Lockland, Ohio, near Cincinnati, was turning out engines which were not in accordance with specifications. These engines were causing the death of some of our student pilots. The committee condemned four hundred of these plane engines. To be equally fair to Curtiss-Wright and to the Army, I made no public announcement of the conditions which our investigator had found. What the committee did was to call in both Curtiss-Wright and the Army and give them each a week or two within which to make their own investigation of the inspection procedures at the Lockland plant. Both reported that they found nothing wrong.

A subcommittee of my group then went to Curtiss-Wright to inspect the plant and hold hearings. Before it had finished, it had heard scores of witnesses, who testified that defective parts and defective engines had passed inspection at the plant and had been turned over to the Army. The Army conducted a second investigation on its own and finally agreed with the facts turned up by the subcommittee. This dangerous and dishonest practice was thus brought to an end.

The Martin bomber was another example. I had an engineering survey made of the B-26 Martin bomber, and it was found that the wingspread was too short. This technical miscalculation had been responsible for a number of fatalities among our Air Force personnel. Glenn Martin, testifying at one of the hearings, said that the blueprints of this plane were already on the board and that he would have to go through with the project.

I told Martin that if the lives of American boys depended upon the planes that were produced for the United States Army Air Force the committee would see to it that no defective ships were purchased.

"Well," Martin replied, "if that's the way you feel about it, we'll change it."

The committee also served notice on the Carnegie-Illinois Steel Corporation, the principal subsidiary of the United States Steel Corporation, that the steel plate made in its Irvin Works for the Navy and the Maritime Commission and Lend-Lease was defective and that the physical tests to which the finished steel plate was subjected to determine its tensile strength were faked and falsified. The company men in charge of the operation with the testing machines testified that about five per cent or more of the tests were deliberately faked and the steel plate falsely reported to be in accordance with specifications. To do this they instructed the testers under them to cheat.

The committee served notice on all such companies that the only excuse it would accept was an early and complete correction.

At the very period when it became clear that some action was necessary to conserve rubber, the civilian production companies indulged in an orgy of consumption, laying in stocks of finished goods at a rate that reached a new high of over a million tons a year by June 1941.

There were three principal causes behind the partial failure of the rubber stockpiling program. The first was the quota restrictions of the International Rubber Regulation Committee. I felt that Jesse Jones, while head of the Reconstruction Finance Corporation, had done a good job of getting these restrictions relaxed, but the relaxation was not obtained soon enough to avoid the critical situation. The second cause was a failure to take full advantage of shipping facilities, and the third was excessive industrial consumption. When the committee analyzed the rubber problem in these terms, the way was made clear for intelligent action by the government.

The committee also encouraged the development of synthetic rubber from corn, soybeans, natural-gas products, coal, and various combinations of these materials. It also discovered that because of shortsighted priority allocation policies raw materials essential to the production of high-octane gasoline fuel for our bombers and fighters were being diverted into the comparatively less urgent synthetic-rubber projects.

These and hundreds of other corrective steps grew out of the month-after-month probing into all areas of the defense effort by the committee. To me, the challenge seemed greater with every month of war that passed.

Although the work of the committee continued uninterrupted throughout the war, its name was never changed from the Special Committee to Investigate the National Defense Program. I remained its chairman until August of 1944, when I submitted the following letter to the President of the Senate:

August 3, 1944

Dear Mr. President:

I herewith submit my resignation as chairman and as a member of the Special Committee of the United States Senate Investigating the National Defense Program.

It is one of the regrets of my lifetime that this had to be done. But frankly, under the present circumstances, I am of the opinion that any statement, hearing or report for which I would be considered responsible would be considered by many to have been motivated by political considerations.

Harry S. Truman

The explanation for this action was, of course, the fact that I had been nominated for the vice-presidency of the United States. Although I was requested unanimously by the other members to stay on as chairman, or at least as a member, I felt that my involvement in the campaign of 1944 might bring the committee into the firing line of politics. I had worked hard for three years to keep it strictly non-political and I wanted to see it remain that way.

At the same time, Hugh Fulton resigned as chief counsel. Senator Mead replaced me as chairman of the committee, and Rudolph Halley, who had held the position of executive assistant to the chief counsel, succeeded Fulton.

In all, the committee had made recommendations resulting in the estimated saving of fifteen billion dollars to the American taxpayers. This had been accomplished at a cost of approximately four hundred thousand dollars, the amount of total appropriations granted for the committee's work. Savings in efficiency, man-hours, and lives could not be calculated, of course, while the preventive influence wielded by the committee kept countless problems from ever developing.

The committee had filed a total of thirty-two reports since its creation on March 1, 1941, and there had never been a dissent to any of these. There had been no factional disputes despite the fact that the committee had functioned through a major national election and was bi-partisan in its membership.

The committee had not attempted to review the strategy of the war or to investigate or to criticize the conduct of military or naval operations. It had been directed by the Senate to conduct a complete investigation of all phases of the program for arming the nation. In accordance with that direction, the committee made a full and impartial study of every aspect of the war program in order to determine whether or not the fullest and most effective utilization was being made of our resources to the end of bringing the war to a successful and early conclusion with the lowest cost in lives.

CHAPTER 13

My experience as chairman of the Special Committee to Investigate the National Defense Program enabled me to develop a practical approach with regard to the scope and function of the congressional committee as an instrument of government.

It is natural for a person whose actions have been questioned to resent being required to account for what he has done. This is true of individuals in government and business when they are subjected to congressional examination. They resort to many subterfuges to avoid or restrict investigation.

Many highly useful jobs have been done by committees of the Congress. The nation has benefited immensely from their work. Sometimes, however, they have been hampered by the claims of some administrators that such investigations were taking too much of their valuable time— that they were already working twenty-four hours a day, seven days a week, on affairs of more importance to the nation. This attitude was often taken by agency heads during the war. The implication was that it would have been much better to abolish most of the committees and to leave the busy administrators free to act as their best judgment dictated.

I do not agree with that attitude. High-ranking administrators often appear before congressional committees at their own request. Since my committee was interested only in obtaining the facts, it would have preferred to get the testimony of witnesses who personally had firsthand knowledge of the facts. We were willing to hear the high-ranking administrators themselves, however, if they preferred to attend, but we seldom requested their testimony.

It is common practice among government officials to attend hearings rather than to content themselves with supplying the facts. They often do so because they wish to take advantage of such occasions by making public statements that consist of long, carefully prepared arguments in their own behalf. These are often mimeographed and distributed to the press, sometimes before the respective committee has even seen them.

The argument that different congressional committees unnecessarily duplicate each other's work is, in my opinion, overemphasized. Some duplication does exist, and much of it is unnecessary. Congress could properly reorganize itself into fewer committees, each with a competent staff, and thereby eliminate some duplication and increase the efficiency of its work. However, it should be borne in mind constantly that one of the principal purposes of an investigation is to obtain and disseminate information so that as many as possible of the members of Congress will have the background necessary for intelligent decisions with respect to legislation.

Also, what looks like duplication because it deals with the same general subject may not be duplication at all. The subject may be so broad in scope that one committee may be investigating for the purpose of determining whether the administrators are competent, and another committee may be trying to determine whether specific legislation to grant additional powers is necessary.

I formed the conviction, however, that certain rules and conditions should be imposed on an investigating committee by the body from which it issues. For example, it should be stated clearly what the power of the committee is to be. The committee chairman should be carefully chosen. He, in turn, should be given every encouragement to select an investigator or counsel who is dependable, able, and above reproach. The committee should concentrate on uncovering facts. At public hearings the committee should know exactly what it wants to find out from each witness.

Witnesses should be interviewed in advance of public hearings so that they may present their case to the committee and so that the committee members may ask pertinent questions. Members not present when these previous interviews are held must, of course, be free to ask questions at the public hearing. A witness should be permitted to answer questions normally, and if he balks, he should be prodded by the record. If an investigation fails in its objective to amass knowledge for legislative purposes, it is a waste of time and public money.

Many congressional committees, in the past and in recent times, have been guilty of departing from their original purposes and jurisdictions. The most outstanding example of misdirected investigation occurred during the Civil War when the Committee on the Conduct of the War attempted to direct military operations in the field. It was this committee that was responsible for making Pope commanding general of the Army of the Potomac, which proved to be an unfortunate decision. Although it was said that, with Pope in command, the army's headquarters would be in the saddle, his appearance on the field was soon followed by the disaster of the Second Battle of Bull Run. Horace Greeley made the remark that the headquarters was in the saddle, to be sure, and that Pope had been sitting on his brains.

This Committee on the Conduct of the War abused witnesses unmercifully. In reading the reports of the hearings of that committee, I was made ashamed of the Congress because of the way General Meade was abused after the drawn battle at Gettysburg. History has since shown that his performance in that turning point of the war was above reproach, but the members of the committee tried to make it look as if he were a traitor for not pursuing Lee's retreating army, when the truth was that his troops and supplies were too exhausted and depleted for any such task.

The special committee never discussed military strategy, although we took testimony from many generals and admirals. The military policy of the United States was entrusted to the President and the Joint Chiefs of Staff and not to any congressional committee. Senators Brewster and Vandenberg tried at times to make another Committee on the Conduct of the War out of our committee by attempting to bring the Congress into control of the operations of the military establishment, but we never permitted that to happen.

I consider the methods used by the House Committee on Un-American Activities to be the most un-American thing in America in its day. The committee had completely forgotten the constitutional rights of the individuals who appeared as witnesses. It made the same mistake as the special committee created in 1859 to investigate John Brown's rebellion: After full-scale war broke out, that committee finally realized it had been picking on the wrong people and making the wrong investigations.

When Pat McCarran became chairman of the Senate Judiciary Committee, that group also began to overstep the bounds of its own authority and to change from its original purpose. In its treatment of witnesses, the McCarran Committee became more of an inquisition than an investigation.

Another misdirected inquiry was conducted by the Special Committee Investigating the Munitions Industry prior to the outbreak of World War II. Under the chairmanship of Senator Gerald P. Nye, this committee made it appear that the munitions manufacturers had caused World War I, and as a result, the Neutrality Act was passed. Because this law placed an embargo on arms shipments to the democratic forces in Spain, it was partly responsible for our losing that country as a potential ally in World War II. The Nye Committee, which was backed by isolationists and "America Firsters," was pure demagoguery in the guise of a congressional investigating committee.

There has been increasing public understanding, I believe, of the necessity for intelligent and energetic investigation by the Congress of the activities of administrative agencies as well as of segments of the American society outside the government. In the future there will undoubtedly be more rather than fewer congressional investigations, and the benefits which the public will obtain from these should be very great. The power of the Congress to investigate may become equal to, if not more important than, its power to legislate.

Early in 1944 some of my friends began to suggest to me that I become a candidate for Vice-President. I had never entertained such an idea, and whenever the suggestion was made I brushed it aside. I was doing the job I wanted to do; it was one that I liked, and I had no desire to interrupt my career in the Senate. As the time for the Democratic convention drew closer, however, my name was mentioned frequently as a possible candidate for the nomination. This disturbed me, for I had repeatedly given notice that I did not want to be a candidate.

In July 1944, as I was about to leave my home in Independence for the opening of the convention in Chicago, the telephone rang. It was Jimmy Byrnes calling from Washington. He told me that President Roosevelt had decided on him as the new nominee for Vice-President, and he asked me if I would nominate him at the convention. I told him that I would be glad to do it if the President wanted him for a running mate.

At the time Byrnes called, Henry Wallace was widely considered to be the leading candidate for the vice-presidential nomination, and there was no doubt that he wanted very much to remain Vice-President. Still a favorite with President Roosevelt, Wallace also had the almost solid support of labor. His only real opposition was in the South, where he was looked upon by many as a dangerous radical. It was in the South that Byrnes expected to get his biggest push. Wallace, moreover, was not popular as Vice-President either in the Senate or with the politicians who ran things in the party organization. Therefore, when Byrnes called to tell me that Roosevelt had decided to have him on his ticket for his fourth term, I took it for granted that all the details had been arranged.

Before I left for Chicago there was another call. It was Alben Barkley, the majority leader of the Senate, asking if I would nominate him for

Vice-President at the convention. I told him that Byrnes had just called me with the same request and that I had already promised to place his name before the convention.

When I arrived in Chicago I had breakfast with Sidney Hillman, who was a power in the labor faction of the convention. I asked him if he would support Byrnes. He said he would not, that there were only two men besides Henry Wallace he would support. They were William O. Douglas, justice of the Supreme Court, and Harry S. Truman, U.S. senator from Missouri. I told him that I was not a candidate and that I had agreed to nominate Byrnes because he told me the President wanted him.

Then I had a meeting with Phil Murray, head of the CIO, and one with A. F. Whitney, head of the Railroad Trainmen. Both expressed themselves exactly as Sidney Hillman had. The next morning William Green, head of the AFL, asked me to breakfast at the Palmer House. He told me that the AFL did not like Wallace and that they had decided to support me. I told him my position with Byrnes and repeated that I was not a candidate.

While we were talking, Senators Tydings and George Radcliffe came over to our table and asked me to come to their table to meet the Maryland delegation to the convention. I went over, thinking perhaps I could drum up some support for Byrnes. Tydings introduced me, however, as the Maryland candidate for Vice-President. All I could do was to explain my position and return to finish my conversation with Green.

I reported all these conversations to Byrnes in detail. Every time I gave him the information Byrnes told me just to wait, that the President would straighten everybody out in plenty of time.

On Tuesday evening of convention week, National Chairman Bob Hannegan came to see me and told me unequivocally that President Roosevelt wanted me to run with him on the ticket. This astonished me greatly, but I was still not convinced. Even when Hannegan showed me a longhand note written on a scratch pad from the President's desk which said, "Bob, it's Truman. F.D.R.," I still could not be sure that this was Roosevelt's intent, although I later learned that the handwriting in the note was the President's own.

One thing that contributed to my confusion was my knowledge of a letter which the President had written earlier in which he stated that he would be satisfied with either Wallace or Douglas. He had also made a public statement to the effect that, if he were a delegate in the convention, he would personally vote for Wallace.

Another fact, which I did not learn until some time later, was that the President had called a meeting, far in advance of the Democratic convention, to discuss with party leaders the selection of a running mate. Among those present at the White House were Bob Hannegan, Ed Pauley, Frank Walker, George Allen, and Ed Flynn. It was at this meeting that Roosevelt told his conferees that he preferred Truman over Wallace, Douglas, or Byrnes, and jotted down the note in longhand which Hannegan was to show me at the convention. At the same meeting he had instructed Walker to notify Byrnes of the decision. I believe, therefore, that Byrnes knew that the President had named me at the time he called me in Independence and asked me to nominate him at the convention.

Meanwhile the Missouri delegation to the convention held its first meeting, and I was named chairman. The first item of business to come up was a resolution endorsing me for Vice-President. In my capacity as presiding officer I ruled the resolution out of order because I was not a candidate. Then someone called me to the door to pass on the admittance of a visitor. While my attention was thus diverted, the vice-chairman of the delegation, Sam Wear, put the motion to a question. I was unanimously endorsed by the Missouri delegation for the nomination to the vice-presidency.

In times gone by the Missourians were always in a knockdown, drag-out fight, over what they wanted to do at Democratic conventions. That was the case in 1896, 1912, 1920, 1924, 1928, and 1932. But this time there was no fight over the choice for either chairman or nominee. I did not understand it.

On Thursday afternoon, the day before the Vice-President was to be nominated, Hannegan called me from his room in the Blackstone Hotel and asked me to come to a meeting of the Democratic leaders. When I arrived there, they all began to put pressure on me to allow my name to be presented to the convention, but I continued to resist.

Hannegan had put in a long-distance telephone call to the President, who was in San Diego at the time. When the connection was made, I sat on one of the twin beds, and Hannegan, with the phone, sat on the other. Whenever Roosevelt used the telephone he always talked in such a strong voice that it was necessary for the listener to hold the receiver away from his ear to avoid being deafened, so I found it possible to hear both ends of the conversation.

"Bob," Roosevelt said, "have you got that fellow lined up yet?"

"No," Bob replied. "He is the contrariest Missouri mule I've ever dealt with."

"Well, you tell him," I heard the President say, "if he wants to break up the Democratic party in the middle of a war, that's his responsibility."

With that, he banged down the phone.

I was completely stunned. I sat for a minute or two and then got up and began walking around the room. All the others were watching me and not saying a word.

"Well," I said finally, "if that is the situation, I'll have to say yes, but why the hell didn't he tell me in the first place?"

My first act was to go over to the Stevens Hotel and report to Byrnes the President's conversation with Hannegan and my decision to do what the President wanted. At this late hour of the convention we had difficulty finding someone to nominate me. I had told all my friends that I was not a candidate, and they were now committed elsewhere. Finally, however, we persuaded Senator Bennett Clark to make the nominating speech. The following day I was chosen by the convention as its nominee for the vice-presidency of the United States.

The President sent the following message:

> From the White House
> Washington
> July 21, 1944

TELEGRAM
Honorable Harry S. Truman
United States Senator
Stevens Hotel
Chicago, Illinois

I send you my heartiest congratulations on your victory. I am, of course, very happy to have you run with me. Let me know your plans. I shall see you soon.

> Franklin D. Roosevelt

After the convention I went to Washington for a visit with President Roosevelt. He told me that because he was so busy in the war effort I would have to do the campaigning for both of us, and we mapped out our program. I then resigned as chairman of the Special Committee to Investigate the National Defense Program and made my plans to devote all my energy to the coming campaign.

The campaign of 1944 was the easiest in which I had ever participated. The Republican candidates never had a chance. As I traveled from one side of the continent to the other telling the people of the accomplishments of the Democratic administrations under President Roosevelt, I found little evidence of any inclination to change leaders during a war. In comparison with my own Senate campaigns, the job was easy. As the Democratic party's candidate for the vice-presidency, I could sincerely pledge my continued support to the policies of the administration. My voting records during both terms in the Senate showed that I had been faithful in support of those policies in the past.

I had no thought that in making this campaign for the President I was in reality doing so as much in my own behalf as in that of Roosevelt's.

At Lamar, Missouri, for instance, on August 31, 1944, I made the following, almost prophetic, statements:

"It takes time for anyone to familiarize himself with a new job. This is particularly true of the presidency of the United States, the most difficult and complex job in the world. Even in peacetime it is well recognized that it takes a new President at least a year to learn the fundamentals of his job.

"We cannot expect any man wholly inexperienced in national and international affairs to readily learn the views, the objectives and the inner thoughts of such divergent personalities as those dominant leaders who have guided the destinies of our courageous allies. There will be no time to learn, and mistakes once made cannot be unmade. Our President has worked with these men during these trying years. He talks their language—the language of nations. He knows the reasons which govern their decisions. Just as he respects them and their opinions, so do they respect him. At no time in our history has the President possessed such knowledge of foreign leaders and their problems. None has ever so completely won their confidence and admiration."

Without suspecting it, I was speaking of the tremendous job which, within a matter of months, was to be my own.

The rest is history. The official vote was 25,602,505, a plurality of 3,596,227 over the Republican ticket. On November 8, 1944, as Vice-President-elect of the United States, while resting at my home in Independence I sent the following telegram to the President:

Honorable Franklin D. Roosevelt
President of the United States, Hyde Park, N.Y.
I am very happy over the overwhelming endorsement which you received. Isolationism is dead. Hope to see you soon.

Harry S. Truman

On January 20, 1945, a snowy Saturday, I stood on the south portico of the White House beside President Roosevelt for the third wartime inauguration in the history of our nation. The first had been Madison's; the second, Lincoln's. A crowd of several thousand had gathered on the White House lawn to witness the ceremony.

As is the custom, I moved first to the front of the platform between the national and the presidential flags to have Henry Wallace, the retiring Vice-President, administer the oath of office to me. In a matter of minutes I was the new Vice-President of the United States. I stepped back, and President Roosevelt took his place at the front of the portico to receive the oath of office for his fourth term from Chief Justice Stone.

There was a post-inaugural White House luncheon after the conclusion of the President's address and the ceremonies. I slipped away from the luncheon a few minutes ahead of time, hitchhiked a ride to Capitol Hill, and telephoned my mother at Grandview. She told me that she had heard the induction ceremony over the radio.

"Now you behave yourself," she warned me.

One of my first duties as presiding officer of the Senate was to swear in Frank P. Briggs of Macon, Missouri, to serve out the two remaining years of my term as senator. Briggs, a newspaper publisher and former state senator, had been appointed by Governor Donnelly.

I enjoyed my new position as Vice-President, but it took me a while to get used to the fact that I no longer had the voting privileges I had enjoyed for ten years as a senator. In the eighty-two days I served as Vice-President I had only one chance to vote. That was on an amendment to limit the Lend-Lease extension bill. I broke the tie and defeated the proposal. The purpose of the amendment was to eliminate presidential power to carry out postwar Lend-Lease deliveries under contracts made during the war.

I was not given many other tasks. Two days after I became Vice-President, Roosevelt left Washington for the Yalta conference, and during the short period I served as Vice-President he was not actually in the capital more than thirty days.

One particular job which I accomplished was to support the President's appointment of Wallace as Secretary of Commerce. By overcoming the opposition of several senators I was able to get the confirmation approved by a narrow vote. In fact, I twice saved Wallace from rejection by the Senate. On one of these occasions his supporters had gained backing for him by agreeing to pass a House-approved measure divorcing the Department of Commerce from the Federal Loan Agency. Jesse Jones had been head of both, and the purpose of this measure was to get Wallace confirmed as Secretary of Commerce only, so that he would have no supervision over the billions of dollars lent by the loan agency. Under these terms some senators who were otherwise opposed to Wallace promised to confirm him as Secretary.

Barkley was supposed to place the House-passed bill immediately before the Senate when it convened. With the bill once passed, the way would be clear for Wallace's confirmation. But when I convened the Senate, Taft quickly demanded recognition and was prepared to move immediate action on Wallace's nomination before the Senate could pass on the saving bill. I recognized Barkley first, however, and the agreed-upon procedure was followed. Otherwise Wallace's confirmation would very probably have been rejected.

The office of Vice-President, according to Woodrow Wilson, is "one of anomalous insignificance and curious uncertainty." While this may have been its history, I did not feel that this was a fair description of what the office should be.

"I want," I told newsmen shortly after being sworn in, "to bring the administration and Congress closer together on the methods of attaining the goal all of us have in common, and if I can create a better understanding, I feel that I can render an important public service."

After taking the oath of office, the first traditional duty of the Vice-President is to make a short inaugural address to the body whose President he is—the United States Senate. His position as presiding officer in the Senate is accorded him by the Constitution. The Senate is thus prevented from choosing its own chairman.

I felt that at all times the Vice-President, in dealing with the Senate, must be a model of tact and forbearance. Custom brings him to include in his inaugural address some praise of the Senate and an appeal for cooperation. Some Vice-Presidents, like John Adams, the first one, adopted a policy of extravagant praise in this inaugural address, and only Andrew Johnson and Charles G. Dawes ever departed from the general policy of addressing the Senate in complimentary terms.

In fact, Dawes made a speech to the Senate which practically ruined him as its presiding officer. On March 4, 1925, after he was sworn in, he took it upon himself to make a kind of inaugural address to the Senate. He criticized Senate rules. He told the Senate members what he, the Vice-President, was going to do with them. He was just being the "Hell and Maria" Dawes he had been in Europe, where he had served so successfully as an important officer in the Service of Supply in World War I. He had done a good job there, but from the time he made that speech in the Senate he had very little influence with that body or any of its members.

I had no procedural problem in my first contact with the Senate as its presiding officer. The rules of the Senate were not new to me. After ten years I knew most of its members well. I spoke their language.

The tradition of vice-presidential deference to the Senate arose primarily because of the fact that the Vice-President himself actually has very little power. He never engages in debate. As presiding officer he may make rulings, but any of these can be appealed and overruled. He does not appoint the committees in the Senate. Only in the period when Calhoun was Vice-President were these appointments made by the President of the Senate, and Calhoun, therefore, was a power in that position. But this power was lost when it came to be the tradition for the Vice-President to take his seat a few days after the beginning of a session.

As a moderator in debate the Vice-President executes only the most rudimentary of powers. He does maintain order and decorum in debate, and it is especially here that whatever tact he possesses is a decided asset.

In this task he is helped and advised by the officers of the Senate, who may save him from traps into which the senators used to like to see their president fall, such as the calling of a senator to order for not speaking to the subject. A senator is privileged to talk on any subject he chooses, whenever he is recognized to speak. This is, unfortunately, one of the loose rules of the Senate.

Among the minor duties of a Vice-President in the Senate is to swear in new senators. Even this task must proceed according to the established ritual. In taking it lightly, Dawes incurred fresh resentment on top of what came to him through his fruitless efforts to change the Senate's rules. On the occasion of his first session with the Senate it was his duty to swear in thirty-two senators-elect. It was customary for the new senators to be conducted to the desk in groups of four, but after less than half of them had been inducted in the usual form, Dawes became impatient and he cried out, "Bring them all up. This is too slow. Bring them on together."

Under the Constitution, the powers of the Vice-President are defined in only one respect: the right to vote in case of a tie. This right, however, has not been exercised very often. A few Vice-Presidents never did have an occasion to vote in the Senate. Others voted only a few times. John Adams voted more often than any other Vice-President, twenty-nine times.

In view of all this, the Vice-President can never exercise open influence in the Senate, but if he is respected personally and if he maintains good relations with the members of the Senate, he can have considerable power behind the scenes. Because the Senate has a president pro tempore to take the chair in his absence, the Vice-President does not have to attend the sessions of the Senate continuously. Thus he may devote part of his time to private meetings, conferences, and other valuable contacts with leaders and committeemen.

A good deal of the Vice-President's functions are social and ceremonial. Very often he acts as a substitute for the President in opening an exposition, dedicating a monument, or in cutting the ribbon to open a new bridge to traffic. Outranking foreign ambassadors, he is almost always the most important guest at a dinner or other social functions. Socially the Vice-President takes precedence over all other officers of the government except the President. I never cared too much for this aspect of my job as Vice-President.

The Vice-President is not an officer of the executive branch of the government and therefore does not attend Cabinet sessions except at the invitation of the President. The history of the office shows that the Vice-President has rarely been used for executive work except where his relations with the President were unusually intimate. I was fortunate to attend the few Cabinet meetings that were held between January and March, to report legislative conditions to the President. I also attended all meetings of the Big Four when they called on the President.

The great importance of the office of Vice-President, of course, lies in the possibility of his succeeding to the presidency. So far in the history of the United States, Presidents have been removed from office only by death. On these occasions the Vice-President has taken the oath of office immediately on notification of the death of the President.

The Constitution provides that the powers and duties of the office of President "shall devolve upon the Vice-President" in case of the removal from office of the President, his resignation, or his inability to discharge his powers and duties. Johnson was in danger of removal by impeachment, and Washington and Wilson were said to have thought of resigning, but the issue of succession under such circumstances has never come up. There were a number of unanswered questions concerning presidential succession. I turned my attention to these shortly after I became President myself.

It has always been my feeling that this office, which is the second highest honor that can be bestowed by the American people, has great inherent and potential dignity that has been sadly neglected. The opportunities afforded by the vice-presidency, particularly the presidency of the Senate, do not come—they are there to be seized. The man who fills the office can choose to do little or he can do much. The Vice-President's influence on legislation depends on his personality and his ability, and especially the respect which he commands from the senators. Here is one instance in which it is the man who makes the office, not the office the man.

Ordinarily a Vice-President has four years to develop these opportunities. I had less than three months. After April 12, 1945, I never again had the time even to speculate on what I might have been able to do with the office of Vice-President. I no longer found myself amid the familiar surroundings of Capitol Hill. I was President.

CHAPTER 14

The presidency of the United States in recent times, even in the prewar period, had become a highly complicated and exacting job. But to this already heavy burden the war had added new and crushing responsibilities. Not only did the President now have to function as Commander in Chief of the armed forces of the United States, but he also had to assume the major share of the leadership of a far-flung coalition of allied nations. As I took the oath of office I was conscious of how vast in scope the presidency had become. Although we were on our way to eventual victory in the Pacific, we still had a long way to go. But by April 1945 the war in Europe was taking a decisive turn.

German resistance had begun to crumble on all fronts by the middle of April. Until almost the end, however, there was talk of a last-ditch stand by the top Nazis and the German Command. It was believed that this stand would revolve about the so-called Redoubt in the mountain areas of Bavaria, Austria, and North Italy. To this region it was expected the Nazi leaders would withdraw with what was left of the SS and other trusted troops, and there they would stage a long-drawn-out resistance. Allied operations for the final phase of the war made provision to head this off. It was rumored that Hitler had left Berlin on April 20 for the Redoubt, but when the American Third and Seventh Armies moved deep into this area they found the Germans had not been able to build this final fortress.

During the last days of April came the linking up of the American and Russian armies, the surrender of the German forces in Italy, and finally the total collapse of German resistance. As our military plans continued to develop with unrivaled speed, frightened Nazi leaders began seeking deals with the Western Allies. The thought of falling into Russian hands drove them into a panic. As the lesser of two evils, they turned to us. One of these attempts at a separate deal had already made some trouble for us with the Russians. In March, General Karl Wolff, the chief SS officer of the German forces in Italy, had started parleys with American OSS agents in Switzerland with a view toward the possible surrender of Kesselring's German army in Italy. Nothing ever came of these parleys except to make the Russians highly suspicious of our motives. Molotov wrote to Ambassador Harriman in Moscow demanding that the negotiations with the Germans be broken off. President Roosevelt cabled Stalin that the Russians were misinformed. He explained that there was no reason why we should not listen to offers by the enemy to surrender to Allied commanders in the field, and that he could not agree to suspend efforts of this sort because Molotov objected. This did not satisfy Stalin, who answered that the Germans had tricked the Allies and had profited by moving three divisions from the Italian front to the Russian front. Actually, those three divisions went to the Western Front, against us. It was not a good situation. Any break with the Russians at this time would have interfered with our advances in Germany.

The Russians were always suspicious of everything and everybody, and Wolff's approach to the Americans and British made them suspect that we were trying to get the German forces in the West to surrender to us while they still continued to fight on the Russian front. The Russians also appeared to be afraid that we would occupy all Germany and leave them on the other side of the Polish border.

At the time this incident occurred the Germans still had a powerful fighting force in Italy, made up of twenty-five German divisions and five Italian Fascist divisions. They were holding strong positions south of the Po, on a line stretching from the west coast near Pisa to the Adriatic near Lake Comacchio, and a surrender at that moment would have been important to us.

The purpose of listening to any German offers by our military command in Italy was not to negotiate but to facilitate an unconditional surrender. But the Germans were hesitant about accepting the terms of surrender upon which we insisted. At Churchill's urging, in order to avoid further friction with the Russians, the Allied commander in Italy, Field Marshal Alexander, was instructed to drop the talks. And the OSS in Switzerland was instructed by our Chiefs of Staff to cease contact with the Germans. We then informed the Russians of our action.

It was not long after this that the Allied forces in Italy jumped off on their final offensive. On April 21 they captured the city of Bologna. On the twenty-third, American units crossed the Po. Soon thereafter the Germans ceased to be an effective force, and Alexander asked for permission to communicate with German officers who would have authority to surrender. This time arrangements were made for the Russians to have a representative on hand. The end came quickly.

On April 28 the terms of surrender were handed to the Germans at Allied headquarters in Italy. These terms were agreed to that same day and signed on the twenty-ninth. General Kislenko and another Russian officer were present. The terms of surrender called for hostilities to cease at noon on May 2. The surrender was to include the Italian Fascist divisions that were part of the German command. By this time Mussolini's puppet Italian Socialist Republic had ceased to exist. Mussolini himself was assassinated in late April by the partisans.

The war in Italy was over, and I sent a message of congratulation to Field Marshal Alexander and to the ranking American commander in that theater, General Mark W. Clark. I used the occasion of the surrender in Italy to warn the Germans and the Japanese that only unconditional surrender could save them from destruction.

"The Allied Armies in Italy," this statement read, "have won the unconditional surrender of German forces on the first European soil to which, from the West, we carried our arms and our determination. The collapse of military tyranny in Italy, however, is no victory in Italy alone, but a part of the general triumph we are expectantly awaiting on the whole continent of Europe. Only folly and chaos can now delay the general capitulation of the everywhere defeated German armies.

"I have dispatched congratulatory messages to the Allied and American officers who led our forces to complete defeat of the Germans in Italy. They deserve our praise for the victory. We have a right to be proud of the success of our armies.

"Let Japan as well as Germany understand the meaning of these events. Unless they are lost in fanaticism or determined upon suicide, they must recognize the meaning of the increasing, swifter-moving power now ready for the capitulation or destruction of the so recently arrogant enemies of mankind."

There was no Russian army in Italy. The German surrender there was consequently made to the Western Allies. Outside Italy the question was different. On all the main fronts the Germans were attempting to make separate surrenders to the Western Allies. There were obvious implications and complications here, for the Nazi leaders and some of their generals were playing a devious game.

It was clear to us that they were trying to create trouble between the Western Allies and Russia, in a last desperate effort to save their necks and salvage as much of their regime as possible. A good indication of this was the Himmler affair.

Himmler, the ruthless head of the Gestapo, approached the Swedish government with a surrender proposition, and Count Bernadotte of the Swedish Foreign Office met him in Lübeck at one o'clock in the morning of April 24. At that meeting Himmler announced himself as being in full power in Germany, the reason being, he explained, that Hitler had suffered a brain hemorrhage and was dying. Himmler then added that he wanted to meet Eisenhower in order to arrange a surrender to the Western Allies only, and asked that the Swedish government arrange the meeting. Himmler pointed out that he expected to continue the fight on the Eastern Front. Reports of this Himmler-Bernadotte conference were sent through the British and American ministers in Stockholm to Churchill and to me. But before the message reached me, Churchill called me on the transatlantic telephone on April 25. We discussed the matter in detail, and we reaffirmed our position that we would consider no separate peace and no partial or conditional surrender.

The Himmler affair created considerable excitement when the story leaked out at the San Francisco conference. I gave little weight, however, to all these last-minute maneuvers by the Nazi leaders. We knew that there was no longer any constituted authority in Germany and that no Nazi leader could speak for the German people or for their armies. Any enemy forces who wanted to surrender could do so, as a tactical matter, to the Allied commanders in the field. Except for local surrenders, there was no question during these last days of anything less than unconditional surrender simultaneously to all three major allies, and military operations continued toward that goal.

In the meantime plans were being made to attack the Germans in Norway in case they continued to hold out. Back in March the Norwegian government had asked Sweden to help expel the Germans by intervening in the war. The Swedish government, however, had declined to go along. They argued that any intervention would result in the certain destruction of Norway by the Germans and would also bring reprisals against her people. Norway expressed irritation over the Swedish assumption that the Swedes knew better than the Norwegians what was good for Norway. They felt they had been led by the Swedes to believe that a favorable answer would be given. Late in April, however, when the end of the war was plainly in sight, there were indications that Sweden might play a part in the liberation of Norway. This was a little bit late, but it could still be important, and on April 25, 1945, Acting Secretary of State Grew reported to me that there was a good possibility that the Swedes would be willing to intervene if a request were made by the American, British, and

Norwegian governments and if no objection were raised by the Soviets. It was thought extremely doubtful, however, that the Swedes would declare war on Germany.

In the last week of the war the Swedish government accepted an Allied proposal that would have amounted to Swedish intervention. It was the Allied plan to attack the German forces in Norway through Swedish territory, but surrender of the German forces in Norway came as this operation was being planned.

German resistance was now crumbling everywhere. On May 1 the German radio announced the death of Hitler. This man, who had brought such infinite misery to the world, had died in the ruins of his Chancellery. The reports I received said he was a suicide. I had expected that many high German officers would take this way out in case of defeat, but I knew that Hitler had never lived by the code of the Prussian officer, and I thought that in his fanaticism he would resist to the very end.

Hitler's monstrous assault on civilization cost the lives of fifteen million people, and he and his regime left countless others maimed in body and soul. But now, at last, the strangle hold this demon of a man had held on the German people had been broken. Throughout the world men could now be certain that his death had brought us closer to the end of fighting and nearer to the return of peace.

When the German surrender came, it was through the military commanders, not through the politically defunct Nazi leaders. And now there was no issue over the terms of unconditional surrender. Germany was in ruins and its armies beaten. Its military leaders knew it and also knew we knew it. But still they preferred to come to the Western Allies for surrender.

On May 2 General Eisenhower reported that General Blumentritt, commanding an army group in northwest Germany, had indicated that he wished to surrender his forces to the British Army. Eisenhower explained that he had given instructions that the surrender must be unconditional and added, "I am treating it as a tactical matter and will inform Russian General Suslaparov accordingly."

The next day, May 3, Eisenhower reported that Blumentritt had not appeared at Field Marshal Montgomery's headquarters and that the Germans now had other intentions. Instead of Blumentritt, Admiral Friedeburg and other high officers had arrived carrying authority from Field Marshal Keitel, chief of the German High Command. They asked Montgomery to accept the surrender of the Twelfth and Twenty-first German Armies then facing the Russians and to permit German refugees to pass through the Allied lines to Schleswig-Holstein. These requests were turned down. The Germans were instructed to inform Keitel that only unconditional surrender could be accepted. Eisenhower said that he had instructed Montgomery that the surrender of Denmark, Holland, the Frisian Islands, Heligoland, and Schleswig-Holstein could be regarded by Montgomery as a tactical matter and the deal closed on the spot.

"If, however," Eisenhower's instructions continued, "any larger offer such as to surrender Norway and forces on other fronts is proposed, the emissaries should be sent at once to my headquarters."

To this Eisenhower added that "General Suslaparov is being informed of above."

On May 4 the Germans surrendered to Montgomery all the German forces in Holland, northwest Germany, and Denmark. Hostilities were to cease at 8 A.M. the next day, May 5. On May 4 Eisenhower reported as follows to the War Department:

"Representative of Doenitz is proceeding to my Headquarters tomorrow apparently to negotiate surrender of remaining enemy forces. I am sending a message to the Russian High Command at once informing them that I propose to instruct this representative to advise his government to surrender to the Russian High Command all enemy forces facing the Russians and to surrender to me those facing this front, including Norway.

"I am suggesting to the Russians that if this is agreeable to them, I suggest further that the surrenders on both fronts be made simultaneously and at the earliest possible hour."

On May 6 Eisenhower described the situation in the following report:

"General Jodl appeared at my headquarters tonight and in company with Admiral Friedeburg continued negotiations with my Chief of Staff and his assistants. It was obvious from the beginning of the discussion that the Germans are stalling for time, their purpose being to evacuate the largest possible number of German soldiers and civilians from the Russian front to within our lines. They continued the effort to surrender this front separately, even stating that no matter what my answer was, they were going to order all German forces remaining on the Western Front to cease firing and to refuse to fire against British or American troops. They asked for a meeting on Tuesday morning for signing final surrender terms with a forty-eight hour interval thereafter in order to get the necessary instructions to all their outlying units. Their actual purpose was merely to gain time. I finally had to inform them that I would break off all negotiations and seal the Western Front preventing by force any further westward movement of German soldiers and civilians, unless they agreed to my terms of surrender. When faced with this ultimatum, they immediately drafted a telegram to Doenitz asking for authority to make a full and complete surrender but specifying that actual fighting would cease 48 hours after the time of signing. Since this solution obviously places the decision as to when fighting would cease in the hands of the Germans, I refused to accept it and stated that all fighting would have to cease on both fronts in 48 hours from midnight tonight or I would carry out my threat. I repeat that their purpose is to continue to make a front against the Russians as long as they possibly can in order to evacuate maximum numbers of Germans into our lines.

"In any event, for all practical purposes fighting will cease almost immediately on this front for the reason that with minor exceptions my troops are on the line I have directed them to occupy.

"If the arrangement goes through as above indicated, I suggest that a proclamation should be made on Tuesday by the governments announcing Wednesday, May 9th, as V-E Day, with a statement that fighting has already largely ceased throughout the front and that by the terms of the agreement hostilities will formally cease on one minute after midnight, night of May 8/9. . . .

"We hope to have a formal signing by tomorrow."

On May 7 Eisenhower reported that a brief instrument of unconditional military surrender had been signed at two forty-one that morning. He said that he was prepared to go to Berlin the next day for the final formal signing, at which Marshal Zhukov would be the Russian representative.

The Russians had serious misgivings as to whether the Germans on their front would in fact surrender, and for that reason Moscow delayed the official announcement of the surrender by one day. We had previously agreed with Stalin that the announcement would be on Tuesday, May 8, at 9 A.M. Washington time. Churchill was now pressing for a day earlier, and the Russians were insisting on a day later. On the seventh Churchill sent messages by phone and cable urging that the formal announcement be made that day. I could see no way of accepting this change unless Stalin agreed. Stalin insisted, however, that the uncertain situation on the Russian front made this difficult. He still preferred May 9, and the final outcome of the several exchanges of messages was that the official announcements of the German unconditional surrender were made at the time originally agreed upon, Tuesday, May 8, at 9 A.M. Washington time.

The German surrender came only a little less than four weeks after I had taken the oath of office as President. On May 7, the night before V-E Day, we moved from Blair House to the White House.

I got up early V-E Day and wrote a letter to Mama and my sister Mary:

May 8, 1945

Dear Mama & Mary:—

I am sixty-one this morning, and I slept in the President's room in the White House last night. They have finished the painting and have some of the furniture in place. I'm hoping it will all be ready for you by Friday. My expensive gold pen doesn't work as well as it should.

This will be a historical day. At 9:00 o'clock this morning I must make a broadcast to the country: announcing the German surrender. The papers were signed yesterday morning and hostilities will cease on all fronts at midnight tonight. Isn't that some birthday present?

Have had one heck of a time with the Prime Minister of Great Britain. He, Stalin and the U.S. President made an agreement to release the news all at once from the three capitals at an hour that would fit us all. We agreed on 9 A.M. Washington time which is 3 P.M. London and 4 P.M. Moscow time.

Mr. Churchill began calling me at daylight to know if we shouldn't make an immediate release without considering the Russians. He was refused and then he kept pushing me to talk to Stalin. He finally had to stick to the agreed plan—but he was mad as a wet hen.

Things have moved at a terrific rate here since April 12. Never a day has gone by that some momentous decision didn't have to be made. So far luck has been with me. I hope it keeps up. It can't stay with me forever however and I hope when the mistake comes it won't be too great to remedy.

We are looking forward to a grand visit with you. I may not be able to come for you as planned but I'm sending the safest finest plane and all kinds of help so please don't disappoint me.

Lots & lots of love to you both.

Harry

By eight thirty-five that morning of May 8 I was in the Executive Office of the White House. I was about to proclaim to the American people the end of the war in Europe. With me at that moment were Mrs. Truman, my daughter Margaret, high United States and British Army and Navy officials, and a number of leaders of the Senate and the House of Representatives.

First I was to receive the press, but before the doors were opened Senator McKellar, president pro tempore of the Senate, greeted me.

"Happy birthday, Mr. President," he said.

I thanked him. The representatives of the press and radio hurried in—unusually silent.

I read them the official announcement:

"This is a solemn but glorious hour. General Eisenhower informs me that the forces of Germany have surrendered to the United Nations. The flags of freedom fly all over Europe.

"For this victory, we join in offering our thanks to the Providence which has guided and sustained us through the dark days of adversity.

Our rejoicing is sobered and subdued by a supreme consciousness of the terrible price we have paid to rid the world of Hitler and his evil band. Let us not forget, my fellow Americans, the sorrow and the heartache which today abide in the homes of so many of our neighbors—neighbors whose most priceless possession has been rendered as a sacrifice to redeem our liberty.

"We can repay the debt which we owe to our God, to our dead, and to our children, only by work, by ceaseless devotion to the responsibilities which lie ahead of us. If I could give you a single watchword for the coming months, that word is work, work and more work. We must work to finish the war. Our victory is only half over."

I then read them another statement in which I informed the Japanese what they could expect, and called their attention to the fact that we were now in a position to turn the greatest war machine in the history of the world loose in the Pacific.

"The Japanese people," this statement warned, "have felt the weight of our land, air and naval attacks. So long as their leaders and the armed forces continue the war, the striking power and intensity of our blows will steadily increase, and will bring utter destruction to Japan's industrial war production, to its shipping, and to everything that supports its military activity.

"The longer the war lasts, the greater will be the suffering and hardships which the people of Japan will undergo—all in vain. Our blows will not cease until the Japanese military and naval forces lay down their arms in *unconditional surrender*.

"Just what does the unconditional surrender of the armed forces of Japan mean for the Japanese people?

"It means the end of the war.

"It means the termination of the influence of the military leaders who brought Japan to the present brink of disaster.

"It means provision for the return of soldiers and sailors to their families, their farms, and their jobs.

"And it means not prolonging the present agony and suffering of the Japanese in the vain hope of victory.

"Unconditional surrender does not mean the extermination or enslavement of the Japanese people."

At nine o'clock, following the press conference, I broadcast an address to the nation, announcing the surrender of Germany and calling upon the people to turn their efforts to the great tasks ahead—first to win the war in the Pacific, and then to win the peace.

I said: "I only wish that Franklin D. Roosevelt had lived to witness this day. General Eisenhower informs me that the forces of Germany have surrendered to the United Nations. The flags of freedom fly over all Europe. . . .

"We must work to bind up the wounds of a suffering world, to build an abiding peace, a peace rooted in justice and in law. We can build such a peace only by hard, toilsome, painstaking work—by understanding and working with our Allies in peace as we have in war.

"The job ahead is no less important, no less urgent, no less difficult than the task which now happily is done.

"I call upon every American to stick to his post until the last battle is won. Until that day, let no man abandon his post or slacken his efforts."

During the course of the war I had listened to many arguments on the question of unconditional surrender, both pro and con. The complete collapse of the German armies and their unconditional surrender had settled the argument by itself.

The three major allies in the war in Europe had agreed on unconditional surrender as far back as 1943. By the time I became President there was a straight-line commitment on it. Churchill and Roosevelt had first announced this at the Casablanca conference in January 1943 as a basic principle for the conduct of the war. Thereafter came frequent official confirmations, straight through to Yalta. At that conference the Allies agreed to bring about, at the earliest possible date, "the unconditional surrender of Germany."

What lay behind this fixed policy of unconditional surrender is clear. When the meeting was held at Yalta, the Allies knew that the complete defeat of Germany was only a matter of time, and they wanted the German people to know that the German armies had been totally defeated in the field as well as in all other respects. Germany at that time had already suffered enormous destruction, but destruction even on such a scale does not necessarily mean military defeat. There must be a collapse of all military effort, and this collapse was what the Allies wanted to impress clearly on the German people.

The Allies had not forgotten what had happened after World War I. When the armistice was signed on November 11, 1918, the German armies were still massed in formation on the Western Front, and this front lay in France and Belgium. Nowhere was there any foreign military on German soil. There had been no fighting in Germany, and even Allied bombers had inflicted nothing more than minor damage on the country.

All this was concrete—something the German people in 1918 could see for themselves. They could not see, and did not recognize, the internal disintegration that was under way in the German armies—a disintegration which, in the face of the overpowering and ever-increasing Allied forces, made further German resistance futile. And in a short time, because of the failure of the German people to recognize these facts, German nationalists were able to contend loudly that Germany had been stabbed in the back by traitors. When it came time to sign the peace treaty in June 1919 there was a great deal of trouble with the Germans. The Nazis made great capital of this betrayal myth. It ʌas one of the main tricks by which Hitler came to power, for the German nation, in the fifteen years that followed World War I, had come to be convinced that they had lost the war by betrayal and not by military defeat. This time, however, unconditional surrender was decided on. The Allies wanted to be sure that there would be no room left for doubt in the German mind as to the reason or the completeness of their military defeat. I am not certain that things always work that way. We have had some defeats ourselves, but in our minds, and over the long years, they have become something less than defeats. If we won the War of 1812, for example, it is not so admitted in English history books.

It seems to me that what happens is that national pride outlives military defeat. It is a delusion to think otherwise. I also think that it is a mistake to insist on unconditional surrender for moral or educational purposes. Any surrender is at the will of the victor, whether the surrender terms be conditional or unconditional. If there is any reason for unconditional surrender, it is only the practical matter of taking over a defeated country and making its control easier.

On the other hand, I am not sure that unconditional surrender would have been pressed unduly if the Germans had quit in time—if Hitler had realized at the proper moment that he was finished and had permitted a new government to take over and submit to the Allies.

A good time for the Germans to surrender would have been after the Russians had driven them from Stalingrad and the Western Allies had landed in Italy and France. Had the Germans surrendered then, it would have meant a quicker recovery for all of Europe and especially for Germany. Furthermore, there would not have been the present division of Germany, which was largely brought about by the presence of great Allied armies in Germany when the war ended.

It is possible that the whole business of surrender will be academic in any large-scale future war, although I do not think so. If, unfortunately, there should be a future war, we can anticipate the absolute devastation of vital parts of one or the other of the belligerent nations, and probably of both of them. Our new and frightfully destructive weapons can surely wipe out the greatest cities. We would probably be dealing in annihilation from the first, and in the event of such a war there would come a time sooner or later—possibly soon after the very first attack—when one of the belligerents would be compelled to ask for terms.

The old question would then confront the victor: Does he want to take over the enemy country completely? If he does, he might find it necessary to fight further, thereby running the risk of atomic-hydrogen attacks on his own territory. And in any event, the power of destruction, vast as it is with the new weapons, does not necessarily do away with political-military objectives such as have always existed in modern war.

Warfare, no matter what weapons it employs, is a means to an end, and if that end can be achieved by negotiated settlements of conditional surrender, there is no need for war. I believe this to be true even in the case of ruthless and terroristic powers ambitious for world conquest.

The thought that frightens me is the possibility of the deliberate annihilation of whole peoples as a political-military objective. There were indications of such madness in the Nazi leadership group, and it could happen elsewhere. Terms of surrender have no meaning here. The only thing that does have meaning, and in all my thinking I have found no alternative, is organized international effort. I know of no other way to meet this terrible menace.

A major difficulty that arises in connection with such a formula as unconditional surrender is that it cuts across the line which should divide political from military decisions. Von Clausewitz long ago pointed out that "war is a continuation of diplomacy by other means," and many of our generals, as well as a large proportion of the public, conclude from this that, once war has begun, all decisions become military in nature. Von Clausewitz, however, said a great deal more than just that easily remembered sentence. He said that both diplomacy and war are merely means to an end and that the nature of that end is a matter for political determination.

My meetings with the Chiefs of Staff were always highly informative and productive. Many complex problems were resolved during these sessions. But the one question never fully answered was whether political considerations took priority over military considerations in the midst of war operations. It is a fact, of course, that the policy of the government determines the policy of the military. The military is always subordinate to the government. But in a situation where the military commanders are convinced that a certain political proposal is militarily too risky or costly or not practical, then the government is bound to take into account the position taken by the military.

We were faced with that kind of problem in the closing phase of the war in Europe. As a result of the rapid advances of our armies on the central front, our operational lines began to outstrip the lines of the occupation zones that had long since been agreed upon. This raised the issue of how far east our armies should go, what lines they should hold when the fighting stopped, and the relation of all this to the occupation zones.

Churchill, on political grounds, pressed for getting a line as far to the east as possible before the fighting ended. Opposed to this policy were our military chiefs, whose arguments were based on military grounds.

At this time it was our objective to destroy all remaining resistance. This was to be achieved by a general advance eastward until our armies met the Russian armies coming westward. In all this there was nothing at all binding on how far our Western Allied armies should go eastward or what lines they should be holding when the fighting stopped. While this matter involved serious political considerations, it also posed a major problem for the military.

All broad strategic plans, wherever they might originate, had to be approved by the Chiefs of Staff and finally by the President. The matter of advances, or of retreats if necessary, was, however, left to the judgment of the field commanders. This enabled them to take advantage of unexpected enemy weaknesses in order to advance as far as their military judgment permitted them to go.

As the war was drawing to a close we were having a great deal of difficulty with our Russian ally. Politically we would have been pleased to see our lines extend as far to the east as possible. We had already found ourselves practically shut out of countries that the Russians had occupied, and we therefore had reason to question their intentions here in Germany. But the specified zones in Germany had been previously agreed upon, and to these zones the British, American, and Russian armies were to withdraw at the end of the war, regardless of where they might be when the fighting stopped. The Russian military commanders, as well as our own, were well aware of the official commitments on these occupation zones.

The matter of occupation zones had first come to my attention in a telegram that Churchill sent me on April 18. It was one of several in which he urged that our armies should push as far to the east as they could reach and firmly hold. Churchill, in fact, had been pressing this point for some time in messages to President Roosevelt. Churchill waged his own battle over it with the military too, particularly with our military chiefs, and had clashed on this general issue with Eisenhower when the plan for the last big offensive was prepared.

This plan called for our troops to stop at the Elbe. The main thrust was to be made by Bradley's Twelfth Army Group, straight across the center of Germany to the Elbe, while Montgomery's Twenty-first Army

Group on the north and Devers' Sixth Army Group on the south would support Bradley's advance by advances in their own sectors. Once Bradley had reached the Elbe, he would turn north to support Montgomery and south to support Devers, in this way aiding in the capture of the Baltic ports as far as Lübeck and as much of Austria as possible.

Churchill wanted the main thrust on the north to be by Montgomery's Twenty-first Army Group reinforced with large American forces. The capture of Berlin, in his belief, should be its great objective. Eisenhower, however, would not give in, and we supported him. Eisenhower maintained that his plan, in conjunction with the Russian armies, would best achieve the over-all objective of crushing German resistance. He objected to the Churchill plan on the grounds that such a procedure would inject political considerations into military operations. Berlin, Eisenhower maintained, might be a matter of prestige, but it was a difficult job to take. Furthermore, Berlin was within the two-hundred-mile agreed-upon Russian occupation zone.

On March 30 General Eisenhower had reported this situation to General Marshall.

"May I point out," his message read, "that Berlin itself is no longer a particularly important objective. Its usefulness to the Germans has been largely destroyed and even their government is preparing to move to another area. What is now important is to gather up our forces for a single drive and this will more quickly bring about the fall of Berlin, the relief of Norway, and the acquisition of the shipping of the Swedish ports than will the scattering around of our efforts."

"The battle of Germany," Marshall replied on March 31, with Roosevelt's approval, "is now at a point where it is up to the field commander to judge the measures which should be taken. To deliberately turn away from the exploitation of the enemy's weakness does not appear sound. The single objective should be quick and complete victory. While recognizing there are factors not of direct concern to SCAEF, the U. S. Chiefs consider his strategic concept is sound and should receive full support. He should continue to communicate freely with the Commander in Chief of the Soviet Army."

Churchill was worried over Russian intentions and wanted all the territory we could get for bargaining purposes after the war. All this, he argued, was part of broad strategy and could not be left out of war plans. For him, Berlin was not just a military matter but a matter of state, to be decided by the heads of government. However, our Chiefs of Staff supported Eisenhower, and Roosevelt would not interfere with the operational plan.

By April 18 the military situation had changed, and this was reflected in Churchill's message to me. On April 12 the advance forces under Bradley had reached the Elbe at Magdeburg, while the Russians were still on the Oder, some eighty miles away.

On April 13 the Russian armies in the south took Vienna, and by the eighteenth their main force was on the outskirts of Berlin. On the same day the U. S. Third Army was entering Czechoslovakia. German resistance was nearing collapse, opening wide areas for possible Allied occupation. On this aspect of the situation Churchill kept pressing.

In his April 18 message Churchill proposed that a directive be issued to the supreme commander, General Eisenhower, on how to act, as our armies would soon meet up with the Russians. The functions of field commanders, he pointed out, related only to what he called tactical zones, and in such areas our troops should hold the line they had reached, except for such tactical deployment as might be necessary against further enemy resistance.

As for the occupation zones, Churchill expressed his willingness to adhere to them, but pointed out that this matter would come up only after V-E Day and that there would be problems to discuss with the Russians. Churchill added that the occupation zones had been decided in some haste at the Quebec conference in 1944, at a time when no one could foresee our great advances in Germany.

This shows conclusively that heads of state should be very careful about horseback agreements, because there is no way of foretelling the final result.

I took some time in answering this message in order to examine the whole situation. I knew what worried Churchill. His experience with the Russians was as trying as ours. The intentions of the Russians to act on their own, without our co-operation, in all the countries they had liberated was evident to us. In fact, on this very day I had sent a protest to Stalin on the Polish situation.

I made a careful study of the subject of occupation zones. As regards Germany, I found that we were clearly committed on specific zones. In the case of Austria, while we were also committed, specific zones had not yet been worked out. Harriman reported from Moscow that Stalin told him that the capture of Vienna now made it necessary to fix the zones of Allied occupation for the city, and Stalin suggested that American, British, and French representatives proceed as soon as possible to Vienna to establish the zones there.

The zones for Germany, however, had been worked out by the European Advisory Commission sitting in London. This commission had been set up in January 1944 to study European questions that arose as the war developed. Ambassador Winant was our representative, Sir William

Strang represented the British, and Gousev, the Soviet Ambassador, the Russians.

This group made joint recommendations, which were sent to each government for its approval, and on September 12, 1944, with aid from the military, had drawn up a rough agreement on the zones. This was accepted in a general way by Roosevelt and Churchill at the Quebec conference which met during that month. No definite arrangements could be made at this conference, however, for the Russians were not present.

In November 1944 the European Advisory Commission submitted a final draft agreement on the zones to be occupied by the three major powers. Each power was to have its own zone, and boundaries of each were specifically delineated, although Berlin was made a special joint zone. At Yalta the zones laid down in this draft agreement were accepted by all three powers. Provision was also made there for a fourth zone, for France, the details to be worked out by the Advisory Commission.

Our commitment on the occupation zones was thus an established fact, and our government had been proceeding on that basis ever since Yalta. Our American Chiefs and the Combined Chiefs of Staff had it in mind in planning their last great offensive, and our Chiefs were already working out plans for the administration of military government in our zone.

A departmental committee was working out general policy. This committee, made up of the Secretaries of State, War, and Treasury, had been set up soon after the Yalta conference, in compliance with President Roosevelt's request that the Yalta decisions be carried forward.

After thus examining the situation, I could see no valid reason for questioning an agreement on which we were so clearly committed, nor could I see any useful purpose in interfering with successful military operations. The only practical thing to do was to stick carefully to our agreement and to try our best to make the Russians carry out their agreements.

It was with this in mind that I replied to Churchill on April 23. This message contained a draft proposal to be sent to Stalin, if Churchill agreed, outlining the procedure to be followed by the armed forces in occupying the various zones.

On the next day I received a reply from Churchill. He was agreeable to most of the text of my proposed message to Stalin but was unhappy over the opening part, in which I proposed that the troops withdraw to their respective zones as soon as the military situation permitted. This meant, he said, that the American troops would have to fall back some one hundred and fifty miles in the center and give up considerable territory to the Russians at a time when other questions remained unsettled.

General Eisenhower, in his message of April 23, gave some indication

of the many problems that were developing in the matter of procedure
with the Russians when they met up with our troops.

". . . I do not quite understand," Eisenhower cabled, "why the Prime
Minister has been so determined to intermingle political and military
considerations in attempting to establish a procedure for the conduct of
our own and Russian troops when a meeting takes place. My original
recommendation submitted to the CC/S was a simple one and I thought
provided a very sensible arrangement.

"One of my concerns in making that proposal was the possibility that
the Russians might arrive in the Danish peninsula before we could fight
our way across the Elbe and I wanted a formula that would take them out
of that region on my request. The only area in which we will be in the
Russian occupation zone is that now held by American troops.

"I really do not anticipate that the Russians will be arbitrary in demanding an instant withdrawal from this region (although I would save
troops for the campaigns on the flanks if they should do so), but if they
should take an arbitrary stand and serve notice that they intend to push
directly ahead to the limits of their occupational zone, the American
forces are going to be badly embarrassed. As I say, I think this fear will
never be realized—but my hope was to protect my subordinate commanders from uncertainties and worry.

"We are working very hard on the redeployment business and on all
our plans for the occupation of the American zone in Germany.

"I telegraphed to you my recommendations on the zone to be allotted
to the French. Smith had a conference with Juin and it develops that the
French are not particularly concerned about giving up the areas we require.

"They are rather upset, though, about the British refusal to allow them
to occupy the Rhineland as far north as Cologne. I suspect there is some
underlying political struggle on this point, of which I am ignorant.

"I note that the redeployment schedule is merely going to intensify
the continuing struggle regarding service troops. To meet the demands
made upon us, our needs in repair and construction companies and many
other units of that type will be greater than ever. At the same time they
will want identical units in the Pacific to prepare for the later arrival of
combat divisions."

Cabling Churchill on April 26, I took occasion to point out that the
armies now in the Soviet zone were American and that any agreement on
withdrawal to the occupation zones would have to be by all three powers.
I also suggested for his consideration a modified version of the message
to Stalin, and the next day he accepted this and sent it on to Stalin. On
the same day I sent a message to Stalin saying that the Churchill com-

munication he had received had my agreement. It was not until May 2 that Stalin answered. Russia, he cabled, would proceed along our proposed lines.

Meanwhile the advance of our forces in Czechoslovakia had added a new aspect to the situation. On April 23 our Embassy in London received a note from the British Foreign Office in which Eden expressed the view that it would be most desirable politically to have Prague liberated by U.S. forces. The note went on to say that the liberation of Czechoslovakia by a Western ally would be of obvious advantage to us and would also help us in establishing our missions in that country.

On April 30 Churchill sent me a message on this matter. He contended that the liberation of Prague and as much else of Czechoslovakia as possible could well affect the postwar situation in that country and possibly in the neighboring countries. Churchill pointed out that while this suggestion was not meant to interfere with the main effort against the Germans it should be brought to Eisenhower's attention.

Churchill added that he had already instructed the British Chiefs of Staff to ask the U. S. Chiefs of Staff to let Eisenhower know that if the opportunity arose to advance into Czechoslovakia he should take advantage of it. Churchill said he hoped this would have my approval.

Our own State Department was impressed with the same idea. Acting Secretary of State Grew sent me a memo suggesting that the Joint Chiefs of Staff be asked to consider the idea seriously. His argument was along familiar lines. If our armies could push to the Moldau River, which runs through Prague, it would give us something to bargain with in our dealings with the Russians.

The Third Army was already deep into Upper Austria, along the Danube, a part of Austria that would probably be part of our occupation zone. Part of this, however, might be claimed by Russia. If we could take the Moldau River in all its length, it would put us in a strong position in dealing with the Soviet government as to both Austria and Czechoslovakia. Grew added that he was fully aware that a decision would have to rest primarily upon military considerations.

I turned to our military leaders for their appraisals of the situation and referred Churchill's suggestion that we take Prague and as much of Czechoslovakia as possible to Eisenhower for his judgment. On May 1 I sent Churchill the following reply:

"General Eisenhower's present attitude, in regard to operations in Czechoslovakia, which meets with my approval, is as follows:

"QUOTE. The Soviet General Staff now contemplates operations into the Vltava Valley. My intention, as soon as current operations permit, is to proceed and destroy any remaining organized German forces.

"If a move into Czechoslovakia is then desirable, and if conditions here permit, our logical initial move would be on Pilsen and Karlsbad. I shall not attempt any move which I deem militarily unwise. UNQUOTE."

Our Chiefs of Staff agreed with Eisenhower. It was always a basic condition of all our military planning that we would not expose our troops to any greater danger than was necessary. Our plans for the advance eastward always had this in mind. The military commanders, General Eisenhower and his staff, decided on how far they could advance without exposing our troops to unnecessary casualties.

Churchill was constantly pressing us to keep the greatest possible military strength in Europe. He wanted as large a force as possible on the continent to counteract the vast Russian armies there. We, however, had to keep in mind that after the defeat of Germany there still remained Japan. To bring Japan to her knees would require the transfer of many troops from Europe to the Pacific. To be sure, I agreed with Churchill that it would be desirable to hold the great cities of Berlin, Prague, and Vienna, but the fact was that, like the countries of eastern Europe, these cities were under Russian control or about to fall under her control. The Russians were in a strong position, and they knew it. On the other hand, if they were firm in their way, we could be firm in ours. And our way was to stick to our agreements and keep insisting that they do the same. And by insisting on orderly procedure, I meant to insist on important details.

There was the matter of Vienna. On April 30 Churchill sent me a message saying he was concerned about Austria. The Russians, without consulting us and in spite of our protests, had established a provisional government in Vienna under Dr. Karl Renner. They were also refusing our missions entry into Vienna.

There was no objection to Renner himself, but Churchill was afraid that the Russians were trying their old trick of organizing a country to suit themselves, and he proposed that we send not troops into Vienna but a protest to Stalin. A draft message for Stalin accompanied Churchill's telegram. I replied to Churchill on the same day, saying I had that day sent a protest to Moscow in line with his thoughts.

"In the spirit of the Yalta declaration on liberated Europe," my message to Stalin said in part, "this Government was preparing with an open mind and in good faith to consult with the Soviet Government about Renner's proposal, when it was surprised to learn through the press that a provisional Austrian government had already been formed in the Soviet-occupied part of Austria. This development could occur in that area only with the full knowledge and permission of the Soviet authorities.

"Yet they failed to consult us or inform us beyond the meager information conveyed in your recent message or to allow time for us to concert with them prior to the establishment of Renner's provisional regime, the details of which we have learned solely from the press.

"We assume that it remains the intention of the Soviet Government that supreme authority in Austria will be exercised by the four powers acting jointly on a basis of equality, through the inter-allied military government envisaged in the proposals for control machinery now before the European Advisory Commission 'until the establishment of an Austrian government recognized by the four powers.'

"In order that we may collaborate with the Soviet authorities effectively in accordance with the Crimea declaration as far as Austria is concerned, it is, in view of this development, all the more necessary that allied representatives proceed at once to Vienna as suggested by Marshal Stalin and that the protocols on zones of occupation and control machinery be completed in EAC without delay."

The Russians were trying their old tactics in Vienna. Our representatives, they said, would be undesirable in Vienna until after the European Advisory Commission had agreed on the zones. It was clear that the Commission could not agree on the zones until there was an examination on the spot. On May 1 Churchill sent a request to Stalin that Allied representatives be permitted to fly to Vienna at once. On May 3 I sent Stalin a similar request.

In the end we made our point. We had insisted on a particular thing being done, as a right under our agreement, and the Russians gave in. I doubt whether we could have gotten anywhere by broad demands. It would have given them too many loopholes.

In a message on May 6 Churchill renewed his plea that we hold our lines, which had been extended by this time into Yugoslavia and Czechoslovakia. I thought the matter had been left to the decision of the military as to where they could safely go and stay. I could feel with Churchill and fully share his views on the problem that lay ahead. But I could not go along with him on method. As before, he wanted us to keep all we could of territory and then show the Russians how much we had to offer or keep back. He observed that the time had come when correspondence was no longer of use and that a meeting of the three heads of government was necessary. I fully agreed with this. On May 9 I sent the following message:

"I am in agreement with your opinion that a meeting of the three heads of government would be desirable in order to get action on the questions of interest to the three governments upon which either a decision or a common understanding have not been reached.

"I very much prefer to have the request for such a tripartite meeting originate from Marshal Stalin and not from either one of us. Perhaps you have means of some kind with which to endeavor to induce Stalin to suggest or request such a meeting.

"In the meantime it is my present intention to adhere to our interpretation of the Yalta agreements, and to stand firmly on our present announced attitude toward all the questions at issue.

"In order to prepare for a possible tripartite meeting in the not distant future, I would be very pleased to have from you a list of the questions that you consider it necessary or desirable for us to bring up for discussion, and also suggestions as to meeting places.

"There should now be no valid excuse for Stalin's refusing to come west towards us.

"In regard to timing, it will be extremely difficult for me to absent myself from Washington before the end of the fiscal year (30 June), but I probably will be able to get away after that date."

On May 12, the thirty-day period of mourning for President Roosevelt was over. The flag on the White House was once more flown at full staff on May 15. We had moved to the White House from Blair House with very little commotion, except that Margaret's piano had to be hoisted through a window of the second-floor living room. Our living quarters in the White House had been repainted. We had given up our apartment on Connecticut Avenue and had shipped some of our furniture to our home in Independence. We were now expecting my mother and my sister Mary Jane to arrive as weekend guests. Had the pressure of events been less, I would have liked to go to Grandview, my mother's home, for Mother's Day. I had planned to have my mother and sister visit us as early as they could after we were settled in the official residence of the President. I now sent the presidential plane, the *Sacred Cow*, to bring them to Washington for Mother's Day. This was Mama's first airplane trip. The plane that brought her was the one that took President Roosevelt to and from his transatlantic conferences. It had a specially built-in elevator to help lift him in and out of the plane.

Mama got a great kick out of the trip. The only thing she did not like was her experience with the elevator. When the plane landed and she was being taken down, the elevator stuck. It had to be pulled back to get her out. She turned to Colonel Myers, the pilot, and said:

"I am going to tell Harry that this plane is no good and I could walk just as easily as I could ride."

By this time a regular passenger stairway had been rolled up to the plane, and I escorted her down myself. When she saw all the reporters and photographers, she turned to me.

"Oh fiddlesticks," she said. "Why didn't you tell me there was going to be all this fuss, and I wouldn't have come."

My mother, who was an unreconstructed rebel, had come to Washington a little concerned about the bed she was going to sleep in, because my brother Vivian had told her several days before she left that the only room available for her at the White House was the Lincoln Room. Vivian told her she would have to sleep in the bed where Lincoln had slept. My mother said to Vivian, "You tell Harry, if he puts me in the room with Lincoln's bed in it I'll sleep on the floor."

Many years ago, when I first joined the National Guard, I went to the farm at Grandview in my new blue uniform. It was a beautiful uniform with red stripes down the pants legs and a red *fourragère* over the shoulder. My good old red-haired grandma, Harriet Louisa Young, looked me over and told me it was a "pretty uniform" but that was the first time a blue uniform had been in the house since the Civil War, and she said please not to come in it again. My mother felt the same way about the uniform, only she did not tell me not to wear it.

But by the time we reached the White House she had been reassured. She was to sleep in the Rose Room, one of the principal guest rooms. This is the room in which all the queens who had ever visited the White House had slept. But my mother took one look at the bed and started walking around the room. This was not for her. The bed was too high and too big, and the surroundings were too fussy, she said. Then she saw the adjoining room, a much smaller room, which was used by ladies-in-waiting to the queens who were guests at the White House. It was cozier and had a single bed in it.

"This is where I'm going to sleep," she decided, and that was her room throughout her stay. It was Mary who took the larger room.

Mama made herself at home very quickly. She got along well with the household help. They fell in love with her and felt at ease with her. She never presumed on the position she had as my mother, and everyone liked her frankness. Mama explored all of the White House. The first day she fell down the stairway at the end of the hall in the East Wing. She was alone at the time and she told no one about it.

The following day—Sunday, May 13—was Mother's Day, and we were to attend religious services in the chapel of the Naval Medical Center at Bethesda, Maryland. Mama said that she did not feel quite up to going to the services, but I did not know at the time that she had had an accident. She kept this a secret for two weeks.

My mother never tried to give me any advice as President. She had a keen interest in politics and she knew what was going on. As a matter of fact, she was a regular reader of the Congressional Record, and she kept up a correspondence with several senators. During her stay at the White House she was interested in everything that was going on. But she did not seem to feel that there was anything special about my being in the White House or about my being President. She thought it was just the natural thing. It did not give her any ideas of grandeur. She was just the same Mama she had always been.

CHAPTER 15

During the ten days before the German surrender I had continuous conversations with the Cabinet and the Chiefs of Staff on what forces and supplies we would send from Europe to the Far East. It was decided that those military divisions and units that had not seen much active service on the fighting front would be the first sent from Europe to the Pacific.

We had to keep in mind that we needed adequate forces of occupation in Europe, not only to maintain law and order in the land of the conquered enemy, but to keep vigil against any sudden eruptions of little would-be Hitlers who might seek to fan the flames of fanatical nationalism.

At the same time we had to keep a watchful eye on our home economy, and I was having detailed plans and studies made on how we could, in an orderly way, go from an economy based on military requirements to a civilian economy.

We also had to reckon with the problem of a devastated Europe where there were starvation and disorganization. War refugees and displaced persons had to be cared for.

The end of the war in Europe necessitated replanning in many fields and redirecting the activities of existing government agencies, civilian as well as military.

Our industrial capacity now was so great that we could supply all fronts simultaneously. Therefore, the end of hostilities in Europe left a large surplus of production facilities. We had to give immediate consideration to converting some of these war production plants to civilian use.

We were now beginning to experience growing shortages in our basic food supplies. At the same time there was an increasing demand for shipment of food abroad. Sugar supplies, for example, had been so seriously drained that we were forced to issue a drastic order cutting consumer rations by twenty-five per cent.

This was the first time in more than twenty years that we had to depend entirely on current production of sugar, all surpluses having been used up.

As shortages grew and rationing became tighter, resentment against the OPA developed in many communities, and strong criticism was voiced in Congress.

On May 1 I called Chester Bowles, the OPA Administrator, to the White House to discuss the situation. Bowles pointed out that criticism and resistance to rationing were making it difficult for him to keep his organization functioning. Many of his top men wanted to quit. Some key men had already left their posts. I told Bowles that I considered the pressure against the OPA due largely to lobbyists working for special interest groups, and I felt that neither the people nor the Congress would turn against the OPA while the war had yet to be won. I commended Bowles for his able, patient, and successful administration and told him that I was issuing that day a public statement showing how OPA had contributed toward the winning of the war and the preservation of economic stability on the home front.

In this statement I stressed the continued need for OPA, even though I understood the natural weariness of the people under rationing and the perfectly normal resentment of businessmen, farmers, and merchants at being told what to charge for their products. But the OPA, touching the life of every citizen, was still urgently needed not only to preserve the economic balance on the home front but also to supplement the badly depleted resources and supplies of our allies. We needed help for millions in the liberated areas if we were to prevent anarchy, riot, and disease.

I knew that the OPA had made mistakes. But I also knew that the price-control program had made an enormous contribution in preventing runaway inflation. Inflation in other countries had brought disorder and tyranny. By curbing inflation in the United States, the OPA had kept our country sound and stable.

This had not been an easy task. Although the vast majority of our citizens put their selfish interests aside during the war, this was not true of some.

John L. Lewis, head of the United Mine Workers, for example, disregarding the fact that we were at war, ordered a strike. Here we were in the midst of one of the gravest conflicts in the history of civilization.

Men were dying in battle. Our citizens were tightening their belts and making every sacrifice to help save the world from tyranny. Compromises and adjustments were being made by management and labor with a minimum of strife. Most labor unions were setting fine examples of give-and-take, and some had assigned their best men to work with the government to prevent industrial dislocation. But John L. Lewis, undisturbed by what it would do to the nation, ordered his coal miners to strike. This strike appeared all the more inexcusable because Lewis seemed more concerned with trying to browbeat the government and intimidate the President of the United States than with the welfare of the mine workers. He seemed to believe that by using hammer-and-tongs methods he could impress other labor unions and so cause them to turn to him for leadership if he were successful in forcing the government to meet his terms.

I would not stand for that. A coal strike would seriously cripple the war effort, and we could not permit it. For Lewis to resort to such action that endangered the national security merely to satisfy a personal craving for power was downright shameful.

The crisis had arisen as a result of a labor dispute between the United Mine Workers of America and the anthracite coal operators. In connection with this, the National War Labor Board had issued an interim order on April 20, 1945. Under this order the parties were required to continue uninterrupted production of coal under the contract terms and conditions formerly in effect until the differences could be resolved.

The War Labor Board held a public hearing on May 1, 1945, and affirmed this order. The operators promptly accepted it. No reply was received from the union, however, and the strike, which was in effect at well over three hundred anthracite coal mines, continued.

It was clear that the coal produced by these mines was essential to the production of war material and for domestic consumption, and the Economic Stabilization Director, William H. Davis, recommended government seizure of the mines to keep production going. The Attorney General and the Secretary of the Interior concurred, as did Fred M. Vinson, head of the Office of War Mobilization.

I approved the recommendation and issued an executive order which directed the Secretary of the Interior, Harold Ickes, to take possession of any and all anthracite coal mines at which there were interruptions or threatened interruptions of operations. Actually this meant that the same people continued to do the work but that they were now working for the government. I have never believed that the government should operate private business, but it must have the means to suppress open defiance such as John L. Lewis's.

This was no time to upset our production and our economy. Serious problems of reconversion would soon face us. Certain phases of our armament and production program had reached levels where government spending and contracts could be cut back. As soon as I saw that this would not interfere with our all-out effort against Japan, I recommended to the Congress on May 2 that it cut $7,445,000,000 from the budget proposed for the fiscal year of 1946. The bulk of this seven billion, I suggested, could come from the reduction of the Maritime Commission's construction activities.

I asked Secretary of the Treasury Morgenthau to make a careful study of our tax situation and to be prepared to discuss with me at an early date possible tax cuts. The next day I received the following note from Secretary Morgenthau:

"I just want to tell you how delighted I was to learn of the retrenchments you have made in Federal expenditures.

"This move on your part will have a most beneficial anti-inflationary effect, and will also be helpful to us in our coming Seventh War Loan Drive."

Throughout the war years our farms had been highly productive. We had been most fortunate in having excellent harvests when we and our allies needed them most. In 1945, however, we were faced with new demands on our farm production. Liberated Europe was virtually starving. Fields in many areas there had not been planted or crops had been destroyed, and in many instances the lateness of the season made it impossible to plant again.

Nevertheless, I disapproved a resolution by Congress to extend deferment to agricultural workers. I felt that in time of war every citizen is under obligation to serve his country. No group should be given special privileges. In my veto message of May 3 I said that Congress had wisely provided in the Selective Training and Service Act of 1940 that no deferment should be made of individuals by occupational groups. In less than three hours the House voted 185 to 177 to override my veto, but this was far below the two thirds necessary, and therefore my veto was sustained.

Moreover, the Southern Hemisphere was experiencing a drought. This meant still further demands on our supplies. In the House of Representatives a committee was set up to investigate the food shortage. It was headed by Clinton P. Anderson of New Mexico. On May 2 I asked Congressman Anderson and his committee to meet with me at the White House. We discussed measures to meet the situation. With Anderson were Congressmen Stephen Pace, Earle C. Clements, Christian A. Herter, Martin Gorski, August H. Andresen, and Hal Holmes.

While swiftly moving events around the world were crowding me for attention, there were enormous housekeeping tasks here at home which also required immediate decisions and actions.

I took up many of these matters at my second meeting with Director of the Budget Harold Smith on May 4.

Commenting on the favorable public reaction to the announced cuts in the budget, I pointed out to Smith, however, that there was some confusion in the public mind as to the difference between reduction in cash expenditures and the lopping off of authorizations for contracts previously approved and no longer needed.

Smith began his report to me by saying that the Red Cross was making urgent representations for a government appropriation of funds to supplement those privately raised by the Red Cross. I told him I was still of the same conviction, and that was that the American Red Cross should not use or spend government funds and should continue to raise money through voluntary contributions.

The Budget Director then brought up the matter of the President's Fund amounting to fifty-nine million dollars, twelve million of which was for unvouchered funds to be used for intelligence work outside this country. I told Smith I did not want the fund enlarged and that I wanted a study made of all the agencies and services engaged in intelligence work.

I told him what my thinking was on the subject of our intelligence activities and my misgivings about some of the fields of these activities. I again wanted to make one thing clear:

"I am very much against building up a Gestapo," I told him.

He asked for instructions with regard to a bill introduced in the Senate appropriating large sums for the building of a network of airports from coast to coast. This was being pushed by Senator Pat McCarran of Nevada and was supported by the Civil Aeronautics Administration.

This was a bad bill, I told him, and the report of the CAA was also bad. I was opposed to it on the grounds that it would lead to "pork barrel" legislation.

I then turned to a situation which I thought required urgent action. This was the reorganization of the executive branch of the government to make it more efficient. There was too much duplication of functions, too much "passing of the buck," and too much confusion and waste. Much of this was inevitable as the war kept piling up additional burdens on the government, but I told Smith I wanted to establish governmental lines so clearly that I would be able to put my finger on the people directly responsible in every situation. It was my intention to delegate responsibility to the properly designated heads of departments and agencies, but I wished to be in a position to see to it that they carried on along the lines of my policy.

I therefore instructed Smith to go ahead and draft a message to the Congress on reorganization legislation, requesting the delegation of the necessary powers to the President to put through needed changes. These proposed changes would, of course, be subject to congressional veto within a specified time. I wanted also to reshape the White House organization and its channels of communications with the other branches of the government. For that reason I asked Smith to make a study of the organizational setup of the President's office as well.

Congress had always had difficulties with problems of reorganization of the government. The legislative branch seldom took the initiative in proposing changes, and a good deal of prodding was necessary to push through the changes we needed. Smith smilingly said this might be a good time to send up reorganization proposals to the Hill because "they are now showering you with expressions of good will and support."

I reminded him, with a little more realism, not to put too much stock in tributes of the moment, much as I appreciated them. Sooner or later I knew such praises would be forgotten in the inevitable tug of wills between the Congress and the President.

I had previously discussed with the Budget Director the reorganization of the Labor Department. I now asked him to make a thorough survey and to complete it by June 16, when there would be a new Secretary of Labor.

I raised the question whether the time had not come to establish a Welfare Department, since the Federal Security Agency had outgrown its original purpose. We needed to extend social security to the white-collar workers and the farmers. Our public health services needed expansion. I thought all these functions might properly come in a new department headed by a Cabinet officer, and I asked Smith to make a survey with that idea in mind.

Concluding our conference, I touched on a subject close to my heart and vital to the future of the nation—the development of river-valley authorities. I told Smith I would come back to this matter at a later date, when I would want him to bring me all the studies he had made on the subject.

A few days after my conference with Smith on government organization I had my first bad experience in the problem of delegating authority.

Leo Crowley, Foreign Economic Administrator, and Joseph C. Grew, Acting Secretary of State, came into my office after the Cabinet meeting on May 8 and said that they had an important order in connection with Lend-Lease which President Roosevelt had approved but not signed. It was an order authorizing the FEA and the State Department to take joint action to cut back the volume of Lend-Lease supplies when Germany surrendered. What they told me made good sense to me; with Germany out of the war, Lend-Lease should be reduced. They asked me to sign it. I reached for my pen and, without reading the document, I signed it.

The storm broke almost at once. The manner in which the order was executed was unfortunate. Crowley interpreted the order literally and placed an embargo on all shipments to Russia and to other European nations, even to the extent of having some of the ships turned around and brought back to American ports for unloading. The British were hardest hit, but the Russians interpreted the move as especially aimed at them. Because we were furnishing Russia with immense quantities of food, clothing, arms, and ammunition, this sudden and abrupt interruption of Lend-Lease aid naturally stirred up a hornets' nest in that country. The Russians complained about our unfriendly attitude. We had unwittingly given Stalin a point of contention which he would undoubtedly bring up every chance he had. Other European governments complained about being cut off too abruptly. The result was that I rescinded the order.

I think Crowley and Grew taught me this lesson early in my administration—that I must always know what is in the documents I sign. That experience brought home to me not only that I had to know exactly where I was going but also that I had to know that my basic policies were being carried out. If I had read the order, as I should have, the incident would not have occurred. But the best time to learn that lesson was right at the beginning of my duties as President.

This was my first experience with the problem of delegating authority but retaining responsibility. The presidency is so tremendous that it is necessary for a President to delegate authority. To be able to do so safely, however, he must have around him people who can be trusted not to arrogate authority to themselves.

Eventually I succeeded in surrounding myself with assistants and associates who would not overstep the bounds of that delegated authority, and they were people I could trust. This is policy on the highest level: it is the operation of the government by the Chief Executive under the law. That is what it amounts to, and when that ceases to be, chaos exists.

In the case of the Lend-Lease matter, a serious situation had been created. The sudden stoppage of Lend-Lease was clearly a case of policy-making on the part of Crowley and Grew. It was perfectly proper and right, of course, to plan for the eventual cutting off of Lend-Lease to Russia and to other countries, but it should have been done on a gradual basis which would not have made it appear as if somebody had been deliberately snubbed. After all, we had extracted an agreement from the Russians at Yalta that they would be in the Japanese war three months after the Germans folded up. There was, at this time, a friendly feeling in America toward Russia because the Russians, though fighting for their own survival, had saved us many lives in the war against the Germans. There were more than a million Japanese deployed in China and ready to carry on war for an indefinite time there. We were eager for the Russians to get into the war with Japan because of their border with China and their railway connections with Europe. Japan controlled all Chinese seaports from Dairen to Hong Kong.

With this situation in mind, I clarified the government's attitude. In a press and radio conference on May 23 I explained that the order behind Crowley's action was intended to be not so much a cancellation of shipments as a gradual readjustment to conditions following the collapse of Germany. I also made it clear that all allocations provided for by treaty or protocol would be delivered and that every commitment would be filled.

When Harry L. Hopkins conferred with Stalin in Moscow on May 27, the Russian leader brought up the subject of Lend-Lease and cited it as an example of the cooling-off attitude of America toward the Soviets after it became obvious that Germany was defeated. Stalin said that the manner in which Lend-Lease had been terminated was unfortunate. He said that if the refusal to continue Lend-Lease was intended as pressure on the Russians in order to soften them up it was a fundamental mistake. Hopkins sought to reassure Stalin that this was not the case.

The Russians were always inclined to be suspicious of every action taken by either Great Britain or the United States. I had found examples of this earlier in reading through a great stack of telegrams which had passed between Churchill and Roosevelt, Churchill and Stalin, and Roosevelt and Stalin on the Polish question, on the situation in Yugoslavia, and on our effort to make peace negotiations with Italy before the defeat of Germany. Repeatedly, messages from Stalin indicated the suspicion that we and the British were determined to make bilateral arrangements, leaving the Russians out. The sudden stoppage of Lend-Lease gave the Russians another chance to accuse the United States of trying to interfere with a three-power approach to peace at their expense. Nevertheless, I continued to hope that we would be able to deal with the Russians in a friendly and co-operative way.

The British also showed immediate signs of anxiety over the prospect of diminishing assistance from the United States after V-E Day. The chief point in the British arguments for continuation of Lend-Lease was based on a conversation between Prime Minister Churchill and President

Roosevelt at their Quebec meeting on September 14, 1944. At that meeting, although President Roosevelt generalized on the willingness of the United States to give all possible aid to the British after Germany was overcome, he made no specific commitments other than those contained in the Lend-Lease Act. He and Churchill agreed, however, to set up an American committee consisting of Secretary of the Treasury Henry Morgenthau, Jr., Under Secretary of State (as he then was) Edward Stettinius, and Foreign Economic Administrator Leo Crowley to consult with a British committee on the international financial position of Great Britain and the Lend-Lease arrangements for the empire.

It was to this committee that the British now directed their appeal. After several months of discussion the Quebec committee had submitted a recommendation to President Roosevelt and then considered itself dissolved. During the latter part of May 1945 Secretary Morgenthau, who had acted as chairman of the committee, notified me that he had received an urgent message from the British Chancellor of the Exchequer, Sir John Anderson, and Mr. Oliver Lyttelton. In this message the British expressed concern that forthcoming Lend-Lease appropriations would not be large enough to cover their needs. They based this on the fact that in preliminary discussions War Department officials had indicated to the British that we did not consider ourselves bound by the principles of the Quebec agreement of the previous autumn.

On May 28 a second and more urgent appeal for continued Lend-Lease aid came from the British government—this one in the form of a personal telegram from Prime Minister Churchill.

"I am distressed," this message read, "to have to bother you with this telegram when so many other graver matters are pending. But the machine has come to a standstill on the subject and it is felt on all sides here that the matter should be referred by me to you.

"When I met President Roosevelt at Quebec in September 1944 we both initialled an agreement about Lend-Lease after the defeat of Germany. In accordance with that agreement a detailed plan was worked out with your administration by the Keynes-Sinclair Mission. It is on this basis that our production plans have been laid.

"I now hear that your War Department has told our people in Washington that they are expecting so large a cut in their forthcoming appropriations for the U. S. Air Corps that supplies to us must be drastically curtailed below the schedule of our requirements as agreed last autumn. These requirements were, of course, subject to subsequent modification in the light of changes in the strategical situation. I am hopeful that our requirements as agreed last autumn can now be reduced, but the details of the reduction depend upon discussions between our respective Chiefs of Staff, which will not have been completed before 31 May. Meanwhile I hope that your people can be told that the principles your predecessor and I agreed on at Quebec will stand, and in particular that the appropriations given to your War Department will be enough to provide for our needs as finally worked out between us."

The need for clarification of Lend-Lease policy on both sides was becoming more evident. On May 31 I received a letter signed by five congressmen—Robert B. Chiperfield, John M. Vorys, Karl E. Mundt, Bartel J. Jonkman, and Lawrence H. Smith—stating that the President's policy on Lend-Lease after V-E Day had been obscured rather than explained by the combined effect of my statement and those of Under Secretary Grew and Leo Crowley. I replied to the congressmen on June 15 and referred them to the following paragraphs from a letter I had sent to the Speaker of the House of Representatives on June 4 concerning Lend-Lease appropriations:

"The war against Japan, like the war against Germany, is a cooperative allied effort. Through Lend-Lease and reverse Lend-Lease we shall continue to pool our resources with those of our allies so that the crushing weight of our combined might may be thrown against our remaining enemy. Where Lend-Lease funds will make the efforts of our allies more effective, we shall use them. Where the redeployment of our troops from Europe or our control over enemy areas requires aid from other nations, Lend-Lease will be available to enable their maximum participation. Similarly, through reverse Lend-Lease we can expect our allies to give us all the assistance possible.

"In the light of changed war conditions, a preliminary review of Lend-Lease assistance to individual nations has been made. Further review will be necessary from time to time in the coming year as the war progresses and the needs and the wartime roles of our allies vary. For this reason any programs proposed must be considered as most tentative.

"Our recent Lend-Lease agreements with France, Belgium and the Netherlands will be carried out by Lend-Lease funds to the fullest extent consistent with changed war conditions and the basic wartime purposes of Lend-Lease aid. Beyond this I propose that these allies be assisted in financing necessary equipment and supplies by the Export-Import Bank."

One of the difficulties was the fact that we could never get Congress to authorize Lend-Lease for the duration of hostilities. Congress would put a time limit on each Lend-Lease appropriation, and the whole process of debate and hearings would have to be repeated every year. Then invariably there would be some bloc either on the floor of the House or the floor of the Senate which would hamper the operation or bring about some readjustment in the administration of Lend-Lease. I could never get Congress to see that by their method they were crippling the war effort.

I had seen it from both ends—as a senator and as President. I discussed this problem with Speaker Sam Rayburn in a language we both understood. I could also talk to the chairman of the Finance Committee, through which the Lend-Lease legislation went, and because of my experience in the Senate I was able to keep out some amendments that would have made the law of no use whatever. In fact, it was the intention of some congressmen to make it of no use.

A great many of the war powers that are delegated to the President when a war is actually going on are made effective for the duration of the war. But Congress is very jealous of its authority to keep the purse strings tight, as in the case of appropriations for Lend-Lease. That is all right in a republic when the republic is not in danger, but it always seemed to me that matters such as Lend-Lease should have been authorized for the duration of hostilities. Nor was this something that I had learned as President. Long before, I had once made such an observation on the floor of the Senate as a result of my investigations with the Truman Committee. It is just common sense, but sometimes common sense doesn't win in legislation.

The Speaker of the House knew what I was driving at, but with 435 congressmen on his hands he had to maneuver all the time to get what was necessary to carry on the government in all its functions. Every Speaker always gets interference from some fellow who wants to make a headline in his home-town paper. Now and then these moves may actually cripple the national welfare, but they may look good to the folks at home, where the situation may not be understood in its entirety.

"I am, of course, in full agreement with you," I said in my answer to the five congressmen, "that the Lend-Lease Act does not authorize aid for purposes of postwar relief, postwar rehabilitation, or postwar reconstruction, and that in the liquidation of any Lend-Lease war supply agreements, articles transferred after they are no longer necessary for the prosecution of the war should be disposed of only on terms of payment."

The matter did not end there, however. At a meeting of the Joint Chiefs of Staff on June 7 the British had been informed that there was no legal authority for further assignment of any Lend-Lease materials except for use in the war against Japan. Admiral William D. Leahy reported to me that the question had come up again in a talk he had with Crowley on June 29 and that the latter was in full agreement with the Joint Chiefs and wanted a positive directive to that effect from the President.

The State Department and the Army, according to Leahy, wanted to continue giving Lend-Lease aid to Europe, particularly to France, for use by French occupation forces in Germany. Fred M. Vinson, as Director of the Office of War Mobilization and Reconversion, sided with the State Department and the Army.

For the year following V-E Day the Lend-Lease budget submitted to Congress included a contingency sum of $935,000,000 for a possible Russian Lend-Lease program. If Russia declined to enter the war against Japan, only a small part of that amount would be necessary to complete our commitments. If Russia entered the war very soon, the amount probably would not be sufficient to meet her requirements for the coming year. I directed the FEA to work very closely with and under the direction of the military authorities in dealing with Russia.

Up to this time we had provided very little in the way of Lend-Lease aid to China because of transportation difficulties. Current requirements were for very large amounts, and it was felt that a substantial part of the supplies requested by China could be effectively used in the war effort. However, because of the difficulties of making deliveries, the amount for the coming year was tentatively limited to five hundred million dollars. If the war developments proved to be such that greater deliveries could be made, the way was left clear to increase China's program substantially.

No direct provision was made in the budget for making Lend-Lease aid available to Italy, but pursuant to arrangements with the Army, Congress approved the transfer of ten million dollars from Lend-Lease appropriations to the Army to permit the continuation of its program for the prevention of disease and unrest for a period of four months beyond August 31, the date to which the Army was financing its own program.

Outside of the fifty million dollars which had meanwhile been authorized for relief in Italy by UNRRA, no funds were available beyond the amount transferred to the Army for its use in dealing with the situation in Italy. This called for a rehabilitation program outside the scope of the Lend-Lease Act.

In Poland, Yugoslavia, Czechoslovakia, and Greece there were no provisions for Lend-Lease because none of these countries was either participating in the war with Japan or aiding in the redeployment of American troops. UNRRA was operating in those countries, and partial immediate relief was being furnished, but no method existed by which these countries might finance the materials and supplies which they needed to restore their industry and transportation facilities.

To meet these conditions, I recommended an expansion of the Export-Import Bank. I suggested an increase of the Bank's lending power to $3,500,000,000, which would make available an additional $2,800,-000,000 that could be loaned during the coming year. This amount, I believed, was sufficient for the needs that could reasonably be met during that period. Once we had some experience in lending this money in post-war Europe, I felt that we would be in a much better position to make an intelligent presentation to the Congress as to the needs of various European countries for financial aid.

It was my plan to go to Congress with a request for funds that would be necessary to meet each year's needs rather than to make long-term commitments that would involve this country in obligations to finance a foreign country by making disbursements over a long period of time.

I made a fundamental distinction between powers that I requested during wartime and those that I expected during peacetime. As I mentioned before in connection with Lend-Lease appropriations, I felt all along that Congress should have given the President authority there for the duration of hostilities instead of renewing the legislation periodically.

When a nation is at war, its leader, who has the responsibility of winning the war, ought to have all the tools available for that purpose. I felt that it was imperative, in dealing with the postwar requirements of Europe, that the United States develop a well-rounded co-ordinated policy rather than attempt to do an unintegrated job through a misuse of Lend-Lease.

When the conflict was all over and we had reached the point where the emergency war powers expired, we would be faced with the problems of rehabilitation of many areas of the world. But a European recovery program would be an entirely different matter from wartime Lend-Lease. I thought at the time that this could be handled on the basis of the information which could be sent to the Congress and reviewed year by year as economic conditions improved.

The story of Lend-Lease is a monument to the genius of Franklin Roosevelt. A President could no more get the Congress to make an outright loan of forty-two billions dollars to foreign countries, even to win a war, than he could fly to the moon, but Roosevelt accomplished the same thing through the idea of Lend-Lease. The money spent for Lend-Lease unquestionably meant the saving of a great many American lives. Every soldier of Russia, England, and Australia who had been equipped by Lend-Lease means to go into that war reduced by that much the dangers that faced our young men in the winning of it. We may never get the money back, but the lives we saved are right here in America.

CHAPTER 16

The thought now uppermost in my mind was how soon we could wind up the war in the Pacific, and it was natural for me to turn to General Marshall and Secretary of War Stimson. From the time of our entry into the war, Marshall had been our chief strategist in Europe and in the Pacific. This country and the free world owe him a debt of gratitude for his brilliant planning and masterly execution. I had the greatest respect also for the experience and judgment of Stimson, who as Secretary of State had once tried to keep Japan out of Manchuria with the machinery then at hand. The machinery—the League of Nations—had been ineffective, and Stimson received no support at home. To his credit, however, he had recognized the danger, although he had been unable to forestall it.

On May 16 I sent for Stimson to review our plans for the campaign against Japan and for rehabilitation in Europe. I stressed the need for speed in the Pacific and expressed the fear of famine in Europe which might lead to chaos. I made it clear also that I was opposed to what was then loosely called the Morgenthau Plan—that is, the reduction of Germany to a wholly agrarian economy. I had never been for that plan even when I was in the Senate, and since reaching the White House I had come to feel even more strongly about it. I thought it was proper to disarm Germany, to dismantle her military might, to punish the war criminals, and to put her under an over-all Allied control until we could restore the peace. But I did not approve of reducing Germany to an agrarian state. Such a program could starve Germany to death. That would have been an act of revenge, and too many peace treaties had been based on that spirit. I was never for the underdog, in turn, becoming the top dog with complete power to act. When the underdog gets power, he too often turns out to be an even more brutal top dog.

I told Stimson of the talks I used to have with my friend Senator Elbert Thomas of Utah. I would point to a map of Europe and trace its breadbasket, with Hungary a cattle country and Rumania and the Ukraine as the wheat area. Up to the northwest lay Western Germany, Northern France, Belgium, and Britain with their coal, iron, and big industries.

The problem, as Senator Thomas and I talked about it, was to help unify Europe by linking up the breadbasket with the industrial centers through a free flow of trade. To facilitate this flow, the Rhine and the Danube could be linked with a vast network of canals which would provide a passage all the way from the North Sea to the Black Sea and the Mediterranean. This would constitute free waterways for trade, while each country bordering on the waterways would have the riparian rights it should have. In addition, it would be possible to extend the free waterways of the world by linking the Rhine-Danube waterways with the Black Sea straits and making the Suez, Kiel, and Panama canals free waterways for merchant ships.

Stimson outlined for me the grand strategy devised by our military planners. The campaign against Japan was based on the assumption that we would not attempt to engage the masses of the Japanese Army in China with our own ground forces. The plans for the campaign being worked out by the Joint Chiefs of Staff would, in their opinion, be adequate for the defeat of Japan without such a sacrifice of American lives as would be involved in a major engagement in China. The plans called for an invasion of the Japanese homeland.

Concerning the rehabilitation of Europe, he observed that there was a strong probability of pestilence and famine throughout central Europe during the following winter. This, he felt, was likely to be followed by political revolution and communistic infiltration. Our defenses against this situation would be the western governments of France, Luxembourg, Belgium, Holland, Denmark, Norway, and Italy. It was vital to keep these countries from being driven to revolution or communism by famine.

It appeared likely that a food shortage would develop in most of these countries even during the summer. Fortunately, however, both Canada and the United States had very large wheat surpluses, and this more immediate problem could probably be solved. This was distinct from the problem of next winter's food supply in central Europe. This was a long-range problem and required careful long-range planning and diplomacy. Stimson opposed any plan that would deprive Germany of the means of building up ultimately a contented Germany interested in following non-

militaristic methods of civilization. This, he knew, would necessarily
involve some industrialization, but a solution had to be found for the
future peaceful existence of the Germans. It was to the interest of the
whole world that they should not be driven by stress of hardship into a
non-democratic and necessarily predatory habit of life.

One of the tragic aftermaths of a world war is the harvest of little
Caesars and their acts of aggression. When the great powers are in conflict, pent-up fanatical nationalisms begin to stir everywhere. This poses
a constant threat to peace, for these little acts of belligerency or aggression—these "little wars"—are frequently fought in the name of liberation. They arise from the natural desire of all people to gain full freedom
—a desire that cannot long be suppressed or denied by a mere show of
force by major powers.

We need patience and understanding in our dealings with people who
have suffered foreign domination or occupation. Unfortunately the wrong
leaders too often undertake the role of liberators. Too many of them turn
out to be men who either lust for power or who are just plain vain or
unstable.

The first world war was followed by a series of bloody conflicts. Now,
even before the end of this second world war, the most violent and destructive war in history, we were facing a variety of belligerent activities
in the name of lost territories, of needed frontier changes, and of national
liberations, and along with these activities came a new crop of little
Caesars.

There were even some nations prepared to risk immediate war in
disputes over mere bits of territory. They invoked national honor, national dignity, and every demagogic appeal, even if the quarrel might lead
to their own destruction. This unreasoning urge to resort to force rather
than submit to the orderly procedure of negotiations created a most trying
situation for the Allies.

These outbreaks were not isolated situations. Frictions developed in
Europe and even involved certain of our allies. Violent resistance movements were developing in North Africa, the Middle East, and the re-
deemed areas of Asia, all in the name of liberation. They sought immediate freedom from the established colonial powers, who were, of course,
our allies in the main war.

We, as a people, have always accepted and encouraged the undeniable
right of a people to determine its own political destiny. It is our own faith
and the foundation of our own political freedom. If this is valid for us, it
must be equally valid for other people. There could be no "ifs" attached
to this right, unless we were to backslide on our political creed. But the

real problem, as I saw it in its application to immediate events, was not one of principle. We accepted the principle of political freedom as our own and believed that it should apply elsewhere as well. The real problem was that of procedure and method.

Amid the shambles of a world breaking down, we were desperately in need of machinery not only to deal with international disputes but also to provide assistance and encouragement to peoples in their peaceful aspirations. I was thinking primarily of a world organized for peace and of our plans for the United Nations.

The difficulties we faced at this time illustrated the need we had for firm and orderly procedure. There was, for example, the case of General de Gaulle and his territorial demands for France.

De Gaulle was a man of dedicated courage who had rendered important services to France in 1940 at a time when French morale had hit bottom. The desire of the French people to regain something of their lost power and prestige was understandable, and Americans found it easy to sympathize with them. De Gaulle's methods of championing French national causes, however, were not always along peaceful lines, and his tendency to use force in pressing national claims made for difficult situations. There was the incident at Stuttgart, for instance, which made little sense except that de Gaulle was determined to force our hand by staking out an occupation zone on his own.

By April 21 the American and French forces under General Devers had approached Stuttgart in their rapid advance to the east. From here the American forces were to turn southeast and head toward the Danube. According to plan, the French were to take Stuttgart and then move to the south while an American unit took over the city. This was agreed to by General de Lattre and General Patch. It was strictly a military arrangement by field commanders.

Having taken the city, however, the French refused to move out, in spite of the agreement. On April 27 General Devers ordered the French to evacuate, but the local French commander replied that he was under orders from General de Gaulle to remain. General Eisenhower's intervention did not move de Gaulle, nor did a message I sent him on May 4. I thereupon ordered our supplies to the French troops cut, and Stuttgart was finally evacuated.

De Gaulle gained nothing by this show of force. Discussions were already under way on the matter of a French zone in Germany, and landgrabbing was out of order. De Gaulle's explanation was not impressive. "Such incidents," he told Ambassador Caffery, "could be avoided if the allies of France would only recognize that questions so closely touching

France as the occupation of German territory should be discussed and decided with her."

Actually the matter of a French zone had been under consideration ever since Yalta, and this zone was to be formed from German territory that was originally regarded as part of our zone. Both the British and we were working to restore France as a power, and discussions were then under way in Paris through our embassies.

A more troublesome incident, however, was the unilateral French attempt to occupy parts of the Aosta Valley in northwest Italy. We were just then denying Tito the right to take over Venezia Giulia by force, and now de Gaulle seized the Italian valley as a national right. Nor did he withdraw his troops until I had threatened, as in the Stuttgart incident, to stop our supplies to the French armies.

The affair started when French troops crossed over into Italy in the last phase of the war and occupied areas which de Gaulle wanted to appropriate as being necessary for what he called "minor frontier adjustments." The French troops were under the Supreme Allied Command and, after V-E Day, Eisenhower ordered their withdrawal to France. The French commander, however, replied that he could not comply without instructions from his government. In the meantime more French troops were coming into the area. French occupation, in fact, was being established, and annexation propaganda was being carried out.

On May 5 the Allied commander in Italy, Marshal Alexander, asked Eisenhower whether he could not get the French to comply with the order he had already issued, as the activities of the French troops were troublesome for the local population. Alexander pointed out that there were bound to be clashes and that this would have a serious effect on the Italian government's position. Caffery, our Ambassador in Paris, was instructed to make representations to de Gaulle. On May 6 Caffery cabled that he had talked with de Gaulle and that the general had said that France had no territorial ambitions in the region other than minor frontier adjustments which he hoped to take up with the Italians amicably at a later date. Reports came to me, however, that the number of French troops in the Aosta Valley was still increasing; that food, already scarce, was being requisitioned; that Italian flags were being taken down; and that notices were being posted asking the Italian population to declare for France and ordering the acceptance of French currency. I received word from the military that United States troops were advancing to the French-Italian frontier control but that this advance was being impeded by passive French resistance, including road blocks.

Our forces were instructed to halt for further orders if hostilities threatened. Ambassador Caffery was instructed to deliver to the French

Foreign Office a strong memorandum on the matter, and the British government informed the French government of its concern over the continued presence of French troops in Italian territory.

De Gaulle's attitude in reply was one of injured dignity. France, he said, was asking only what was her due. About the same time he began to hint that if another Big Three conference was held he should be invited to take part as an equal of Stalin, Churchill, and myself. To prove this claim to the status of a great power, he demanded that French troops should be included in the forces that would deliver the final blow to the empire of Japan. Their weapons and equipment, of course, were to be furnished by us. And as to the movement of French troops, de Gaulle told General Eisenhower that with the end of the war with Germany this had become a wholly French matter.

Official relations with France were becoming seriously strained, and my own feelings about General de Gaulle were less and less friendly when, on May 18, and at de Gaulle's request, I received the French Foreign Minister, Georges Bidault. I was happy to see him because he was a French patriot who would understand our concern about Allied-French tension. I knew his record in the resistance movement. I told him that I had always been interested in France and that almost every American had a high regard for the French people. I said we wanted to do everything we possibly could to see France get back on her feet and become a great power. I told him that the United States was moved by the strongest ties of friendship dating back to the foundation of this nation. A strong France would represent a gain to the world. I told Bidault the people of the United States had accepted a reduction in their requirements of essential food items in order to permit increased shipments to the liberated countries of Europe, including France. I informed him that the United States was reaffirming its readiness to relinquish to France a part of the American zone of occupation in Germany and that only the details remained to be worked out.

The French Foreign Minister raised the question of French military participation in the war against Japan. He was very anxious to have me commit myself on help in transporting French troops to the Pacific.

I told him the matter of transportation would depend entirely on the strategic disposition of troops under the American general in command and our ability to find facilities and supplies for the shipping of troops. I wanted Bidault to understand clearly that if French troops were used we would have to have prior agreement from the French that they would be under our command. I added that I would insist on the condition that the French troops obey the orders of our commanding general. We were now going through an unhappy experience in the European Theater, and

I had no wish to see it repeated. I told Bidault I did not like what was happening and that I would lay all the cards on the table:

Unless France carried out her commitments, I explained, and unless French troops were instructed to obey the order of the general under whom they were serving, we could not possibly furnish transportation, equipment, planes, and other matériel for them to use.

This was a difficult session and one that I did not enjoy, but it served to clear up our position. Without impairing our warm regard for the French people, I wanted de Gaulle to know that we did not like what he was doing and that all French forces in northwest Italy should be withdrawn. I ended my meeting with Bidault by telling him that I would be happy to welcome General de Gaulle to the United States.

Bidault understood my attitude, and he expressed the opinion that the matter could be straightened out. But Ambassador Caffery reported on June 4 that the general was in no mood to reason and that all he would talk about to the Ambassador when he saw him were the "humiliations" to which he said the French were being subjected. He said that all he wanted on the Italian border was a minor rectification of the boundary, but when Caffery asked him why he did not take his troops out of the area he said, "There would be another humiliation for us."

Caffery was instructed to stress our traditional friendship. We had no intention to humiliate France. But at a time when we were lecturing Russia on keeping her agreements, and telling Tito how to behave in territorial matters, the unilateral French tactics were embarrassing as well as potentially dangerous.

However, there was no improvement in the Franco-Italian situation. French troops were actively obstructing the Allied military government in the area. Administrative officers who had been installed by the AMG —that is, by the British and ourselves—were actually ordered expelled by the French general, and Allied posters and proclamations were being torn down by French soldiers.

On June 5 I took the situation up with the Chiefs of Staff and with the State Department. After the meeting I ordered that further issues of munitions and equipment to the French troops be stopped.

I also sent a message to General de Gaulle in which I expressed my surprise at the language used by his commander, General Doyen, to General Crittenberger. The French commander had actually threatened to have his troops fight the American troops who had come into the area under orders from the Supreme Command.

I notified de Gaulle that no more supplies would be issued to the French Army until its withdrawal from Aosta Valley. I prepared a public statement for release to the American press, declaring that I was stopping shipment of supplies to the French because of their threat to use these munitions against American soldiers. I forwarded this statement to Churchill for his concurrence. Churchill agreed. However, I decided to hold up publication of the statement in view of the extreme sensitivity of the French at the time and to see what de Gaulle would do in response to my direct message to him.

Commenting on my action to withhold publication of my statement to the press, Churchill cabled on June 6 that "the publication of your message would have led to the overthrow of de Gaulle, who after five long years of experience I am convinced is the worst enemy of France in her troubles." Churchill said he considered General de Gaulle "one of the greatest dangers to European peace. No one has more need than Britain of French friendship, but I am sure that in the long run no understanding will be reached with General de Gaulle."

My message to de Gaulle brought results. The general agreed to withdraw French troops from Aosta.

Meanwhile new problems involving de Gaulle had developed in the Near East, where the French had formerly held Syria and Lebanon as League of Nations mandates. In the course of World War II the Allies recognized Syria and Lebanon as independent countries. They were now members of the United Nations and had their representatives in San Francisco. In the spring of 1945 de Gaulle began to press these two nations for special concessions of a political, cultural, and military nature which would put them under French domination. French troops were landed in both Syria and Lebanon to back up de Gaulle's demands. By late May violence had broken out, including the shelling of Damascus and other communities in Syria.

The United States cabled a protest to the de Gaulle government asking that in dealing with the Levant states they be treated as fully sovereign and independent members of the family of nations. President Shukri el Quwatli of Syria made a strong appeal to me for help, saying French bombs had been dropped on unarmed cities because, he said, "we refused to grant special privileges to France."

In trying to restore French colonial interests in the Levant, de Gaulle had come up against a hornets' nest and did not know how to get out of it without losing face. Once de Gaulle got involved, the question of prestige kept him there until he was forced out.

Secretary Stettinius at San Francisco advised me that the Levant situation was threatening to disrupt the San Francisco conference because of the anger of the representatives of the Arab countries and most of the other small countries who were united in opposition to the French tactics. The small countries, Stettinius said, saw the affair as a preview of what might happen if the veto power were granted to the five major countries. The representatives of the small states felt that if the United Nations were now functioning and France had the veto power she could stop any action on behalf of independent Syria and Lebanon.

Prime Minister Churchill cabled me on May 30 that severe fighting threatened the security of the whole Middle East and our communications for the war against Japan. The British Prime Minister asked my approval for the British to intervene with troops in order to stop the fighting and restore order. I cabled Churchill that his proposed plan for action to end the conflict had my approval.

The British government then instructed its commanding officer in the Middle East, General Sir Bernard Paget, to restore order. General Paget asked the French commander to issue a cease-fire order, and the French commander gave the order to end the fighting.

On June 2 the State Department received a note dated June 1 from Soviet Russia on the Levant situation. The Russian note must have been written before the Russians had received the State Department messages to Moscow outlining the American position. On this occasion the Soviet position seems to have paralleled the American and came at a time when Churchill and I had already agreed on a course of action to curb de Gaulle. Order returned to the two countries when the British guaranteed the governments of Syria and Lebanon against the new pressures from the French, and in a matter of weeks our Minister in Damascus reported that withdrawal of all foreign troops was recommended.

We had another explosive situation on our hands that could become serious, and that was in the Trieste area. This was brought on by the nationalistic ambitions of the partisan leader, Tito. Allied and Russian support had enabled Tito to campaign successfully against the Germans and to establish himself as the head of the Yugoslav National Provisional Government. Tito was a Communist, but he combined with his communism an appeal to the ardent nationalism of the Yugoslav peoples. In the name of Yugoslav nationalism he was laying claim to the important seaport of Trieste and the surrounding area of Venezia Giulia.

In this area populations and language groups are intermingled. The city of Trieste is overwhelmingly Italian in population, while the surrounding countryside is inhabited primarily by Slovenes, one of the nationalities that compose Yugoslavia. Slovene and Croat settlements are also to be found in the border sections of the Austrian provinces of Styria and Carinthia, and Tito was moving troops into these sections with the idea of obtaining them for Yugoslavia.

Trieste was particularly important because it is a major port forming an outlet into the Adriatic for the entire surrounding region, as well as for landlocked Austria and other portions of the Danube River basin.

The Allied plan called for all these contested areas to be occupied by forces under Field Marshal Alexander's command. The Allied forces at the time were driving into north Italy and would shortly have to spread out in order to seize such important centers as Milan and Turin.

On April 27 Churchill cabled me, saying:

"The plan for the Anglo-American occupation of Venezia Giulia has been hanging fire in Washington for a considerable time, with the result that Field Marshal Alexander is still without orders. I should therefore be most grateful if you would give your personal attention to this. . . . It seems to me vital to get Trieste if we can do so in the easy manner proposed, and to run the risks inherent in these kinds of political-military operations. . . . The great thing is to be there before Tito's guerillas are in occupation. Therefore it does not seem to me there is a minute to lose. The actual status of Trieste can be determined at leisure. Possession is nine points of the law. I beg you for an early decision."

I consulted with the Joint Chiefs of Staff and wired Churchill that "the Combined Chiefs of Staff with my approval authorized Alexander to accomplish what I understand to be your idea regarding Trieste and other areas formerly under Italian rule as a matter of military necessity."

Alexander was instructed to establish Allied military government in Venezia Giulia and in the areas to the north which, until 1919, had been Austrian territory. He was told that the successful working out of the plan depended on Soviet co-operation and that the United States and Britain were considering the best method of seeking such co-operation and subsequent Yugoslav agreement to the plan, but that in the meantime he should carry out the plan if military necessity "so requires even before Soviet and Yugoslav agreements have been obtained."

On April 30 I received Churchill's comment on the instruction cabled to Alexander.

"The military part," he said, "seems to me very good; but it is surely a delusion to suppose the Yugoslav government, with the Soviet government behind them, would agree to our entering or taking control of Venezia Giulia including Fiume, etc. They will undoubtedly try to overrun all this territory and will claim and occupy the ports of Trieste, Pola and Fiume, and once they get there I do not think they will go. No one is more keen than I to play absolutely fair with the Soviet on matters of the surrender of the German armies. . . . On the other hand we have never undertaken to be limited in our advances to clear Italy, including these Adriatic Provinces, of the Germans by the approval either of the Yugoslavs or of the Russians, nor to report to them the military movements our commanders think it right to make. . . . We are as much en-

titled to move freely into Trieste, if we can get there, as were the Russians
to win their way into Vienna. We ought if possible to get there first and
then talk about the rest of the Province. After all the basic principle on
which we have been working is that territorial changes must be left for
the peace or armistice settlement.

"I therefore hope that Alexander will be left to carry out the plan,
which the Chiefs of the Combined Staffs have approved, as quickly and
as secretly as possible and that above all we shall try to take possession
of Trieste from the sea before informing the Russians or Yugoslavs,
assuming of course that the Supreme Commander considers that it can
be successfully accomplished with the amphibious and other forces at
his disposal. . . ."

I thought it necessary and appropriate at this point to make our position clear to Churchill. I cabled him that same day, April 30, as follows:

"It seems to me that Field Marshal Alexander has all the guidance he
needs from the Combined Chiefs of Staff. I agree that in the operational
phase when he is endeavoring to establish his lines of communication to
Austria and to establish his control over Trieste and Pola, there is no
need for obtaining prior Russian consent. I note that before his task
force enters Venezia Giulia Alexander will inform Marshal Tito of his
intentions and explain to Tito that if any of his forces remain in that area
they must necessarily come under Alexander's command. Alexander is
directed to communicate with the Combined Chiefs of Staff before taking
further action in the area in question if the Yugoslav forces there fail to
cooperate. I think this is important for I wish to avoid having American
forces used to fight Yugoslavs or being used in combat in the Balkan
political arena."

I was trying to be extremely careful not to get us mixed up in a Balkan
turmoil. The Balkans had long been a source of trouble and war. I believed that if the political situation in the Balkans could be adjusted so
that Hungary, Yugoslavia, Rumania, and Bulgaria, as well as Poland and
Austria, could all have governments of their own people's choosing, with
no outside interference, this would help us in our plans for peace.

I did not want to become involved in the Balkans in a way that could
lead us into another world conflict. In any case, I was anxious to get the
Russians into the war against Japan as soon as possible, thus saving the
lives of countless Americans.

Churchill, on the other hand, was always anxious to do what he could
to save British control of the eastern Mediterranean area in order to
maintain Great Britain's influence in Greece, Egypt, and the Middle East.
I could not blame Churchill for the position he took. Had I been in his
place, I might probably have been inclined to do as he wanted to do.

General Marshall and I, in discussing each military phase, agreed that if we were to win the peace after winning the war, we had to have Russian help. I was trying to get Churchill in a frame of mind to forget the old power politics and get a United Nations organization to work.

It had long been evident that the northern frontiers of Italy would be in dispute. In September 1944, at the Quebec conference, President Roosevelt had approved a plan that would leave the final disposition of disputed areas on Italy's borders to a final peace settlement. Meanwhile, however, Allied military government was to be established in Italy with her 1939 frontiers under Allied control, and it was on this basis that the directive of April 20 had been sent to Field Marshal Alexander to maintain Allied and military government in areas along the Italian northern frontier likely to be disputed, including Venezia Giulia.

Alexander had discussed the Allied occupation plans with Tito in Belgrade in February 1945. Tito had accepted this plan, which provided that local authorities, whatever their nationalities, would come under the Allied military government. Russia had been informed of the British-American position on Venezia Giulia on March 19. The Russians had not dissented. Now, however, Tito claimed that because conditions had changed since the time he made the agreement with Alexander he would no longer observe it. He informed Alexander that he intended to occupy Venezia Giulia up to the Austrian border, but that he would allow the Allies the use of the port of Trieste and of the railway to Austria. But when Alexander's troops reached the cities of Trieste, Monfalcone, and Gorizia, they found that Tito's forces were ahead of them and that Tito was continuing to pour Yugoslav troops into the entire area east of the Isonzo River. Furthermore, he persisted in his claim that this area was his exclusive operational theater. His forces were also setting up the administration of the area, and Alexander's forces were unable to establish an Allied military government, even in the portion of the three cities they had entered. And finally, the formation of a Slovene government at Trieste was actually announced.

The Italian government became increasingly alarmed, fearing that Tito's action would play into the hands of subversive groups in Italy. On May 7 our Ambassador in Rome, Alexander Kirk, reported that east of the Isonzo River a Yugoslav military government was in full control. All public buildings had been occupied and Yugoslav flags were flying over them. Italian names of towns had even been replaced by Yugoslav names. A large number of persons, including the Italian Archbishop of Gorizia, had been arrested and removed.

Two days later Ambassador Kirk reported growing tension in Italy, and Premier Bonomi complained that the Italian Communists were claiming Tito's action had the approval of the Allies. The American government never for a moment considered that Trieste should go to Yugoslavia. That was Roosevelt's position, and it was mine. Tito was now plainly determined to use force to gain his territorial objective instead of waiting for a peace conference to settle all boundary claims. I therefore called the Chiefs of Staff and representatives of the State Department to a special conference at the White House. I then cabled Churchill on May 11 and issued a directive to the Joint Chiefs of Staff. The cable to Churchill follows:

"Since sending you my telegram of April 30 I have become increasingly concerned over the implication of Tito's actions in Venezia Giulia. You are no doubt receiving the same reports which indicate that he has no intention of abandoning the territory or of permitting a peaceful solution of this century old problem as part of a general pacific postwar settlement. I have come to the conclusion that we must decide now whether we should uphold the fundamental principles of territorial settlement by orderly process against force, intimidation or blackmail. It seems that Tito has an identical claim ready for South Austria, in Carinthia and Styria and may have similar designs on parts of Hungary and Greece if his methods in Venezia Giulia succeed. Although the stability of Italy and the future orientation of that country with respect to Russia may well be at stake the present issue, as I see it, is not a question of taking sides in a dispute between Italy and Yugoslavia or of becoming involved in internal Balkan politics. The problem is essentially one of deciding whether our two countries are going to permit our Allies to engage in uncontrolled land-grabbing or tactics which are all too reminiscent of those of Hitler and Japan. Yugoslav occupation of Trieste, the key to that area and a vital outlet for large areas of central Europe, would, as I know you will agree, have more far-reaching consequences than the immediate territory involved. . . . I suggest we instruct our ambassadors at Belgrade to inform Tito along these lines: that Venezia Giulia is only one of the many territorial problems in Europe to be solved in the general peace settlement. The doctrine of solution by conquest and by unilateral proclamation of sovereignty through occupation, the method used by the enemy with such tragic consequences, has been definitely and solemnly repudiated by the Allied Governments participating in this war. . . . The plan of Allied military government for Venezia Giulia was adopted precisely to achieve a peaceful and lasting solution of a problem of admitted complexities. It is designed to safeguard the interests of the peoples involved. . . . With these considerations in mind, and in view of the previous general agreement of the Yugoslav Government to the plans proposed for this region, my Government has instructed me to inform you that it expects that the Yugoslav Government will immediately agree to the control by the Supreme Allied Commander in the Mediterranean of the region which must include Trieste, Gorizia, Monfalcone and Fola, and issue appropriate instructions to the Yugoslav forces in the region in question to cooperate with the Allied commanders in the establishment of military government in that area under the authority of the Allied commander. . . ."

On May 12 Churchill replied:

"I agree with every word you say, and will work with all my strength on the line you propose. . . . If it is handled firmly before our strength is dispersed Europe may be saved from another blood-bath. Otherwise the whole fruits of our victory may be cast away and none of the purposes of World Organisation to prevent territorial aggression and future wars will be attained. . . ."

Churchill agreed to have the British Ambassador join ours in the representation to Tito, but he made a plea for a standstill order on the withdrawal of American troops from Europe. He wanted me to commit myself to the maintenance under Alexander's command of the same number of American divisions he then had.

I could not make any such commitments. Victory over Japan would require the transfer of troops from Europe to the Pacific, and this movement had already been started. There was also strong pressure building up throughout our country to "bring the boys back home." The American people wanted nothing more at that moment than to end the war. I cabled Churchill that I could not consider a standstill order unless further developments should make it necessary. "Unless Tito's forces should attack," I wrote, "it is impossible for me to involve this country in another war."

Churchill, in his reply, said, "I quite understand your wishing to wait further developments before deciding on such serious steps and that we should await the result of our message to Tito. I am not quite clear about your sentence 'unless Tito's forces should attack, it is impossible, etc.' I thought, from your number 34, that if he were recalcitrant, we should have to push his infiltrations east of the line *you* have prescribed. I presume his prolonged intrusion into these regions would, if persisted in, constitute 'an attack.' I believe myself he will give in and conform to our wishes, especially when he realizes we are in deadly earnest. Anyhow I agree we must wait until he replies."

On the following day, May 13, Churchill cabled again, proposing that I join him in a message to Stalin with regard to the Trieste situation. I agreed, and in a joint message we set out in full the background of the controversy and informed Stalin of the sharp note that had been sent to Belgrade. On May 16 I cabled Churchill again as follows:

"I am pleased with your agreement that we should await results of our messages to Tito before deciding upon further action.

"To clarify understanding of my message beginning, QUOTE: Unless Tito should attack, it is impossible, etc., UNQUOTE, it means definitely that I am unable and unwilling to involve this country in a war with the Yugoslavs unless they should attack us, in which case we would be justified in using our Allied forces to throw them back to a distance that would preclude further attack on our troops."

Churchill replied on May 19, saying that in view of the completely negative response to our note by Tito he thought such action as Alexander might have to take could not be considered a war with Yugoslavia. He did not think we should wait on a clear-cut act of aggression before taking action because it might be possible for Yugoslav units so to isolate Allied elements that they would be completely helpless.

"There should be no question," I answered, "about our commanders taking essential precautions to prevent their forces from being placed in an untenable position. However, I think we should make very clear to our leaders that this should be done with maximum precautions to insure that the overt act, if any, comes from Tito's forces."

I then suggested new instructions to be sent to Eisenhower and Alexander to reinforce the front-line troops in and around Trieste. I again emphasized that "I must not have any avoidable interference with the redeployment of American forces to the Pacific."

The Yugoslavs continued to push their occupation attempts. On May 17 Field Marshal Alexander sent a message to General Eisenhower saying that the situation had seriously deteriorated and that the Yugoslav activities could not be controlled without the use of force.

Several days before, I had called in the Chiefs of Staff. I wanted to know what forces were available in the immediate area in case it became necessary for us to make a show of strength. I believed that all that it was necessary for us to do to impress Tito was to show such overpowering strength that he would back down before undertaking anything foolhardy. Through General Marshall I asked General Eisenhower if he could send three divisions to the Brenner Pass or above Trieste. I asked Admiral King whether he could send some units of the Mediterranean fleet to the Adriatic and how long it would take to get there. I told him to alert the necessary ships. I asked Arnold what air squadrons he could move, and I asked him to alert them.

General Marshall reported that Eisenhower was prepared to dispatch General Patton with up to five armored divisions to the Brenner Pass and, if necessary, into Italy. Admiral King reported that units of the Mediterranean fleet had been alerted to steam into the Adriatic, and General

Arnold told me that several Air Force squadrons were ready to move at a moment's notice.

Once again I addressed myself to Stalin. "Through the Embassy in Moscow," I cabled him on May 20, "I have been keeping you informed of the American position on the interim administration of the Venezia Giulia. In particular your Government was given copies of the recent American and British notes to Marshal Tito which proposed, in accordance with the previous understanding reached in February between Field Marshal Alexander and Marshal Tito, that the Supreme Allied Commander should exercise control in an area including Trieste, Monfalcone, Gorizia and Pola in order not to prejudice any final disposition through occupation by either claimant. We have now had a reply from Marshal Tito which is entirely unsatisfactory in that he states that his government is not prepared 'to renounce the right of the Yugoslav Army holding the territory up to the Isonzo River.' As regards the administration of the area he offers a solution which cannot be reconciled with the principles we have enunciated. Meanwhile the proximity of Alexander's and Tito's troops in undefined areas of occupation and the dual nature of control thus created are fraught with danger. . . . We cannot consider this simply in the light of an Italian-Yugoslav boundary dispute but must regard it as a question of principle involving the pacific settlement of territorial disputes and the foundation of a lasting peace in Europe. We will not now or in the future take or permit any action in respect to this territory which does not fully take into account legitimate Yugoslav claims and the contribution which Yugoslav forces made to the victory over Germany won at such great cost to us all. We cannot however accept any compromise upon the principles of an orderly and just settlement and are so informing Marshal Tito.

"I know you will agree that we must stand firm on the issue of principle and I hope that we can count on your influence also to assist in bringing about the provisional settlement outlined in our recent note to Marshal Tito. After Field Marshal Alexander has extended his authority in the Venezia Giulia east of the line indicated in our note and tranquility has thus been restored, we could then continue in the spirit of our Yalta understandings looking towards further adjustments of the problem."

I notified Churchill of this move, and he replied that he would send a similar message to Stalin. He said: "Our firm attitude will be of value in our discussions with Stalin. It seems to me that the need for our triple meeting at the earliest possible moment is very great."

I answered Churchill that I would be able, in another week or so, to advise him when and where I might be able to attend such a high-level meeting. I thanked him for the British support of my message to Stalin, adding that "I indulge in a hope that U.J. will use his influence to assist in reaching a settlement of the Tito problem in Venezia Giulia."

Stalin's answer to my message came on May 23. It disappointed me. The Russian Premier backed Tito in his claims and hoped that the conflict would be terminated *by our acceptance of the Yugoslav position.* Stalin wrote:

"I have received on May 21 your message on the question of Istria-Trieste. Somewhat earlier I have also received from you, through Mr. Kennan, the text of the message transmitted by the American Ambassador in Belgrade to the Yugoslav Government on the same question. Thank you for this information.

"In regard to the essence of the question I have to say the following:

"Your opinion, that this question is of principle and that in respect to the territory of Istria-Trieste no action should be allowed which will not fully consider the lawful claims of Yugoslavia and the contribution made by the Yugoslav armed forces to the common cause of the Allies in the struggle against Hitlerite Germany, seems to be quite correct. It goes without saying that the future of this territory, the majority of whose population is Yugoslavian, should be determined during the peace adjustment. However, at the present time the question under consideration is the temporary military occupation of this territory. In this respect it is necessary, in my opinion, to take into consideration the fact that it is the Allied Yugoslav troops who have driven the German invaders from the territory of Istria-Trieste, thereby rendering an important service to the common cause of the Allies. By virtue of this circumstance only it would not be fair and would be an undeserved insult for the Yugoslav Army and the Yugoslav people to refuse Yugoslavia the right to occupy the territory retaken from the enemy after the Yugoslav people has made so many sacrifices in the struggle for the national rights of Yugoslavia and for the common cause of the United Nations. It seems to me that the correct solution of this question is the one which would provide that the Yugoslav troops remain in the region of Istria-Trieste as well as the Yugoslav administration functioning at the present time in this region. At the same time in this region be established a control of the Allied Supreme Commander, and, on mutual agreement between Field Marshal Alexander and Marshal Tito, a demarcation line be drawn. By accepting these proposals the question of administration in the region of Istria-Trieste would also receive a correct solution.

"As the Yugoslav population is in majority on this territory and already in the period of German occupation a local Yugoslav administration was being formed, which at the present time enjoys the confidence of the local population, the present situation should be taken into consideration. By subordinating the already existing Yugoslavian civilian administration in this region to the Yugoslav military command the question of administrative direction of this territory would be appropriately regulated.

"I would like to hope that the misunderstanding regarding the situation of the region Istria-Trieste, arisen among the Governments of the United States and Great Britain on the one hand and the Yugoslav Government on the other, will be eliminated and the whole matter will be favorably settled."

Field Marshal Alexander showed a great deal of patience throughout the crisis. But on the one occasion when he spoke his mind, he compared Tito to Hitler and Mussolini. The Yugoslavs and the Russians alike raised storms of indignant protest over this incident.

Later in May, Tito advised us that he would agree to Allied control of Trieste and Venezia Giulia if Yugoslav military units could remain in the Allied occupied area, if Yugoslav representatives could participate in Allied military government, and if our military administration would act through the civil authorties Tito had already set up in the area. This counterproposal was unworkable, as well as unacceptable from a military standpoint to Field Marshal Alexander, but it kept the door open to further negotiations. That was what I wanted, and talks continued despite irritating local incidents. Then on May 29 Dr. Ivan Subašić, the Yugoslav Foreign Minister, called on me, accompanied by the Yugoslav Ambassador. Dr. Subašić had been at the San Francisco conference and was on his way back to Belgrade. He was a leader in the Croatian Peasant party, had been Prime Minister in the government-in-exile, and now represented the fusion element in the new Tito government. He made a fine impression on me. I talked very plainly to him and to the Ambassador. The Allies, I told them, intended to extend an impartial military administration to some of the disputed territory of Venezia Giulia without prejudice to the final disposition of the area, and we expected the Yugoslav government to co-operate, as a member of the United Nations. Tito, I pointed out, had already violated the Yalta agreement by setting up a totalitarian regime and was now trying to extend it to Venezia Giulia by force. If Tito persisted in this, we would meet him with overwhelming force, and the time had come for a decision. I let Dr. Subašić know that we now had completed a draft agreement and would soon present it to Tito, expecting him to co-operate without further obstructionist tactics.

On June 9 an agreement was finally signed making two military occupation zones out of Venezia Giulia. The western zone, known as Zone A and including the city of Trieste, was placed under Anglo-American occupation, and the eastern zone, known as Zone B, was to be under Yugoslav occupation. The line of demarcation had been worked out by General Sir Frederick Morgan, Alexander's chief of staff, in agreement with the Yugoslavs, and this line became known as the Morgan Line. Yugoslav troops were to be withdrawn to their own zone, and the Allied commander was to decide on the use of all civil authorities in our zone. Both zones were to be considered as temporary occupation areas and as not affecting the ultimate territorial settlement.

Getting supplementary agreement needed to implement military and technical details of this agreement met with further difficulties.

Now, on June 21, Stalin took up Tito's case.

"The tone," he said, "of the ultimatum of the declaration which was presented to the Yugoslav Government by Anglo-American representatives on June 2, was . . . unexpected for the Soviet Government. How is it possible to believe that such methods will provide strong positive results? . . . I, as before, hope that in respect to Trieste-Istria the just Yugoslav interests will be satisfied."

I cabled Stalin on June 25, explaining the course of the negotiations in detail and assuring him that any still unexplained questions could be discussed at our forthcoming meeting. Trieste was one of many problems that would have to be taken up at this meeting. Throughout May and June many difficulties developed between the Russians and ourselves and the British. At Yalta, President Roosevelt had agreed to a policy for the re-establishment of free governments for the liberated countries of Europe under inter-Allied supervision. But in Bulgaria and Rumania, with the advancing Soviet armies, Communist governments were imposed by the Russian military commanders.

I received a firsthand report of conditions in these two countries on May 2, when Acting Secretary of State Grew brought our representatives on the two respective Allied Control Commissions to my office. They were Brigadier General Cortlandt Van Rensselaer Schuyler and Major General John A. Crane.

In Rumania, General Schuyler informed me, the Russians were running the Allied Control Commission without consulting the British and American members. The government was a minority government dominated by the Communist party, which, the general estimated, represented less than ten per cent of the Rumanian population. The vast majority of the Rumanian people, he said, did not want either the government they had or any other form of communism. The Communist party, however, was using every means possible to gain full control of the governmental machinery, and the opposition groups under young King Michael and the leaders of the majority parties were becoming ineffectual.

Economically Rumania was being tied closely to the Russian state—through reparations payments, through the transfer of property said by the Russians to have been German-owned, and through the surrender of industrial equipment as "war trophies." Furthermore, Rumania was being kept almost entirely cut off from trade relations with other nations, and this made her increasingly dependent on Russia for exports and imports alike.

In Bulgaria, General Crane reported, the situation was as bad. The American representatives there were treated almost as if they were captives. No American was allowed outside the capital city of Sofia without a Russian going with him, and usually such escorts could not be found unless the American was of the highest rank. Every ounce of supplies or mail brought in for the American mission required Russian permission and was subject to Russian inspection on arrival. As far as the Allied Control Commission was concerned, the American member was not only without a voice but was unable even to get copies of the directives that were being issued in the name of the Commission of which he was a member.

Since September 1944, when the Russians had entered the country, the government of Bulgaria had been totally dominated by the Communists, who had gained complete control of the police and of the Army and had succeeded in suppressing all opposition sentiment in the press by labeling it "Fascist."

From Churchill I learned that the representatives of the British had painted a similar, disturbing picture to him. On the other hand, Winston Churchill himself revealed that in October 1944 he had proposed to Stalin that Rumania and Bulgaria be considered as lying within the Russian sphere of influence, and Russian dominance in these two countries had thus been recognized.

On the basis of this information I instructed the State Department to remind the Russian government of its obligation under the Yalta agreement and to ask that restrictions of movement on American representatives of the Allied Control Commissions be removed.

In Poland the situation was different. Negotiations there were still going on about the composition of the provisional government. I considered it essential that agreement be reached on the Polish provisional government before we could grant diplomatic recognition to Poland and agree to her appearance at the San Francisco conference. On May 4 I cabled Stalin:

"Replying to your message of 24 April, Prime Minister Churchill has sent me a copy of his message to you of April 28. Since you are aware of the position of the United States Government from the messages you have received from President Roosevelt and myself, I need hardly tell you that in regard to the reorganization of the Polish Government I agree with the views Mr. Churchill has expressed in his message of April 28. This government still considers that the Crimea decisions constitute a fair basis for the settlement of the Polish question and should be carried out.

"The meetings of the three foreign secretaries on the Polish matter have not yet produced a formula which is satisfactory. I consider it of the utmost importance that a satisfactory solution of the problem be worked out as soon as possible. I must tell you that any suggestion that the representatives of the Warsaw Provisional Government be invited to San Francisco, conditionally or otherwise, is wholly unacceptable to the United States Government. To do so would be the acceptance by the United States Government of the present Warsaw Provisional Government as representative of Poland which would be tantamount to the abandonment of the Yalta agreement."

Stalin's reply to Churchill's message, which I had endorsed, came on May 6.

"Unless," he wrote, "the provisional government which is now functioning in Poland and which enjoys the support and confidence of the majority of the Polish people is taken as the foundation of the future government of national unity, there is no possibility of envisaging a successful solution of the problem set before us by the Crimea Conference."

Because Poland occupied a "peculiar position" as a neighbor of Russia, Stalin argued that the Soviet Union was entitled to insist that the future government should be made up of men who would be actively promoting friendly relations between the two countries. It was not enough, he said, to exclude only those "extremely unfriendly toward Russia," as Churchill had suggested.

"We insist and shall insist," Stalin continued, "that there should be brought into consultation on the formation of the future Polish government only those persons who have actively shown a friendly attitude toward the Soviet Union and who are honestly and sincerely prepared to cooperate with the Soviet State."

He concluded with the statement that the Anglo-American position was so plainly contrary to his that agreement on the issue seemed impossible.

Churchill's reaction was that nothing could be accomplished by further correspondence and that as soon as possible there should be a meeting of the three heads of government.

In my reply I informed Churchill that I would welcome an opportunity to meet with him and Stalin. But I wanted the initiative to come from

Stalin and I told the Prime Minister that it would not be convenient for me to leave Washington before the end of the fiscal year.

Churchill replied on May 11:

"I think we should offer an invitation jointly or severally at the same moment to Stalin to meet us at some agreed unshattered town in Germany for a tripartite meeting in July. We should not rendezvous at any place within the present Russian military zone. . . . I do not know at the moment when our general election will be, but I do not see any reason why it should influence your movements or mine where public duty calls. If you will entertain the idea of coming over here in the early days of July, His Majesty will send you the most cordial invitation and you will have a great reception from the British nation. . . . I should of course bring with me representatives of both parties in our state and both would use exactly the same language about foreign affairs as we are closely agreed. Therefore I urge your coming here in the earliest days of July and that we leave together to meet U.J. at wherever is the best point outside Russian-occupied territory to which he can be induced to come. Meanwhile I earnestly hope that the American front will not recede from the now agreed tactical lines.

"I doubt very much whether any enticements will get a proposal for a tripartite meeting out of Stalin. But I think he would respond to an invitation. If not, what are we to do?

"I rejoice that your present intention is to adhere to our rightful interpretation of the Yalta agreements and to stand firmly on our present announced attitude towards all the questions at issue.

"Mr. President, in these next two months the gravest matters in the world will be decided. May I add that I have derived a great feeling of confidence from the correspondence we have interchanged. . . ."

On May 12 I replied to Churchill:

"I would much prefer to have Stalin propose the meeting and believe it is worth while to endeavor, through our Ambassadors, to induce him to propose the meeting. If such an effort fails, we can then consider our issuing an invitation jointly or severally.

"When and if such a meeting is arranged, it appears to me that in order to avoid any suspicion of our 'ganging up' it would be advantageous for us to proceed to the meeting place separately.

"When the conference ends, if my duties here do not make it impossible, I shall be very pleased to make a visit to England where you and I may discuss fully our common interests and problems.

"I am fully in agreement that the next few months will decide questions of the greatest consequence to the whole world."

CHAPTER 17

It was inevitable that Roosevelt's death would raise questions about the working relationship between the heads of government of Great Britain, Russia, and the United States. In a number of conferences and frequent meetings, a personal knowledge and estimate of each other had grown up between Roosevelt and Churchill and among Roosevelt, Churchill, and Stalin. It was natural that a new relationship would have to be established by me and that I would have to meet with Churchill and Stalin. But it was impossible for such a meeting to take place while I was under an enormous burden of work involving so many critical decisions. Apart from that, I wanted to be fully informed about the attitudes of Churchill and Stalin and what changes the death of Roosevelt may have made in their outlook. At the same time I wanted to get word to Churchill and Stalin through a trusted representative of Roosevelt that there had been no change in the basic policies of the United States.

On May 4 I saw Hopkins again, for the first time since our return from Hyde Park and the graveside of President Roosevelt.

While on the journey to and from Hyde Park, Hopkins and I had continued our talks about Russia. I suggested to Hopkins the possibility of his going on a personal mission for me to Stalin. I inquired about his health, asking whether he thought he would be strong enough to undertake the journey. Hopkins at that time said he would have to talk to his doctor and said, "Why don't you send Harriman back on a special mission since he is already our Ambassador there?" I had seen Harriman several times between my talks with Hopkins. Harriman suggested that

I send Hopkins to Moscow because Hopkins was a link between Roosevelt and Stalin. Since Hopkins had raised the question with me of his health, I told Harriman that I was thinking of him to take a special message to Stalin. Harriman replied that he thought that because Hopkins was very close to Roosevelt he would be in a better position to impress on Stalin that we intended to carry out the Roosevelt policies.

Now, as I shook hands with Hopkins, I saw that he was still a sick man. But Hopkins was a man of courage, and since I was disturbed at the trend of Russian developments, especially since my meeting with Molotov, I presumed again to raise the subject of his undertaking a mission to Stalin.

Hopkins said he understood the urgency of the situation and that he was prepared to go. He asked me when Harriman was planning to return to Moscow. I told him I expected Harriman to return to Washington from San Francisco within a week, when I would talk over with him the Russian situation and his returning to his post. I asked Hopkins to see me the following day for further discussion of the mission. I also asked him to study with the State Department all the latest Russian developments.

This gave me the opportunity of sounding out Cordell Hull, Jimmy Byrnes, and others not only about this particular mission by Hopkins to Moscow but about sending the former U.S. Ambassador to Russia, Joseph E. Davies, on a special mission to London.

The State Department opposed the idea of sending Hopkins and so did Byrnes. Cordell Hull told me Hopkins was an excellent choice for the mission.

On May 19 Hopkins came to the White House for final instructions. I had telegraphed Stalin that day as follows:

"I am sure you are as aware as I am of the difficulty of dealing by exchange of messages with the complicated and important questions with which we are faced. Pending the possibility of our meeting I am therefore sending Mr. Harry Hopkins with Ambassador Harriman to Moscow in order that they may have an opportunity of discussing personally with you these matters. Following these talks Mr. Hopkins will return immediately to Washington in order to report personally to me. They plan to arrive in Moscow about May 26. I would appreciate your letting me know if this time is convenient for you."

I asked Hopkins to tell Stalin that I was anxious to have a fair understanding with the Russian government, that we never made commitments which we did not expect to carry out to the letter, and that we expected Stalin to carry out his agreements. I made it plain to Hopkins that in talking to Stalin he was free to use diplomatic language or a baseball bat if he thought that was the proper approach. I further instructed him to tell Stalin that I would be glad to see him personally and that I thought it was now his turn to come to the United States, as our President had been to Russia.

The following evening I saw Joseph E. Davies and told him that our plans were now definite to send Hopkins to Moscow and that therefore I wanted Davies himself to go to London. I said that Hopkins would arrive in Moscow on May 26, and I asked Davies to arrange to be in London at the same time.

Two days later, on May 21, I received the following message from Stalin:

"I have received your message regarding the arrival of Mr. Hopkins and Ambassador Harriman in Moscow by May 26. I readily accept your proposal to meet Mr. Hopkins and Ambassador Harriman. The date—May 26 is quite convenient for me."

On May 22 I replied to Stalin:

"I was most pleased to receive your wire in regard to Mr. Hopkins' visit. I feel that it is wiser that I make an announcement of his proposed visit to Moscow following his departure from the United States rather than risk having it leak out and become the subject of speculation in the press. Mr. Hopkins plans to leave tomorrow morning, May 23, and later in the day I propose to announce to the press that he is proceeding to Moscow with Ambassador Harriman to talk over with you matters now in discussion between the Soviet and the United States Government."

The same day I cabled Churchill:

"I am asking Mr. Joseph E. Davies to come to see you prior to the pending conference between you, Marshal Stalin and myself. There are a number of matters that I want him to explore with you which I would prefer not to handle by cable. Mr. Davies will be in London probably the 25th. I would appreciate it if you could see him at your convenience."

Churchill replied:

"I shall be delighted to see Mr. Davies as soon as he arrives."

On May 23 I made public the news of the special missions of Hopkins to Moscow and Davies to London.

I had asked Ambassador Harriman, who was to accompany Hopkins, to proceed in advance to London and see Churchill. I thought it best to have Harriman fill Churchill in on the nature of the Hopkins mission. Harriman dined privately with the British Prime Minister on May 22. The next day Churchill ended the wartime coalition and formed a new interim government. This meant a general election would soon be held.

Harriman cabled me on May 23 from Paris, where he was to be joined by Hopkins, and reported that Churchill was pleased that Hopkins was going to Moscow. Harriman said the resignation of his government and the coming election were much in Churchill's mind. The Prime Minister, he said, was gravely concerned over the developments with Russia and felt that it was of the utmost importance to go through firmly with the situation in Venezia Giulia. He believed, however, that issues such as Poland could not be settled until "you and he" met with Stalin. Churchill asked Harriman to assure me that he would not take any position in regard to Russia which did not have our full support and that "he is ready to come and meet you anywhere at any time you are prepared to see him."

Ambassador Davies held his private talks with Prime Minister Churchill from May 26 to May 29 at Chequers and at No. 10 Downing Street. Davies did not cable me any details of his meetings with the British Prime Minister, preferring to report to me in person. However, on May 31 I had a cable from Churchill referring to his talks with Davies, but raising a puzzling question.

Churchill said that he was hoping I would soon be able to let him know the date "of the meeting of 'the three.'" The Prime Minister said his talks with Davies were agreeable, as he would report to me on his return. Then Churchill made the surprising statement that he would not be prepared to attend a meeting which was a continuation of a conference between myself and Stalin and that "the three" should meet simultaneously and on equal terms.

I had at no time proposed seeing Stalin alone at any separate conference. What I was anxious to do was to get Stalin and Churchill and myself at the same table and maintain the unity we had during the war. Unity was even more necessary to keep the peace. I had even rejected the idea of meeting Churchill alone. Churchill intimated through regular channels that he would like to see me before we had a meeting with Stalin. He considered coming over to Washington and the two of us going back together. In my judgment that would have been a serious mistake at a time when we were trying to settle things with Stalin. Stalin was always fearful that the British and ourselves would gang up on him. We did not want that. We wanted world peace, and we needed the three powers working together to get it. Of course, since I was not personally acquainted with either Stalin or Churchill, I had intended that when we arrived at our meeting place I would have an opportunity to see each separately. In this way I would become better acquainted with them and be able to size them up, and they too would get a chance to size me up.

I intended to wait to see if Davies could shed more light on this cable of Churchill's. On June 5 Davies came to report to me. I asked Acting Secretary of State Grew, Admiral Leahy, and Justice Byrnes to join us on this occasion.

Davies made his report orally, then submitted it in writing. He had represented my position and the policy of the United States with accuracy, carrying out instructions with exceptional skill.

Davies told me that he had talked with the Prime Minister alone for approximately eight hours. Their first talk had been at Chequers from eleven o'clock Saturday night until four-thirty Sunday morning. The talks were resumed in Churchill's bedroom Sunday morning at eleven o'clock (he sitting up in his bed) and lasted until one-thirty lunch, and were again resumed later in the afternoon and on the following Tuesday at No. 10 Downing Street.

Davies told Churchill that I was gravely concerned over the serious deterioration in the relations of the Soviets with both Britain and the United States and that I believed that without continued unity of the Big Three there could be no reasonable prospect of peace. Davies told the Prime Minister my position was that every agreement made by President Roosevelt would be scrupulously supported by me and that if there were differences of opinion as to what these agreements were I wanted them cleared up.

"It is the President's conviction," Davies said to Churchill, "that the paramount objective now must be to conserve peace after victory. He conceives it to be the duty of the three nations which won the war to leave honorably nothing undone in an effort to solve their differences, and through continued unity make possible a just and durable peace structure.

"The President has reason to believe that the situation is the more serious because of Soviet suspicion that Britain and the U.S., along with the United Nations, are now 'ganging up' on them. Such suspicion in fact is unjustified, and ought to be dispelled. That requires the establishment of confidence in the good faith and reliability of the parties, which comes only through frank discussions and the opportunity to know and estimate each other.

"On that score the President is at a disadvantage in contrast to that which the Prime Minister and Marshal Stalin enjoy. The Prime Minister and Mr. Eden both have had the benefit of frequent contacts and friendly association with Marshal Stalin and Commissar Molotov. It is the President's desire, therefore, in view of the responsibility which he must assume, to have a similar opportunity to know the Marshal and to have Marshal Stalin come to know him. . . .

"The President therefore," explained Davies, "desires an opportunity to meet the Marshal before the scheduled forthcoming meeting. He feels certain that the Prime Minister will appreciate the reasonableness of his position and facilitate such arrangement."

At this point I saw how the Prime Minister might have taken this suggestion to mean that I desired to have a preliminary meeting with Stalin first. I had no such idea in mind. What Davies was to convey was that before the meeting got formally under way I planned visits with Stalin, as well as with Churchill, on the spot and in private in order to get better acquainted with both of them personally.

I took immediate steps to clear this point up with Churchill, advising him of my intent to discuss no business with either him or Stalin separately.

Davies then proceeded to report on Churchill's analysis of the European situation. Davies said that he was struck by the bitterness of Churchill's tone as he discussed de Gaulle, Tito, and Stalin. Davies said, "Churchill elaborated at length and with great emphasis and emotion on the grave dangers which would arise with the withdrawal of American troops from Europe. It would be a 'terrible thing' if the American army were vacated from Europe. Europe would be prostrate and at the mercy of the Red Army and of communism."

At this point I interrupted Davies to say that I had no such thing in mind, that we would withdraw only the troops we could spare from Europe for our war in the Pacific. We were committed to the rehabilitation of Europe, and there was to be no abandonment this time.

Hopkins and Harriman saw Stalin and Molotov on May 26. Hopkins reported that Stalin was as anxious to meet with Churchill and me as we were to meet him. A number of important conferences followed, and talks continued until June 7. Hopkins sent me a daily report by cable, keeping me completely informed. This enabled me to take up with Churchill a number of problems affecting the three governments.

One of the first results of Hopkins' mission was to set the date and place for the meeting of Stalin, Churchill, and myself.

In his first report to me Hopkins cabled on May 27:

"We outlined at great length the gravity of the feeling in America and expressed as forcibly as we could the point of view that you wished us to convey. The importance of the Polish business was put on the line specifically. Stalin listened with the utmost attention to our description of the present state of American public opinion and gave us the impression that he also was disturbed at the drift of events. . . ."

The Russian dictator, Harriman later reported, showed that he did not fully understand the basis of the difficulties. He took the offensive in complaining "about our misdeeds and aggressively indicated that if we did not wish to deal on a friendly basis with the Soviet Union, she was strong enough to look after herself." Nevertheless, he was glad to see Hopkins and accepted unquestioningly the fact that I had sent him as an indication of my desire to work with the Russians.

On May 28 Hopkins informed me that Stalin told him he would meet me at any time I wished and that there would be adequate quarters for such a meeting in the suburbs of Berlin.

In reply I instructed Hopkins to inform Stalin that I perceived no objection to meeting in the Berlin area and that about the fifteenth of July appeared to be a practicable date for me. I so informed Churchill, who in reply once again pleaded for mid-June. Stalin, in turn, agreed to July 15. Churchill argued for early July, but at last the three of us agreed that the date would be July 15 and the place Babelsberg, a suburb of Potsdam.

"Hopkins did a first-rate job," Harriman said in a message to me, "in presenting your views to Stalin, and in explaining the most important matters—particularly Poland—which were causing us concern. I am afraid," Harriman continued, "that Stalin does not and never will fully understand our interest in a free Poland as a matter of principle. The Russian Premier is a realist in all of his actions, and it is hard for him to appreciate our faith in abstract principles. It is difficult for him to understand why we should want to interfere with Soviet policy in a country like Poland which he considers so important to Russia's security unless we have some ulterior motive. He does, however, appreciate that he must deal with the position we have taken. . . ."

Hopkins reported that Stalin was ready to talk business at once as to the names of the Poles both in London and in Poland proper who were not members of the Lublin government but who would be invited to Moscow to meet with the Polish Commission and consult about the organization of a temporary government for Poland. Hopkins therefore proposed a list of three Poles from London and five from within Poland, all of whom had previously been approved by the British and ourselves. Stalin indicated that he wanted three or four from the existing provisional government in Poland, but under no circumstances more than four. Hopkins thought that this tentative list was satisfactory and urged that I approve it. I did so in a telephone conversation with Hopkins on June 1.

In the meantime messages were going back and forth between Washington and London. We examined the list of names in detail. We tried to reconcile the position of the Polish government-in-exile, our own attitude, and Stalin's intentions. Finally an agreement was reached, and Hopkins, in his last meeting with Stalin on June 6, was able to bring this matter to a conclusion.

This did not settle the Polish problem. All that was accomplished was to break the deadlock between ourselves and the Russians over the Polish problem.

Before Hopkins left for Moscow, I had impressed upon him the need for getting as early a date as possible on Russia's entry into the war against Japan. Hopkins had been with Roosevelt at Yalta and knew of Russia's commitment there to move against Japan after the war in Europe was ended. On May 28 Hopkins and Harriman got from Stalin a very important declaration which Hopkins cabled me.

"Harriman and I saw Stalin and Molotov for the third time last night," Hopkins said. "Following are the important results:

"The Soviet Army will be properly deployed on the Manchurian positions by August 8th.

"Stalin repeated the statement he made at Yalta that the Russian people must have a good reason for going to war and that depended on the willingness of China to agree to the Yalta proposals.

"He stated for the first time that he was willing to take these proposals up directly with Soong when he comes to Moscow. He wants to see Soong not later than July first and expects us to take matter up at the same time with Chiang Kai-shek. Because of Stalin's statements about the Far East which follow, this procedure seems most desirable from our point of view.

"He left no doubt in our mind that he intends to attack during August. It is therefore important that Soong come here not later than July 1st. Stalin is ready to see him any time now.

"Stalin made categorical statement that he would do everything he could to promote unification of China under the leadership of Chiang Kai-shek. He further stated that this leadership should continue after the war because no one else was strong enough. He specifically stated no communist leader was strong enough to unify China. He proposes to back the Generalissimo in spite of the reservations he expressed about him.

"He repeated all of his statements made at Yalta, that he wanted a unified and stable China and wanted China to control all of Manchuria as part of a United China. He stated categorically that he had no territorial claims against China and mentioned specifically Manchuria and Sinkiang and that he would respect Chinese sovereignty in all areas his troops entered to fight the Japanese.

"Stalin stated that he would welcome representatives of the Generalissimo to be with his troops entering Manchuria in order to facilitate the organization of Chinese administration in Manchuria.

"Stalin agreed with America's 'open door' policy and went out of his way to indicate that the United States was the only power with the resources to aid China economically after the war. He observed that Russia would have all it could do to provide for the internal economy of the Soviet Union for many years to come.

"Stalin agreed that there should be a trusteeship for Korea, under China, Great Britain, the Soviet Union and the United States."

As to Japan, Hopkins reported that Stalin preferred to go through with unconditional surrender in order to destroy the military might and forces of Japan once and for all. He felt, however, that if we stuck to unconditional surrender the Japanese would not give up and we would have to destroy them as we did Germany. If they offered to surrender, however, in an effort to seek softer terms, the Allies should depart from the announced policy of unconditional surrender and be prepared to accept a modified surrender. He visualized imposing our will through occupation forces, thereby gaining substantially the same results unconditional surrender would be expected to bring. He added that Russia would expect to share in the actual occupation of Japan and that he wanted an agreement with us and the British as to zones of occupation, as well as an understanding among the Allies as to areas of operation in Manchuria and China.

I cabled Hopkins on May 31:

"We will inform Soong of Stalin's desire to see him in Moscow not later than July first and will provide the necessary air transportation.

"At the time of Soong's arrival in Moscow, I will take up with Chiang the conditions stated at the Yalta Conference."

Hopkins' last talk with Stalin was about voting procedure in the United Nations. It was clear, Hopkins reported, that Stalin had not understood the issues involved. After Hopkins cleared up the issues, Stalin accepted our position, despite the opposition of Molotov, whom he waved aside. But Stalin pointed out that he did not consider that "a country is virtuous because it is small," and that small nations had been responsible for some of the world's troubles. He expressed emphatically his unwillingness to allow the Soviet Union's interests to be affected by such countries.

I was reassured to learn from Hopkins that Stalin had confirmed the understanding reached at Yalta about Russia's entry into the war against Japan. Our military experts had estimated that an invasion of Japan would cost at least five hundred thousand American casualties even if the Japanese forces then in Asia were held on the Chinese mainland. Russian entry into the war against Japan was highly important to us.

At Yalta, Roosevelt, Churchill, and Stalin had agreed that the Japanese should be deprived of all the conquests they had made since 1894. These included certain territories and privileges that had been Russian before the Russo-Japanese War of 1904–5. Since this agreement involved Chinese interests and seaports, the United States had agreed to obtain the concurrence of the Chinese government.

Our Ambassador to China, General Patrick Hurley, sent me several long cables in which he detailed our experience in China during the war and what Roosevelt told him about the Yalta agreements as they affected China. Hurley reported that he had been able to talk to Chiang Kai-shek about all the matters involved without, however, revealing to him anything about the Yalta accord. The Ambassador wired me on May 10 that, with the exception of two words in the accord about the port city of Dairen, he was "convinced that he [Chiang Kai-shek] will agree to every one of the requirements." These two words were "lease" and "preeminent," which had a bad connotation to the Chinese people.

"Both Roosevelt and Stalin advised me," Hurley's message read, "that it was agreed between them that I would not open the subject of the Yalta decision with Chiang Kai-shek until the signal was given me by Stalin. Stalin said he would give me carte blanche and let me use my own judgment as to when and how to present the subject. However, both Harriman and I were of the opinion that it would be best to delay the presentation because of the possibility of leakage which in turn might bring undesirable results. I explained this to Stalin and it was finally decided that I am not to present the subject to Chiang Kai-shek until we have advised Stalin that, in our opinion, the time is opportune and until we have received the signal from him."

Hurley now raised the point that the time was opportune for this move, and he asked me to instruct him to ask Stalin for his approval to tell the generalissimo about the Far Eastern decisions that had been reached at Yalta.

On May 12 I sent this message to Hurley:

"Please continue your efforts to accomplish the purposes outlined to you by President Roosevelt.

"I am informed in regard to your previous reports of the attitude of the imperialist governments in China, and hope that the agreement with Churchill and Stalin reported by you may result in the establishment of a free united democratic Chinese Government.

"In regard to the 'prelude' to the Yalta agreement on the future conduct of the Pacific war, it is not appropriate at the present time for you to give any information to the Chinese Government.

"When it is appropriate and promising of advantage to the common cause, you will be advised to inform the Chinese Government of the particulars of arrangements that may be in effect at that time.

"We will endeavor to get to Chiang Kai-shek, through you at the earliest practicable date, all the available information on this subject that can be disclosed without damage to the overall prospect."

Ambassador Hurley had been entrusted by President Roosevelt with two specific missions in addition to his duties as Ambassador to China. The first was to bring Churchill and Stalin to an agreement on the policy that the United States had been pursuing in China. This policy was to take all necessary action to bring about unification under the national government of all anti-Japanese armed forces in China and to endorse the aspirations of the Chinese people for the establishment of a free, united, democratic Chinese government. The second mission was to continue to insist that China furnish her own leadership, make her own decisions, and be responsible for her own policies and thus work out her own destiny in her own way.

Our efforts to strengthen and sustain China in her war program involved many operations and included delicate diplomatic negotiations. To achieve this end we had placed American advisers in China, had provided top-level military and economic advice, and had given extensive credits to the Chinese. On May 14, 1945, Foreign Minister T. V. Soong, who had called on me once before, came to see me to get the release of a balance of two hundred million dollars in gold still due the Chinese from the half-billion-dollar credit approved by the Congress in January 1942. Soong said that this gold was now needed to bolster the Chinese economy, because China was suffering from acute inflation.

My information showed that Chinese prices, over a period of seven years, had increased at an average rate of about ten per cent per month and that during the last three months these increases had risen at a rate of over thirty per cent a month. As a result of these price increases China kept issuing more currency, and inflation had reached a "galloping" stage.

The Treasury and the State Department recommended that we advance this gold in keeping with our agreement, although I felt that what China needed more were urgent financial and economic reforms. I therefore approved the shipment of the gold to China. I also approved a letter by Secretary of the Treasury Morgenthau to Dr. Soong stating the American government's position. The Secretary's letter pointed out that the purpose of the half-billion-dollar financial aid to China, and particularly the agreement in July 1943 to ship gold to China, was to assist in anti-inflationary programs which would strengthen confidence in the Chinese government and its finances and thereby help maintain the Chinese economy.

"It is the opinion of this Government," the Secretary wrote, "that the sale of gold by China has not proved effective in combating inflation.

"Also the manner in which the gold sales had been conducted and subsequent public criticism of them in China are not conducive to achieving the purposes for which American financial aid was granted.

"Therefore, we ask the Chinese government to consider carefully the matters proposed in the United States Treasury memorandum of May 8, 1945—in particular the suggestion that China constitute a half billion dollar fund for combating inflation and stabilizing the currency from its foreign exchange assets.

"This step would be of considerable benefit now and in the future and it would inspire confidence in the Chinese government's handling of its difficult economic situation. . . .

"The carrying out of effective reforms will do more to insure confidence among the people and give a measure of stability to the present economic and financial situation than the gold program. . . ."

On June 4, after I had heard from Hopkins that Stalin was now ready to talk to the Chinese, I cabled Ambassador Hurley.

"You may expect in the near future," my message read in part, "instructions to endeavor to obtain approval by Chiang Kai-shek of a military-political matter of the highest importance that, if it is approved, will radically and favorably change the entire military picture in your area.

"For your information, only, Soong is going to Moscow to discuss the same matter."

My message concluded: "To avoid leakage of highly secret information, the above mentioned instructions to you will be delayed until shortly prior to Soong's arrival in Russia."

On June 7 Stettinius notified me from San Francisco that Dr. Soong was flying to see me.

I received Soong at 11 A.M. on June 9. The Chinese Foreign Minister was accompanied by Acting Secretary of State Grew.

Stalin, I told Soong, claimed he had no territorial demands against China and favored a unified China under the leadership of Chiang Kai-shek. But Stalin wanted to restore to Russia her former rights in the Pacific which Japan had taken from her in 1904, and he wanted agreement with China in this matter before Russia would participate in the war against Japan.

Following this meeting with Soong, I directed the Acting Secretary of State to cable Ambassador Hurley as follows:

You are aware of an agreement made in February[1] that the President would take measures to obtain from Chiang Kai-shek his concurrence in the understanding of the Soviet Government stated herewith following.

---

[1] By Roosevelt at Yalta.

Stalin wishes to discuss his proposals directly with Soong in Moscow before the first of July.

1. Stalin has made to us a categorical statement that he will do everything he can to promote unification under the leadership of Chiang Kai-shek.

2. That this leadership should continue after the war.

3. That he wants a unified stable China and wants China to control all of Manchuria as a part of a United China.

4. That he has no territorial claims against China, and that he will respect Chinese sovereignty in all areas his troops enter to fight the Japanese.

5. That he will welcome representatives of the Generalissimo to be with his troops in Manchuria in order to facilitate the organization of Chinese administration in Manchuria.

6. That he agrees with America's "open door" policy in China.

7. That he agrees to a trusteeship for Korea under China, Great Britain, the Soviet Union, and the United States.

The conditions for Soviet participation in the war against Japan are as follows, and if these conditions are met, a Soviet attack will be made in August:

"1. The status quo in Outer-Mongolia (The Mongolian People's Republic) shall be preserved;

"2. The former rights of Russia violated by the treacherous attack of Japan in 1904 shall be restored, viz:

"(a) The southern part of Sakhalin as well as all the islands adjacent to it shall be returned to the Soviet Union,

"(b) the commercial port of Dairen shall be internationalized, the preeminent interests of the Soviet Union in this port being safeguarded and the lease of Port Arthur as a naval base of the USSR restored,

"(c) The Chinese-Eastern Railroad and the South Manchurian Railroad which provides an outlet to Dairen shall be jointly operated by the establishment of a joint Soviet-Chinese company it being understood that the preeminent interests of the Soviet Union shall be safeguarded and that China shall retain full sovereignty in Manchuria.

"3. The Kurile Islands shall be handed over to the Soviet Union.

"4. The Soviet Union is ready to conclude with the National Government of China a pact of friendship and alliance between the USSR and China in order to render assistance to China with its armed forces for the purpose of liberating China from the Japanese yoke."

Inform Chiang Kai-shek that President Roosevelt at Yalta agreed to support these Soviet claims upon the entry of Russia in the war against Japan. I am also in agreement.

T. V. Soong has been given this information.

You are hereby directed to take up this matter with Chiang on June fifteenth and to make every effort to obtain his approval.

On June 14 I again met with Dr. Soong before he left for Chungking. Grew and Charles E. Bohlen were present. I revealed to Dr. Soong some of the important points of the conversation between Harry Hopkins and Marshal Stalin in Moscow.

Dr. Soong replied that he was glad to hear what I had told him but that he wished to call my attention to a few points that would have to be cleared up. The Yalta understanding, he said, called for the re-establishment of the Russian rights in Manchuria which had been lost as a result of the Russian-Japanese War of 1904.

Soong said that in two treaties made in 1924 the Soviet government had renounced all special concessions, leases, and privileges, including extraterritoriality. He added that it would be necessary to clarify all these points with Stalin when he went to Moscow, including the meaning of the term "preeminent interests" of the Soviet Union in the port of Dairen. The most difficult item of the Soviet demands, Soong pointed out, was the lease of Port Arthur. The Chinese government and people had come to feel very strongly opposed to any re-establishment of the old system of special leased ports in China, and it would be difficult to accept the Russian position on this point.

I explained to Soong, as I had done previously, that I was anxious to see the Soviet Union come into the war against Japan early enough to shorten the war and thus save countless American and Chinese lives. But while this was my chief concern at the moment, I told him I wanted him to know that I would do nothing that would harm the interests of China, our friend in the Far East.

I was extremely anxious, I told him, to avoid setting up tinderboxes either in the Far East or in Europe which might cause future trouble and wars. Soong replied that he was happy to hear this statement, remarking that there was no nation in the world that China regarded more as a friend than the United States.

I then cabled Stalin this message:

"T. V. Soong departed by airplane today for Moscow via Chungking.

"He will arrive Moscow before July first to discuss details of arrangements for Soviet-Chinese agreements.

"Ambassador Hurley has been directed to inform Chiang Kai-shek on June fifteenth of Soviet conditions and to make every effort to obtain Generalissimo's agreement therewith. Hurley is directed to inform Chiang Kai-shek that the Yalta agreement will have the support of the United States Government."

I also cabled Churchill a similar message, to which the British Prime Minister responded: "I entirely agree and welcome these arrangements."

CHAPTER 18

My first act as President of the United States had been to reaffirm the American desire for a world organization to keep the peace. Within a few minutes of my taking the oath of office I announced that the United States would take part in the San Francisco conference with no delay in the schedule or change in the arrangements.

I wanted to make it clear that I attached the greatest importance to the establishment of international machinery for the prevention of war and the maintenance of peace. I knew many of the pitfalls and stumbling blocks we could encounter in setting up such an organization, but I also knew that in a world without such machinery we would be forever doomed to the fear of destruction. It was important for us to make a start, no matter how imperfect. Even the constitutional structure of our own country had to undergo many trials and changes, including a bloody conflict, before we achieved a workable union.

I had hoped that someday we could build an international organization that would eventually work on the same basis as the union of the United States. I had made a study of the "Grand Design" of King Henry IV of France. This plan called for a kind of federation of sovereign states in Europe to act in concert to prevent wars. This, as far as I know, was the first practicable international organization ever suggested. Woodrow Wilson must have thought of it when he planned the League of Nations. King Henry IV is supposed to have discussed the idea with King James I of England and was on his way to Germany to talk about his plan when he was unfortunately assassinated. There are some who claim that Henry did not originate the idea but had borrowed it from the Duc de Sully, his Minister of Finance. I am of the opinion that Henry was the man who actually conceived it.

I had also read carefully all of Woodrow Wilson's writings and speeches on the League of Nations. I followed closely the debates in the Senate on the Versailles treaty and saw how a small group of what Woodrow Wilson called "willful men" in the Senate had managed to prevent American participation in the League of Nations.

Roosevelt had shared with me his determination to avoid the experience of Woodrow Wilson by getting in advance the participation and consent of leaders of both parties. In order to ensure acceptance by the Senate, Roosevelt and I had both insisted that the Republican as well as Democratic ranking members of the Senate and House foreign relations committees be included in the delegation to the United Nations Conference in San Francisco. This procedure of having the Senate and House represented in the delegation had been followed at Dumbarton Oaks, where the essence of the Charter had been worked out for submission to the San Francisco conference.

Before the American delegation left for San Francisco, I conferred with them and had numerous meetings with individual members. I told them what I had in mind and exchanged views with them on some of the basic aims. We were agreed that we ought to strive for an organization to which all nations would delegate enough powers to prevent another world war. This was not going to be easy. At the same time we knew the Charter of the proposed organization had to be acceptable to the United States Senate. We did not want to run the risk of another League of Nations tragedy, with the United States standing in isolation on the side lines. I specifically instructed Secretary of State Stettinius to consult Senators Connally and Vandenberg on every move he made in order to get full agreement. If he could not get those men to go along, he was to call me, and I would try to resolve the issues by telephoning them personally. I asked Stettinius to keep in constant touch with me by telephone or telegram. He was to telephone me at the conclusion of each day and night session. He was not to hesitate to call me at any hour, and because of this arrangement all important matters were referred to me either for my suggestions or approval.

Stettinius always conferred with the delegation before calling me, and he was consequently able to give me messages or suggestions from individual members. Furthermore, I frequently talked to Senators Connally and Vandenberg, who were the ranking members of the Senate Foreign Relations Committee. I wanted these two key figures to have direct access to me at all times, and I wanted the benefit of their counsel and experience.

Throughout the long discussions I was always trying to work out a way to keep Russia and Great Britain in harmony with our own aims. It was obvious that unless the United States, Great Britain, and Russia worked together within the framework of the United Nations we could not secure the peace of the world. I opposed yielding on fundamental principles, but I was ready to compromise on minor issues if they threatened to deadlock the conference.

I always kept in mind our own history and experience in the evolution of our Constitution. It took many years and a number of amendments and compromises to make our Constitution work. It would take years for an international organization to work effectively. It would involve experience, often disagreeable and painful, in the matter of give-and-take among sovereign nations. It would take much more time and patience to work out a world constitution than it would to create a charter for an individual nation. And it would try the souls of many a statesman before a workable arrangement could be achieved. But I always considered statesmen to be more expendable than soldiers.

The American delegation to San Francisco carried with it several directives unanimously agreed upon by its members and approved by me. Proposals made at Dumbarton Oaks in the fall of 1944 were to serve as a framework for the drafting of a United Nations charter, but some changes had been proposed by our delegation, who, through the Secretary of State, had submitted them to me for consideration and approval. I went over these proposed changes. They were adopted and, with my approval, constituted a directive and working guide for the conference. The changes had grown out of many meetings by the delegation and my talks with them. These talks began on my second day in office, April 13, when I received a comprehensive report from Secretary Stettinius.

Stettinius informed me that the delegation, as appointed by President Roosevelt,[1] had been meeting daily to review the substance of the Dumbarton Oaks proposals and to consider what changes, if any, should be advanced by me at San Francisco or supported by us there if advanced by others. For instance, the delegation would accept the Vandenberg proposal to include references to justice and international law in the Charter. The final recommended changes of the delegation, Stettinius told me, would be submitted to me for consideration and approval.

It had been agreed at Yalta that the United States, Britain, Russia, China, and France would draw up a new trusteeship system to replace

[1]In addition to Stettinius as chairman, it consisted of former Secretary of State Cordell Hull, senior adviser; Senator Tom Connally; Senator Arthur H. Vandenberg; Congressman Sol Bloom; Congressman Charles A. Eaton; Commander Harold Stassen; and Dean Virginia Gildersleeve.

the mandate system of the League of Nations. These five nations were to make up the permanent membership of the Security Council. This trusteeship machinery would be made a part of the Charter. But no specific territories to be placed under trusteeships were to be discussed at San Francisco, since they were to be dealt with as part of the peace settlements. Because of the importance of certain strategic areas in the Pacific to our future security a question had arisen as to the wisdom of discussing the subject at all at this time. This matter, Stettinius said, had been referred to President Roosevelt a few days before his death with the recommendation that he review the matter with the Secretaries of State, War, and Navy on his return from Warm Springs, and he had agreed to do this.

The trusteeship problem was one of long standing. It had become more pressing as the end of the war approached. President Roosevelt and those responsible for the security and defense of America faced a twofold problem: first, the future of dependent peoples everywhere, but specifically in areas freed from the enemy; and, second, the disposition of the islands in the Pacific used by the Japanese as military and naval bases during the war. These were the Marshalls, the Marianas, and the Carolines, together including some hundreds of islands and clusters containing a native population of about fifty thousand. Their total area was small— roughly eight hundred and fifty square miles—but they stretched over a great area of the western Pacific. In the hands of a hostile power they could again be used to shut us out of that area and block us off from the Philippines and Guam, as well as from the British and Dutch possessions in that portion of the world. They could also be used to threaten our lines of communication with New Zealand and Australia. These islands had come under Japanese control at the end of World War I, and promptly thereafter they had been fortified and closed to non-Japanese. As bases for Japanese operations, they made much trouble for us during the war, and we were consequently interested in them not only as trusteeships but, in the case of some, as special strategic areas within a trusteeship system. With victory in the Pacific now assured as American forces drove the Japanese from one after another of their island strongholds, peacetime control of these islands assumed growing importance in the development of American postwar policies.

In earlier meetings with Cabinet members on the question of trusteeships, I found that the State Department held views that differed from those of the War and Navy Departments. I listened carefully to both points of view. In the end I sustained the Army and Navy chiefs on the major issue of the security of the bases. But I also saw the validity of the ideal for which the State Department was contending—that the United Nations should not be barred from the local territories beyond the bases, if at any time the United Nations should want to look into the social and economic conditions on these islands. The United States would never emulate the policy of Japan in the areas that were given her under mandate by the League of Nations. We thus assured full protection to our nation against a future Pacific aggressor and, at the same time, laid the foundation for future self-government of the island people.

My attitude was always that while it was necessary for us to control certain islands in the Pacific until peace was established, these territories should not be closed to the rest of the world. I believed we should set up civil governments as soon as possible to replace the military governments. Some of the military objected, but while I remained President I intended to try to get as near to self-government as we could wherever we had the responsibility. We had done this in Cuba. We were about to do it in the Philippines, and this was also to be our aim in Puerto Rico.

I had always been opposed to colonialism. Whatever justification may be cited at any stage, colonialism in any form is hateful to Americans. America fought her own war of liberation against colonialism, and we shall always regard with sympathy and understanding the desire of people everywhere to be free of colonial bondage. The intention of President Roosevelt and the Congress to give early freedom to the Philippines was an expression of this policy as well as of the will of the American people, and I was determined to carry it through to speedy fulfillment.

I wanted to see the brave Filipinos back on their feet and thriving as citizens of a free and successful republic. I hoped that by making the Philippines as free as we had made Cuba it would have an effect on British, Dutch, and French policy in their Far Eastern affairs.

I still believed in Woodrow Wilson's philosophy of "self-determination."

There was some opposition to taking up the question of Philippine independence at this time. There were those who felt that this was one of many questions in the Pacific that had better wait for solution after the war. Special interests also were heard from. They wanted time to get control of certain resources for their own exploitation. Even Secretary of the Interior Ickes had strongly opposed early independence, taking a vigorous stand on the matter, first with President Roosevelt and then with me. He went so far, in fact, as to ask me to postpone my first meeting with President Osmeña on April 19. He exhibited the same violent opposition with me as he did with Roosevelt, to whom he had written at Warm Springs that if independence were granted at an early date, he wanted to be relieved of all responsibility for the Philippines.

I rejected Ickes' capricious position and I was determined to set up the necessary machinery to expedite Philippine independence. Ickes was to have no part in this procedure. I had seen President Osmeña on April 19. A second appointment with him was set for May 4, and I intended to express to him my determination to carry out our announced policy.

President Osmeña had been one of the last official visitors received by Roosevelt at Warm Springs. He was there on April 5 when Roosevelt held a press conference, during which he told of talks he had had with Osmeña.

"We are absolutely unchanged," Roosevelt had said at that time, "in our policy of two years ago for immediate Filipino independence."

Prior to my second meeting with Osmeña, I had informed General MacArthur at Manila of my plans to hasten the granting of full independence to the Philippines and that it was my intention to appoint a special commission to be headed by Senator Tydings to go to Manila and report on conditions in the islands rather than to send a high commissioner or a special envoy. General Marshall reported to me that General MacArthur had replied that he was in full agreement with the plan proposed.

When I received President Osmeña at noon on May 4 we quickly got down to business. I again stated my intention of carrying out all of our promises and pledges and added that I was in favor of the earliest possible independence date. I informed him that I had talked with Senator Tydings and had asked him to proceed to Manila as head of a commission to report to me on conditions in the Philippines. President Osmeña expressed his deep gratitude to the American people and said he felt this was an important date for the people of his country.

The following day I issued a statement on the Philippines.

"I have had several discussions with President Osmeña on the subject of Philippine independence," this statement read in part. "These discussions were started by President Roosevelt.

"As a result of the discussions I have had with the President of the Philippines, I am prepared to endorse and carry through to their conclusion the policies laid down by President Roosevelt respecting the Islands and the independence of the Filipino people.

"The date of independence will be advanced as soon as practicable in pursuance of the policy outlined by Congress in S. J. Resolution 93. The Filipino people, whose heroic and loyal stand in this war has won the affection and admiration of the American people, will be fully assisted by the United States in the great problem of rehabilitation and reconstruction which lies ahead.

"In view of the special relationship between the United States and the Philippines as created by S. J. Resolution 93, I believe that suitable reciprocal trade between the two countries should continue for such time, after independence, as may be necessary to provide the new Republic

with a fair opportunity to secure its economic freedom and independence
—a permanent blessing for the patriotic people of the Philippines.

"To assist me in the attainment of these objectives and with concurrence of President Osmeña, I am asking Senator Millard Tydings of
Maryland, chairman of the Filipino Rehabilitation Commission, to proceed to Manila as my special envoy to examine conditions there and
report his recommendations to me.

"It will be my constant endeavor to be of assistance to the Philippines.
I will be only too happy to see to it that the close friendship between our
two peoples, developed through many years of fruitful association, is
maintained and strengthened.

"I hope to be able to accept the invitation of President Osmeña to visit
Manila at the inauguration of the Philippine Republic."

President Osmeña came to see me again on May 14 to sign an agreement to permit the United States to have military and naval bases in the
islands. The Philippine Islands are a vital strategic center in the Pacific,
and we were anxious that a military agreement with the Philippines be
concluded in order that we might in the future continue to protect them
against outside attack. The Filipinos themselves were equally anxious to
have this protection, because without it the republic we were helping to
establish might sometime find itself helpless.

On April 19 Secretary of State Stettinius brought me a set of recommendations unanimously agreed to by our delegation in San Francisco. I
discussed these, section by section, with him and then approved them in
the following form as a general working directive for the delegation:

Subject: *Charter for the International Organization.*
The American Delegation to the United Nations Conference on International Organization is unanimously agreed that we should propose a few
alterations in the Dumbarton Oaks Proposals during the San Francisco Conference. We will reserve our final positions on all of these, of course, until
we learn the views of other governments. The most important points involved:

PURPOSES
1. Inclusion of a statement that the organization should act in accordance
with the principles of justice and equity in adjusting or settling disputes, and
that the organization should foster the development of international law.
2. Inclusion of a statement on the promotion of respect for human rights
and fundamental freedoms (in the Dumbarton Oaks Proposals this is stated
in the chapter on economic and social cooperation only).

PRINCIPLES
1. Change the expression "sovereign equality of peace-loving states" to
"the sovereign equality of all member states."
2. Make clearer that members must refrain from using any but peaceful

means in settling their disputes and must use such means pursuant to the provisions of the Charter.

THE GENERAL ASSEMBLY

1. Clarify to show that the General Assembly can at all times *discuss* any question bearing on the maintenance of peace and security, and that the limitation on its power to make recommendations concerning matters which are being dealt with by the Security Council should be confined to *specific* recommendations.

2. Give the General Assembly power to determine the qualifications of membership, and to admit new members by its own action unless the Security Council interposes objections for reasons of security.

3. Apportionment by the General Assembly of expenses among the members should be on the basis of an appropriate proration.

4. Add to recommendatory powers, so it can make recommendations relative to the promotion of measures to establish justice, to foster the observance of human rights and fundamental freedoms, and to encourage the development of rules of international law.

5. Extend power to recommend measures for peaceful adjustment to include situations likely to violate the principles enunciated in the Atlantic Charter and situations arising out of any treaties or international engagements.

THE SECURITY COUNCIL

1. Eliminate provision that regional subcommittees of the Military Staff Committee can be established.

MAINTENANCE OF PEACE AND SECURITY

1. Propose that the exclusion from the scope of the Security Council in peaceful settlement of matters within the domestic jurisdiction of a state should be stated without the present qualification that those matters must be ones which "by international law" are "solely" within domestic jurisdiction.

AMENDMENTS

We should hold to the present proposals, but serious consideration is being given to proposing or supporting a possible additional provision to the following effect:

"A general conference of the members of the United Nations may be held at a date and place to be fixed by a two-thirds vote of the General Assembly with the concurrence of the Security Council, for the purpose of reviewing the Charter. Each member shall have one vote in the Conference. Any alterations of the Charter recommended by a two-thirds vote of the Conference shall take effect when ratified in accordance with their respective constitutional processes by the members of the organization having permanent membership on the Security Council and by a majority of the other members of the Organization."

QUESTIONS DEFERRED

We have been considering, but have deferred, making decisions on the following questions:

1. Wording of the Preamble.
2. Defining the right of self-defense.

3. Possible changes in the wording in the chapter on economic and social cooperation.

4. Possible withdrawal provision.

I agreed that it would be best for us to reserve our final position on all questions until we learned the views of other governments. We did not want to confront our neighbor governments of Central and South America and Canada with a *fait accompli*. It was a case of giving them a chance to say, "We don't like this or that."

We were particularly anxious to be sure that the Western Hemisphere nations and the British Commonwealth were in agreement. We felt that if we had that sort of backing we would get almost anything we wanted to build an international organization that would work.

I emphasized to Stettinius the importance of the point dealing with a declaration on human rights. I felt very strongly about the need for a world "bill of rights," something on the order of our own.

On the question of the powers to be vested in the General Assembly, I told Stettinius that I felt that if a veto were to be used in the Security Council by some stubborn big power that wanted to block efforts toward the solution of peace, then the Assembly ought to have some way of dealing with the problem. I thought the best way to do this was in the same manner that any question can be raised in our own House of Representatives or Senate. However, the big powers were agreed on the right of any one of the five permanent members of the Council to an absolute veto, mainly on the assumption that unity on any important decision was essential between those powers. In the present world setup sovereign powers are very jealous of their rights. We had to recognize this as a condition and to seek united action through compromise.

It has always been my hope that independent nations would sometime be able to work out a world parliamentary setup along the lines of the Senate and the House of Representatives of the United States. I knew, however, that this was not possible at this stage of national sovereign rivalries. We had to find some way of pooling whatever power the nations were willing to delegate to prevent aggression and keep the peace. That is what I had in mind, and not so much the details of the final shape it had to take.

I also thought it was necessary to find a way to make amendments to the Charter. Unless a constitution can be amended as conditions change, it will become obsolete and cease to be a workable instrument of government. Most of our states have had several constitutions, and all of them have had revisions and amendments. The Constitution of the United States itself had twenty-one amendments added by 1945. In my discussions with our delegates I frequently pointed to our own Constitution, not only as a model, but as a good analogy of what happens in the growth and development of a constitution and a government.

In drafting the Charter of the United Nations it was well for us to keep in mind our own history. If we could not achieve a perfect document at San Francisco, we surely could provide for such changes and amendments as time would prove necessary in making it work to keep the peace.

I have always believed that, once the sovereign nations of the world united in a world organization and gave it a reasonable chance to work, peace would become a reality.

The San Francisco conference opened on April 25, 1945. It was not possible for me to be in attendance, but Secretary of State Stettinius kept me closely informed on the proceedings.

I had instructed our delegation to cast the American vote for the Russian proposal that White Russia and the Ukraine, two member republics of the Soviet Union, be admitted to initial membership in the proposed world organization.

On April 27 the Steering Committee of the conference agreed to admit the Ukrainian and White Russian republics as members of the United Nations. When President Roosevelt agreed at Yalta with Churchill and Stalin to support the Russian claims of the Ukrainian and White Russian republics to be members, he said his objective was to keep the Russians in a negotiating mood. In talking to me about his decision at Yalta, Roosevelt told me that he wanted the Russians to go along as one of the great powers to help build the United Nations. He said that when Stalin first brought up the matter of additional votes the Russian leader wanted sixteen votes. He wanted one vote for each of the sixteen republics of the U.S.S.R. Roosevelt said, "I then countered with the proposal that we have forty-eight votes, one for each of our forty-eight sovereign states. That ended it. Stalin did not bring up his proposal for sixteen votes again."

My idea was that all sovereign nations should ultimately belong to the United Nations. We were, of course, still at war with the Axis nations, but I believed that after peace treaties had been concluded they too would be admitted in the regular way in which the Charter would provide. No peace-loving nation was to be barred.

At the same session of the Steering Committee the persistently troublesome question of Poland came up again, and Stettinius reported that Molotov had moved that the provisional Polish government be invited to the conference. It was the Russian position that the Yalta decision for the reorganization of the Polish government should be carried out but that Poland should not be excluded from the conference just because the implementation of this decision had been delayed.

Stettinius replied that the United States Government could not accept Molotov's proposal until the new Polish government was constituted in accordance with the Crimea decision. Eden made a strong statement endorsing the United States position, adding that his government had no means of knowing whether the provisional government was supported by the Polish people, since Britain had not been permitted to send representatives into Poland.

Molotov then moved that the question be referred to the Executive Committee for preliminary consideration, but New Zealand and Venezuelan delegates urged that the question be settled by the three interested powers rather than referred to the Executive Committee. The United States chairman, however, pointed out that under the Yalta agreement the conference had no right to consider this question until the Polish government had been reorganized.

Molotov declared that the Soviet government had a right to raise this question at the conference and wished to refer it to the Executive Committee. At this stage Mr. Spaak of Belgium saved the situation by delivering a stirring speech expressing his dismay that even before the conference had started this most delicate and controversial question should be raised. He expressed the fear that at this rate the conference would never get down to business, and then proposed a resolution expressing the desire of the conference that Poland be represented as soon as its government had been recognized by the sponsoring powers. After prolonged and rather acrimonious discussion Molotov stated that he would not press for a vote on his own motion, and the motion proposed by Spaak was adopted, thirty-one nations voting in favor and none against.

The position taken by our delegation was in keeping with our policy. I felt very strongly about the refusal to reorganize the Polish government in keeping with the Yalta agreement, and we would oppose Poland's becoming a member of the United Nations until this was done. But Molotov would not let the matter rest.

On May 1 the admission of the two Soviet republics was approved unanimously in the Executive Committee and then approved by acclamation in the plenary session of the conference. On the same day the question of Argentina's participation in the conference was raised. This was brought before the Executive Committee by the Mexican and Chilean delegations, and the proposal was supported by the other Latin-American delegations.

Molotov spoke up in opposition, seeking to use the occasion to further the Polish claim to participation in the conference. He argued that Argentina had helped the enemy throughout the war and that if Argentina was invited and Poland was not it would be a blow to the prestige of the conference. Australia's Foreign Minister Evatt recommended delay and reference to the next meeting of the committee. He felt that Argentina was pro-Fascist and had opposed the United Nations in the war. Nevertheless, he recognized that the return of Argentina to the community of nations was of the first importance and she should probably be admitted.

Stettinius stated that the American republics wished to have Argentina represented at San Francisco and that the United States was in entire accord with the desire of her sister republics.

Molotov wanted to refer the question to the four sponsoring powers for preliminary consideration, but Eden said that he saw no use in putting off the decision. The Mexican motion proposing participation of Argentina in the conference was then put to a vote and approved nine to three. Russia, Yugoslavia, and Czechoslovakia voted in the negative, and China and Iran did not vote.

The same question was discussed at length in the Steering Committee later the same morning, and Molotov took the same position, making every effort to link the Argentine and the Polish questions. However, the Soviet motion that the matter be delayed was defeated seven to twenty-five, and an Ecuadorian motion that Argentina be admitted to the conference was passed twenty-nine to five. Those opposing Ecuador's motion were Russia, Czechoslovakia, Yugoslavia, Belgium, and Greece.

The same issue was raised in the plenary session. Once again the same motions were presented, and the Soviet motion was defeated and the Latin-American motion approved by votes closely similar to those recorded in the Steering Committee.

The United States had refused to recognize the Farrell government in Argentina for over a year because of its pro-Axis activities and because of its failure to comply with inter-American undertakings for the defense of the continent. On April 9, however, Argentina had been readmitted to the inter-American association, and we had recognized the Farrell government after it declared war on the Axis powers.

I felt the action Argentina had taken was of the "band-wagon" variety but had instructed Stettinius to support the admission of Argentina at the opportune time in order to promote Western Hemisphere solidarity.

On May 3 Rosenman and Stettinius met with Eden and Molotov to discuss the treatment of war criminals. Judge Rosenman presented the American proposal for an agreement among the United States, United Kingdom, U.S.S.R., and France.

On the preceding day, May 2, I had announced the appointment of Associate Justice Robert H. Jackson of the Supreme Court of the United States as representative of the United States and its chief of counsel in the preparation and prosecution of charges against the European Axis war criminals. This government was committed from the earliest days of the war to the policy of punishing war criminals. In August 1942 President Roosevelt had sounded a warning to the Nazis that "the time will come when they shall have to stand in the courts of law in the very countries which they are now oppressing and answer for their acts." And on October 7, 1942, he had declared "the intention of this government that the successful close of the war shall include provisions for the surrender to the United Nations of war criminals." Roosevelt had also stated that the United States was prepared to co-operate with the British and other governments in establishing a United Nations commission for the investigation of war crimes.

Judge Rosenman, who was now in San Francisco, had served as Roosevelt's personal representative in London at meetings with the British on war criminals. After I became President, Rosenman told me that in these talks it had been tentatively agreed that where any war criminal could be clearly identified he should be sent back to the country in which his crime had been committed, to be tried and punished by that country. The six or more top criminals (the original list had included Hitler, Mussolini, Goering, Goebbels, Himmler, and von Ribbentrop) were to be given a special trial before a mixed military tribunal. This tribunal was to consist of four officers—one each from the United States, the United Kingdom, the Soviet Union, and France (with perhaps an additional three representing all of the other smaller United Nations).

The trial would consist of filing against them a bill of arraignment in which the crimes against humanity which these men had committed would be set out in documentary form—such as the formal Nazi decrees against minorities; excerpts from *Mein Kampf;* photographs of concentration camps, torture chambers, crematories, etc. The bill of arraignment would be so fully documented that oral evidence would be practically unnecessary. The criminals would be given a copy of these charges and an opportunity to be heard in their own defense—the time of which would be fixed in advance so that the trial could not be protracted.

The vast number of other war criminals whose identity could not be established by competent proof, or against whom evidence would not be obtainable, would be reached by trials of the organizations to which they had belonged—the Gestapo, for example, as well as the SS and similar organizations.

The British war Cabinet, Rosenman informed me, held a special meeting on this subject the same day the late President died, but before the news of his death had been received. Rosenman left London immediately upon learning the news but had been advised by the Lord Chancellor that the British war Cabinet was generally in approval with the tentative agreement but had unanimously disapproved of the trial of the six top criminals. Their view was that these criminals should not be given a trial but should be dealt with politically by agreement of the four major powers and shot forthwith. Furthermore, Prime Minister Churchill had told Rosenman that he personally held this same opinion and that he had so stated to Marshal Stalin at the time of the Moscow Declaration, but that Stalin had insisted on a trial.

I told Rosenman that I did not believe in a political disposition of these top criminals but believed that some kind of trial should be accorded them. I then asked Judge Rosenman to go to San Francisco and take the matter up with Molotov and Eden.

In San Francisco, Rosenman told Eden and Molotov that we proposed an international military tribunal to try the Nazi leaders, as well as such organizations as the Gestapo and the SS, on the charge of engaging in a criminal conspiracy. He also informed them that we opposed the political punishment of the top Nazi leaders as had been suggested by the British.

Eden stated that the British war Cabinet had recently changed its position, because many of the top Nazis had already committed suicide, or had been killed, and no doubt many more would follow before any trial could be held. While the war Cabinet still saw no objection to a formal state trial, they were prepared to agree to a judicial trial if Russia and the United States favored that method. To this Molotov made no comment. On May 6 Judge Rosenman wired me:

"We are making progress. The representatives of France, Russia and Britain now seem to be generally agreed with us on setting up an international military tribunal of one representative of each; a trial rather than political disposition of the major criminals; and a committee of four chiefs of counsel, one from each of the powers."

The voting procedure of the Security Council, as proposed by the sponsoring powers, was now coming under attack from practically all the smaller countries, according to a message from Stettinius on May 21. Their target was the veto right of the great powers, which was based on an agreement that had been reached at Yalta.

Under this agreement the United States, the United Kingdom, the U.S.S.R., China, and France would have a veto in the Security Council wherever the question of military or economic sanctions was involved. All of our experts, civil and military, favored it, and without such a veto no arrangement would have passed the Senate. There was great pressure from the small nations to amend the voting procedure adopted at Yalta, particularly with respect to peaceful settlement procedures and the ratification of amendments to the Charter. On peaceful settlements this would have meant that unanimity among the five powers, if not involved in the dispute, would not be required. Our delegation was willing to agree to this if the Soviets were prepared to accept it. On the other hand, our delegation recommended that unless the Soviets were willing to accept the change the Yalta formula be adhered to. And, in any event, our delegates felt that there should be no change on Charter amendments.

On May 8 Molotov left San Francisco for Moscow.

"Molotov departed this morning in good spirits," Stettinius reported to me, "returning to Moscow via Alaska and Siberia. As he boarded his plane he particularly asked that his compliments be presented to you.

"Eden has told me in confidence this morning that he had received a message from the Prime Minister saying that because of the domestic-political situation in England he wanted both him and Attlee to return to London immediately. Eden feels they will have to go in a few days but he has assured me he will finish out the week here.

"Averell Harriman will be leaving for Washington this afternoon and will report to you immediately on his arrival. . . ."

After May 9 the meetings of the sponsoring powers were referred to as the Big Five, as France had joined all such discussions. The conference was making progress, having completed all of its preliminary arrangements and discussions. The main work was now in the hands of the different committees.

The question of the veto power in the Council was emerging as the single outstanding issue of the conference.

The committee dealing with the General Assembly meanwhile approved the Vandenberg amendment, which had been proposed by the sponsoring powers. This empowered the Assembly to recommend measures for the peaceful adjustment of any situation, regardless of origin, that was likely to impair the general welfare of friendly relations among nations or that resulted from the violation of the principles and purposes of the Charter.

On May 22 I asked Stettinius to return to Washington to see me. I wanted to go over the major issues still before the conference and discuss the setting of an early terminating date.

Progress being made at San Francisco was very encouraging. I was reassured to find that a conference involving so many nations and special interests had produced very few crises despite some tense moments of debate.

Our delegation was doing an excellent job. They were greatly aided by the ground broken at Dumbarton Oaks and the preliminary discussions on the United Nations in which the key figures of the United States Senate had been consulted. The meeting at Chapultepec also brought into harmony our Latin-American neighbors, and they went to San Francisco ready to co-operate on a world organization.

With the Secretary of State, who arrived in Washington on May 23, I examined each of the issues still pending before the conference, and I told Stettinius that we would stand by the Yalta formula on voting in the Security Council. We were committed to this formula, and we would abide by it.

On the right of withdrawal from the United Nations then being discussed, I agreed with the two senators, Vandenberg and Connally, that the right of any nation to withdraw should not be specifically prohibited, but at the same time I agreed with the delegates that an amendment to that effect at this stage would not be advisable.

I disapproved the recommendation that we should insist on voluntary jurisdiction for the World Court. I felt that if we were going to have a court it ought to be a court that would work, with compulsory jurisdiction. Consequently Stettinius was instructed to strive for a formula that would make possible, at least eventually, compulsory jurisdiction of the International Court of Justice.

One of the items then pending was the date for concluding the conference. There had been suggestions that the conference adjourn temporarily because some of the key foreign ministers—Molotov, Eden, and Soong, for example—had had to leave for urgent duties elsewhere. I was opposed to postponement on any ground until the conference had finished its important task of framing a charter, which would then have to be submitted to the many nations for ratification. Adjournment for even a short period might imperil the smooth progress and complicate the work already achieved. I therefore instructed Stettinius to keep working for and to aim at adjournment in early June.

In the course of the conference the heads of the delegations from the four sponsoring governments—the United States, Great Britain, the Soviet Union, and China—and of France, had developed the practice of consulting among themselves on outstanding issues. By June 1 the number of points still to be settled had been substantially reduced, but the thorniest of them all—that of voting procedure in the Security Council—still remained. Stettinius advised me that he was certain that, once this issue was cleared away, other points, such as the procedure for electing the Secretary General and the judges of the International Court of Justice, and the establishment of a Preparatory Commission, would be solved without undue difficulty.

The controversy over the voting procedure of the Security Council seemed to have reached an impasse. The real issue at stake was whether the discussion and consideration of a dispute could be stopped by the veto of any permanent member of the Council. The Russians insisted on the veto right, while we, together with the British, the Chinese, and the French, were opposed. We felt that such a use of the veto would make freedom of discussion impossible in the Council.

On the morning of June 2 Stettinius reported the situation to me by phone and, in outlining the problem, raised the question whether Stalin really knew what the position of his delegation involved. Stettinius observed that on previous occasions it had been found that Stalin had not always been informed of the instructions that had been issued by the Kremlin, and that on occasion it had been Molotov himself who had failed to inform his superior.

Since Harry Hopkins was then in Moscow talking with Stalin, Stettinius suggested that we make a direct approach and see if the deadlock could not be broken in that way. I told Stettinius to send a message to Ambassador Harriman and Hopkins, asking them to place the matter of the voting procedure of the Security Council before the Russian Premier.

On June 6 I heard from Hopkins that he had talked that day with Stalin about our position on the veto aspects of the voting procedure.

"We . . . laid out to him," Hopkins' message read, "the impasse at San Francisco over the voting procedure. Stalin had not understood the issues. After considerable discussion in which Molotov took an active part, Stalin overruled Molotov and agreed that the American position was acceptable to him. Harriman should be informed if Gromyko does not receive instructions promptly."

This meant the end of a deadlock that had threatened to disrupt the whole conference.

The next day Stettinius reported that Gromyko had received instructions from Moscow and that his government agreed with our position on the voting procedure.

Thus complete agreement had been reached among the four sponsoring powers and France on the voting procedure, so that no single state would be able to prevent the hearing of a dispute by the Security Council.

Now that this issue had been settled, it was agreed that every effort would be made to bring the conference to a close on Saturday, June 23. But we were to encounter another delay. Once again the Russians blocked agreement, and we had to go over the heads of the delegation by taking up the problem with Moscow. Moscow again accepted our position. What was involved was the right of the General Assembly, in which all the member nations would be represented, to free discussion of all matters and to make recommendations to the Security Council. This had become a symbol of the share the smaller nations were to have in the United Nations.

The position of the smaller nations was expressed in a proposed amendment to the Charter which provided that "The General Assembly shall have the right to discuss any matter within the sphere of international relations, and [subject to specified exceptions] . . . to make recommendations to the members of the organization or to the Security Council or both on any such matters."

Stettinius informed me that there was a big majority behind this proposal. On June 4 Gromyko had announced to the heads of the delegations that Russia would insist on having this paragraph taken out. The Australian Minister, Herbert Evatt, made a strong speech in defense of the proposal and, generally, on behalf of the smaller nations. Stettinius, in reporting to me, said that support for this proposal had grown stronger because it gave a voice to the smaller nations, who felt that they were being overshadowed by the dominant position of the Security Council and especially by the veto privilege of the permanent members.

The Russians objected, and I instructed Stettinius to take the matter up directly with Molotov, saying that if that did not help I would talk to Stalin directly.

Stettinius sent his message to Molotov on June 18. I left Washington on June 19 for the West Coast after a stopover in the state of Washington, as I had agreed to go to San Francisco to address the United Nations Conference on its closing day. Molotov's reply was forwarded to me at Olympia, Washington. It suggested a small change in the original Russian position, but it was unacceptable. I instructed Stettinius to try again.

Molotov finally accepted a compromise solution which provided that the General Assembly had the right to discuss any questions relating to the matters of international peace and security, unless it was already being dealt with by the Security Council, and to make recommendations to the members of the United Nations or the Security Council or both on such questions. The last road block in the path of the Charter of the United Nations had now been removed.

I arrived by the *Sacred Cow* from Olympia on the afternoon of June 25. I was given a wonderful reception by the people of San Francisco, who turned out a million strong as I motored into the city from the airport at Hamilton Field. I stayed at the Fairmont Hotel with the American delegation and held a reception that evening for the delegates of the conference.

About three o'clock the following day I went with Secretary of State Stettinius and the other members of the United States delegation to the Veterans' War Memorial Building to witness the signing of the Charter. We were escorted to the stage of the main auditorium of the building, where the flags of all the United Nations formed an impressive backdrop.

I took my position on the right of the Secretary of State, who sat down at a circular table. On it lay the books that contained the new Charter in the five official languages of the organization. When the Secretary signed on behalf of the United States, I stepped over to shake his hand and to thank him for his good work.

Senator Tom Connally signed next, followed by the other members of the American delegation, including Cordell Hull, who signed in Washington. I thanked each of them individually for their part in this historic achievement, and we then proceeded to the Opera House, where I addressed the final session of the plenary conference.

"The Charter of the United Nations," I said, "which you have just signed is a solid structure upon which we can build a better world. History will honor you for it. Between the victory in Europe and the final victory in Japan, in this most destructive of all wars, you have won a victory against war itself.

"It was the hope of such a Charter that helped sustain the courage of stricken peoples through the darkest days of the war. For it is a declaration of great faith by the nations of the earth—faith that war is not inevitable, faith that peace can be maintained.

"If we had had this Charter a few years ago—and above all, the will to use it—millions now dead would be alive. If we should falter in the future in our will to use it, millions now living will surely die.

"It has already been said by many that this is only a first step to a lasting peace. That is true. The important thing is that all our thinking and all our actions be based on the realization that it is in fact only a first step. Let us all have it firmly in mind that we start today from a good beginning and, with our eye always on the final objective, let us march forward.

"The Constitution of my own country came from a Convention which —like this one—was made up of delegates with many different views. Like this Charter, our Constitution came from a free and sometimes bitter exchange of conflicting opinions. When it was adopted, no one regarded it as a perfect document. But it grew and developed and expanded. And upon it there was built a bigger, a better, a more perfect union.

"This Charter, like our own Constitution, will be expanded and improved as time goes on. No one claims that it is now a final or a perfect instrument. It has not been poured into any fixed mold. Changing world conditions will require readjustments—but they will be the readjustments of peace and not of war.

"That we now have this Charter at all is a great wonder. It is also a cause for profound thanksgiving to Almighty God, Who has brought us so far in our search for peace through world organization.

"There were many who doubted that agreement could ever be reached by these fifty countries differing so much in race and religion, in language and culture. But these differences were all forgotten in one unshakable unity of determination—to find a way to end wars.

"Out of all the arguments and disputes, and different points of view, a way was found to agree. Here in the spotlight of full publicity, in the tradition of liberty-loving people, opinions were expressed openly and freely. The faith and the hope of fifty peaceful nations were laid before this world forum. Differences were overcome. This Charter was not the work of any single nation or group of nations, large or small. It was the result of a spirit of give-and-take, of tolerance for the views and interests of others.

"It was proof that nations, like men, can state their differences, can face them, and then can find common ground on which to stand. That is the essence of democracy; that is the essence of keeping the peace in the future. By your agreement, the way was shown toward future agreement in the years to come.

"This Conference owes its success largely to the fact that you have kept your minds firmly on the main objective. You had the single job of writing a constitution—a charter for peace. And you stayed on that job.

"In spite of the many distractions which came to you in the form of daily problems and disputes about such matters as new boundaries, control of Germany, peace settlements, reparations, war criminals, the form of government of some of the European countries—in spite of all these, you continued in the task of framing this document.

"Those problems and scores of others, which will arise, are all difficult. They are complicated. They are controversial and dangerous.

"But with united spirit we met and solved even more difficult problems during the war. And with the same spirit, if we keep to our principles and never forsake our objectives, the problems we now face and those to come will also be solved.

"We have tested the principle of cooperation in this war and have found that it works. Through the pooling of resources, through joint and combined military command, through constant staff meetings, we have shown what united strength can do in war. That united strength forced Germany to surrender. United strength will force Japan to surrender. . . .

"What you have accomplished in San Francisco shows how well the lessons of military and economic cooperation have been learned. You have created a great instrument for peace and security and human progress in the world.

"The world must now use it.

"If we fail to use it, we shall betray all those who have died in order that we might meet here in freedom and safety to create it.

"If we seek to use it selfishly—for the advantage of any one nation or any small group of nations—we shall be equally guilty of that betrayal.

"The successful use of this instrument will require the united will and firm determination of the free peoples who have created it. The job will tax the moral strength and fibre of us all.

"We all have to recognize—no matter how great our strength—that we must deny ourselves the license to do always as we please. No one nation, no regional group, can or should expect any special privilege which harms any other nation. If any nation would keep security for itself, it must be ready and willing to share security with all. That is the price which each nation will have to pay for world peace. Unless we are all willing to pay that price, no organization for world peace can accomplish its purpose.

"And what a reasonable price that is!

"Out of this conflict have come powerful military nations, now fully trained and equipped for war. But they have no right to dominate the world. It is rather the duty of these powerful nations to assume the responsibility for leadership toward a world of peace. That is why we have here resolved that power and strength shall be used not to wage war, but to keep the world at peace, and free from the fear of war.

"By their own example the strong nations of the world should lead the way to international justice. That principle of justice is the foundation stone of this Charter. That principle is the guiding spirit by which it must be carried out—not by words alone but by continued concrete acts of good will.

"There is a time for making plans—and there is a time for action. The time for action is now. Let us, therefore, each in his own nation and according to its own way, seek immediate approval of this Charter—and make it a living thing.

"I shall send this Charter to the United States Senate at once. I am sure that the overwhelming sentiment of the people of my country and of their representatives in the Senate is in favor of immediate ratification.

"A just and lasting peace cannot be attained by diplomatic agreement alone, or by military cooperation alone. Experience has shown how deeply the seeds of war are planted by economic rivalry and by social injustice. The Charter recognizes this fact for it has provided for economic and social cooperation as well. It has provided for this cooperation as part of the very heart of the entire compact.

"It has set up machinery of international cooperation which men and nations of good will can use to help correct economic and social causes for conflict.

"Artificial and uneconomic trade barriers should be removed—to the end that the standard of living of as many people as possible throughout the world may be raised. For Freedom from Want is one of the basic Four Freedoms toward which we all strive. The large and powerful nations of the world must assume leadership in this economic field as in all others.

"Under this document we have good reason to expect the framing of an international bill of rights, acceptable to all the nations involved. That bill of rights will be as much a part of international life as our own Bill of Rights is a part of our Constitution. The Charter is dedicated to the achievement and observance of human rights and fundamental freedoms. Unless we can attain those objectives for all men and women everywhere—without regard to race, language or religion—we cannot have permanent peace and security.

"With this Charter the world can begin to look forward to the time when all worthy human beings may be permitted to live decently as free people.

"The world has learned again that nations, like individuals, must know the truth if they would be free—must read and hear the truth, learn and teach the truth.

"We must set up an effective agency for constant and thorough interchange of thought and ideas. For there lies the road to a better and more tolerant understanding among nations and among peoples.

"All Fascism did not die with Mussolini. Hitler is finished—but the seed spread by his disordered mind have firm root in too many fanatical brains. It is easier to remove tyrants and destroy concentration camps than it is to kill the ideas which gave them birth and strength. Victory on the battlefield was essential, but it was not enough. For a good peace, a lasting peace, the decent peoples of the earth must remain determined to strike down the evil spirit which has hung over the world for the last decade.

"The forces of reaction and tyranny all over the world will try to keep the United Nations from remaining united. Even while the military machine of the Axis was being destroyed in Europe—even down to its very end—they still tried to divide us.

"They failed. But they will try again.

"They are trying even now. To divide and conquer was—and still is—their plan. They still try to make one Ally suspect the other, hate the other, desert the other.

"But I know I speak for every one of you when I say that the United Nations will remain united. They will not be divided by propaganda either before the Japanese surrender—or after.

"This occasion shows again the continuity of history.

"By this Charter, you have given reality to the ideal of that great statesman of a generation ago—Woodrow Wilson.

"By this Charter, you have moved toward the goal for which that gallant leader in this second world struggle worked and fought and gave his life—Franklin D. Roosevelt.

"By this Charter, you have realized the objectives of many men of vision in your own countries who have devoted their lives to the cause of world organization for peace.

"Upon all of us, in all our countries, is now laid the duty of transforming into action these words which you have written. Upon our decisive action rests the hope of those who have fallen, those now living, those yet unborn—the hope for a world of free countries—with decent standards of living—which will work and cooperate in a friendly civilized community of nations.

"This new structure of peace is rising upon strong foundations.

"Let us not fail to grasp this supreme chance to establish a world-wide rule of reason—to create an enduring peace under the guidance of God."

Six days later I stepped to the rostrum in the Senate Chamber of the Capitol in Washington and presented the Charter to the Senate of the United States for ratification.

With events crowding and work piling up on me, I had not been able to write Mama since her visit to the White House. But on June 13, before breakfast, I wrote:

Dear Mama & Mary:—It is just two months last night since I took the oath of office—and what a two months! The next two years can't hold any more. I don't dare think of facing the next two months let alone two years. I have to take things as they come and make every decision on the basis of the facts as I have them and then go on from there; then forget that one and take the next.

I guess you are both glad to be in the house and sort of settled once more.

Wish I could drop in on you as I once did without upsetting the apple cart—but I can't.

Your trip here was a grand success and so was the Texas trip. As long as we all behave as we have the first two months, Mr. President will get through the next two years all right.

I am having breakfast with Mr. Hopkins, Mr. Davies and Admiral Leahy this morning to discuss Russian, German, Italian and British affairs. It ought to be an interesting breakfast and maybe a headache—you never can tell. . . .

It is rather lonesome here in this old barn without anyone. I am all alone—but I get a lot of work done. It is now seven A.M. and I've been up an hour. Went to bed at 11:30 after reading dispatches, letters, reports, etc. The clocks have all decided it's seven o'clock. One with a hoarse voice leads off. It is a little one which sits on my study mantel. Like most small people it has a big voice. Then comes the gold clock on the bedroom mantel. I swiped it out of the Madam's sitting room after she left. The ship's clock in Mrs. Wallace's room bangs away in that crazy sailor count of bells. And then the old grandpa clock in the hall comes out with the high squeaky voice you remember—the biggest clock with the highest pitch. Like fat tenors you know. The clock on my study mantel is the one you had in the Rose Room.

We're getting straightened up. I've moved my desk between the windows, and they've put the drapes in my bedroom and Bess' bedroom. When we get all straightened up, you'll have to come and see us again.

Take care of yourselves and let me hear from you.

Love to you both.

Harry

On June 16 I found time to write Mama and Mary another letter.

Dear Mama & Mary:—The deed came day before yesterday and that gives you a rent free home for the rest of your life anyway—and that goes for you both. So now take good care of yourselves and live as long as you can—"forever" the Mesopotamian Kings used to say to each other—"O King, live forever." But they never did, only in statuary, and vandals usually carried that off to decorate some other building than the king's tomb or used it for a hitching post.

I am having a strenuous time. Every day I see some notable of some sort, pin medals on heroes and make world shaking decisions. It seems to agree with me for I've gained twelve pounds since last January: I guess it's because I have nothing to look forward to but retirement. . . .

Had a dozen people over for dinner last evening—just the military aide and his wife and kids and the Naval aide and his wife and Marine sergeant boy—a nice kid by the way—and John Snyder and his wife and lovely daughter. She's about Margie's age. Vaughan's daughter is about sixteen and his boy is ten—13 at the table.

Three generals came in to see me yesterday and General Patch gave me Herr Goering's baton. I always get those dirty Nazis mixed up but it makes no difference. Anyway it's the fat Marshal's insignia of office. It is about a foot and a half long, made of ivory inlaid with gold eagles and iron crosses with diamond studded end caps and platinum rings around it for engraving. Must have cost several thousand dollars—maybe forty—to make. Can you imagine a fat pig like that strutting around with a forty thousand dollar bauble—at the poor taxpayer's expense and making 'em like it? It goes to a military museum.

Monday I entertain Eisenhower, a real man. Tuesday I go to Olympia, Washington—Saturday a week from today San Francisco, Sunday back here, Monday June 25th appear in the Senate and Wed. 27th Independence, 28th K.C. and home for a few days and July 3rd Governors Conference at Mackinac, Mich., and then get ready to go to Berlin. How would you like to be the President des Etats Unis? It's a hell of a life.

Love to you both.

Harry

Before leaving for the West Coast I had rushed off this letter on June 19:

Dear Mama & Mary:—I am all packed up and ready to go to the plane for Washington State. Will send you a line or two. The deed was OK. I get all the mail but don't get a chance to answer it specifically. The papers usually tell all I'm doing anyway.

It makes no difference about the Daily Record publishing the deed to the house. That is to be expected. They publish everything recorded and it doesn't make any difference. There's nothing they can say about me that hasn't been said all over and they can't do me any harm now.

Tried to call you Sunday but could get no answer. Guess you were at Mrs. Lester's. Hope you had a good time.

I'll stop at home on the way back. Love to you both.

Harry

P.S. Had a big shindig for Gen. Eisenhower last night. About 110 there. It was quite a party. Mostly soldiers. The Supreme Court and the Cabinet were there too as was the staff—the Presidential Staff I mean—both civil and military. It was a gaudy affair if gold braid counts. . . .

Too bad about old Sam. I sent Delsie a telegram.

Sam was the son of Aunt Caroline Simpson. This good old black woman had been our cook and washwoman. All of us called her Auntie. We were all as fond of her as we were of our kinfolks. She was the mother of three boys and two girls with whom we grew up. Sam was the oldest boy and big and fat. Everyone called him Fat Sam. I had made him fireman at the county home when I was on the county court of Jackson County. He supported his mother and Delsie, his crippled sister. The other two boys were married and had families of their own. When Auntie died, we all felt as if we'd lost a member of the family, and we felt the same way when Sam died.

I wrote Mama again on June 22, shortly after I arrived in Olympia:

Dear Mama & Mary:—Well, we arrived safely day before yesterday (the day before that) after 12½ hours continuous flying. Rather rough on the last end because of sunshine on plowed fields.

Have been going at a terrific gait all the time. Gave a nice looking soldier boy a Congressional Medal on Wednesday and went fishing on Thursday. The

Dept. of the Interior gave us their fishing boat—a nice yacht built for Herbert Hoover when he was Sec. of Commerce in 1926. We caught no fish but Senator Magnuson bought one from a couple of real fishermen in a row boat for picture-taking purposes. Fish weren't interested in our bait I guess. Got a good sunburning and had a lot of fun—also saw some beautiful scenery on Puget Sound.

We are going to Mt. Rainier today. It is 14,200 feet high and a very beautiful mountain. Looks like a big ice cream cone from here—seventy-five miles away.

Mon's sister's husband died day before yesterday and put a damper on our party. But Mon wouldn't leave us.

We go to San Francisco on Monday and will start for home on Tuesday after my speech. Hope you are both well. We'll be at the Fairmont Hotel. Hope to be in Independence next Wednesday at 2 P.M.

Will do better next time.

Love to you both.

Harry

CHAPTER 19

The end of war and the effort by the Allies to restore order in Europe brought on many unexpected difficulties. The early stages of the occupation of Germany and Austria resulted in new tensions. Under the terms of the unconditional surrender of Germany, the Allies had absolute authority and complete control. But the major problem was how to work out occupational arrangements that would be satisfactory to each of the Allies.

There was no German government except for a group at Flensburg under Admiral Doenitz, who claimed to be the acting authority of the Reich. We paid no attention to Doenitz, although our Army kept a vigilant eye on him.

In Austria we faced a Russian occupation with their usual "provisional government" setup which was completely under Russian control and which claimed to represent all of Austria. We protested to the Soviet government that the provisional government in Vienna had been formed without consultation with the Americans, the British, and the French. The American chargé in Moscow had been instructed to inform the Soviet government "that while we do not object to the establishment of native local administration in occupied areas, we do object to the Soviet government permitting the establishment of a government claiming to represent all of Austria, including the American occupied zone. Full consultation should have taken place and effective consultation will be possible only when allied representatives arrive in Vienna and joint control begins. Until then the American government is not associated with and accepts no responsibilities for measures taken in the Vienna area."

The chargé was instructed also to restate the American position regarding the zone of Vienna and to point out "that it is the Soviet government which has been refusing to follow the German precedents and subdivide Greater Vienna in a manner which will give us the facilities we require."

Both in Germany and in Austria the major task facing us was to set up control machinery and to arrange for the withdrawal of the Allied troops to their respective zones. In Austria none of this work had been done. In Germany, however, the preparatory work on occupation and control had already been completed by the European Advisory Commission. Only Soviet approval was needed before the details of organization in each zone could be made public.

It was our plan, to which the British had agreed, to dissolve the combined headquarters of General Eisenhower (SHAEF) as soon as the zones of occupation were established. Eisenhower would then be placed in charge of the American zone, Montgomery would take over the zone allocated to the British, and a French general would be in command of that portion of the original American sector which was to become a French zone. These three Allied officers, together with the commander of the Russian zone, would form the Allied Control Council for all Germany.

On May 10 General Eisenhower recommended that the dissolution of SHAEF take place as soon as the American, British, and French forces had occupied their respective zones.

On May 11 Churchill cabled me urging that our forces be kept on the farthest advanced lines they had reached. In spite of the fact that he agreed to the occupation zones, he asserted that the Allies ought not withdraw from the positions they had reached until we had been satisfied about Poland and other problems we had with the Russians.

Churchill followed this note with other messages on the subject of the withdrawal of our troops. He said he was disturbed by our plans for redeployment to the Pacific and asked for a standstill order on the movement of American forces. But we were still in the midst of a major war in the Pacific, and our troops were needed there. Furthermore, there was public clamor at home for the return of troops not going to the Pacific.

I had already indicated to Churchill my intention to live up to the commitments we had entered into with regard to the zones of occupation, and we had no intention of extending ourselves beyond those zones. I took this position after consultations with our military chiefs. Russian tactics and aims were, of course, of much concern to us, and I agreed with Churchill on the seriousness of the situation. But I could not agree to going back on our commitments. Apart from that, there were powerful military considerations which we could not and should not disregard.

Churchill and I exchanged a number of messages about these matters, and on May 16 I addressed a message to Stalin, who was still refusing to permit our troops to enter Vienna.

"I am unable to understand," my message read, "why the Soviet authorities are now refusing to permit American and Allied representatives to proceed to Vienna, contrary to the good suggestion you made to Ambassador Harriman on April 13 that representatives go there to study the Vienna zones of occupation, in order that the agreements on the occupation of Austria now pending in the European Advisory Commission may be completed.

"Intelligent arrangement of the Vienna zones would be greatly facilitated by an examination and discussion on the spot by the military authorities who will later be responsible for smooth operation of the inter-Allied administration of Austria. For example, the Soviet representative in the European Advisory Commission has recently proposed that the air comunication needs of the American forces be met by placing under American administration the airport at Tulen, 20 kilometers northwest of Vienna, in lieu of an airport in Vienna itself. However, neither he nor we know the precise dimensions or conditions of this airport, and to give his proposal proper consideration we should be permitted to survey it.

"Since the area to be zoned is no longer in enemy occupation it seems only reasonable to examine it, as you suggested, in order to facilitate completion of the agreements in the European Advisory Commission. Continued refusal of the Soviet authorities to permit this, in spite of your original suggestion, would not be understood by the American public.

"I therefore hope that you will yourself let me know whether you will issue the necessary instructions to Marshal Tolbukhin to facilitate a survey by the Allied representative of those Vienna areas which are now under discussion in the European Advisory Commission."

Stalin's reply reached me on the eighteenth.

"I have received your message of May 17," it read, "regarding the trip of American and Allied military representatives to Vienna. It is true that I agreed in principle to the arrival in Vienna of the said representatives, but, of course, I had in mind that by the time of arrival there of the said representatives a necessary understanding will be reached on the question of the zones of occupation of Austria and that the zones themselves will be specified by the European Consultative Commission.

"As it was agreed upon among Mr. Churchill, President Roosevelt and myself such questions are entirely within the competency of the European Consultative Commission. I still adhere to this point of view at the present time. Therefore it would not be possible to agree that the question about zones of occupation and other questions concerning the situation in Austria be transferred for consideration to Vienna.

"I do not object, however, against a trip of the American and Allied representatives to Vienna for the purpose of acquainting themselves on the spot with the situation of the city and for preparing proposals regarding the zones of occupation in Vienna. In accordance with this necessary instructions will be given to Marshal Tolbukhin.

"Besides, it should be kept in mind that the American military representatives could arrive in Vienna by the end of May or the beginning of June, when Marshal Tolbukhin, who is at present on his way to Moscow, will return to Vienna."

Our problem in Germany now was to get the Allied Control Council into operation. Germany was in effect being run by local military commanders. There was the danger of complete economic and social collapse of the country. Therefore, it was imperative that there be established at the earliest possible moment a council to make policy for Germany as a whole and to direct the administration of Greater Berlin.

On May 22 the United States, Britain, Russia, and France approved the formal declaration of defeat of Germany drawn up by the European Advisory Commission. The four military commanders would meet in Berlin early in June to sign this document and would remain there to work out the details of Control Council machinery.

In approving these plans, it was my purpose that Germany would be treated as one country, eventually to be placed under one government that would be subject to checks by the Allied Control Council in order to prevent a re-emergence of Nazism and Prussian militarism. At this time Admiral Doenitz was placed under arrest as one of the top Nazi leaders listed by the War Crimes Commission.

Acting Secretary of State Grew reported to me that in a discussion on May 16 between General Eisenhower and Churchill, General Eisenhower pressed for an early control by the Allied Control Council for Germany even though the Russian representative might have to refer everything to Moscow.

Eisenhower expressed the view and position taken by Churchill:

"Although Churchill agreed that this matter should receive urgent consideration he feels that SHAEF should be responsible for the control of Germany until some other body is established to take over. He did not appear to be in any real hurry about this matter. Churchill stated full agreement with the British Foreign Office memorandum which among other things pointed out that the need to establish some German government was becoming ever more apparent. Churchill stated that the Allies should not assume full responsibility for Germany but should only take measures to prevent Germany from ever being able to start another war. German problems should be handled by Germans and some of the German generals now held by us might be employed for this purpose since they would be obeyed by the German people. Among other points mentioned by Churchill were a reduction in rations for non-working prisoners of war and a statement that German war equipment, particularly aircraft, should not be destroyed but should be kept to equip liberated nations."

On June 2 General Eisenhower, as head of SHAEF, cabled the Combined Chiefs of Staff, asking for instructions on the date of withdrawal of our remaining troops to the designated zones of occupation. His telegram read:

"It is anticipated that one of the questions which will be raised at Berlin meeting to sign and issue declaration will be date on which our forces will begin their withdrawal from Russian zone. It is possible that Russians may establish such withdrawal as a corollary to the establishment of the Control Council on a functioning basis in Berlin and to turning over the several zones in Berlin to the forces to occupy these zones. Any cause for delay in the establishment of Control Council due to the delay in withdrawal would be attributed to us and might well develop strong public reaction. We have as yet no instructions covering such withdrawal. It is believed desirable that separate instructions be given to me as American commander and to the British commander prior to Berlin meeting as to how we should reply to this question if it is raised."

The Chiefs of Staff, with my approval, instructed General Eisenhower on June 3:

"The question of withdrawal to our own zones should not be a condition precedent to establishment of the Control Council on a functioning basis and turning over of zones in Berlin. If Russians raise the point, you should state in substance that the matter of withdrawal of forces to their own zones is one of the items to be worked out in the Control Council. As to the actual movement of U.S. forces, you should state that this, in your view, is primarily a military matter; its timing will be in accordance with U.S. ability to withdraw their forces from other than their own zone and British and Russian ability to take over."

On June 4 Churchill again urged against the withdrawal of American troops to the designated occupation zones. He said that he viewed "with profound misgivings the retreat of the American army to our line of occupation in the Central Sector, thus bringing Soviet power into the heart of Western Europe and the descent of an iron curtain between us and everything to the eastward." He hoped "that this retreat, if it has to be made, would be accompanied by the settlement of many great things which would be the true foundation of world peace. Nothing really important has been settled yet, and you and I will have to bear great responsibility for the future."

On June 5 the declaration of the defeat of Germany was signed in Berlin by the commanders of the four Allied armies. At the meeting the Russians made it plain that they felt that the Allied troops should be redistributed into their respective zones and that a governmental decision regarding the delimitation of those zones had to be made before the Control Council was organized. The State Department reported to me on June 8 that "General Eisenhower forcefully pointed out that Allied Military Government had become a fact in Germany through the signature by the commanders of the four-power declaration on establishing supreme authority. . . . The meeting terminated with agreement that the problem of redistribution of forces is one to be settled by government decision and that each commander would refer the question to his respective government for action."

The State Department report, quoting Eisenhower's political adviser, Ambassador Murphy, concluded:

"Murphy secretly informs the Department that he believes General Eisenhower does not consider it wise to retain our forces in the Russian zone nor does he feel that it would be productive of advantages. Murphy personally believes that there is no ground for any discouragement in these developments and on the contrary finds definite progress has been made. He is convinced that the Soviets regard the Control Council as necessary and its operation as redounding to their interest.

"Marshal Zhukov has accepted General Eisenhower's invitation to visit him on June 10 at Frankfurt."

Hopkins, on his return from his meeting with Stalin, stopped off at Frankfurt, Germany, to talk to Eisenhower. On June 8 he informed me that he had discussed the Russian situation in Germany with Eisenhower and got the general's impression of his talk with Zhukov. Hopkins was convinced "that present indeterminate status of the date for withdrawal of Allied Troops from area assigned to the Russians is certain to be misunderstood by Russia as well as at home."

Hopkins stressed the fact that Allied control machinery could not be started until Allied troops had withdrawn from territory included in the Russian area of occupation and that any delay in the establishment of control machinery would interfere seriously with the development of governmental administrative machinery for Germany. Hopkins suggested that "as a concurrent condition to our withdrawal we should specify a simultaneous movement of our troops to Berlin under an agreement between the respective commanders which would provide us unrestricted access to our Berlin area from Bremen and Frankfurt by air, rail and highway on agreed routes."

I informed Churchill of my decision to withdraw American troops from the Russian zone beginning June 21.

"In consideration of the tripartite agreement," I cabled him, "as to zones of occupation in Germany, approved by President Roosevelt after long consideration and detailed discussion with you, I am unable to delay the withdrawal of American troops from the Soviet zone in order to use pressure in the settlement of other problems.

"Advice of the highest reliability is received that the Allied Control Council cannot begin to function until Allied troops withdraw from the Russian Zone.

"I am also convinced that the Military Government now exercised by the Allied Supreme Commander should, without delay, be terminated and divided between Eisenhower and Montgomery, each to function in the zone occupied by his own troops.

"I am advised that it would be highly disadvantageous to our relations with the Soviet to postpone action in this matter until our meeting in July.

"I therefore propose to send the following message to Stalin:

"QUOTE. Now that the unconditional defeat of Germany has been announced and the Control Council for Germany has had its first meeting, I propose that we should at once issue definite instruction which will get forces into their respective zones and will initiate orderly administration of the defeated territory. As to Germany, I am ready to have instructions issued to all American troops to begin withdrawal into their own zone on 21 June in accordance with arrangements between the respective commanders, including in these arrangements simultaneous movement of the national garrisons into Greater Berlin and provision of free access by air, road, and rail from Frankfurt and Bremen to Berlin for U.S. forces.

"As to Austria, it seems that arrangements can be completed more quickly and satisfactorily by making our commanders on the spot responsible for determining the definition of zones both in Austria itself and in the Vienna area and the readjustment of forces, referring to their respective governments only those matters that they are unable to resolve between themselves. I consider the settlement of the Austrian problem as of equal urgency to the German matter.

"If you agree with the foregoing, I propose that appropriate instructions be issued at once to our respective commanders. UNQUOTE."

Churchill's reply arrived on June 14. In it he said that "obviously we are obliged to conform to your decision," and that the necessary instructions would be issued.

Churchill added:

"It is not correct to state that the tripartite agreement about zones of occupation in Germany was the subject of 'long consideration and detailed discussion' between me and President Roosevelt. References made to them at OCTAGON[1] were brief and concerned only the Anglo-American arrangements which the President did not wish to raise by correspondence beforehand. These were remitted to the Combined Chiefs of Staff and were certainly acceptable to them."

Churchill suggested a change in the wording of the next to the last paragraph of my message to Marshal Stalin, and offered the following version:

"I consider the settlement of the Austrian problem is of equal urgency to the German matter. The redistribution of forces into occupation zones which have been agreed in principle by the EAC [European Advisory Commission], the movement of the national garrisons into Vienna, and the establishment of the Allied Commission for Austria should take place simultaneously with these developments in Germany. I therefore attach the utmost importance to settling the outstanding Austrian problems, in order that the whole arrangement of German and Austrian affairs can be put into operation simultaneously. I hope that the recent visit of American, British, and French missions to Vienna will result in the EAC being able to take the necessary remaining decisions to this end without delay."

He said he attached particular importance to having the Russians evacuate that part of the British zone in Austria which they were then holding at the same time that the British and American forces pulled back from the Russian zone in Germany.

Churchill added, "I sincerely hope that your action will in the long run make for a lasting peace in Europe."

I accepted in full Churchill's suggested changes to my proposed message to Stalin and sent it the same day. Churchill advised me the following day that he had sent a message to Stalin endorsing my views and advising him that the British government would also order withdrawal from the Russian zone on June 21.

In spite of previous Russian pressure for our quick evacuation from the Russian zone, Stalin suddenly and surprisingly proposed a slight postponement. The Russian Premier preferred an even later date than the one I had suggested. Stalin had a parade on his mind.

---

[1] Code name for second Quebec conference.

"I have received your message," his cable read, "regarding the expediting of removal of Allied troops into appropriate zones in Germany and Austria.

"To my regret I have to say that your proposal to begin the removal of American troops into their zone and the entry of American troops into Berlin on June 21 meets with certain difficulties as, beginning with June 19, Marshal Zhukov and all of our other troop commanders are invited to Moscow to the session of the Supreme Soviet as well as for the organization of a parade and for the participation in the parade on June 24. Not mentioning the fact that not all the districts of Berlin have been cleared of mines and that this clearing cannot be finished before the end of June. As Marshal Zhukov and other commanders of Soviet troops are not able to return from Moscow to Germany before June 28th–30th, I would like to request that the removal of the troops begin on July 1 when the commanders will be back and the clearing of the mines completed.

"As regards Austria—the above-stated in respect to the summons of Soviet commanders to Moscow and the date of their return to Vienna applies to them as well. Besides it is necessary that in the nearest future the European Consultative Commission complete its work on the establishment of zones of occupation of Austria and Vienna as this work has not been completed up to the present time. In view of the stated circumstances the allocation of appropriate troops to their zones in Austria should also be postponed until July 1.

"Besides, in respect to Germany as well as to Austria, it would be necessary, right now, to determine the zones of occupation by the French troops.

"On our part all necessary measures will be taken in Germany and Austria in accordance with the above-stated plan."

On June 18 I replied to Stalin:

"I have issued instructions to the American commanders to begin the movement on July 1 as requested by you. It is assumed that American troops will be in Berlin at an earlier date in sufficient number to accomplish their duties in preparation for our conference."

I then directed General Marshall to instruct the American commander to begin the evacuation movement on July 1 and for his information sent him copies of the messages exchanged between Stalin and myself.

With the date for evacuation set for July 1, the movement of our troops and the final details were now matters for the commanding general to carry out.

The agreement among Roosevelt, Churchill, and Stalin on how they would handle Germany was being kept. My intention was always to carry out to the letter all agreements entered into by Roosevelt with our allies. The main purpose was to set up a joint government of Germany consisting of the three powers and France.

My aim was a unified Germany with a centralized government in Berlin. In the case of Austria, I hoped for a unified country with its own government in Vienna. It was my own opinion that it would be silly if these arrangements were to lead to an isolated Berlin and Vienna to which we would have no access. I asked Stalin, with Churchill's backing, in my cable of June 14 for free access by air, road, and rail to Berlin and to Vienna as part of the withdrawal of troops previously agreed to by Roosevelt, Churchill, and Stalin.

At my forthcoming meeting with Churchill and Stalin I intended to call for the setting up of a centralized Allied-controlled government. I was opposed to the breaking up of Germany into several Allied segments. It was our plan that transportation, communications, and finance would be administered on a national basis for all of Germany under Allied control. At no time did I believe that Germany should be split into several rival territorial divisions or that its capital should become an island shut off from the rest of the country.

On June 25 General Marshall advised General Eisenhower of our thinking about access rights to Berlin. General McNarney and General Deane, who was head of the military mission to Russia, were also advised.

"It will be noted," Marshall cabled them, "that the proposed . . . directive . . . contains no action to obtain transit rights to Berlin and Vienna on a combined basis. In accordance with the President's message to Stalin . . . these should be arranged with Russian commanders concerned simultaneously with arrangements for other adjustments, by Eisenhower for Berlin and Clark for Vienna. It is assumed that appropriate Russian commanders have been instructed accordingly . . . and it is desired that Deane confirm this with the Soviet staff."

On the following day Deane cabled:

"This afternoon attempted to get confirmation that Soviet commanders have been instructed regarding free access to Berlin and Vienna, as directed in . . . While Lt. General Slavin was unable to give me an immediate reply, from the way he talked I do not anticipate there will be any difficulty in the matter. I will inform you immediately upon receipt of an official reply."

On June 25 General Deane advised Marshall, Eisenhower, and McNarney by cable from Moscow:

"I have requested General Antonov by letter to confirm fact that

Soviet Commanders have been authorized to agree with American Commanders on freedom of access by road, rail and air to Berlin and Vienna as directed in your . . . of 25 June. Will meet with either Antonov or his representative today and hope to get an answer at that time."

On June 27 Deane reported that Marshal Zhukov had been empowered to negotiate for the Russians with General Clay, deputy to General Eisenhower.

General Deane informed Marshall in a cable on June 28, "It is my opinion that when our representatives meet with Zhukov there will be little difficulty in arranging for free access for our troops to Berlin, and that, if I am correct in this, the same principle will apply to Vienna. . . ."

The Soviet agreed to provide unrestricted use by the Allies of the standard-gauge railroad from Goslar to Berlin via Magdeburg. The Allies were also given the use of the Hanau-Magdeburg-Berlin autobahn but were refused free use of the Berlin-Frankfurt autobahn. The Allies were to have an air lane some twenty miles wide from Berlin to Magdeburg and two lanes from Magdeburg to Frankfurt.

With the redistribution of forces into the occupation areas, clearing the way to establish Allied control over Germany, we could now consider the principles by which we would deal with the defeated enemy.

There had been considerable discussion in this country about whether we should make a "hard" or a "soft" peace with Germany. Most of us agreed that Germany should be deprived of the capacity ever to commit aggression again, and in that sense we wanted the peace to be "hard." At the same time, we remembered that after 1919 Germany was so enfeebled that only American money made it possible to pay the reparations that had been imposed.

The subject of reparations was, of course, one of the most critical aspects of this entire question. At Yalta it became apparent that the Russians did not share the views that we and the British held with regard to reparations. At the Yalta conference the Soviets had asked that a flat twenty billion dollars be extracted from the German economy to compensate the nations on the Allied side for their losses, and that fifty per cent of this amount be allocated to the U.S.S.R.

Neither the United States nor Great Britain had been willing to fix a monetary value or to agree to this Russian formula for allocation. In the end, it was agreed that the entire problem of "compensation for damages," as President Roosevelt preferred to call it, would be referred to an Allied commission on reparations. This group was to meet in Moscow in time to prepare proposals for the next meeting of the heads of state.

To lay the groundwork for American participation in the work of this commission, an interdepartmental committee, under Assistant Secretary of State Will Clayton, had been at work since February. Dr. Isador Lubin had been designated as our representative on the Allied Reparations Commission, and he had begun to assemble a small staff. Their planning was well under way.

Lubin was an able public servant of high intelligence. But in the light of the difficulties that had arisen with the Soviets over the application of the Yalta agreement on Poland, I felt that the position required a tough bargainer, someone who could be as tough as Molotov. For this reason I asked Edwin W. Pauley to become my personal representative in reparations matters, while Dr. Lubin agreed to assist him as associate representative of the United States on the Allied Commission.

Pauley was well prepared for the job not only by reason of a long career in business but as a student of economics, and he understood my attitude on the reparations question.

I was deeply concerned that the peace to be written should not carry within it the kind of self-defeating provisions that would enable another Hitler to rise to power. I wanted to work out a peace settlement that would be lasting.

It was already becoming apparent that we would be called upon to give aid, on a large scale, to many of the war-devastated areas. Judge Rosenman had just returned from an extensive inspection of the economic and, especially, the food situation in western Europe. His comprehensive report to me made it plain that help was badly needed and that it would have to come from us.

In England, France, Belgium, and Norway the prospects appeared equally bleak. Food supplies were critical; on the continent the return of acreage to agricultural use was hindered by the widespread presence of mines and explosives in the fields; everywhere fuel, transportation, and industrial plants were far below minimum needs. Added to this was the presence on the continent of several million persons displaced by the war, and in England and on the continent alike an alarming lack of shelter.

As our armies had advanced into Germany, it had become evident that the situation there was desperate. It seemed unlikely that much could be extracted from Germany beyond war machinery proper without reducing the country to the reliefer's role. Germany would have to be fed, and I was determined to see that it would not once again be charity altogether from us that fed her.

These considerations were reflected in the instructions Pauley was given. This document had been worked out by Clayton's committee, and I approved it on May 18.

"It is and has been fundamental United States policy," it read in part, "that Germany's war potential be destroyed, and its resurgence as far as possible prevented, by removal or destruction of German plants, equipment and other property." But we also instructed our delegation to oppose "any reparations plan based on the assumption that the United States or any other country will finance directly or indirectly any reconstruction in Germany or reparation by Germany."

Since the Soviets would be occupying Eastern Germany, the source of most of Germany's food, while we and the British would hold the area in which most of the industrial strength was to be found, we instructed Pauley to see that the burden of reparations would, as far as possible, be divided equally among the several zones of occupation. Our delegation was further directed to press for the principle that, to the maximum extent possible, reparations should be taken from the national wealth of Germany existing at the time of the collapse, with primary emphasis upon removal of industrial machinery, equipment, and plants. The German people were to be deprived of the ability to make war but should be left with sufficient means to provide a minimum subsistence level without sustained outside (which could only mean American) relief.

But if there were to be continuing reparations from current production, we would insist that the "first charge" principle be observed. That is, we wanted those exports that were necessary to maintain minimum production to be charged against the imports necessary to feed the country before anything went for reparations.

Pauley was also directed to seek agreement on the scope of war booty, reimbursement for occupation costs, and restitution. Since the definition of these terms would have an important effect on the amount of materials available for reparations purposes, agreement on these points was essential.

The food situation in Europe gave me increasing cause for concern. The Department of Agriculture's experts came up with an estimate that continental Europe alone, not including the British Isles, would need twelve million tons of food during the next year to prevent large-scale starvation. Production for 1946, they calculated, would be five to ten per cent below that for 1945, the lowest since prewar days. Our own farm yields were less promising for this year than they had been since the war began. I thought it might be desirable and useful to consult with former President Herbert Hoover on this situation. I invited him to visit with me and give me the benefit of his rich experience in the field of food relief. When he came, I had a most pleasant and satisfactory meeting with him. He helped me to review the world food-distribution problem, which he knew from one end to the other. The former President was pleased to be able to make a personal contribution to the settlement of the aftermath of the war.

Meanwhile the Pauley mission had proceeded to Moscow for the meetings of the Allied Reparations Commission. Pauley had assembled a notable group of men. It was a bi-partisan group, including President Robert Gordon Sproul of the University of California, Dr. Luther Gulick, and a number of experts drawn from business and government.

Pauley arrived in Moscow as the Moscow radio broadcast a sharp attack on "U.S. industrialists who are doing their utmost to restore German heavy industry." It was not until June 21 that the Commission met. After our delegation presented a statement of eight principles embodying our position, the Soviet representative presented the plan of his government. This called for withdrawals to be made from the existing national wealth of Germany for two years. Thereafter, annual deliveries from current production would continue over a ten-year period and, in addition, there would be wide utilization of German labor. Furthermore, there would be a fixed sum total for all reparations in the amount of twenty billion dollars, exclusive of labor. The Russians proposed that the Commission proceed first to plan for the withdrawal of national wealth and then pass to the other items on the Soviet agenda. Our delegation asked for data that would support the twenty-billion-dollar figure, a request that had originally been made at Yalta, but none was forthcoming. In fact, the Russians, unwilling to make any concessions, prevented, by delaying tactics, any further meetings of the full Commission.

The Steering Committee of the Commission decided on a compromise for the allocation of shares from the total of reparations. The Russians had proposed that they receive fifty per cent, the United States and the United Kingdom together forty per cent, and all other nations ten per cent. The British were interested in having their claim spelled out separately, and we made the point that the claims of nations not represented in the Commission should not be prejudged. The compromise provided for a ratio of 56-22-22 among the three powers present and deferred until later the determination of what other nations were to get. Then, whatever would go to the other nations would be prorated against the three major powers on the same basis of 56-22-22.

Pauley's discussions in Moscow, on which he kept me constantly advised, took place while there were increasing reports that wholesale removals of plants and equipment were under way in the Soviet zone of Germany. The Russians chose to interpret the words "war booty" in a manner that included any plant or equipment ever used to supply the armed forces of the defeated enemy. Under modern war conditions that made the definition nearly all-inclusive.

Meanwhile at Moscow, any attempt to agree on a definition was frustrated by Russian refusal to consider anything until the plan for the initial withdrawal from national wealth had been worked out. When we thought of withdrawals from the national wealth of Germany, we naturally thought of a Germany of pre-World War II dimensions. With this in mind we had asked, and had received, Russian agreement to the basic proposition that, for purposes of reparations, Germany would be treated as an economic whole. Even while this principle was being agreed to at Moscow, however, a sizeable portion of German territory had been placed under the administration of Poland and had thus been withdrawn from the area from which reparations might be taken. Since this portion of Germany, along with the zone occupied by the Russians, had contributed the bulk of prewar Germany's food supply, the effect this change would have on the German economy was bound to be drastic. Nor could the worsening economic condition of all Europe be separated from our thinking on reparations. Germany was as thoroughly devastated as any part of Europe, but millions of persons displaced by the war aggravated the problems.

Joseph C. Grew, Acting Secretary of State, reported to me in June that the State Department, at the suggestion of Secretary Morgenthau, was planning to send Earl G. Harrison, a former immigration commissioner and dean of the University of Pennsylvania Law School, to Europe to look into the problems and needs of displaced persons, especially those who were considered "non-repatriable." Grew told me that the majority of the displaced persons were being returned by the military authorities in Europe to their respective countries. There remained, however, the Jewish survivors of Nazi persecution and such other groups as Poles and nationals of the Baltic states whose return was being delayed by political reasons.

I approved of the proposed mission and on June 22 wrote directly to Harrison. I told him that it was important to the early restoration of peace and order in Europe that plans be developed to meet the needs of those who, for justifiable reasons, could not return to their countries of former residence.

It became apparent, because of Russian non-cooperation, that each occupying power would have to look to its own zone for reparations claims.

Pauley was to join the staff at Potsdam, both as my representative for reparations and as economic adviser. The progress report Pauley submitted to me before the Potsdam discussions began was a well-prepared document. It was a clear analysis of the Moscow talks and stated the issues that had to be resolved. One of these was the basic difference in attitude between us and the Russians on the question of forced labor. At the suggestion of Justice Jackson, our chief counsel for the war crimes trials, instructions to Pauley affirmed our refusal to accept any reparations for ourselves in the form of labor. In addition, we took the position that compulsory labor should not be imposed by any of the victors except upon individuals judicially convicted as war criminals.

I had held a number of conferences with Justice Jackson and Judge Rosenman in order to set the keynote for our policy on the legal questions of our dealings with Germany.

On June 6 Justice Jackson sent me a progress report. This report expressed decisions and opinions previously considered in conferences I had had with Justice Jackson. This report set the keynote for our policy:

"Fair hearings for the accused are, of course, required to make sure that we punish only the right men for the right reasons.

"But the procedure of these hearings may properly bar obstructive and dilatory tactics resorted to by defendants in our ordinary criminal trials.

"Nor should such a defense be recognized as the obsolete doctrine that a head of state is immune from legal liability. There is more than a suspicion that this idea is a relic of the doctrine of the divine right of kings.

"It is, in any event, inconsistent with the position we take toward our own officials, who are frequently brought to court at the suit of citizens who allege their rights to have been invaded.

"We do not accept the paradox that legal responsibility should be the least where power is the greatest.

"We stand on the principle of responsible government declared some three centuries ago to King James by Lord Chief Justice Coke, who proclaimed that even a King is still 'under God and the law.' . . .

"Whom will we accuse and put to their defense? We will accuse a large number of individuals and officials who were in authority in the government, in the military establishment, including the General Staff, and in the financial, industrial and economic life of Germany who by all civilized standards are provable to be common criminals.

"We also propose to establish the criminal character of several voluntary organizations which have played a cruel and controlling part in subjugating first the German people and then their neighbors.

"It is not, of course, suggested that a person should be judged a criminal merely because he voted for certain candidates or maintained political affiliations in the sense that we in America support political parties. The organizations which we will accuse have no resemblance to our political parties.

"Organizations such as the Gestapo and the S.S. were direct action units, and were recruited from volunteers accepted only because of aptitude for, and fanatical devotion to, their violent purposes. . . .

"Our case against the major defendants is concerned with the Nazi master plan, not with individual barbarities and perversions which occurred independently of any central plan.

"The groundwork of our case must be factually authentic and constitute a well-documented history of what we are convinced was a grand, concerted pattern to incite and commit the aggressions and barbarities which have shocked the world.

"We must not forget that when the Nazi plans were boldly proclaimed, they were so extravagant that the world refused to take them seriously.

"Unless we write the record of this movement with clarity and precision, we cannot blame the future if in days of peace it finds incredible the accusatory generalities uttered during the war. We must establish incredible events by credible evidence. . . .

"Those acts which offended the conscience of our people were criminal by standards generally accepted in all civilized countries, and I believe that we may proceed to punish those responsible in full accord with both our own traditions of fairness and with standards of just conduct which have been internationally accepted.

"I think also that through these trials we should be able to establish that a process of retribution by law awaits those who in the future similarly attack civilization. . . .

"Our people have been waiting for these trials in the spirit of Woodrow Wilson, who hoped to 'give to international law the kind of vitality which it can only have if it is a real expression of our moral judgment.' . . ."

Jackson concluded: "May I add that your personal encouragement and support have been a source of strength and inspiration to every member of my staff, as well as to me, as we go forward with a task so immense that it can never be done completely or perfectly, but which we hope to do acceptably."

314

CHAPTER 20

We were now rushing plans to concentrate the preponderance of our military might and energy in the final drive to
end the war in the Pacific. We were doing this at a time when our military
and political experts in Europe were tackling the enormously complicated
task of rebuilding Europe and peace in the West.

The war in the Pacific had been hard and costly in the years since
December 7, 1941. We had come a long way back from Pearl Harbor and
Bataan. From Australia and New Caledonia in the south and island bases
on Hawaii in the eastern Pacific, our forces had fought their way back to
the Philippines and to the last island chain before the Japanese home
islands. Okinawa and Iwo Jima had been defended fiercely by the enemy,
and our loss of lives had been very heavy. But we now had bases from
which direct attacks could be launched on Japan. We also knew that the
closer we came to the home islands the more determined and fanatical
would be the resistance. There were still more than four million men in
the Japanese armed forces to defend the main Japanese islands, Korea,
Manchuria, and North China. The Japanese were also building up a
"National Volunteer Army" at home for a last-ditch stand.

The Chiefs of Staff were grim in their estimates of the cost in casualties
we would have to pay to invade the Japanese mainland.

As our forces in the Pacific were pushing ahead, paying a heavy toll in
lives, the urgency of getting Russia into the war became more compelling.
Russia's entry into the war would mean the saving of hundreds of thousands of American casualties.

That was one of the compelling reasons that would take me out of the country to a meeting with Stalin and Churchill. And this is why we were urging the Chinese and the Russians to conclude an accord on the basis of the Roosevelt, Churchill, and Stalin agreement at Yalta.

There was no way for us to get troops into China to drive the Japanese from the Chinese mainland. Our hope always was to get enough Russian troops into Manchuria to push the Japanese out. That was the only way it could be done at this time.

In China our entire wartime policy had been designed to keep the people united in the fight against Japan. Ambassador Hurley had reported to me on May 20, "We have succeeded in having the National Government recognize the Chinese Communist armed party as a political party by appointing a Chinese Communist as a delegate to represent the National Government at San Francisco. The Communists recognized the National Government by accepting the appointment. We have visited with the Communist leaders in their own territory. We have brought about conferences between the Communist and National leaders in which they seem to have eliminated some of their conflicts. In the controversy between the Government and the Communist Party, we had two major objectives:

"(1) to avoid what appeared to be an immediately impending civil war;

"(2) to unite the Communist and National Government armies under one commander to fight Japan . . ."

Since Russia's entry into the war depended a great deal upon the outcome of the negotiations between Stalin and Chinese Foreign Minister Soong, I asked Ambassador Harriman to keep me closely informed of the progress of the talks to be held in Moscow.

Soong arrived in the Russian capital on June 30 and was received by Stalin that day. Stalin began the conversations by insisting that the Chinese recognize the independence of Outer Mongolia. Soong replied that China could not agree to the cession of territory, that it would complicate the question of Tibet, and that no government of China could last if it ceded Outer Mongolia. He later explained to Harriman that this was a matter of principle that was deeply embedded in Chinese psychology, and that although they realized that they could not then exercise sovereignty over Outer Mongolia the Chinese would be unwilling to support a government which gave up for all time Chinese claims to this territory.

Harriman reported that Soong informed him that Stalin had suggested a secret agreement on the independence of Outer Mongolia which might be published after the defeat of Japan. Soong objected but cabled Chiang Kai-shek for instructions. He also asked Harriman what the understanding of President Roosevelt had been on this point and said that he understood that I interpreted the Russian proposal in the same manner that he, Soong, did. Nevertheless, he asked Harriman to telegraph urgently to ascertain what the United States Government's interpretation was.

As the talks continued, Soong told Harriman, difficulties arose on the matter of ports and railroads. Stalin made demands that extended his earlier ones, and proposed that the ownership of the Chinese Eastern and South Manchuria railroads should be Russian; that they should be operated by a joint Soviet-Chinese board, but that the management should be Russian.

"Soong," Harriman cabled, "contended that the ownership of the railroads should be Chinese, and that they should be operated by a Soviet-Chinese company with joint responsibility and a mixed management partly Chinese and partly Russian. Stalin indicated that he was interested only in the main lines and not in the subsidiary lines. Molotov however raised the question of control of the coal production for the operation of the railroad. Stalin agreed that Russia should have the right to move troops only in time of war or in preparation for threat of war.

"Stalin further agreed that Russia should not have the right to station troops in Manchuria. As regards the port of Dairen, Stalin interpreted 'internationalization' as meaning that it should be subject to Chinese and Russian control; that no other country was to be involved, that Russia should have a preeminent interest, and that there should be a Russian management. The revenues of the port should go half to Russia and half to China. Soong maintained that the port should be a free port under Chinese administration with some Russian technical assistance and with full rights for Russia to use the port freely. As to Port Arthur, Stalin agreed to eliminate the word 'lease' and work out some basis by which both countries could have naval facilities. Stalin proposed that the agreement regarding the railroads and ports should be for a forty-five year period . . . On the question of the sovereignty of China in Manchuria, Soong was reassured by Stalin's statements. Stalin agreed that representatives of the Chinese National Government should accompany the Red Army when it advanced into Manchuria to organize the government. Stalin told Soong it was important for the National Government to appoint competent individuals. Stalin inquired regarding the National Government's attitude towards the Communists, and Soong told him that the Generalissimo was prepared to bring Communist representation into the government but the Kuomintang should be in control. Soong says that Stalin appeared to agree in principle but there was no detailed discussion or agreement as to the understanding to be reached with the Communists. . . .

"As to Korea, Stalin confirmed to Soong his agreement to establishing a four power trusteeship. Molotov interjected that this was an unusual arrangement with no parallel and that therefore it would be necessary to come to a detailed understanding. Stalin stated that there should be no foreign troops or foreign policy in Korea. Soong understands that the Russians have 2 Korean divisions trained in Siberia. He believes that these troops will be left in Korea and that there will be Soviet trained political personnel who will also be brought into the country. Under those conditions he is fearful that even with a four power trusteeship the Soviets will obtain domination of Korean affairs."

On July 4 I instructed Secretary of State Byrnes to inform Harriman that the United States did not want to act as interpreter on any point in the Yalta agreement during the present discussions in Moscow. Harriman was told, however, that he could "informally" confirm to Soong his understanding that in so far as the United States was concerned there was no discussion of interpretation of the wording of the Yalta decision relating to the status of Outer Mongolia and that in the absence of such discussion the accepted meaning of the words as written would be that the present factual and juridical status of Outer Mongolia was to be preserved.

"For your information only," the message to Harriman concluded, "the status quo as we understand it is that while the *de jure* sovereignty of Outer Mongolia remains vested in China, *de facto* this sovereignty is not exercised. The United States Government in conformity with the Nine Power Treaty of 1922 has carefully refrained from any indication that it considered the outlying dependencies of China, such as Outer Mongolia, in a different status from the remainder of China."

On July 6 Harriman was instructed to inform the Russians and the Chinese that our government, being a party to the Yalta agreement, expected to be consulted before any final agreement was concluded between the Russians and the Chinese.

Further, we proposed at an appropriate time to make clear to the Soviet and Chinese governments that we would expect assurances that any arrangements made between the governments of the Soviet Union and China would cover the right of equal access by nationals of all peace-loving nations to the port facilities of Dairen and participation by them in transportation privileges on the railways, and would preclude practical denial of equality of economic opportunity, as was the case during the period of Japanese control.

We were pleased, we told Harriman, to note that Soong was reassured by Stalin's statements in regard to the sovereignty of China and Manchuria and also that Stalin agreed that Russia should not have the right to station troops in Manchuria. As to Stalin's proposal that the ownership of the principal railroads in Manchuria should be Russian, our understanding of the Yalta agreement, Harriman was informed, was that they should be jointly operated by the Soviet Union and China and that there was no provision providing for exclusive Soviet ownership.

On July 7 Ambassador Hurley transmitted a message to me from Generalissimo Chiang Kai-shek:

"Last night Chiang held a long conference with his advisers after which he cabled to Soong instructions substance of which is as follows:

"China will agree to recognize the independence of the Mongolian People's Republic after the war if the Soviet agrees fully to respect the sovereignty and territorial and administrative integrity. The Soviet would be offered the joint use of Port Arthur but not joint control. Dairen will be made a free port but under Chinese administration. The two railroads will be jointly operated but remain under Chinese ownership and sovereignty. The Soviet agrees not to give any support to the Chinese Communists or to rebellious elements in Sinkiang. . . .

"The Generalissimo said that these are the 'maximum concessions' which China can make. . . .

"The Generalissimo was anxious that the concessions he is willing to make be made known to the President immediately."

From July 9 to July 13 Harriman had daily talks with Soong, who reported to him all the details of his negotiations with Stalin and Molotov. These cables were sent to me on the U.S.S. *Augusta* as I sailed for the Potsdam meeting. In these cables I was informed that Stalin submitted drafts of four agreements containing the Russian proposals. These were a general treaty of friendship and alliance and agreements on the independence of Outer Mongolia, the ports of Dairen and Port Arthur, and the operation of the Manchurian railroads.

The proposal on Outer Mongolia led to an extended argument, neither of the parties being willing to yield. Soong sent the text to Chungking for instructions. Chiang Kai-shek made a counterproposal that if Stalin would give full recognition to Chinese sovereignty in Manchuria and agree to withdraw all moral and material aid from the Chinese Communists and the Sinkiang rebels, then Chiang would agree to have a plebiscite held in Outer Mongolia after the war to determine the status of the area.

On the question of Port Arthur and Dairen, the main point of disagreement was over the Soviet demand that the civil administration of the two port cities should be controlled by them. The Russians wanted Port Arthur, which was to be a military port for the joint use of the Russians and the Chinese, to be placed directly under their control. In Dairen, which was to be open to all nations, the Russians wanted a joint board for the administration of city and port, with a Russian chairman and a Russian as chief administrative officer. There was also a conflict of views on the term of years, the Chinese wanting it limited to twenty, while the Russians wanted forty years.

Stalin was always asking for as much as he could get. The Chinese National Government had not exercised any authority in Outer Mongolia, in a large part of Manchuria, in Dairen, or in Port Arthur for many years.

On July 10 Stalin accepted the Chinese compromise proposal on Outer Mongolia, with a Russian promise not to support either the rebels in Sinkiang or the Communists in China. Stalin denied that there had been any such support in the past. Soong told Harriman that Stalin "categorically stated that he would support only the National Government in China and that all the military forces of China must come under the government's control." Soong outlined the conditions the National Government was ready to grant the Communists, and Stalin made no adverse comment.

The question of Russian military control of the two ports and the Manchurian railroads remained unsettled. Stalin insisted that the majority of the directors of the railroads should be Russian and that the military zone under Russian control should include both Port Arthur and Dairen. Soong offered Port Arthur and the area south of Dairen.

"Soong then suggested to Stalin," Harriman cabled me, "that he return to Chungking to consult the Generalissimo over the points still at issue. Stalin said, however, that it was better to come to agreement before he met you at Berlin as he wished to decide with you the date of his entry into the war. Another meeting has been arranged therefore for the night of the 12th. Soong intends to outline in detail the maximum concessions he is authorized to make along the above lines. If no agreement is reached, he will return to Chungking to consult the Generalissimo."

The meeting resulted in no agreement, and Soong returned to Chungking, saying he was prepared to return to Moscow any time Stalin wished.

On July 20 Chiang Kai-shek, after discussing with Soong his talks with Stalin, cabled me:

"Although China was not represented at the Yalta Conference, you, Mr. President, will realize that we have gone the limit to fulfill the Yalta formula. We have even gone beyond it in the case of Outer Mongolia, we have gone as far as the public opinion of China will stand. We may even have already gone beyond the limit that the Chinese people will support. I trust in your conversations with Generalissimo Stalin you would impress on him the eminently reasonable stand we have taken, so that he will not insist on the impossible."

On July 23 I telegraphed Chiang Kai-shek from Potsdam:

"I asked that you carry out the Yalta agreement, but I had not asked that you make any concession in excess of that agreement. If you and Generalissimo Stalin differ as to the correct interpretation of the Yalta agreement, I hope you will arrange for Soong to return to Moscow and continue your efforts to reach complete understanding."

Stalin's tactics in the Chinese negotiations followed the now familiar pattern he employed in the Polish question. Months of delaying tactics by the Russians and the sharp exchanges between Washington, London, and Moscow had hampered and almost destroyed the machinery set up at Yalta to reorganize the provisional Polish government.

At Yalta a commission had been set up "to consult with members of the Polish Provisional Government and with Democratic leaders in Poland and abroad concerning the reorganization of the Polish Provisional Government on a broader democratic basis with the inclusion of democratic leaders from Poland itself and Poles from abroad." This was on February 11, 1945. It was four months to the day from the time the commission was created before it could get around even to issuing invitations.

The commission, consisting of Molotov for Russia, Harriman for the United States, and Clark Kerr for Britain, sent out the invitations on June 11, with a request that recipients arrive in Moscow by June 15 to form a Polish Provisional Government of National Unity.

Then came a sudden Moscow announcement that sixteen Polish democratic leaders who had been previously arrested under outrageous circumstances would now be tried. This was provocative and discouraging. The deliberate timing of events by the U.S.S.R. in order to confront the negotiators with a *fait accompli* at the very outset of discussions was fast becoming part of the habitual pattern of Russian tactics.

I remembered other occasions. In 1941, just as Polish Premier Sikorski arrived in Moscow, it was announced suddenly that all Poles of Ukrainian or White Russian descent would be considered Soviet citizens and not Poles. Later, when Mikolajczyk was en route from London to Moscow on his first visit after the war, the Lublin government was set up. While he was en route for his second visit, the Lublin government received formal Soviet recognition, and just before Molotov left Moscow to attend the San Francisco conference and to discuss the Polish question with me, the U.S.S.R. signed its twenty-year pact with the Lublin regime. It was all a part of the Russian game.

Despite the fact that the suddenly announced trials were calculated to put a damper on the Poles, the Moscow meetings were held, and the delegates succeeded in reaching satisfactory agreements among themselves. The agreements provided for a broadening of the provisional government by the admission of Mikolajczyk, Grabski, Witos, Stanczyk, and others who had thus far remained outside the Warsaw government.

Harriman reported to me that the settlement was reached because of the concern which all non-Lublin Poles felt over the current situation in Poland, a concern which made them ready to accept any compromise providing some hope for Polish independence and freedom for the individual.

Their agreement, however, was only a beginning. Both Ambassadors Harriman and Clark Kerr, speaking for their governments, made it clear that the formation of the Provisional Government of National Unity was only the first step in carrying out the Yalta agreement. This, they pointed out, would not be fulfilled until truly free elections were held in Poland. Harriman asked and received a pledge from the principal parties to maintain the basic agreement until free elections were held. He also asked for assurances that freedom of assembly and discussion would be granted prior to elections and that amnesty would be given persons accused of political offenses. President Bierut gave Harriman private assurances that he expected eighty per cent of the political prisoners in Poland to be released.

I directed the Secretary of State to inform the Polish Foreign Minister that the United States would recognize the new government as soon as there was an official announcement that it was functioning in Poland. On June 30 Acting Secretary of State Grew informed me that the Prime Minister of the new Polish Provisional Government of National Unity had addressed a message to me stating that the new government had been formed on June 28 in conformity with the Crimea decision, and that he requested in the name of the new government that we establish diplomatic relations between our two countries and exchange ambassadors.

Ambassador Harriman also reported that in his opinion the new government had in fact been formed in conformity with the Crimea decision and that we should therefore carry out our obligation to recognize it. I decided that no useful purpose would be served by further delay, and I addressed a message on July 2 to Churchill regarding simultaneous recognition of the Polish government by our two countries.

"Ambassador Harriman has informed me," my message read. "and I concur that the new Polish Provisional Government of National Unity has been established in conformity with the Crimea decision. As you know, the new government has addressed parallel communications to us requesting that we accord recognition.

"On the basis of the assurances given by the new government and on the recommendations of Ambassador Harriman, I plan to accord recognition to the new government to become effective at 7 P.M. Eastern War Time on July 3.

"I feel that now the matter has moved this far forward any further delay would serve no useful purpose and might even prove embarrassing to both of us. I hope, therefore, you will agree to accord recognition simultaneously with us."

Churchill replied the following day, expressing surprise that he should have only "a few hours'" notice of my decision to recognize the new Polish government. He pointed out that the old Polish government was located in London and that it had under its control a Polish army of 170,000 men, whose attitude had to be considered. He was prepared to recognize the new government, but "we should hope that some consideration could be shown to us in meeting difficulties which you, in no way, share. We had been hoping to give the London Poles at least twenty-four hours' notice, which seems only reasonable, as they have to tell all their employees about their immediate future, and that three months' salary will be paid."

Accordingly he asked me to postpone my announcement until July 4. I replied to the Prime Minister:

"In view of the reasons given by you I concur with your suggestion that we delay temporarily the recognition of the new Polish government.

"The twenty-four hour delay suggested by you would mean that we would accord recognition on Independence Day. I, therefore, suggest and hope you will concur that we postpone recognition for forty-eight hours; that is, until 7 P.M. Eastern War Time, July 5. . . .

"In order that there may be no unwarranted speculation regarding the delay in recognition, I propose to advise Ambassador Harriman today that for administrative reasons due to my absence from Washington and the advent of the national holiday, we shall not be in a position to accord recognition of the new government until July 5. I am instructing him to advise the Polish Ambassador in Moscow in confidence that we shall recognize the government on July 5.

"Unless I hear from you to the contrary, we shall go ahead with this plan so that we may both recognize simultaneously the new government on July 5."

Churchill agreed, and I announced on July 5 that diplomatic relations had been established with the Polish Provisional Government of National Unity.

In preparation for the conference with Churchill and Stalin, I was going over in my mind the purposes for which I was traveling to Potsdam. Of course my immediate purpose was to get the Russians into the war against Japan as soon as possible, but my main objective was to come out with a working relationship to prevent another world catastrophe.

I was thinking of our experience at the close of World War I. At that time President Wilson tried to work out a way to prevent another world war. He was the most popular man in the history of the country at the time he went to Europe and when he came back. But unfortunately there were men in Congress who, jealous of Wilson's popularity, began to undermine his efforts. In a way he aided his opponents, for he took none of the leaders in the Senate into his confidence. Instead, he waited until he came back with the treaty and then, with too little regard for the feeling on Capitol Hill, presented it to the Congress. It was my opinion that if President Wilson had had the leaders of the Congress in his confidence all the time and had trusted them he would not have been defeated on the League of Nations. The fact was that he did not like many of them, and very few were his close personal friends.

I had made up my mind to work in close co-operation with Congress and, in the working out of a settlement of World War II, to avoid the mistakes which had led to the disillusionment of the American people. There was one pitfall I intended to avoid. We did not intend to pay, under any circumstances, the reparations bill for Europe. We wanted a European recovery plan that would put Europe on its feet. We did not intend to send billions of dollars to Russia just because there was no possible way for Germany to pay vast reparations—although morally she should have been made to pay.

I was trying to profit by the mistakes of Woodrow Wilson as well as by those of Jefferson Davis and Abraham Lincoln. I hoped that we would come out of this war with a going world organization for peace and, at the same time, that we could help get our friends and allies back on their economic feet.

Every President must have a Cabinet of his own choosing. But in time of national emergency continuity of government is of paramount importance. Such continuity helps a succeeding administration to maintain the existing contacts with Congress. That is why, at my first meeting with the Roosevelt Cabinet, I asked all the members to stay on. Eventually there had to be changes. I needed time to get to know each member who had agreed to stay on. I also needed time to familiarize myself with all the urgent business confronting the government.

I knew that several members of the Cabinet had planned to leave even prior to the death of Roosevelt. I knew others would prefer to leave now that Roosevelt was gone, because of the special relationship they had established with him.

When I took office, these were the members of the Cabinet:

Secretary of State—Edward R. Stettinius, Jr.
Secretary of the Treasury—Henry Morgenthau, Jr.
Secretary of War—Henry L. Stimson
Attorney General—Francis Biddle
Secretary of the Navy—James Forrestal
Postmaster General—Frank C. Walker
Secretary of Agriculture—Claude R. Wickard
Secretary of the Interior—Harold L. Ickes
Secretary of Commerce—Henry L. Wallace
Secretary of Labor—Miss Frances Perkins

The first Cabinet member whose resignation I accepted was Frank C. Walker, the Postmaster General. I announced his retirement, to be effective June 30, and appointed Robert E. Hannegan, chairman of the Democratic National Committee, his successor. Walker had wanted to quit long before. As a matter of fact, before I was elected Vice-President, Walker had asked me to come down to the Postmaster General's office one day. He told me that President Roosevelt wanted me to be chairman of the Democratic National Committee and asked me if I would take it.

I told Walker that I was in the United States Senate and was chairman of the Special Committee to Investigate the National Defense Program, which I thought was making a contribution to the winning of the war. While the offer was a great compliment, I did not feel that I could accept it.

I went back to the Senate and discussed the matter with Senators Carl Hatch and Mon Wallgren, and they both came to the conclusion that I had made the right decision. I also talked it over with Alben Barkley at the same time. All of this was in preparation for Walker to resign, both as chairman of the Democratic National Committee and as Postmaster General. Roosevelt had promised to let him quit and said he would appoint Hannegan in his place. Hannegan had been chairman of the St. Louis Democratic Committee, and when a vacancy came about in St. Louis for a collector of internal revenue, Bennett Clark and I discussed the idea of recommending him to President Roosevelt. After Hannegan had been collector for some time, Morgenthau selected him as Commissioner of Internal Revenue, calling him the best collector of internal revenue in the country.

Therefore, when Walker insisted on retiring after President Roosevelt's death, I decided on Hannegan to succeed him.

On May 23 I announced three additional changes in the membership of the Cabinet: the resignation of Francis Biddle as Attorney General and the appointment of Tom C. Clark to succeed him; the resignation of Frances Perkins as Secretary of Labor and the appointment of Lewis B. Schwellenbach to succeed her; and the resignation of Claude R. Wickard as Secretary of Agriculture and the appointment of his successor, Clinton P. Anderson.

Like Walker's, these resignations would take effect on June 30.

Miss Perkins was among the first to come and tell me that she no longer wanted to stay in the Cabinet. She said that she needed a rest. I told her that I would be happy to have her remain in the Cabinet. She was a very able administrator. I always thought she made a good Secretary. She was liked very much and trusted by labor, and she was also well thought of by many of the industrialists.

Lewis Schwellenbach was a federal judge in the state of Washington when I asked him to head up the Department of Labor. He had been a senator from 1935 to 1940, and at the time of his appointment as Secretary of Labor he seemed to me to be the best man for that office. I told him that I wanted to make a real Labor Department and that he was going to have plenty of work and trouble to deal with. A great many of the Labor Department functions had been absorbed during the war, and I was anxious to restore it to the place for which it was originally intended. Schwellenbach was in agreement with me on this. He was an able lawyer and federal judge, a good senator, and a real, honest-to-goodness liberal. We saw right down the same alley on public policy.

Francis Biddle had been a good Attorney General, and there was no ill feeling between us. I did not ask him to quit. He quit voluntarily. I do not believe that he was as well satisfied with me as a liberal President as he had been with my predecessor. This was his right. People are entitled to their own opinions as to policy, things, or people, and they have a right to express those opinions.

I asked Biddle whom he would recommend to take his place, and he suggested Tom Clark, who, of course, was strongly endorsed by the whole Texas delegation, including Sam Rayburn and Tom Connally, in all of whom I had the utmost confidence.

When I conferred with Clark regarding his appointment, I expressed to him my ideas of how I wanted him to run the Department of Justice. I emphasized to him the need to be vigilant to maintain the rights of individuals under the provisions of the Bill of Rights. I asked him to call a meeting of the district attorneys of the United States. I told them, when we met, that while they were enforcement officers of the government it was their duty to see also that rights of the citizens were protected. I pointed out the danger of prosecuting officers becoming persecuting officers. They are there not only for the purpose of enforcing the law in the interest of the government of the United States, but also to be sure that the rights of individuals under the Constitution are fully protected. I emphasized this so much that Tom Clark thought I was "hipped" on the subject—and I was. Particularly in time of war, there is danger of encroachments on the civil rights of the people. There are always some officials who will take advantage of war powers and do things they could not possibly do in time of peace.

The appointment of a new Secretary of Agriculture became necessary when I appointed Claude Wickard to be head of the Rural Electrification Administration. He had told me he would like to be head of the REA and did not want to remain any longer as Secretary of Agriculture. I was very much surprised that he asked for the new office, and I gave it to him because I knew he was well fitted for it.

Clinton Anderson was on the special committee of the House of Representatives to investigate food shortages and had been instrumental in the passage of a great deal of legislation in the House. I invited him to breakfast at the White House one morning and asked him if he would consider being Secretary of Agriculture, and he accepted.

The reconstituted Cabinet resulted in an unprecedented situation in that five members were from west of the Mississippi. These included Secretary of Commerce Henry Wallace, Iowa; Secretary of Labor Schwellenbach, Washington; Attorney General Clark, Texas; Postmaster General Hannegan, Missouri; and Secretary of Agiculture Anderson, New Mexico.

Two more important changes, the fifth and sixth in the Cabinet following my accession to the presidency, came about at the end of June and during the first days of July. These were the appointments of James F. Byrnes to succeed Edward R. Stettinius, Jr., as Secretary of State, and the appointment of Fred M. Vinson to replace Henry Morgenthau, Jr., as Secretary of the Treasury.

Stettinius had submitted his resignation at the close of the San Francisco conference, and I had persuaded him to become the United States member of the Security Council of the United Nations.

I announced the appointment of Byrnes as Secretary of State on June 30. Byrnes took the oath of office three days later in my office at the White House.

After I took office as President, Byrnes had immediately come to Washington and offered his services. I decided upon his appointment as Secretary of State at that time and offered him the appointment as we were returning from Roosevelt's funeral at Hyde Park. It was agreed that out of consideration for Stettinius no announcement would be made until the close of the United Nations meeting in San Francisco.

Secretary Morgenthau called upon me at the White House on July 5 to submit his resignation. His letter of resignation and my reply were made public later that day at a press and radio conference. The previous fall he had attended the Quebec meeting of Roosevelt, Churchill, and Mackenzie King and had worked on a plan to eliminate the industrial potential of Germany by making Germany strictly a pastoral and agricultural community. This is what became known as the Morgenthau Plan. Those of us who looked into it did not think much of this plan. I did not like it. When he found out I was going to Potsdam in July, Secretary Morgenthau came in to ask if he could go with me. I told him I thought the Secretary of the Treasury was badly needed in the United States—much more so than in Potsdam. He replied that it was necessary for him to go and that if he could not he would have to quit.

"All right," I replied, "if that is the way you feel, I'll accept your resignation right now." And I did. That was the end of the conversation and the end of the Morgenthau Plan.

Although Morgenthau and I were personally friendly, it would be difficult for me to evaluate him as Secretary of the Treasury because I had too few contacts with him. I always had the impression that Mr. Roosevelt was his own Secretary of the Treasury.

No announcement of a successor to Morgenthau was made immediately, as it was intended that this should be withheld until my return from the Potsdam conference, for which I was to leave Washington the following night. I decided, however, to make the announcement shortly before leaving the White House on the night of July 6 that Fred Vinson, the Director of the Office of War Mobilization and Reconversion, would be nominated upon my return from Europe.

A second letter from Morgenthau was later transmitted to me at Potsdam by wireless. In that letter Morgenthau urged that the appointment of Vinson be made without delay. As a result, I ordered the nomination of Vinson sent to the Senate on July 16. It was confirmed the next day, and the new Secretary was commissioned on July 18. He took the oath of office and entered upon his duties on July 23.

I had not been very closely associated with Vinson until after he became an assistant to President Roosevelt as head of OWMR. He had been chairman of the tax subcommittee of the Ways and Means Committee in the House of Representatives and had been instrumental in implementing the tax policy of the administration. I knew Vinson socially, but after I went down to the White House and became better acquainted with him I became highly appreciative of his capacity as an administrator and of his ability to see clearly through a situation as it arose. I valued his judgment and advice very highly, and until he was appointed to the

Supreme Court he was in on nearly every conference on every subject.

By mid-July all that remained of the Cabinet which had served under President Roosevelt were four men: Secretary of Commerce Henry Wallace, Secretary of the Interior Harold L. Ickes, Secretary of the Navy James Forrestal, and Secretary of War Henry L. Stimson. At this time my Cabinet was made up of men who had had government experience and most of whom had had political experience along with it.

I consider political experience absolutely necessary, because a man who understands politics understands free government. Our government is by the consent of the people, and you have to convince a majority of the people that what you are trying to do is right and in their interest. If you are not a politician, you cannot do it.

I had previously outlined to the members of the Cabinet my views as to the position I believed they should occupy in the administration of the executive branch of the government. I explained that, in my opinion, the Cabinet was like a board of directors appointed by the President to help him carry out policies of the government; that in many instances the Cabinet could be of great help to the President ,by offering advice, whether he liked it or not.

At a meeting on May 18 I related a story about President Lincoln and his Cabinet. In a discussion of the Emancipation Proclamation, all of the members of Lincoln's Cabinet opposed the issuance of the proclamation. Lincoln put the question to the entire Cabinet, and they voted "No." Lincoln told them that was all very well, but the President voted "Aye," and that was the way it was going to be.

I had some very definite ideas on the status of the Cabinet and what it was intended to be. In Washington's administration there were only four members of the Cabinet: Secretary of State, Secretary of the Treasury, Secretary of War, and Attorney General, and those were all that were needed at that time. As the country grew, the size of the Cabinet expanded too, so that today there are ten members. The Secretaries of the President's Cabinet are the civilian heads of the executive branch of the government. They are responsible to the President for carrying out the directions and the policies of the executive branch, as the law provides.

Lincoln had a great deal of trouble with his Cabinet because some of them got it into their heads that they, and not the President, were the policy-makers. James K. Polk had the same difficulty with his Cabinet. Franklin Roosevelt never had any difficulty with his Cabinet for the simple reason that he himself, in my opinion, spent too much time doing the work that should have been delegated to the Cabinet. He was his own Secretary of State nearly all the time he was President. He was his own Secretary of the Treasury. And when it came to the operation of military affairs, he was his own Secretary of War and Secretary of the Navy.

Roosevelt had his own way of working with his Cabinet. All Presidents have. Roosevelt liked to meet with individual members before a full Cabinet meeting. He frequently discussed the same matters with two or more Cabinet members individually even though they were not responsible personally. This was his way of obtaining different views, but it often engendered rivalry and conflict within the Cabinet.

I believed that the best way to obtain different views, without encouraging rivalries among individual members, was to have complete airings in the open at full Cabinet meetings. When difficulties arose among members of the Cabinet, I had those difficulties brought out frankly and settled.

I would, of course, see Cabinet members individually, but theirs were special problems that affected only their own departments. Many decisions were made by me in consultation with one or more Cabinet members.

I believed that members of the Cabinet were there for a purpose and that when the President outlined his policies to the Cabinet it was their business to carry out his directions. I initiated that plan, and it worked reasonably well.

When a Cabinet member speaks publicly, he usually speaks on authorization of the President, in which case he speaks for the President. If he takes it upon himself to announce a policy that is contrary to the policy the President wants carried out, he can cause a great deal of trouble. I was always careful to discuss all matters of policy in open Cabinet meetings where all members were present, but when it was necessary to elaborate on anything special, they had access to me at any time.

However, once a policy is established, it is the policy of the President of the United States and nobody else. That is the way it has to be if the operation of government is going to be orderly. The President is elected for that purpose; his office is a constitutional one. He is the Chief Executive of the Republic and Commander in Chief of the armed forces.

Cabinet positions, on the other hand, are created by law at the request of the President to help him carry out his duties as Chief Executive under the Constitution. It is a very satisfactory arrangement if the President keeps his hands on the reins and knows exactly what goes on in each department. That he has to do if he is to be successful.

Our political setup is something unique in the history of the world, and it is a matter with which the President himself must be entirely familiar. He must know where he is going and why he is going there, and the manner in which he puts his policies into effect is a matter which he discusses with his Cabinet and all his advisers. It is really a most interesting procedure that has to be followed by a President when he is trying his best to run the government in the interest of all the people.

There is a difference between Cabinet members and presidential advisers. The President may have an adviser who is not a Cabinet member, although all Cabinet members are advisers. There are some special issues on which the President needs detailed information from experts, and it is customary to try to discover the man who is best informed on these detailed matters. For instance, when we set up a scientific commission of any sort, it is necessary to find out the scientists who are best informed on the subject. Then it is necessary to find administrators who understand administration and who are willing to take advice from scientists who are doing the work. The President naturally has to consult with them. Sometimes the Congress makes an effort to rob the President of his appointive powers. I would never stand for it.

In one instance I had interviews with a senator on that very subject, and I told him that, unless legislation was drawn up in such a manner as not to infringe in any way on the powers of the President, the bill would never be signed. He made the statement that I didn't have the education to know anything about science. "Well," I said, "I think I know a little more about the Constitution than you do, Senator, and as long as I am here I am going to support it as I have sworn to do." I got the bill in the form I wanted, and then I signed it, but it took a long time.

The most important Cabinet officer is the Secretary of State. He is the direct representative of the President for all foreign ambassadors. He is also in charge of American ambassadors to foreign countries. He must not only be well informed on world affairs, but he must be a man who can distinguish the wheat from the chaff in the reports that come from all these countries.

The President, of course, must be prepared to support his Cabinet members when they need backing. This is especially true with regard to the Secretary of State. It is immensely important that these two men— the President and the Secretary of State—understand each other completely and that they know what their respective roles are. The Secretary of State should never at any time come to think that he is the man in the White House, and the President should not try to be the Secretary of State.

On July 3, the day after I went to the Senate to submit in person the United Nations Charter, I wrote a letter to Mama and Mary:

. . . Went to the Senate yesterday, and you should have seen the carrying on they did. I could hardly shut 'em up so I could speak. And they did the same thing after I finished. Some said the Senate never did carry on so over a President or anybody else. Well anyway, I believe we'll carry the Charter with all but two votes. Hiram Johnson and Curly Brooks, I believe, will be the only ones against it. Won't that be great?

I am getting ready to go see Stalin & Churchill, and it is a chore. I have to take my tuxedo, tails . . . preacher coat, high hat, low hat and hard hat as well as sundry other things.

I have a brief case all filled up with information on past conferences and suggestions on what I'm to do and say. Wish I didn't have to go, but I do and it can't be stopped now.

Hope you are both well. I sent a check today. Will leave Friday night, but you can keep on writing to me; they'll send me a pouch by air every day.

Love to you both.

Harry

CHAPTER 21

When a President of the United States leaves Washington, even on a short trip, many special operations and people are set in motion. But when he travels overseas under wartime conditions, it is a vast undertaking. It is hard to picture all that is involved in getting a President off to a conference such as the one I was about to attend in Potsdam. The fact that this was to be a meeting with heads of other governments called for extraordinary planning of transportation, housing, protection and security, communications, protocol, and staffs.

I had always been in the habit of making my own traveling arrangements—driving my own car, buying my own railroad tickets, carrying my own bags—but as President none of these things was possible. I had to do a great deal of traveling as President, but wherever I went I was accompanied by at least a part of the executive branch of the government. There was never a time when I could not be reached immediately by Washington. To facilitate this, special communications arrangements had to be made, and I always had to have staff assistants with me.

For the Potsdam conference, Cabinet officers, ambassadors, the Chiefs of Staff, the White House staff, the State Department, the Army, Navy, and the Air Force, the Treasury and the Secret Service, all had a share in the working out of arrangements. Many of them had to take part in the work of the conference. The White House, in a sense, had to be moved to Potsdam for the duration of the conference. I wanted to take Fred Vinson with me, but he and I thought it best for him to remain in Washington, for if anything were to happen to Byrnes and me, Vinson, as Secretary of the Treasury, would be the successor to the office of the President.

The President of the United States can never escape being a public figure, and when he travels, Secret Service agents travel ahead of him to inspect the route that he will follow, the vehicles he is to use, and the buildings he intends to enter.

I decided to make the journey aboard a naval vessel, since I felt I would be better able aboard ship to study the many documents that had been assembled for my information. There would be an opportunity as well to consult with my advisers without interference by the usual White House routine. And I needed to have uninterrupted communications with Washington for transacting government business and to keep in touch with London and Moscow. Arrangements had to be closely co-ordinated with the preparations of the British and the Russians, and exchanges of messages were a continuing process.

During the early stages of preparation I cabled Harriman to inform Stalin that "Eisenhower has been directed to make advance arrangements for accommodations and conference space for American members of the forthcoming conference. He has not yet been informed of the names or number of Americans who will be in my party. I intend to take with me my Chiefs of Staff, the Secretary of State with his assistants, two or three other officials of high rank, [and] Secret Service men. As soon as the number and names are known, I will send them for your information."

On the same day Churchill cabled me suggesting that we use the code word TERMINAL for the Potsdam conference. I agreed. In another message Churchill advised me that King George VI would be traveling in France and Germany, inspecting British troops. Churchill said he understood that General Eisenhower hoped the King would visit SHAEF. Since this visit would take place during the progress of the Potsdam conference, it was His Majesty's desire, Churchill said, to come to Berlin for a day, adding that of course the King would not take any part in the discussions. Churchill said it was his idea that the King would arrive in the British sector and, if convenient to Marshal Stalin, would lunch with the Russians. In the evening there would be a dinner in the British sector at which the King and I, as heads of states, and Stalin would meet. The British Prime Minister said he hoped I would visit London immediately after the Potsdam meeting.

In reply I cabled Churchill that "I will be very pleased to agree to any arrangements you may make to accomplish His Majesty's desires during his projected visit in Berlin. It is my intention to visit London en route home from the conference. . . ."

Stalin finally agreed on the housing plans for the conference, which was to take place in the Russian sector. Stalin said, "The delegations will be housed as you propose in your message and as was arranged in the

Crimea. Each delegation will have its own closed territory under a regime regulated at the discretion of the head of the delegation. The area in which the three delegations will be housed is Babelsberg, southeast of Potsdam. There will be a fourth building for the joint session—the Palace of the German Crown Prince in Potsdam.

"Marshal Zhukov will be in Berlin on June 28th. The advance parties of Montgomery and Eisenhower should be sent in about this time to reconnoitre and take over the buildings in Babelsberg. Montgomery's and Eisenhower's advance parties will be able to obtain on the spot all the necessary information and further details about the buildings from General Kruglov, who is known to your people from Yalta."

The Russians were a little slow in permitting our advance detachments to enter Berlin for the necessary preparatory work, but once our advance parties had arrived and inspected the facilities assigned to us, they reported them entirely satisfactory. The local Russian commanders had little authority to act, and time and again questions of detail had to be referred to Moscow before adjustments could be made.

I had an unusually long list of callers on July 6, the day of my departure for Potsdam, including several members of Congress and government officials as well as the French Ambassador, Henri Bonnet. There was a concert by the Army Air Forces band on the south lawn of the White House in the evening, and I walked from the White House to the lawn to attend it.

Members of the Cabinet and other government officials were among the guests, only a few of whom knew that I would be on my way within a few hours. I left the White House by automobile for the Union Station and boarded a train for Newport News, Virginia, where the heavy cruiser U.S.S. *Augusta* was waiting to take me to Europe.

No public announcement was made of my departure for obvious security reasons. The special train which had been made up for the presidential party of fifty-three assistants, advisers, newsmen, and help arrived at the *Augusta's* berth in Newport News just before six o'clock in the morning on July 7. I went aboard at once.

At my previous request, nothing more than the customary Navy honors of side boys, guard of the day, and "piping over the side" were rendered. Captain James H. Foskett, commanding officer of the *Augusta,* was at the quarter-deck to meet me and showed me to the admiral's cabin in "flag country," where I was to live during the cruise.

Within an hour after we arrived at dockside, the *Augusta* was under way, and with her, as we left Hampton Roads, was the heavy cruiser *Philadelphia*. These two ships formed Task Force 68, commanded by Rear Admiral Allan R. McCann, who was charged with the mission of transporting the President of the United States and his party to Europe and back. No other escort, either ship or air, was used.

The *Philadelphia* went ahead of us and made a smooth path in what otherwise would have been a rough sea, so that those of us who were not good sailors did not suffer from seasickness.

As soon as we had passed the swept channel leading through the mine field at the entrance of Chesapeake Bay and reached the open sea, the *Augusta* held an abandon-ship drill.

I went to my station, the No. 2 motor whaleboat on the portside of the well deck, and took part in the drill. I had always had great respect for the efficiency with which our naval vessels are operated, and as long as I was aboard ship I wanted to fit into the routine as much as it was possible.

With the hostilities in the Atlantic ended, the ships of our task force were not darkened at night and, except for extra-vigilant lookout watches, the passage to Europe was made under normal cruising conditions.

A part of each day was devoted to conferences with Secretary Byrnes and Admiral Leahy, shaping up the agenda for the forthcoming conference and preparing a written brief on the problems that were expected to be brought up at the meetings. Most of the afternoons on the voyage were spent in this way.

It was a wonderful crossing. The *Augusta* had a fine band which played during the dinner hour each evening. There were movies every night in Secretary Byrnes's cabin. I was up early every morning to take some exercise on the deck and spent a good deal of time talking with the members of the crew. I also ate a meal in every mess aboard the ship, taking my place in the "chow lines" with my aluminum tray along with the men.

The third day out the *Augusta* left formation to take position for a gunnery exercise. The *Philadelphia* was used as target ship. This was what was called an offset practice—that is, the deflection sight scales in the gun directors controlling the fire, as well as on the guns concerned, were offset so that the fall of shot was four degrees to the right of the line of the target. Thus, while the fire was actually directed at the target ship, the shots landed some five hundred yards or more astern the *Philadelphia*. I witnessed the practice from the navigating bridge through binoculars that had also been offset to the same degree as had the fire-control instruments, causing actual misses to appear as hits on the target ship.

On the same day the first news stories by correspondents accompanying the party were released for publication and transmitted to Washington by high-speed circuit. Press Secretary Ross had hoped that all information concerning my trip could be withheld until the party was safely ashore at Antwerp, but a news leak in Washington had occurred the night before when a columnist broke the story on a radio newscast, and it was no longer considered necessary to hold up release of the stories submitted by the White House correspondents on board.

On July 14, our eighth day under way, we entered the English Channel, where we were met by the light cruiser H.M.S. *Birmingham* and six destroyers. They escorted us along the southern coast of England, and as we passed Dover we were so very close inshore that I got an excellent view of the famous White Cliffs. I was much impressed by the joining-up maneuvers of the escort force, and signaled Rear Admiral Cunninghame Graham, the British commander, my appreciation and admiration of the beauty and precision of the maneuver.

As we entered the North Sea, the H.M.S. *Birmingham* and the destroyers, which had proceeded ahead of us, reversed course and passed us to port, in column with the cruiser leading. As each ship passed the *Augusta,* the crews "cheered ship." Officers and men were in ranks along the port rail, and each ship's crew appeared to shout in unison, "Three cheers for the President of the United States." Later I received this message from Admiral Cunninghame Graham: "It has been a great honor to us to have had the privilege of escorting you through the English Channel. On behalf of all officers and men of the escorting force I ask you to accept our sincere good wishes."

On the last night of the voyage we were forced to restrict our speed to ten knots because of mine fields in the North Sea and wreck buoys marking the location of sunken Axis and Allied ships. I was up early the next morning, which was Sunday, to watch the hundreds of wildly enthusiastic Belgians and Hollanders who thronged the little towns along the Schelde Estuary and cheered our ships as we passed by. It was clear that the news of our arrival was no secret. As we passed Flushing, Holland, I received a message of greeting from the burgomaster.

Just above Antwerp we passed an American Army camp, where we observed thousands of GI's waiting for ships to take them home. At one turn in the river there were no cheers from the persons who watched the *Augusta* standing in to shore. These were a large group of German prisoners of war, cooped up behind barbed wire in an Allied prison camp.

It was difficult to realize that I was looking upon the scene of a devastating war which had just ended. Along the riverbanks I saw very little evidence of damage caused by the war. Everything appeared peaceful and in order, and large herds of fat cattle could be seen grazing in the green meadows along our way.

But as the *Augusta* moved slowly into the harbor of Antwerp and proceeded to the municipal dock, I could see something of the war's devastation in the wreckage from bombing. The *Augusta* moored at 10:04

A.M. on July 15, and the *Philadelphia* tied up astern. We had come 3,387 miles from Newport News in nine days.

During the nine days I had spent at sea I had been in constant touch with developments at home and in other parts of the world through the unique facilities which had been set up aboard ship.

The office of the first lieutenant of the *Augusta* had been made over into a communications center which was complete in every detail. This was designated as the Advance Map Room, corresponding to the Map Room in the White House.

Here messages were received and transmitted in virtually the same volume and with the same dispatch as at the White House itself. For all practical purposes, the Advance Map Room was the White House during the time the *Augusta* was under way.

Among the messages I received was one from the British Ambassador to Washington, Lord Halifax, forwarding a message from Churchill.

Great Britain had had a general election on July 5 (although the results would not be known until July 26, to allow a three-week period for the counting of the soldier vote). The future of the government was at stake and could have an important bearing on the forthcoming conference. Churchill expressed the belief that his government would obtain a majority but added, "As you know, electioneering is full of surprises." He said it was "most unlikely" in any event that he would resign on an adverse declaration of the poll unless it amounted to a very extreme expression of national displeasure. He would await the result of a confidence vote in the House of Commons on the King's speech and would take his dismissal from the House of Commons. Churchill went on to say that the King would not open Parliament until August 8, and a parliamentary session would not take place before August 10. But he advised me that the political members of the British delegation would quit the conference on July 25 in order to await the results of the poll in England. This, he said, would avoid any possible embarrassment when the results were made known. But the British delegation could return to Berlin on July 27, and he said that he personally would be able to stay there, if necessary, until about August 5 or 6. Churchill added that whatever happened in England the conference should not be hurried. He recalled that the Crimea conference was somewhat abruptly curtailed.

At Antwerp a special communications plane was waiting to pick up mail pouches from the ship for Washington, D.C., and one of the letters it carried back was to my mother and my sister.

July 12, 1945

Dear Mama & Mary:—I hope you are both well and that everything is all right with you. It is with me. We left Norfolk at 7 A.M. last Sunday, July 7, on a nice sunny morning, and the trip has been most pleasant and restful. Went to church at 10:30 with officers and men. Sat around on the deck with Mr. Byrnes and Adm. Leahy most of the morning and took a nap in the afternoon.

Saw a picture show that night—we have one every night. On Monday, inspected the ship from top to bottom. Found a boy on board whose name is Lawrence Truman. He comes from Owensborough, Ky., and is the great grandson of our grandfather's brother. He's a nice boy and has green eyes just like Margaret's. Looks about her age.

We had target practice on Monday firing eight inch, five inch and forty millimeter guns. Right interesting to an artillery man. I've had various meals with officers mess, warrant officers and petty officers. Tonight I eat with the crew.

We'll land Sunday, and this will be mailed then. I wish this trip was over. I hate it. But it has to be done.

The King of England has asked me to call, as have the Kings of Denmark and Norway. But I think I'll come home with all speed when the show's over in Berlin. Take care of yourselves. Love to you both.

Harry

Just before I went ashore from the U.S.S. *Augusta,* I received a welcoming party that included the American Ambassador to Belgium and Mrs. Charles Sawyer, General Eisenhower, Admiral Stark, General Lee, General Surles, General Koenig, J. H. Keeley, Consul General to Belgium, Rear Admiral McCann, and Captain Kelly Thomas, British naval officer in charge at Antwerp. A representative of the Prince Regent of Belgium also greeted me as I landed to begin the thirty-five-mile motor trip to the airport northwest of Brussels.

The evidences of war's destruction were less marked along the road than in the city of Antwerp, but I saw many bombed-out homes and factories and temporary wooden bridges. Most of the damage here, I was told, was done by V-bombs. We passed Breendonck, which was reputed to be the Germans' biggest and most feared concentration camp for Belgians during the war.

The road from Antwerp to Brussels was guarded by soldiers from the 137th Infantry Regiment, 35th Division—the division in which I had served as a captain during World War I. The route was lined with spectators—mostly Belgians just recently liberated from the Germans—who came to watch our forty-car caravan.

Shortly after noon we arrived at the airfield. A military band and four hundred picked men of the 137th Infantry Regiment performed a brief honor ceremony, and then I reviewed the honor guard. Each man in the guard was a "five-star" combat man. I talked with several of them before boarding my plane, the *Sacred Cow.* Two other C-54's were waiting to take the members of the presidential party, which split into three groups for the flight to Berlin.

I was told that Secretary Byrnes took the controls of the No. 2 plane while en route from Kassel to Magdeburg. Those two cities, as viewed from the air, appeared to be completely destroyed. I could not see a single house that was left standing in either town. The German countryside, however, seemed to be under cultivation and presented a beautiful appearance.

After a flight of about three hours and a half we landed at Gatow airfield, ten miles from Babelsberg. I was greeted at the airfield by a large delegation including Secretary of War Stimson, Assistant Secretary McCloy, Assistant Secretaries Clayton and Dunn, Ambassadors Harriman, Pauley, and Murphy, Fleet Admiral King, Minister Lubin, Lieutenant General Clay, Major General Floyd Parks, and Soviet Ambassadors Gromyko and Gousev. Honors were accorded by a detachment from the 2nd Armored "Hell on Wheels" Division, following which I inspected the honor guard. Then another automobile caravan took us to our quarters in Babelsberg, passing through a section of Potsdam on the way. A part of the road we took was guarded by American and British troops, but the greater part was patrolled by green-capped Soviet frontier guardsmen, this being a Russian-controlled zone. In less than thirty minutes we had arrived at our final destination.

Babelsberg lies about twelve miles southwest of Berlin, between Berlin and Potsdam. It is in a thickly wooded area along winding Tetlow Canal and Griebnitz Lake. The town was quite popular with the Germans as a summer resort and was also the seat of Germany's movie colony before the war. My quarters was a three-story stucco residence at No. 2 Kaiserstrasse which had formerly been the home of the head of the German movie colony. The building, which was promptly designated as the "Little White House," although it was painted yellow, was right on the lake and was surrounded on three sides by groves of trees and shrubbery forming a very beautiful garden that reached down to the lake. The house had been stripped of its furnishings during the war but had been refurnished by the Russians. Quartered in the house with me were Secretary Byrnes, Admiral Leahy, Press Secretary Ross, General Vaughan, Captain McMahon, Commodore Vardaman, Chip Bohlen, and others. A map room and communications center had been installed with direct wire service to Frankfurt and Washington. The Joint Chiefs of Staff and State Department parties also lived in Babelsberg in close proximity to the Little White House.

Prime Minister Churchill lived at 23 Ringstrasse in Babelsberg, about two blocks from my residence. His was a similarly large house. Generalissimo Stalin also resided at Babelsberg, about a mile from the Little White

House, on the way to Cecilienhof, where the conference sessions were to be held.

The day had been long and strenuous, and I retired early. It was the following morning, July 16, when I met Prime Minister Churchill for the first time. He came to call on me, but I did not feel that I was meeting a stranger. I had seen him on several occasions when he had been in Washington for conferences with Roosevelt, although I had not talked to him then. We had had a number of telephone conversations since I had been President, and in that way a personal contact had already been made.

I had an instant liking for this man who had done so much for his own country and for the Allied cause. There was something very open and genuine about the way he greeted me.

Accompanying Churchill on this social visit were his daughter Mary, Anthony Eden, Sir Alexander Cadogan, and Commander C. R. Thompson, naval aide to the Prime Minister. No business of the conference was discussed. I did tell the Prime Minister that I had an agenda which I would like to present at the meeting and asked him if he had one. He said, "No, I don't need one." Then we talked briefly about the latest news in the Pacific.

Churchill and I never had a serious disagreement about anything, although we argued about a great many things. He was very grateful to the United States for what we had done, and he was a very great admirer of Roosevelt. On the fundamentals of great principles we were in complete agreement.

I liked to listen to him talk. But he wasn't very fond of music—at least my kind of music.

Later that day I wrote Mama and Mary my second letter since leaving Washington:

July 16, 1945

Dear Mama & Mary:—Arrived in Berlin yesterday afternoon about three o'clock and was met by all the Foreign Ministers and high ranking officials of Great Britain and Russia and a special contingent of American soldiers whom I had to inspect. We then came to a beautiful house on a lake in Potsdam, which formerly belonged to the head of the movie colony. It is said that he had been sent back to Russia—for what purpose I don't know.

I had a very pleasant visit with the Prime Minister of England this morning, and I am expecting a visit from Marshal Stalin either this afternoon or tomorrow. I hope I shall have an opportunity to write more in detail later, but I want to get this off to you so as to get it in the pouch that is to leave here this afternoon.

If you will address your letters to the White House with instructions that they be forwarded on to me, I will get them promptly.

Lots of love to you both.

Harry

The arrival of Marshal Stalin from Moscow was delayed because of a slight heart attack which he had suffered—this was a well-kept secret. He was due to arrive on the following day.

I took advantage of this unscheduled delay in the opening of the conference to make a motor tour of Berlin. Our motor convoy left Babelsberg early in the afternoon and soon turned onto the famous autobahn, heading north for what was left of the German capital.

About halfway to the city we found the entire American 2nd Armored Division deployed along one side of the highway for my inspection. We stopped, honors were rendered by a band and honor guard, and I left the sedan in which I had been riding and entered an open half-track reconnaissance car. In this I passed down the long line of men and vehicles, which comprised what was at that time the largest armored division in the world. Men and tanks were arrayed down the highway in front of me as far as the eye could see. The line was so long it took twenty-two minutes to ride from the beginning to the end of it.

Our motorcade then drove to the center of Berlin and turned to drive down Wilhelmstrasse to the remains of the Reich Chancellery, where Hitler had so often harangued his Nazi followers. I never saw such destruction. "That's what happens," I said, "when a man overreaches himself."

The remainder of our drive took us past the Tiergarten, the ruins of the Reichstag, the German Foreign Office, the Sports Palace, and dozens of other sites which had been world-famous before the war. Now they were nothing more than piles of stone and rubble. A more depressing sight than that of the ruined buildings was the long, never-ending procession of old men, women, and children wandering aimlessly along the autobahn and the country roads carrying, pushing, or pulling what was left of their belongings. In that two-hour drive I saw evidence of a great world tragedy, and I was thankful that the United States had been spared the unbelievable devastation of this war.

The next day I met Stalin for the first time. He came to pay a visit at the Little White House shortly after his arrival at Babelsberg. He was accompanied by Molotov and by Pavlov, who acted as interpreter. Secretary Byrnes and Admiral Leahy were present, and Charles E. Bohlen acted as my interpreter.

Stalin apologized for being late, saying that his health was not as good as it used to be. It was about eleven o'clock when he came, and I asked him to stay for lunch. He said he could not, but I insisted.

"You could if you wanted to," I told him.

He stayed. We continued our conversation through lunch. I was impressed by him and talked to him straight from the shoulder. He looked me in the eye when he spoke, and I felt hopeful that we could reach an agreement that would be satisfactory to the world and to ourselves.

I was surprised at Stalin's stature—he was not over five feet five or six inches tall. When we had pictures taken, he would usually stand on the step above me. Churchill would do the same thing. They were both shorter than I. I had heard that Stalin had a withered arm, but it was not noticeable. What I most especially noticed were his eyes, his face, and his expression.

I was pleased with my first visit with Stalin. He seemed to be in a good humor. He was extremely polite, and when he was ready to leave he told me that he had enjoyed the visit. He invited me to call on him, and I promised him I would.

CHAPTER 22

Shortly before five o'clock on the afternoon of July 17 I arrived at Cecilienhof Palace in Potsdam for the opening session of the conference. Cecilienhof had been the country estate of the former Crown Prince Wilhelm. It was a two-story brownstone house of four wings with a courtyard in the center—a courtyard which was now brilliantly carpeted with a twenty-four-foot red star of geraniums, pink roses, and hydrangeas planted by the Soviets. The flags of the three Allied nations were flying over the main entrance to the palace.

Cecilienhof had been used as a hospital during the war by both the Germans and the Soviets. It had been stripped of all its furnishings, but the Russians had done an impressive job in refurnishing and refitting it for the conference. The furniture and furnishings had been brought in from Moscow. There were separate suites for the Prime Minister, the generalissimo, and myself, and each delegation had a retiring room and offices.

The place for the meetings was a big room, about forty by sixty feet, at one end of which was a balcony. Near the center of the room was a large round table twelve or fourteen feet in diameter, around which were chairs for the principal delegates from each of the three governments. I had a place on one side of the table with Byrnes, former Ambassador Joseph E. Davies, and Leahy, and my interpreter, Bohlen, sat next to me. Immediately behind me were other members of my staff. Stalin sat part way around the table to my right with Molotov, Vishinsky, and his interpreter. Behind him were members of his military and civilian staffs. Churchill was similarly placed to my left, where he sat with Eden, Clement Attlee, and several others of his staff. This arrangement permitted any persons coming in with information to have easy access to the delegations of the governments with which they were connected.

Guards were placed unobtrusively in strategic spots in the room. The guards were made up of the Secret Service or their equivalent of each of the three governments. Around the palace and its gardens armed men policed the conference.

Present at the opening meeting were:

For Russia: Premier Stalin, Molotov, Vishinsky, Ambassador Gromyko, Ambassador Gouseve, Novikov, Sobolev, and the translator, Pavlov.

For Great Britain: Prime Minister Churchill, Anthony Eden, Clement Attlee, Sir Alexander Cadogan, Ambassador Clark Kerr, Sir William Strang, and Major Birse, the interpreter.

For the United States: the President, Secretary Byrnes, Admiral Leahy, Ambassadors Harriman, Pauley, and Davies, Assistant Secretaries Dunn and Clayton, Benjamin Cohen, H. Freeman Matthews, and the interpreter, Charles E. Bohlen.

At ten minutes past five the Potsdam conference was officially called to order. Premier Stalin opened the meeting by suggesting that I be asked to serve as the presiding officer. Churchill seconded the motion. I thanked them both for this courtesy.

The general purpose of this first meeting was to draw up the agenda of items which would be discussed in detail at subsequent meetings. I thereupon stated that I had some concrete proposals to lay before the conference. My first proposal was to establish a Council of Foreign Ministers. I said that we should not repeat the mistakes that we made in the peace settlements of World War I.

"One of the most urgent problems in the field of foreign relations facing us today," I pointed out, "is the establishment of some procedure and machinery for the development of peace negotiations and territorial settlements without which the existing confusion, political and economic stagnation will continue to the serious detriment of Europe and the world.

"The experience at Versailles following the last war does not encourage the hope that a full formal peace conference can succeed without preliminary preparation."

I proposed that the Council be made up of the foreign ministers of Great Britain, Russia, China, France, and the United States. These countries were the permanent members of the Security Council of the United Nations. I suggested that this Council meet as soon as possible after our meeting.

Churchill suggested that the proposal be referred to Foreign Secretaries Byrnes, Eden, and Molotov for study.

Stalin agreed with that procedure but said he was not clear about the inclusion of China in a Council of Foreign Ministers to deal with the European peace.

I told Stalin that his question could be discussed by the foreign ministers and then referred back to us.

I then placed my second proposal before the conference. This dealt with the control of Germany during the initial period. I explained that the United States believed that the Control Council should begin to function at once. I submitted a statement of proposed political and economic principles under which Germany would be controlled. This document, copies of which I passed to Stalin and Churchill, outlined the basic principles that should guide the Control Council:

Complete disarmament of Germany and the elimination or control of all German industry that could be used for military production.

The German people should be made to feel that they had suffered a total military defeat and that they could not escape responsibility for what they had brought upon themselves.

The National Socialist party and all Nazi institutions should be destroyed, and all Nazi officials removed.

Preparations should be made for the eventual reconstruction of German political life on a democratic basis and for eventual peaceful cooperation in international life by Germany.

Nazi laws of the Hitler regime which established discriminations on grounds of race, creed, or political opinion should be abolished.

War criminals and those who had participated in planning or carrying on Nazi enterprises involving or resulting in atrocities or war crimes should be arrested and brought to judgment.

Economic controls should be imposed only in so far as they were necessary to the accomplishment of these ends. Germany, I stressed, should be treated as a single economic unit.

This proposal was not discussed but was referred to the foreign secretaries with instructions to report back to us the following day.

I then submitted the following statement, which I read:

"In the Yalta Declaration on liberated Europe signed February 11, 1945, the three governments assumed certain obligations in regard to the liberated peoples of Europe and the peoples of the former Axis satellite states. Since the Yalta Conference, the obligations assumed under this declaration have not been carried out. In the opinion of the United States Government the continued failure to implement these obligations would be regarded throughout the world as evidence of lack of unity between the three great powers, and would undermine confidence in the sincerity of their declared aims.

"The United States Government proposes, therefore, that the following steps to carry out the obligations of the Declaration be agreed upon at this meeting:

"1. The three Allied Governments should agree on necessity of the immediate reorganization of the present governments in Rumania and Bulgaria, in conformity with Clause (C) of the third paragraph of the Yalta Declaration on liberated Europe.

"2. That there be immediate consultation to work out any procedures which may be necessary for the reorganization of these governments to include representatives of all significant democratic elements. Diplomatic recognition shall be accorded and peace treaties concluded with those countries as soon as such reorganization has taken place.

"3. That in conformity with the obligations contained in Clause (D) of the third paragraph of the Declaration on liberated Europe, the three governments consider how best to assist any interim governments in the holding of free and unfettered elections. Such assistance is immediately required in the case of Greece, and will in due course undoubtedly be required in Rumania and Bulgaria, and possibly other countries."

Churchill then spoke up. He said he wanted time to read and study the document and that probably he generally concurred in it.

My final suggestion for the agenda concerned a revision of our policy toward Italy. I explained that because the Italians had entered the war against Japan I thought the time had come to admit Italy into the United Nations, and I wished to submit a proposal looking toward the establishment of peace with Italy.

Churchill interrupted. He pointed out that we were preparing to deal with very important policies too hastily. The British, he said, were attacked by Italy in 1940 at the time France was going down, which was described by President Roosevelt as "a stab in the back." The British, he said, fought the Italians for some time before the United States entered the war. At a most critical time the British were obliged to send sorely needed troops to Africa, and they had fought two years on those shores until the arrival of the American forces, he added. He also pointed out that the British had suffered heavy naval losses in the war with Italy in the Mediterranean.

Churchill suggested that I proceed with the presentation of my proposal. Stalin agreed. I then submitted a document on Italy which stated in part:

"The objectives of the three governments with regard to Italy are directed towards her early political independence and economic recovery, and the right of the Italian people ultimately to choose their own form of government. . . .

"Under an interim arrangement, control of Italy should be retained only to cover Allied military requirements, so long as Allied forces remain in Italy and to safeguard the equitable settlement of territorial disputes."

After submitting the four American proposals, I said that although I considered these questions of the highest importance I wanted it understood that I might add other items to the agenda. Turning to Churchill and Stalin, I expressed my appreciation for the honor of being designated chairman and said that I would welcome any proposals or suggestions they had in mind. I added that I was glad to be at this conference. I had come with some trepidation, I said, realizing that I had to succeed a man who really was irreplaceable. I was aware that President Roosevelt had been on the friendliest terms with both the Prime Minister and Premier Stalin, and I said that I was hopeful of meriting that same friendship and good will.

Churchill replied that he felt certain that both he and Stalin wished to renew with me the regard and affection which they had had for President Roosevelt, and that he had every hope and confidence that the ties between our nations and us personally would increase.

Stalin, on behalf of the whole Russian delegation, expressed the desire to join in the sentiments expressed by the Prime Minister.

Churchill then proposed that we go ahead with the simple question of the agenda and either deal with the items or refer them to the foreign ministers. The British, Churchill said, wished to add the Polish problem to the agenda.

Stalin spoke next. He set forth the questions Russia wished to discuss. These dealt with (1) the division of the German merchant fleet and Navy; (2) reparations; (3) trusteeships for Russia under the United Nations Charter; (4) relations with the Axis satellite states; (5) the Franco regime in Spain. At this point in the outline of his proposals the Russian leader digressed to declare that the Spanish regime did not originate in Spain but was imported and forced on the Spanish people by Germany and Italy. It was a danger to the United Nations, he said, and he thought it would be well to create conditions that would enable the Spanish people to establish the regime they wanted.

Churchill pointed out to Stalin that "we are only discussing things to go on the agenda," but agreed that the matter of Spain should be added.

Stalin continued his list with (6) the question of Tangier; (7) the problem of Syria and Lebanon; and (8) the Polish question, involving the determination of Poland's western frontier and the liquidation of the London government-in-exile.

Churchill agreed that all aspects of the Polish question should be taken up. He stated that he was sure the Premier and I would realize that Britain had been the home of the Polish government and the base from which the Polish armies were maintained and paid. He said that, although all three of us might have the same objectives, the British would have a harder task than the other two powers because they would have the details to handle. They did not wish to release large numbers of soldiers in their midst without making proper provision for them, he added. He observed that it was important to continue to carry out the Yalta agreement and that he attached great importance to the Polish elections in order that the will of the Polish people would be reflected. He added that the British delegation were submitting their proposed agenda in writing, and suggested that the foreign secretaries meet that night and agree on the items we would discuss the following day. Stalin and I agreed.

Churchill remarked, "The foreign ministers can prepare a menu for us better than we could at this table, so tomorrow we will have prepared for us the points which are most agreeable—or, perhaps I should say, the least disagreeable."

Stalin rejoined that all the same we would not escape the disagreeable ones.

Before adjourning the first session, I asked if there were any further suggestions. Stalin brought up the question of the Council of Foreign Ministers which I had proposed at the beginning of the meeting. He objected to the inclusion of China.

I explained that China had been suggested as a member of the proposed Council because she was one of the five members of the Security Council.

Stalin wanted to know if the quarterly meeting of the foreign secretaries, which had been in effect ever since Yalta, was not to continue.

I reminded him that the arrangement at Yalta was a temporary one.

Churchill said that he had found the quarterly meetings of the foreign secretaries very helpful in advising his government. He added that he considered it a complication to bring China into the Council and questioned the advisability of bringing in from the other part of the world a country which had contributed little to the defeat of the enemy in Europe.

I then explained that the problems to be considered by the Council would be quite different from those that would arise in the ordinary meetings of the foreign secretaries. The Council I was proposing was for certain distinct and specific purposes. These were: to draw up for submission to the United Nations treaties of peace with Italy, Rumania, Bulgaria, and Hungary, and to propose settlements of territorial questions outstanding on the termination of the war in Europe. The Council was also to be used for the preparation of a peace settlement for Germany.

Stalin commented that this would be a "conference to prepare for the future peace conference" and that this Council would deal with postwar reparations and decide on the date for the peace conference.

I replied that the date could be fixed when we felt we were adequately prepared to hold the peace conference.

Churchill said that he could foresee no difficulty in reconciling our different objectives. Until the Japanese were defeated, he said, there would be difficulties in China's having an important role in settling the tangled problems of Europe—"the volcano from which war springs." It was possible, he stated, that while the Council was sitting the war with Japan would end; then China could come into the world peace conference. Until that time, he said, China would have only an intellectual interest in the peace settlements.

I said that I would not object to the exclusion of China from the Council until the war with Japan was ended. At Stalin's suggestion I referred the whole question to the foreign ministers to consider and submit recommendations to us at a later date.

Stalin quipped, "As all the questions are to be discussed by the foreign ministers, we shall have nothing to do."

Stalin's wry humor was frequently in evidence during the meeting. When Churchill suggested that the foreign ministers look into the question of there being four or five members on the Council, the Russian interrupted him to say, "Or three members?"

I told Stalin and Churchill that we should discuss the next day some of those points on which we could come to a conclusion. Churchill replied that the secretaries should give us three or four points—enough to keep us busy.

I said I did not want just to discuss. I wanted to decide.

Churchill asked if I wanted something in the bag each day.

He was as right as he could be. I was there to get something accomplished, and if we could not do that, I meant to go back home. I proposed that we meet at four o'clock instead of five in order to get more done during the time we would be meeting. The others agreed to this. I then proposed we adjourn.

Stalin agreed to the adjournment but said there was one question he would like to raise first: Why did Churchill refuse to give Russia her share of the German fleet?

Churchill explained that he thought the fleet should be destroyed or shared, saying that weapons of war are horrible things and that the captured vessels should be sunk.

Whereupon Stalin said, "Let us divide it," adding, "If Mr. Churchill wishes, he can sink his share."

With that, the first meeting of the Potsdam conference adjourned.

After that first meeting with Churchill and Stalin, I returned to my temporary home at Babelsberg with some confidence. I hoped that Stalin was a man who would keep his agreements. We had much to learn on this subject. Because the Russians had made immense sacrifices in men and materials—over five million men killed in action, more millions slain and starved wantonly by Hitler in his invasion of the Ukraine—we hoped that Russia would join wholeheartedly in a plan for world peace.

I did not underestimate the difficulties before us. I realized that as chairman I would be faced with many problems arising out of the conflict of interests. I knew that Stalin and Churchill each would have special interests that might clash and distract us.

Stalin, I knew, wanted the Black Sea straits for Russia, as had all the czars before him. Churchill was determined that Britain should keep and even strengthen her control of the Mediterranean. I knew that I was dealing with two men of entirely different temperaments, attitudes, and backgrounds. Churchill was great in argument. His command of the spoken word is hard to equal. Stalin was not given to long speeches. He would reduce arguments quickly to the question of power and had little patience with any other kind of approach.

I was pleased with the orderly manner in which the interpreters conducted their very essential functions. These three men had been at all the conferences before and were masters at their jobs. There was no difficulty at all in understanding what was being said. Bohlen would translate for me when I talked, Pavlov would translate while Stalin was speaking, and Major Birse would translate Churchill's words for the Russians. We would slow down from time to time so the interpreters could translate each sentence. If there was any disagreement among the interpreters as to the proper Russian word for the English equivalent, they would settle it right there while Stalin would sit back and grin. There were times when I suspected he really understood English.

Following the adjournment of the first meeting, we were invited into a large banquet room in Cecilienhof Palace, where the Russians entertained at a lavish buffet dinner spread on a tremendous table about twenty feet wide and thirty feet long. The table was set with everything you could think of—goose liver, caviar, all sorts of meats, cheeses, chicken, turkey, duck, wines, and spirits. The major-domo in charge was from Moscow's leading hotel. He spoke English and was very careful to show the greatest respect for all the heads of government and their foreign ministers.

On our way back to Babelsberg it was necessary for us to drive through various parts of the Russian zone. Admiral Leahy and Secretary Byrnes were with me, and at one of the crossings our car was stopped by a Russian lieutenant. The delay was no more than a matter of minutes, for we were quickly identified by other Russian officers arriving on the scene. These officers proceeded to scare the life out of the lieutenant for making such a blunder. Leahy turned to me and said, "I'll bet that lieutenant is shot in the morning."

I worked late that evening on a big batch of mail that had arrived from Washington. At 11 P.M. my nephew, Harry Truman, arrived for a few days' visit. He is the son of my brother Vivian, and I had mentioned to General Lee a few days earlier in Antwerp that my nephew was in the European Theater and that I would like to see him. They found him on board the *Queen Elizabeth* in Glasgow Harbor ready to sail for home, but General Lee got him off the ship in time and had him flown to Babelsberg. I introduced him to all the heads of government and the members of my party, and after three days Sergeant Truman was put on our communications plane, which carried mail between Washington and Potsdam, and was flown to the United States. He arrived at Norfolk ahead of the rest of his outfit and joined them as they left the *Queen Elizabeth*.

On the morning of the eighteenth, after a conference with my advisers, I walked to the British Prime Minister's residence for a return visit. Later I went to Marshal Stalin's quarters to return his call, and by four o'clock in the afternoon I arrived at Cecilienhof Palace for the second meeting of the conference.

Churchill opened the second meeting of the conference by raising a question of the relation of the press to the conference. At Teheran, he said, it was difficult for the press to have access to the conference, while at Yalta it had been impossible. But here, he complained, there were many representatives of the press outside the well-guarded fortress in which the conference was taking place, and they were raising a great cry in the world press regarding the inadequacy of their access to information.

"Who let them in?" Stalin shouted in a loud voice.

Churchill told the Premier that the press was being kept outside the compound. If his colleagues agreed, Churchill said he was willing to have a talk with the press, not to explain the work of the meeting, but rather why the press must be excluded.

I saw no need for this. I pointed out that each delegation had a press representative here and suggested that it be left to them to handle. We were still at war in the Pacific, and many delicate problems remained to be settled in Europe, and we therefore could not open the proceedings to the press.

Churchill agreed, saying, "I only offered myself as the lamb and, in any event, I would only go if the generalissimo agreed to rescue me."

I think Churchill enjoyed the reaction of his colleagues to the dramatic suggestion of his acting as spokesman in a situation such as this one.

At this second meeting I placed on the agenda three topics submitted to the conference by the foreign ministers. The first dealt with a redraft of the American proposal for setting up a Council of Foreign Ministers. It provided that the Council be made up of those countries which had already signed terms of surrender with the enemy. This left the door open for China to participate in the Council later at the close of the war with Japan. Therefore, this proposal was acceptable to us. The make-up of the Council of Foreign Ministers and the procedure for peace settlements were agreed to unanimously.

In the discussion on the submission of all treaties to the United Nations, Stalin observed that this made no difference, as "the three powers would represent the interests of all."

That was Stalin's viewpoint all the way. His viewpoint was that Russia, Britain, and the United States would settle world affairs and that it was nobody else's business. I felt very strongly that participation of all nations, small and large, was just as important to world peace as that of the Big Three. It was my policy and purpose to make the United Nations a going and vital organization.

I then asked Secretary Byrnes to read the foreign ministers' report on the American proposal on policy toward Germany. Byrnes said the political and economic experts had not yet completed their work. The foreign ministers recommended, however, that the heads of government hold an exploratory discussion on the political questions dealing with the occupation of Germany.

Churchill remarked that the word "Germany" was used repeatedly and asked what was meant by the term. If it meant prewar Germany, he was in agreement.

Stalin replied, "Germany is what she has become after the war. No other Germany exists now. Austria is not a part of Germany."

I proposed that we consider the Germany of 1937.

Stalin then suggested that we add, "Minus what Germany lost in 1945."

Germany had lost all in 1945, I said to Stalin. The generalissimo referred to the Sudetenland, which Germany had taken from Czechoslovakia, and asked if his colleagues were proposing that this be considered part of Germany. I replied that I was suggesting the Germany of 1937.

Stalin agreed that from a formal point of view Germany might be considered in this way. He suggested that the western frontier of Poland be fixed now and that the question would then become clear.

I said that this could best be done when it had been decided what to do with Germany.

Stalin, obviously stalling, said that Germany was a country with no government and with no definite frontier. It had no frontier guards, no troops. The country was broken up into four occupation zones.

I repeated that the Germany of 1937 would give us a starting point.

Stalin replied that as a starting point he would accept the Germany of 1937.

Churchill said he agreed.

As chairman I ruled that the Germany of the Versailles Treaty as it existed in 1937 would be the basis of discussion.

Churchill drew attention to a clause in the document which covered the destruction of arms, implements of war, etc., in Germany. There were many things, he said, that should not be destroyed, such as wind tunnels and other technical facilities.

Stalin said that the Russians were not barbarians and that they would not destroy research institutions.

All this, of course, was before Manchuria. We were to see later what the Russians would do with the technical facilities of a conquered country. Even in Berlin they showed evidence of lack of association with civilized facilities. They robbed houses of such rare items as fine old grandfather clocks, often putting them in the bottoms of wagons and throwing heavy objects on top of them. They would smash art objects in the same way.

We now turned to a discussion of the Polish question. Stalin introduced a Russian draft proposal on Poland. The substance of this was that the conference should call upon all member governments of the United Nations to withdraw recognition from the Polish government-in-exile in London and that all assets of that government would be transferred to the provisional government in Warsaw. The Russian draft proposed placing all Polish armed forces under the control of the Warsaw government and left it up to that government to dispose of them.

What the Russians wanted to accomplish with this proposal was plain: They wished to get all the property and equipment of the 150,000 men in the Polish Army for the Warsaw regime, although this equipment had originally been supplied by Great Britain and the United States.

Churchill immediately pointed out that the burden of this proposal would fall most heavily on Britain. The United Kingdom had received the Poles when they were driven out by the Germans. He did not remind the Russian Premier that Russian connivance had made this possible. There was no property of any kind or extent belonging to the old Polish government, he added. There were twenty million pounds of gold in London and Canada which was frozen and was the ultimate property of the Polish national state. There was a Polish embassy vacated by the old Ambassador, he said, which was available to the Ambassador of the new government as soon as they sent one, and "the sooner the better."

Churchill talked at length about the contribution the Polish forces had made to the Allied victory over the Axis, and added that Britain had pledged her honor to these men. He told us that he had said in Parliament that if there were Polish soldiers who had fought with the Allies and did not wish to return to Poland, Great Britain would receive them as British subjects.

"We cannot cast adrift men who have been brothers in arms," he declared.

He hoped that most of them would want to go back to their own country, but he felt that there should be reassurances that they would be safe there in the pursuit of their livelihoods. Subject to these reservations, he said, he was in agreement with the Russian proposal and would be pleased to have it passed on to the foreign secretaries for study.

Stalin said that he appreciated the difficulties of the British and that there was no intention on the part of Russia to make the British position more complicated. He merely wished to put an end to the former Polish government in London. Stalin offered to withdraw any part of the Russian draft which Churchill felt would complicate the British position.

I said I wanted an agreement on the Polish question, but what I was particularly interested in was free elections for Poland, as assured by the Yalta agreement.

Stalin replied that the Polish government had never refused to hold elections. He suggested that the question be referred to the foreign secretaries, and Churchill and I agreed.

That was all of the agenda for the second meeting, and the session adjourned at six o'clock, after meeting only an hour and forty-five minutes. I felt that some progress had been made, but I was beginning to grow impatient for more action and fewer words.

Late that night I talked with Mrs. Truman in Independence via transatlantic radiotelephone. It was the first call from Berlin to America since 1942. The connection was just as clear as if it had been between Independence and Washington. I learned later that the calls were routed over Signal Corps circuits through Frankfurt and London to New York and from there to Independence.

CHAPTER 23

At the third session, on July 19, I asked Anthony Eden to present the agenda prepared by the foreign ministers for our discussion. He submitted a revised draft of the political agreement on Germany, and it was accepted by Churchill, Stalin, and myself. The other subjects on the agenda included the disposition of the German naval and merchant fleet; Franco Spain; the situation in Yugoslavia; and the removal of oil equipment from Rumania.

On the question of the disposition of the German fleet, I said that we had to make a distinction between what was reparations and what was war booty. The merchant fleet, I said, should be classified as reparations, and the matter therefore would eventually be referred to the Reparations Commission. Our interest in the merchant fleet, I declared, was to make use of it in the Japanese war zone.

Stalin said that war material taken by armies in the course of a war is booty. Armies that laid down their arms and surrendered, he said, turned in their arms as booty. He applied the same thing to the German Navy; when the fleet was surrendered to the three powers, it therefore became booty. It was possible, however, Stalin continued, to discuss the question whether the merchant fleet was booty or reparations. Regarding the Navy, he said, there was no question about the matter. He recalled the case of Italy, in which both naval and merchant fleets had been treated as booty, and no question had been raised.

Churchill said he hoped we could solve the problem by agreement at the conference. He was speaking only of the German war fleet. He said that the British had the whole of the German merchant fleet in their keeping at the present time.

Churchill pointed out that the U-boats had a limited legal use and that the Germans had used them in contravention of the international agreements on this subject. As many of them as possible, in his opinion, should be destroyed and the remainder shared equally. With respect to the other naval vessels, he thought they should be divided equally, provided a general agreement was achieved at the conference. He said he did not feel that a nation as great and as mighty as Russia should be denied a share. As it took so long to build new vessels, he said, these vessels would be a means of developing a Russian navy and training personnel and would facilitate showing the Russian flag on the ocean.

Churchill continued his summary of the problems by saying that he felt that all ships should be used to contribute to the ending of the war with Japan.

I said that I would be agreeable to a three-way division of the German merchant and naval fleets, but that I should like it to be done after the war in the Pacific was over. I emphasized that we needed these ships not only for the conduct of the war but also to haul food and supplies for the rehabilitation of Europe, and even to our Russian ally, to Greece, and to other countries. We would need every bomb and every ton of food that could be moved by ship.

Stalin asked me what I thought about the German Navy.

I told him that I was ready to dispose of Germany's naval vessels right then. "When the war with Japan is over," I said, "the United States will have both merchant and naval ships for sale." But I did not want the situation disturbed until Japan had been defeated.

Stalin inquired, "Are not the Russians to wage war against Japan?"

I replied that when Russia was ready to fight Japan she would be taken into the shipping pool the same as the others. I added that we were eager to have Russia in the shipping pool with us.

Churchill suggested that the vessels could be earmarked, "if they had any ears when the Japanese war was over"; if any were damaged, they could be made good from our general resources. He said that he must avow himself as a supporter of the request of Marshal Stalin that the Russians receive a share of these war and merchant vessels. The only alternative, he said, was the sinking of the naval vessels, which, he felt, would be a harsh procedure when "one of our trusty allies has a desire for them."

I observed that we were not apart on this question.

Stalin said that of course it was not possible to depict the Russians as having the intention to interfere with the war against Japan, and the matter could not be put in a way to imply that they were to receive a gift from the Allies. They were not after a gift, he asserted.

Churchill and I reminded him that neither of us had mentioned such a thing.

Stalin continued by asking that the matter be cleared up as to whether Russia was to have the right to claim one third of the German merchant and naval fleet. If one third was allocated to Russia, he promised, he would raise no objection to its use in the war against Japan.

It was agreed, as proposed by Churchill, that the matter would be settled at the end of the conference.

Stalin said there was one other thing he should like to see accomplished. His representatives were not allowed to see the German fleet. The Russians had set up a commission to deal with this question, he said, but they were not allowed to see the fleet, nor were they even given a list of the vessels. He requested a list and permission to inspect the ships.

Churchill replied that it was quite possible, but the British would want reciprocal facilities to be given them to see German installations in the Baltic. He believed that the Russians had obtained forty-five German U-boats in Danzig. He suggested an interchange of inspections.

Stalin observed that these submarines were damaged and out of use but that he could arrange for Churchill's people to see them.

"All we want is reciprocity," Churchill replied.

I said that so far as the United States zone in Germany was concerned the Russians were at liberty to see anything they wanted to see but that we, too, would expect reciprocity. I was trying to pave the way for the Reparations Commission to see everything that had been captured by the Russians in the territory they had taken over. I had already had a glimpse of what was happening to materials that had been captured from Germany by the Russians. In the Russian zone of Berlin, which was the industrial zone of the city, I had seen where the Russians had torn the plants up and taken everything out of them. They had loaded the industrial facilities on flatcars, and in many instances the cars were standing on a sidetrack. The material was rusting and disintegrating. Very soon it would be of no use to anybody.

I suggested that we move on to the question of Spain. Churchill said that his government had a strong distaste for General Franco and his government. But, he said, there was more to Spanish policy than drawing rude cartoons of Franco. He revealed that Franco had written him a letter proposing that they join each other to organize the Western states against "that terrible country Russia." With the approval of the British Cabinet, Churchill said he had sent Franco a chilly reply and that a copy of this reply had been sent to Molotov.

Stalin said he had received a copy of the British reply to Franco.

Churchill went on to say that he saw some difficulty in Stalin's proposal, particularly in regard to the breaking off of all relations with Franco Spain. He said that he was against interfering in the affairs of a country which had not molested the Allies and believed it was a dangerous principle to break off relations because of Spain's internal conduct. He would deplore anything, he said, that might lead Spain back into civil war. He pointed out that the United Nations Charter had a provision against interference in the domestic affairs of a nation, and that it would be inconsistent, while preparing to ratify that Charter, to resort to action that would be prohibited under it.

I made it clear that I had no love for Franco and also that I had no desire to have any part in starting another civil war in Spain. There had been enough wars in Europe. I said that I would be happy to recognize another government in Spain but that I thought Spain itself must settle that question.

Stalin said that this was no internal affair, because the Franco regime had been imposed on the Spanish people by Hitler and Mussolini. He said he believed that his colleagues had no love for Franco and that he did not propose to renew civil war in Spain either. If breaking relations was too severe a demonstration, he asked if there were not some other more flexible means by which the Big Three could let the Spanish people know that the three governments were in sympathy with the people of Spain and not Franco. He said it was presumed that the Big Three could settle such questions and that we could not pass by this cancer in Europe. If we remained silent, he warned, it might be considered that we sanctioned Franco.

Churchill reiterated his opposition to breaking relations. He referred to the valuable trade relations which Britain maintained with Spain. Unless he were convinced, he said, that breaking relations would bring about the desired result, he did not want this old and well-established trade with Spain stopped. He fully understood the feeling of Marshal Stalin, he said, when Franco had had the audacity to send a Spanish Blue Division to Russia. Russia was in a different position, he admitted, because she had been molested. He pointed out that the Spaniards had refrained from taking action against the British at a time when such intervention could have been disastrous. During the Torch operation, he said, merely opening fire on the ships in the area of Gibraltar would have done the British great harm. But the Spaniards would have been doomed if they had dared to take such action against the Allies.

Stalin suggested that the foreign secretaries try to find some means of making it clear that the heads of the three governments were not in favor of the Franco regime.

I agreed with this suggestion, but Churchill wanted the matter settled by the heads of government.

Stalin pointed out that it would be settled by the three of us. The foreign ministers would only give it preliminary study.

Churchill said he did not think this was advisable.

The discussion ranged ahead in seesaw fashion, with both the Premier and the Prime Minister restating their earlier arguments. I saw that there was no chance for agreement on this issue at the moment and suggested that we pass on to something else upon which we could come to a decision and that we come back to the Spanish question at a later session.

Stalin again suggested that it be referred to the foreign ministers for their consideration. Churchill again balked on this point and insisted that the heads of state simply leave the question without decision. I pointed out that we could return to it at any time.

We turned our attention next to Yugoslavia. Stalin said that we could not discuss this question because the Yugoslavs were not present to be heard, and they were allies.

Eden spoke up to say that the Big Three had agreed upon a declaration at Yalta, although no Yugoslavs were present.

Stalin replied that when they met at Yalta there had been two Yugoslav governments, but now there was one legitimate government.

Churchill inquired if Stalin meant the government of Tito or that of Subašić. He said that the Yugoslavs were in extreme disagreement.

Stalin replied that this was the first time he had heard about it. He proposed that this information be verified and that Yugoslav representatives be summoned to tell them about the situation.

I asked whether, on the basis of the Prime Minister's information, we should send for the Yugoslav representatives.

Churchill answered that the Tito-Subašić agreement had not been carried out and that he was disappointed at the way things had turned out in Yugoslavia since the Yalta decisions.

Stalin charged that Churchill was going on with the discussion without answering the presiding officer's question. Then followed an exchange between Churchill and Stalin concerning the calling of the Yugoslav representatives.

I felt that I had heard enough of this. I told Churchill and Stalin that I had come to the conference as a representative of the United States to discuss world affairs. I did not come there to hold a police court hearing on something that was already settled or which would eventually be settled by the United Nations. If we started that, I said, we would become involved in trying to settle every political difficulty and would have to hold hearings for a succession of representatives, including de Gaulle,

Franco, and others. I told them frankly that I did not wish to waste time listening to grievances but wanted to deal with the problems which the three heads of government had come to settle. I said that if they did not get to the main issues I was going to pack up and go home. I meant just that.

Stalin laughed heartily and said he did not blame the President for wanting to go home; he wanted to go home too.

Churchill said he thought that the United States was interested in carrying out the Yalta agreement. Great allowances had to be made for Tito, he said, in view of the great disturbances in that country.

I replied that I not only desired to see the Yalta Declaration carried out but that, in so far as the United States was concerned, I intended to carry it out to the letter. I observed that we, too, had received complaints about Yugoslavia. I suggested that the matter of Yugoslavia be postponed so that we could go ahead with other and more urgent problems before us.

Our final topic on the agenda for the day had to do with British and American oil equipment in Rumania.

Churchill said that the British had submitted a paper on this subject which they thought the foreign ministers could agree upon, and suggested that since it was a rather detailed question it be referred to them first.

Stalin said he thought this was a trifling matter which could be settled through diplomatic channels without raising it at this conference. Since it had been brought up, however, he wished to rectify one misstatement, he said. No British property had been taken by the Soviet Union in Rumania, he declared. The property of some of these oil companies had been obtained in Germany, but the Germans had captured it and had used it against the Allies. The Russians, Stalin admitted, removed some quantity of this type of equipment because the Germans had destroyed the Soviet oil industry. He repeated that this was a trifling matter with which the conference should not be troubled.

The reason Stalin insisted that this was a "trifling matter" was that he had obtained possession of equipment that belonged to the United States and Great Britain. It was funny to watch him. Every time there was something like this, where the Russians had stolen the coffin and disposed of the body, he was always very careful to insist that it be settled through diplomatic channels. But where it was a matter of Franco Spain and Yugoslavia, he was very anxious that the matter be put out on the table and settled. I saw what was going on, and that is why I made my "police court" statement when I did.

Churchill stated that the disposition of British and American oil equipment was not a trifling matter. It was true, he agreed, that the Germans had stolen pipe from the British, but it was pipe which the British had bought and paid for. If the Soviet Union took some of this pipe, the Prime Minister asserted, and was considering it as reparations, then Rumania should reimburse the British for it.

I observed that the United States was involved in a similar situation with regard to American oil companies.

Stalin had nothing more to say on this subject.

It was agreed that the matter would be referred to the foreign ministers, and this concluded the third meeting.

On the evening following the third afternoon session I entertained at a state dinner held in the Little White House. Guests at the dinner, in addition to Churchill and Stalin, were Byrnes, Attlee, Molotov, Leahy, Vishinsky, Cadogan, Harriman, Gromyko, Lord Cherwell, Pauley, Davies, Sobolev, Bohlen, Pavlov, and Birse.

Music was by a special concert orchestra. The pianist, Sergeant Eugene List, played Chopin's great Waltz in A-Flat Major, Opus 42, and several Chopin nocturnes. Stalin was a Chopin fan. Churchill did not care much for that kind of music. Stalin was so delighted by the Chopin waltz and nocturnes that he rose from the dinner table, walked over to Sergeant List, shook his hand, drank a toast to him, and asked him to play more. The Prime Minister also complimented List. I took a hand in the musical program, and when I was asked to play the piano, I offered Paderewski's Minuet in G, one of my favorites. Since I had been told previously that Stalin was fond of Chopin, I had asked Sergeant List to brush up on his Chopin. He sent for the score of the Waltz in A-Flat Major and practiced it for a week before the dinner. The piano was not a good concert instrument, but List did a good job anyway.

This was the first of several informal gatherings among the heads of the three governments. These social occasions helped to promote a friendly atmosphere among the men who had come to Berlin to settle problems which demanded the utmost in co-operation if they were to be solved.

The following day, July 20, I drove to the United States Group Control Council headquarters in Berlin to participate in the official raising of the Stars and Stripes over Berlin. The ceremonies were held in the courtyard of the buildings which had formerly been the home of the German Air Defense Command for Berlin. Honors were accorded by an Army band and an honor guard from Company E of the 41st Infantry. In the party with me were Secretary Stimson, Assistant Secretary McCloy, and Generals Eisenhower, Bradley, Patton, and Clay.

As the flag was officially raised over the U.S.-controlled section of Berlin—the same flag, incidentally, which had flown over the United

States Capitol in Washington when war was declared against Germany and which had been taken to Rome after that city's capture—I made the following remarks:

"General Eisenhower, officers, and men: This is an historic occasion. We have conclusively proved that a free people can successfully look after the affairs of the world. We are here today to raise the flag of victory over the capital of our greatest adversary. In doing this, we must remember that in raising this flag we are raising it in the name of the people of the United States who are looking forward to a better world, a peaceful world, a world in which all the people will have an opportunity to enjoy the good things in life and not just a few at the top. Let's not forget that we are fighting for peace and for the welfare of mankind. We are not fighting for conquest. There is not one piece of territory or one thing of a monetary nature that we want out of this war. We want peace and prosperity for the world as a whole. We want to see the time come when we can do the things in peace that we have been able to do in war. If we can put this tremendous machine of ours, which has made this victory possible, to work for peace, we could look forward to the greatest age in the history of mankind. That is what we propose to do."

I left the scene of the flag-raising immediately after the ceremony and proceeded to Cecilienhof Palace, where I called the fourth meeting of the Potsdam conference to order at 4:05 P.M.

In keeping with the practice which had been established by the foreign ministers of taking turns in reporting their meetings to the Big Three, Molotov presented the agenda for the fourth session. He reported that the foreign ministers had a long discussion on the subject of Bulgaria, Rumania, and Greece in connection with the working out of the Yalta decision concerning supervision of elections, but that they had not arrived at an agreement.

I interrupted the Soviet secretary to say that I had no desire to "supervise" elections in the liberated countries and that I thought "observe" would be a better word.

Churchill intervened also to state that the British had not contemplated control of the elections and did not wish to have responsibility for them. They merely wanted to know how the elections were being conductd in these countries.

Turning next to the question of policy toward Italy, I stated that I stood behind the draft which I had submitted at the opening session. This called for a series of simple obligations to replace the surrender terms so that Italy might be freed of occupation restrictions while the peace treaty was still in preparation.

Stalin said that he had no objections in principle to the United States proposals, but he wanted the same treatment to be extended to the other German satellites—Finland, Hungary, Rumania, and Bulgaria.

I said that I had brought up Italy first because she surrendered first, and the surrender terms imposed on Italy had been more harsh than those imposed on the other satellite states. I suggested that we take care of Italy first, then take up the others.

Churchill was reluctant to abandon the terms of the Italian surrender and made a long speech on the subject. He said the Italian government intended to hold elections before winter. While he agreed that a start should be made on the work of preparing a peace treaty, he did not think a final conclusion should be reached until the Italian government rested on a recognized democratic base. He said he was not in full agreement with my position to replace surrender terms with undertakings which the Italian people were not prepared to assume. The proposed undertakings, he felt, did not cover the future of the Italian fleet, reparations, colonies, and other details. He feared that the British would lose their rights under the surrender. Finally, he stated that the terms of surrender were signed by the Dominions, and they would have to be consulted. He did not wish to go further than to assent to the preparation of a peace treaty.

Churchill always found it necessary in cases of this kind, particularly where the Mediterranean was involved, to make long statements like this and then agree to what had already been done. The Mediterranean at that time was extremely vital to the British because it was the highway to India and Australia. He was apparently making a record for use later by the British when the peace treaties were really and actually negotiated. He did the same thing when we were talking about Franco and Spain. On several occasions when Churchill was discussing something at length, Stalin would lean on his elbow, pull on his mustache, and say, "Why don't you agree? The Americans agree, and we agree. You will agree eventually, so why don't you do it now?" Then the argument would stop. Churchill in the end would agree, but he had to make a speech about it first.

Stalin stated that the question of Italy and that of the satellite countries were questions of great policy. The purpose of such a policy was to separate these countries from Germany. There were two methods by which this could be done, he said. One was the use of force, but this would not be enough, he felt. If we used force alone, he warned, we would create a medium that would favor the association of these countries with Germany. Therefore, he concluded, it was expedient to add force to a policy that would wean the satellite nations from Germany. That would be the only means, he explained, of rallying the satellites around us. All considerations of revenge, all complaints of suffering were relatively unimportant, he said, compared with these considerations of high policy. He said he had no objection in principle to the proposal by me, but he asserted that there might be some improvements of a drafting nature.

Stalin observed that Italy had committed great sins. It had committed some sins against the Russians. The Italians had fought on the Don and in the Ukraine, he pointed out, but it would be incorrect to be guided by injuries or feelings of retribution. Such feelings, he said, were poor advisers in politics. In politics, he continued, we should be guided by the calculation of forces. The question then was whether we wanted Italy on the side of the United Nations. This determined everything, in his opinion, and the same principle applied to the other satellites.

While Stalin was capable of making speeches about the German satellites—Bulgaria, Italy, Hungary—he always had his iron heel on those satellites which his Army had occupied so they could not turn around. His iron-heel policy had been extended to Estonia, Latvia, Lithuania, Poland, Bulgaria, Hungary, Rumania, and Czechoslovakia.

Stalin pointed out that there had been many difficulties and sacrifices caused them by the satellite states. Rumania had used twenty-two divisions against them. At the termination of the war Hungary had twenty-six divisions, and still greater injuries were caused them by Finland. Of course, he said, if it had not been for the help of Finland, Germany could not have maintained the blockade at Leningrad. Finland had moved twenty-four divisions against Soviet troops. Bulgaria, he thought, should be punished for causing alarm to the Allies, Yugoslavia, and Greece. The armistice terms provided for reparations to be paid to these two countries, and he told us "not to worry, for the Russians would compel this payment."

What he meant was that the Russians would steal it if they could not get it any other way.

Stalin continued to speak for a considerable time. It was about the longest speech he was to make in the whole conference. He never used notes, although he might turn to Molotov or Vishinsky once in a while. He would talk for about five minutes, then Pavlov would translate. Stalin knew exactly what he wanted to say and what he wanted to obtain. He spoke in a quiet, inoffensive way.

I stated that, as I understood the position, I had made a concrete proposal. The armistice agreement with Italy had been signed by the three governments represented here. The same was true of the other armistice arrangements. I had made a proposition, I repeated, with regard to Italy, and Marshal Stalin had made a proposal with regard to the others.

Stalin interrupted to point out that the dominions had not signed these agreements.

Eden replied that the three countries had signed in the names of all the other United Nations.

I interrupted at this point to state that I would like to keep the argument to the questions which we had been discussing. On the agenda of our meeting, I said, there had been the suggestion of a statement of policy on Italy; Marshal Stalin had raised the question of Rumania, Bulgaria, and Finland.

I thought that agreement could be reached on all of these satellite countries. The United States policy in this matter, I explained, was for bringing about a feeling of peace in the world, and this did not have to wait a final peace conference for the world as a whole.

My country, I said, was faced with a situation where it must spend enormous sums of money because of conditions in the countries of Europe. With reference to the question of reparations from Italy, I reminded the Premier and the Prime Minister that the United States was spending from seven hundred and fifty million dollars to a billion dollars to feed Italy this winter. The United States was rich, I conceded, but it could not forever pour out its resources for the help of others without getting some results toward peace for its efforts.

Unless we were able to help get these governments on a self-supporting basis, I warned, the United States would not be able to continue to maintain them indefinitely when they should be able to help themselves. The Big Three, I said, must try at this meeting to prepare conditions that would bring about a situation in which these countries could help themselves.

Our discussion of Italian policy followed the course of most subjects we had touched on so far: It was referred to the foreign secretaries for study and was then to be reported back to us.

The next point on the agenda was the situation in Austria, particularly in Vienna.

Churchill complained that the British had not even been allowed to enter the sector assigned to them in Vienna because of intervention by Russian troops.

Stalin replied that only yesterday agreement had been reached on zones inside Vienna. As far as he was concerned the movement of troops into Vienna could begin at once.

Churchill said he was glad the matter was settled at last.

After the session adjourned, I returned immediately to Babelsberg, where I was pleased to find Colonel L. Curtis Tiernan, Chief of Army Chaplains in the European Theater, at the Little White House. Monsignor Tiernan had been chaplain of the 129th Field Artillery of the 35th Division, in which I had served during World War I. During the night rides of my field artillery outfit (I was C.O. of Battery D) Monsignor Tiernan—or the Padre, as we all affectionately called him—would ride with me at the head of the outfit, and we would discuss all the ills of the world, both political and religious. He is one of the best-informed men I have ever known and one of the kindliest. He is a good man, and that says everything necessary about him. The monsignor was stationed in Paris during World War II. When I first landed at Antwerp, I had asked that he be brought to Potsdam for a visit. He spent several days with me at the Little White House.

Our fifth session, on July 21, opened with a statement on the Polish question. Secretary Byrnes reported that the foreign ministers had been unable to reach agreement and wished to refer the matter to the heads of government for final decision. Churchill and I, without much debate, were able to get Stalin to accept two paragraphs in the proposed declaration on Poland which Molotov had previously blocked in the foreign secretaries' meeting. One of these recognized the principle that the liabilities of the former Polish government should be taken into account in determining Polish assets abroad, mainly in England and the United States, which would be turned over to the Warsaw regime. The second of Stalin's concessions involved a specific statement that press observers would be admitted to the Polish elections.

The next important question on the agenda was that of the Polish western frontier. I began by saying that I wanted to make a general statement regarding the Polish frontiers. I said it had been decided at Yalta that Germany would be occupied by the Soviet Union, the United Kingdom, the United States, and France, and that the Polish frontiers would be favorably considered by the four governments but that final settlement of the frontiers would be effected at the peace conference. I reminded Churchill and Stalin that at our first meeting we had agreed to use the 1937 boundaries of Germany as a point of departure. I pointed out that the three governments had decided upon zones of occupation in Germany. The boundaries of these zones had been set, and the Americans and the British had already gone into the areas assigned to them. It now appeared, I said, as if another occupying government was being assigned a zone in Germany. This was being done without consultation, I charged, and if the Poles were actually to occupy this zone, an agreement on it should have been reached. I added that I failed to see how reparations or other questions could be decided if Germany were carved up. I made it clear that I was very friendly toward the Polish provisional government, and I felt that full agreement could probably be reached on what the Soviet government desired, but I wanted to be consulted.

Stalin replied that the Yalta decision was that the eastern frontiers of Poland should follow the Curzon Line. In regard to the western frontiers, it had been decided at Yalta that Poland should receive cessions of territory in the north and west. He said it had also been decided that a new Polish government should consult at the appropriate time on the final settlement of the western frontiers.

I agreed that this was a correct statement of the Yalta decision but that it was not correct to assign a zone of occupation to the Poles.

Stalin declared that it was not accurate to say that the Russians had given the Poles a zone of occupation without agreement. What had happened, he explained, was that the German population in these areas had followed the German Army to the west, and the Poles had remained. The Red Army, he said, had needed local administration in this territory. It could not clear out enemy agents and fight a war and set up an administration at the same time, and he was unable to see what harm had been done by the establishment of a Polish administration where only Poles remained.

I replied that I had no objection to an expression of opinion regarding the western frontier, but I wanted it distinctly understood that the zones of occupation would be exactly as established by previous agreement at Yalta. Any other course, I warned, would make reparations very difficult, particularly if part of the German territory was gone before agreement was reached on what reparations should be.

Stalin boasted that the Soviet Union was not afraid of the reparations question and would, if necessary, renounce reparations entirely.

In response to this, I observed that however this matter was handled the United States would get no reparations—that what we were trying to do was to keep from paying the reparations bill from the U. S. Treasury, as we had done after World War I.

Stalin then said that no frontiers had been ceded at Yalta except for the provision that Poland would receive territory. The western frontier question was open, and the Soviet Union was not bound.

I turned to Stalin. "You are not?" I asked.

"No," replied Stalin.

Churchill remarked that he had a good deal to say about the actual line but gathered that it was not yet the time for saying it.

I agreed that it was not possible for the heads of government to settle this question. It was a matter for the peace conference.

Stalin expressed the opinion that it would be very difficult to restore a German administration in this area of East Prussia. He said that he wanted me to understand the Russian conception, to which the Russians had adhered both in war and during the occupation. According to this view, an army fights in war and cares only for its efforts to win the war. To enable an army to win and advance, it must have a quiet rear. It fights well if the rear is quiet, and better if the rear is friendly.

Even if the Germans had not fled, he went on, it would have been very difficult to set up a German administration in this area because the majority of the population was Polish. The Poles who were there, he contended, had received the Soviet Army enthusiastically, and it was only natural that the Soviet government should have set up an administration of friends, especially since the Russian Army was still fighting to win the war. He insisted there was no other way out. Soviet action, he said, did not imply that the Russians had settled the question themselves. Perhaps, he suggested, the whole question should be suspended.

Churchill raised a doubt as to whether the question could be suspended and added that there was also the question of supply. This was very urgent because the region under discussion was a very important source of food from which Germany was to be fed.

Stalin asked who would work to produce the grain and who would plow the fields.

I pointed out that the question was not one of who occupied an area but a question of the occupation of Germany. We should occupy our zone, the British theirs, the French theirs, and the Russians should occupy theirs. There was no objection, I said, to discussing the western frontiers of Poland, and I added that I did not believe we were far apart on this matter.

Stalin insisted that on paper these areas constituted German territory, but for all practical purposes they were actually Polish territories since there was no German population.

I took issue with that by remarking that nine million Germans seemed like a big population to me.

Stalin maintained, however, that all the Germans had fled westward.

Churchill observed that if this were true, consideration should be given to the means of feeding them in the regions to which they had fled. The produce of the land they had left, he added, was not yet available to nourish Germany.

He went on to say that it was his understanding that under the full Polish plan put forward by the Soviet government one quarter of the total arable land of 1937 Germany would be alienated from the German area on which food and reparations were based. This was tremendous. It appeared, he continued, that three to four million people would be moved, but the prewar population of that territory had been eight and a quarter million. It was a serious matter, he concluded, to effect whole-sale transfers of German populations and burden the remainder of Germany with their care if their food supply had been alienated.

I interjected to ask where we would be if we should give France the Saar and the Ruhr.

Stalin replied that the Soviet government had not made a decision in regard to French claims, but it had done so in regard to the western frontier of Poland. He added that he fully appreciated the difficulties that would arise in transferring this territory from the Germans to the Poles, but that the German people were principally to blame for these difficulties. Churchill, he said, had quoted the figure of eight and a quarter million as the population of this area. It should be remembered, Stalin said, that there had been several "call-ups" during the war and that the rest of the population had left before the Soviet Army arrived. He emphasized that no single German remained in the territory to be given Poland.

"Of course not," Admiral Leahy whispered to me. "The Bolshies have killed all of them!"

Stalin went on to say that between the Oder and the Vistula the Germans had quitted their fields, which were now being cultivated by the Poles. It was unlikely, he said, that the Poles would agree to the return of these Germans.

Of course I knew that Stalin was misrepresenting the facts. The Soviets had taken the Polish territory east of the Curzon Line, and they were now trying to compensate Poland at the expense of the other three occupying powers. I would not stand for it, nor would Churchill. I was of the opinion that the Russians had killed the German population or had chased them into our zones.

I was getting tired of sitting and listening to endless debate on matters that could not be settled at this conference yet took up precious time. I was anxious also to avoid any sharpening of the verbal clashes in view of the more immediate and urgent questions that needed to be settled. I was becoming very impatient, and on a number of occasions I felt like blowing the roof off the palace.

When Stalin concluded, I said that I wanted to declare again that the occupation zones in Germany should be occupied as agreed upon. The question of whether the Poles should have part of Germany, I said, could not be settled here.

The argument continued between Stalin and Churchill.

At last I intervened to say that it seemed to be an accomplished fact that a large piece of Germany had been given to the Poles. The Silesian coal mines, I pointed out, were a part of Germany for reparations and feeding purposes, and these were now in Polish hands. We could talk about boundaries and reparations and feeding problems, but the Poles, I emphasized, had no right to take this territory and remove it from the German economy. Simply stated, I said, the case was this: Were the zones valid until peace terms had been signed, or were we going to give Germany away piecemeal?

Stalin recapitulated his claims for Polish control of the arable lands and the coal mines of Silesia, saying that his policy was to make things difficult for the Germans so that German power would not rise again. It was better to make difficulties for the Germans, he reasoned, than for the Poles.

I replied that it was bad to create difficulties for the Allies.

Stalin asserted that the less industry there was in Germany the greater would be the market for American and British goods. Germany was a dangerous business rival, he said, unless we kept her on her knees. Churchill remarked that we did not wish to be confronted by a mass of starving people. Stalin assured him, "There will be none."

Clement Attlee then spoke at some length, taking the same view that Churchill and I had taken.

It seemed to me that nothing remained to be said except to repeat in all frankness where I stood: I could not agree to the separation of the eastern part of Germany.

Stalin, too, apparently had decided there was nothing to be gained by continuing this discussion.

"Are we through?" he asked abruptly.

Churchill suggested that we were hardly through but that we should turn now to more agreeable things.

I announced that the conference had apparently reached an impasse on this matter and that the session was adjourned.

That evening Stalin gave a state dinner. It was quite an occasion, and I described parts of it in a letter to Mama and Mary two days later:

Berlin, July 23, 1945
Dear Mama & Mary:—Your letter of the 16th came yesterday and those of the 17th and 19th came this morning. I am most happy to hear from you. I suppose the radio keeps you well informed on my movements.

The conference has met every day since the 17th. Many things have been accomplished and many more which should be accomplished have not been acted upon. But we have time yet to get most of them in some sort of shape for a peace conference.

Stalin gave his state dinner night before last, and it was a wow. Started with caviar and vodka and wound up with watermelon and champagne, with smoked fish, fresh fish, venison, chicken, duck and all sorts of vegetables in between. There was a toast every five minutes until at least twenty-five had been drunk. I ate very little and drank less, but it was a colorful and enjoyable occasion.

When I had Stalin & Churchill here for dinner, I think I told you that a young sergeant named List from Philadelphia played the piano, and a boy from the Metropolitan Orchestra played the violin. They are the best we have, and they are very good. Stalin sent to Moscow and brought on his two best pianists and two female violinists. They were excellent. Played Chopin, Liszt, Tschaikowsky and all the rest. I congratulated him and them on their ability. . . . It was a nice dinner. . . .

I was seated next to Stalin, and I noticed that he drank from a tiny glass that held about a thimbleful. He emptied it frequently and replenished it from a bottle he kept handy. I assumed that it was vodka, which everybody else was being served, and I began to wonder how Stalin could drink so much of that powerful beverage. Finally I asked him, and he looked at me and grinned. Then he leaned over to his interpreter and said, "Tell the President it is French wine, because since my heart attack I can't drink the way I used to."

CHAPTER 24

July 22 was Sunday, but we had decided to continue the daily conferences without interruption. During the morning, accompanied by my old friend, Colonel and Monsignor Tiernan, and my military and naval aides, I attended Protestant church service in the Colosseum Building, a former film laboratory in the Babelsberg area. This service was conducted by Lieutenant Colonel Lawrence Nelson. An hour later I attended a second service in the same building, a Catholic mass conducted by Colonel Tiernan. I returned to the Little White House for lunch, and shortly thereafter Prime Minister Churchill called on me and we conferred for about an hour. After attending to some urgent mail for Washington, I left for Cecilienhof Palace and called to order the sixth meeting of the conference at 5 P.M.

Our discussion was resumed where it had left off the day before, with the question of Poland's western frontier and Prime Minister Churchill restating his reasons for refusing to accept Stalin's proposal to cede the eastern territory of Germany to Poland. Stalin, in turn, challenged the Prime Minister's reasoning with the same arguments he had previously advanced.

I then read a portion of the Yalta Declaration concerning Poland's western frontier and reminded them that this agreement had been reached by President Roosevelt, Marshal Stalin, and Prime Minister Churchill. I added that I was in complete accord with it and wished to make the point clear that Poland now had been assigned a zone of occupation in Germany without any consultation among the three powers. While I did not object to Poland being assigned a zone, I did not like the manner in which it had been done. Our main problem here, I repeated, was that of the occupation of Germany by the four authorized powers. That, I said, was my position yesterday, that was my position today, and that would be my position tomorrow.

Stalin said that if we were not bored with the question of frontiers he would like to point out that the exact character of the Yalta decision was that we were bound to receive the opinion of the Polish government on the question of its western frontiers. As we were not in agreement with the Polish proposal, we should hear the representatives of the new Polish government. If the heads of government did not wish to hear them, then the foreign ministers should hear them.

Stalin said that he wished to remind Mr. Churchill, as well as others who had been at the Crimea conference, that the view held by the President and Mr. Churchill with regard to the western frontier and with which he did not agree was that the line should begin from the estuary of the Oder and follow the Oder to where it is joined by the Eastern Neisse. He had insisted on the line of the Western Neisse. The plan proposed by President Roosevelt and Prime Minister Churchill, said Stalin, left the town of Stettin on the German side, as well as Breslau and the region west of Breslau.

At this point Stalin walked around the table and showed me this line on a map.

Stalin said the question to be settled was that of the frontier and not that of a temporary line. We could settle the matter, and we could put it off, but we could not ignore it.

Churchill agreed that the matter could not be settled without the Poles, unless, of course, we accepted the Polish proposal. Stalin then turned to me and said that in regard to my observation that a fifth country was now occupying Germany, he wished to state that if anyone was to blame, it was not just the Poles—circumstances and the Russians were to blame.

I replied that that was exactly what I had been talking about. I then agreed that the Polish representatives could come to Potsdam and be heard by the foreign ministers, who would report to us.

It was now agreed that as presiding officer I should issue an invitation to the Poles to send representatives to the foreign ministers' meeting at Potsdam in an effort to reach some kind of practical solution to the problem of boundaries which could last until the matter was finally settled at the peace conference.

Molotov now brought up the subject of trusteeships and said that the San Francisco conference had settled, in principle, a trusteeship system, and there was now the question of the disposition of specific territories, such as Italy's colonies and also, perhaps, Korea.

Molotov went on to say that he had learned from the foreign press that Italy had lost its colonies, and the question was who had received them, and where had this matter been decided? Churchill replied by referring to the heavy losses which the British had suffered and the victories which the British Army had achieved by "conquering alone all of the colonies of Italy except Tunis."

I turned to the Prime Minister and repeated, "All?"

Churchill explained that when he referred to Italian colonies he meant Libya, Cyrenaica, and Tripoli. The British had conquered these at a time when they were under heavy attacks and were without help, he said, at least during the early part. Molotov interjected that Berlin had been conquered by the Red Army.

Churchill, ignoring Molotov, continued, saying that they were not expecting any gain out of this war. British losses had been terrible, although not so heavy in human life as those of their gallant Soviet ally. They came out of the war, however, a great debtor to the world. In spite of the heavy losses they had suffered, they had made no territorial claims—no Koenigsberg—no Baltic states—nothing. With regard to the Italian colonies, he said he regarded Italy as having lost them, but this did not preclude the peace conference from considering whether some of these colonies should be restored to Italy. He was not declaring himself in favor of restoration but was willing to discuss it. At present, Churchill said, the British held these colonies. He wanted to know who wanted them. If there were claimants, said Churchill, they should put forward their claims.

I said that the United States did not want them, nor did we want a trusteeship over them.

Molotov said that the Soviet proposal had been submitted in writing and that they would like the conference to consider them. Churchill asked what did the Soviet allies want? Did Stalin wish to put forward a claim to one of these Italian colonies?

Stalin replied that they would like to learn whether this conference was going to deal with the question of whether Italy was to lose these colonies. In such an event, they could decide to what states they would be transferred for trusteeship.

Churchill said he had not considered the possibility of the Soviet Union desiring a large tract of the African shore. If that were the case, it would have to be considered in relation to many other problems.

Stalin declared that at San Francisco the Soviet delegation had stated that they were anxious to receive mandates for certain territories, and the matter was now set forth in the Russian paper.

I pointed out that the Soviet proposal was a matter for the foreign ministers to discuss and that I had no objection to this.

Churchill said he had no objection either, and it was agreed that the question of trusteeships be referred to the foreign ministers. We turned our attention to the question of Turkey.

Churchill said there was an admitted need to modify the old Montreux Convention regarding Turkey, and he had frequently expressed his readiness to welcome an arrangement for the free movement of Russian ships through the Black Sea and back. But he wished to impress on Marshal Stalin the importance of not alarming Turkey. Turkey was very much alarmed, he said, by a strong concentration of Bulgarian and Soviet troops in Bulgaria, by continuous attacks in the Soviet press, and by the conversations between the Turkish Ambassador and Mr. Molotov in which modifications of Turkey's eastern frontier were mentioned, as well as a Soviet base in the straits.

Molotov explained that the Turkish government had taken the initiative through the Turkish Ambassador in Moscow and had proposed an alliance with Russia. In 1921, he said, a portion of Russian territory had been torn from Soviet Armenia and Soviet Georgia, and he had insisted that this question be settled before the conclusion of a treaty of alliance.

Churchill challenged the right of the Russians to consider the matter of the Black Sea straits as one in which no one had a voice except themselves and Turkey. Molotov replied that similar treaties had existed between Russia and Turkey in the past, and he cited the treaties of 1805 and 1833.

Churchill said he would have to ask his staff to look up these ancient treaties. He said that the British were not prepared to push Turkey to accept such proposals from Russia.

I said that I was not ready to express an opinion and suggested that we defer consideration of the question until necessary study could be given to it. This was agreed to.

After an exchange between Churchill and Molotov on the question of the treatment of Russian prisoners in Italy, I adjourned the meeting.

We met the following day, July 23, for the seventh meeting of the conference. The agenda for that day involved four controversial territories: Turkey, Koenigsberg, Syria and Lebanon, and Iran. Other questions which had been passed over or referred to the foreign ministers were in the drafting stage or still under study by heads of state, the secretaries, and boards of experts assembled at Potsdam. Military talks were going on between the Chiefs of Staff. The sessions of the Big Three were only a part of the continuous round of discussions and consultations which were going on at all hours in the area of the conference.

Churchill spoke first, reaffirming his position that he could not consent to the establishment of a Russian base in the straits, adding that he did not think Turkey would agree to that proposal.

Stalin declared that Churchill had been mistaken in saying that the Russians had frightened the Turks by concentrating too many troops in Bulgaria. Russia had fewer troops in Bulgaria, he said, than the British had in Greece. Churchill inquired how many Stalin thought the British had in Greece. Stalin replied, "Five divisions." Churchill said there were only two.

Stalin inquired about armored units and asked how strong the British divisions were.

Churchill said they had about forty thousand troops altogether in Greece.

Stalin replied that they had only about thirty thousand in Bulgaria.

Churchill said he hoped that the meeting would hear Field Marshal Alexander, as he preferred that he give the figures, to which Stalin replied that he was not seeking for accuracy and that he believed Churchill "one hundred per cent." But the Turks, with twenty-three divisions of their own, had nothing to fear from the Russians, he said. He explained that, as to the rectification of the frontier, perhaps it was the possible restoration of the prewar frontiers that had existed under the Czar that had frightened the Turks. He said that he had in mind the area of Kars, formerly in Armenia, as well as Ardahan, formerly in Georgia, and asserted that rectification of the frontier would not have been brought up at all if the Turks had not suggested an alliance with Russia. An alliance meant that both countries would defend mutually the frontiers between them and, in the Russian opinion, the frontiers in the area mentioned were incorrect, and they told the Turks that these would have to be rectified in the event of an alliance. If this was not agreeable to the Turks, he said, the question of an alliance would be dropped. He would like to know what there was to be afraid of.

With regard to the Black Sea straits, Stalin said Russia regarded the Montreux Convention as inimical. Under this treaty, he complained, Turkey had the right to block the straits not only if Turkey were at war but if it seemed to Turkey that there was a threat of war. The result was, he continued, that a small state supported by Great Britain held a great state by the throat and gave it no outlet. He could imagine what commotion there would be in England if a similar regime existed in Gibraltar or in the Suez Canal, or what a commotion there would be in the United States if such a regime existed with regard to the Panama Canal. The point at issue, he concluded, was to give Soviet shipping the possibility to pass to and from the Black Sea freely. As Turkey was too weak to guarantee the possibility of free passage in case complications arose, the Soviet Union would like to see the straits defended by force.

I said that the attitude of the American government was that the Montreux Convention should be revised. I thought, however, that the straits should be a free waterway open to the whole world and that they should be guaranteed by all of us. I had come to the conclusion, I said, after a long study of history, that all the wars of the last two hundred years had originated in the area from the Black Sea to the Baltic and from the eastern frontier of France to the western frontier of Russia. In the last two instances the peace of the whole world had been overturned—by Austria in World War I and by Germany in this war. I thought it should be the business of this conference and of the coming peace conference to see that this did not happen again.

I announced that I was presenting a paper proposing free access to all the seas of the world by Russia and by all other countries. I was offering as a solution of the straits problem the suggestion that the Kiel Canal in Germany, the Rhine-Danube waterway from the North Sea to the Black Sea, the Black Sea straits, the Suez Canal, and the Panama Canal be made free waterways for the passage of freight and passengers of all countries, except for the fees for their necessary operation and maintenance.

I went on to say that we did not want the world to engage in another war in twenty-five years over the straits or the Danube. I said that our only ambition was to have a Europe that was sound economically and that could support itself. I wanted to see a Europe that would make Russia, England, France, and all other countries in it secure, prosperous, and happy, and with which the United States could trade and be happy as well as prosperous. I felt that my proposal was a step in that direction.

I said that the question of territorial concessions was a Turkish and Russian dispute which they would have to settle themselves and which the marshal had said he was willing to do. But the question of the Black Sea straits, I pointed out, concerned the United States and the rest of the world.

Churchill expressed agreement with Stalin's proposal for revision of the Montreux Convention to give Russia freedom of navigation in the straits by merchant and warships alike in peace and war. He said he also agreed with my proposal that this should be guaranteed by all of us. A guarantee by the great powers and the powers interested would certainly be effective. He earnestly hoped that the marshal would accept this alternative in contrast to that of a base in the straits in close proximity to Constantinople.

With regard to the other waterways, the British were in full accord with the general line that I had taken in my statement. Churchill thought that the Kiel Canal should certainly be free and open and guaranteed by all the great powers. He attached great importance to the free navigation of the Danube and the Rhine. He felt that there was a great measure of agreement among the three powers on this subject.

I said there was no doubt concerning agreement on the question of revising the Montreux Convention.

Stalin said he wished to withhold any statement of opinion regarding my proposal, since he would want to read it attentively before discussing it. Stalin next brought up the question of the city of Koenigsberg, pointing out that this question had been discussed at the Teheran conference. The Russians complained that all their seaports in the Baltic froze over for a period each year and that they felt it necessary to have at least one ice-free port at the expense of Germany. Stalin added that the Russians had suffered so much at the hands of Germany that they were anxious to have some piece of German territory as some small satisfaction to tens of millions of Soviet citizens. This had been agreed to, he said, by Roosevelt and Churchill at Teheran, and he was anxious to see this agreement approved at this conference.

I said that I was ready to agree in principle, although it would be necessary to study the population affected and other related questions. Churchill also agreed to the concession of an ice-free port to Russia. The only question, he said, was that of the legal occasion to transfer. The Soviet draft on this subject, he pointed out, would require each of us to admit that East Prussia did not exist and also to admit that the Koenigsberg area was not under the authority of the Allied Control Council in Germany. The draft, he pointed out, would commit us to the recognition of the incorporation of Lithuania into the Soviet Union. He pointed out that all these matters really belonged to the final peace settlement, but he wished to assure the marshal of his continued support of the Russian position in that part of the world. Stalin agreed that the matter would be settled at the peace conference and added that Russia was satisfied that the British and American governments approved.

Molotov then announced that the Russian delegation wished to submit a paper on the question of Syria and Lebanon and proposed that the situation in these two countries be considered by a four-power conference of representatives of the United States, Great Britain, the U.S.S.R., and France, with the consent of France to be first obtained.

Churchill said that the burden of defending Syria and Lebanon had fallen upon the shoulders of the British. At the time they entered Syria and Lebanon to throw out the Germans and the troops of Vichy, he said, they had made an arrangement with the French in which they both recognized Syria and Lebanon. The British, he pointed out, had told General de Gaulle that the moment he made a satisfactory treaty with Syria and Lebanon the British would withdraw their troops. He explained that if the British withdrew their troops now, it would lead to the massacre of the French civilians and the small number of troops there. This, he warned, would cause a great outbreak of turbulence and warfare in the Arab world which might affect Egypt too, and thus seriously endanger communication lines through the Suez Canal which were now being used by the Allies in the war against Japan. He expressed confidence that an agreement could be reached with the French in which de Gaulle should guarantee the independence of Syria and Lebanon and which would reserve for the French some of their cultural and commercial interests in this territory. He summed up his remarks by stating that the British would not welcome a proposal for a four-power conference on this question, which concerned only Britain, France, and the areas of Syria and Lebanon. The whole burden had been borne by the British, except for diplomatic approval of the United States which they had enjoyed. The British would not welcome the whole matter being reviewed by a body of this kind. Of course, if the United States wanted to take their place, that would be a different matter.

I replied, "No, thanks."

I pointed out that when this controversy arose there had been an exchange of correspondence between the Prime Minister and myself. The Prime Minister had offered to keep British troops in that region to stop the outbreak of war, I explained, and I had asked him to do so immediately in order to protect our line of communication to the Far East through the Suez Canal. I thought, however, that no country should have a special privilege such as that being considered for France. The French, I said, did not deserve a special position after the way they had stirred up all this trouble. All countries should have equal rights, I stated.

Stalin replied by noting our reluctance to have the matter discussed by a four-power group and then withdrew the Russian proposal.

This brought us to the last point on the agenda for the day—the situation in Iran.

Churchill said that the British had submitted a paper on the subject, and he would like to hear the views of the others.

Stalin remarked that the British proposals were based on the presumption that the term for the presence of Allied troops in Iran had expired. The Soviets were proceeding on the assumption, he said, that the term would not expire until after the termination of the war against Japan. He pointed out that this was stipulated by the treaty. Nevertheless, he said, the Soviet delegation concurred with the proposal that troops be withdrawn from Teheran, and he suggested that we let it go at that.

I said that we had been ready to withdraw for a long time but that we had many supplies in Iran and wished to guard them for use in the war against Japan.

Stalin said that the Russian delegation had no objection to the presence of American and British troops in Iran, but he felt that troops in Teheran might be withdrawn.

I said I thought there were no American troops in Teheran.

Stalin said that, even if there were, the Russians had no objection. He proposed that they confine themselves to the immediate withdrawal from Teheran.

Churchill said that the British were anxious to have the removal of troops continue on both sides because they had promised to withdraw when the German war was over.

Stalin said that he would have to think this over. The treaty, he said, required that troops be withdrawn not later than six months after the termination of the war with Germany and her associates, and that included Japan. They had until six months after the completion of the war with Japan. This gave us plenty of time, Stalin said.

Churchill suggested that we accept the proposal to withdraw from Teheran and that we let the foreign ministers take another look at the matter when they met.

I observed that the United States was proceeding with its withdrawal because we needed our troops in the Far East. I estimated that we could be out of Iran in sixty days.

Stalin then remarked that the United States was fully entitled to look after her supplies. "So as to rid the United States of any worries," he added, "we promise you that no action will be taken by us against Iran."

I thanked the marshal for this statement.

At this point British Field Marshal Alexander entered the room and shook hands with Marshal Stalin and with me. The conversation that followed had to do with the occupation of Vienna, a subject that had first come up during our fourth session. Churchill observed that with respect to the zones allotted to British and American troops, it appeared that in the British zone of Vienna there were five hundred thousand people. They would not be able to undertake the feeding of these five hundred thousand, he said, because the feeding grounds of Vienna lay to the east of the city. He suggested, therefore, a provisional arrangement under which the Russians would go on feeding them until a more permanent arrangement could be worked out. Field Marshal Alexander then supplied some additional information on the food situation in Vienna.

I said that there were about three hundred and seventy-five thousand people in our zone and that our transport system was almost totally engaged in handling supplies in the Japanese war and in supplying Italy, France, Russia, and other countries in Europe.

Stalin asked several questions and informed us that there was a temporary agreement with the Austrian government of Dr. Renner under which the Russians were going to supply some food to the Austrians. He promised to look further into the matter and to let us know within a few days what additional help he could give in the feeding of the Austrian capital.

Churchill then brought up the matter of the British elections. He informed Stalin and me that Mr. Attlee and he would have to be in London on the following Thursday for the elections and that they would take Eden with them. They would be back for the evening sitting on July 27. "Or some of us will be back," he added. He asked if we could meet on the Wednesday morning before his departure. This was agreed to, and it was also agreed that the foreign ministers would continue to meet and that, in Eden's absence, Sir Alexander Cadogan would represent him.

The meeting then adjourned, and at eight o'clock that evening I walked with Secretary Byrnes and Admiral Leahy to Churchill's residence, where we attended a state dinner given by the Prime Minister in honor of Generalissimo Stalin and myself.

The following morning—it was July 24—Admirals Leahy and King and Generals Marshall, Arnold, and Somervell accompanied me to the British headquarters to go over the military strategy for the next stages of the war with Japan.

On the British side, in addition to Churchill, there were Lord Leathers, the Minister of War Transport; Field Marshal Sir Alan F. Brooke; Marshal of the Royal Air Force Sir Charles F. A. Portal; Admiral of the Fleet Sir Andrew B. Cunningham; General Sir Hastings L. Ismay; Field Marshal Sir H. M. Wilson; and Major General R. E. Laycock.

The British and American Chiefs of Staff had held daily meetings since our arrival at Potsdam and now placed before us the draft of their final report to Churchill and me. We examined it paragraph by paragraph. The unconditional surrender of Japan at the earliest possible moment was the main objective of the strategy. Churchill and I approved the report in full. Some of the main strategic aims as stated in this report were:

In cooperation with other Allies to bring about at the earliest possible date the defeat of Japan by: lowering Japanese ability and will to resist, by establishing sea and air blockades, conducting intensive air bombardment, and destroying Japanese air and venal strength; invading and seizing objectives in the Japanese home islands as the main effort; conducting such operations against objectives other than the Japanese home islands as will contribute to the main effort; establishing absolute military control of Japan; and liberating Japanese-occupied territory if required;

In cooperation with other Allies to establish and maintain, as necessary, military control of Germany and Austria;

The invasion of Japan and operations directly connected therewith would be the supreme operations in the war against Japan; forces and resources would be allocated on the required scale to assure that invasion would be accomplished at the earliest practicable date. No other operations would be undertaken which might hazard the success of, or delay of, these main operations;

Russian entry into the war against Japan should be encouraged. Such aid to her war-making capacity as might be necessary should be provided;

Such measures as might be necessary and practicable should be taken in order to aid the war effort of China as an effective ally against Japan;

The control of operation strategy in the Pacific theater would remain in the hands of the United States Chiefs of Staff;

The United States Chiefs of Staff would provide the British Chiefs of Staff with full and timely information as to their future plans and intentions;

In the event the U.S.S.R. entered the war against Japan, the strategy to be pursued should be discussed between the parties concerned;

The British Pacific Fleet would participate as at present planned;

A British very long range bomber force of 10 squadrons, increasing to 20 squadrons when more airfields became available, participate;

It was agreed that the appropriate British commanders and staff should visit Admiral Nimitz and General MacArthur and draw up with them a plan for submission to the Combined Chiefs of Staff;

For the purpose of planning production and the allocation of manpower, the planning date for the end of organized resistance by Japan should be 15 November 1946 and this date should be adjusted periodically to conform to the courses of the war.

That same day, in the afternoon, the Combined Chiefs met for the first and only time with the Russian Chiefs of Staff: General Antonov, the Red Army Chief of Staff; Admiral of the Fleet Kuznetsov of the People's Commissariat for the Navy; and Marshal of Aviation Fallalev, the Chief of the Soviet Air Staff. Antonov was accompanied by his deputy, Lieutenant General Slavin. Admiral Leahy presided at the meeting, and later he and General Marshall gave me a detailed report.

The primary purpose was to co-ordinate strategy in the Far East, an important step toward bringing Russia into the war on our side. General Antonov reported that Soviet troops were being concentrated in the Far East in order to be ready to start operations against the Japanese in the latter half of August. The exact date, he informed our military leaders, would depend on the satisfactory completion of the negotiations with the Chinese.

Antonov defined the Russian objective in the Far East to be the destruction of the Japanese in Manchuria and the occupation of the Liaotung Peninsula. After the defeat of the Japanese, he said, it was the intention of the Soviets to withdraw all Russian troops from Manchuria.

General Marshall then informed the Russians of the general disposition of Japanese troop strength as known to us. He gave them a very general picture of our position in the Pacific and discussed some possible courses of action open to the Japanese. Admiral King and General Arnold discussed the effect of sea and air activities against the Japanese forces.

General Antonov showed particular interest in any intentions we might have to undertake operations against the Kuriles or in Korea. He was told by Admiral King that we would not be able to operate against the Kuriles but that a line of communications could be maintained through that island chain without the seizure of any of the islands.

General Marshall stated that we had no present plans for amphibious operations against Korea. From our point of view, he explained, such a move would require an undue amount of shipping, and it was the belief of our experts that Korea could be brought under control without difficulty once our aircraft could operate from fields on the Japanese island of Kyushu.

Admiral Leahy reported that the meeting was friendly.

Another meeting was held two days later, on July 26, but with only the Americans and the Russians present. The primary purpose was to receive the Russian answers to a number of questions of detail which General Marshall had given them. In their answers the Russians agreed to the establishment of weather stations at Petropavlovsk and Khabarovsk and, although initially reluctant, they agreed at the meeting that American personnel should man these stations.

Agreement was also reached on lines to mark off areas of operation for the respective air and naval forces. These ran generally from the northern tip of Japan across extreme northern Korea. No lines were set up for land operations since it was not anticipated by our military leaders that we would carry out operations to Korea.

The two military groups also agreed to exchange liaison groups, including a Soviet military mission in Washington, and to make designated ports and airfields in Siberia available to our units for repair needs and emergency use. The Russians took pains to point out that all these agreements would become effective only upon Russia's entry into the war against Japan, but the general atmosphere of this meeting, like the one before, was one of co-operation and friendship.

At the eighth session of the heads of government, on July 24, we were again dealing with the question of peace treaties and interim arrangements with Italy and the other satellites. I had agreed to include the eastern satellites in a redraft of my original proposal, and this new version was now placed before us by Secretary Byrnes.

The bitterest debate of the conference now developed, the point at issue being that Stalin wanted us to recognize the puppet governments he had installed in the satellite countries overrun by the Russian armies.

Stalin said an abnormal distinction was being drawn between Italy and the other satellite states, as if Rumania, Bulgaria, Hungary, and Finland belonged in the category of leprous states. In such a distinction he saw a danger that attempts would be made to discredit the Soviet Union and asked whether the Italian government was any more democratic or responsible than the governments of the other countries. No democratic elections had been held in Italy, he said.

I replied to Stalin that everybody had free access to Italy—the United States, Great Britain, the Soviet Union, and other nations—but we had not been able to have free access to Rumania, Bulgaria, and Hungary, and had not been able to get information concerning them. When Rumania, Bulgaria, and Hungary were set up on a basis giving us free access to them, I declared, then we would recognize them, but not sooner. I said I was asking for the reorganization of the other satellite governments along democratic lines, as had been agreed upon at Yalta.

Stalin objected to the words "responsible and democratic governments" in the draft, saying that they should be deleted, since they served to discredit these countries. I pointed out that this language was necessary to show that the only way in which they could obtain our support for entry into the United Nations was for them to have democratic governments. Stalin said that these were not fascist governments. There was a far less democratic government in Argentina, he pointed out, which in spite of this had been admitted to the United Nations.

Churchill said he would like to put in a plea for Italy. He said he had considerable sympathy for Italy because there was no censorship there, there had been a considerable growth of freedom, and now the north was going to have democratic elections. He did not see why the Big Three should not discuss peace with them. With regard to Rumania, and particularly to Bulgaria, he added, the British knew nothing. Their mission in Bucharest, he asserted, had been penned up with a closeness approaching internment.

Stalin broke in to ask if it were really possible for Churchill to cite such facts that had not been verified.

Churchill said that the British knew this by their representatives there. Stalin would be very much astonished, he stated, to read a long catalogue of difficulties encountered by their mission there. An iron fence, he charged, had come down around them.

Stalin interrupted to exclaim, "All fairy tales." Churchill rejoined that statesmen could call one another's statements fairy tales if they wished. He expressed complete confidence in his representatives in Bucharest and said that the conditions in the British mission there had caused him the greatest distress.

I stated that, in the case of the United States, we had been much concerned about the many difficulties encountered by our missions in Rumania and Bulgaria.

The exchange continued sharp and lengthy, and I suggested that the question again be referred to the foreign ministers for redrafting.

Next on the agenda was a renewal of the discussion regarding the Black Sea straits. I inquired if my paper on inland waterways had been considered.

Stalin remarked that this paper did not deal with the question of Turkey and the straits but dealt with the Danube and the Rhine. The Soviet delegation, he said, would like to receive a reply to their proposal of a Russo-Turkish treaty regarding the Black Sea straits. I replied that it was my wish that the two questions be considered together.

Stalin said he was afraid that we would not be able to reach an agreement in regard to the straits, since our views differed so widely. He suggested that we postpone the question and take up the next one.

Churchill said he understood that it was agreed that freedom in the Black Sea straits should be approved and guaranteed by the Big Three and other powers. He observed that my proposal to join in an organization to free the waterways of the world was, to his mind, a remarkable and important fact.

I stated that the Prime Minister had clearly presented the position of the United States in this matter and agreed with him that this would be a big step.

Churchill said he hoped that the guarantee proposed by the President would be considered by Stalin as more than a substitute for fortification of the straits.

Molotov asked if the Suez Canal was operated under such a principle.

Churchill rejoined that it was open in war and in peace to all.

Molotov asked whether the Suez Canal were under the same international control as was proposed for the Black Sea straits.

Churchill observed that this question had not been raised.

Molotov retorted, "I'm raising it." If it was such a good rule, he said, why not apply it to the Suez?

Churchill explained that the British had an arrangement with which they were satisfied and under which they had operated for some seventy years without complaints.

Molotov charged that there had been a lot of complaints. "You should ask Egypt," he said.

Eden intervened to point out that Egypt had signed the treaty with England.

Molotov said that the British had asserted that international control was better.

Molotov did a lot of talking at Potsdam. He and Stalin, along with Trotsky and Lenin, were among the old Bolsheviki of the 1917 Revolution. Molotov would take the bit in his teeth and talk as if he were the Russian state, until Stalin would smile and say a few words to him in Russian, and he would change his tune.

I often felt that Molotov kept some facts from Stalin or that he would not give him all the facts until he had to. It was always harder to get agreement out of Molotov than out of Stalin. Where Stalin could smile and relax at times, Molotov always gave the impression that he was constantly pressing.

Churchill said that the suggestion of international control of the inland waterways had been made to meet the Russian position that Russia should be able to move freely in and out of the Black Sea, and that his government was prepared to join in a guarantee with other nations and was prepared to press it on Turkey. Freedom of the seas could be attained in this way without trouble to Turkey, he said. He agreed that the question must be put off, but he hoped that the "tremendous fact that they had heard at this meeting" should not be underestimated by their Russian friends.

I said I wished to make clear my understanding of an international guarantee of the freedom of the straits; it meant that any nation had free ingress for any purpose whatever. I did not contemplate any fortifications of any kind, I added.

We agreed that each of us would study the problem of the straits.

Before proceeding with any further business, I pointed out that the conference would have to be wound up in not more than a week or ten days and that a communiqué would have to be prepared. I proposed that a committee be appointed to start working on it and suggested that the foreign ministers make a proposal to us on the following day.

I stated that I was anxious to do as much work as possible, because when there was nothing more upon which we could agree I was returning home. I had a great deal of business waiting for me in Washington, I added.

Churchill said that he could not stay longer than August 6, as both he and Mr. Attlee would have to be in England by the eighth for the new Parliament.

The occupation of Vienna was the final item for our consideration. Stalin announced that he had talked to Marshal Konev and that the U.S.S.R. was ready to continue to issue rations to all zones in Vienna until such time as the British and Americans found it possible to make some other arrangements.

I had come to Potsdam with a draft of an ultimatum calling upon the Japanese to surrender which I intended to discuss with Churchill. This was to be a joint declaration by the heads of government of the United States, the United Kingdom, and China. I waited until the Joint Chiefs of Staff had reached an agreement on our military strategy before I gave him a copy of the draft on July 24. Churchill was as anxious as I was for the Russians to come into the Japanese war. He felt, as did our military leaders, that Russia's entry would hasten Japanese defeat. At the same time, Churchill agreed quickly to the principle of the proposed declaration and said he would take the copy with him for further study of the text.

Stalin could not, of course, be a party to the proclamation itself since he was still at peace with Japan, but I considered it desirable to advise him of the move we intended to make. I spoke to him privately about this in the course of the conference meeting.

Churchill and I agreed that Chiang Kai-shek should be asked to join in the issuance of the document and that China should be listed as one of the sponsoring governments. Accordingly I sent the text of the proposed document to Ambassador Hurley at Chungking with instructions to obtain the generalissimo's concurrence without delay. The message went through naval channels and also through the Army's signal setup. But for more than twenty-four hours there was neither reply nor acknowledgment. Churchill was about to return to London to learn the results of the election, but before he left he transmitted his approval of the wording of the proclamation and agreed to have me issue the document at my discretion.

July 25 was the day Winston Churchill would have to leave the conference, and Stalin and I, to accommodate him, had agreed to meet in the morning. Before we went into this, the ninth meeting of the conference, Churchill, Stalin, and I posed in the palace garden for the first formal photographs of the conference.

The ninth session got under way with a discussion of the now familiar topic of Poland's western frontier. Churchill said that he had had a talk with President Bierut and that Mr. Eden had seen the Polish delegation for two hours last evening. The Poles were all in agreement, he reported, that about one and one half million Germans were left in the area in the west which was under discussion.

I observed that this was true. I added that the Secretary of State, Mr. Byrnes, had talked with the Poles and expected to have more talks with them.

Churchill said that he thought the question of transfer of populations from Germany and Czechoslovakia and Poland should be discussed. He pointed out that the Poles were evacuating Germans from an occupational zone. This area was part of the Russian zone, and Poles were driving the Germans out. He felt that this ought not to be done without consideration being given to the question of food supply, reparations, and other matters which had not yet been decided. The result was that the Poles had little food and fuel, he said, and that the British had a mass of population thrown on them.

Stalin remarked that we should appreciate the position in which the Poles found themselves. They were taking revenge on the Germans, he said, for the injuries the Germans had caused them in the course of centuries. Churchill pointed out that their revenge took the form of throwing the Germans into the American and British zones to be fed.

I expressed full agreement with the Prime Minister that this should not be tolerated. If the Poles were to have a zone, I repeated, this matter should be considered very carefully. The occupying powers of Germany were Great Britain, the Soviet Union, France, and the United States. If the Poles were in a zone, they were responsible to the Soviet Union for it. I stated that I wanted to be as helpful as I could, and the position I had taken was that the frontier should be fixed at the peace conference.

At this point I thought it necessary to tell what my powers as President were with respect to the question of the treaty of peace. When we were discussing matters appropriate for inclusion in the peace treaties, I stated, I wanted all to understand that under the Constitution of the United States a treaty could be concluded only with the consent of the United States Senate. I assured them that when I supported a proposal at the conference I would use my best efforts to support the matter when it came up for consideration in the Senate. This did not preclude, however, my coming back and saying that I considered the political sentiment in the United States was such that I could not press the matter without the danger of injuring our mutual relations. I explained that I was making these remarks not in order to change the basis of any discussion with my colleagues, nor to change the basis upon which the discussions with President Roosevelt had been held, but to make clear what my constitutional powers were. I had to consider these matters, I continued, from the standpoint of the people of the United States, and I wished to be able to be in a position to get the best arrangements approved by the Senate. I concluded by saying that I was convinced that world peace could be maintained only by the co-operation of the three major powers present at the table.

Stalin inquired if my remarks referred only to the peace treaties or to the whole discussion. I replied that I was referring only to those agreements or treaties that had to go to the Senate for ratification. I had large war powers, I pointed out, but I did not wish to abuse these powers to the point where they might endanger the conclusion of peace. Furthermore, I explained, I always wanted to have the full support of the American people for my policies.

Stalin said that he understood. Churchill, I know, understood.

Stalin took the position that, in the discussion of German supplies and production, coal and steel were much more important than food. Stalin, I could see, saw his opportunity here to bargain for access to the resources of the Ruhr basin. And now he argued that the yield of this German industrial area should be made available to all of Germany, as Churchill argued that East German food supplies should be.

Churchill replied that the British themselves were short of coal because they were exporting to Holland, France, and Belgium. They were denying themselves to supply these countries; the coming winter would be the most nearly fireless one of the war for the people of England.

Stalin replied that the Russian situation was still worse than that of the British. The Russians had lost more than five million men in this war and were short of coal and other things. He was afraid, he said, that if he started describing the situation in Russia he would make Churchill burst into tears.

Churchill insisted that he was still eager to barter coal from the Ruhr in exchange for food for the German population, and Stalin agreed that this question must be discussed. Churchill replied that he did not expect a decision today but he hoped for one soon. Furthermore, he did not think we should consider that we had yet solved the major problems. So far as he was concerned we had only exchanged views.

A few more interchanges followed, and Churchill, referring to his departure the following day for the British elections, announced that he had finished.

"What a pity," Stalin quipped.

"I hope to be back," Churchill replied.

Stalin remarked in reply that, judging from the expression on Mr. Attlee's face, he did not think Mr. Attlee was looking forward to taking over Churchill's authority.

With the end of the ninth meeting the conference was adjourned until the return of the British delegation from England.

At the time Churchill left for London, we were still without an answer from Chiang Kai-shek. The message to him had met with more than its share of difficulties. First there had been a delay in its transmission at the Honolulu communications center. Then heavy traffic between Honolulu and Guam had slowed its way. But it had finally reached Hurley at 8:35 P.M. Chungking time.

Ambassador Hurley radioed that the statement to the Japanese people had been delivered to Prime Minister Soong, but the generalissimo was out of Chungking, in the mountains across the Yangtze River. He said the message would be translated and delivered to Chiang that night. Hurley then described the difficulty of reaching Chiang: "The translation was not finished until after midnight. We then had difficulty in procuring a ferry across the Yangtze. The prime minister declined to go out to Yellow Mountain with me in the night. This morning, K. C. Wu, Assistant Minister of Foreign Relations, accompanied me to the General-issimo's residence at Yellow Mountain. The Generalissimo read the translation carefully, and then K. C. Wu interpreted my explanation of the necessity for immediate concurrence. The Generalissimo was kindly and courteous throughout. After he had told me that he concurred in the proclamation, Dr. Wang Shih-chieh, the Minister of Information, arrived at the conference. It became necessary to explain the whole situation again to Wang. Incidentally, Wang is to succeed the Prime Minister as Minister of Foreign Relations. When Chiang Kai-shek had approved the message of concurrence, we found the telephone out of order. It was necessary for me to return to Chungking to contact facilities to make transmission to you. . . ."

Chiang Kai-shek had concurred with one reservation: He wanted us to change the order in which we listed the heads of the three sponsoring governments in order to put him ahead of the British Prime Minister, because it would help him at home. The proclamation was changed to accommodate Chiang Kai-shek.

At nine-twenty on the night of July 26 I issued the joint proclamation from Berlin. This was the ultimatum that came to be known as the "Potsdam Declaration." I directed the Office of War Information in Washington to begin immediately to get this message to the Japanese people in every possible way. Here is the Proclamation:

PROCLAMATION BY HEADS OF GOVERNMENTS,
UNITED STATES, UNITED KINGDOM, AND CHINA

(1) We—the President of the United States, the President of the National Government of the Republic of China, and the Prime Minister of Great

Britain, representing the hundreds of millions of our countrymen, have conferred and agree that Japan shall be given an opportunity to end this war.

(2) The prodigious land, sea and air forces of the United States, the British Empire and of China, many times reinforced by their armies and air fleets from the west, are poised to strike the final blows upon Japan. This military power is sustained and inspired by the determination of all the Allied Nations to prosecute the war against Japan until she ceases to resist.

(3) The result of the futile and senseless German resistance to the might of the aroused free peoples of the world stands forth in awful clarity as an example to the people of Japan. The might that now converges on Japan is immeasurably greater than that which, when applied to the resisting Nazis, necessarily laid waste to the lands, the industry and the method of life of the whole German people. The full application of our military power, backed by our resolve, *will* mean the inevitable and complete destruction of the Japanese armed forces and just as inevitably the utter devastation of the Japanese homeland.

(4) The time has come for Japan to decide whether she will continue to be controlled by those self-willed militaristic advisers whose unintelligent calculations have brought the Empire of Japan to the threshold of annihilation, or whether she will follow the path of reason.

(5) Following are our terms. We will not deviate from them. There are no alternatives. We shall brook no delay.

(6) There must be eliminated for all time the authority and influence of those who have deceived and misled the people of Japan into embarking on world conquest, for we insist that a new order of peace, security and justice will be impossible until irresponsible militarism is driven from the world.

(7) Until such a new order is established *and* until there is convincing proof that Japan's war-making power is destroyed, points in Japanese territory to be designated by the Allies shall be occupied to secure the achievement of the basic objectives we are here setting forth.

(8) The terms of the Cairo Declaration shall be carried out and Japanese sovereignty shall be limited to the islands of Honshu, Hokkaido, Kyushu, Shikoku and such minor islands as we determine.

(9) The Japanese military forces, after being completely disarmed, shall be permitted to return to their homes with the opportunity to lead peaceful and productive lives.

(10) We do not intend that the Japanese shall be enslaved as a race or destroyed as a nation, but stern justice shall be meted out to all war criminals, including those who have visited cruelties upon our prisoners. The Japanese Government shall remove all obstacles to the revival and strengthening of democratic tendencies among the Japanese people. Freedom of speech, of religion, and of thought, as well as respect for the fundamental human rights shall be established.

(11) Japan shall be permitted to maintain such industries as will sustain her economy and permit the exaction of just reparations in kind, but not those which would enable her to re-arm for war. To this end, access to, as distinguished from control of, raw materials shall be permitted. Eventual Japanese participation in world trade relations shall be permitted.

(12) The occupying forces of the Allies shall be withdrawn from Japan as soon as these objectives have been accomplished and there has been estab-

lished in accordance with the freely expressed will of the Japanese people a peacefully inclined and responsible government.

(13) We call upon the government of Japan to proclaim now the unconditional surrender of all Japanese armed forces, and to provide proper and adequate assurances of their good faith in such action. The alternative for Japan is prompt and utter destruction.

As there was no meeting on July 26, I left early in the morning by plane for Frankfurt. General Eisenhower, Lieutenant General Wade H. Haislip, Major General Harold R. Bull, and Brigadier General Doyle O. Hickey greeted me and the members of my party at the airport in Frankfurt.

I began my inspection of the various units of the 3rd Armored Division under General Hickey's command as we drove through Frankfurt in an open car. The various units were lined up alongside the road for a distance of approximately thirty miles.

Arriving at the town of Heppenheim, I was greeted by an honor guard from the 84th Infantry Division, known as the "Railsplitters." This division was under Major General A. R. Bolling's command. After the honors, the hundred-piece band of the 84th Division softly played "The Missouri Waltz" while I inspected the guard of honor. After addressing a few remarks to the guard, I entered General Eisenhower's armored car and with General Bolling we began the long drive to the latter's headquarters in Weinheim.

The route led through several very picturesque little German villages that seemed to be totally unscathed by the ravages of war. As a war reminder, however, there remained signs along the road that read, "Mineswept to ditch."

Just before noon we arrived at General Bolling's headquarters, a beautiful château that had formerly been the home of German royalty. The house was handsomely furnished, and apparently nothing had been altered to change its original appearance. In one corner of the main room hung a red flag inscribed, "Russian 32nd Cavalry Smolensk Division Greets the 84th Railsplitter Division," which the Soviets had presented to General Bolling when the two Allied divisions had met on the Elbe.

After luncheon at General Bolling's headquarters, where I visited with a cousin of mine, Colonel L. W. Truman, General Bolling's chief of staff, I resumed my inspection of the 84th Division. In the first group were about four hundred and fifty men, all from Missouri. As I walked down the line I singled out several of the men to inquire what their home towns were and to discover what mutual acquaintances we might have.

After a brief talk to the group I ended by telling them that I did not want to keep them in the hot sun any longer to listen to me, since

I was not running for office and since they couldn't vote for me anyway.

Continuing in the armored vehicle, we drove along the road with men of the 84th Division lining both sides of the road in single file for a distance of more than seven miles. Then we left the area and returned to Frankfurt via the autobahn. The German autobahns by-pass all cities, and we were told that the Germans had no speed laws for traffic using them.

Arriving in Frankfurt, I visited General Eisenhower's headquarters. The big yellow building composed of many wings, slightly reminiscent of the Pentagon in Washington, was noticeably unbombed amid Frankfurt's general desolation. It once housed the central offices of the vast I. G. Farben industries.

Returning to the airport, I made presentation of the Distinguished Service Medal to four high-ranking officers of the United Kingdom Army and Air Forces for exceptionally meritorious service. After the presentation, the same units that had greeted me in the morning passed in review before their Commander in Chief. Our plane left immediately for Gatow airport, and by 7 P.M. I was back in Babelsberg.

Captain John B. Ross, son of my press secretary, Charles Ross, and Major Alfred K. Lee, a personal friend of mine and son of former Congressman Frank Lee, were dinner guests at the Little White House that evening. Captain Ross spent several days in Babelsberg visiting with his father. Other callers included General Marshall and Ambassador Harriman.

On the same day I received the following invitation from Prime Minister Churchill in London:

"Assuming your departure would be 6th or 7th it would be very agreeable if you would come by air to Plymouth and join Augusta there. Your privacy between the airfield and the ship would be carefully protected. The King feels he would not like you to touch our shores without having an opportunity of meeting you. He would therefore be in a British cruiser in Plymouth Sound and would be very glad if you would lunch with him. He would then pay a return visit to the Augusta before she sailed. I hope these arrangements will be convenient to you."

I replied: "I fully expect to get away from Terminal earlier than August 6th and I will give you as much advance notice as possible.

"Your permission to join the Augusta at Plymouth is accepted with appreciation. I will be very much pleased to meet with the expressed desires of His Majesty at Plymouth if my necessity for early departure for Washington meets entirely with his convenience."

On the following day, July 27, there was again no meeting of the conference, since the British delegation had not yet returned to Babelsberg.

I worked on my mail during the forenoon and conferred during the day with Secretary Byrnes and Admiral Leahy. Joseph Davies called on me during the early evening, and that night Judge Samuel I. Rosenman, special assistant to the President, arrived from Washington and joined our party. At "Colors" I was so impressed with the quality of the bugling as the flag was lowered that I walked across the lawn to congratulate the buglers personally. That evening I also enjoyed the piano playing of Sergeant List.

On July 28 I wrote my mother and sister Mary:

Dear Mama & Mary:—Well here another week has gone, and I'm still in the Godforsaken country awaiting the return of a new British Prime Minister. I had hoped we'd be finished by now, but there are some loose ends to clean up, and we must meet again to do it. . . .

I went to Frankfurt and inspected two American divisions on Thursday, the 3rd Armored and 84th Infantry Divisions.

Lewis Truman, Ralph's boy, is the Chief of Staff and Asst. Div. Commander of the 84th. He is a nice boy and a good officer. He is a full Colonel now. I saw a lot of Missourians and a lot of good American soldiers. In most of the regiments they had the Missourians all in one place. I saw men from all over the state and talked to them.

When we were going through the 3rd Armored I made the remark that I'd seen a lot of Missourians but no South Carolinians, kidding Mr. Byrnes, who was in the car behind me. The soldier who was driving the car stood it as long as he could and finally, much to the pained surprise of the General who was riding with me, spoke up and said he was from Mr. Byrnes' home town, Spartanburg. I stopped the caravan and brought Jim up and introduced him. The kid lived just around the corner from him.

That part of Germany where we made the inspection looks much different from Berlin and its surrounding territory. The children and the people looked well fed and seemed in better spirits.

The big towns like Frankfurt and Darmstadt were destroyed, but the small ones are intact. It is awful to see what the bombs did to the towns, railroads, and bridges. To think that millions of Russians, Poles, English and Americans were slaughtered all for the folly of one crazy egotist by the name of Hitler. I hope it won't happen again.

There was a lieutenant in one of those Missouri artillery outfits I inspected named Hitler. He was from St. Louis. We had lunch with the 84th Division, finished the inspection and went back to Frankfurt where I pinned some four medals on 3 Englishmen and a Canadian.

It was the best day I've had here. Hope you are both well. I am hoping to leave here some day soon. Maybe next Tuesday or Wednesday.

Love to you both.

Harry

CHAPTER 25

On the afternoon of July 28 the heads of the British delegation returned, although Winston Churchill and Anthony
Eden were no longer among them. Their party had suffered a decisive
defeat in the elections, and as a result the Conservative Cabinet had resigned.

The new Prime Minister was Clement Attlee, and with him, as Foreign
Minister, came Ernest Bevin. The two, accompanied by Sir Alexander
Cadogan, Permanent Under Secretary for Foreign Affairs, called on me
at the Little White House shortly after they arrived from London. The
main purpose of their visit was to introduce Bevin. Secretary Byrnes
and Admiral Leahy were with me. The new Prime Minister had been
present at the conference from the beginning and I had come to know
him well. Attlee had a deep understanding of the world's problems,
and I knew there would be no interruption in our common efforts.

Bevin appeared to me to be a tough person to deal with, but after I
became better acquainted with him I found that he was a reasonable man
with a good mind and a clear head. He was anxious to do all he could
for the peace of the world and to maintain friendship and understanding between Great Britain and the United States.

As Attlee and Bevin took their chairs at the round table for the tenth
meeting of the conference, it was a dramatic demonstration of the stable
and peaceful way in which a democracy changes its government.

Two days had passed without meetings between the heads of government, and because the new Prime Minister and his associates had arrived

so late from London, we decided to hold our first night meeting, convening at ten-fifteen at Cecilienhof.

Stalin said he wished to make an announcement before we went into the business of the meeting. He stated that the Russian delegation had received a proposal from Japan and that although the Soviet delegation had not been officially informed when the Anglo-American ultimatum was drawn up against Japan, nevertheless he wished to keep the Allies informed of an overture on the part of Japan.

The Russian interpreter then read for Stalin a communication from the Japanese Ambassador to Moscow, Saito, which was, in substance, as follows:

"On July 13 the ambassador had had the honor to submit a proposal of the Japanese Government to send Prince Konoye to Moscow. He had received the reply of the Soviet Government which did not see the possibility of giving a definite reply to the approach because no definite proposal had been made. In order to make the matter more precise, he was communicating the following: The mission of Prince Konoye was to ask the Soviet Government to take part in mediation to end the present war and to transmit the complete Japanese case in this respect. He would also be empowered to negotiate with respect to Soviet-Japanese relations during the war and after the war. Simultaneously, he wished to repeat that Prince Konoye was especially charged by his Majesty, the Emperor, to convey to the Soviet Government that it was exclusively the desire of His Majesty to avoid more bloodshed by the parties engaged in the war. In view of the foregoing, he hoped that the Soviet Government would give favorable attention to his request and would give its consent to the arrival of the mission. He added that the Soviet Government was aware of the position which Prince Konoye occupied in Japan."

Stalin had told me, shortly after our arrival in Potsdam, that the Japanese had asked the Kremlin if it would be possible for Prince Konoye to come to Moscow. The Russians, so Stalin had informed me, had replied that they could not answer such a request until they knew what he wanted to talk about. It now appeared that the Japanese had sent another message, advising the Soviet government that Prince Konoye would request Russian mediation and that he was acting on behalf of the Emperor, who wanted to prevent further bloodshed in the war.

After the interpreter finished reading the Japanese message to Russia, Stalin declared that there was nothing new in it except that it was more definite than the previous approach and that it would receive a more definite answer than was the case the last time. The answer would be in the negative, he said.

I thanked Marshal Stalin. Our ultimatum to the Japanese people of

July 26 was broadcast continuously and also had been sent through the customary neutral diplomatic channels; that is, through the intermediaries of Switzerland and Sweden. No formal reply had come from the Japanese. But on this day, July 28, when Stalin had the Japanese message read to the conference, our radio monitors reported that Radio Tokyo had reaffirmed the Japanese government's determination to fight. Our proclamation had been referred to as "unworthy of consideration," "absurd," and "presumptuous."

I then opened the meeting for business, stating that the Soviet delegation had two questions to discuss.

Attlee interjected to express regret that the "domestic occurrences" in Great Britain had interfered with the work of the conference and said that he was prepared to stay as long as necessary to complete this work.

We then went ahead with the business, the first of which involved the drafting of the agreement on the recognition of Italy and the eastern satellites, Bulgaria, Rumania, and Hungary. The three foreign secretaries found that they could not agree among themselves on just what it was that the heads of government had agreed to. The Russians said it was one thing, the British said it was another, and Jimmy Byrnes could only report that "the United States has unfortunately found that if it agrees with the Soviet delegation, the British delegation does not agree, and if it agrees with the British, then the Soviet disagrees."

It was decided, after the British and Russian views had been restated, to pass over the question of recognition of Italy and the satellite states.

I next introduced the matter of Italian reparations, pointing out that the United States had found it necessary, with the government of Great Britain, to contribute five hundred million dollars for the feeding and rehabilitation of Italy. We recognized, I added, that much more would be needed to keep Italy from starving, and I made it plain that the United States did not intend to provide money for the payment of reparations. If there were war plants that the Soviets needed, I said, we agreed that they should take them, but our contributions made to support Italy should have first claim on exports and removals.

Stalin said that it was possible to agree not to exact reparations from Austria, but the Soviet people would not understand if the same treatment was applied to Italy. Austria did not have her own armed forces, but Italy had sent her army as far as the Volga to devastate his country.

I replied that if any reparations could be obtained from Italy I was perfectly willing but that the United States could not spend money to rehabilitate Italy just to enable her to pay reparations to other countries. Stalin replied that he understood this but that he referred to the moral right of the Soviet Union to reparations as being based on the fact that for three and a half years its territory had been occupied and much devastation caused. In Rumania, Hungary, and Finland, he observed, the Russians had found equipment which would constitute a sum of three hundred million dollars for reparations. What sum, Stalin asked, was Italy prepared to pay in the form of equipment which might be available?

I answered that I would not even venture a guess and that, in any event, America was not interested in reparations for anybody.

Stalin said the answer could be postponed, but Bevin inquired if the Russian plan for collecting reparations from Italy was based on the assumption that the supplies furnished by the United States and Great Britain would be protected.

"I do not wish," Stalin replied, "to ignore the interests of America."

Attlee expressed his agreement with me and also his full sympathy for the Russian people in the suffering they had undergone. He reminded Stalin, however, that Britain had also suffered from attacks by Italy. The marshal, he said, could imagine the feelings of the British people if Italy had to pay reparations which actually came from Britain and America. He had no objection to military equipment being taken as reparations, but the fact was that Italy had to receive help in order to live.

Stalin replied that he would be willing to take equipment as reparations.

"Military equipment?" Bevin shot back.

"Yes," Stalin agreed, "military equipment."

Attlee asked if this would be once-and-for-all removals and not levies on war production.

"Yes," Stalin replied, "once-for-all removals."

Bevin, continuing the cross-examination, inquired if this meant military equipment having no peacetime value.

Stalin replied that military factories could be used for any purpose, and added that he had in mind the same type of equipment that was taken from Germany. Attlee said that it should be equipment having no peacetime usefulness. Stalin answered that all equipment could be adjusted for peacetime production. The Soviet Union was adjusting theirs now, he continued, since all such equipment was capable of peacetime uses.

Bevin observed that it was difficult to tell what the Russians would take away or to define the effect that removal of equipment might have on the economic life of a nation. Stalin admitted the difficulty, but he said he wanted only a decision recognizing the principle. The sum of reparations asked by Russia, he went on, could be reduced.

I said that I thought we were not far apart on the principle. What I wanted to protect, I insisted, was the help we were giving to Italy, and I added that I did not intend that help to be drained away for reparations to Russia.

Stalin expressed his agreement and assured me that the Russians "do not want to touch the advances the United States was making to Italy."

Bevin inquired if it were not then a question of priorities. The first priority, he suggested, should be given to what Great Britain and the United States had supplied to Italy, and the second claim would be reparations. Stalin said he wanted to give no bonus to aggressors without their paying at least a small part of the damage they had caused. I said I agreed with that. At five minutes past midnight the meeting was adjourned.

When I returned to the Little White House I immediately went to the Advance Map Room to look over the dispatches that had been coming in from Washington reporting the debate in the Senate on the ratification of the United Nations Charter. A message from the White House in Washington informed me, "Debate on the United Nations Charter has gone smoothly. Approximately 40 members of the Senate have spoken during the week. No difficulties have arisen. Every indication now that the Senate will vote on the Charter this afternoon and adjourn tonight. Hiram Johnson is in the hospital. Wheeler and La Follette have already stated publicly that they will vote for the Charter, and from present indications both Shipstead and Langer will also vote for the Charter. At the opening of this morning's session, McKellar read the President's message relative to the matter of forces being authorized under a joint resolution rather than a treaty. This has had a favorable affect.

"Will wire you again immediately after vote has been taken."

On July 27, the day before, I had sent a message to the president pro tempore of the Senate, Senator McKellar, to help dispel a doubt about the mutual-defense provisions of the Charter. The White House reported that this letter had helped solidify Senate support for the treaty.

A message had gone from the Advance Map Room to Washington saying, "President, Secretary of State and all the staff are eagerly awaiting your flash on the Charter. They wish to be notified regardless of the hour. There is a Big Three meeting late tonight and the hope is that the President can inform Stalin and Attlee at that meeting."

Before I turned in for the night a flash came to me from Stettinius, announcing: "Senate has just ratified the United Nations Charter 89 to 2. Senators Langer and Shipstead voted against ratification."

With this announcement that the Untied States Senate had supported me in my pledge of full co-operation with the peace-loving nations of the world within the framework of the United Nations, I immediately wrote out the following statement for the press, to be released simultaneously in Berlin and Washington:

"It is deeply gratifying that the Senate has ratified the United Nations Charter by virtually unanimous vote. The action of the Senate substantially advances the cause of world peace."

The next day, July 29, was my second Sunday in Germany, and I again attended Protestant services at the Colosseum. When I returned to my quarters at Babelsberg I found Mr. Molotov and his interpreter, Mr. Calounsky, waiting to see me. Molotov came to inform me that Premier Stalin had caught a cold and that his doctors had ordered him not to leave his residence. For that reason, Molotov said, the Premier would not be able to attend a meeting of the conference today.

Molotov then told me that he wanted to discuss some of the issues that should come up at the next meeting of the conference. I agreed to his request and sent for Secretary Byrnes, Admiral Leahy, and Chip Bohlen, my interpreter. Our meeting lasted about an hour. Molotov began by saying that he would like to go over the problems that were proving difficult in the conference discussions. Secretary Byrnes pointed out that there were two principal questions which, in his opinion, remained outstanding and that if a decision could be reached on these it would be possible to consider winding up the Big Three conference. These were: the Polish western boundary and German reparations.

Secretary Byrnes then handed Molotov a copy of the United States proposal for fixing the western boundary of Poland, which read in part as follows:

"The three Heads of Government agree that, pending the final determination of Poland's western frontier, the former German territory east of a line running from the Baltic Sea through Swinemunde, to west of Stettin to the Oder and thence along the Oder River to the confluence of the eastern Neisse River and along the eastern Neisse to the Czechoslovak frontier, including that portion of East Prussia not placed under the administration of the Union of Soviet Socialist Republics in accordance with the understanding reached at this conference and including the area of the former free city of Danzig shall be under the administration of the Polish State and for such purposes should not be considered as part of the Soviet zone of occupation in Germany."

Molotov objected, saying that under the proposal the area between the Eastern and Western Neisse would not be included under Polish administration, and stated that Marshal Stalin probably would not approve it for that reason.

I said that I thought this proposal would be agreeable to the Soviet delegation, since in my opinion it represented a very large concession on our part, and that I hoped Mr. Molotov would submit it to Marshal Stalin. He replied that he would, of course, do so.

We then turned to a discussion of reparations from Germany. Molotov wanted to know what amount of equipment would be turned over from the Ruhr. He said he was prepared to demand a fixed sum, such as two billion dollars, from the Ruhr or five or six million tons of equipment. Secretary Byrnes said that our experts felt it was impossible to put any specific dollar value or tonnage on the equipment which would be available but that our proposal was to offer the Soviet Union twenty-five per cent of the total equipment considered available from the Ruhr.

Molotov said that twenty-five per cent of an undetermined figure meant very little and added that the Soviet delegation wished to have a fixed sum or quantity agreed upon. Byrnes replied that at Yalta the Russians had suggested a total of twenty billion dollars for reparations from Germany, of which ten billion would go to the Soviet Union. These figures, he pointed out, had no relation to reality and offered a very good illustration of the danger of attempting to fix sums prematurely. He added that if we were to do that now, in the absence of sufficient data, the Soviet government might charge six months from now, if the figure turned out to be incorrect, that we were going back on the agreement reached at the Potsdam conference.

At this point I made it clear to Molotov that what we were trying to do was to arrive at a workable plan for reparations and that I would be inclined to have the Soviet Union receive fifty per cent of the total.

There was also some discussion on the division of the German merchant and naval fleets, and I expressed my opinion that we had already reached agreement that Russia was to get one third of the Navy now and that the merchant fleet was to be utilized in the war against Japan, with one third earmarked for the Soviet Union.

Molotov said he wished to take up one final matter with us in behalf of Premier Stalin, and that was the immediate cause of the Soviet entry into the Japanese war. He said that the Soviet government considered that the best method would be for the United States, England, and the other allies in the Far Eastern war to address a formal request to the Soviet government for its entry into the war. He said that this could be based on the refusal of the Japanese to accept the recent ultimatum to surrender and could be made on the basis of shortening the war and saving lives. Molotov said that of course the Soviet government was assuming that the agreement with the Chinese would be signed before the Soviet Union entered the war.

The proposal came as a surprise to me. I told Molotov that I would have to give the Soviet suggestion careful examination. The Russian commissar then left to report our discussion to Marshal Stalin.

We informed the British of the talk when Prime Minister Attlee, Mr. Bevin, and Sir Alexander Cadogan called at the Little White House later that day to confer with me and Secretary Byrnes.

On the following day, July 30, there was again no meeting of the heads of state, because Stalin was still indisposed. I spent most of the day on military matters in conference with Secretary Forrestal, General Eisenhower, Admiral Cooke, Admiral Cochrane, General Clay, Commodore Schade, and Captain E. B. Taylor. I took time to sign papers and to go over messages and mail from Washington—and to write to my mother and sister:

Dear Mama & Mary:—The conference has been prolonged by the English elections and by the illness of Stalin. Mr. Stalin has been unable to leave his house for a couple of days. I really think he's not so sick but disappointed over the English elections. I think we'll be able to get along all right though.

Attlee has been here with Churchill all the time, and he has been Deputy Prime Minister in Churchill's cabinet, so we ought to be able to proceed all right. We've had one meeting since the English came back and will have one today. If we can get a couple of major agreements over tomorrow and a few minor ones the next day, we can probably leave here Thursday or Friday, and I ought to be back in Washington by Thursday or Friday, Aug. 9th or 10th. Let's hope so anyway. You never saw such pig-headed people as are the Russians. I hope I never have to hold another conference with them—but, of course, I will.

If we get done Thursday we'll fly to Plymouth in England and leave from there. That will save two days on the ocean because it takes so long to get out of the English Channel when we leave from Antwerp.

I will have to lunch with the English King aboard a British cruiser, and then he'll have to return the call to my ship, and then we'll sail for home. I'd rather fly just as Harry did. I could be home a week sooner. But they all yell their heads off when I talk of flying.

I surely hope you are both well. Will keep you informed.

Love to you both.

Harry

From the time Stalin suggested, through Molotov, on July 29 that the United States, along with the other allies, address a formal request to the Soviet government for its entry into the war against Japan, I had been giving the matter careful thought. I had conferred with Prime Minister Attlee and with my advisers at length on the Russian proposal.

I did not like this proposal for one important reason. I saw in it a cynical diplomatic move to make Russia's entry at this time appear to be the decisive factor to bring about victory. At Yalta, Russia had agreed, and here at Potsdam she reaffirmed her commitment, to enter the war against Japan three months after V-E Day, provided that Russia and China had previously concluded a treaty of mutual assistance. There were no other conditions, and certainly none obliging the United States and the Allies to provide Russia with a reason for breaking with Japan. Our military advisers had strongly urged that Russia should be brought into the war in order to neutralize the large Japanese forces on the China mainland and thus save thousands of American and Allied lives. But I was not willing to let Russia reap the fruits of a long and bitter and gallant effort in which she had had no part.

After further consultation with the military and our British ally there was no question that Russia was bound to enter the war under the obligations the Soviet Union had undertaken at Moscow in October 1943 and recently under the Charter of the United Nations. With these facts and conditions in mind, I was now prepared to address a letter to Stalin. On July 31 I wrote Stalin as follows:

In response to your suggestion that I write you a letter as to the Far Eastern situation, I am attaching a form letter which I propose to send you at your convenience after you notify me you have reached an agreement with the Government of China. If this is satisfactory to you, you can let me know immediately when you have reached such agreement, and I will wire you the letter, to be used as you see fit. I will also send you by fastest courier the official letter signed by me. If you decide to use it, it will be all right. However, if you decide to issue a statement basing your action on other ground or for any other reason prefer not to use this letter, it will be satisfactory to me. I leave it to your good judgment.

Harry S. Truman

The form letter read as follows:

July 31, 1945

Dear Generalissimo Stalin:

Paragraph 5 of the Declaration signed at Moscow October 30, 1943, by the United States, the Soviet Union, the United Kingdom and China, provides:

"5. That for the purpose of maintaining international peace and security pending the reestablishment of law and order and the inauguration of a system of general security, they will consult with one another and as occasion requires with other members of the United Nations with a view to joint action on behalf of the community of nations."

Article 106 of the proposed Charter of the United Nations provides:

"Pending the coming into force of such special agreements referred to in Article 43 as in the opinion of the Security Council enable it to begin the exercise of its responsibilities under Article 42, the parties to the Four-Nation Declaration, signed at Moscow, October 30, 1943, and France, shall, in accordance with the provisions of paragraph 5 of that Declaration, consult with one another and as occasion requires with other Members of the United Nations with a view to such joint action on behalf of the Organization as may be necessary for the purpose of maintaining international peace and security."

Article 103 of the Charter provides:

"In the event of a conflict between the obligations of the Members of the United Nations under the present Charter and their obligations under any other international agreement, their obligations under the present Charter shall prevail."

Though the Charter has not been formally ratified, at San Francisco it was agreed to by the Representatives of the Union of Soviet Socialist Republics and the Soviet government will be one of the permanent members of the Security Council.

It seems to me that under the terms of the Moscow Declaration and the provisions of the Charter, above referred to, it would be proper for the Soviet Union to indicate its willingness to consult and cooperate with other great powers now at war with Japan with a view to joint action on behalf of the community of nations to maintain peace and security.

Sincerely yours,

. . . .

The Potsdam conference was now drawing to a close. The eleventh meeting was held on July 31, and on August 1, which turned out to be the last day of the conference, we held two sessions. We were now trying to get agreement on questions on which there had been sharp differences of opinion.

Our delegation sponsored a proposal to combine three of the major issues: reparations, Poland's western frontier, and satellite membership in the United Nations.

Stalin at once protested, saying that these questions were not connected and dealt with different subjects. Secretary of State Byrnes said that of course they were different subjects, but they had been before the conference for weeks without agreement having been reached. They were now being linked together because, he said, the American delegation was no longer willing to consider the one without the others in order to speed action on all three.

Stalin said the most debatable question was that of reparations from Germany. He said he was ready to accept the American position that no definite figure be set for reparations and that each country exact reparations from its own zone. Stalin also agreed that a determination was to be made within six months as to the share of equipment Russia was to get from the western zones. But Stalin and Molotov were persistently difficult about fixing the exact percentage of the reparations the Russians would get from the British, French, and American zones. Since most of the reparations would come from the Ruhr area, which lay within the British zone of occupation, Bevin fought to reduce the Russian percentages. He eventually yielded to Stalin's figure of fifteen and ten per cent. The fifteen per cent would apply to commodities in exchange from Russia, and the ten per cent would constitute outright reparations. We had previously agreed to that figure. Bevin said that the percentage the Soviets were asking, plus reparations from their own zone, would give them more than fifty per cent. Stalin insisted that it was less than fifty per cent. With the formula finally agreed upon, I appointed a committee composed of two representatives from each of the three governments to draw up a text.

I announced that the next question on the agenda was the second of the three proposals submitted in the United States paper—that of the western frontier of Poland. Byrnes read the United States proposal, which provided that the Poles were to have provisional administration of the area bounded by the Oder and the Western Neisse.

Bevin stated that his instructions were to hold out for the Eastern Neisse. He wanted to know if the zone would be handed over to the Poles entirely and if Soviet troops would be completely withdrawn. Bevin added that, according to the United States proposal, the territory would be under the Polish state and not part of the Soviet zone of occupation or responsibility.

I interrupted to say that cession of territory was subject to the peace treaty and that the American plan concerned only the temporary administration of this area. Bevin said it was his understanding then that the area would still technically remain under Allied military control. Otherwise, he said, we would be transferring territory before the peace conference. If it were a question of outright transfer, he said, he would first have to get the approval of the French. Stalin replied that this concerned the Russian zone and that the French had nothing to do with it.

Bevin asked if the British could give away pieces of their zone without approval from the other governments. Stalin replied that in the case of Poland it could be done, because we were dealing with a state which had no western border. This was the only such situation in the world, he asserted.

Bevin pointed out that the authority of the Control Council was to extend over the whole of Germany with its 1937 boundaries. He questioned whether any transfer could be made without consulting the Control Council.

Byrnes stated that we all understood that the cession of territory was left to the peace conference. Here was a situation, he said, where Poland was administering with Soviet consent a good part of this territory. Under the United States proposal, he explained, the three powers would agree to the administration in the interim by Poland in order that there would be no further dispute between them in regard to the administration of the area by the Polish provisional government. He added that it was not necessary that the Poles have a representative on the Control Council.

After another exchange of views I declared that we were all agreed on the Polish question. Stalin said, "Stettin is in the Polish territory." Bevin said, "Yes, we should inform the French." And it was agreed to inform the French.

I then asked Byrnes to speak on the third United States proposal. Our terms of admission of states to the United Nations were quickly adopted with two minor changes in the wording as requested by the Soviet delegation.

The next topic on the agenda was that of economic principles for the control of Germany. Bevin proposed that we pass over this question until we had decided the question of political principles. This was agreed upon. Molotov pointed out that the Soviets had circulated a paper on the Ruhr, in which the Ruhr was contemplated as a part of Germany. I stated that there was no doubt in my mind that the Ruhr was a part of Germany.

Bevin inquired why the matter was raised. Stalin replied that it was brought up because at Teheran the point had been raised that the Ruhr region should be separated from Germany under the control of the great powers. Several months afterward, he said, he had discussed the question with the British on the occasion of Churchill's visit to Moscow, and it had been said then that perhaps it would be a good thing to establish the Ruhr under an international control. This discussion was a consequence of the consideration of the general dismemberment of Germany. Since that time, Stalin continued, the views of the great powers had changed, and dismemberment of Germany was considered inadvisable. The Russian delegation would like to know, he asked, if it was agreed that the Ruhr should not be detached.

I repeated that the Ruhr was a part of Germany, and it would be under the administration of the Control Council. Stalin said the Soviets agreed but thought it should be mentioned somewhere. He asked if the British delegation agreed. Bevin said he could not agree on the question without further consideration. The internationalization of the Ruhr to reduce the war potential of Germany had been discussed, he was aware, but he felt that the region should remain under the administration of the Control Council until it should be disposed of otherwise. He wanted to discuss the matter with his government and was willing that it should be referred to the Council of Foreign Ministers. This was agreed upon.

The twelfth meeting of the Potsdam conference convened at four o'clock in the afternoon on August 1, my last day at Potsdam. Byrnes said the foreign ministers had not been able to complete the draft on reparations because there was no agreement by the Big Three on Russia's claim to German gold and foreign assets.

Stalin declared that an agreement might be possible on these lines: The Russians, he proposed, would not claim the gold which their allies had found in Germany. But with regard to shares and foreign investments, he suggested a demarcation line between the Soviet and western zones of occupation, with everything west of that line going to the Allies and everything east of that line going to the Russians.

I inquired if he meant a line running from the Baltic to the Adriatic. Stalin replied that he did, giving as an example that German investments in Rumania and Hungary would go to the Russians.

There followed a prolonged exchange between Bevin and Stalin in which the British Foreign Minister attempted to exact from the Russian Premier definitions of Russian claims to various types of German holdings in different geographical areas, but without much success.

It was finally agreed to accept the demarcation proposed by the Soviet delegation for the determination of reparations from German assets. Stalin said that he thought this decision should be put in the protocol but not published. I objected at once. I could see no reason for this secrecy, and I said so. Stalin thereupon withdrew his suggestion.

We were not misled by Stalin's concessions on minor and sometimes only procedural points. When pressed on basic issues, he would resort to diversionary tactics, and on one occasion he said, "What can I do if I am not ready to make a decision?"

I then called on Secretary Byrnes to report on the question regarding war criminals. Byrnes said the draft was ready except for the listing of specific names, and he suggested that the listing be left to the prosecutor. Stalin insisted that names were necessary. If we were going to try industrialists, he said, the people should know. He said that was why the Russians had included the name of Krupp. I remarked that I did not like any of the Nazi war criminals and that by naming some of them we might lead the others to think they would escape.

Stalin said that they were mentioned only as examples and that public opinion was interested in this matter. People were wondering why Hess was living so comfortably in England, he said. Attlee said, "You need not worry about that." Stalin replied that what was important was the opinion of the people in the occupied countries. Bevin said that if there was any doubt about Hess he could give an undertaking that Hess would be handed over, and he added that the British would also send along a bill for his keep.

Stalin said he wanted advance delivery. Attlee replied that he had already received advance delivery on some of them. He had Goebbels, he observed. Stalin said he personally needed no undertaking. He was anxious to satisfy public opinion.

I stated that, as Marshal Stalin knew, the United States had appointed one of its most able jurists to the commission set up to deal with this question and that Justice Jackson had advised me that it would be a handicap to him if persons were named before the commission was ready to bring them to trial, which I expected would be within thirty days. All of these people, I said, would be named in the indictment, and the marshal need not worry, for they would be tried and punished.

Stalin said he would be satisfied with just three names. Attlee suggested Hitler as one of them. Stalin replied that we did not have Hitler at our disposition but that he had no objection to naming him. Then he suggested that perhaps we could announce that within one month the first list of war criminals would be published. This was agreed upon.

We went on to examine the various points on which the conference committees had agreed, and one after another we gave them our approval. And at last only the final communiqué and protocol remained for a session that was to be held later that day. In this connection I asked that the communiqué mention my proposal for the international control of waterways, but Stalin objected, saying that there was already enough in the protocol. I pointed out, however, that the subject had been considered by the conference and that I wanted it included in the communiqué.

Stalin still objected. The question, he contended, had not been mentioned in a list of questions submitted before the conference, and the Russians were not in a position to discuss it. We should not be in a hurry to dispose of the matter. I said that I had not asked that it be disposed of but that it be referred to the Council of Foreign Ministers. This had been done, and I now asked that this be stated in the communiqué.

Stalin pointed out that there was nothing in the communiqué in regard to the Black Sea straits. The question of inland waterways was raised in connection with the question of the Black Sea straits, he observed, and he wanted to know why it should be given preference. In reply, I remarked that the question of the Black Sea straits would be mentioned. But Stalin insisted that this would make the communiqué and the protocol too long. I stated that I was trying to prevent a situation in which it could be charged that secret agreements had been concluded at the conference. Stalin said that the answer was that there were no secret agreements.

"Are we finished?" he asked.

"I don't think so," I replied.

Secretary Byrnes said he wished to remind us that we had agreed to refer the document under discussion to the Council of Foreign Ministers. As long as that had been done, he asked, why could we not agree to state it? If it was not in the communiqué, he pointed out, we would not want to make a statement in the United States about it.

Stalin said that at Teheran and at previous conferences there were two kinds of decisions. One kind was included in the protocol, and these were greater than those published in the communiqué, but this did not mean that they were secret, he stated. It meant that there was no need to publish them. Decisions of a formal nature, not affecting the substance of the question, should not be mentioned in the communiqué, he said, but only in the protocol.

I said that I had no objection if this applied to all questions but that I wanted to be free to mention this matter of inland waterways in any statement I might have to make before the Senate.

The afternoon meeting then adjourned.

The final meeting, the thirteenth, was scheduled to convene at nine o'clock that evening, but it was delayed until 10:40 P.M. to permit the various delegations more time to complete drafts of the two major documents growing out of the conference—the protocol and the communiqué.

A protocol is a formal record of understandings reached by the parties to a conference. At the Potsdam meeting there were no secrets. I had made up my mind from the beginning that I would enter into no secret agreements, and there was none.

In this final meeting much time was taken up by changes in wording and minor amendments to the texts of both the protocol and the communiqué. For instance, Molotov suggested an amendment to the text concerning the western frontier of Poland. In the paragraph which stated that the line ran from the Baltic Sea through Swinemünde, he suggested the substitution of the words "west of" instead of "through."

"How far west?" I asked.

Stalin suggested the words "immediately west of," and the change was approved. Molotov then wished to make another change in the wording of the same document. Instead of the words "subject to examination by experts" he suggested the words "exact line on ground should be established by experts of the U.S.S.R. and Poland."

Bevin stated that this was asking too much. The British could not cut themselves out of this, he added. Stalin observed that the question concerned the frontiers of Russia and Poland, and Bevin admitted this fact, but he pointed out that the line must be recognized by the United Nations. He went on to say that the British and Americans had agreed to support this line at the peace settlement but that we had not agreed to accept a line established by the Russians and Poles.

Stalin pointed out that the conditions for establishing the boundary were given in the document, and all that remained was to establish the exact frontier. This would mean only a variation of a kilometer or so, he remarked, "including a village here or there."

Attlee argued that the amendment proposed by Molotov would anticipate the work of the peace conference. He wished to have a commission of experts appointed by the peace conference to lay out the frontier between Poland and Russia.

Stalin replied that he just could not understand this attitude. He asked who it was the British thought should be on the commission of experts—British, Americans, or Australians? He agreed, however, to let the old wording stand, and the Russian proposal was dropped.

Prolonged and petty bickering continued on the final wording of the protocol. I was getting very impatient, as I had many times before in these sessions, with all the repetition and beating around the bush, but I restrained myself because I saw that we were very slowly making progress in the right direction. I did not see why they could not come right to the point and get it over with instead of doing so much talking.

At last the protocol was agreed to by the heads of the three governments, and the remaining business of this final session was the communiqué. Here, however, Stalin took the position that, after listing the big decisions, the small ones would spoil the communiqué. He said we need not keep our decisions secret, but he just did not want the minor decisions in the communiqué.

Bevin inquired if he could speak of these decisions in the House of Commons. "Of course," Stalin replied.

A number of minor verbal suggestions were made—mostly by Bevin—and discussed. At one point, when Bevin criticized the English phraseology of the communiqué, Stalin said that whatever English was acceptable to the Americans was acceptable to the Russians.

The draft of the communiqué was finally approved, but now the Soviet delegation raised the question of who should sign first. At the previous two conferences of the Big Three, they pointed out, the Prime Minister or the President had been first to sign the communiqué. According to the procedure of rotation, Stalin said he felt that his signature should come first on the Potsdam document.

"You can sign any time you want to," I said. "I don't care who signs first."

Attlee remarked that he was in favor of alphabetical preference.

"That way," he said jokingly, "I would score over Marshal Zhukov."

Release time for the communiqué was agreed for 9:30 G.M.T. the following day, August 2. This was 5:30 P.M. Washington time. It would, of course, be released simultaneously in London and Moscow.

I then stated that there was no further business and that the conference was now ready to adjourn. I expressed the hope that our next meeting together might be in Washington.

Someone said, "God willing." It was Stalin.

It was three o'clock in the morning when the Potsdam conference formally adjourned. The delegates from the three nations spent some time in saying good-bys, and at 4 A.M. I left Cecilienhof with my party and returned to the Little White House. Shortly thereafter I left Babelsberg for the airport at Gatow on the first leg of my journey home.

The Potsdam conference had kept me away from the United States for nearly a month, and I was anxious to get back to Washington to report to the American people. As I left for home I felt that we had achieved several important agreements. But more important were some of the conclusions I had reached in my own mind and a realization of what I had to do in shaping future foreign policy.

En route home I wrote a report to the people to be given by radio on my return. In this statement I summarized the principal achievements of the conference. Among these was the establishment of the Council of Foreign Ministers as a consultative body of the five principal governments.

Another important agreement was the adoption of the formula for reparations. We were not making the mistake again of exacting reparations and then lending the money to pay for them. We intended to make it possible for Germany to develop into a decent nation and to take her place in the civilized world.

We had agreed on a compromise on the frontiers of Poland, which was the best we were able to get, but we had accepted it only subject to a final determination by the peace conference.

There were many reasons for my going to Potsdam, but the most urgent, to my mind, was to get from Stalin a personal reaffirmation of Russia's entry into the war against Japan, a matter which our military chiefs were most anxious to clinch. This I was able to get from Stalin in the very first days of the conference. We were at war, and all military arrangements had to be kept secret, and for this reason it was omitted from the official communiqué at the end of the conference. This was the only secret agreement made at Potsdam.

But the personal meeting with Stalin and the Russians had more significance for me, because it enabled me to see at first hand what we and the West had to face in the future.

At Potsdam the Russians had pledged their signature on a document that promised co-operation and peaceful development in Europe. I had already seen that the Russians were relentless bargainers, forever pressing for every advantage for themselves. It did not seem possible that only a few miles from the war-shattered seat of Nazi power the head of any government would not bend every effort to attain a real peace. Yet I was not altogether disillusioned to find now that the Russians were not in earnest about peace. It was clear that the Russian foreign policy was based on the conclusion that we were heading for a major depression, and they were already planning to take advantage of our setback.

Anxious as we were to have Russia in the war against Japan, the experience at Potsdam now made me determined that I would not allow the Russians any part in the control of Japan. Our experience with them in Germany and in Bulgaria, Rumania, Hungary, and Poland was such that I decided to take no chances in a joint setup with the Russians. As I reflected on the situation during my trip home, I made up my mind that General MacArthur would be given complete command and control after victory in Japan. We were not going to be disturbed by Russian tactics in the Pacific.

Force is the only thing the Russians understand. And while I was hopeful that Russia might someday be persuaded to work in co-operation for peace, I knew that the Russians should not be allowed to get into any control of Japan.

The persistent way in which Stalin blocked one of the war-preventative measures I had proposed showed how his mind worked and what he was after. I had proposed the internationalization of all the principal waterways. Stalin did not want this. What Stalin wanted was control of the Black Sea straits and the Danube. The Russians were planning world conquest.

In a physical sense I found the conference to be exacting. Churchill and Stalin were given to late hours, while I was an early riser. This made my days extra long, and they were filled, in addition to the formal sessions, with long rounds of preparatory conferences with my advisers, with the study of documents pertaining to the meetings, and with work that was required on many state papers sent on from Washington. A President of the United States takes his office with him wherever he goes, and the number of details that require his attention never ends.

I was glad to be on my way home.

Arrangements had been made for me to fly to England, where I would board the *Augusta* in Plymouth Harbor and where I would have a brief meeting with King George VI. But there was considerable fog when we arrived over the southern coast of England.

Commodore Vardaman, my naval aide, had made arrangements for us to land at the airfield at St. Mawgan and had notified all the towns along the forty-mile route to Plymouth that our party would pass that way. But when we were over Harrowbeer, where the weather was fine, I asked the pilot of the *Sacred Cow* whether we could land at this airport near Plymouth. He said we could, and we did. It upset the naval aide, but it saved us two hours! This also thwarted the plans of a reception committee of the United States military personnel at St. Mawgan, but it was not long before transportation was assembled and we were in a motorcade en route to the city of Plymouth. I went directly by barge to the U.S.S. *Augusta,* which was anchored in Plymouth Roads, and arrived on board just before noon.

Soon after I was settled in my quarters Ambassador Winant, Admiral Stark, General Lee, and Admiral McCann came aboard to pay their respects and to make a short visit. They had been waiting for me at St. Mawgan but had hurried to Plymouth when they learned of our landing at Harrowbeer.

Shortly after noon I left the *Augusta* with Secretary Byrnes and Admiral Leahy for the H.M.S. *Renown,* which was anchored nearby. King George VI had come down from London by train during the morning and was aboard the *Renown,* waiting to welcome me to England. The British ship accorded the customary high honors as I arrived, and I was greeted personally by the King, who extended his hand to me and said, "Welcome to my country."

I was impressed with the King as a good man. In the course of my visit with him I found him to be well informed on all that was taking place, and he gave me the impression of a man with great common sense.

After lunching with the King, I returned to the *Augusta* and within a few minutes the British monarch came aboard with his royal party to return my visit. He inspected the marine guard and made a brief tour of inspection of personnel on the weather decks forward. We then retired to my quarters, where we had a very pleasant visit for about thirty minutes. The King and his party then left, accompanied by full honors, and the U.S.S. *Augusta* immediately got under way. While we were talking, the King had asked me to autograph White House cards for the Queen and his daughters, and he, in turn, signed a card for my daughter Margaret.

As we were leaving Plymouth Roads a message from the *Renown* was received by the quartermasters of the *Augusta.*

From the King to the President [I read when it was handed to me]. It has been a very real pleasure to me to meet you during your all too brief visit to my country after your recent labors in the great causes to which the Allied Nations are pledged. I send you my best wishes for your homeward voyage and for your safe return.

George R.I.

"From the President to the King," I replied. "My hearty thanks for your generous expressions. It has been a delightful experience to visit you and your country. I am sure that our two nations will cooperate in peace as they are now cooperating so effectively in war."

I had declined invitations to visit Denmark, Norway, and France after the Potsdam conference and to make an extended visit to England, because I felt it my duty to return to the United States as quickly as possible. I had consented to the short visit to England when it had been explained to me that by having the U.S.S. *Augusta* leave Antwerp and proceed to Plymouth I could spend six hours at Plymouth and still be twenty-four hours ahead of schedule. I expressed my desire to arrive at our port of debarkation, Newport News, as soon as practicable, and speed for the return trip was set at 26.5 knots, which was the maximum speed at which our escort ship, the U.S.S. *Philadelphia,* could make the trip without refueling.

On the second day out I had the following message sent to Washington:

3 August 1945

Please have telegraph office send following telegram to Mrs. Truman:

"I left Plymouth yesterday afternoon and am now well out on the Atlantic enjoying good weather and smooth seas. Will advise you tomorrow of our date of arrival.

"Harry"

CHAPTER 26

The historic message of the first explosion of an atomic bomb was flashed to me in a message from Secretary of War Stimson on the morning of July 16. The most secret and the most daring enterprise of the war had succeeded. We were now in possession of a weapon that would not only revolutionize war but could alter the course of history and civilization. This news reached me at Potsdam the day after I had arrived for the conference of the Big Three.

Preparations were being rushed for the test atomic explosion at Alamogordo, New Mexico, at the time I had to leave for Europe, and on the voyage over I had been anxiously awaiting word on the results. I had been told of many predictions by the scientists, but no one was certain of the outcome of this full-scale atomic explosion. As I read the message from Stimson, I realized that the test not only met the most optimistic expectation of the scientists but that the United States had in its possession an explosive force of unparalleled power.

Stimson flew from Frankfurt to Potsdam the next day to see me and brought with him the full details of the test. I received him at once and called in Secretary of State Byrnes, Admiral Leahy, General Marshall, General Arnold, and Admiral King to join us at my office at the Little White House. We reviewed our military strategy in the light of this revolutionary development. We were not ready to make use of this weapon against the Japanese, although we did not know as yet what effect the new weapon might have, physically or psychologically, when used against the enemy. For that reason the military advised that we go ahead with the existing military plans for the invasion of the Japanese home islands.

At Potsdam, as elsewhere, the secret of the atomic bomb was kept closely guarded. We did not extend the very small circle of Americans who knew about it. Churchill naturally knew about the atomic bomb project from its very beginning, because it had involved the pooling of British and American technical skill.

On July 24 I casually mentioned to Stalin that we had a new weapon of unusual destructive force. The Russian Premier showed no special interest. All he said was that he was glad to hear it and hoped we would make "good use of it against the Japanese."

A month before the test explosion of the atomic bomb the service Secretaries and the Joint Chiefs of Staff had laid their detailed plans for the defeat of Japan before me for approval. There had apparently been some differences of opinion as to the best route to be followed, but these had evidently been reconciled, for when General Marshall had presented his plan for a two-phase invasion of Japan, Admiral King and General Arnold had supported the proposal heartily.

The Army plan envisaged an amphibious landing in the fall of 1945 on the island of Kyushu, the southernmost of the Japanese home islands. This would be accomplished by our Sixth Army, under the command of General Walter Krueger. The first landing would then be followed approximately four months later by a second great invasion, which would be carried out by our Eighth and Tenth Armies, followed by the First Army transferred from Europe, all of which would go ashore in the Kanto plains area near Tokyo. In all, it had been estimated that it would require until the late fall of 1946 to bring Japan to her knees.

This was a formidable conception, and all of us realized fully that the fighting would be fierce and the losses heavy. But it was hoped that some of Japan's forces would continue to be preoccupied in China and others would be prevented from reinforcing the home islands if Russia were to enter the war.

There was, of course, always the possibility that the Japanese might choose to surrender sooner. Our air and fleet units had begun to inflict heavy damage on industrial and urban sites in Japan proper. Except in China, the armies of the Mikado had been pushed back everywhere in relentless successions of defeats.

Acting Secretary of State Grew had spoken to me in late May about issuing a proclamation that would urge the Japanese to surrender but would assure them that we would permit the Emperor to remain as head of the state. Grew backed this with arguments taken from his ten years' experience as our Ambassador in Japan, and I told him that I had already given thought to this matter myself and that it seemed to me a sound idea. Grew had a draft of a proclamation with him, and I instructed him to send it by the customary channels to the Joint Chiefs and the State-War-Navy Co-ordinating Committee in order that we might get the opinions of all concerned before I made my decision.

On June 18 Grew reported that the proposal had met with the approval of his Cabinet colleagues and of the Joint Chiefs. The military leaders also discussed the subject with me when they reported the same day. Grew, however, favored issuing the proclamation at once, to coincide with the closing of the campaign on Okinawa, while the service chiefs were of the opinion that we should wait until we were ready to follow a Japanese refusal with the actual assault of our invasion forces.

It was my decision then that the proclamation to Japan should be issued from the forthcoming conference at Potsdam. This, I believed, would clearly demonstrate to Japan and to the world that the Allies were united in their purpose. By that time, also, we might know more about two matters of significance for our future effort: the participation of the Soviet Union and the atomic bomb. We knew that the bomb would receive its first test in mid-July. If the test of the bomb was successful, I wanted to afford Japan a clear chance to end the fighting before we made use of this newly gained power. If the test should fail, then it would be even more important to us to bring about a surrender before we had to make a physical conquest of Japan. General Marshall told me that it might cost half a million American lives to force the enemy's surrender on his home grounds.

But the test was now successful. The entire development of the atomic bomb had been dictated by military considerations. The idea of the atomic bomb had been suggested to President Roosevelt by the famous and brilliant Dr. Albert Einstein, and its development turned out to be a vast undertaking. It was the achievement of the combined efforts of science, industry, labor, and the military, and it had no parallel in history. The men in charge and their staffs worked under extremely high pressure, and the whole enormous task required the services of more than one hundred thousand men and immense quantities of material. It required over two and a half years and necessitated the expenditure of two and a half billions of dollars.

Only a handful of the thousands of men who worked in these plants knew what they were producing. So strict was the secrecy imposed that even some of the highest-ranking officials in Washington had not the slightest idea of what was going on. I did not. Before 1939 it had been generally agreed among scientists that it was theoretically possible to release energy from the atom. In 1940 we had begun to pool with Great Britain all scientific knowledge useful to war, although Britain was at war at that time and we were not. Following this—in 1942—we learned that the Germans were at work on a method to harness atomic energy for use as a weapon of war. This, we understood, was to be added to the V-1 and V-2 rockets with which they hoped to conquer the world. They failed, of course, and for this we can thank Providence. But now a race was on to make the atomic bomb—a race that became "the battle of the laboratories."

It was under the general policy of pooling knowledge between our nation and Great Britain that research on the atomic bomb started in such feverish secrecy. American and British scientists joined in the race against the Germans. We in America had available a great number of distinguished scientists in many related fields of knowledge, and we also had another great advantage. We could provide the tremendous industrial and economic resources required for the project—a vastly expensive project—without injury to our war production program. Furthermore, our plants were far removed from the reach of enemy bombing. Britain, whose scientists had initiated the project and were contributing much of the original atomic data, was constantly exposed to enemy bombing and, when she started the atomic research, also faced the possibility of invasion.

For these reasons Roosevelt and Churchill agreed to pool the research and concentrate all of the work on the development of the project within the United States. Working together with the British, we thus made it possible to achieve a great scientific triumph in the field of atomic energy. Nevertheless, basic and historic as this event was, it had to be considered at the time as relatively incidental to the far-flung war we were fighting in the Pacific at terrible cost in American lives.

We could hope for a miracle, but the daily tragedy of a bitter war crowded in on us. We labored to construct a weapon of such overpowering force that the enemy could be forced to yield swiftly once we could resort to it. This was the primary aim of our secret and vast effort. But we also had to carry out the enormous effort of our basic and traditional military plans.

The task of creating the atomic bomb had been entrusted to a special unit of the Army Corps of Engineers, the so-called Manhattan District, headed by Major General Leslie R. Groves. The primary effort, however, had come from British and American scientists working in laboratories and offices scattered throughout the nation.

Dr. J. Robert Oppenheimer, the distinguished physicist from the University of California, had set up the key establishment in the whole process at Los Alamos, New Mexico. More than any other one man, Oppenheimer is to be credited with the achievement of the completed bomb.

My own knowledge of these developments had come about only after I became President, when Secretary Stimson had given me the full story. He had told me at that time that the project was nearing completion and that a bomb could be expected within another four months. It was at his suggestion, too, that I had then set up a committee of top men and had asked them to study with great care the implications the new weapon might have for us.

Secretary Stimson headed this group as chairman, and the other members were George L. Harrison, president of the New York Life Insurance Company, who was then serving as a special assistant to the Secretary of War; James F. Byrnes, as my personal representative; Ralph A. Bard, Under Secretary of the Navy; Assistant Secretary William L. Clayton for the State Department; and three of our most renowned scientists—Dr. Vannevar Bush, president of the Carnegie Institution of Washington and Director of the Office of Scientific Research and Development; Dr. Karl T. Compton, president of the Massachusetts Institute of Technology and Chief of Field Service in the Office of Scientific Research and Development; and Dr. James B. Conant, president of Harvard University and chairman of the National Defense Research Committee.

This committee was assisted by a group of scientists, of whom those most prominently connected with the development of the atomic bomb were Dr. Oppenheimer, Dr. Arthur H. Compton, Dr. E. O. Lawrence, and the Italian-born Dr. Enrico Fermi. The conclusions reached by these men, both in the advisory committee of scientists and in the larger committee, were brought to me by Secretary Stimson on June 1.

It was their recommendation that the bomb be used against the enemy as soon as it could be done. They recommended further that it should be used without specific warning and against a target that would clearly show its devastating strength. I had realized, of course, that an atomic bomb explosion would inflict damage and casualties beyond imagination. On the other hand, the scientific advisers of the committee reported, "We can propose no technical demonstration likely to bring an end to the war; we see no acceptable alternative to direct military use." It was their conclusion that no technical demonstration they might propose, such as over a deserted island, would be likely to bring the war to an end. It had to be used against an enemy target.

The final decision of where and when to use the atomic bomb was up to me. Let there be no mistake about it. I regarded the bomb as a military weapon and never had any doubt that it should be used. The top military advisers to the President recommended its use, and when I talked to Churchill he unhesitatingly told me that he favored the use of the atomic bomb if it might aid to end the war.

In deciding to use this bomb I wanted to make sure that it would be used as a weapon of war in the manner prescribed by the laws of war. That meant that I wanted it dropped on a military target. I had told Stimson that the bomb should be dropped as nearly as possibly upon a war production center of prime military importance.

Stimson's staff had prepared a list of cities in Japan that might serve as targets. Kyoto, though favored by General Arnold as a center of military activity, was eliminated when Secretary Stimson pointed out that it was a cultural and religious shrine of the Japanese.

Four cities were finally recommended as targets: Hiroshima, Kokura, Niigata, and Nagasaki. They were listed in that order as targets for the first attack. The order of selection was in accordance with the military importance of these cities, but allowance would be given for weather conditions at the time of the bombing. Before the selected targets were approved as proper for military purposes, I personally went over them in detail with Stimson, Marshall, and Arnold, and we discussed the matter of timing and the final choice of the first target.

General Spaatz, who commanded the Strategic Air Forces, which would deliver the bomb on the target, was given some latitude as to when and on which of the four targets the bomb would be dropped. That was necessary because of weather and other operational considerations. In order to get preparations under way, the War Department was given orders to instruct General Spaatz that the first bomb would be dropped as soon after August 3 as weather would permit. The order to General Spaatz read as follows:

24 July 1945

TO: General Carl Spaatz
Commanding General
United States Army Strategic Air Forces

1. The 509 Composite Group, 20th Air Force will deliver its first special bomb as soon as weather will permit visual bombing after about 3 August 1945 on one of the targets: Hiroshima, Kokura, Niigata and Nagasaki. To carry military and civilian scientific personnel from the War Department to observe and record the effects of the explosion of the bomb, additional aircraft will accompany the airplane carrying the bomb. The observing planes will stay several miles distant from the point of impact of the bomb.

2. Additional bombs will be delivered on the above targets as soon as made ready by the project staff. Further instructions will be issued concerning targets other than those listed above.

3. Dissemination of any and all information concerning the use of the weapon against Japan is reserved to the Secretary of War and the President of the United States. No communique on the subject or release of information will be issued by Commanders in the field without specific prior authority. Any news stories will be sent to the War Department for special clearance.

4. The foregoing directive is issued to you by direction and with the approval of the Secretary of War and the Chief of Staff, U.S.A. It is desired that you personally deliver one copy of this directive to General MacArthur and one copy to Admiral Nimitz for their information.

> /s/ Thos. T. Handy
> General, GSC
> Acting Chief of Staff

With this order the wheels were set in motion for the first use of an atomic weapon against a military target. I had made the decision. I also instructed Stimson that the order would stand unless I notified him that the Japanese reply to our ultimatum was acceptable.

A specialized B-29 unit, known as the 509th Composite Group, had been selected for the task, and seven of the modified B-29's, with pilots and crews, were ready and waiting for orders. Meanwhile ships and planes were rushing the materials for the bomb and specialists to assemble them to the Pacific island of Tinian in the Marianas.

On July 28 Radio Tokyo announced that the Japanese government would continue to fight. There was no formal reply to the joint ultimatum of the United States, the United Kingdom, and China. There was no alternative now. The bomb was scheduled to be dropped after August 3 unless Japan surrendered before that day.

On August 6, the fourth day of the journey home from Potsdam, came the historic news that shook the world. I was eating lunch with members of the *Augusta's* crew when Captain Frank Graham, White House Map Room watch officer, handed me the following message:

> Following info regarding Manhattan received. "Hiroshima bombed visually with only one tenth cover at 052315A. There was no fighter opposition and no flak. Parsons reports 15 minutes after drop as follows: 'Results clear cut successful in all respects. Visible effects greater than in any test. Conditions normal in airplane following delivery.'"

I was greatly moved. I telephoned Byrnes aboard ship to give him the news and then said to the group of sailors around me, "This is the greatest thing in history. It's time for us to get home."

A few minutes later a second message was handed to me. It read as follows:

> TO THE PRESIDENT
> FROM THE SECRETARY OF WAR
> Big bomb dropped on Hiroshima August 5 at 7:15 P.M. Washington time. First reports indicate complete success which was even more conspicuous than earlier test.

When I had read this I signaled to the crew in the mess hall that I wished to say something. I then told them of the dropping of a powerful new bomb which used an explosive twenty thousand times as powerful as a ton of TNT. I went to the wardroom, where I told the officers, who were at lunch, what had happened. I could not keep back my expectation that the Pacific war might now be brought to a speedy end.

A few minutes later the ship's radio receivers began to carry news bulletins from Washington about the atomic bomb, as well as a broadcast of the statement I had authorized just before leaving Germany. Shortly afterward I called a press conference of the correspondents on board and told them something of the long program of research and development that lay behind this successful assault.

My statements on the atomic bomb, which had been released in Washington by Stimson, read in part as follows:

". . . But the greatest marvel is not the size of the enterprise, its secrecy, nor its cost, but the achievement of scientific brains in putting together infinitely complex pieces of knowledge held by many men in different fields of science into a workable plan. And hardly less marvelous has been the capacity of industry to design, and of labor to operate, the machines and methods to do things never done before, so that the brain child of many minds came forth in physical shape and performed as it was supposed to do. Both science and industry worked under the direction of the United States Army, which achieved a unique success in managing so diverse a problem in the advancement of knowledge in an amazingly short time. It is doubtful if such another combination could be got together in the world. What has been done is the greatest achievement of organized science in history. It was done under high pressure and without failure.

"We are now prepared to obliterate more rapidly and completely every productive enterprise the Japanese have above ground in any city. We shall destroy their docks, their factories, and their communications. Let there be no mistake; we shall completely destroy Japan's power to make war.

"It was to spare the Japanese people from utter destruction that the ultimatum of July 26 was issued at Potsdam. Their leaders promptly rejected that ultimatum. If they do not now accept our terms, they may expect a rain of ruin from the air, the like of which has never been seen on this earth. Behind this air attack will follow sea and land forces in such numbers and power as they have not yet seen and with the fighting skill of which they are already well aware.

". . . The fact that we can release atomic energy ushers in a new era in man's understanding of nature's forces. Atomic energy may in the future supplement the power that now comes from coal, oil, and falling water, but at present it cannot be produced on a basis to compete with them commercially. Before that comes there must be a long period of intensive research.

"It has never been the habit of the scientists of this country or the policy of this Government to withhold from the world scientific knowledge. Normally, therefore, everything about the work with atomic energy would be made public.

"But under present circumstances it is not intended to divulge the technical processes of production or all the military applications, pending further examination of possible methods of protecting us and the rest of the world from the danger of sudden destruction.

"I shall recommend that the Congress of the United States consider promptly the establishment of an appropriate commission to control the production and use of atomic power within the United States.

"I shall give further consideration and make further recommendations to the Congress as to how atomic power can become a powerful and forceful influence towards the maintenance of world peace."

Still no surrender offer came. An order was issued to General Spaatz to continue operations as planned unless otherwise instructed.

On the afternoon of August 7 the U.S.S. *Augusta* completed a record run from Europe and entered Chesapeake Bay. As soon as the ship was moored alongside the dock at Newport News I disembarked and entered a special train which left immediately for Washington. By 11 P.M. I was back at the White House, where other members of the Cabinet were on hand to greet me and to welcome me back home. It had been a month since I left the White House, and I had traveled a total of 9,346 miles.

The Russian-Chinese negotiations were resumed shortly after the Potsdam conference when Stalin returned to Moscow. Prime Minister Soong, accompanied by the new Chinese Foreign Minister, Wang Shih-chieh, bringing further instructions from Chiang Kai-shek, went back to the Russian capital from Chungking.

Ambassador Harriman, who also had returned to his post in Moscow, was kept fully informed by Soong on the details of the talks and continued to report to me. Some of the messages had reached me on the *Augusta.*

On August 5 I instructed Secretary Byrnes, aboard the *Augusta,* to send new directions to Ambassador Harriman. I asked that Harriman tell Stalin that we believed Soong had already met the Yalta requirements. And we would request that no agreement be made involving further concessions by China, Harriman was advised through Byrnes, that might adversely affect our interests, "particularly with reference to the inclusion of the Port of Dairen in the Soviet military zone, without consultation with us. It should be recalled that President Roosevelt declined to agree to Soviet original proposal for a lease of Dairen and insisted on its internationalization as a free port. Because of our interest in the open door policy we would be opposed to the inclusion of the Port of Dairen in the Soviet military zone or its use as a Soviet naval base."

I was not too hopeful about the renewed talks between Soong and Stalin. Ambassador Hurley in Chungking reported that the Russians had added a new demand, that China should agree not to fortify any islands for a hundred miles south of Port Arthur. The Chinese were determined to reject this new demand. On the other hand, Chiang Kai-shek had authorized Soong to agree to the inclusion in the Soviet military zone around Port Arthur of the area that had once been leased by the czarist Russian government, although he still insisted that Dairen and the connecting railroad be exempted.

Stalin accepted this formula and also agreed to the face-saving device of a Chinese-Russian military commission to supervise the port at Port Arthur, although the administration of the city and the port would be in the hands of the Russians. He insisted, however, that Dairen also had to be under a mixed commission with a Soviet official in charge of the operation of the port, and at the first conference that followed Soong's return to Moscow, Stalin also introduced a topic that had not been brought up before.

"Stalin then raised the question of 'war trophies,' " Harriman reported, "and indicated that some of the Japanese properties, including the shares of some Japanese enterprises, should be considered as Soviet war trophies in areas occupied by the Red Army. Soong inquired exactly what Stalin had in mind, but Stalin was evasive and left the matter for future discussion. This was the first time this subject has been mentioned to Soong, and it has never been raised with us. If the Soviets define war trophies as they did in connection with Germany, including also shares of Japanese enterprises, it would be possible for the Soviets to strip Manchuria of certain of its industries and to obtain permanently complete industrial domination of Manchuria. I understand the Japanese have taken possession of and developed most of the heavy and light industries in Manchuria. I request urgent instructions as to our position on this question, particularly if Stalin should raise the matter with me. This is another case where Stalin has increased his appetite, and I recommend that we resist his demands for shares of stock of Japanese enterprises and restrict the definition of war booty to matériel that has been historically so regarded in accordance with the United States' definition submitted at Potsdam. As to reparations, I recommend that our position should be that all Japanese property whether in Manchuria or elsewhere should be available to all countries who have suffered damage by Japanese aggression to be allocated by agreement between the powers. As this subject has now been raised, I am fearful that unless we make our position plain at this time the Soviets will contend that they have the right to define unilaterally war trophies within the areas occupied by the Red Army. I have consulted Ambassador Pauley, and he concurs in these recommendations. . . ."

I was keeping a close watch on the Russian-Chinese negotiations. It was our hope that despite the long-drawn-out negotiations our two wartime allies might reach agreement. Stalin had said that Russia would not come into the war against Japan until she had concluded an agreement with China. It was for this reason that I urged Chiang Kai-shek to continue the talks in Moscow.

Without warning, while Russian-Chinese negotiations were still far from agreement, Molotov sent for Ambassador Harriman on August 8 and announced to him that the Soviet Union would consider itself at war with Japan as of August 9. This move did not surprise us. Our dropping of the atomic bomb on Japan had forced Russia to reconsider her position in the Far East. The message from Harriman informing me of this sudden switch by the Russians reached me early in the afternoon of August 8, and I promptly called a special press conference. Admiral Leahy and Secretary Byrnes were present when I met the correspondents. There were only four sentences to my announcement:

"I have only a simple announcement to make. I can't hold a regular press conference today, but this announcement is so important I thought I would like to call you in. Russia has declared war on Japan. That is all."

The following day Harriman reported further on the Russian decision:

"When Molotov informed the British ambassador and me last evening that the Soviet Union would consider itself in a state of war with Japan as of August 9 he emphasized that although at one time it was thought that this action could not take place until mid-August the Soviet Government had now strictly lived up to its promise to enter Pacific War 3 months after the defeat of Germany. In reply to an inquiry made by the British ambassador as to how the Japanese ambassador had reacted to the statement handed him at 5 o'clock, Molotov first explained that Sato was a 'kind hearted man' and that he had always had good relations with him. Molotov continued that Sato inquired as to what the Soviet statement meant with respect to the words 'to deliver the people from further sacrifices and suffering and to enable the Japanese people to avoid those dangers and destruction which Germany had undergone.' Molotov replied that the Soviet Government wished to shorten the duration of the war and decrease sacrifices. Sato then remarked that the Pacific war would not be of long duration."

In another message Harriman reported that the Russians were not wasting any time in bringing their forces into action.

"I saw Stalin and Molotov this evening," this second message read. "Stalin said that his advance troops had already crossed the frontiers of Manchuria both from the west and the east not meeting heavy resistance on any front and had advanced 10 or 12 kilometers in some sections. The main forces were starting across the frontier as we spoke. He said that there were 3 main attacks from the west, one south towards Heilar, the second east from Outer Mongolia towards Solun, and the third, a cavalry column, through the Gobi desert toward South Manchuria. In the Vladivostok area there was one drive west toward Grodekovo. He explained that his objectives from all directions were Harbin and Chang-chun. He said that his forces from the north in the Khabarovsk area were being held to attack when the enemy has been compelled to weaken their forces defending that front. He said further that they had not yet attacked in Sakhalin but were prepared to do so later. In discussing the Japanese situation he said that he thought the Japanese were looking for a pretext to set up a government that would surrender and he thought that the atomic bomb might give this pretext. He showed great interest in the atomic bomb and said that it could mean the end of war and aggression but that the secret would have to be well kept. He said that they had found in Berlin laboratories in which the Germans were working on the breaking of the atom but that he did not find that they had come to any results. Soviet scientists had also been working on the problem but had not been able to solve it."

On August 9 the second atom bomb was dropped, this time on Nagasaki. We gave the Japanese three days in which to make up their minds to surrender, and the bombing would have been held off another two days had weather permitted. During those three days we indicated that we meant business. On August 7 the 20th Air Force sent out a bomber force of some one hundred and thirty B-29's, and on the eighth it reported four hundred and twenty B-29's in day and night attacks. The choice of targets for the second atom bomb was first Kokura, with Nagasaki second. The third city on the list, Niigata, had been ruled out as too distant. By the time Kokura was reached the weather had closed in, and after three runs over the spot without a glimpse of the target, with gas running short, a try was made for the second choice, Nagasaki. There, too, the weather had closed in, but an opening in the clouds gave the bombardier his chance, and Nagasaki was successfully bombed.

This second demonstration of the power of the atomic bomb apparently threw Tokyo into a panic, for the next morning brought the first indication that the Japanese Empire was ready to surrender.

CHAPTER 27

On August 10, at seven thirty-three in the morning, our radio monitors heard this news item being given out over Radio Tokyo:

"The Japanese Government today addressed the following communication to the Swiss and Swedish Governments respectively for transmission to the United States, Great Britain, China and the Soviet Union:

" 'In obedience to the gracious command of His Majesty the Emperor, who, ever anxious to enhance the cause of world peace, desires earnestly to bring about an early termination of hostilities with a view to saving mankind from the calamities to be imposed on them by further continuation of the war, the Japanese Government several weeks ago asked the Soviet Government, with which neutral relations then prevailed, to render good offices in restoring peace vis-à-vis the enemy powers.

" 'Unfortunately, these efforts in the interest of peace having failed, the Japanese Government, in conformity with the august wish of His Majesty to restore the general peace and desiring to put an end to the untold sufferings engendered by the war, have decided on the following:

" 'The Japanese Government is ready to accept the terms enumerated in the joint declaration which was issued at Potsdam, July 26, 1945, by the Heads of Government of the United States, Great Britain, and China, and later subscribed to by the Soviet Government, with the understanding that said declaration does not comprise any demand which prejudices the prerogatives of His Majesty as a sovereign ruler.

" 'The Japanese Government hopes sincerely that this understanding is warranted and desires keenly that an explicit indication to that effect will be speedily forthcoming.' "

This was not an official communication, but it was enough notice of Japanese intention to permit us to discuss what our reply should be. I asked Admiral Leahy to have Secretaries Byrnes, Stimson, and Forrestal come to my office at nine o'clock to confer on the next step to be taken.

When the four had arrived, I turned to each in turn and asked his opinion on these questions: Were we to treat this message from Tokyo as an acceptance of the Potsdam Declaration? There had been many in this country who felt that the Emperor was an integral part of that Japanese system which we were pledged to destroy. Could we continue the Emperor and yet expect to eliminate the warlike spirit in Japan? Could we even consider a message with so large a "but" as the kind of unconditional surrender we had fought for?

Secretary Stimson had always expressed the opinion that it would be to our advantage to retain the Emperor. He urged the same point now. We needed, as he saw it, to keep the only symbol of authority which all Japanese acknowledged. Admiral Leahy also recommended that we accept the Japanese proposal if for no other reason than that we would be able to use the Emperor in effecting the surrender. Secretary Byrnes was less certain that we should accept anything short of an unequivocal declaration of surrender. He argued that in the present position it should be the United States and not Japan that should state conditions. Secretary of the Navy Forrestal offered the suggestion that we might in our reply indicate willingness to accept, yet define the terms of surrender in such a manner that the intents and purposes of the Potsdam Declaration would be clearly accomplished.

I asked Byrnes to draft a reply that might convey such an understanding. The Cabinet officers then returned to their respective departments. Shortly before noon Secretary Byrnes came back to the White House, bringing with him the official communication from the Japanese government which had just been received from the Swiss legation. It was identical with the earlier radio transmission, except for an added paragraph that informed us that the same request had also been forwarded, through neutral intermediaries, to the governments of China, Great Britain, and the U.S.S.R.

Byrnes also submitted for my approval a draft of a proposed reply to be sent to Japan. I asked the Secretary of State to stay for lunch, while I summoned a Cabinet meeting for two o'clock. During lunch we worked out an urgent communication to go to the British, Russian, and Chinese governments to get their concurrence to the answer we proposed to send to Japan and were joined by Admiral Leahy, who helped with the drafting.

At two o'clock the Cabinet convened, and I read them the text of the

Japanese note. Then Byrnes presented the proposed reply and indicated by what procedure we would seek the approval of our allies. We dispatched identical messages to London, Moscow, and Chungking, and in each of these we instructed our Ambassador to make immediate delivery of the message to impress upon the recipients that speed was of the essence. The message we enclosed read, in part, as follows:

"With regard to the Japanese Government's message accepting the terms of the Potsdam proclamation but containing the statement 'with the undertanding that the said declaration does not comprise any demand which prejudices the prerogatives of His Majesty as a sovereign ruler'— our position is as follows:

" 'From the moment of surrender the authority of the Emperor and the Japanese Government to rule the state shall be subject to the Supreme Commander of the Allied Powers who will take such steps as he deems proper to effectuate the surrender terms.

" 'The Emperor and the Japanese High Command will be required to sign the surrender terms necessary to carry out the provisions of the Potsdam Declaration, to issue orders to all the armed forces of Japan to cease hostilities and to surrender their arms, and to issue such other orders as the Supreme Commander may require to give effect to the surrender terms.

" 'Immediately upon the surrender the Japanese Government shall transport prisoners of war and civilian internees to places of safety, as directed, where they can be quickly placed aboard allied transports.

" 'The ultimate form of government of Japan shall, in accordance with the Potsdam Declaration, be established by the freely expressed will of the Japanese people.

" 'The armed forces of the Allied Powers will remain in Japan until the purposes set forth in the Potsdam Declaration are achieved.' "

The message to London left the White House at three forty-five Eastern War Time; it was received by our Embassy in London at four fifty-eight, our time, and was in the Foreign Secretary's hands thirty minutes later. The British answer was received in Washington at nine forty-eight that evening.

Attlee and Bevin agreed but expressed doubts that it would be wise to ask the Emperor personally to sign the surrender terms. They therefore suggested this change in the language of the proposed reply:

"The Emperor shall authorize and ensure the signature by the Government of Japan and the Japanese General Headquarters of the surrender terms necessary to carry out the provisions of the Potsdam Declaration, and shall issue his commands to all the Japanese military, naval, and air authorities and to all the forces under their control wherever located to cease active operations and to surrender their arms, etc. as in your draft."

Ambassador Winant also reported that Mr. Churchill had telephoned him, saying that he agreed entirely with our approach.

Our message to Chiang Kai-shek brought us this reply, which my naval aide brought to me at seven thirty-five on the morning of August 11:

"President Truman: I concur in all the conditions and join you in your reply to the Japanese Government on the acceptance of the Potsdam proclamation. I especially concur in the condition to require the Emperor and the Japanese High Command to sign the surrender terms and issue orders to make surrender effective. I also concur in the condition requiring that the ultimate form of government of Japan shall be in accordance with the freely expressed will of the Japanese people. This latter is a condition which I have expressed over a period of years. Chiang Kai-shek."

Ambassador Harriman's report of the reaction in Moscow was handed me when I arose that morning:

"The British Ambassador and I were with Molotov when your . . . message . . . was delivered to me. Molotov was in process of inquiring what the attitudes of our respective governments were to the Japanese Government's proposal. He informed us that the Soviet attitude towards it was 'skeptical' since the Soviets did not consider it unconditional surrender, and that the Soviet forces, therefore, were continuing their advance into Manchuria. As this was shortly after midnight, he emphasized that it was the third day of the Soviet campaign which would continue. He gave me the definite impression that he was quite willing to have the war continue.

"Your message then arrived, and it was translated to him. His reaction was noncommittal and suggested that he would give me an answer tomorrow. I told him that this would not be satisfactory and that we wished it tonight. He thereupon agreed to take it up with his Government and attempt to give me an answer tonight. If I do not hear from him in a reasonable time, I will telephone him and keep you informed of the developments."

A second message from Harriman followed shortly.

"Molotov asked the British Ambassador and me to call again," Harriman cabled. "He handed us the following statement:

" 'The Soviet Government agrees to the draft reply of the Allied Powers proposed by the United States Government to the statement of the Japanese Government concerning surrender.

" 'The Soviet Government considers that the above mentioned reply should be presented in the name of the principal powers waging war with Japan.

" 'The Soviet Government also considers that, in case of an affirmative reply from the Japanese Government, the Allied Powers should reach an agreement on the candidacy or candidacies for representation of the Allied High Command to which the Japanese Emperor and the Japanese Government are to be subordinated.

" 'August 11, 1945, 2:00 A.M., Moscow time.

" 'On the authority of the Government of the U.S.S.R., signed: V. Molotov.'

"I took a firm exception to the last paragraph and said that in my opinion my Government would never agree to it. I pointed out this was a qualification of the Soviet Government's acceptance of our proposal and that it gave the Soviet Government veto power on the selection of the Allied High Command. In answer to my inquiry as to his meaning, he finally suggested that the High Command might consist of two persons, both an American and a Soviet general, specifying Marshal Vasilevsky by name. I stated that it was unthinkable that the supreme commander could be other than American.

"After a most heated discussion he insisted that I send his communication to my government. I maintained, however, that in my opinion it would be unacceptable.

"When I reached my office, I found Pavlov, Molotov's secretary, on the telephone, advising me that Molotov had consulted Stalin. He said that there had been a misunderstanding and that only consultation had been intended and not the necessity of reaching an agreement. I pointed out to the secretary that I believed the words 'or candidacies' would also be unacceptable and asked him to convey this message to Molotov. Within a very few minutes he called back stating that Stalin had agreed to the deletion of these words. He agreed to confirm this in writing.

"The last paragraph will, therefore, read 'The Soviet Government also considers that, in case of an affirmative reply from the Japanese Government, the Allied Powers should consult on the candidacy for representation of the Allied High Command to which the Japanese Emperor and the Japanese Government are to be subordinated.'

"I would appreciate advice as to whether the Soviet reply as now amended is acceptable."

Harriman was, of course, expressing our set policy. The State, War and Navy Co-ordinating Committee had some time ago formulated our position on the postwar control of Japan, and I had approved it. We wanted Japan controlled by an American commander, acting on behalf of the

Allies, who might co-ordinate their desires through a conference or council which we proposed to call the Far Eastern Advisory Commission.

I was determined that the Japanese occupation should not follow in the footsteps of our German experience. I did not want divided control or separate zones. I did not want to give the Russians any opportunity to behave as they had in Germany and Austria. I wanted the country administered in such a manner that it could be restored to its place in the society of nations. I had impressed these thoughts strongly on all our officials at Potsdam. Thus Harriman, who was there, was able to speak up at once when Molotov tried to change the basic policy for Japan.

With the concurrence of the three governments received, we were now ready to dispatch a formal reply to the Japanese. We accepted the change proposed by the British but altered one phrase in it to make it clearer. Where the British had proposed that we say "The Emperor shall authorize and ensure the signature, etc.," we put "The Emperor will be required to authorize and ensure . . ."

The completed message, dated August 11, was handed to Herr Max Grassli, the Chargé d'Affaires of Switzerland, by Secretary Byrnes, to be transmitted to Tokyo by way of Berne. The war was, of course, not at an end. Admiral Nimitz had sent out an order to the Pacific fleet that must have been typical of many:

"The public announcement by the Japanese of counter proposals for the termination of the war must not be permitted to affect vigilance against Japanese attacks. Neither the Japanese nor Allied Forces have stopped fighting. Take precautions against treachery even if local or general surrender should be suddenly announced. Maintain all current reconnaissance and patrols. Offensive action shall be continued unless otherwise specifically directed."

General Arnold sent out an order to the Strategic Air Forces to drop leaflets over centers of population in Japan to advise the people there of the status of the peace negotiations.

Meanwhile in Washington a message was prepared to inform our allies of the selection of General Douglas MacArthur to be the Supreme Commander in Japan. In the same message I proposed that the new Supreme Commander should instruct the Japanese to surrender their forces in Southeast Asia to Admiral Lord Louis Mountbatten, the Supreme Commander in that area; those forces facing the Russians, to the Soviet High Commander in the Far East; and all other forces in China, to Generalissimo Chiang Kai-shek.

Steps were also taken to disseminate the acceptance of our terms by the Japanese as quickly as possible. The State Department prepared identical messages to go to the Soviet, British, and Chinese governments that would require nothing but the insertion of the time and date the reply was received. With these steps completed, there remained nothing to do but to await that reply.

The next day—August 12—was a Sunday, but I spent nearly the entire day in my office, frequently joined by the Secretary of State and the heads of the armed forces. The place was beleaguered by press and radio people, and large crowds gathered outside the White House and in Lafayette Park. A report that the Japanese had accepted was circulated early in the evening, but it turned out to be false.

In the midst of this I wrote my sister Mary.

Dear Mary: This is your birthday, and I had intended to have a letter there this morning. But conditions here have been such that it was impossible to get it done. I surely hope you have a happy one. Margaret should be out with some presents, and I mailed you one from Germany.

I have a beautiful Belgian luncheon set for Mama and some handkerchiefs for Luella and a Swiss watch for Martha Ann. I also have a present for Gilbert.

Since I landed last Tuesday there hasn't been a minute. The speech, the Russian entry into the war, the Jap surrender offer and the usual business of the President's office have kept me busy night and day.

It seems that things are going all right. Nearly every crisis seems to be the worst one, but after it's over, it isn't so bad. . . .

Happy birthday and lots of love,

Harry

In the meantime I received word from Stalin, Chiang Kai-shek, and Attlee that the selection of Douglas MacArthur to be the Supreme Commander for the Allied powers met with their approval. Despite these agreements, however, there were also ominous notes. Ambassador Pauley, who was in Moscow on another—futile—attempt to find agreement on reparations matters with the Russians, urged quick action in the Far East to prevent Russian excesses:

"Conclusions I have reached," a message from him read, "through discussions on reparations and otherwise (I repeat otherwise) lead me to the belief that our forces should occupy quickly as much of the industrial areas of Korea and Manchuria as we can, starting at the southerly tip and progressing northward. I am assuming all of this will be done at no risk of American lives after organized hostilities have ceased, and occupancy to continue until satisfactory agreements have been reached between the nations concerned with respect to reparations and territorial rights or other concessions."

Harriman similarly urged us to counter Russian intransigence with action.

"While at Potsdam," he cabled, "General Marshall and Admiral King told me of the proposed landings in Korea and Dairen if the Japanese gave in prior to Soviet troops occupying these areas.

"Considering the way Stalin is behaving in increasing his demands on Soong I recommend that these landings be made to accept surrender of the Japanese troops at least on the Kwantung Peninsula and in Korea. I cannot see that we are under any obligation to the Soviets to respect any zone of Soviet military operation."

Complications were also beginning to arise in China. Hurley reported that the Communists were seeking to take the greatest possible advantage of the impending Japanese collapse. In a detailed message he told the State Department that General Chu Teh, commanding general of the Chinese Communist forces, had broadcast an order that any "anti-Japanese armed force" in the liberated areas could, on the basis of the Potsdam proclamation, deliver an ultimatum to the enemy troops or their headquarters in the nearby cities, towns, or communication centers, ordering them to hand over their arms within a certain limit of time. After being thus disarmed, they would be treated according to the regulations governing the preferential treatment of war prisoners and their lives would be protected. He also proclaimed that his troops had the right to enter and occupy any city, town, or communication center occupied by the enemy or the puppets, carry on military management there to maintain order, and appoint a commissioner to look after the administrative affairs of the locality.

This order was clearly in open defiance of Chiang Kai-shek's government and in conflict with the Potsdam Declaration, which designated the governments to which surrender was to be made.

"If the United States," Ambassador Hurley cabled, "and the United Nations permit an armed belligerent political party in China to accept surrender of the Japanese and to acquire Japanese arms, a fratricidal war in China will thereby be made certain. I have already suggested that in the terms of surrender Japan be required to surrender all Japanese arms in China, including Japanese arms that are in the hands of Japanese soldiers, Chinese puppet troops supporting Japan, and Chinese partisan organizations operating with Japan, to the National Government of China. We have also recommended that the terms of surrender should penalize Japan for any attempt to arm any belligerent forces within China against the National Government. . . .

"General Wedemeyer has shown me his report to the Chief of Staff setting out his opinion of the situation that will prevail if the Japanese are allowed to surrender their arms to the Communist armed party. I concur in General Wedemeyer's report and recommend that the State Department urge that the surrender terms provide that none of the Japanese arms will be surrendered to the Chinese Communist armed party."

These messages from Moscow and Chungking did not, of course, raise new issues. The preceding months had shown us that Stalin and his colleagues did not view matters in the same light we did. The delicate balance in China between the forces of Chiang Kai-shek and those of the Chinese Communists had been the subject of many discussions among our policy experts. But the opportunity of the moment was to put an end to the years of war. A dictator can use his soldiers as soulless pawns, but in a government like ours, the voice of the people must be heeded; and the American people wanted nothing more in that summer of 1945 than to end the fighting and bring the boys back home.

On August 12 the Joint Chiefs of Staff studied drafts of the letters of instruction that were to go to General MacArthur. I approved the documents the following day, with one change: Whereas the draft called for only one signature on the surrender documents to represent the Allies, that of the Supreme Commander, I instructed the Joint Chiefs to tell MacArthur that, after his signature on behalf of all the Allies, each of the four major powers' representatives should affix his signature.

August 13 passed without word from the Japanese. On the morning of August 14, however, Commodore Vardaman brought word that a coded cable from Tokyo had been received in Berne. That should be the answer we were waiting for. Byrnes came over after breakfast, and we checked the steps to be taken if—as we were confident—the Japanese had accepted. Shortly before noon, too, the Secretary of State called Mr. Harrison, our Minister in Berne, to find out what the message from Tokyo had contained. It turned out that it was not an answer to our message at all, and the wait continued.

At three o'clock Byrnes informed me that he had just learned that a code message was then being received in Berne from Tokyo. At five minutes after four he put through a call to Harrison, who gave him the answer we wanted: Japan had surrendered!

Byrnes now called Bevin, Harriman, and Hurley and arranged for the news to be announced at the same time, seven o'clock Washington time, in the four capitals.

At 6 P.M. the Swiss Chargé d'Affaires in Washington delivered the formal reply to Byrnes, who brought it at once to the White House. Here are the words that ended the war:

August 14, 1945

Sir:

I have the honor to refer to your note of August 11, in which you requested me to transmit to my Government the reply of the Governments of the United States, the United Kingdom, the Union of Soviet Socialist Republics, and

China to the message from the Japanese Government which was communicated in my note of August 10.

At 20:10 today (Swiss time) the Japanese Minister to Switzerland conveyed the following written statement to the Swiss Government for transmission to the Allied Governments:

"Communication of the Japanese Government of August 14, 1945, addressed to the Governments of the United States, Great Britain, the Soviet Union, and China:

"With reference to the Japanese Government's note of August 10, regarding their acceptance of the provisions of the Potsdam declaration and the reply of the Governments of the United States, Great Britain, the Soviet Union, and China sent by American Secretary of State Byrnes under the date of August 11, the Japanese Government have the honor to communicate to the Governments of the four powers as follows:

"1. His Majesty the Emperor has issued an Imperial rescript regarding Japanese acceptance of the provisions of the Potsdam declaration.

"2. His Majesty the Emperor is prepared to authorize and ensure the signature by his Government and the Imperial General Headquarters of the necessary terms for carrying out the provisions of the Potsdam declaration. His Majesty is also prepared to issue his commands to all the military, naval, and air authorities of Japan and all the forces under their control wherever located to cease active operations, to surrender arms and to issue such other orders as may be required by the Supreme Commander of the Allied Forces for the execution of the above-mentioned terms."

Accept, Sir, the renewed assurances of my highest consideration.

/s/ Grassli
Chargé d'Affaires ad
interim of Switzerland

The Honorable
James F. Byrnes
Secretary of State

At 7 P.M. the White House correspondents gathered in my office. Mrs. Truman was with me, and most of the members of the Cabinet were present. I had also asked a former Cabinet member to join me on this momentous occasion. Cordell Hull, now seriously ill and for many years a most distinguished Secretary of State, did not arrive until the conference was nearly over, but I was glad that we could include him in the official picture that was taken of the event. He had done much to make this day possible.

When everybody was in, I stood behind my desk and read this statement:

"I have received this afternoon a message from the Japanese Government in reply to the message forwarded to that Government by the Secretary of State on August eleventh. I deem this reply a full acceptance of the Potsdam Declaration which specifies the unconditional surrender of Japan. In the reply there is no qualification.

"Arrangements are now being made for the formal signing of the surrender terms at the earliest possible moment.

"General Douglas MacArthur has been appointed the Supreme Allied Commander to receive the Japanese surrender. Great Britain, Russia and China will be represented by high-ranking officers.

"Meantime, the Allied armed forces have been ordered to suspend offensive action.

"The proclamation of V-J Day must wait upon the formal signing of the surrender terms by Japan. . . ."

The remainder of the statement was the text of the Japanese note.

The correspondents shouted congratulations as they rushed out the doors to flash the word to their papers. Mrs. Truman and I went out to the fountain on the north lawn. A vast crowd had assembled outside the gates, and when I made a V sign in the manner of Churchill, a great cheer went up. I remained outside only a few minutes and then went back into the White House and called my mother at her home in Grandview, Missouri.

Around eight o'clock the crowds outside were still growing, and I went out on the north portico and spoke a few words through a loudspeaker that had been set up there. This was a most significant and dramatic moment, and I felt deeply moved by the excitement, perhaps as much as were the crowds that were celebrating in cities and towns all over the nation.

We had won the war. It was my hope now that the people of Germany and Japan could be rehabilitated under the occupation. The United States, as I had stated at Berlin, wanted no territory, no reparations. Peace and happiness for all countries were the goals toward which we would work and for which we had fought. No nation in the history of the world had taken such a position in complete victory. No nation with the military power of the United States of America had been so generous to its enemies and so helpful to its friends. Maybe the teachings of the Sermon on the Mount could be put into effect.

CHAPTER 28

The guns were silenced. The war was over. I was thinking
of President Roosevelt, who had not lived to see this day.
He would have rejoiced in the fulfillment of the pledge he had given the
nation when war was forced upon us in December 1941. I reached for
the telephone and called Mrs. Roosevelt. I told her that in this hour of
triumph I wished that it had been President Roosevelt, and not I, who
had given the message to our people.

I had previously issued an order giving all federal employees a two-day
holiday in recognition of their faithful service throughout the war years.
At a press conference I announced an immediate cut in the monthly draft
quota from eighty thousand to fifty thousand. But beyond these orders
an infinite number of details remained to be attended to. As was to be
expected, the end of hostilities brought with it a mass of new problems.

The theaters of military operation had been notified of the surrender
by a message that left the Pentagon as I made my announcement at the
press conference.

"The following directive received from the President is repeated to you
for necessary action," this message read.

" 'The Government of Japan having on 14 August accepted the Allied
Governments' demand for surrender, you are hereby directed to suspend
offensive operations against Japanese Military and Naval forces insofar
as is consistent with the safety of Allied forces in your area.' "

Thus our field commanders were told to cease fighting, and in a separate message the beginning of the occupation phase was marked.

"From Marshall to MacArthur, info Nimitz, Deane and Wedemeyer . . . ," this second message read. "You are hereby officially notified of Japanese capitulation. Your directive as Supreme Commander for the Allied Forces is effective with receipt of this message."

The directive to MacArthur, which I had approved on August 13, read as follows:

DIRECTIVE TO THE SUPREME COMMANDER FOR THE ALLIED POWERS INSTRU-MENTS FOR THE SURRENDER OF JAPAN ISSUED BY THE PRESIDENT OF THE UNITED STATES

1. In accordance with the agreement among the Governments of the United States, Chinese Republic, United Kingdom, and Union of Soviet Socialist Republics to designate a Supreme Commander for the Allied Powers for the purpose of enforcing the surrender of Japan, you are hereby designated as the Supreme Commander for the Allied Powers.

2. You will require the issuance of a proclamation signed by the Emperor authorizing his representatives to sign the instrument of surrender. The proclamation to be signed should be substantially in the form appended hereto. You will take the necessary steps to require and receive from the duly authorized representative of the Japanese Emperor, the Japanese Government, and the Japanese Imperial General Headquarters the signed instrument of surrender. The text of the instrument is appended hereto. You will accept the surrender for the four Governments concerned and in the interests of the other United Nations at war with Japan.

3. I have asked the heads of state of China, Great Britain, and the Union of Soviet Socialist Republics each to designate a representative who may be present with you at the time and place of surrender. I have designated Fleet Admiral Chester W. Nimitz to be present as the United States representative for this purpose. As soon as I have received the other designations you will be advised. You will make the appropriate arrangements.

4. Having accepted the general surrender of the Japanese armed forces, you will require the Japanese Imperial General Headquarters to issue general orders which will instruct Japanese commanders wherever situated as to the mechanics of surrender and other details effectuating the surrender. You will effect any necessary coordination of arrangements with the Japanese Imperial General Headquarters with regard to the surrender to the Allied Commanders concerned of Japanese armed forces abroad.

5. From the moment of the surrender, the authority of the Emperor and Japanese Government to rule the state will be subject to you and you will take such steps as you deem proper to effectuate the surrender terms.

6. You will exercise supreme command over all land, sea and air forces which may be allocated for enforcement in Japan of the surrender terms by the Allied Powers concerned.

7. Your appointment as Supreme Commander for the Allied Powers is effective upon receipt of this directive.

Copies of this directive were at once transmitted to Attlee, Stalin, and Chiang Kai-shek. The same was done with General Order No. 1, the order which we expected the Emperor to issue. My message on this subject informed the other governments that changes might be made in this

General Order by the Joint Chiefs of Staff and that minor modifications might be made by General MacArthur if local circumstances made it necessary. Mainly, this General Order was a directive to the Japanese forces in the field to lay down their arms and, specifically, to whom they were to surrender. In China, Formosa, and in Indo-China north of the 16th parallel they were to surrender to Chiang Kai-shek. In Manchuria, Korea north of 38°, and on Karafuto, the surrender would be received by the Russian commander. In Southeast Asia, from 16° north in Indo-China south and from Burma to the Solomons, the Allied representatives were to be either Lord Mountbatten or the Australian commander, with the exact line of demarcation to be fixed between them. In Japan and the Philippines, and in Korea south of the 38th parallel of North Latitude, General MacArthur would accept the surrender; elsewhere in the Pacific it would be Admiral Nimitz.

With this General Order we moved from general principles to their practical applications, and at once the difficulties began to arise.

From Generalissimo Stalin came this reply, dated August 16, 1945:

"I have received your message with the 'General Order No. 1.' Principally I have no objections against the contents of the order keeping in view that the Liaotung Peninsula is a composite part of Manchuria. However, I suggest to introduce the following corrections into the 'General Order No. 1':

"1. To include in the region of surrender of Japanese armed forces to Soviet troops all the Kurile Islands which, in accordance with the decisions of the three powers in the Crimea, have to come into possession of the Soviet Union.

"2. To include in the region of surrender of the Japanese armed forces to Soviet troops the northern part of the Island Hokkaido which adjoins in the north to the La Perouse Strait which is between Karafuto and Hokkaido. The demarcation line between the northern and southern half of the Hokkaido Island should be on the line leading from the city Kushiro on the eastern coast of the island to the city of Rumoi on the western coast of the island including the named cities into the northern half of the island.

"This latter proposal has a special meaning for the Russian public opinion. As it is known, the Japanese in 1919–1921 held under occupation of their troops the whole Soviet Far East. The Russian public opinion would be seriously offended if the Russian troops would not have an occupation region in some part of the Japanese proper territory.

"I greatly wish that my modest suggestions as stated above would not meet any objections."

The correspondence that followed was not unlike the sharp exchanges we had had with the Russians over Polish and Yugoslav problems. The exchange covered a period of nearly two weeks.

In answer to Stalin's request I cabled him on August 18 as follows:

"Replying to your message of August 16, I agree to your request to modify General Order No. 1 to include all the Kurile Islands in the area to be surrendered to the Commander in Chief of the Soviet Forces in the Far East. However, I should like it to be understood that the United States Government desires air base rights for land and sea aircraft on some one of the Kurile Islands, preferably in the central group, for military purposes and for commercial use. I should be glad if you would advise me that you will agree to such an arrangement, the location and other details to be worked out through the appointment of special representatives of our two governments for this purpose.

"Regarding your suggestion as to the surrender of Japanese forces on the Island Hokkaido to Soviet forces, it is my intention and arrangements have been made for the surrender of Japanese forces on all the islands of Japan proper, Hokkaido, Honshu, Shikoku and Kyushu to General Mac-Arthur.

"General MacArthur will employ Allied token forces, which, of course, includes Soviet forces, in so much of a temporary occupation of Japan proper as he considers it necessary to occupy in order to accomplish our Allied surrender terms."

Stalin cabled his reply on August 22:

"I have received your message of August 18.

"1. I understand the contents of your message in the sense that you refuse to satisfy the request of the Soviet Union for the inclusion of the northern part of the Island Hokkaido in the region of surrender of the Japanese armed forces to the Soviet troops. I have to say that I and my colleagues did not expect such an answer from you.

"2. As regards your demand for a permanent aviation base on one of the Kurile Islands which, in accordance with the Crimea decision of the three powers, have to come into possession of the Soviet Union, I consider it my duty to tell you in this respect the following.

"First, I have to remind you that such a measure was not provided for by the decision of the three powers neither in the Crimea, nor in Berlin, and in no way does it ensue from the adopted there resolutions. Second, demands of such a nature are usually laid before either a conquered state, or such an allied state which is in no position to defend with its own means certain parts of its territory and, in view of this, expresses readiness to grant its Ally an appropriate base. I do not believe that the Soviet Union could be included among such states. Third, as your message does not state any motives for a demand to grant a permanent base I have to tell you frankly that neither I, nor my colleagues understand what circumstances prompted such a demand to be made of the Soviet Union."

My first inclination was to let this message with its strong undercurrent of antagonism go unanswered. However, on August 25 I sent Stalin a mildly conciliatory reply:

"In response to your message of August 22, 1945, as far as the base on the Kurile Islands is concerned, my idea was that use of landing rights in the central Kuriles during the occupation of Japan would be an important contribution to the cooperative action we will be taking in connection with the carrying out of the Japanese surrender terms as it would afford another route for air connection with the United States for emergency use during the period of occupation of Japan.

"I also felt no hesitancy in bringing up the matter of landing facilities for commercial use. You evidently misunderstood my message because you refer to it as a demand usually laid before a conquered state or an allied state unable to defend parts of its territory. I was not speaking about any territory of the Soviet Republic. I was speaking of the Kurile Islands, Japanese territory, disposition of which must be made at a peace settlement. I was advised that my predecessor agreed to support in the peace settlement the Soviet acquisition of those Islands. I did not consider it offensive when you asked me to confirm that agreement. When you expect our support for your desire for permanent possession of all the Kurile Islands I cannot see why you consider it offensive if I ask for consideration of a request for landing rights on only one of those islands. I consider the request for discussion all the more reasonable because of the close and cordial relations existing between our two governments and between us personally. While I believe early discussion of these matters would be helpful, I will not press it if you do not wish to discuss them now."

Harriman delivered this message the same evening and further explained our position to Stalin. Following his meeting with Stalin, Ambassador Harriman cabled me on August 27:

"As I had an engagement to see Stalin this evening, I handed him your message of August 27 regarding landing rights in the Kuriles. After it was translated to him, he questioned me about some of the points. Sticking to the text of your message, I explained on a map the reasons why landing rights were of importance. He said that he now understood the reasons for the request, would consult his associates and then reply. He told me that he had understood from your first message that a permanent fortified military base was requested which penetrated the Soviet outer defenses. I got the impression that he considered landing rights during the occupational period as being reasonable, but I got no impression as to his reaction on the permanent facilities for commercial use. . . .

"Stalin was quite cold at the beginning of our talk, but as it progressed he became entirely cordial and kept me for over an hour talking about the procedure that General MacArthur was pursuing for the Japanese surrender and other matters of general interest. I will report this more fully in the morning."

A few days later—August 30—a direct message from Stalin confirmed Harriman's impressions:

"I have received your message of August 27. I am glad that the misunderstandings, that slipped into our correspondence, have cleared away. I was not in the least offended by your proposal but experienced a state of perplexity because I, as it is now clear, have misunderstood you.

"I, of course, agree with your proposal to secure for the United States the right of landing on our airdromes on one of the Kurile Islands in emergency cases in the period of occupation of Japan.

"I also consent that a possibility be provided on a Soviet airdrome on one of the Kurile Islands for landing of commercial planes. The Soviet Government expects reciprocity on the part of the United States in respect to the right of landing of Soviet commercial planes on an American airdrome on one of the Aleutian Islands. It is the case that the present aviation route from Siberia across Canada to the United States of America does not satisfy us because of its long stretch. We prefer a shorter route from the Kurile Islands through the Aleutian Islands, as an intermediate point, to Seattle."

Stalin was trying to bring to Japan the same kind of divided rule which the circumstances and necessities of the military situation had forced upon us in Germany. He also renewed his efforts to have the unified Supreme Command arrangement modified. Interestingly enough, this was done through military rather than diplomatic channels, probably in the hope that General MacArthur could be persuaded to make changes that might appear to him to be minor. Like all important messages from and to the theater commanders, these, too, passed through the White House Map Room and were brought to my attention by Admiral Leahy.

First, a message from General Deane of our military mission in Moscow was sent to General Marshall and General MacArthur:

"Antonov called on me early this morning and handed me the following letter which he wishes transmitted to General MacArthur:

" 'After reading your letter of 19 August 1945 which contained the Instrument of Surrender of Japan, the General Staff of the Red Army considers it necessary to include in this instrument the following amendments:

" '1. Change paragraph three to read:

" 'We hereby command all Japanese Forces wherever situated and the

Japanese people to cease hostilities forthwith, to preserve and save from damage all ships, aircrafts, and military and civil property and to comply with all requirements which may be imposed by the Supreme Commander for the Allied Powers *and by the separate allied high commands in their respective theaters of operations* or by agencies of the Japanese government at their direction.

" '2. Change paragraph five to read:

" 'We hereby command all civil, military and naval officials to obey and enforce all proclamations, orders and directives deemed by the Supreme Commander for the Allied Powers *and by the separate allied high commands in their respective theaters of operation* to be proper to effectuate this surrender and issued by *them* or under *their* authority and we direct all such officials to remain at their posts and to continue to perform their noncombatant duties unless specifically relieved by *the Supreme Commander for the Allied Powers or by the Separate Allied High Commander in their respective theaters or under their authority*.

" '3. Change paragraph eight to read:

" 'The authority of the Emperor and the Japanese Government to rule the state shall be subject to the Supreme Commander for the Allied Powers *or to such organization as the Allied Powers may create for these purposes* who will take such steps as *they* deem proper to effectuate these terms of surrender.'

"Antonov stated that the above amendments had the approval of Generalissimo Stalin. . . ."

I have italicized here the changes for which the Russians were asking. If we had agreed to them, it would have meant our approval of everything and anything the Russians might want to do in Manchuria, and it would have opened the door for them to press for a Control Council type of occupation in Japan. MacArthur's reply referred the Russians, as was proper, to the governmental level, and on August 27 General Antonov wrote to say that "if these corrections may create any sort of difficulty for General MacArthur, then the General Staff of the Red Army will not insist on these corrections."

Neither in Stalin's message to me nor in Antonov's to MacArthur nor in any other communication from the Russians was there any comment or question regarding the line of demarcation for the occupation of Korea. The 38th parallel, which was destined to loom so large in later years, was not debated over nor bargained for by either side. When General Order No. 1 was submitted to me for approval, it provided that south of Latitude 38° North the surrender should be accepted by our forces and north of that line by the Russians. I was told that Secretary Byrnes had suggested that American forces receive the surrender as far north as practicable. The Army authorities, however, were faced with the insurmountable obstacles of both distance and lack of manpower. Even the 38th parallel was too far for any American troops to reach if the Russians had chosen to disagree. If we had been guided solely by how far north we could get our troops if there was opposition, the line would have had to be drawn considerably farther south on the peninsula. By drawing it along the 38th parallel, our military assured us of the opportunity to receive the surrender in Korea's ancient capital city, Seoul. Of course there was no thought at the time other than to provide a convenient allocation of responsibility for the acceptance of the Japanese surrender. All previous discussions on the subject of Korea had shown the Russians agreed with us that Korea should pass through a trusteeship phase before attaining independence.

There had also been the possibility of objections to the Korean arrangements from China, for Korea had been under Chinese control before the Sino-Japanese war of 1894, and on several occasions China had shown some inclinations to claim it again. But no objections were forthcoming. The government of Chiang Kai-shek was beginning to see surrender problems nearer home. The most serious of these was that the Chinese Communists had the advantage of having their military forces located where Japanese troops could be reached.

The Communist commander, Chu Teh, forwarded a lengthy document to General Wedemeyer for transmission to Washington. In this he sought to prove that the Communists, and not the Chungking government, had carried the burden of war in China and that they properly deserved to be represented at the surrender ceremony with General MacArthur. He also contended that they were rightfully entitled to receive local surrenders within China.

From this and other facts it became clear, as Wedemeyer said in a telegram the same day to MacArthur and Nimitz, that "the problem of orderly surrender of the bulk of Japanese troops in the China theater with the preservation of law and order in presently Japanese occupied areas resolves itself to one of rapidly deploying Central Government troops into strategic areas." In other words, Chiang Kai-shek needed our help to get his troops to the points where the principal Japanese forces were ready to surrender. Otherwise, the Chinese Communists would get their arms and, incidentally, would come to occupy the territory the Japanese were holding.

Chiang's second problem was Manchuria. This area had been extended by the Japanese to include the province of Jehol. Chiang naturally wanted to restore Manchuria to its former limits, which would mean that while the Russians would accept the surrender in Manchuria proper, Chinese forces would do so in Jehol. We, however, could do little more than point out to Chiang that the Russians were then in fact in Jehol and that General Order No. 1 authorized them to accept the surrender in the "Soviet area of operations."

By comparison, the controversy that developed over the British crown colony of Hong Kong might today seem of much less importance, but it agitated the Chinese no less. Chiang Kai-shek claimed Hong Kong to be in the area in which Japanese forces were to surrender to him as generalissimo of the China Theater. The British were willing to have Chiang send a representative to be present on the occasion of the surrender of Japanese forces in Hong Kong, but they would not accept any interpretation of General Order No. 1 as meaning that Hong Kong, as British territory, was included in the expression "within China."

In his message to me on the surrender of Hong Kong, Attlee pointed out that the Joint Chiefs of Staff and the Chinese government had been notified that a British naval force was then on its way to release Hong Kong from Japanese occupation, to bring aid to prisoners and internees situated in the colony, and to restore British administration. "It may be that the Japanese commanders on the spot," Attlee said, "may regard Hong Kong as being 'within China,' and I therefore request you to instruct the Allied Supreme Commander, General of the Army MacArthur, to order the Japanese High Command to ensure that the Japanese local commanders in the British Colony of Hong Kong shall surrender to the commander of the British naval force on his arrival."

President Roosevelt had made no commitment, but he had intimated that he would not block possible efforts of the Chinese after the war to negotiate for the return of Hong Kong to the Chinese. This was in line with our general policy of encouraging the termination of extraterritorial rights and foreign settlements in China. But while we considered the matter open to discussion, we still adhered to our recognition of the established rights, and General MacArthur was instructed to arrange for the surrender of Hong Kong to the British commander. Secretary of State Byrnes informed T. V. Soong of this action, stating that it did not in any way represent United States views regarding the future status of Hong Kong.

Chiang Kai-shek was unwilling to accept this arrangement, and he addressed himself to me personally.

"My dear Mr. President," he wrote. "On August 20 I received the following memorandum from His Excellency the British Ambassador in Chungking:

" 'His Majesty's Embassy learns that Dr. T. V. Soong has been informed by the United States Secretary of State in Washington of the action contemplated for the recovery of Hong Kong by a British naval force.

" 'The Embassy has been instructed to inform His Excellency the President of the Republic of China that the British service authorities concerned have been given the appropriate instructions, in order that full military coordination may be effected with the Chinese High Command on operational matters connected with assistance and support through the Hong Kong area to Chinese and United States forces engaged against the enemy or involved in securing the surrender of Japanese forces in contiguous areas.'

"In delivering the memorandum, the British Ambassador informed Dr. K. C. Wu, Vice Minister of Foreign Affairs, that you had wired Prime Minister Attlee that the United States has no objection to the recovery of Hong Kong by a British naval force. The British Ambassador also stated that you had authorized the British to accept surrender of Japanese troops in the 'areas' of Hong Kong. We have not heard from Dr. Soong or from you, Mr. President, any word that affirms or denies the claim made by the British. If you have not sent such a telegram to the British I would strongly advise against any unilateral alteration of the terms of the Potsdam Declaration and the surrender terms already issued by the Supreme Commander for the Allied Powers. A change now in the surrender order could create a bad precedent that might have more serious consequences in places other than Hong Kong. The British should conform to the general order and refrain from landing troops on Hong Kong or attempting to accept the surrender of Japanese in this theater.

"If you have already sent the telegram to Prime Minister Attlee as stated by the British Ambassador, in order to avoid causing you embarrassment, I make the following proposal. The Japanese forces in Hong Kong should surrender to my representative in a ceremony in which both American and British representatives will be invited to participate. After the surrender the British will be authorized by me to land troops for the reoccupation of the island of Hong Kong. The British should not, under any pretext, land any troops on the mainland of China. It is with reluctance that I make the above concession. I hope that Your Excellency will support this position and that you will obtain reply before I make definite arrangements with His Majesty's Government."

My reply, which also was in the form of a personal letter, began by quoting verbatim and in full what I had sent to Attlee on the subject of Hong Kong, and then continued:

"I had assumed that Premier Soong would inform you of the views expressed in my message to the Prime Minister.

"The situation with regard to the Japanese surrender at Hong Kong presents a problem which is to my mind primarily a military matter of an operational character. No question arises with regard to British sovereignty in the area and it is my understanding that you do not desire to raise such a question. It was with these considerations in mind that I prepared the message to Prime Minister Attlee quoted above. It seems reasonable that, where it is practicable to do so, surrender by Japanese forces should be to the authorities of that nation exercising sovereignty in the area. In the case of Hong Kong, it appears to me quite practicable to effect military coordination between the British and yourself on operational matters which would make feasible the surrender of the Japanese at Hong Kong to British military authorities.

"I sincerely hope, my dear Generalissimo, that you will be able to see this matter in the same light as I do and that, in the spirit of cooperation and understanding which has characterized the relations between our Governments and peoples for so many years, you will see your way clear to authorize the military coordination with the British, which I have recommended, in order that appropriate instructions can be given General MacArthur to arrange for the surrender of Hong Kong to a British commander.

"I fully appreciate the motives which prompted you to make the proposal contained in your message to me but I believe that, taking into account all factors, the procedure which I have proposed provides a reasonable solution."

Chiang Kai-shek was still unwilling to concede the main point. He wanted Hong Kong to be received on his behalf, as a part of China. But he realized that he could no more get to Hong Kong with his own forces than he could reach North China and Manchuria without aid from us. This was his reply, on August 23, to my message:

"My dear Mr. President: I have received your message transmitted by Ambassador Hurley in regard to the surrender at Hong Kong. In compliance with your request and in deference to your suggestion on military coordination between China and Britain on operational matters connected with Hong Kong, I have notified the British that as Supreme Commander of this theater I agree to delegate my authority to a British commander to accept the surrender of Japanese forces in Hong Kong. I will also designate a Chinese and an American officer to participate in the acceptance of surrender there, and I have asked the British to effect the necessary military coordination on operational matters beforehand with my Chief of Staff, General Wedemeyer, and the Chinese Board of Military Operations. Difficult as it is for me to make these concessions, Mr. President, I have done so out of my great desire to cooperate with you in every way possible."

I thought Chiang's concession was quite reasonable, and I thought also that it would settle the matter. In fact, I sent him a personal message of appreciation for his considerate action. On the morning of August 27, however, a long message arrived from Ambassador Hurley reporting that the difficulties were far from resolved, and that afternoon I received another message from Chiang Kai-shek:

"My dear Mr. President: Out of my great desire to cooperate with you, I informed you on August 23 that I had notified the British that as Supreme Commander of this theater I agreed to delegate my authority to a British Commander to accept the surrender of the Japanese forces in Hong Kong. On August 23 I received your most cordial and encouraging reply transmitted by Ambassador Hurley, which is in full as follows:

" 'Please accept this expression of my appreciation of your considerate action in regard to the surrender of the Japanese in Hong Kong to a British Commander by which action you eased a difficult situation.'

"Today the British Government has addressed the following verbal communication to me through its Ambassador in Chungking:

" 'His Majesty's Government are anxious to reach a mutually satisfactory arrangement. They do not doubt that the Generalissimo will understand their feelings that Great Britain must reestablish status quo in Hong Kong after the defeat of Japan. Therefore, they must regret that they are unable to accept the suggestion of the Generalissimo that the officer of the British forces should accept surrender on this British territory as the Generalissimo's Delegate. They welcome the Chinese representative and also the American representative. Surrender will be accepted by a British officer who would be empowered for this purpose under General Order No. 1. The Chinese and American officers designated by the Generalissimo will attend as representatives of the Supreme Commander of the China Theater. On the assumption that there is a surrender document, they would sign as witnesses.'

"The British Ambassador further informed me that his government has designated Rear Admiral C. H. J. Harcourt as the commander to accept the surrender of the Japanese at Hong Kong.

"I told the British Ambassador that I could not subscribe to the position taken by the British Government in this matter. The British desire to reestablish status quo in Hong Kong has never been affected since from the very beginning I have assured them that it is not the intention of this government to send Chinese troops to occupy Hong Kong. Hong Kong is not included in the areas to be surrendered to the British, according to General Order No. One. Hong Kong lies definitely within the China Theater. As Supreme Commander of this theater, I have my duties to fulfill and the agreements with the Allies to observe. I have made the concession to delegate my authority to a British Commander to accept the surrender there purely out of my desire to keep friendly relations with our Allies. And in making this concession, I have your concurrence and approval. To go beyond that on my part would be neither in accordance with the agreements of the Allied powers nor compatible with my duties as Supreme Commander of this theater.

"I have also notified the British Ambassador that since Rear Admiral Harcourt has been nominated by his government to accept the surrender of the Japanese in Hong Kong, I do delegate my authority to him as from today.

"As the American people and you, Mr. President, have always shown the highest regard for fair dealing and scrupulous observance of agreements in international relations, I trust that you will support me in this position and instruct General MacArthur to issue the necessary instructions to Admiral Harcourt."

Hurley's description of his interview with Chiang Kai-shek served to make the picture of the generalissimo's annoyance even more vivid. "He said," Hurley reported, "that every intimation he has received from the British has been accompanied by a threat of force not in regard to Hong Kong and Kowloon alone, but in regard to other parts of China. The Generalissimo stated that he considers the British attitude imperialistic, domineering and unbecoming a member of the United Nations. . . ."

Much as I deplored this friction between two of our allies, there seemed to be little else that could be done by us. The British naval unit was already on the way to Hong Kong, and eventually (on September 16) Admiral Harcourt received the surrender there of the Japanese. No mention of the generalissimo was made at the ceremony, but Chiang's headquarters listed it as one of the several surrenders to be effected to him. I had taken no further action in the matter.

CHAPTER 29

While London, Moscow, Chungking, and Washington were busy with agreements and disagreements that arose in connection with the Japanese surrender, a steady stream of messages from Guam and Manila reported the progress of our forces toward the occupation of the Japanese mainland and the formal surrender that was to be accepted there.

As soon as the first word had been received that the Japanese were ready to accept the Potsdam terms, Admiral Leahy and General Marshall had asked me where I thought the formal surrender should take place. I suggested, without hesitation, that the official act of surrender should take place in Tokyo Bay, aboard a naval vessel, and that ship to be the U.S.S. *Missouri*. I thought it wise to hold the ceremony within view of the Japanese capital in order to impress the fact of defeat on the Japanese people, but it also seemed desirable to remain offshore until we could be assured that there would be no last-minute outbursts of fanaticism.

My choice of the *Missouri* was an obvious one. She was one of the newest and most powerful battleships in our fleet; she had been named after my own state; my daughter Margaret had christened her, and I had spoken on that occasion.

The Japanese surrender was to be a momentous occasion for the American people, and I wanted as many of them as possible to share it. As early as August 13 I had given these instructions to the Joint Chiefs of Staff:

"It is my desire that the formal signing of the Japanese surrender should be an open news event and that free and competitive news coverage should be permitted by the news reporters present.

"It is my desire also that the Allied Military and Naval Officers present at the formal signature of surrender be given full status as representatives of their governments and of their services—land, sea, and air; and that they be accorded every possible consideration.

"Please instruct General MacArthur accordingly."

But these were not only days of rejoicing and celebration. We were not unmindful of the divine Providence that had enabled us to prevail. August 19 was declared a day of prayer in a proclamation which I issued:

The war lords of Japan and the Japanese armed forces have surrendered. They have surrendered unconditionally. Three months after victory in Europe victory has come in the East.

The cruel war of aggression which Japan started eight years ago to spread the forces of evil over the Pacific has resulted in her total defeat.

This is the end of the grandiose schemes of the dictators to enslave the peoples of the world, destroy their civilization, and institute a new era of darkness and degradation. This day is a new beginning in the history of freedom on this earth.

Our global victory has come from the courage and stamina and spirit of free men and women united in determination to fight.

It has come from the massive strength of arms and materials created by peace-loving peoples who knew that unless they won, decency in the world would end.

It has come from millions of peaceful citizens all over the world—turned soldiers almost overnight—who showed a ruthless enemy that they were not afraid to fight and to die, and that they knew how to win.

It has come with the help of God, Who was with us in the early days of adversity and disaster, and Who has now brought us to this glorious day of triumph.

Let us give thanks to Him, and remember that we have now dedicated ourselves to follow in His ways to a lasting and just peace and to a better world.

NOW, THEREFORE, I, HARRY S. TRUMAN, President of the United States of America, do hereby appoint Sunday, August 19, 1945, to be a day of prayer.

I call upon the people of the United States, of all faiths, to unite in offering their thanks to God for the victory we have won, and in praying that He will support and guide us into the paths of peace.

I also call upon my countrymen to dedicate this day of prayer to the memory of those who have given their lives to make possible our victory.

IN WITNESS WHEREOF, I have hereunto set my hand and caused the seal of the United States of America to be affixed.

DONE at the city of Washington, this sixteenth day of August, in the year of our Lord nineteen hundred and forty-five, and of the Independence of the United States of America the one hundred and seventieth.

(SEAL)

HARRY S. TRUMAN

By the President:
JAMES F. BYRNES
Secretary of State

In the meantime General MacArthur had been informed of our official reply to the Japanese surrender and had been told what procedure to follow in establishing contact with the defeated enemy.

FROM: Marshall
TO: MacArthur

State Department has received official Japanese acceptance of surrender demands and is replying, through the intermediary power, to the Japanese as follows:

"1. Direct prompt cessation of hostilities by Japanese forces, informing the Supreme Commander for the Allied Powers of the effective date and hour of such cessation.

"2. Send emissaries at once to the Supreme Commander for the Allied Powers with information of the disposition of the Japanese forces and commanders, and fully empowered to make arrangements directed by the Supreme Commander for the Allied Powers to enable him and his accompanying force to arrive at the place designated by him to receive the formal surrender.

"For the purpose of receiving such surrender and carrying it into effect, General of the Army Douglas MacArthur has been designated as the Supreme Commander for the Allied Powers, and he will notify the Japanese Government of time, place and other details of formal surrender."

You will take the necessary action indicated by the foregoing, keeping all concerned informed. . . .

General MacArthur then radioed a message to the Japanese ordering them to send representatives to him at Manila. This was the first of a number of radio exchanges between his headquarters and Tokyo, preparing the way for the formal surrender and the arrival of the occupation troops. As these messages went back and forth, copies passed across my desk to keep me constantly posted on MacArthur's progress. MacArthur's first message to the Japanese was as follows:

FROM SUPREME COMMANDER FOR THE ALLIED POWERS TO THE JAPANESE EMPEROR, THE JAPANESE IMPERIAL GOVERNMENT, THE JAPANESE GENERAL HEADQUARTERS

I have been designated as the Supreme Commander for the Allied Powers (The United States, the Republic of China, United Kingdom, and the Union of Soviet Socialist Republics) and empowered to arrange directly with the Japanese authorities for the cessation of hostilities at the earliest practicable date. It is desired that a radio station in the Tokyo area be officially designated for continuous use in handling radio communications between this headquarters and your headquarters. Your reply to this message should give the call signs, frequencies and station designation.

It is desired that the radio communication with my headquarters in Manila be handled in English text. Pending designation by you of a station in the Tokyo area for use as above indicated, Station JUM on frequency 13705 kilocycles will be used for this purpose, and WTZ Manila will answer on 15965 kilocycles.

Upon receipt of this message, acknowledge.

In a second message the newly appointed Supreme Commander instructed the Japanese to send a delegation to Manila by way of the Ryukyus in order to receive his detailed directive for the formal acceptance of the surrender.

The Japanese replied by radio. They reported that the Emperor had issued an imperial order to all his armed forces to cease hostilities. They asked permission to dispatch members of the imperial family to outlying troop headquarters to convey this order and assure that it would be obeyed.

On August 17 the Japanese GHQ complained that the Russians were still carrying out attacks and asked MacArthur to intervene.

There followed a flow of messages exchanged between Manila and Tokyo. I was being kept informed of these exchanges and of the progress of arrangements. The Japanese emissaries left by plane for MacArthur's headquarters and returned to Japan with the documents which had been sent to MacArthur from Washington for the formal surrender—the Proclamation by the Emperor, the Instrument of Surrender, and General Order No. 1. In addition, they were given MacArthur's own "Requirements for entry of the Supreme Commander."

On August 20 the Japanese reported difficulties in China where various local commanders were taking it upon themselves to effect the surrender in their own manner. MacArthur was requested to send officials to China to investigate and advise on "the actual situation."

On August 21 the Japanese informed the Supreme Commander that they had accepted the "good offices and cooperation" of the International Red Cross in handling the Allied prisoners of war in Japan. This, they suggested, would make it unnecessary to dispatch special contact teams ahead of the principal occupation forces.

As the actual date of surrender neared, the messages increased. There were Japanese requests for clearance of mercy shipments to outlying islands, courier flights by small aircraft, changes in radio frequencies and identification signals—it was apparent that the Japanese wished to avoid anything that might give offense to the Allies and thus cause the fighting to flare up again.

Meanwhile in Washington we were working on policy directives for the occupation. We expected that control over the conduct of the occupation would become the subject of some differences among the Allies and wanted to fix our position.

On August 18 I approved a memorandum establishing this government's basic policy with regard to the military occupation of Japan. The key point of this policy was that the actual control of occupied Japan should be under our direction. We recognized that others of the United

Nations had taken part in the war against Japan and were entitled to take part in the determination of policies, but just as we were expected to furnish the major share of the occupation forces, so did we also want to reserve for ourselves the controlling voice in the occupation. We were determined that the occupation should be run on a centralized control basis and that there should be no division of the Japanese nation into zones.

There were many touchy areas among our allies in connection with the procedures of the formal surrender. In the initial instructions to Mac-Arthur it was specified that, besides himself as Supreme Commander, the surrender document would be signed by the other three representatives of the four powers that had joined in the Potsdam Declaration. The British, however, were anxious to satisfy the demands for participation that came from their Dominions, especially Australia. The Foreign Minister there, Mr. Evatt, had made some strong public statements demanding that his country be heard in any dealings with Japan.

On August 18, therefore, I sent word to MacArthur that, in addition to representatives of the United States, Great Britain, China, and the Soviet Union, representatives of Australia, Canada, France, New Zealand, and the Netherlands had been invited to be present at the acceptance of the Japanese surrender and for him to make the necessary arrangements.

Immediately after the surrender, we had received a communication from the Japanese through the Swiss which undertook to suggest to us how the occupation could be made most effective. This was the message:

"The Japanese Government would like to be permitted to state to the governments of America, Great Britain, China and the Soviet Union what they most earnestly desire with reference to the execution of certain provisions of the Potsdam Declaration. This may be done possibly at the time of the signature, but fearing that they may not be able to find an appropriate opportunity they take the liberty of addressing to the governments of the four powers through the good offices of Switzerland.

"Primo—in view of the fact that the purpose of occupation as mentioned in the Potsdam Proclamation is solely to secure the achievement of the basic objectives set forth in the said proclamation, the Japanese Government sincerely desire that the four powers, relying upon the good faith of the Japanese Government, will facilitate discharge by the Japanese Government of their obligations so as to forestall any unnecessary complications. It is earnestly solicited that:

"In case of the entry of Allied fleets or troops in Japan proper the Japanese Government be notified in advance so that arrangements can be made for reception.

"The number of the points in Japanese territory to be designated by the Allies for occupation be limited to minimum number, selection of the points be made in such a manner as to leave such a city as Tokyo unoccupied, and the forces to be stationed at each point be made as small as possible.

"Secundo—disarming of the Japanese forces being a most delicate task as it involves over three millions of officers and men overseas and having direct bearing on their honor, the Japanese Government will, of course, take utmost pains. But it is suggested that the best and the most effective method would be that under the command of his Majesty the Emperor the Japanese forces are allowed to disarm themselves and surrender arms of their own accord. Disarming of the Japanese forces on the continent be carried out beginning on the front line and in successive stages.

"In connection with the disarming it is hoped that Article 35 of the Hague Convention will be applied and the honor of the soldier will be respected, permitting them, for instance, to wear swords. Further, the Japanese Government be given to understand the Allies have no intention to employ disarmed Japanese soldiers for compulsory labor. It is sincerely hoped that shipment and transportation facilities necessary for the evacuation of the soldiers to their homeland will be speedily provided.

"Tertio—since some forces are located in remote places difficult to communicate the Imperial order, it is desired that a reasonable time be allowed before the cessation of hostilities.

"Quarto—the Allies will be good enough quickly to take necessary steps or extend to us facilities for the shipment of indispensable food stuffs and medical supplies to Japanese Forces in distant islands and for the transport of wounded soldiers from those islands."

Some of the things the Japanese were asking in this letter we would of course do. They were just matters of common decency in dealing with a defeated enemy. But we could not begin the occupation by bargaining over its terms. We were the victors. The Japanese were the losers. They had to know that "unconditional surrender" was not a matter for negotiations. On my instructions, Secretary Byrnes sent a coldly formal reply:

"Such information as the Japanese Government requires to carry out the surrender arrangements will be communicated by the Supreme Commander at appropriate times determined by him. The four Allied Powers have subscribed to the Potsdam Declaration which assures the return to the homeland to peaceful occupations of all Japanese Armed Forces who surrender to United States commanders, Generalissimo Chiang Kai-shek, Admiral the Lord Louis Mountbatten and Soviet commanders as directed by the Supreme Commander for the Allied Powers. This return will be

arranged through the Supreme Commander and will take place after the
Japanese Armed Forces have been disarmed by the Allied commanders
to whom they surrender and when Japanese and other transportation
can be made available."

In order to make clear to the Japanese as well as to General Mac-
Arthur what the scope of the Supreme Commander's authority was to be,
I sat down with Admiral Leahy and General Marshall, and together we
drafted a statement that was forwarded to MacArthur shortly after he
arrived in Japan. Later, at MacArthur's request, I granted him permission to publish this communication:

6 September 1945

TO MACARTHUR FROM THE JOINT CHIEFS OF STAFF
The following exposition of your authority as Supreme Commander for the
Allied Powers has been approved by the President:
1. The authority of the Emperor and the Japanese Government to rule the
state is subordinate to you as Supreme Commander for the Allied Powers.
You will exercise your authority as you deem proper to carry out your mission. Our relations with Japan do not rest on a contractual basis, but on an
unconditional surrender. Since your authority is supreme, you will not entertain any question on the part of the Japanese as to its scope.
2. Control of Japan shall be exercised through the Japanese Government
to the extent that such an arrangement produces satisfactory results. This does
not prejudice your right to act directly if required. You may enforce the
orders issued by you by the employment of such measures as you deem necessary, including the use of force.
3. The statement of intentions contained in the Potsdam Declaration will
be given full effect. It will not be given effect, however, because we consider
ourselves bound in a contractual relationship with Japan as a result of that
document. It will be respected and given effect because the Potsdam Declaration forms a part of our policy stated in good faith with relation to Japan
and with relation to peace and security in the Far East.

Meanwhile MacArthur had perfected his plans for the formal surrender ceremony, and on August 21 he forwarded a detailed schedule to the
Japanese government. But the violent storms that struck the home islands
of Japan on August 22 forced a short postponement of MacArthur's
schedule.

All preparations for the surrender ceremony were by now well under
way. It was apparent that the Japanese were going to be entirely co-
operative, and all their messages indicated a strong desire to accommodate the victors. Interestingly enough, Stalin did not share this opinion.
He would have handled the situation quite differently. Ambassador Harriman reported Stalin's comments on our plans.

"For your information as a matter of general interest," he cabled, "in
my conversation with Stalin on August 27 he showed great interest in and
asked me about the setting for the Japanese surrender. When I told him

as much as I knew about it, he commented that there were considerable risks, the Japanese were treacherous people and there were many 'crazy cutthroats' left. He said he would have taken some hostages to protect against incidents. He suggested that it would have been more advisable to order all Japanese ships, airplanes, etc., to Manila and then have the Japanese come to MacArthur's headquarters to sign the surrender. When I explained the desirability of bringing home to the Japanese their defeat by having the surrender signed in the heart of Japan, he stated that the large armada must be very impressive. It was risky but if there were no incidents the armada and the troops landed by air would be a most impressive demonstration of strength to the Japanese people."

I decided that I would speak to the nation in connection with the surrender ceremony, and on August 28 MacArthur was so informed. At the last minute it took some frantic exchanges between Tokyo and Washington to get the timing fixed—amid a flurry of other messages that sought to unsnarl some details that had become confused. The Dutch, for instance, had given us the name of General Van Oyen to act as their representative, but on August 30 MacArthur reported, "now arrives Admiral Helfrich senior officer in this region and CINC of Netherlands Forces in the East" with word from his government that he was to be its authorized representative. Then, too, the Russians wanted to send a press and radio party and seemed to feel that they would not be welcome unless MacArthur had approved of each and every name included.

While these matters of military protocol were being adjusted, the following messages were exchanged in order to co-ordinate the timing of the surrender ceremony with the timing of my broadcast:

TO MACARTHUR FROM THE JOINT CHIEFS OF STAFF
The President desires that if it is practicable the actual signing of the instrument of surrender be accomplished not later than ten or eleven o'clock A.M. Tokyo time in order that his announcement from here may follow without delay.
A reply by telegraph is requested.

FROM MACARTHUR TO MARSHALL
Actual details of surrender ceremony . . . are to be arranged immediately after my landing in Tokyo area. I am certain that the President's desires as to hour of signing can be accomplished. Will confirm the hour immediately upon conclusion of preliminary meeting.

FROM: The War Department
TO: General MacArthur
The President hopes that the signing of the Japanese surrender will be arranged so that it will be concluded at about 10:00 P.M. Washington time (E.W.T.). He has approved the following procedure, recommended by United States networks:

1. A radio pickup from the U.S.S. *Missouri,* giving a simple direct description of the actual signing ceremonies, with announcement of the name of each participant as he signs. At the close the announcer would say that the surrender had been completed and add, "We take you now to the White House in Washington."

2. The President will then immediately address the nation.

3. At the end of the President's remarks the broadcasts will be switched back to the U.S.S. *Missouri* for remarks by General MacArthur and Admiral Nimitz.

The President hopes that the time for the surrender ceremony will be fixed as far in advance as possible so that the radio companies may have ample time for their arrangements and for advertising the broadcast.

FROM MACARTHUR TO MARSHALL

Arrangements made for completion of surrender ceremony on *Missouri* at 10301 September 2d.

Radio broadcast, press dispatches and all publicity released simultaneously here at that hour.

FROM: General MacArthur
TO: War Department

Arrangements in general accordance with your instructions have been made. As reported . . . the ceremony will go on the air at 10301 on the second. It will be impracticable after the President's address to switch the broadcast back to the *Missouri* for speeches by General MacArthur and Admiral Nimitz. As previously directed they will be made on later broadcasts.

FROM: General MacArthur
TO: The War Department

Arrangements have now been made for short address by MacArthur and Nimitz to follow immediately the address of the President.

FROM: The Naval Aide to the President
TO: General MacArthur

Request verification immediately of 10301 2 September as time of surrender ceremony. Also request estimated time radio circut will switch to White House for President's broadcast.

FROM: Naval Aide to the President
TO: General MacArthur

Reference my message about broadcast of surrender ceremony. Conflicting reports received here are confusing to press and public. Please confirm by urgent message your previous statement that broadcast of surrender ceremony will begin 1030 Item September 2. Please estimate time broadcast will be switched from Tokyo to Washington for President's address. Please also advise whether actual signing will take place during Tokyo broadcast or will broadcast only consist of a description of what has taken place.

FROM: Supreme Commander for the Allied Powers
TO: Naval Aide to the President

In reply your message broadcast of surrender ceremony will begin at 1030 I, 2 September. Switch to White House for President's broadcast estimated between 1045 I and 1055 I.

FROM: U.S.S. Ancon Communications Center
for General MacArthur's
Headquarters afloat
TO: Naval Aide to the President

Surrender ceremony broadcast description of events taking place starts at 0130 G.M.T. until 0145 G.M.T. Switch to White House comes at 0145 G.M.T.

FROM: U.S.S. Ancon
FOR: Naval Aide to the President

Length of surrender ceremony broadcast 26½ minutes. This supersedes previous information stating 15 minutes length. Program schedule to start 0130Z.

On the evening of September 1 (September 2 Tokyo time), I, like millions of my fellow citizens, listened to the description of the proceedings aboard the *Missouri*.

I was thinking of the history of previous occasions when dictators and absolute rulers had brought disaster to their people and their countries. There had been Philip II of Spain and his armada, the destruction of which was the beginning of the end for Spain as a world power. Then there was Louis XIV and the Battle of Blenheim; Napoleon and Waterloo; the Kaiser; Hitler; and—now—the war lords of Japan. This second surrender of World War II marked the ignominious defeat and downfall of the second of the world's cruelest dictatorial governments.

I was wondering that night if the world, and particularly ourselves, had learned anything—whether we would profit from our terrible mistakes of World War I or would we repeat them. I was in the midst of these thoughts when the announcer in Tokyo Bay switched the broadcast to the White House, and I spoke to the nation.

"My fellow Americans," I said. "The thoughts and hopes of all America—indeed of all the civilized world—are centered tonight on the battleship *Missouri*. There on that small piece of American soil anchored in Tokyo Harbor the Japanese have just officially laid down their arms. They have signed terms of unconditional surrender.

"Four years ago the thoughts and fears of the whole civilized world were centered on another piece of American soil—Pearl Harbor. The mighty threat to civilization which began there is now laid to rest. It was a long road to Tokyo—and a bloody one.

"We shall not forget Pearl Harbor.

"The Japanese militarists will not forget the U.S.S. *Missouri*.

"The evil done by the Japanese war lords can never be repaired or forgotten. But their power to destroy and kill has been taken from them. Their armies and what is left of their navy are now impotent.

"To all of us there comes first a sense of gratitude to Almighty God who sustained us and our Allies in the dark days of grave danger, who made us to grow from weakness into the strongest fighting force in history, and who now has seen us overcome the forces of tyranny that sought to destroy His civilization.

"God grant that in our pride of the hour we may not forget the hard tasks that are still before us; that we may approach these with the same courage, zeal and patience with which we faced the trials and problems of the past four years.

"Our first thoughts, of course—thoughts of gratefulness and deep obligation—go out to those of our loved ones who have been killed or maimed in this terrible war. On land and sea and in the air, American men and women have given their lives so that this day of ultimate victory might come and assure the survival of a civilized world. No victory can make good their loss.

"We think of those whom death in this war has hurt, taking from them husbands, sons, brothers and sisters whom they loved. No victory can bring back the faces they longed to see.

"Only the knowledge that the victory, which these sacrifices made possible, will be wisely used can give them any comfort. It is our responsibility—ours, the living—to see to it that this victory shall be a monument worthy of the dead who died to win it.

"We think of all the millions of men and women in our armed forces and merchant marine all over the world who, after years of sacrifice and hardship and peril, have been spared by Providence from harm.

"We think of all the men and women and children who during these years have carried on at home, in lonesomeness and anxiety and fear.

"Our thoughts go out to the millions of American workers and businessmen, to our farmers and miners—to all who have built up this country's fighting strength, and who have shipped to our Allies the means to resist and overcome the enemy.

"Our thoughts go out to our civil servants and to the thousands of Americans who, at personal sacrifice, have come to serve in our government during these trying years; to the members of the selective service boards and ration boards; to the civilian defense and Red Cross workers; to the men and women in the USO and in the entertainment world—to all those who have helped in this cooperative struggle to preserve liberty and decency in the world.

"We think of our departed gallant leader, Franklin D. Roosevelt, defender of democracy, architect of world peace and cooperation.

"And our thoughts go out to our gallant Allies in this war; to those who resisted the invaders; to those who were not strong enough to hold out, but who nevertheless kept the fires of resistance alive within the souls of their people; to those who stood up against great odds and held the line, until the United Nations together were able to supply the arms and the men with which to overcome the forces of evil.

"This is a victory of more than arms alone. This is a victory of liberty over tyranny.

"From our war plants rolled the tanks and planes which blasted their way to the heart of our enemies; from our shipyards sprang the ships which bridged all the oceans of the world for our weapons and supplies; from our farms came the food and fibre for our armies and navies and for our Allies in all the corners of the earth; from our mines and factories came the raw materials and the finished products which gave us the equipment to overcome our enemies.

"But back of it all were the will and spirit and determination of a free people—who know what freedom is, and who know that it is worth whatever price they had to pay to preserve it.

"It was the spirit of liberty which gave us our armed strength and which made our men invincible in battle. We now know that that spirit of liberty, the freedom of the individual, and the personal dignity of man are the strongest and toughest and most enduring forces in the world.

"And so on V-J Day, we take renewed faith and pride in our own way of life. We have had our day of rejoicing over this victory. We have had our day of prayer and devotion. Now let us set aside V-J Day as one of renewed consecration to the principles which have made us the strongest nation on earth and which, in this war, we have striven so mightily to preserve.

"Those principles provide the faith, the hope and the opportunity which help men to improve themselves and their lot. Liberty does not make all men perfect nor all society secure. But it has provided more solid progress and happiness and decency for more people than any other philosophy of government in history. And this day has shown again that it provides the greatest strength and the greatest power which man has ever reached.

"We know that under it we can meet the hard problems of peace which have come upon us. A free people with free Allies, who can develop an atomic bomb, can use the same skill and energy and determination to overcome all the difficulties ahead.

"Victory always has its burdens and its responsibilities as well as its rejoicing.

"But we face the future and all its dangers with great confidence and great hope. America can build for itself a future of employment and security. Together with the United Nations, it can build a world of peace founded on justice and fair dealing and tolerance.

"As President of the United States, I proclaim Sunday, September second, 1945, to be V-J Day—the day of formal surrender by Japan. It is not yet the day for the formal proclamation of the end of the war or of the cessation of hostilities. But it is a day which we Americans shall always remember as a day of retribution—as we remember that other day, the day of infamy.

"From this day we move forward. We move toward a new era of security at home. With the other United Nations we move toward a new and better world of peace and international goodwill and cooperation.

"God's help has brought us to this day of victory. With His help we will attain that peace and prosperity for ourselves and all the world in the years ahead."

CHAPTER 30

In times of war the duties and responsibilities of the Commander in Chief take precedence over other obligations of the presidency. But with hostilities over, the emphasis had now shifted to domestic problems and political leadership. On the home front we faced a multitude of postwar adjustments. Our position of world leadership brought with it new responsibilities and staggering obligations, and it was up to us to manage our affairs at home so that our foreign policy could be conducted on the broad scope required to help shape the future peace of the world.

Among the many things that demanded urgent attention was the world's great need for food. It was this problem that I had in mind when I reported by radio to the American people on conditions abroad.

"Europe today is hungry," I said. "I am not talking about Germans; I am talking about the people of countries which were overrun and devastated by the Germans and, particularly, about the people of western Europe.

"As the winter comes on, the distress will increase. Unless we do what we can to help, we may lose next winter what we won at such terrible costs last spring. Desperate men are liable to destroy the structure of their society to find in the wreckage some substitute for hope. If we let Europe go cold and hungry, we may lose some of the foundations of order on which the hope for worldwide peace must rest."

That was the literal truth. It had been apparent since early spring that growing needs for food by the people in the ruined countries of Europe, the growing consumption by the armed forces, and a threatened shortage in the crops at home would call for drastic action.

One of the first steps I had taken in an effort to co-ordinate all activities of the various government agencies affecting the food supply produced or conserved in the homes of America was to appoint a Director of Home Food Supply. For this job I had chosen Paul C. Stark of Louisiana, Missouri, who had served during the war with the National Victory Garden Institute. I had been impressed with the enterprise with which he had conducted the campaign for "victory" gardens. He had even tried to put one on the White House lawn.

To bolster the work of this new office, I had appealed directly to the American people on June 2 for greater home production and for greater conservation of food so that we could allocate more to help feed the hungry millions of Europe. I had also combined the War Food Administration with the Department of Agriculture in order to make more effective use of existing machinery in carrying out the food program.

In order to get as many facts as possible, I had called upon the services of experts to study the problem of feeding Europe and to make recommendations. Foremost among these was former President Herbert Hoover, who had done such a remarkable job in food relief after World War I. I invited President Hoover to visit the White House, his first call there since 1932, and in a pleasant meeting on May 28 he gave me some very constructive ideas. I had also issued invitations to Alf Landon of Kansas, former Republican candidate for President, and Governor Thomas E. Dewey of New York to discuss the situation.

Evidence of an impending food crisis in Europe had been coming to me in reports from our own people abroad, and in messages—many tragically urgent—from the leaders of other countries. England, Belgium, and other countries that had for many years depended largely on imports to feed their crowded populations were now in worse straits than they had ever been before. Much of their agricultural production had been either destroyed or made idle by the war. They had lost much of the shipping which, in former years, had enabled them to bring food products from abroad, and their foreign exchange balances had been depleted by military requirements and the enormous reduction in their exports.

Some of the problems involved in the food crisis were highly complicated. If, for instance, Belgium and France should be forced to turn to Argentina to buy meat, the prices there would rise sharply, and this would hurt the British, who had long obtained much of their meat there. With this in mind, the British suggested in June 1945 that we release portions of our European military surplus food stocks to the French and Belgians. Their assumption was that the reduction of our military forces in Europe meant that the food already shipped to Europe for these troops would be available. I had to point out to the British, however, that we needed these supplies to feed the huge numbers of German prisoners who had fallen into our hands.

The meat situation in our own country had become so tight in the spring of 1945 that the amounts available to civilians in our urban areas had actually dropped below the British per capita consumption. Nevertheless, in order to supply the most urgent needs of France and Belgium, I arranged to have fifty million pounds of meat shipped to them. I hoped that this would relieve, to a degree, the pressure on British buying in the Argentine. At the same time I called Winston Churchill's attention to certain other implications of the food situation.

"I do not feel that we can properly allocate meat to France and Belgium," I cabled him on June 23, "and ignore the rest of Europe. If we can find any meat, there must be at least a semblance of uniformity in its allocation."

It would have been better for all concerned if the problem could have been entrusted to a world-wide organization. But the United Nations Organization was only then being fashioned, and in this formative stage it could not be expected to assume that responsibility.

The role of the United Nations Relief and Rehabilitation Administration—UNRRA—was negligibly small in western Europe, although it was doing a big job in Greece. A major difficulty was that when UNRRA had been established in Atlantic City in 1943 its purpose was not clearly defined. While it was organized to meet the needs of countries unable to provide their own relief and rehabilitation, there was no fixed limit of the field of rehabilitation into which UNRRA was entitled to go. And there was no clear distinction as to the scope and functions of its combined food boards. In addition to this, congressional appropriations for use by UNRRA were delayed and, with the United States being the largest financial supporter of the organization, its operations were obviously limited until funds could be made available.

On October 16, 1945, the United Nations formally established an organization specifically designed to cope with the international food problem. This was the Food and Agriculture Organization, which was set up to gather and evaluate information on the known needs of people for food and to link that with the means for satisfying those needs. Basically, however, its function was an educative one, and the burden of doing something concrete about the starving populations of Europe still rested on the United States. At the FAO's first conference in Quebec on October 16, Secretary of Agriculture Clinton Anderson headed up the United States delegation and kept me supplied with information from that source.

Despite the preparations that the United States made in 1945 in an effort to avert a world food crisis, the threat of famine became almost global during the ensuing winter. More people faced starvation and even death for want of food during the year following the war than during all the war years combined. America enjoyed a near-record production of food and a record crop of wheat, but the wheat crops of Europe and North Africa and the rice crops of the Far East proved to be much shorter than anticipated. Not only the disruption of war but also extreme droughts in many parts of the world created a food crisis that gave promise of being the worst in modern times.

Information we had showed that, while Americans were living on a diet of about thirty-three hundred calories per person per day, more than one hundred and twenty-five million Europeans were subsisting on less than two thousand a day, and in some parts of Europe large groups were sometimes able to obtain no more than one thousand calories. World food production per capita was about twelve per cent below prewar production. In Europe, however, it was about twenty-five per cent below normal, and in Japan it was only fractionally better.

In many parts of the Orient the situation was even more critical than in the worst areas of Europe. In the Philippines production declined even more than in Japan. We were actually shipping sugar to the Philippines which normally export large quantities of it. In India and the Far East, where ninety-five per cent of the world's rice is normally produced, production was fifteen per cent below normal because of drought and the cumulative effects of war. The greatest reduction was in Burma, Siam, and in Indo-China, the world's largest exporter of rice.

The British estimated that in the first half of 1946 there would probably be a deficit of nearly seven million tons between available supplies of wheat and the quantities that the different importing countries had asked for. In addition, it appeared that large quantities of wheat might also be necessary to make good a shortage of rice which was at that time estimated at between one and two million tons.

The crux of the wheat problem lay not so much in the actual quantity of wheat in the various wheat-producing countries as in its collection from farms, its transport to the ports, and its shipment from there. Prime Minister Attlee cabled me on January 4, 1946, that unless the maximum quantities that could be spared were exported from all producing countries there was grave danger of widespread famine in Europe and Asia during the next few months. He emphasized, too, that the effects of this would spread far beyond the national boundaries of the countries concerned and would undoubtedly make infinitely more difficult the work of building a sound peace through the United Nations. For this reason he pleaded for my personal and active interest.

I instructed Secretary Anderson and other Cabinet officers and members of my staff to work closely with the British experts so that we could get a clear picture of the needs and a program to meet them. On February 6, 1946, I announced a nine-point emergency program in the hope that mass starvation could be prevented. The measures to be taken were as follows:

"(1) The appropriate agencies of this Government will immediately inaugurate a vigorous campaign to secure the full cooperation of all consumers in conserving food, particularly bread. Additional emphasis will be placed upon the cooperation of bakers and retailers in reducing waste of bread in distribution channels.

"(2) The use of wheat in the direct production of alcohol and beer will be discontinued; the use of other grains for the production of beverage alcohol will be limited, beginning March 1, to five days' consumption a month; and the use of other grains for the production of beer will be limited to an aggregate quantity equal to that used for this purpose in 1940 which was three per cent less than the quantity used in 1945. This will save for food about 20 million bushels of grain by June 30, 1946.

"(3) The wheat flour extraction rate (the quantity of flour produced from each bushel of wheat) will be raised to 80 per cent for the duration of the emergency. Also, steps will be taken to limit the distribution of flour to amounts essential for current civilian distribution. This will save about 25 million bushels of wheat during the first half of 1946.

"(4) The Department of Agriculture will control millers' inventories of wheat and bakers' and distributors' inventories of flour. The inventory controls will be designed to maintain the wheat and flour being held for civilian use at the minimum necessary for distribution purposes.

"(5) Specific preference will be given to the rail movement of wheat, corn, meat, and other essential foods in order promptly to export maximum quantities to the destinations where most needed.

"(6) The Department of Agriculture will exercise direct control over exports of wheat and flour to facilitate movement to destinations of greatest need.

"(7) Necessary steps will be taken to export during this calendar year, 375,000 tons of fats and oil, 1.6 billion pounds of meat, of which one billion pounds is to be made available during the first half of 1946, and to increase the exports of dairy products, particularly cheese and evaporated milk.

"(8) The War and Navy Departments already have aided materially the movement of Philippine copra (the raw material from which cocoanut oil is produced) by releasing 200 LCM and J boats for the interisland trade in the Philippines. These Departments and the War Shipping Administration will take immediate steps to make available the additional ships needed for this purpose.

"(9) The Department of Agriculture will develop additional ways in which grain now being used in the feeding of livestock and poultry could be conserved for use as human food. These steps may include means to obtain the rapid marketing of heavy hogs, preferably all those over 225 pounds, and of beef cattle with a moderate rather than a high degree of finish; to encourage the culling of poultry flocks; to prevent excessive chick production; and to encourage more economical feeding of dairy cattle. Regulations to limit wheat inventories of feed manufacturers and to restrict the use of wheat in feed will be prepared."

Only two days before this program was announced, Prime Minister Attlee had given me a vivid picture of the measure of hardship the British people would have to undergo.

"The Minister of Food has reported to me and the Cabinet," the Prime Minister's message read, "the results of his recent discussions in Washington with you and your Secretary of Agriculture on the serious world shortage of wheat and rice. I am most grateful to you for the help which you gave in those discussions and for the directions which you have issued since.

"We recognize that heavy sacrifices must be made to help the less fortunate peoples of the world. We ourselves accept the reduction of nearly a quarter of a million tons in United Kingdom wheat imports for the first half of 1946, although the consequences for us will be very serious. We shall have to reduce our stocks far below the safety level, and run the risk of interference with internal distribution of flour and bread if there is any irregularity in the arrival of imports. We shall have to increase the extraction rate of flour from 80% to 85% and return to the darker bread which we accepted as a wartime necessity but hoped we had discarded with the end of hostilities. We shall also have to reduce our fat ration from eight ounces to seven ounces a week which is lower than at any time during the war. This is a direct consequence of the wheat shortage; since as a result of drought and other disasters in Madras, Mysore, Bombay and Punjab, India fears a recurrence of famine worse than the Bengal famine of 1943 and is unable to rely on the imports of wheat and rice which she needs. Consequently she will have to use for food in India ground nuts which she would have otherwise exported to us for fats manufacture.

"The decision to increase our flour extraction rate, coupled with the decision taken at Washington to divert coarse grains from animal to human use, will substantially reduce our supplies of meat, bacon and eggs. Our plans for reestablishing our livestock herds will suffer a heavy setback and a considerable slaughter of pigs and poultry will be inevitable. Finally, we shall have to launch a vigorous publicity campaign to economize to the utmost all food, particularly bread, and to encourage increased sowings this spring of crops to be harvested during the coming summer.

"Sir Ben Smith will broadcast this grim story to the British public on Tuesday evening. The further sacrifices for which he must call will be a severe strain on our people, who have been looking forward to some relaxation of the standards of austerity which they have cheerfully accepted throughout the war.

"Then when we look further ahead the outlook is little better. Even after the next harvest, European production will be far below prewar figures and the demand from Far Eastern countries will not be reduced. And world stocks will have been exhausted by our efforts to meet the crisis in 1946.

"I am sending a personal cable to the Prime Ministers of Canada and Australia urging them to take all possible measures to increase the export of wheat by raising the extraction rate, curtailing the use of wheat for feeding animals and preventing all waste. I am also asking them to increase their wheat acreage for the next harvest.

"The people of this country will be strengthened in their determination to face the new hardships demanded of them by the knowledge that other countries are making similar exertions. And I am sure that the governments of Canada and Australia will also be greatly influenced in their attitude to my appeal by the measures adopted by your government to increase wheat exports from the United States. We greatly value the steps which you have already taken; but, knowing your deep concern in this problem which is bound to affect all our postwar settlements, I venture to ask you to consider whether you can make still further contributions on the following lines.

"If it were possible for you to increase your flour extraction rate, this would not only provide a major increase in the supplies of wheat available for export, but would also give a most valuable lead to other exporting countries. Our extraction rate, as I have said, will have to be raised to 85% and as a result of the allocations proposed in the Washington discussions it is clear that all countries in Europe will have to adopt a figure of at least 80%, and in many cases higher.

"Secondly, to meet the continuing shortage next year, I hope that you will do everything possible to increase your wheat acreage, especially as carry-over stocks will be so small.

"Thirdly, since Sir Ben Smith's return from Washington, there has been a serious deterioration in the food situation in Asia, especially in India, and we are facing a grave world shortage of rice. We have decided to continue our policy of not issuing rice for the civil population in this country and we are urging European countries to do the same. If your country could provide some contribution from its own rice resources, it would be of great assistance in stemming the flood of famine in the East and would materially assist in reducing demands for wheat.

"The world will pass through a period of great strain and hardship before we see the next harvest. I fear that thousands may die of starvation and many more thousands may suffer severely from hunger.

"It is for these reasons, Mr. President, that I make this earnest appeal for your continued help in mitigating the disasters which threaten the world."

When my nine-point program was made public on February 6, Attlee sent me a message of "warm thanks and appreciation," but a few weeks later he cabled urgently that the cereal situation had become even worse as the result of later estimates of both supply and demand. India had suffered a disastrous crop failure as a result of monsoons and would need imports of over four million tons of wheat or rice to maintain even a very inadequate minimum ration.

Attlee urged me to take steps to increase the United States wheat acreage. This, he felt, would make an immense difference to the world's welfare in the next fifteen months, and he closed his long message by asking my assistance on three points in particular.

"First," he wrote, "I hope you will join with us in ensuring that demands for importing countries throughout the world are kept to the minimum that are really essential.

"Secondly, it is most important to stimulate planting of rice for the next harvest. The prospect for next year seems to me almost as bleak for rice as it is for wheat. However hard we try, I think it unlikely that it will be possible to step up production in Asiatic countries to anything like prewar levels. As in the case of wheat, there will again be no stocks to fall back on and again there seems to be virtually no danger of oversupply. If you agree with this view, anything you can do to secure increased plantings in the United States and in the many areas of United States influence throughout the world would be most valuable.

"Thirdly, it would help materially if you could find means of reducing the consumption of rice in the United States. . . ."

In the light of this appeal I decided to ask a number of distinguished citizens to serve on a Famine Emergency Committee, and I was glad when former President Herbert Hoover consented to act as honorary chairman of the group. Along with twelve other members of the newly organized committee, Hoover met with me at the White House on March 1 to discuss the food situation. Secretary of Commerce Wallace and Secretary of Agriculture Anderson also sat in on the conference, and I told the group that I thought it was the most important meeting we had held in the White House since I had been President.

Mr. Hoover said that famine had always been the inevitable aftermath of war. The last great reservoir from which starvation could be halted, he pointed out, was in the United States, and he expressed confidence that the American people would respond to this great obligation again, as they had done after World War I.

I asked the former President if he could arrange to go at once to make a detailed study of conditions in the famine areas of the world, and he said he could.

The most immediate need was for wheat to be shipped to western Europe to tide those countries over until their own harvests began to come in. On April 9 the Famine Emergency Committee advised me that the crisis was more severe than when the committee had first met with me. Loadings of wheat in the first quarter of the year had fallen 313,000 tons below the goal of three million tons which had been set. Another report from the Secretary of Agriculture informed me that bread consumption in the United States was continuing at a high rate. Another fact was that, while feeding of wheat to livestock showed some reduction, it still continued at a considerable rate in spite of efforts made thus far to cut it to a minimum. It was clear that, unless effective measures were taken promptly to get wheat moving off the farms and to check its domestic consumption for bread and for feed, the United States would fall lamentably short of its goal for helping to feed the famine countries.

Additional difficulties in coping with the food problem were posed by the development of black markets. But I was certain that if we could get all the facts to the American people so that they would understand how buying from the black market was taking food from the starving, they would end such operations of their own volition.

Strikes in industries which affected the production and transportation of food supplies also complicated the famine relief program, and here again I felt that an educational program on the part of the government would go far in persuading labor and management to make extraordinary efforts to compose their differences.

While I approved the enforcement of stricter measures to increase the availability of food exports, I put the greatest emphasis on the importance of the personal responsibility of every citizen for food conservation and for co-operation on the part of the people of the United States in overcoming the famine situation around the world. I felt this so strongly that on April 18, 1946, I dispatched the following telegram to Mr. Hoover, who was then in Egypt making his survey of famine conditions:

"An urgent need has developed in this country to bring forcibly and dramatically to public attention, as a spur to the Food-For-Famine-Effort, the facts about conditions in Europe which your visit and inquiries have brought to light.

"Therefore, I wish to suggest the advisability of your return to the United States immediately after completion of the engagement in Cairo, in order to bring directly home to the American people your eye witness account of the necessity for greater assistance from this country.

"This would make your trip to India, China and Japan by way of the United States.

"The Famine Emergency Committee in session yesterday with representatives of the Government Departments concerned, including the Departments of State, Agriculture and Commerce, felt that with only seventy-five days left in the current phase of the Famine Relief Program, nothing should be left undone that can increase public response in ways to draw more wheat from the farms and to save more food in homes and eating places. Arrangements would be made for a large meeting in New York City and for others elsewhere."

Hoover replied that he wished to continue his travels directly to India and the Orient, returning to the United States in two weeks. I, of course, deferred to his wishes, but I felt that a nationwide radio appeal was necessary, and I decided to make it on April 19.

"It is my duty," I said in part, "to join my voice with the voices of humanity everywhere in behalf of the starving millions of human beings all over the world. We have a high responsibility, as Americans, to go to their rescue.

"I appointed the Famine Emergency Committee to make sure that we do all we can to help starving people. We are particularly grateful to former President Hoover for undertaking a survey of the situation in Europe. The messages he has sent back have driven home again and again the desperate plight of the people over there. We cannot doubt that at this moment many people in the famine-stricken homes of Europe and Asia are dying of hunger.

"America is faced with a solemn obligation. Long ago we promised to do our full part. Now we cannot ignore the cry of hungry children. Surely we will not turn our backs on the millions of human beings begging for just a crust of bread. The warm heart of America will respond to the greatest threat of mass starvation in the history of mankind."

Some of the immediate measures I put into effect to get grain off farms and into ships included:

(1) A government-paid bonus of thirty cents above the ceiling for each bushel of wheat delivered by farmers before May 25, and a similar bonus for fifty bushels of corn;

(2) a cut in flour milling for domestic use to seventy-five per cent of that ground in the corresponding 1945 period, the remaining twenty-five per cent to be earmarked for export;

(3) a 25 per cent reduction in use of wheat by bakers and food manufacturers; and

(4) government purchase of an unlimited amount of oatmeal and whole oats for export.

I also had the Federal Trade Commission look into the subject of wasteful trade practices in the milling and baking industries in order to guard against any unnecessary loss of life-saving grains.

On May 13 Mr. Hoover returned from his 35,000-mile trip around the world with his report on the food needs of twenty-two famine-ridden countries. The dominant need of the world, his report showed, was still cereals, particularly wheat and rice. The world grain deficit, he was able to report, had been reduced from the eleven million tons which had been the estimate at the beginning of his tour to 3,600,000 tons, but the survey showed that only constant effort could prevent mass starvation.

Mr. Hoover's report outlined a country-by-country, month-by-month minimum program of required cereal imports to the deficit and famine areas from May 1 to September 30, 1946, which was invaluable to me in planning the measures that had to be taken for the months ahead. And, too, Mr. Hoover accepted my proposal that he round out his world-wide survey by going to South America as our "food ambassador" to enlist the support of the Latin republics in the universal emergency.

These combined efforts on the part of government administrators, transportation companies, food producers and handlers, and American consumers paid off. By June 27 I was able to announce to the public that in six months the United States had shipped over five and a half million tons of bread grains to help feed the hungry people of other lands. Three weeks later we met our half-year goal of six million tons. There had been no mass starvation, but I felt compelled to warn the nation that the crisis was not past by any means. Europe was facing another winter, and it was not expected that her harvests would have much effect on the general food situation. The chief hope for survival there still seemed to depend upon America's ability and willingness to produce enough for the people of every country not yet recovered from the aftermath of the war.

The British economy was seriously hurt by the loss of her foreign markets, on which she had always depended. We used Lend-Lease in part to offset Britain's economic plight. When the temporary arrangement of Lend-Lease was terminated at the end of the war—since it was a war measure—Britain's economic difficulties became critical. Winston Churchill had on several occasions approached me with specific questions that pointed up the need for some postwar economic arrangement between the United States and Great Britain. He first suggested the financial conversations in a letter to me dated July 24, 1945, which discussed various phases of the postwar economic situation. One of these problems he brought up had to do with our decision on the munitions schedules. Our decision was that no shipments would be made hereafter except on what was needed for direct use against Japan, and "with Washington officials interpreting this in the narrowest possible sense," said Churchill, "this has reduced munitions supplies almost to the vanishing point, and has put us in a very difficult position."

He went on to say that this and other questions were linked up closely with the general postwar economic arrangements which would have to be worked out before the war ended and that he would like to send a special delegation to Washington as soon as convenient.

I replied to Churchill from Babelsberg, Germany, on July 29:

"In accordance with my letter of July 25, I enclose a copy of a memorandum directive on the issuance of Lend-Lease Munitions, which I have today sent to the Joint Chiefs of Staff. This directive eliminates the delivery of Lend-Lease material for the occupation of Axis countries. In other respects I believe it adequately covers your expressed desires.

"I have noted the suggestion in the letter of July 24, that postwar economic arrangements be discussed in Washington, say in September. Mr. W. L. Clayton, Assistant Secretary of State, will be in London shortly for the UNRRA Council meeting, and I have instructed him to engage in informal conversations with your people about these matters. When he has reported to me in Washington, we shall be able to decide upon arrangements for further discussions with your representatives."

After Attlee succeeded Churchill, he and I exchanged letters dealing with postwar financial problems. Attlee was fully informed of the discussions I had had with Churchill; nevertheless, it apparently came as a shock to the British government when on August 21 I directed that Lend-Lease should be closed out.

With the collapse of Japan on August 14 and the end of hostilities in the Pacific Theater, the purpose for which Lend-Lease had been adopted was at an end. Accordingly, on August 21, I announced that I had directed the Foreign Economic Administration to take steps immediately to discontinue all Lend-Lease operations and to notify the foreign governments receiving Lend-Lease of this action. The direction also ordered the cancellation of all outstanding contracts for Lend-Lease, except where Allied governments were willing to agree to take them over, or where it was in the interest of the United States to complete them.

Two days after the announcement, I held a press and radio conference at which questions were asked as to the reasons for the action in view of some published statements that it was a direct blow at the British government.

"That is not true at all," I said. "The reason is that the bill passed by Congress defined Lend-Lease as a weapon of war, and after we ceased to be at war it is no longer necessary. I happened to be Vice-President at the time the law was extended, and I made such a promise. I am merely living up to the promise I made as Vice-President of the United States."

The next day, August 24, Prime Minister Clement Attlee told the House of Commons that the termination of Lend-Lease had placed Great Britain in a "very serious financial position." He announced that the Earl of Halifax, Lord Keynes, and other British government experts were leaving for Washington to discuss the matter with United States officials. Winston Churchill, now the leader of His Majesty's loyal opposition, termed Attlee's statement "very grave disquieting news."

On the same day Foreign Economic Administrator Crowley emphasized that the discontinuance of Lend-Lease was not a matter of discretion with the President or himself and that British officials knew it had to end with the close of the war.

Secretary of the Treasury Vinson, in a memorandum to me on August 22, had already suggested that the end of Lend-Lease would cause certain of the Allied governments, and particularly the United Kingdom, to present special claims for financial aid. In the same note he observed that the liquidation of Lend-Lease and the negotiation of new financial arrangements to maintain a flow of essential supplies to Allied and liberated countries presented new problems to his department. Such negotiations, he pointed out, would affect the State Department, the Foreign Economic Administration, and the Treasury. He suggested, therefore, that a subcommittee be set up, with Secretary of State Byrnes, Crowley, and himself as members, to study the new problems that would arise in the aftermath of Lend-Lease and to make recommendations to the President through the Financial Council, which had been set up under the Bretton Woods legislation and in whose purview all such matters belonged. I approved Vinson's suggestion and requested that the subcommittee be organized to proceed along the lines he proposed.

With the end of Lend-Lease, the time had also come to consider dissolving the Foreign Economic Administration and redistributing its functions among the regular departments. Later in August, Secretary of the Treasury Vinson submitted to me a tentative outline for redistributing the functions of FEA. Crowley submitted a more detailed plan embodying the same suggestions. When the FEA had been formed in 1943 as a wartime agency, the move had involved a merger of all or parts of forty-three different agencies. The functions and services with which it was charged were such that they could not be stopped suddenly. A reasonable period would be required in which to effect a transfer of these functions without serious loss of efficiency in the government. Thus, when I issued an Executive Order on September 27 terminating the FEA, I stipulated that the transfer of each function should be completed not later than December 31, 1945.

As one of its last acts FEA requested the governments that had received Lend-Lease aid to furnish the United States with an inventory of the Lend-Lease materials which they had on hand on V-J Day.

From its inception in 1941 to the end of 1945, total Lend-Lease aid from this country to the Allies amounted to $46,040,000,000. Of this amount, $1,895,000,000 was shipped during the final four months of 1945. Tangible goods and services accounted for $43,952,000,000 of the total, while the remainder was for use of production facilities in the United States, for transfer to federal agencies, and for other charges and expenses. Reverse lend-lease—that is, materials furnished to the United States by other governments—during the same period amounted to something over six billion dollars. Great Britain and Russia together received ninety-four per cent of all Lend-Lease aid, with Great Britain getting by far the larger share—sixty-nine per cent. However, most of the reverse lend-lease—four billion dollars—came from Britain.

While Russia was not the chief recipient of American Lend-Lease supplies, hers certainly presented the widest variety of requirements. Our North Atlantic convoys delivered complete rolling mills, tire plants, petroleum refineries, electric power plants, railroad block-signal systems, chemical factories, railroad locomotives and cars, explosives, food, machinery, metals, trucks and other vehicles, and munitions to the Soviets, not to mention $1,647,000 worth of buttons.

The total given to Russia added up to more than eleven billion dollars. I had planned to discuss with the Russians at Potsdam some method of adjusting this huge account, but there was no opportunity except for some preliminary talks about it. The British, however, had all along been most anxious to discuss postwar financial matters, and at Potsdam, Churchill proposed that such talks be held. I had agreed to this, and Assistant

Secretary of State Will Clayton went to London to help lay the ground-work for such a conference.

These discussions with Clayton were informal and preliminary to actual negotiations. Lord Keynes, for the British, emphasized the handling of the accumulated balances of British currency frozen in various countries and the continuing problem of deficits after V-J Day. He explained that the balances were an obstacle to new borrowing and said the British believed that current sterling balances had to be made fully convertible through an adequate loan from the United States.

Clayton told the British officials that American public opinion would probably support a line of credit of three billion dollars on liberal terms if a satisfactory over-all commercial policy agreement could be reached. Such an agreement, he said, would have to include elimination of the dollar pool and cover tariffs, cartels, quotas, discrimination, and other details.

The State Department strongly supported Clayton's insistence at the outset on tying financial and commercial policy discussions together. We believed that international finance and trade were inextricably meshed and that the only chance of making a really satisfactory credit arrangement was to provide financial assistance for two or three years of transition and agree upon trade arrangements that would make for the sort of economic world in which the British and other nations would be able to service their borrowings. Our delegation at the London discussions made it clear that the British should not expect to obtain financial assistance in the form of free grants, but that the United States was prepared to extend liberal credits on moderate terms.

The so-called "United States-United Kingdom Economic Negotiations" were initiated in Washington on September 11. Heading the British delegation were Lord Keynes and Lord Halifax. The American side was represented on the "top committee" by Assistant Secretary of State Clayton and Secretary of the Treasury Vinson. The "top committee" set up the committee structure for the negotiations. This structure included a financial committee to handle the monetary questions.

From the beginning of the discussions of the financial committee there was general agreement that the United States must furnish substantial aid to Great Britain in order to enable the latter nation to base its foreign economic policy on a multilateral basis rather than upon a sterling bloc arrangement. There was no agreement, however, on (1) the facts of the British position, (2) the amount of the line of credit which the United States should offer in order to improve this position, (3) the terms of repayment on which the line of credit should be offered, and (4) the other terms that should be tied to the credit.

Negotiations on these matters required the attention of the financial committee from late September to early December, even though the British delegation was more willing to make concessions than the London conversations had indicated. Secretary of the Treasury Vinson kept me currently informed on the progress of these talks.

Our technical experts thought that the British had overstated the seriousness of the United Kingdom's financial position. The British estimated a deficit in the balance of payments of $3,100,000,000 at the end of 1946, but the American estimate was only $2,300,000,000; and where the British predicted a deficit of five to six billion dollars by the end of 1948, the American estimate was only $3,300,000,000. Our representatives also arrived at a higher figure than that given by the British officials for the United Kingdom's gold and dollar holdings as of June 30, 1945. The true financial status of our chief ally was therefore never agreed upon, although it was obviously serious.

It took several months before agreement was reached on the amount of the loan. Lord Keynes stated on September 20 that the minimum aid which his country needed from the United States was five billion dollars and that six billion would be a safer amount. There was a difference of opinion, however, within the United States delegation. Assistant Secretary of State Clayton recommended four billion dollars, while Secretary of the Treasury Vinson believed that $3,100,000,000 should be the maximum amount offered in view of the British statement that payments to service the credit could not exceed $100,000,000 a year. He wrote to me that he did not feel we were justified in giving the British a fifty-year loan without interest, which is what they were asking.

After protracted negotiations the American delegation agreed on a figure of $3,500,000,000 as a fair minimum and four billion dollars as a maximum to be offered. It was in the final stages of the conference that I decided upon a figure halfway between these two positions—$3,750,-000,000. Although Lord Keynes had written Secretary Vinson that the United Kingdom "could not successfully implement the clauses" most desired by the United States in the final agreements with less than four billion dollars, the British delegation accepted $3,750,000,000 when it became apparent that we would go no higher.

The terms of the loan were fixed at two per cent per annum by the American delegation. The British had requested that two billion dollars of the loan be interest-free, with the remainder repayable at two per cent, but the American delegation adhered to its early decision that the line of credit should not be interest-free. However, the inclusion of a five-year grace period before the beginning of interest payments in reality reduced the interest rate to 1.63 per cent. A further concession to Great Britain was an agreement to waive payment of interest for any year in which that government should prove, in terms of a predetermined formula, that it was unable to pay.

Other matters agreed upon before the conclusion of the twelve-week conference included an advance of $672,000,000 to Great Britain to enable her to wind up Lend-Lease operations, a commitment by the United Kingdom to proceed at once to reduce the amount of her debt (between three and four million pounds) to sterling bloc countries, and a promise by the British to back a multilateral trade program in subsequent negotiations.

At the close of the Anglo-American financial talks there was some misgiving expressed on both sides of the Atlantic. There was criticism that the loan was insufficient and criticism that it was extravagant, and Uncle Sam was cartooned both as Santa Claus and as Shylock. It was a transaction that called for a good deal of understanding of all the factors involved, and it represented a crucial stage in British-American relations, particularly in so far as public opinion on both sides was concerned.

The significance of these financial agreements, as I mentioned in my State of the Union message to the Congress on January 21, 1946, was that they would contribute to easing the transition problems of one of our major partners in the war.

My view was that, in the long run, our economic prosperity and the prosperity of the whole world were best served by the elimination of artificial barriers to international trade, whether in the form of unreasonable tariffs or tariff preferences or commercial quotas or embargoes on the restrictive practices of cartels.

On January 30, in a special message to the Congress, I urged prompt passage of the required legislation to make available the funds necessary to extend the line of credit to Great Britain. I defined the position of the financial agreement as one more achievement in carrying out the spirit of the Bretton Woods Agreements Act which the Seventy-ninth Congress had passed and which President Roosevelt had called "the cornerstone for international economic co-operation."

The British loan bill reached my desk on July 15, 1946. I signed it into law on that date, with the statement that "the loan serves our immediate and long-range interests by helping to restore world trade. At the same time it enables Great Britain to cooperate in creating a pattern of mutually beneficial economic relations among the nations of the world."

I made it clear that this agreement between the United States and Great Britain was in no way directed against any other country. The system of trade we sought was open on the same fair terms to all the United Nations.

CHAPTER 31

The conduct of the war and the management of foreign affairs had crowded into my life with such speed and insistence that I could not find all the time I needed to devote to domestic matters.

The San Francisco conference, the surrender of Germany, the Potsdam conference, the birth of the atomic age, the surrender of Japan—all these transpired within a period of just four months.

All the immediate domestic problems of converting back to a peace economy had to be taken care of in the midst of these and other events of major significance that followed the collapse of the Axis. Each of these events, even for a President who had been in office for many years, would have been a time-consuming job requiring weeks of preparation and consultation.

For me, who had been suddenly catapulted into the midst of world-shaking episodes, who had to learn about the past at the same time that I had to act for the present and plan for the future, too little time was left for long-range domestic planning.

On September 6, 1945, I sent to the Congress one of the most important messages of my administration. It contained the twenty-one points of domestic legislation which, in effect, constituted the platform of my administration.

This twenty-one-point message marked the beginning of the "Fair Deal," and September 6, 1945, is the date that symbolizes for me my assumption of the office of President in my own right. It was on that day and with this message that I first spelled out the details of the program of liberalism and progressivism which was to be the foundation of my administration. It was my opportunity as President to advocate the political principles and economic philosophy which I had expressed in the Senate and which I had followed all my political life.

In a sense, my twenty-one-point message was like a combination of a first inaugural and a first State of the Union message—it was to set the tone and direction for the rest of my administration and the goals toward which I would try to lead the nation. In my senatorial experience I had followed the leadership and the political and economic program of Franklin Roosevelt. I had campaigned and been elected on Roosevelt's platform. As a delegate to the Democratic convention I had helped to write the platform of 1944. Now it became my responsibility to lead—to recommend legislation, to administer the government, and to use the prestige and power of the presidency to induce sound social and political action.

I had given these matters considerable thought during my first four months in office, even though war matters and foreign-policy problems had occupied most of my time. I actually started work on this comprehensive program while I was on my way home from the Potsdam conference. Judge Samuel I. Rosenman, the counsel to the President, had joined me at the conference and, returning home with me, was helping me prepare my report to the Congress and to the nation on the recently adjourned Big Three conference. One evening in my cabin aboard the *Augusta,* as I was putting the finishing touches on my report, I said to Rosenman:

"Sam, one of the first things I want to do after we get home and make this report is to get busy on my domestic program. I would like to submit most of it at the same time instead of on a piecemeal basis. Ordinarily that would be done in a State of the Union message next January, but I cannot wait that long. What I think I will do is to send up a message as soon as we can get one up. Will you start to get together the material and perhaps get up a rough draft?"

Judge Rosenman had been counsel to Franklin Roosevelt as governor and as President, and his personal friend and adviser for almost two decades. He was familiar with the facts and the philosophy of the New Deal, and I had persuaded him to stay on with me as counsel to the President.

"Fine," he replied. "What in general are the things you would like to say?" And he reached for a pencil and pad. I reviewed to him my views on the social and economic problems that had faced the nation before the collapse of the early thirties, and my views on the measures which the Roosevelt administration had taken for economic recovery and social reform. I spoke then of my own plans and policies for future legislation—

the general direction in which I thought the United States ought to go in the years after the war. As we discussed these long-range policies and the legislation I was suggesting to carry them out, Rosenman leaned forward.

"You know, Mr. President," he said eagerly, "this is the most exciting and pleasant surprise I have had in a long time."

"How is that?" I asked.

"Well," he replied, "I suppose I have been listening too much to rumors about what you are going to do—rumors which come from some of your conservative friends, and particularly from some of your former colleagues up on Capitol Hill. They say you are going to be quite a shock to those who followed Roosevelt—that the New Deal is as good as dead —that we are all going back to 'normalcy' and that a good part of the so-called 'Roosevelt nonsense' is now over. In other words, that the conservative wing of the party has now taken charge. I never really believed any of that in view of your long voting record in the Senate—on the basis of which President Roosevelt was so anxious that you become the vice-presidential candidate, just in case anything happened to him.

"But this seems to settle it," he continued. "This really sets forth a progressive political philosophy and a liberal program of action that will fix the theme for your whole term in office. It is one thing to vote for this kind of a program when you are following the head of your party; it is quite another to be the head of a party and recommend and fight for it."

My attention to the framing of this important message, however, was interrupted by the sudden capitulation of Japan and the international problems that were involved. It was not until the end of August that I could get around to it again. By that time Rosenman had prepared a rough draft, and it had been on my desk for several days. It was a good beginning, too, and I worked on it for ten days—adding sections, eliminating some points, and editing the document thoroughly. I sent the final revised version to the printer, and when the galley proofs were ready I called Clark Clifford, John Steelman, John Snyder, Charlie Ross, and several other advisers. With Rosenman, we went over the proofs point by point, and many suggestions were made, some of which were adopted. Then I had the corrected proofs sent to the various agencies and Cabinet members for their comments. In this manner I gave all the major officers in the executive branch a voice in the formulation of the message.

Most of my advisers agreed with the message, but some of my more conservative associates advised me against this definite commitment to such liberal measures. One of these was John Snyder, who at that time was Director of War Mobilization and Reconversion. Privately he expressed his disagreement to me in the frankest and most explicit terms. But his loyalty and friendship for me kept him from voicing any public opposition. I listened very carefully to Snyder's advice, for it has always been my policy to hear all sides on every question before coming to a decision, and now I listened particularly because of the high regard I had for Snyder's judgment.

Early in my administration I set out to achieve a balance between conservative and liberal points of view among the members of my Cabinet and other advisers. I wanted to be exposed to opposite poles of opinion in forming my own conclusions and making my own decisions on basic policy matters. With this in mind I listened to various objections to the contents of the message, but I saw little reason to change it. On September 6—four days after my proclamation of V-J Day—I sent the twenty-one points up to the Congress.

I considered the time of Congress' reconvening as one of great emergency, as I stated at the beginning of the message. Reconversion from a wartime economy to one of peace raised great problems, and in the message I outlined the policy that had been laid down for re-establishing an expanded peacetime industry, trade, and agriculture as quickly as possible. I stated that I would follow eight specific policies:

(1) Demobilize as soon as possible the armed forces no longer needed;

(2) cancel and settle war contracts as quickly as possible;

(3) clear the war plants in order to permit contracts to proceed with peacetime production;

(4) hold the line on prices and rents until fair competition could operate to prevent inflation and undue hardship on consumers;

(5) hold wages in line where their increase would cause inflationary price rises;

(6) remove all possible wartime government controls in order to speed and encourage reconversion and expansion;

(7) keep only those controls that were necessary to help reconversion and expansion by preventing bottlenecks, shortages of material, and inflation; and

(8) prevent rapid decrease of wage incomes or purchasing power.

This was an ambitious program, and to show that it was not unrealistic I described in detail each of the twenty-one points and the legislative steps required to carry out the policies.

One of the key items in the program was the recommendation for a national reassertion of the right to work for every American citizen able and willing to work. It was a declaration of the ultimate duty of government to use all of its resources if supply-and-demand methods should fail to prevent prolonged unemployment. I felt that in normal times we had to look first to private enterprise to provide jobs and that the government should do all it could to inspire enterprise with confidence. But that confidence, I emphasized in the message, would have to come mainly from deeds, not words.

I asked for speedy action on the full-employment legislation to assure sustained confidence in our economy and prosperity. And I recommended legislation that would provide the machinery for a continuous full-employment policy based on the co-operation of industry, agriculture, and labor, and between the Congress and the Chief Executive, and between the people and their government.

I was convinced that along with full employment there had to be equal opportunity for all races, religions, and colors. This fundamental of our political philosophy should also be an integral part of our economy. The Fair Employment Practices Committee, which had operated during the war, was continuing through the transition period. I had already requested legislation placing this committee on a permanent basis, and I repeated that recommendation in the twenty-one-point message.

This was one of the lengthiest messages that a President had ever sent to the Congress. Containing approximately sixteen thousand words, it was the longest one since 1901, when Theodore Roosevelt had addressed the Congress with a twenty-thousand-word message. I did not attempt to deliver it in person but had printed copies sent to every member of the House and the Senate. The actual reading of the message was done by reading clerks in both Houses.

On October 4, 1945, I sent a letter to various Cabinet members and agency heads, assigning to each specific responsibility for legislative measures necessary to carry out those portions of the message that properly fell within the department or agency affected. I asked from each a brief report on current developments on the first and fifteenth day of each month.

The message, in its formal proposals and in its language, contained the rudiments of the Fair Deal program. But within ten weeks after it was read before the Congress I sent up several more messages, each adding new recommendations to be included in the Fair Deal. The new elements dealt with health insurance and prepaid medical care, nationalization of atomic energy, the development of the St. Lawrence seaway project, and federal aid to education.

The proposals I submitted in my first comprehensive domestic message were designed to be as liberal and as far-reaching as the prewar 1940 Democratic campaign. I was also determined to carry out the campaign pledges of 1944 to which Roosevelt and I were committed.

This legislative program promulgated in 1945 became the domestic goal of the administration. It was a reminder to the Democratic party, to the country, and to the Congress that progress in government lies along the road of sound reform in our private-enterprise system and that progressive democracy has to continue to keep pace with changing conditions.

High on my list of priorities in the reconversion program was organizing the machinery of government to meet the new needs and responsibilities that had arisen. I had realized long before I became President that a reorganization of the executive branch was desirable and, in some respects, necessary. Common sense told me that a better-organized executive branch would operate more efficiently. History records many instances of former Presidents urging the Congress to provide the necessary legislation to make the executive branch operate along more efficient lines. My own experience had already demonstrated to me that substantial progress could be made in this respect through action initiated by the President.

The Reorganization Act of 1939 provided a method for improving the organization of the executive branch of the government and of the executive agencies. This act enabled the President to initiate improvements and changes subject only to disapproval by each of the two Houses of Congress within a period of sixty days. There was also the First War Powers Act of 1941, which empowered the President to make necessary adjustments in the organization of the executive branch in relation to the conduct of the war. These two pieces of legislation provided the basis for many of the changes which President Roosevelt made during the war years.

The problem I now faced was that the First War Powers Act would expire automatically six months after the end of the war. I saw the need for legislation generally similar to the Reorganization Act of 1939 that would be of a permanent character and broad enough to include all executive departments and agencies, yet flexible enough to permit any form of adjustment that might be necessary.

On May 24, 1945, I had sent a message to Congress requesting such legislation. I was advised by congressional leaders in June that action on my proposal would be delayed until the Congress had reconvened in the fall. In my message to the Congress of September 6, therefore, I again pointed out the urgent need for increased presidential authority over executive agencies. After some debate in both the House and the Senate, most of which concerned the exemption of specified agencies from the provisions of the act, a compromise bill was sent to me, and I signed it on December 20.

I had already issued executive orders abolishing a number of the wartime agencies. Many of these had been created by executive orders and were scheduled to terminate at the end of the war or at the President's pleasure. Included in the list of the agencies terminated were the National War Labor Board, the Foreign Economic Administration, the War Production Board, the Office of Economic Stabilization, the Office of Censorship, the Office of Defense Transportation, the Office of War Information, the Petroleum Administration for War, and the War Shipping Administration. Others were retained for specially needed services during the reconversion period.

One problem with which I was particularly concerned in regard to strengthening the executive branch had to do with the existing vacancy in the office of the Vice-President. I felt that the law governing the order of succession to the office of Chief Executive needed to be changed so that only an elective official of the government might succeed to the presidency upon the death of the President or his inability to fill the post. Under the Presidential Succession Act of 1886, the Secretary of State was next in line after the President and Vice-President. Other members of the Cabinet then followed in order under that law. Since the members of the Cabinet are all presidential appointees, the law gave me the power to appoint my own successor until a new Vice-President could be elected almost four years later. This is a power which I believe no President ought to possess.

Inasmuch as the President and Vice-President are the only officers of the government elected by all the voters of the United States, I felt that the Speaker of the House of Representatives most nearly represents selection by the people, because, as a member of the House, he is elected to the Congress by the voters of his district, and as Speaker, he is chosen by a majority of the representatives from all of the states. Accordingly, I had recommended a bill providing for these changes early in my administration. It was passed by the House on June 29, 1945, but it failed to pass the Senate. Finally the bill passed and became law. I believe some way should be found to elect a successor to the Vice-President when he takes over the office of President. It seems to me that presidential electors or the House of Representatives could function in such an election. I think the electors would probably do a better job of it.

But as we were shaping our plans to tighten up the executive branch, we had to deal with the major problem of inflation. Four days after the surrender of Japan I had issued what amounted to a declaration of war against this new enemy of the United States. In an Executive Order on August 18, 1945, I set forth the guiding policies of the administration for stabilizing the economy during the reconversion period.

The order, which had its authority in the Emergency Price Control Act of 1942 and the Stabilization Act of the same year, called upon the Office of Price Administration and the Secretary of Agriculture to work directly with the Director of Economic Stabilization to take all the steps necessary to keep the cost of living and the general level of prices from going up. I proposed several specific measures for combating both inflationary and deflationary influences.

The fact was that the administration was not seeking more government controls, but fewer. In a radio address on October 30 I made the statement that we should drop as quickly as practicable wartime government controls and that we must get back to the free operation of our competitive system. I made it clear that the only workable alternative to government price controls was the wholehearted co-operation of business, labor, industry, agriculture, the Congress, and the American public. We were ready to go along with a concerted voluntary program to fight inflation rather than resort to the use of controls. Inflationary pressures were still great, and danger signals were pointing to a further building up through the winter and spring.

By December it was obvious that decontrol of prices would not work, at least until the emergency was less threatening. When the Second War Powers Act was extended for six months by the Congress during the last week of December, this brief extension would not meet the full needs. The economy was certain to be plagued by war-born shortages for a considerable time, and I urged further legislation to cover the period after June 30, 1946.

Despite the promises that had been made for the co-operation and teamwork of all parties involved in holding the line against inflation, I had to report to the Congress in my radio talk to the people on January 3, 1946, that not all these promises had been kept. It would be necessary to extend price and rent controls before their expiration date, June 30. In that message I sounded the warning that pressure groups were at work in the Congress and outside, constantly pushing, lobbying, and arguing for the end of price controls regardless of the consequences.

Realizing that price-control adjustments would be necessary in certain cases where the Price Administrator should find that an industry was in a position of real hardship as a consequence of an approved increase in wages or salaries, I issued an Executive Order on February 14 that permitted such temporary adjustments. It was my desire to be fair to all sides, and the purpose of this order was to allow producers to increase prices in those instances where an increase was justifiable. This was an emergency increase only and required the joint approval of the Price Administrator, the Director of Economic Stabilization, and the Director of War Mobilization and Reconversion.

The Office of Economic Stabilization had been abolished soon after the end of the war, but the growing economic problems made it necessary that I re-establish that wartime agency. On February 25 I signed the order calling it back into being and charged it with the responsibility for the administration of the government's wage and price policy. Chester Bowles resigned as head of OPA to become Director of the Office of Economic Stabilization, and Paul Porter succeeded him as Price Administrator.

The obstructionist tactics of special privilege groups continued to impede our natural reconversion to stable prices. I understood their methods and their objectives from the beginning and tried to expose them at every opportunity. In an address to the Federal Council of Churches of Christ in America, which I made at Columbus, Ohio, on March 6, I said, "If certain interests were not so greedy for gold, there would be less pressure and lobbying to induce the Congress to allow the Price Control Act to expire, or to keep down minimum wages, or to permit further concentration of economic power." These were strong words, but they were true.

As the date of expiration of the law drew nearer, I made another appeal in a public statement on April 3 for early extension of price control and for stabilization laws, which were desperately needed. Without them, I warned, our progress would be turned into economic chaos. However, the bill which Congress was then writing would not work. It would, in fact, throw the doors wide open to inflation. Nevertheless, the House passed it, and it seemed destined for Senate approval as well.

Chester Bowles, who had supported me in my opposition to this "amended" price-control legislation, flatly charged that under the new bill effective control of prices and rents would be impossible. He submitted his resignation as Director of the Office of Economic Stabilization on June 28, stating, as one of his reasons, "Clearly I could not remain here in any event to administer the inflationary bill which the Congress is about to present for your signature."

"In accepting your resignation," I replied in part, "I want to assure you, and at the same time every American, that this administration will never give up the fight. We shall continue the battle against inflation with every weapon at our disposal, and shall not rest until this country has reached permanent high levels of production, prosperity and employment."

On June 29 I vetoed House Resolution 6042 amending the price-control laws and extending them for another year. I did so because under this bill it was not a choice between continued price stability and inflation, but a choice between inflation with a statute and inflation without one.

My fundamental objection to the bill was to the numerous amendments that would raise the price of essential cost-of-living commodities. The most damaging of these was the price-raising amendment for manufacturers introduced by Senator Taft and operating in conjunction with the revised price-raising amendment for distributors introduced by Senator Wherry. While giving the delusion of protection, the bill would permit prices to pyramid spectacularly, thus providing a sure formula for inflation.

Reminding the Congress that since September 6, 1945, I had continued to request an extension of price-control legislation without crippling amendments, I now asked on behalf of the American people a resolution by the Congress continuing the current controls for the short period of time necessary to write a workable bill. I also explained to the nation by radio my reasons for considering this bill inadequate. I announced that I had submitted to the Congress a plan for price-control legislation which we regarded as fair and effective. I called upon every businessman, every producer, and every landlord to adhere to existing regulations even though for a short period they might not have the effect of law. I also requested every employee of the OPA to stay at his battle station and continue the effort to make price control a success until the Congress adopted the kind of bill that could be made to work.

It was necessary for me to issue an Executive Order on July 1 providing for the continuation of certain functions and powers of the OPA which did not terminate with the expiration of the Price Control and Stabilization Acts. These functions and powers were delegated under Title III of the Second War Powers Act, which was, of course, still in effect. The order did not cover prices or rents.

I was asked at a press conference held on July 17 for a group of editors and executives of the McGraw-Hill Publishing Company if I thought that the figures of rising prices since July 1 had borne out the predictions I had made in my veto speech. I replied that, according to the figures in the New York *Journal of Commerce,* it was very conclusively proven. I stated that I was sure that prices were going higher unless we got an OPA bill soon.

What had actually happened was revealed in a report to me from the Bureau of Labor Statistics. As a result of the price spurt following the failure of the Congress to renew the Price Control Act, the index of prices had risen twenty-five per cent during the first sixteen days of July. Steel scrap, copper, tin, rubber, burlap, and sugar were the only commodities in the index to show no price change since June 28. Most of these commodities, however, had their prices set by the government; without them, the index showed an increase of thirty-five per cent in prices for all twenty-eight commodities listed.

On July 25 I signed a new act which extended the price-control law for another year, but I sent a message to the Congress explaining that I was approving the bill with reluctance. While it corrected some of the graver abuses of the Taft-Wherry amendments, it still fell far short of giving the government the necessary machinery for assuring the stability of prices. It was, nevertheless, a better bill than the one I had vetoed.

The threat of inflation not only presented one of the biggest domestic problems during the reconversion period, but it also created other economic conditions which caused me a great deal of concern. I was especially anxious about the effect which the attitude of several business groups toward price and rent control might have on production and employment.

I knew that full production would be our greatest weapon against inflation. But if manufacturers and producers chose to hold back goods and products in anticipation of higher prices, which inevitably prevail in postwar periods, they would slow down production and create needless unemployment.

That was my reason for requesting, in the twenty-one-point message to the Congress on September 6, 1945, full-employment legislation. My objective was to carry out, during the reconversion period, the economic bill of rights which had been formulated by President Roosevelt.

By full employment I meant the opportunity to get a good peacetime job for every worker who was ready, able, and willing to take one. Making jobs, or making people work, was in no sense a part of the full-employment program. I did feel, however, that it was the responsibility of the government to inspire private enterprise with confidence by giving assurances that all the facts about full employment and opportunity would be gathered periodically for the use of all; assurance of stability and consistency in public policy, so that enterprise could plan better by knowing what the government intended to do; assurance that every governmental policy and program would be pointed to promote maximum production and employment in private enterprise; and assurance that priority would be given to doing those things first which stimulated normal employment most.

When I first proposed full-employment legislation, it was with the thought that we might have from two to eight million people out of work in this country, if the pattern of the 1920's was any guide. No one really knew what would happen as far as American production and employment were concerned. But I wanted to exert every effort to prevent the terrible unemployment experiences of past decades.

The full-employment item was one of the twenty-one points on which I particularly wanted swift action, because the problem promised to grow as soon as wartime production was curtailed and demobilization was stepped up. I urged John McCormack, the House majority leader, to speed the bill along, as the following letter indicates:

October 29, 1945

Dear John:

I am most anxious that the House Committee on Expenditures of Executive Departments report out the Full Employment legislation. Such legislation is of the utmost urgency and importance to the future of our nation.

I feel sure that the people in every state of the Union are for this kind of measure and are looking to their Congress to act.

It is already two and a half months since Japan surrendered. Reconversion of our plant to peacetime production is well along. The future is rushing toward us.

It is not enough to make a transition to temporary prosperity. We cannot repeat the mistakes made after the last war. This time we must build on a more solid foundation. We must take those steps now that will move us with firm purpose toward full employment and keep us there.

There are some who say, "Let's wait and see what happens." Such a course would be the height of recklessness. We must look ahead. If we wait for protracted mass unemployment to come upon us, we face another disaster. To no major situation has it been more applicable that "an ounce of prevention is worth a pound of cure."

It is time that the people be reassured by the Congress that the government stands for full employment, full production and prosperity, not unemployment and relief.

I have talked to hundreds of workers and hundreds of our veterans. These men and women who have worked and fought to defend our American institutions expect us to take the steps necessary to translate their victory on the battlefield to peacetime jobs with security and opportunity.

Full employment legislation has the firm and complete support of my administration. The Senate has already passed such legislation, and I am sure that the House will want to make its position clear to the American people at the first possible opportunity.

I do not refer to any specific bill. I refer to the general purposes and principles of full employment legislation.

If this legislation could be reported out of committee so that it could be passed by the Congress by Thanksgiving, it would give that day particular significance for millions of American families who remember only too well the dark days of the depression, and want reassurance that we shall never again have another 1932.

Very sincerely,
Harry S. Truman

I was able to report at my November 29 press conference that total employment had already returned to the V-J Day level, after the greatest part of layoffs from war plants had been completed. Unemployment was so far less than had been expected, and employment in non-war activities was increasing at a satisfactory rate. Three and a half million men and women had been demobilized, and ninety-three per cent of our plants had been reconverted from wartime to peacetime production.

By January 1946 the picture was even brighter. Despite numerous strikes and lockouts, fifty-two million workers were already employed in civilian jobs. With full employment calculated by some at 53,500,000 jobs, it seemed that this goal would be reached much sooner than had been expected. There were still two million unemployed, but these represented no more than the fractional unemployment percentage which the country would have even with full employment.

The real problem was not how to *achieve* full employment. It was how to *maintain* it. That was the purpose of the Employment Act of 1946, which I signed on February 20.

While the full-employment bill had undergone some considerable changes in the process of being shaped into law, it still retained the essential features of my original proposal. The bill made it the responsibility of the federal government to co-ordinate and utilize all its plans, functions, and resources for the purpose of maintaining conditions under which there would be afforded useful employment opportunities, including self-employment, for those seeking to work.

The act included a significant provision to facilitate co-operation between the Executive and the Congress in the formulation of policies and to accomplish the purpose of the act. It established a joint congressional committee consisting of seven members of the Senate and seven members of the House to study and report to the Congress on the President's recommendations regarding the employment program.

While the measure was concerned primarily with the problems of unemployment and economic depression, one of its major provisions authorized the establishment of a Council of Economic Advisers within the Executive Office of the President. The job of the three-man council was to help the administration decide what the government should do to help the nation's economy function smoothly and prosperously. The council was also assigned the duty of assisting and advising the President in the preparation of an economic report to be submitted to the Congress within sixty days after the beginning of each regular session.

Even before passage of the act, I had discussed plans for the economic council with the Director of the Bureau of the Budget, with whom the council would, of course, have to work very closely. But it was not until July 1946 that the membership was named. I appointed Dr. John Davidson Clark, Leon H. Keyserling, and Edwin G. Nourse, the latter to act as chairman.

Dr. Clark came to the White House from the University of Nebraska, where he had been dean of the School of Business Administration. He had had a long career as a lawyer and had been a vice-president of the Standard Oil Company of Indiana.

Leon Keyserling was a product of the New Deal. A Harvard law graduate, he had come to Washington in 1933, first as a lawyer with the AAA. At the time of his appointment to the Council of Economic Advisers he was the general counsel of the National Housing Agency.

Dr. Nourse was the vice-president of the Brookings Institution, a distinguished and highly respected research organization in Washington. Earlier he had spent several years teaching economics and agricultural economics in the Middle West.

These were eminently qualified men. They differed greatly in point of view and, in the years ahead, were to disagree sharply. I knew this when I appointed them. I believe that I was well advised in their selection by the very fact that they were not all of one mind.

In accordance with the provisions of the act, I transmitted an economic message at the beginning of each regular session of Congress. We fully realized that neither this legislation nor the machinery it established would automatically give the nation full employment and full production, or full protection from economic depression. That was a goal that could be achieved only by the concerted efforts of all segments of our society in co-operation with the government. But the full-employment act did give us a clear-cut declaration of national policy to enable us to attain many of our desired objectives. It gave positive expression to a deep-seated desire of the American people for a sustained attack upon the perennial problem of mass unemployment.

A proposed statement by Secretary of the Treasury Fred Vinson for my use in connection with the signing of the Employment Act of 1946, which I did not use at the time, but which is still in my files, contains the following paragraph, which reflects the hope and the confidence with which I regarded this legislation:

"Occasionally, as we pore through the pages of history, we are struck by the fact that some incident, little noted at the time, profoundly affects the whole subsequent course of events. I venture the prediction that history, someday, will so record the enactment of the Employment Act of 1946."

CHAPTER 32

Labor unrest is inevitable in a free economy; it is part of the struggle for adjustment to shifting economic conditions. The labor unrest that developed during the closing months of the war and mushroomed into violence during the early period of my administration presented one of the most difficult and persistent of all the domestic problems I faced as President of the United States.

My attitude toward labor had consistently been one of sympathy and support. This is evident in my voting record in the Senate over a period of ten years. And later, as Vice-President and then as Chief Executive, I was deeply aware of the serious problems that were certain to confront labor when the war came to an end and during the period of industrial reconversion that followed.

With the return of millions of servicemen to the ranks of labor, the workers in industry and business were faced with redeployment of manpower, with reductions in overtime pay, curtailment of wartime production, and the consequent threat of competition for jobs. Questions of seniority rights came to be involved with the rights of veterans returning to their jobs. And under these new conditions many disputes arose— many of them legitimate—regarding wage increases commensurate with increased profits and with rising costs of living in the postwar period.

These were real problems, affecting one of the largest segments of our population. I always favored pay increases and other benefits where they could be effected without raising prices and encouraging inflation. I worked to restore to labor the free collective bargaining process of which it had been deprived during the war years. But it was also my responsibility as Chief Executive to see that the public was not injured by private fights between labor and management or among the unions themselves. I intervened in these disputes only when it became apparent that the economic welfare or security of the nation as a whole was jeopardized.

Such action on my part was first made necessary just eighteen days after I took the oath of office as President, when on April 30, 1945, John L. Lewis ordered seventy-two thousand anthracite coal miners out on strike after efforts to obtain a satisfactory contract with the mine operators had failed. As Commander in Chief, I viewed any stoppages in any of the basic industries as direct threats to the war effort and the national security. On May 3 I issued an Executive Order placing the affected mines under the temporary possession and control of the Department of the Interior.

The coal strike in May of 1945 was only the beginning. Even though Lewis accepted a compromise agreement from the operators for a daily wage increase of $1.37½ for the anthracite miners, work stoppages persisted in the form of absenteeism and repeated wildcat strikes. By the middle of summer we lost more than twelve million tons of coal.

I was gravely concerned about the coal situation in Europe, and in June I sent a message to Prime Minister Churchill:

"The coal famine which threatens Europe this coming winter has impressed me with the great urgency of directing our military authorities in Germany to exert every effort to increase German coal production and to furnish for export the whole quantity over and above minimum German needs.

"From all the reports which reach me, I believe that without immediate concentration on the production of German coal we will have turmoil and unrest in the very areas of western Europe on which the whole stability of the continent depends.

"Similar representation should be made to France and Belgium to take drastic steps to increase their production within their own boundaries.

"I, therefore, propose to send the following directive to General Eisenhower. Before dispatching it I should like to have your agreement that a similar directive will be sent by you to General Montgomery.

"I am sending a similar communication to the Provisional French Government to cover the production in the Saar region. . . .

"QUOTE: Directive to the American Commander in Chief in Europe.

"Unless large quantities of coal are made available to liberated Europe in forthcoming months, there is grave danger of such political and economic chaos as to prejudice the redeployment of Allied troops and to jeopardize the achievement of the restoration of economic stability which is the necessary basis for a firm and just peace. Coal for western Europe in adequate quantities cannot, as a practical matter, be obtained from any source other than Germany. It is a matter of great urgency that Germany be made to produce for export to other European nations the coal which they must have to support economic life on at least a minimum basis.

"You are therefore directed, in your capacity of Commanding General of United States Forces in Germany and as United States member of the Allied Control Council, to take all steps necessary to achieve the following objectives:

"To make available for export from Germany out of the production of the coal mines in western Germany, a minimum of 10 million tons of coal during 1945, and a further 15 million tons by the end of April 1946 . . . subordinate only to requirements necessary to ensure the safety, security, health, maintenance and operation of the occupying forces and the speedy redeployment of the Allied Forces from Germany. . . .

"It is recognized that the carrying out of the above policies with respect to German coal may cause unemployment, unrest and dissatisfaction among Germans of a magnitude which may necessitate firm and rigorous action. Any action required to control the situation will be fully supported. UNQUOTE."

On July 27 I sent the following letter to Marshal Stalin, enclosing the same directive, seeking a common policy with respect to the coal crisis:

"An acute coal famine threatens Europe this winter unless German coal in substantial quantities can be made available for export. Despite our own shortage of coal, internal transportation and ocean shipping, we are now shipping coal to Europe as an emergency measure in order to provide some relief in the present crisis. It is obvious, however, that with our large commitment of industrial and military resources in the war against Japan, the quantities of coal which we can make available to Europe will be inadequate to cover pressing European needs. To meet these needs all possible measures should immediately be taken to increase coal production in Germany and to make the maximum quantities available for export.

"In order to avoid delay, I have directed the United States Commander in Chief to take the necessary measures in his zone of occupation. I understand that the British and French Governments have issued similar directives to their respective commanders in Germany. A copy of the directive to General Eisenhower is attached.

"I am most anxious that a common policy in respect to coal should be followed by the four occupying powers, and I have therefore instructed General Eisenhower to discuss the policy set forth in the above directive at the Allied Control Council at the earliest possible date. I trust that the Soviet Government will see their way to joining with us in this policy. It is my hope that they will be prepared to instruct their commander in chief to take similar action in the portions of Germany occupied by the Soviet forces, and to proceed with the formulation in the Control Council of a coal production and export program for Germany as a whole."

Stalin's reply came two days later:

"I have received your memorandum of July 27 concerning German coal and a copy of your directive to General Eisenhower.

"The important question set forth in your memorandum concerning the use of German coal to satisfy European needs will be subject to appropriate study. The Government of the United States will be informed of the point of view of the Soviet Government on this question.

"I must however state that we should avoid a situation arising whereby the taking of measures on the export of German coal would lead to any disturbances in Germany, concerning which mention is made in your directive to General Eisenhower—and this seems to me fully possible and necessary from the point of view of the interests of the Allied Governments."

By the autumn of 1945 the labor situation in the United States was assuming serious proportions. Strikes were spreading once more through the coal mines, until twenty-eight thousand miners were idle. The issue this time involved union demands for recognition as collective bargaining agents for supervisory employees. Walkouts in the oil and lumber industries were crippling the reconversion program. In the Detroit area, labor disturbances were halting automobile production in one plant after another, culminating in the United Automobile Workers' strike against General Motors. This was the first strike of such magnitude following the war and involved 175,000 workers and plants in nineteen states. Strikes were also threatening the steel industry and the railroads. In scores of smaller industries in various parts of the country strikes were widespread and occasionally violent during the latter half of 1945.

While I realized that these turbulent conditions were largely a manifestation of labor's readjustment from wartime to peacetime economy, it was also clear to me that the time had come for action on the part of the government. I had decided long before becoming President that the country needed a national wage policy, effective mediation machinery, and other remedial legislation which would protect the rightful interests of labor, of management, and of the public.

Under the Smith-Connally Act of 1943 I had the authority as President to seize for government operation essential strike-bound industries, and I invoked the law in a number of cases. But it was not adequate legislation, because it provided no means to prevent strikes and had the undesirable effect in some instances of dramatizing strike threats. Even the co-author of the bill, Representative Howard W. Smith of Virginia, proposed repeal of the act in October of 1945.

The increasing labor difficulties of the postwar period were the subject of many discussions with the Cabinet in meetings during October and November 1945. I decided to invite the leaders of labor and management to meet in Washington to work out a new approach toward solving the industrial crisis.

I sent letters to William Green, president of the American Federation of Labor; Ira Mosher, president of the National Association of Manufacturers; Philip Murray, president of the Congress of Industrial Organizations; and Eric Johnston, president of the United States Chamber of Commerce. Thirty-six delegates were appointed to represent the interests of both labor and management, and a conference got under way in the Labor Department auditorium on November 5.

I opened the conference with an appeal to the delegates to set up among themselves a definite policy in the field of labor relations. I recommended that such a policy be based on four fundamentals: (1) genuine collective bargaining; (2) use of impartial machinery for reaching decisions where bargaining fails; (3) peaceful negotiation of contracts and methods of peaceful adjustment of disputes arising under these agreements; and (4) a substitute for inter-union jurisdictional strikes.

Emphasizing that this was not a government conference but a conference of representatives of labor and management chosen by their own leaders, I warned that failure to produce any workable recommendations on how to avoid work stoppages would mean legislation by the Congress.

After three weeks of deliberations, the conference adjourned without making any recommendations, and I went before the Congress on December 3 with a request for immediate legislation. The plan I recommended called for the establishment of fact-finding boards which would be directed to make a thorough investigation of all the facts involved in each dispute. They would be empowered to subpoena all records which the boards should deem relevant to the case. A cooling-off period of thirty days, during which strikes would be outlawed, would be required while the fact-finding boards were being named and the investigations made.

In order to avoid delay in the settlement of the automobile, oil, and meat-packing strikes, and to cope with the threatened steel strike before the Congress would have a chance to pass such legislation, I set up such fact-finding boards by Executive Order. While these did not have the statutory power I hoped the Congress would soon authorize, I felt that the

American people would expect the employer and the employees in each case to co-operate with the boards as fully as if appropriate legislation had already been passed.

The unions—particularly the United Mine Workers—reacted violently to the plan as a restriction of the right to strike and as compulsory arbitration. It was, of course, neither of these. It was simply an attempt at peaceful mediation of labor-management disputes by eliminating the harmful effects on the public and on the national economy of prolonged work stoppages. With 265,000 workers idle in the United States at the time I made the proposal, the need for such action was obvious. Furthermore, the value of the fact-finding boards in bringing the truth before the public was proved many times. In the steel strike of January and February 1946, the findings of the board were instrumental in bringing about a settlement even though the board's recommendations were not adhered to. Following the steel agreement, the 113-day-old United Automobile Workers' strike against General Motors was concluded without the need for a meeting at the White House.

It was evident, however, that statutory authority was needed to enforce the recommendations of fact-finding boards and to forbid striking during the mediation period. In repeated messages to the Congress I asked for the quick passage of such legislation. Instead, the trend in the House was toward harsh, restrictive anti-labor measures that would do more harm than good.

In the spring of 1946 two crises in labor developed which eclipsed all preceding ones in their direct effect on the public. One of these involved the railroad industry and the other the coal industry. On May 23, 1946, the railroad unions called out on strike three hundred thousand members from most of the major lines across the country. I had been conferring with the twenty unions involved as far back as February in order that every effort be made to avert a rail strike, and when it became evident that the railroad operators and the union representatives were unable to agree, I submitted a compromise proposition to the parties concerned.

Eighteen of the unions in the dispute accepted my proposed settlement, as did the operators. It was an offer of an increase of eighteen and a half cents per hour in wages plus certain changes in rules by the arbitration and emergency boards. Two men, however—Alvanley Johnston, president of the Brotherhood of Locomotive Engineers, and A. F. Whitney, president of the Brotherhood of Railway Trainmen—rejected my compromise offer and refused to arbitrate the matter for their unions.

After three conferences in the White House with these men, who would not meet with the operators in the presence of the representatives of the other eighteen unions, I saw that this was no contest between labor and management but one between a small group of men and their government. Johnston and Whitney said, despite my appeals to them, that they were determined to strike.

"You are not going to tie up the country," I told them. "If this is the way you want it, we'll stop you."

On May 24, the day following the start of the strike, I went before the American people in a nationwide radio broadcast and related the facts. I announced that unless operation of the railroads was resumed at once I would call upon the Army to assist the Office of Defense Transportation in operating the trains, and I added that I would appear before the Congress on the next day with a message on the subject.

In a joint session of the Congress on May 25 I requested strong emergency legislation that would authorize the institution of injunctive or mandatory proceedings against any union leader, forbidding him from encouraging or inciting members to leave their work or to refuse to return to work, that would deprive workers of their seniority rights who without good cause persisted in striking against the government, that would provide criminal penalties against employers and union leaders who violated the provisions of the act, and that would authorize the President to draft into the armed forces all workers who were on strike against their government.

These were drastic measures. They were against the principles I believed in, and I proposed them only as a desperate resort in an extreme emergency where leaders defiantly called the workers out in a strike against the government.

Halfway through my message to the Congress I was interrupted by Leslie Biffle, Secretary of the Senate, who handed me a note announcing that the railroad strike had been settled on the terms of the compromise proposal previously accepted by all except these two unions.

I was relieved and I was glad that a quick end was thus brought to the railroad strike. But even more satisfying was the fact that the settlement was in conformity with the National Railway Labor Act. Under this act the recommendations of the emergency board are enforceable, and it was upon these recommendations that I had based my compromise proposal to both sides.

I knew from the beginning of the difficulty with the railroad unions that an attempt was being made by some of the unions to circumvent the Railway Labor Act. That is another reason why I felt justified in asking for the emergency strike legislation. Senator Wayne Morse of Oregon declared at the time that I had fixed the whole thing in advance, and he accused me from the floor of the Senate of putting on a "ham act." Later, however, when he learned the facts, he apologized for his statement and requested that his apology be printed in the Congressional Record. I have always held Wayne Morse in high regard, and this forthright act made me respect him all the more.

Meanwhile, on the coal scene, John L. Lewis was negotiating once more for a new contract—this time for the bituminous coal miners. As early as March 1946 the parleys between Lewis and the operators showed that no agreement was in prospect. Lewis was demanding a welfare fund, to come from a royalty on coal, of which he was to have exclusive control. It was a new grab for more power on the part of the miners' boss; the miners at this time were not asking for wage increases. When negotiations bogged down, Lewis ordered four hundred thousand coal miners to walk out of the bituminous fields on April 1. The country was once more faced with an emergency situation.

I called Lewis to the White House six times from March to May, along with Charles O'Neill, spokesman for the coal operators, in an effort to bring the two factions together. At the May 10 Cabinet meeting I stated that Lewis had promised that the strike would not last more than a few days. But Lewis failed to keep his word. I told the Cabinet that it was ironical that Lewis was now making safety and welfare the primary issues of the coal strike when for ten years he had opposed the inclusion of safety features in the union contracts.

The coal strike showed once more the desperate need for legislation to safeguard the nation against precipitous strikes. But I also feared the danger that in such legislation there would be ill-considered punitive measures against labor. Six months earlier I had, for that reason, recommended fact-finding boards as a legal instrument. The Congress had not acted on my proposal. What Congress did pass was the Case Bill, which was placed on my desk for approval on June 11. I studied the bill carefully and concluded that it would not help to stop strikes. I therefore vetoed it. My principal objections were: (1) it would encourage quick strikes; (2) it superimposed a five-man board over the Conciliation Service, which had been so effective since 1913 in settling strikes. It had settled ten strikes a day during the reconversion period; (3) the bill provided a clause for mediation which I felt was too punitive to encourage mediation; (4) its new provision for a cooling-off period was one of the main points of my proposed legislation still before the Congress; and (5) the bill took away from the Secretary of Labor all responsibility for the operation of the mediation board, leaving only the appointment of members by the President.

In my veto message I said the proposals that I had made to the Congress would be a more effective way to deal with strikes, and my veto was sustained by the House.

During this soft-coal strike of 1946 the mines had been shut down for forty-five days at a cost of ninety million tons of coal. At this point the government stepped in to take over operations in May. However, we continued negotiating with Lewis until we reached an agreement on joint control of the welfare fund and other issues in dispute.

Five months passed without serious incident, when Lewis began to find fault with his contract. He demanded that the agreement be reopened, implying that the miners would go on strike again if negotiations were refused.

On November 14 the government delivered to Lewis a written proposal containing the details of a plan under which the operators and miners could negotiate their differences without interrupting the operation of the mines. I did not feel that the federal government could replace private management as a bargaining agent without interfering with true collective bargaining between labor and management.

The government had taken over the bituminous mines in May only after it became clearly evident that this was the only available means of averting an economic disaster to the country. I was eager that the mines be returned as early as possible to private operation, and the owners stated that they, too, were eager to regain control of their properties. Lewis, however, held out for a new contract and encouraged his miners to lay down their tools. On November 21 the country was once again plunged into a general coal strike—this time against the government of the United States.

I had instructed the Justice Department to seek a temporary injunction restraining Lewis's action in calling the strike. Federal Judge T. Alan Goldsborough issued the injunction against the United Mine Workers' chief, ordering him to cancel notice of the termination of the contract. When Lewis refused to comply with the injunction, he was summoned before Judge Goldsborough to show cause for his failure to obey the court injunction. On December 4 Lewis was found guilty of civil and criminal contempt of court. His personal fine was fixed at ten thousand dollars, and the United Mine Workers Union was fined a total of three and a half million dollars. Seventeen days after he had called the costliest strike in his career, Lewis ordered the miners to return to work.

Tempers were running high, especially within the ranks of labor. This is one of the many telegrams that came to the White House. It was sent by one of the railroad brotherhoods on December 8, 1946.

Whatever temporary sense of exaltation may prevail among government officials today upon the return of American citizens to their jobs in the mine pits must be obliterated when calm regard and due weight are given to the fact that the result has been achieved by governmental utilization of the malevolent and illegal process of injunction in a labor dispute. Working men throughout the country feel nothing but revulsion toward the invasions upon their fundamental freedoms recently sponsored by the government and approved by the Federal Court in the United Mine Workers' case.

The employment of the anti-labor injunction by the oligarchy of the Federal Courts as a weapon of oppression on labor was rebuked and invalidated by Congress more than fourteen years ago. And until the recent resort to the procedure of injunction the spirit and intent of the law have been in most part respected. Not only does recourse to injunction in labor controversies flaunt Congressional mandate; it is a despoliation of the constitutional guarantees of free speech and assembly and a violation of the constitutional prohibition against involuntary servitude. But what is more insidious, the efforts led by the government to enforce economic servitude on the miners, so loudly applauded by press and radio, give impetus and momentum to the program now being spawned by reactionary capitalism to deprive labor of gains hard won over the years and to impose savage and drastic restraints upon our people.

We, the Associations of General Grievance Committees of the Brotherhood of Locomotive Firemen and Enginemen in the United States, in meeting at Cleveland, Ohio, on behalf of our members, unanimously condemn recourse to injunction by the government and employers in labor disputes as being un-American and unlawful; and we denounce any program, whether pursued in the courts or in the legislatures, designed to inhibit American working men in the free exercise of constitutional privileges.

D. B. Robertson, President

This was my reply on December 11:

My dear Mr. Robertson:

There is no exaltation in the office of the President of the United States—sorrow is the proper word. There should be, however, a sense of shame in all the hearts of all the leaders of labor for the manner in which Mr. Lewis attempted to defy the Government. His action is in line with the action of Whitney and Johnston last fall and does labor no credit.

Lewis had the best contract he ever had in his life. I myself forced him to take the safety measures in that contract for which he had never fought before. He knew, and his men know, that the contract with the Solid Fuels Administrator was for the duration of Government operation. He attempted to pull a dirty political trick and it backfired; but he succeeded in giving labor generally a black eye, which will do labor no good in the new Republican Congress.

We used the weapons that we had at hand in order to fight a rebellion against the Government, and I am here to tell you that I expect to use whatever powers the President and the Government have, when the law and the Government are defied by an arbitrary dictator, such as Lewis.

Eighteen of the Railroad Brotherhoods have always been my friends, and I have always been theirs, as I have been a friend to labor in my whole political career; but there are certain segments of labor who have been anything but friends and cooperators with me in this terrible reconversion period through which we have been passing.

I think you are taking an absolutely wrong viewpoint on the court procedure, which was necessary to take against Mr. Lewis, and I am sorry to see you do it.

I am going to need all the help and cooperation I can possibly get to keep labor from getting its throat cut in this Congress. When Murray and Green and able leaders, like yourself, condone the action of Lewis you are not helping yourselves either with me or with the Congress.

Sincerely yours,
Harry S. Truman

Lewis had failed in an attempt to bluff the government. It was, as I saw it, a challenge by the head of the United Mine Workers against the authority of the United States. As a political maneuver, the strategy employed by Lewis was successful to a degree. By calling for a strike just five days before the congressional elections of 1946, he may have contributed to the turnover in the Congress which he was anxious to bring about. But instead of helping to elect a sympathetic Congress, Lewis soon learned that he was faced with a reactionary-controlled group in the Eightieth Congress, which soon was to produce the Taft-Hartley Act, to which the mine leader was bitterly opposed. His political victory in 1946 proved to be a Pyrrhic one.

While there were some continuing disturbances between labor and management following the railroad and coal strikes of 1946—most notable of which were the maritime union and telephone strikes—there was a general slackening of major disputes during the closing months of 1946 and the first half of 1947.

CHAPTER 33

Americans hate war. But once they are provoked to defend themselves against those who threaten their security, they mobilize with unparalleled swiftness and energy. While the battle is on there is no sacrifice of men or treasure too great for them to make.

Once hostilities are over, Americans are as spontaneous and as headlong in their eagerness to return to civilian life. No people in history have been known to disengage themselves so quickly from the ways of war.

This impatience is the expression of a deeply rooted national ideal to want to live at peace. But the tragic experience following World War I taught us that this admirable trait could lead to catastrophe. We needed to temper and adjust the rate of the demobilization of our forces so we would be able to meet our new obligations in the world.

The fighting in Europe had hardly ended when pressure began to build up for the release of men in the armed forces. With the end of hostilities in the Pacific, the public demand for the discharge of the millions of men in the service became insistent.

A "point" system for determining eligibility for discharge on the basis of length of service, combat duty, time overseas, and parenthood credit was put into effect shortly after V-E Day, and on the eve of the Japanese surrender General Marshall sent me a memorandum setting forth the problem and how he proposed to handle it.

The War Department was confronted with the question of the morale of the soldiers who had undergone the longest and most difficult service, Marshall pointed out, and therefore they should be the first to be demobilized and have the first chance at civilian jobs. If this policy was to be put into effect, there were many service units with "low scores" that had already returned home from Europe that ought to be sent to the Pacific. We would have to do this in order to meet General MacArthur's requirements for occupational troops.

In any event, Marshall told me, many of these low-point units would have to be held in service for some time as a reserve pending the development of events, and other low-point men already returned to the United States would be substituted in the Army administrative establishment in order to release for demobilization the high-point men still in service there.

The Army's plan was to stop at once the flow of low-point units from Europe. Instead, high-point units in Europe would be sent home for demobilization. If this plan was followed, Marshall reported, there would be no cause for criticizing the policy of demobilization in so far as the men in Europe were concerned. While the Pacific Theater would still have a huge operational job to complete, the flow of high-point men home from there would continue, and low-point replacements would be sent out as they were needed. The soldiers who had fought so long in the Pacific would, in this way, have the same opportunities as those who had fought in Europe.

Nevertheless, the criticisms came. On August 23, only nine days after the capitulation of Japan, I took occasion to point out at a press conference that there had already been considerable criticism of the demobilization program. I explained, however, that I had conferred with the Secretaries of War and Navy, Chief of Staff General Marshall, and Chief of Naval Operations Admiral King, and that I was convinced that they were doing everything possible to expedite the undertaking.

At the August 31 meeting of the Cabinet I asked Under Secretary of War Patterson to express his views on the movement of military personnel from foreign theaters. He stated that all that could be done to get men home as soon as possible was being done. The Army, he said, had plans for the movement of five and a half million men back to the United States by July 1, 1946. Under Secretary of the Navy Gates reported at the same meeting that the Navy would be demobilizing at the rate of 260,000 per month after the program got under way.

Nevertheless, the demand for speedier demobilization continued to increase. On September 18 I issued a statement assuring the American people that the return of servicemen from the fighting fronts of the world to their homes was proceeding as fast as the circumstances permitted. In less than one month after the day of Japan's surrender the number of men discharged each day from the Army had risen from 4,200 to more than 15,200. Our soldiers were being returned to civilian life at a rate in excess of 650 per hour. This rate, I announced, would be steadily increased to more than 25,000 discharges per day by January 1946.

Only those who were in a position to understand the over-all operation could realize what an enormous task confronted the government in demobilizing and redeploying almost twelve million men within a period of a few months. While our own numbers were staggering when it was considered what they meant in terms of ships, rail transport, and the extensive staffs required to carry out processing before discharge, our problem was compounded by the obligation to consider the demobilization needs of our Allies, particularly Great Britain.

Since early in the war we had been making full use of Britain's three largest vessels—the *Queen Mary,* the *Queen Elizabeth,* and the *Aquitania*—for the transportation of American troops to and from the battle areas. In October 1945, however, the British government requested the return of these ships, or provision of equivalent American transport facilities. Prime Minister Attlee called my attention to the fact that many of their men had been on active service and away from their homes for five or more years and that the demands for their early return, now that hostilities were over, had become loud and insistent. The Prime Minister also reminded me that the arrangement to loan us the two *Queens* and the *Aquitania* had been conditioned solely on the urgency of redeploying American forces for the war against Japan. With the unexpected early termination of the Japanese war, Attlee pointed out, these conditions had ceased to exist.

The British fully realized the desire on the part of the American people to welcome back their soldiers and airmen who had been fighting in Europe. Their own urgent necessities, however, said Attlee, now compelled them to request us to loan them, in return for the *Queens* and the *Aquitania,* an equivalent "personnel lift" in American-controlled troopships for use between India and Australia and the United Kingdom.

Our Chiefs of Staff had told the British that they regretted "that the necessity to return U.S. forces from Europe as expeditiously as possible requires all lifts scheduled under present agreements to December, 1945, and that therefore they are unable to provide assistance in U.S. controlled troop shipping before the end of 1945." On the other hand, I was impressed by Attlee's cable. "I shall speak with the utmost frankness," his message concluded. "While so many of our troops overseas are awaiting repatriation after nearly six years of war and of separation from their families, I cannot continue to justify to the British public the use of our three biggest ships in the American service. I am reluctant to suggest the return of the Queens and the Aquitania. I must, however, ask you most earnestly, Mr. President, to provide us in the immediate future with an equivalent lift for these three ships."

There could be no doubt that Attlee was right, and I cabled him:

"I have directed the Joint Chiefs of Staff to return to you the two Queens and the Aquitania or to provide equivalent personnel lift, the details to be worked out with your staff representatives here."

The progress of our own demobilization program was reviewed at a Cabinet meeting on October 26. Secretary of the Navy Forrestal and Secretary of War Patterson outlined the program and expressed the warning that its acceleration threatened to jeopardize our strategic position in the midst of the postwar tensions that were building up around the world. I agreed entirely with this view and stated at that meeting that, so far as I was concerned, the program we were following was no longer demobilization—it was disintegration of our armed forces.

Despite the dangerous speed with which the program was being carried out, public pressure on me and on the heads of the services for even faster demobilization continued to mount. Many letters from parents and appeals from organizations came to me pleading for the release of various groups. Members of the Congress were reminding me that their constituencies were bombarding them with telegrams and letters. On January 8, 1946, I issued a statement in which I said that, while I recognized the anxiety and impatience of families, it was just not possible to discharge every member of the armed forces promptly. I pointed out that the Army had already released more than four and three quarter million men and women since the European fighting had stopped. The Navy, out of a peak strength of three and a half million, had returned almost a million and a quarter persons to civilian life. From the Marine Corps, which totaled nearly 486,000 at the end of the war, more than 183,000 had been discharged. The Coast Guard had demobilized over 74,000 of its 180,000 men.

I sympathized with parents still waiting for their sons, and with the wives and children longing to see their husbands and fathers again. I knew that many young men were eager to continue their education or return to their jobs. But my overriding responsibility as President of the United States was the security and welfare of the nation as a whole. We had an obligation as a leading nation to build a firm foundation for the future peace of the world. The future of the country was as much at stake as it had been in the days of the war.

On April 17, 1946, at a press conference in the White House, I called attention to the fact that discharges in the Army had reached nearly seven million. I termed this "the most remarkable demobilization in the history of the world, or 'disintegration,' if you want to call it that."

Our frenzied demobilization, in fact, grew out of our antagonism toward maintaining a large standing army. There was only one alternative, in my opinion, and that was a prepared soldier-citizenry. I have held this view for thirty years—ever since World War I. From the beginning of my administration in 1945 I had publicly favored a program of military training for boys and young men. At a press conference on August 16 I was asked if I would propose peacetime conscription. I replied that I would ask the Congress to enact a program of universal training for American youth.

At a Cabinet meeting on August 31 I presented a detailed preliminary plan for national military security which included universal training. I asked for the views and recommendations of each member of the Cabinet, and the general reaction was favorable. I have always believed that military preparedness is necessary to national security. History has proved that many times. President Washington instituted the first military policy of the United States when he recommended a universal draft as a guarantee of basic minimum military protection for the Republic against aggressors. Washington's policy was not implemented until 1917, when President Wilson authorized the first compulsory draft. During the nation's other great crisis in the 1860's, the lack of a firm military policy resulted in disgraceful draft riots and mob actions and in the corrupt practice of selling draft exemptions to individuals who could raise the required sum.

I told the Cabinet that the time had come to initiate a new military policy. If we were to maintain leadership among other nations, we must continue to be strong in a military way.

In the twenty-one-point message on domestic legislation of September 6, 1945, I notified the Congress that I would soon communicate further with respect to a long-range program of national military security, and on October 22 I sent to Capitol Hill my recommendations concerning one aspect of that program—universal training. What I was proposing, in brief, was a system of universal training during peacetime which would provide this country with a well-trained and effectively organized citizen reserve to reinforce the professional armed forces in times of danger as decided upon by the Congress. I pointed out that the latent strength of our untrained citizenry was no longer sufficient protection and that if attack should come again, as it did at Pearl Harbor, we could never again count on the luxury of time with which to arm ourselves and strike back. Our geographic security was forever gone—gone with the advent of the atomic bomb, the rocket, and modern airborne armies.

I recommended that we create a postwar military organization that would contain three basic elements: (1) a comparatively small Army, Navy, and Marine Corps; (2) a greatly strengthened National Guard and Organized Reserve for the Army, Navy, and Marine Corps; and (3) a General Reserve composed of all the male citizens of the United States who had received training. This General Reserve would be provided by adoption of a plan for universal military training, but members would have no obligation to serve at home or abroad unless called to the service by an act of the Congress.

The plan was thoroughly democratic and was not intended to take the place of the Selective Service System. Young men who received training under the plan would not be members of the armed services, but civilians who could be mobilized into the armed services in time of danger only to augment the strength of the regular and reserve forces. I suggested a period of training for one year for eighteen-year-olds, with no exemptions except for total physical disqualification. After one year of training, the trainee would become a member of the General Reserve for six years and, subsequently, would be placed in a secondary reserve status.

This was not a military training program in the conventional sense. The military phase was incidental to what I had in mind. While the training was to offer every qualified young man a chance to perfect himself for the service of his country in some military capacity, I envisioned a program that would at the same time provide ample opportunity for self-improvement. Part of the training was calculated to develop skills that could be used in civilian life, to raise the physical standards of the nation's manpower, to lower the illiteracy rate, to develop citizenship responsibilities, and to foster the moral and spiritual welfare of our young people.

These were not theoretical goals. This was what was unique about the plan I contemplated—it was a universal training program, not just a military program. The educational and special training benefits were strong arguments in themselves for immediate legislation setting up the universal training program. But the basic reason for my proposed plan was still to guarantee the safety and freedom of the United States against any potential aggressor.

I am certain that if we had had a training program for American youth we would not have had a rejection of thirty-four per cent of our young men because of physical defects. That is what we had among those drafted and those who volunteered during World War II.

I am sure that a large part of that thirty-four per cent could have been made physically fit and self-supporting with the right sort of treatment. At the same time, under this plan we could teach citizenship to the teen-agers and help show them how to get along with their fellow men and still stick to their own individual beliefs.

I am morally certain that if Congress had gone into the program thoroughly in 1945, when I first recommended it, we would have had a pool of basically trained men which would have made the Soviets hesitate in their program of expansion in certain strategic parts of the world.

Housing was one of the acute postwar problems with which I had to deal. More than a million families were living "doubled up" with other families in the fall of 1945 because of a critical housing shortage. This shortage had been building up over a period of years. We entered the war with a housing deficit, and the war had served to widen the gap. At the same time that building materials and manpower were engaged in the all-out war effort instead of home construction, marriages increased at far above the normal rate. Wars have always stimulated marriages, and with the return of millions of veterans and the additional marriages that followed, the immediate demand for new housing was far in excess of the industry's capacity to produce.

In October I directed the Federal Public Housing Authority to release for sale the 320,000 temporary housing units which the government had erected around war plants now shut down, along with 35,000 trailers. These units, which were sold at no more than the cost to tear them down, helped provide some emergency relief but of course had little effect on alleviating the general shortage. Nothing less than several years of peak production would really solve the problem. It would take time to get the construction industry into full operation, and I knew that we would do well to have more than 500,000 housing units built in 1946. Veterans were given preference in all federal housing units, but it was impossible to meet their needs at once or to solve the housing problems of millions of war workers and others who were still confronted with substandard or inadequate conditions.

In December 1945 I asked for a report on the housing situation from the Office of War Mobilization and Reconversion, and an outline of what was being done. John W. Snyder, OWMR Director, advised me that his agency was taking energetic action under a six-point program. The six objectives were: (1) to increase the supply of building materials; (2) to strengthen inventory controls to prevent hoarding; (3) to strengthen price controls over building materials; (4) to discourage unsound lending practices and speculation; (5) to enlist industry support in increasing production and fighting inflation; and (6) to provide information and advisory service on home values to the public.

Under this program the executive agencies had combined their powers to meet emergency situations. Price increases, special manpower recruiting by the United States Employment Service, priorities and allocations of machinery and material were authorized in cases where more production was needed. During 1945 residential building rose from $56,000,000 in June—normally a peak month—to $125,000,000 in December, although this level was still extremely low in relation to the country's home-building needs.

The federal government instituted a series of meetings with industry and with community groups during December in an effort to come to grips with the problem on a co-operative basis. Other meetings were held with home-financing institutions, with real estate boards, and with consumer groups. The National Housing Administrator requested the mayors of all communities with severe housing problems to set up emergency housing committees to work with the federal government for emergency relief in their areas.

In addition to this program, I encouraged a speed-up in the release of surplus housing units and building materials held by the government, with preference for veterans. I favored a regulation establishing priorities on building materials which would channel about fifty per cent of all building materials into housing units costing ten thousand dollars or less. Recognizing the threat of inflation in the field of housing to be the most menacing in our economy, I requested ceiling prices on old and new housing, curbs on unsound lending practices, and rent control.

To carry out these policies I appointed Wilson Wyatt, formerly mayor of Louisville, to the new position of Housing Expediter in the Office of War Mobilization and Reconversion. To Wyatt was assigned the responsibility for co-ordinating and expediting the housing program and for recommending new steps that might be needed to meet new problems. I wanted him to search out all bottlenecks at whatever level of industry or government they might be concealed, and to break them in order to make the machinery of housing production run as smoothly and as speedily as possible.

In reviewing the housing situation in my talk to the people on January 3, 1946, I said: "Of the three major components which make up our standard of living—food, clothing, and housing—housing presents our most difficult problem." I cited to the Congress our need for about five million additional homes at once, although the greatest number of homes that had ever been built in one year before the war was less than one million. It was clear, I told the Congress, that this was an emergency problem that demanded an emergency method of solution. And five weeks later I presented to the Congress a veterans' emergency housing program, with the request that legislation be promptly enacted for carrying out the program.

Meanwhile the shortage had become acute, particularly where veterans and their families were concerned. Thousands were finding it impossible to obtain adequate housing, in spite of our best efforts to facilitate new construction. Feeling that every effort at relief was worth while, I discussed the matter with representatives of the Protestant, Catholic, and Jewish faiths and suggested a nationwide "Share the Housing" drive to be conducted through the churches of the land.

Finally, on May 22, the emergency housing bill to provide for the construction of 2,700,000 homes for veterans within two years became law. The original proposal submitted by Representative Wright Patman had undergone considerable abuse in both Houses of the Congress before reaching my desk in amended form, but it was nevertheless the first effective legislation designed specifically to cope with the housing shortage. The heart of the program was the appropriation of $400,000,000 for subsidies to spur production of bottleneck materials. The act also increased by one million dollars the government's authority to insure home loans through private capital, thus protecting lenders against risks incurred by selling homes on small down payments.

This was only emergency legislation, and its provisions were not designed to take care of the long-range residential building needs. A permanent law which would implement the construction of fifteen million homes over a ten-year period was being worked on by the Congress. This was the Wagner-Ellender-Taft bill providing government loans to small-income builders, slum clearance, and other general inducements to low-cost housing construction. I urged Representative Brent Spence, chairman of the House Committee on Banking and Currency, to take quick action to help solve the problem, but despite my warning and Spence's tireless efforts, the months dragged by with no decisive action from the Congress. By October the nation was confronted with an emergency unique in its history.

The minimum goal set by Housing Expediter Wyatt for new construction in 1946 had been 1,200,000 homes—mostly for veterans. In October he reported 708,000 started and 350,000 completed. Wyatt had performed prodigiously in accomplishing this, but there were many handicaps with which he had to reckon.

The chief deterrent to faster construction was the failure of the Congress to provide the enabling legislation. It had pared $200,000,000 for subsidies from the emergency housing act before approving it in May. It had failed to give prompt enactment to the Wagner-Ellender-Taft bill to provide low-cost housing. It had refused to approve price ceilings on existing housing and had allowed the OPA to expire. Other almost insurmountable handicaps cropped up in the form of material shortages, work stoppages, and the persistent lobbying in Washington by groups from the real estate, lumber, contracting, and other special interests.

It became necessary for me to issue a proclamation on October 25 declaring a state of emergency because of the housing shortage and authorizing free importation of lumber into the country.

CHAPTER 34

War weariness leads to easy illusions. It was natural for
people everywhere, when fighting ended, to hope that peace
and harmony would come at once and without too much effort. But keeping the peace is a vast undertaking, and constant vigilance and effort are
needed to keep conflicting interests from destroying it.

Many differences among the Allies had been subordinated during the
war, but now that the common enemy was defeated, the problems of
peace had brought these differences to the surface. We had already discovered how difficult the Russians could be, but in the months that immediately followed the war this was revealed even further.

Secretary Byrnes went to London in September to attend the first meeting of the Council of Foreign Ministers set up by the Potsdam conference,
and at this meeting Molotov proved to be much more difficult than he
had ever been. On September 22, eleven days after the opening of the
conference, Byrnes felt compelled to ask me to intervene personally with
Stalin to prevent a breakup of the meeting.

I was spending a brief weekend at Jefferson Island in Chesapeake Bay
when I received a message from Admiral Leahy through the code room
aboard the *Williamsburg*. The admiral had just held a teletype conversation with Secretary Byrnes in London during which the Secretary of State
reported that on the first day of the conference it had been unanimously
agreed that France and China would participate in discussions but could
not vote on matters which did not directly concern them. Now, however,
Molotov declared that he would attend no further meetings unless France
and China were excluded from all matters where they were not directly

concerned as signatories of an armistice agreement. Byrnes believed this to be only an excuse for Molotov to leave the conference and that the fact was that he was angry because the United States and Britain would not recognize Rumania. Byrnes suggested that I wire Stalin immediately, asking him to communicate with Molotov and not allow the Council to be broken up. Since I was en route to the *Williamsburg* at the time the teletype conversation took place, Byrnes and Leahy, realizing that the situation could not wait until my arrival at the ship, took the unusual step of anticipating my approval and agreed on a message to be sent to Stalin in my name. This read as follows:

"I am informed that Mr. Molotov is considering withdrawing from the Council of Foreign Ministers in London because of difficulty in reaching agreement as to the participation of France and China in discussions of the Balkan situation.

"I urgently request that you communicate with Mr. Molotov telling him that because of the bad effect it would have on world peace he should not permit the Council to be broken up."

I was informed of this action by Byrnes and Leahy immediately upon my arrival at the *Williamsburg,* and I sent word to Leahy that I approved the message to Stalin. Meanwhile Leahy had another teletype conversation with London in which Byrnes suggested that a more specific message be sent to Stalin. This was the second message:

"The Secretary of State has fully informed me of the difficulty encountered at the Council of Foreign Ministers.

"I agree that under a strict interpretation of the language of the Potsdam Agreement, France and China have not the right to participate in the construction of peace treaties unless they are signatories to the surrender terms or unless they are invited under paragraph 3 (2) of the Potsdam Agreement which provides that members of the Council other than the signatories may by agreement be invited to participate when matters directly concerning them are under discussion.

"It is my recollection that at the conference table at Potsdam it was agreed during the discussion that members not signatory could be present and participate in the discussion but could not vote. It seems the first day the Council met, it was unanimously agreed that members not signatories could participate in the discussion, but could not vote. If we now change this rule and deny France and China because they are not signatories to the surrender the right even to discuss a matter in which they state they are interested, I fear it will create a bad impression. It will be charged that the three big powers are denying other members of the Council an opportunity even to present their views.

"Can't we agree to regard the unanimous action of the Council on the opening day as an invitation to France and China to participate under the Potsdam Agreement? This is too small a matter to disrupt the work of the Council and delay progress toward peace and better understanding."

In approving this message, I instructed Leahy to send the full text of both messages to Prime Minister Attlee at once. Later that day I received a copy of a message which Attlee had sent to Stalin. It enumerated in more detail than my message the difficulties that had developed and ended with this appeal to the Russian leader: ". . . I earnestly hope that you will agree to authorize your delegation to adhere to the decision taken on September 11. After all it is peace we are endeavoring to establish, which is more important than procedure."

Stalin replied in two messages. In the first one he noted that he was still awaiting a reply to his own inquiry from Molotov but commented on the issue in such a way that it was plain that he would not concede anything. The second message, sent the following day, after he had heard from Molotov, made it clear that he intended to stand his ground. Here are these two messages:

FOR THE PRESIDENT FROM GENERALISSIMO STALIN, 22 SEPTEMBER 1945.
I received your message.
I inquired Molotov, but have not yet his answer. I became acquainted with the matter and came to a conclusion that if the question relates to the participation of France and China in the settlement of the Balkan affairs, these governments, according to the exact meaning of the decisions of the Berlin conference, must not be invited to participate.

FROM GENERALISSIMO J. V. STALIN TO PRESIDENT H. S. TRUMAN.
I have received your second message regarding the Council of Ministers.
I have received today a reply from Mr. V. M. Molotov who informed me that he is acting in accordance with the decision of the Berlin Conference and considers that this decision should not be violated. On my part, I have to remind you that at the Berlin Conference neither a decision was adopted nor was it agreed among us that the members of the Council who did not sign the terms of surrender could participate in the discussions but could not vote. I consider that the position of Molotov to adhere strictly to the decision of the Berlin Conference cannot make a bad impression and should not offend anybody.
September 24, 1945.

I saw no reason for further immediate communication with Stalin on this subject. The conference adjourned on October 2. The newspapers called it a failure. But I do not feel that all such conferences should be expected always to produce immediate tangible results. It was another stage in our efforts to reach an ultimate understanding if we could. In politics, national or international, we often spend a good deal of time trying to find out just where we stand with the other parties. I have always felt that it does not help to keep a running box score on international events. Nor do I think it is ever helpful to have the newspapers shout "Failure!" when our diplomatic discussions do not result in the full retreat of the other nations. There are many issues that cannot be solved by the surrender of either side but only through a reasonable compromise which does not sacrifice principles.

Russia was proving herself equally difficult in the Pacific. The British had raised no objections to the manner in which we handled the occupation in Japan and Korea. But Russia had, up to now, declined to take any part in the meetings of the Far Eastern Advisory Commission, which had been convened in Washington in the fall. We had been unable to arrive at any formula to bring about Russian co-operation in the occupation of Japan.

This occupation was succeeding beyond our expectations. Dr. Karl T. Compton, the distinguished president of the Massachusetts Institute of Technology, had spent some time in Japan in order to learn what advances Japanese scientists and technicians had made in the course of the war. Upon his return he came to the White House and gave me a most enlightening account of the success of our occupation, which I asked him then to reduce to a memorandum.

"We were all very much surprised," he wrote in his report, "at the apparent absence of rancor and the apparent eagerness of practically all the Japanese with whom we had contact to help us and to show us what they had been doing. We attributed this to several factors, such as (a) their inferiority complex which impels them to seek recognition and appreciation of their accomplishments, (b) the fact that the emperor had ordered their cooperation and hence they could give it without feeling of disgrace or disloyalty, (c) the fact that they have actually been a nation of serfs under a feudal system in which the military were the overlords. The ordinary civilian in Japan has therefore been shifted in obedience from one overlord to another, in the present case our own forces of occupation. To many of them this shift means very little provided their opportunities for livelihood are maintained under the new regime. General MacArthur stresses this latter factor."

Edwin A. Locke, Jr., whom I had sent on an economic mission to China, had stopped off in Japan to talk with MacArthur.

"General MacArthur," Locke wrote me on October 19, 1945, "gave considerable emphasis to the influence of Russia on Japanese affairs, expressing concern over 'underground Communist agitation' in Japan. Many of the so-called liberal elements of Japan are Communistic, he stated, and in his opinion, Japanese Communism is dominated from Moscow."

Locke also reported that "General MacArthur mentioned several times his difficulty in obtaining what he felt were prompt and understanding responses to cabled messages sent to Washington by the Supreme Allied Command." The general also told Locke that, in his opinion, policies relative to the control of Japan should for the most part be made in Tokyo rather than in Washington. The general "spoke feelingly" of the problems created for him by policy pronouncements made in Washington without prior consultation with him.

Washington, however, had cause to complain in turn about pronouncements made by General MacArthur without any clearance by his superiors in the national capital. On September 17, for instance, he gave·out word that the strength of the occupation forces could be pared to 200,000 men. The Joint Chiefs of Staff, the State Department, and I first learned of this announcement through the press. This was not only embarrassing but actually affected the position the administration could take, both at home and abroad.

Twice—first on September 17 and again on October 19—I had Marshall invite MacArthur to return to the States to receive the plaudits of a grateful nation. I felt that he was entitled to the same honors that had been given to General Eisenhower. And, like Eisenhower, he could have returned to his post after a brief sojourn here. But the general declined.

The first message sent General MacArthur by General Marshall was as follows:

"When the situation in Japan permits I suggest that you make a visit home. Undoubtedly a series of welcome celebrations will be proposed. This would amount to visits to several representative cities throughout the United States, including a stop in your state. Admiral Leahy has communicated with you in reference to a request from the Governor of Wisconsin that you come home there. In Washington the Congress would certainly invite you to address a joint session and there would be a reception or dinner by the President. Following all this you will probably want to consider a period of rest. Available is a completely staffed deluxe cottage at Ashford General Hospital which was formerly the Greenbriar Hotel at White Sulphur Springs, West Virginia. I believe your return should best be timed with the hearings of the Congressional Committees on the postwar national defense. They have indicated their desire to have you testify. I understand these hearings will be conducted during late October and November.

"Please let me have your views concerning such a proposed visit together with your desires. It would be well to consider bringing back in your party some representative enlisted men, as well as officers and naval officers in addition to members of your staff."

On September 19 General MacArthur replied:

"Appreciate very much your message. I naturally look forward to a visit home, from which I have been absent more than eight years. The delicate and difficult situation which prevails here, however, would make it unwise for me to leave until conditions are far more stabilized than at present. I believe a considerable period of time must elapse before I can safely leave.

"I am deeply grateful for the courtesies that have been planned. When I do return, I would hope to bring with me as a group such officers as Krueger, Kenney, Kinkaid, Sutherland, Eichelberger, Whitehead, Barbey and others. I would not wish to return on such a visit without these men whose magnificently united efforts so largely brought about the defeat of Japan. Such a visit home, symbolizing the contribution to victory made by the commands with which I have been associated, would make me very desirous of avoiding complications in any way involved in appearances before Congressional committees on any extraneous issues such as postwar organization or any other matters. It would completely negative the character of the trip, involving me in controversial issues which I do not feel I should undertake at that time and under such circumstances."

On October 19, 1945, I instructed Marshall to send this second message to General MacArthur:

"The President has asked me to inform you that he wishes you to understand that he would like you to make a trip home at such time you feel that you can safely leave your duties. Our liaison contact with Congress indicated that as soon as they have something fairly definite about your plans they wish to extend you a formal invitation to return and address the Congress in joint session. I shall do nothing further until I hear from you."

Two days later General MacArthur cabled:

"I am deeply grateful and most appreciative of the general action of Congress and the sympathetic attitude of the President and yourself. Nothing ordinarily would please me more than to accept this invitation without delay. A realization however of the extraordinarily dangerous and inherently inflammable situation which exists here compels me to suggest that this visit be delayed. The desperation of the coming winter here cannot be overestimated. I would feel that I were failing in my duty and obligations were I to delegate this responsibility. Be assured that as soon as I feel conditions are safe I shall report myself with a heart full of thanks and gratitude. Please convey this message to the President."

MacArthur's conversation with Locke had also revealed that the general was increasingly concerned over developments in Korea. Reports which I had received from that country had indeed been discouraging. The 38th parallel, fixed originally as a mere convenience to decide who should accept the Japanese surrender in a given locality, had become a rigid boundary, with the Russians to the north permitting none of our people to see what was going on. Korea, instead of being helped to become a free and independent nation, was on the way to being divided. And there were reports that both in Korea and Manchuria the Russians were stripping the factories and shipping the machinery to Russia. I therefore sent for Ed Pauley to make a study of reparations in the Far East. I asked him to find out for me, on the spot, whether the reports we received from Korea and Manchuria were correct.

On the other side of the world trouble was beginning to brew in Greece. That country had been occupied by the Germans after a truly heroic resistance. It had suffered badly during the war, and its recovery was dangerously slow. It is more than likely that only the aid which UNRRA furnished had prevented a complete collapse.

Greece occupied a highly sensitive position. To the north, all its neighbors had fallen under the sway of the Communists, and even within Greece there was evidence that the Communists were ready to take over, with help from Communists abroad, whenever the situation degenerated from instability to chaos. State Department reports to me described the situation in Greece in the fall of 1945 this way: "Severe inflation, high governmental expenditure and low revenue, disrupted Civil Service, stagnant industry and trade, and widespread unemployment."

The British, after V-E Day, had assumed the principal responsibility for aid to Greece, but it became evident that our help would be needed. I was unwilling to put American money into Greece, however, until there was some indication that the Greeks themselves would act to get their house in order. I authorized the State Department to inform the British government of our position and to send a note to the government of Greece that would urge them to adopt a program of economic stabilization. I added that the extent to which we would help would depend on the effectiveness of the Greek action.

In the Middle East the situation in Iran had suddenly taken a turn for the worse. That country had served as a vital connecting link between us and the Russians during the war, especially in the earlier years, when it was important to reinforce Russian resistance against Hitler with Lend-Lease supplies. To secure the supply line, Russian troops had been stationed in northern Iran, and British and American forces were garrisoned in the southern part of the country. Early in September I had received the first reports of Russian actions that appeared to be undue interference in Iran's internal affairs. Russian Army units were apparently stopping Iranian police from moving into areas where the Tudeh party, the local version of the Communists, was making trouble. Later that month I was informed by the State Department that the Iranian province of Azerbaijan, which adjoins Soviet territory, was torn by unrest. A movement for autonomy seemed under way which was encouraged, if not actually inspired, by the Russians.

Agreement had been reached at the London conference of the Council of Foreign Ministers that all foreign troops should be withdrawn from Iran not later than March 2, 1946. But reports reaching me in October told of additional Russian troops being sent in. It all seemed to add up to a planned move on the part of the Russians to get at least northern Iran under their control. Together with the threat of a Communist coup in Greece, this began to look like a giant pincers movement against the oil-rich areas of the Near East and the warm-water ports of the Mediterranean.

These were ominous signs which called for every effort we could make through the United Nations to compel the Russians to carry out the London agreement and get out of Iran.

While these tensions were building up in Europe and in Asia, our policy was to act swiftly and decisively wherever trouble developed.

Ever since Hiroshima I had never stopped thinking about the frightful implications of the atomic bomb. We knew that this revolutionary scientific creation could destroy civilization unless put under control and placed at the service of mankind. On August 8, 1945, I received a message from Prime Minister Attlee, who suggested that we issue a joint statement that might serve to reassure the world.

"There is widespread anxiety," he observed, "as to whether the new power will be used to serve or to destroy civilization." The economic effects of the discovery would probably not reveal themselves for some years, he pointed out, but its influence on international relations would be immediate. He urged, therefore, that we, as heads of the two governments, should without delay make a joint declaration of our intentions to utilize the existence of this great power "not for our own ends, but as trustees for humanity in the interests of all peoples in order to promote peace and justice to the world."

In my reply I assured the Prime Minister that I shared his views entirely. In fact, I had already prepared, for inclusion in my radio report to the nation on the Potsdam Conference, a declaration that it was our intention to make the new force of atomic energy into a weapon for peace.

Attlee cabled at once that "this statement . . . in fact amounts to a declaration of intentions of the kind I had in mind. In these circumstances I think that any joint declaration should wait until the means of control and the implications in the field of international relations have been more fully considered between those concerned." Attlee advised that he intended to issue a statement for his government that would conclude with this declaration:

"President Truman in his broadcast of August 9th has spoken of the preparation of plans for the future control of the bomb, and of a request to Congress to cooperate to the end that its production and use may be controlled and that its power may be made an overwhelming influence towards world peace. It is the intention of His Majesty's Government to put all their efforts into the promotion of the objects thus foreshadowed, and they will lend their full cooperation to the end."

We now had to find some way to control this new force. The destruction at Hiroshima and Nagasaki was lesson enough to me. The world could not afford to risk war with atomic weapons. But until a practical and foolproof method of control could be found, it was important to retain the advantage which possession of the bomb had given us. In other words, it was now more than ever necessary to guard and maintain the secrecy of the bomb, and I issued the following order to the principal officials concerned as soon as hostilities in the Pacific ended:

15 August 1945

MEMORANDUM FOR
　The Secretary of State
　The Secretary of War
　The Secretary of the Navy
　The Joint Chiefs of Staff
　The Director of the Office of Scientific Research and Development

Appropriate departments of the Government and the Joint Chiefs of Staff are hereby directed to take such steps as are necessary to prevent the release of any information in regard to the development, design or production of the atomic bomb; or in regard to its employment in military or naval warfare, except with the specific approval of the President in each instance.

Vigilance at the various installations of the Manhattan District was intensified. The basic facts about nuclear reactions—long known to world scientists—were made public in the Smyth report. But our possession of the secret of harnessing atomic energy already had far-reaching effects on our relations with other nations.

On September 11 Secretary Stimson sent me a memorandum setting forth his views on the atomic bomb and our relations with the Russians. Secretary Stimson had given a great deal of thought to this subject, since he had played an important role in the development of atomic energy. He proposed that the United States make a direct approach to Russia with a view of reaching some agreement about the future use of atomic bombs. "In my judgment," he wrote, "the Soviets would be more apt to respond sincerely to a direct and forthright approach made by the United States on this subject than would be the case if the approach were made as part of a general international scheme, or if the approach were made after a succession of expressed or implied threats in our peace negotiations.

"My idea of an approach to the Soviets would be a direct proposal after discussion with the British that we would be prepared in effect to enter an arrangement with the Russians, the general purpose of which would be to control and limit the use of the atomic bomb as an instrument of war and so far as possible to direct and encourage the development of atomic power for peaceful and humanitarian purpose. Such an approach might more specifically lead to the proposal that we would stop work on the further improvement in, or manufacture of, the bomb as a military weapon, provided the Russians and the British would agree to do likewise. It might also provide that we would be willing to impound what bombs we now have in the United States provided the Russians and the British would agree with us that in no event will they or we use a bomb as an instrument of war unless all three governments agree to that use. We might also consider including in the arrangement a covenant with the U.K. and the Soviets providing for the exchange of benefits of future developments whereby atomic energy may be applied on a mutually satisfactory basis for commercial or humanitarian purposes."

Stimson did not propose that we "turn the bomb over" to Russia. As far as I was concerned, this was not a matter for discussion. I had decided that the secret of the manufacture of the weapon would remain a secret with us. At the weekly Cabinet luncheon on September 18 I started a discussion of atomic energy, as a result of which I decided that there would be one item only on the agenda of the next formal Cabinet meeting on September 21, and that was atomic energy.

This was Secretary Stimson's last Cabinet meeting. His resignation was already in my hands, and immediately after the meeting ended, he left Washington, thus ending one of the most distinguished careers of public service to this nation. I was sorry to see him go. Stimson was an honest man. As was said of Enoch, he was a just man. He had the ability to express his views in plain language. I respected and trusted him.

I opened the meeting by calling on Stimson to present his views to the Cabinet. In his statement he pointed out that the future of atomic energy would fall into two major areas: the further pursuit of scientific investigation, and the application of the newly won knowledge to industrial uses. It was his opinion that the scientific secrets were in fact not secrets—not in the sense in which the ordnance or weapon developments could be kept secret. The problem, Stimson said, was how to treat these secrets in order to assure the safety of the world, and he thereupon put forward the proposal contained in his memorandum to me.

Under Secretary of State Dean Acheson, sitting in for Byrnes, who was in London, expressed general agreement with Stimson. He said safeguards were needed in any mutual sharing of scientific knowledge. American scientists would have to be fully informed of Soviet developments so that there would be no one-sided exchange in which we gave information and received none in return. He said the United Nations could not function in the atomic energy field without agreement among the United States, Great Britain, and Russia.

Secretary of the Treasury Fred M. Vinson took strong issue with the Secretary of War. Why, he asked, if we wanted to share any part of our knowledge of atomic energy, would we not also want to share all the military secrets? He was opposed to that, and he expressed fear that an exchange of information would be a one-sided affair, with our receiving little or nothing in return. Attorney General Clark agreed with Vinson. He said he saw no reason, with the world situation as it was, for sharing our secrets.

I interrupted to point out that we were not discussing the question of giving the secret of the bomb itself to the Russians or to anyone else, but the best methods of controlling bomb warfare and the exchange only of scientific information.

Postmaster General Bob Hannegan expressed his respect for Stimson's judgment and supported his position. Secretary of the Navy Forrestal declared that the problem had a military as well as a civilian aspect and that both needed to be considered. He said that no precipitate action should be taken before further study, and he offered to submit a memorandum on the subject. I thanked him for this suggestion, and I asked the others present to submit written memoranda fully expressing their views. Secretary of Agriculture Anderson then went on with the discussion, saying that he was strongly opposed to revealing any scientific or commercial secrets any more than we should reveal the military secret of atomic energy. He added that he did not trust the Russians or their willingness to reciprocate in any arrangement. Henry Wallace said he wanted to know whether we were to follow the line of bitterness, as he put it, or the line of peace. He said that scientific progress could not be held down by man-made laws.

Under Secretary of War Robert Patterson, whom I would name a few days later to succeed Stimson, expressed agreement with Stimson. Secretary of Labor Schwellenbach, Major General Philip B. Fleming, Administrator of the Federal Works Agency, and Paul McNutt expressed more or less agreement with Stimson.

Leo Crowley said that it would be difficult to divorce other aspects of atomic energy from the bomb, and Julius Krug expressed the opinion that we ought to delay any decision for six months, to permit a general cooling off. John Snyder and Senator McKellar stated that they shared this view. The discussion had been lively, and it was this kind of interchange of opinion that I liked to see at Cabinet meetings. This Cabinet meeting showed that honest men can honestly disagree, and a frank and open argument of this kind is the best form of free expression in which a President can get all points of view needed for him to make decisions. The decisions had to be mine to make.

I had asked also for a memorandum from Dr. Vannevar Bush, Director of the Office of Scientific Research and Development, and one from the Joint Chiefs of Staff. Dr. Bush said he believed a proposal to Russia for exchange of scientific information would open the door to international collaboration in the field of atomic energy and eventually to effective control, the alternative being an atomic bomb race.

"The move does not involve 'giving away the secret of the atomic bomb,' " wrote Dr. Bush. "That secret resides principally in the details of construction of the bombs themselves, and in the manufacturing processes. What is given and what is received is scientific knowledge. Under an attempted closed system, and scientific espionage, it is probable that Russia would benefit to a considerable degree by our scientific progress, and we would benefit little by hers. Moreover, we cannot keep scientific secrets from Russia without also keeping them from the major portion of American scientists.

"We have a problem before us," added Dr. Bush. "Can we work with Russia and trust Russia? To some extent this move would enable us to find out. But the general advantage is that this move, when it became known, would announce to the world that we wish to proceed down the path of international good will and understanding."

Admiral Leahy sent me a memorandum incorporating the views of the Chiefs of Staff, although this did not reach me until a few weeks later. But I had already discussed the problems of atomic energy with Admiral Leahy, General Marshall, and the other Chiefs of Staff, and their views were known to me as I studied all the memoranda I had asked for at the Cabinet meeting of September 21.

The Joint Chiefs of Staff recommended that the United States retain all existing secrets with respect to the atomic weapons. Although the principles of nuclear physics underlying atomic explosives are widely known throughout the world, they said, many of the technical procedures and manufacturing processes used for atomic weapons were still secret. And in the absence of agreement among the great powers on fundamental international political problems, they said, they felt the release of information on atomic weapons would speed up an atomic armament race and expose the United States to greater danger. The Chiefs of Staff urged that steps of "political nature should be promptly and vigorously pressed during the probably limited period of American monopoly" to bring about international control for restricting or outlawing the use of atomic weapons. "The possibility," they concluded, "that other nations may succeed in developing atomic weapons in the not too distant future suggests that the question of political controls is a matter of immediate importance."

CHAPTER 35

        The news that I had held a Cabinet meeting to discuss atomic energy quickly led to false reports alleging there had been a sharp division in the Cabinet on the question of "giving the bomb to the Russians." Following the Cabinet meeting I had spent the weekend at Jefferson Island with a number of congressmen and government leaders, and on my return to Washington I was asked by a White House correspondent if I had approved or disapproved the "Wallace proposal." Some stories were published that Henry Wallace had led off the Cabinet discussion by calling for the surrender of the bomb's secret. I replied that Wallace had made no such proposal, adding that whatever was done with the bomb was a matter on which I, and I alone, would make the decision.

        As a matter of fact, I had already decided that atomic energy would require drastic controls, both at home and internationally. On September 19 I had asked Senators Connally, Vandenberg, and Lucas to come to my office, and I outlined for them, in general terms, what I had in mind. I told them that I wanted atomic energy developments at home to be under the control of a government agency. This was too important a development to be made the subject of profit-seeking. Most of all, further progress and development would require capital expenditures which, outside of government, could be found only under monopolistic conditions, and I was firmly opposed to any private monopoly in the field of atomic energy. I also told the senators that I hoped to start talks with our British and Canadian partners in this venture, looking toward some plan for international control. I was anxious to keep partisanship out of the discussion of the area of atomic energy policy, just as I always sought to keep foreign policy bi-partisan.

On October 3 I sent to the Congress a message urging that a national policy for atomic energy be enacted into law. Here is what I said:

"Almost two months have passed since the atomic bomb was used against Japan. That bomb did not win the war, but it certainly shortened the war. We know that it saved the lives of untold thousands of American and Allied soldiers who would otherwise have been killed in battle.

"The discovery of the means of releasing atomic energy began a new era in the history of civilization. The scientific and industrial knowledge on which this discovery rests does not relate merely to another weapon. It may someday prove to be more revolutionary in the development of human society than the invention of the wheel, the use of metals, or steam or internal combustion engines.

"Never in history has society been confronted with a power so full of potential danger and at the same time so full of promise for the future of man and for the peace of the world. I think I express the faith of the American people when I say that we can use the knowledge we have won, not for the devastation of war, but for the future welfare of humanity.

"To accomplish that objective we must proceed along two fronts—the domestic and the international.

"The first and the most urgent step is the determination of our domestic policy for the control, use and development of atomic energy within the United States.

"We cannot postpone decisions in this field. The enormous investment which we have made to produce the bomb has given us the two vast industrial plants in Washington and Tennessee and the many associated works throughout the country. It has brought together a vast organization of scientists, executives, industrial engineers and skilled workers—a national asset of inestimable value.

"The powers which the Congress wisely gave to the Government to wage war were adequate to permit the creation and development of this enterprise as a war project. Now that our enemies have surrendered, we should take immediate action to provide for the future use of this huge investment in brains and plant. I am informed that many of the people on whom depend the continued successful operation of the plants and the further development of atomic knowledge are getting ready to return to their normal pursuits. In many cases these people are considering leaving the project largely because of uncertainty concerning future national policy in this field. Prompt action to establish national policy will go a long way toward keeping a strong organization intact.

"It is equally necessary to direct future research and to establish control of the basic raw materials essential to the development of this power whether it is to be used for purposes of peace or war. Atomic force in ignorant or evil hands could inflict untold disaster upon the nation and the world. Society cannot hope even to protect itself—much less to realize the benefits of the discovery—unless prompt action is taken to guard against the hazards of misuse.

"I therefore urge, as a first measure in a program of utilizing our knowledge for the benefit of society, that the Congress enact legislation to fix a policy with respect to our existing plants, and to control all sources of atomic energy and all activities connected with its development and use in the United States.

"The legislation should give jurisdiction for these purposes to an Atomic Energy Commission with members appointed by the President with the advice and consent of the Senate.

"The Congress should lay down the basic principles for all the activities of the Commission, the objectives of which should be the promotion of the national welfare, securing the national defense, safeguarding world peace and the acquisition of further knowledge concerning atomic energy.

"The people of the United States know that the overwhelming power we have developed in this war is due in large measure to American science and American industry, consisting of management and labor. We believe that our science and industry owe their strength to the spirit of free inquiry and the spirit of free enterprise that characterize our country. The Commission, therefore, in carrying out its functions should interfere as little as possible with private research and private enterprise, and should use as much as possible existing institutions and agencies. The observance of this policy is our best guarantee of maintaining the pre-eminence in science and industry upon which our national well-being depends.

"All land and mineral deposits owned by the United States which constitute sources of atomic energy, and all stock piles of materials from which energy may be derived, and all plants or other property of the United States connected with its development and use should be transferred to the supervision and control of the Commission.

"The Commission should be authorized to acquire at a fair price, by purchase or condemnation, any minerals or other materials from which the sources of atomic energy can be derived, and also any land containing such minerals or materials which are not already owned by the United States.

"The power to purchase should include real and personal property outside the limits of the United States.

"The Commission should also be authorized to conduct all necessary research, experimentation, and operations for the further development and use of atomic energy for military, industrial, scientific or medical purposes. In these activities it should, of course, use existing private and public institutions and agencies to the fullest practicable extent.

"Under appropriate safeguards, the Commission should also be permitted to license any property available to the Commission for research, development and exploitation in the field of atomic energy. Among other things, such licensing should be conditioned of course upon a policy of widespread distribution of peacetime products on equitable terms which will prevent monopoly.

"In order to establish effective control and security, it should be declared unlawful to produce or use the substances comprising the sources of atomic energy or to import or export them except under conditions prescribed by the Commission.

"Finally, the Commission should be authorized to establish security regulations governing the handling of all information, material, and equipment under its jurisdiction. Suitable penalties should be prescribed for violating the security regulations of the Commission or any of the other terms of the Act.

"The measures which I have suggested may seem drastic and far-reaching, but the discovery with which we are dealing involves forces of nature too dangerous to fit into any of our usual concepts.

"The other phase of the problem is the question of the international control and development of this newly discovered energy.

"In international relations as in domestic affairs, the release of atomic energy constitutes a new force too revolutionary to consider in the framework of old ideas. We can no longer rely on the slow progress of time to develop a program of control among nations. Civilization demands that we shall reach at the earliest possible date a satisfactory arrangement for the control of this discovery in order that it may become a powerful and forceful influence towards the maintenance of world peace instead of an instrument of destruction.

"Scientific opinion appears to be practically unanimous that the essential theoretical knowledge upon which the discovery is based is already widely known. There is also substantial agreement that foreign research can come abreast of our present theoretical knowledge in time.

"The hope of civilization lies in international arrangements looking, if possible, to the renunciation of the use and development of the atomic bomb, and directing and encouraging the use of atomic energy and all future scientific information toward peaceful and humanitarian ends. The difficulties in working out such arrangements are great. The alternative to overcoming these difficulties, however, may be a desperate armament race which might well end in disaster. Discussion of the international problem cannot be safely delayed until the United Nations Organization is functioning and in a position adequately to deal with it.

"I therefore propose to initiate discussions, first with our associates in this discovery, Great Britain and Canada, and then with other nations, in an effort to effect agreement on the conditions under which cooperation might replace rivalry in the field of atomic power.

"I desire to emphasize that these discussions will not be concerned with disclosures relating to the manufacturing processes leading to the production of the atomic bomb itself. They will constitute an effort to work out arrangements covering the terms under which international collaboration and exchange of scientific information might safely proceed.

"The outcome of the discussions will be reported to the Congress as soon as possible, and any resulting agreements requiring Congressional action will be submitted to the Congress.

"But regardless of the course of discussions in the international field, I believe it is essential that legislation along the lines I have indicated be adopted as promptly as possible to insure the necessary research in, and development and control of, the production and use of atomic energy."

The following day a bill was introduced in the Congress with the stated intention of putting my program into effect. This was the May-Johnson bill, and few legislative proposals have ever had so stormy a trail to follow. A question immediately arose as to which committee the bill should be referred. I had given to the State Department the responsibility of looking after atomic energy legislation. But on Capitol Hill a significant battle took place between the Military and Foreign Affairs committees to take charge of the bill, resulting in an unfortunate delay.

At a press conference a week later I made another statement on atomic policy. I had promised some time earlier to attend the Pemiscot County Fair at Caruthersville, Missouri, an event that I had rarely missed in the years since my election to the Senate. While on this trip I stopped at Linda Lodge on Reelfoot Lake, near Tiptonville, Tennessee, and the press conference was held on the porch of the lodge.

The first question asked ran something like this: "Mr. President, you made a statement, as near as I can remember, in your speech at the fair that when the nations of the world learn to put total world progress ahead of individual national gain, then we could put this great discovery of the release of atomic energy to work and make the world a better place to live in. Would it be correct to interpret your position there as meaning that the atomic secret would not be shared unless and until we had positive assurance that the world has progressed to that point?"

To this I answered: "No, that would not be true, for this reason. The scientific knowledge that resulted in the atomic bomb is already world-wide knowledge. It is only the know-how of putting that knowledge practically to work that is our secret; just the same as know-how in the construction of the B-29, and the plane soon to follow the B-29, the greatest long-distance bomber in the world, and the mass production of automobiles. So far as the scientific knowledge is concerned, all the scientists know the answer, but how to put it to work—that is our secret."

The reporter then asked: "What I am getting at is, would it apply to letting them in on the know-how?"

I replied: "Well, I don't think it would do any good to let them in on the know-how, because I don't think they could do it, anyway. You would have to have the industrial plant and our engineering ability to do the job, as well as the scientific knowledge, and there isn't any reason for trying to keep the scientific knowledge covered up, because all the great scientists in every country know it; but the practical know-how is our ability to do the job. If they catch up with us on that, they will have to get it on their own hook, just as we did."

The reporter: "You mean, then, that we will not share that knowledge with our Allies?"

I replied: "Just the same as we haven't shared any of our engineering secrets. But so far as the scientific knowledge is concerned, they all know that, anyway."

The reporter kept on: "But so far as the bomb secret is concerned, we will not share that?"

I answered: "Not the know-how of putting it together, let's put it that way."

Meanwhile the groundwork had already been laid for the international discussions. I talked to the British Ambassador, Lord Halifax, about my plans, and he informed me that Prime Minister Attlee, too, was deeply preoccupied about the future of atomic energy in international relations.

On September 25 Attlee sent me a long letter in which he suggested that we hold joint discussions on the future of our atomic partnership. The emergence of the new weapon, the British Prime Minister said, meant not a quantitative but a qualitative change in the nature of warfare. The new weapon carried destructiveness far beyond anything the world had previously known, and no effective defense against it appeared in sight. Attlee noted, too, that the process was basically known to scientists of all nations and that development of usable weapons by nations not friendly to our two countries had to be expected. It was futile, he thought, to talk in terms of peaceful uses only, for he had been informed, he said, that "the harnessing of atomic energy as a source of power cannot be achieved without the simultaneous production of material capable of being used in a bomb."

The responsible statesmen of the world, the Prime Minister continued, were therefore faced with decisions that would affect the very survival of civilization. The question he was asking himself, he said, as he and his associates were planning the future of their nation, was, "Am I to plan for a peaceful or a warlike world?"

He explained that he believed he saw the hope of a peaceful world in the framework that had been erected at San Francisco, but this, he felt, was only a first step. "Now, it seems to us," he added, "that the building, the framework of which was erected at San Francisco, must be carried much further if it is to be an effective shelter for humanity."

He asked me to find an early occasion when he and I might sit down together and discuss this momentous problem. Attlee's suggestion was in line with my own idea to meet with him and the Canadian Prime Minister, Mackenzie King. I therefore invited both Attlee and King to visit Washington in November.

One of the problems that obviously bothered the British leader was the extent to which we would be willing to share our atomic knowledge. The basic arrangement between ourselves and the British was still the understanding which President Roosevelt and Prime Minister Churchill had reached at Quebec in August 1943. At that time it had been agreed that there should be a Combined Policy Committee, consisting of three Americans and three British members. This would serve as the channel through which atomic information would be exchanged. What was to be shared was described by the agreement in this manner:

". . . (b) There shall be complete interchange of information and ideas on all sections of the project between members of the Policy Committee and their immediate advisers.

"(c) In the field of scientific research and development there shall be full and effective interchange of information and ideas between those in the two countries engaged in the same sections of the field.

"(d) In the field of design, construction and operation of large-scale plants, interchange of information and ideas shall be regulated by such *ad hoc* arrangements as may, in each section of the field, appear to be necessary or desirable if the project is to be brought to fruition at the earliest moment. Such *ad hoc* arrangements shall be subject to the approval of the Policy Committee."

In a clarifying memorandum prepared for me by the State Department the meaning and understanding of this language was set out in further detail:

"It is quite clear on the face of the document that information concerning all scientific research and development was to be completely shared, but that information concerning manufacturing know-how was to be shared only if necessary to bring the project to speedy fruition and then only to the extent approved by the Policy Committee.

"There is only one possible basis for disagreement. It might be argued that manufacturing information is included within subparagraph (b) which provides for the complete interchange of information and ideas on all sections of the project between members of the Policy Committee and their immediate technical advisers.

"The history of the negotiations preceding the execution of the agreement, however, refute this interpretation of subparagraph (b).

"A draft of the agreement, in the same form in which it was eventually executed, was submitted on August 4, 1943, by Sir John Anderson, the chief British negotiator, to Dr. Bush, the chief American negotiator.

"On August 6, 1943, Dr. Bush acknowledged receipt and approval of Sir John's draft and made these statements of interpretation:

" 'In order that we may be sure that there is now no misundertanding I will comment on a few points. . . . It is our understanding that while the members of the Policy Committee will have access to all general information about all phases of the effort, the interchange of information about the detail of manufacture or construction of plants or of any final weapon will be governed by the provisions of (d), and that your suggested provision (b) merely is intended to provide that members of the Committee may interchange with their immediate scientific advisers the information they may have, in view of the fact that in some cases members of the Committee may not themselves be scientists.'

"In response to this letter of interpretation, Sir John stated in a letter to Dr. Bush of this same date:

" 'Thank you so much for your letter of the 6th August which is entirely satisfactory from my point of view.' "

Of course, throughout the war, we had thought of this problem entirely in the light of its military purposes—the production of the bomb. It had been a joint enterprise, but, by virtue of the fact that it had been located in the United States and the major part of the personnel and resources used were American, the manufacturing processes were not known to our British partners. But now, apparently, the nature of the partnership had to be readjusted. We were no longer striving for a limited objective of producing a weapon. We were to plan for the continued and peaceful use of an unprecedented force. The November discussions with Attlee were to provide him and me with an opportunity to exchange thoughts and ideas on this matter.

There were other important matters I wanted to discuss with Attlee.

These were financial and economic matters and the Palestinian problem. By then it had become clear that Great Britain would require major assistance in her work of reconstruction and rehabilitation. The British had at first indicated that they would like to have a loan of five billion dollars, without interest, repayable at one hundred million dollars a year, and our Treasury had countered with a proposal for a loan of three and a half billion dollars, at two per cent interest, payable over a fifty-year period and with deferment of payments in economically bad years. In the talks that followed between the British and us our differences had been considerably narrowed, but agreement still remained to be reached before we could submit the loan proposal.

In return for the loan, we wanted the British to relinquish many of the trade agreements by which the United States and many other countries had been placed at a disadvantage as against the countries of the British Commonwealth and the so-called sterling bloc, and in this connection some differences remained to be ironed out.

Shortly before Attlee's arrival in the United States I had chosen the occasion of Navy Day to make a foreign-policy statement. The day was October 27, 1945, and the place Central Park in New York. Earlier in the day it had been my privilege to be present and make a brief address at the ceremonies marking the commissioning of the aircraft carrier *Franklin D. Roosevelt.*

This was my first official visit as President to the City of New York, and I was given a warm and friendly welcome as our caravan of cars made its way up Broadway amid showers of ticker tape and confetti from the windows of the office buildings. Mayor La Guardia introduced me. I paid tribute to our Navy and then stated the principle which guided us in relation to the rest of the world:

"The foreign policy of the United States is based firmly on fundamental principles of righteousness and justice. In carrying out those principles we shall firmly adhere to what we believe to be right; and we shall not give our approval to any compromises with evil.

"But we know that we cannot attain perfection in this world overnight. We shall not let our search for perfection obstruct our steady progress toward international cooperation. We must be prepared to fulfill our responsibilities as best we can, within the framework of our fundamental principles, even though we have to operate in an imperfect world.

"Let me restate the fundamentals of that foreign policy of the United States:

"1. We seek no territorial expansion or selfish advantage. We have no plans for aggression against any other state, large or small. We have no objective which need clash with the peaceful aims of any other nation.

"2. We believe in the eventual return of sovereign rights and self-government to all peoples who have been deprived of them by force.

"3. We shall approve no territorial changes in any friendly part of the world unless they accord with the freely expressed wishes of the people concerned.

"4. We believe that all peoples who are prepared for self-government should be permitted to choose their own form of government by their our freely expressed choice, without interference from any foreign source. That is true in Europe, in Asia, in Africa, as well as in the Western Hemisphere.

"5. By the combined and cooperative action of our war allies, we shall help the defeated enemy states establish peaceful democratic governments of their own free choice. And we shall try to attain a world in which Nazism, Fascism and military aggression cannot exist.

"6. We shall refuse to recognize any government imposed upon any nation by the force of any foreign power. In some cases it may be impossible to prevent forceful imposition of such a government. But the United States will not recognize any such government.

"7. We believe that all nations should have the freedom of the seas and equal rights to the navigation of boundary rivers and waterways and of rivers and waterways which pass through more than one country.

"8. We believe that all states which are accepted in the society of nations should have access on equal terms to the trade and the raw materials of the world.

"9. We believe that the sovereign states of the Western Hemisphere, without interference from outside the Western Hemisphere, must work together as good neighbors in the solution of their common problems.

"10. We believe that full economic collaboration between all nations, great and small, is essential to the improvement of living conditions all over the world, and to the establishment of freedom from fear and freedom from want.

"11. We shall continue to strive to promote freedom of expression and freedom of religion throughout the peace-loving areas of the world.

"12. We are convinced that the preservation of peace between nations requires a United Nations Organization composed of all the peace-loving nations of the world who are willing jointly to use force if necessary to insure peace.

"That is the foreign policy which guides the United States now. That is the foreign policy with which it confidently faces the future."

At my conference with Attlee and Mackenzie King a foundation was drafted for a sound plan of international control of atomic energy. Our discussions got under way on November 11, the day after Attlee's arrival.

I told the two Prime Ministers that, so far as I could speak for the government of the United States, I believed that a free exchange of scientific knowledge would be essential to the peace of the world.

I explained that what I meant by "free exchange of scientific information" was that scientists of all countries should be allowed to visit freely with one another and that free inspection of the plans for atomic energy's use in peacetime pursuits should be the policy of every country. But I stressed that this would not necessarily mean that the engineering and production know-how should be made freely available, any more than we would make freely available any of our trade secrets.

I informed the two Prime Ministers that legislation was then pending in the Congress of the United States for the domestic control of atomic energy for peacetime purposes. It was my view, I said, that the control of atomic energy for destructive purposes should be lodged in the United Nations when we had become absolutely sure that the confidence of each nation in the good faith of the other was well founded. This, I suggested, might make it necessary to abandon the veto power in the Security Council.

Both Attlee and Mackenzie King then gave their views, and I was pleased that they were essentially in agreement with me.

This first conference was held with only the three of us present, but we met again in the afternoon of the same day, November 10, with our principal advisers. I had Secretary Byrnes and Admiral Leahy with me, and Attlee was accompanied by Lord Halifax and Sir John Anderson. Mr. Lester Pearson, the Canadian Ambassador in Washington, was with Mr. King.

Mr. Attlee led off the conversation by substantially stating the premises as I had outlined them in our morning talk, and Mr. King followed with a statement of his concurring views. Secretary Byrnes gave expression to the difficulties that would be encountered in trying to put such an agreement in words that could be clearly understood by all parties concerned.

All present were of the opinion that there should be free interchange of scientific knowledge and free inspection of industrial plants devoted to the manufacture of atomic energy for peacetime uses, but also that there should be agreement on these matters before any exchanges were made. Mr. Byrnes and the British and Canadian ambassadors were instructed to make an effort to put the views as mutually agreed upon in writing and to submit them to the three heads of government for consideration.

The discussion then turned to the problem of Palestine, but since there seemed to be more than superficial differences, it was decided to take this up later during the British Prime Minister's stay.

The Far Eastern situation was discussed, and agreement was reached on some basic points of policy. With regard to Japan, it was decided that if Russia should continue to stay away from the Advisory Council for Japan, the Council should go ahead and work without the Russians. On Korea it was agreed that immediate steps would be taken by our countries to set up a trusteeship under the direction of Great Britain, Russia, China, and the United States. We also discussed the disturbances in China, the two Prime Ministers concurring with my view that the government of Chiang Kai-shek, as the lawful government of the country, should receive continued support but without involving any of our countries in a possible civil war in China.

The spirit of our discussions is perhaps best illustrated by the informal remarks which Clement Attlee and I exchanged at the state dinner given for him and Mr. King at the White House on November 10. After the toasts had been exchanged, I rose to say a few words:

"It is a very great privilege for me tonight, as the President of the United States, to be host to the Prime Ministers of Great Britain and Canada, and the representatives of the other Commonwealths of the British Empire; and I want to say a few things that are, I think, in the hearts of all of us.

"We, I know, are striving for a world order, and a world peace, in which nations will feel as the British Commonwealth of Nations does, and as the forty-eight states in the United States feel. The objective of the United States, I think, has been stated both by the President of the United States and by the Secretary of State, in words which all of us can understand. We are trying heroically to implement the program which was started by Woodrow Wilson, was carried forward by Franklin Roosevelt, and was finally consummated at San Francisco by a delegation made up of members of the Senate and the House and citizens at large, without political complexion.

"One of the great things of the British Empire is that when they have a foreign policy—and they always have one—the British people are behind that foreign policy no matter which government is in power. That was amply illustrated at the Potsdam conference which started with Winston Churchill as Prime Minister of Great Britain and ended with our guest of honor tonight as the Prime Minister of Great Britain. And there was no break in the negotiations. Mr. Attlee was there with Mr. Churchill from the beginning. He knew the aims of the conference, and when he came back as Prime Minister, things went on just as they had started.

"I am hoping that the United States of America can implement a foreign policy which will be the policy of the people of the United States and not the policy of any political party.

"The Prime Minister of Great Britain and the Prime Minister of Canada are here to discuss with the Secretary of State and the President of the United States a program for the use of atomic energy, and for the implementing of a peace program that will be world-wide and continuous, and that will include every nation in the world without exception.

"We are going at our conference prayerfully. We are hoping that agreements and policies will come out of those conferences which will make the United Nations Organization a living, moving, active program."

Clement Attlee responded also informally:

"Mr. President and gentlemen: I am extraordinarily glad to be here this evening at this historic occasion, and in this great White House, and to be your guest tonight.

"I heard what you said with great interest, Mr. President, of the need for having a foreign policy—a foreign policy for Britain, a foreign policy for the United States of America—but it seems to me today that what we need most of all is a universal foreign policy, a foreign policy that is directed not to any immediate aim of any particular country, but a foreign policy that is conceived in the interest of all the people of the world. That does not mean that we don't take into account our particular differences, but it seems to me today that our overriding interests of world civilization come first.

"We all stand here for freedom, but we know that freedom may be attacked from many sides. Freedom needs to be retranslated every generation. Things that menace one epoch pass away; something else may menace it in another.

"We all here believe in democracy. We have come out of the war in a great fight for freedom and democracy. And I think that, standing here today with the United States of America and the representatives of the British Commonwealth of Nations, we can all take pride in our freedom; but I think we must beware of attributing that entirely to our own virtues. It has also something to do with our geographic positions, and we have to have a little charity towards others who are less happily placed.

"We, for years, have had the Channel to protect us; you, for years, have had the Atlantic—but as we know today, the discoveries of science are transcending seas and transcending oceans. We must not let anything rob us of our freedom, and of our democracy. Rather, we must try to see whether we cannot give to all nations that kind of security in which through long years on both sides of the Atlantic we worked up in practice, that most difficult of all forms of government—democracy, about the only form of government that is worthy of free men.

"And I hope, Mr. President, that our meeting today—this week—in which we shall take counsel together, will lead us on to help in bringing about what I believe is the supreme need today—the lifting of the bonds of fear from the human spirit, and the setting free of the human spirit, so that science, instead of a menace, as it is being looked on today, shall be looked on as something that is throwing open wide the gate to a fuller life for all of us.

"It is my earnest desire, Mr. President, in meeting with you here today, that you and I and Mr. King, and all others with whom we shall be talking, will keep ever in mind that what we are out for today is to try and devise a world policy of the common man."

When our discussions were concluded on November 15, I called the press and radio correspondents into my office and, in the presence of Attlee and King, read them the declaration we had agreed on:

THE PRESIDENT OF THE UNITED STATES, THE PRIME MINISTER OF THE UNITED KINGDOM, AND THE PRIME MINISTER OF CANADA HAVE ISSUED THE FOLLOWING STATEMENT:

1. We recognize that the application of recent scientific discoveries to the methods and practice of war has placed at the disposal of mankind means of destruction hitherto unknown, against which there can be no adequate military defense, and in the employment of which no single nation can in fact have a monopoly.

2. We desire to emphasize that the responsibility for devising means to ensure that the new discoveries shall be used for the benefit of mankind, instead of as a means of destruction, rests not on our nations alone, but upon the whole civilized world. Nevertheless, the progress that we have made in the development and use of atomic energy demands that we take an initiative in the matter, and we have accordingly met together to consider the possibility of international action:

(a) To prevent the use of atomic energy for destructive purposes.

(b) To promote the use of recent and future advances in scientific knowledge, particularly in the utilization of atomic energy, for peaceful and humanitarian ends.

3. We are aware that the only complete protection for the civilized world from the destructive use of scientific knowledge lies in the prevention of war. No system of safeguards that can be devised will of itself provide an effective guarantee against production of atomic weapons by a nation bent on aggression. Nor can we ignore the possibility of the development of other weapons, or of new methods of warfare, which may constitute as great a threat to civilization as the military use of atomic energy.

4. Representing, as we do, the three countries which possess the knowledge essential to the use of atomic energy, we declare at the outset our willingness, as a first contribution, to proceed with the exchange of fundamental scientific information and the interchange of scientists and scientific literature for peaceful ends with any nation that will fully reciprocate.

5. We believe that the fruits of scientific research should be made available to all nations, and that freedom of investigation and free interchange of ideas are essential to the progress of knowledge. In pursuance of this policy, the basic scientific information essential to the development of atomic energy for peaceful purposes has already been made available to the world. It is our intention that all further information of this character that may become available from time to time shall be similarly treated. We trust that other nations will adopt the same policy, thereby creating an atmosphere of reciprocal confidence in which political agreement and cooperation will flourish.

6. We have considered the question of the disclosure of detailed information concerning the practical industrial application of atomic energy. The military exploitation of atomic energy depends, in large part, upon the same methods and processes as would be required for industrial uses.

We are not convinced that the spreading of the specialized information regarding the practical application of atomic energy, before it is possible to devise effective, reciprocal, and enforceable safeguards acceptable to all nations, would contribute to a constructive solution of the problem of the atomic bomb. On the contrary, we think it might have the opposite effect. We are, however, prepared to share, on a reciprocal basis with others of the United Nations, detailed information concerning the practical industrial application of atomic energy just as soon as effective enforceable safeguards against its use for destructive purposes can be devised.

7. In order to attain the most effective means of entirely eliminating the use of atomic energy for destructive purposes and promoting its widest use for industrial and humanitarian purposes, we are of the opinion that at the earliest practicable date a Commission should be set up under the United Nations Organization to prepare recommendations for submission to the Organization.

The Commission should be instructed to proceed with the utmost dispatch and should be authorized to submit recommendations from time to time dealing with separate phases of its work.

In particular the Commission should make specific proposals:

(a) For extending between all nations the exchange of basic scientific information for peaceful ends;

(b) For control of atomic energy to the extent necessary to ensure its use only for peaceful purposes;

(c) For the elimination from national armaments of atomic weapons and of all other major weapons adaptable to mass destruction;

(d) For effective safeguards by way of inspection and other means to protect complying states against the hazards of violations and evasions.

8. The work of the Commission should proceed by separate stages, the successful completion of each one of which will develop the necessary confidence of the world before the next stage is undertaken. Specifically, it is considered that the Commission might well devote its attention first to the wide exchange of scientists and scientific information, and as a second stage to the development of full knowledge concerning natural resources of raw materials.

9. Faced with the terrible realities of the application of science to destruction, every nation will realize more urgently than before the overwhelming need to maintain the rule of law among nations and to banish the scourge of war from the earth. This can only be brought about by giving

wholehearted support to the United Nations Organization, and by con-
solidating and extending its authority, thus creating conditions of mutual
trust in which all peoples will be free to devote themselves to the arts of
peace. It is our firm resolve to work without reservation to achieve these
ends.

The City of Washington
THE WHITE HOUSE
November 15, 1945

> Harry S. Truman
> President of the United States
>
> C. R. Attlee
> Prime Minister of the United Kingdom
>
> W. L. Mackenzie King
> Prime Minister of Canada

In addition to this agreed declaration, the three of us also signed a
brief memorandum that read as follows:

"1. We desire that there should be full and effective cooperation in
the field of atomic energy between the United States, the United Kingdom
and Canada.

"2. We agree that the Combined Policy Committee and the Combined
Development Trust should be continued in a suitable form.

"3. We request the Combined Policy Committee to consider and recommend to us appropriate arrangements for this purpose."

By this memorandum we pledged ourselves to continue the wartime
collaboration that had brought us to a successful outcome. I gave the
Cabinet a detailed account of my conversations with the two Prime
Ministers at the Cabinet meeting on November 16 and asked for their
comments. All the members present thought that this agreement was a
step in the right direction. Secretary Wallace expressed some doubts
about the device of a U.N. commission. Vinson and Clark, in line with
the position they had taken at our earlier discussion of atomic energy,
wanted to be assured that there was no intention on my part to reveal
any of the "know-how." Forrestal thought that this agreement would
"make the U.N.O. a living thing." All agreed, however, that to refer the
problem of atomic energy to the United Nations would give that organization a chance to prove itself.

CHAPTER 36

Typical of our impatience in the fall of 1945, with the capitulation of Japan, was the rush of wartime officials in key government posts to return to civilian life. Despite the urgent jobs that still had to be done in the transition from war to peace, officials in great numbers in all ranks were submitting resignations. It was a major headache to replace those who were leaving. The sensitivity to criticism of men in government service grows as war fades into the background.

Public officials live in glass houses. They are subject at any time to attacks in Congress or in the press. There are few people willing to expose themselves to such hazards, especially those who have been used to private business careers. And government salaries, even for top positions, are small compared to what is paid by business. But fortunately, during the critical years that followed, we did have men who were able and willing to pass up the inducements of private life and business in their devotion to the public good. These men deserve the highest consideration when the history of their country is finally written.

Under the Constitution the President of the United States is alone responsible for the faithful execution of the laws. Our government is fixed on the basis that the President is the only person in the executive branch who has the final authority. Everyone else in the executive branch is an agent of the President. There are some people, and sometimes members of Congress and the press, who get mixed up in their thinking about the powers of the President. The important fact to remember is that the President is the only person in the executive branch who has final authority, and if he does not exercise it, we may be in trouble. If he exercises his authority wisely, that is good for the country. If he does not exercise it wisely, that is too bad, but it is better than not exercising it at all.

Yet our government is so vast that branches of the administrative machinery do not always tie in smoothly with the White House. The Cabinet presents the principal medium through which the President controls his administration. I made it a point always to listen to Cabinet officers at length and with care, especially when their points of view differed from mine.

I never allowed myself to forget that the final responsibility was mine. I would ask the Cabinet to share their counsel with me, even encouraging disagreement and argument to sharpen up the different points of view. On major issues I would frequently ask them to vote, and I expected the Cabinet officers to be frank and candid in expressing their opinions to me. At the same time, I insisted that they keep me informed of the major activities of their departments in order to make certain that they supported the policy once I had made a decision.

If a Cabinet member could not support the policy I had laid down, I tried to work out an understanding with him. But I could not permit, any more than any President can, such difference of opinion to be aired in public by a dissenting member of the Cabinet. In late 1945 and during 1946 there were three occasions when I found myself faced with a problem of this kind. The first of these involved the Secretary of State.

James F. Byrnes could look back upon a career of almost unequaled experience in government. As a senator, he had been a leader of the administration forces. He had seen service on the highest court of the nation. From there, President Roosevelt had called him to the executive branch, making him, in effect, the Assistant President in charge of domestic economy. In political circles it was known that Byrnes had hoped to be chosen as Roosevelt's running mate in 1944.

In his executive position during the war years Byrnes had enjoyed unprecedented freedom of action. President Roosevelt had delegated to him whatever necessary powers could be marshaled to keep the nation's economy behind the war effort. This arrangement had left President Roosevelt free to devote his time and energies mainly to the conduct of the war and to foreign relations. But this delegation of presidential powers had an extraordinary influence on Byrnes. It caused him to believe that, as an official of the executive branch of the government, he could have a completely free hand within his own sphere of duty. In fact, he came to think that his judgment was better than the President's.

More and more during the fall of 1945 I came to feel that in his role as Secretary of State Byrnes was beginning to think of himself as an Assistant President in full charge of foreign policy. Apparently he failed to realize that, under the Constitution, the President is required to assume all responsibility for the conduct of foreign affairs. The President cannot abdicate that responsibility, and he cannot turn it over to anyone else.

A Secretary of State should never have the illusion that he is President of the United States. Some Secretaries of State have had such illusions, but they would never admit it. There have been some Presidents, of course, who acted as if they were Secretaries of State. They are not and cannot be, and they will get into trouble if they try. The primary function of the Secretary of State is to be the President's personal adviser on foreign affairs. He has to run a department which should have skilled and experienced men to get the best information possible on any subject or problem that affects the relations with other governments. The Secretary of State obtains, if he can, the very best advice from people who live with the problems of foreign affairs so that he may present it to the President. The President then must make the basic decisions, but he must be kept constantly informed of all major developments. A President cannot tolerate a Secretary of State who keeps important matters away from him until five minutes before a decision has to be made. Certainly a President cannot permit a Secretary of State to make policy decisions for him.

The conference of the Council of Foreign Ministers at Moscow in December 1945 produced a situation that made it necessary for me to make it plain to Byrnes that he was not carrying out the foreign policy I had laid down and that, in effect, he was assuming the responsibilities of the President.

Hardly had Byrnes left on his trip to the Russian capital when, on December 14, I was asked by Senator Tom Connally if I could see him and the other members of the Senate Atomic Energy Committee. Byrnes, it appeared, had met with a number of senators the day before and had informed them that it was his plan to secure Russian concurrence at the forthcoming conference to the proposal of setting up an Atomic Energy Commission under the United Nations—the plan on which Attlee, Mackenzie King, and I had agreed the previous month.

The Senate committee members were greatly disturbed by the conversation they had had with the Secretary of State. They said they had received the impression from him that he would discuss, and perhaps agree to, the turnover of certain atomic energy information even before there had been any agreement on safeguards and inspections against the abuse of such information. Senator Vandenberg told me that he feared Byrnes might make such an agreement because the directive under which he traveled—and which had been drawn up on Byrnes's own instructions in the State Department—made it possible for him to discuss any portion of the proposal independently of other sections.

I immediately informed the senators that there was no intention by the administration to disclose any scientific information during the Moscow conference, nor would there be any final commitment there on the turnover of such information. I made it clear that I had no thought of releasing any information regarding the bomb itself until the American people could be assured that there were adequate arrangements for inspection and safeguards.

I instructed Under Secretary of State Acheson to send a message to Byrnes to inform him of this meeting with the senators.

"The President," Acheson cabled, "explained that you had no intention whatever of disclosing any scientific information in the course of your present mission. It was explained further that you intended primarily to discuss in Moscow the matter of securing Soviet support for the establishment of the United Nations Commission.

"The President," Acheson added, "made it clear that any proposals advanced would be referred here before agreement was reached and that he had no intention of agreeing to disclose any information regarding the bomb at this time or unless and until arrangements for inspection and safeguards could be worked out."

Secretary of State Byrnes replied on December 17:

"I do not intend presenting any proposal outside of the framework of the three power declaration. . . ."

I heard no more from the Secretary of State until Christmas Eve, when he sent me the following message through Ambassador Harriman:

"We have reached complete agreement as to the peace conference and resumption of the work on peace treaties with Italy and enemy Balkan states. China has concurred. We have not definitely heard attitude of France but I hope to talk with Bidault this afternoon and secure the agreement of France.

"In my first conversation with Stalin on the peace conference he supported Molotov's position but later Stalin telephoned making concessions which made possible our agreement. As a result of a long conference with Stalin yesterday afternoon, I now hope that we can make forward step toward settling the Rumanian-Bulgarian problems. We also discussed the Chinese situation, Iran and atomic energy. As a result of our conversation, I hope that we will this afternoon be able to reach some agreement on these issues. Yesterday Molotov held out for complete subordination of the Atomic Energy Commission to the Security Council, making it a subordinate agency of the Council, and objected to any reference to a plan being developed by stages. We are in general accord as to Far Eastern issues. The situation is encouraging and I hope that today we can reach final agreement on the questions outstanding and wind up our work tomorrow."

This message told me very little that the newspaper correspondents had not already reported from Moscow. This was not what I considered a proper account by a Cabinet member to the President. It was more like one partner in a business telling the other that his business trip was progressing well and not to worry.

I was in Independence, Missouri, on December 27 when the next word from Byrnes reached me. Charles Ross, my press secretary, informed me from Washington that a message had been received from the Secretary of State. Byrnes had asked that the White House arrange for him to address the American people over all the networks so that he might report on the results of the conference. What those results were I did not yet know.

A little after ten that night the text of the State Department's communiqué on the Moscow conference was brought to me. It had been released in Washington, by Byrnes's orders, an hour earlier.

I did not like what I read. There was not a word about Iran or any other place where the Soviets were on the march. We had gained only an empty promise of further talks.

I returned to Washington from Independence the next day, December 28. Almost immediately upon my arrival Senator Arthur H. Vandenberg, the ranking Republican member of the Foreign Relations Committee, who had previously telephoned me at Independence about the Byrnes communiqué, came to see me. Under Secretary of State Dean Acheson, whom I had called to the White House, was present while I talked to the senator. Vandenberg's main concern was with the section in the communiqué in which the three foreign ministers agreed to take up, "in stages," the question of international control of atomic energy. The communiqué listed four points that would deserve consideration, the last point being the provision of inspections and safeguards against abuse of atomic power information. The senator read this to mean that we might dicuss, or consent to, the sharing of atomic information before any safeguards might have been agreed on to protect the nation's interests. I assured him that as long as I was President no production secrets of the bomb would be given away until there was international agreement on a system of inspection.

Acheson and Vandenberg helped me draft a statement for release to the press. In this statement I wanted to clear up the meaning of the Moscow agreement as it related to atomic energy. I thought that it was most urgent that there be no misunderstanding about our determination to ensure proper safeguards.

Once this was done, I went directly to the presidential yacht *Williamsburg* for a cruise which was to be devoted mainly to the preparation of a radio address to the nation which I had scheduled for January 3. I had asked a number of my advisers to join me aboard the yacht so that we might have time to discuss problems of domestic policy. We were anchored at Quantico, Virginia, the next day when Press Secretary Charles Ross received a telephone call from Byrnes. The Secretary of State had just arrived in Washington and wanted to know if everything was set up for the four-network broadcast he had requested.

I was sitting next to Ross as he took this call.

"Who's on the phone?" I asked.

"Byrnes," he replied.

I told him what to say in reply, and he turned back to the telephone.

"The President asks me to tell you," he said, "that you had better come down here posthaste and make your report to the President before you do anything else."

By five o'clock that afternoon Byrnes had reached Quantico and the *Williamsburg*.

We went into my stateroom when he arrived, and I closed the door behind us. I told him that I did not like the way in which I had been left in the dark about the Moscow conference. I told him that, as President, I intended to know what progress we were making and what we were doing in foreign negotiations. I said that it was shocking that a communiqué should be issued in Washington announcing a foreign-policy development of major importance that I had never heard of. I said I would not tolerate a repetition of such conduct.

Byrnes sought to put the blame mostly on his subordinates. He said that he had expected them to keep me informed. But he now admitted that he should have attended to it personally.

Byrnes left a collection of documents on the conference with me, and I agreed to study them at once. As I went through these papers it became abundantly clear to me that the successes of the Moscow conference were unreal. I could see that the Russians had given us no more than a general promise that they would be willing to sit down to talk again about the control of atomic energy. There was not a word in the communiqué to suggest that the Russians might be willing to change their ways in Iran—where the situation was rapidly becoming very serious—or anywhere else. Byrnes, I concluded after studying the entire record, had taken it upon himself to move the foreign policy of the United States in a direction to which I could not, and would not, agree. Moreover, he had undertaken this on his own initiative without consulting or informing the President.

I knew that it was time to make things perfectly clear between the Secretary of State and myself. I wanted to do it without delay, without publicity, and in writing. So I wrote out in longhand a letter to Byrnes, and when he came to the White House on January 5 I read it to him as he sat at my desk in the Oval Room:

My dear Jim:

I have been considering some of our difficulties. As you know, I would like to pursue a policy of delegating authority to the members of the Cabinet in their various fields and then back them up in the results. But in doing that and in carrying out that policy I do not intend to turn over the complete authority of the President nor to forgo the President's prerogative to make the final decision.

Therefore it is absolutely necessary that the President should be kept fully informed on what is taking place. This is vitally necessary when negotiations are taking place in a foreign capital, or even in another city than Washington. This procedure is necessary in domestic affairs and it is vital in foreign affairs. At San Francisco no agreements or compromises were ever agreed to without my approval. At London you were in constant touch with me and communication was established daily if necessary. I only saw you for a possible thirty minutes the night before you left after your interview with the Senate committee.

I received no communication from you directly while you were in Moscow. The only message I had from you came as a reply to one which I had Under Secretary Acheson send to you about my interview with the Senate Committee on Atomic Energy.

The protocol was not submitted to me, nor was the communiqué. I was completely in the dark on the whole conference until I requested you to come to the *Williamsburg* and inform me. The communiqué was released before I ever saw it.

Now I have infinite confidence in you and in your ability but there should be a complete understanding between us on procedure. Hence this memorandum.

For the first time I read the Ethridge letter this morning. It is full of information on Rumania and Bulgaria and confirms our previous information on those two police states. I am not going to agree to the recognition of those governments unless they are radically changed.

I think we ought to protest with all the vigor of which we are capable against the Russian program in Iran. There is no justification for it. It is a parallel to the program of Russia in Latvia, Estonia and Lithuania. It is also in line with the high-handed and arbitrary manner in which Russia acted in Poland.

At Potsdam we were faced with an accomplished fact and were by circumstances almost forced to agree to Russian occupation of Eastern Poland and the occupation of that part of Germany east of the Oder River by Poland. It was a high-handed outrage.

At the time we were anxious for Russian entry into the Japanese War. Of course we found later that we didn't need Russia there and that the Russians have been a headache to us ever since.

When you went to Moscow you were faced with another accomplished fact in Iran. Another outrage if I ever saw one.

Iran was our ally in the war. Iran was Russia's ally in the war. Iran agreed to the free passage of arms, ammunition and other supplies running into the millions of tons across her territory from the Persian Gulf to the Caspian Sea. Without these supplies furnished by the United States, Russia would have been ignominiously defeated. Yet now Russia stirs up rebellion and keeps troops on the soil of her friend and ally—Iran.

There isn't a doubt in my mind that Russia intends an invasion of Turkey and the seizure of the Black Sea Straits to the Mediterranean. Unless Russia is faced with an iron fist and strong language another war is in the making. Only one language do they understand—"how many divisions have you?"

I do not think we should play compromise any longer. We should refuse to recognize Rumania and Bulgaria until they comply with our requirements; we should let our position on Iran be known in no uncertain terms and we should continue to insist on the internationalization of the Kiel Canal, the Rhine-Danube waterway and the Black Sea Straits and we should maintain complete control of Japan and the Pacific. We should rehabilitate China and create a strong central government there. We should do the same for Korea.

Then we should insist on the return of our ships from Russia and force a settlement of the Lend-Lease debt of Russia.

I'm tired of babying the Soviets.

Byrnes accepted my decision. He did not ask to be relieved or express a desire to quit. It was not until some months later that he came to me and suggested that his health would not allow him to stay on. He agreed to remain through the negotiations of the peace treaties that were to grow out of his Moscow commitments. Throughout the remainder of 1946, however, it was understood between him and me that he would quit whenever I could designate his successor. I knew all that time whom I wanted for the job. It was General Marshall. But the general was on a vital assignment in China that had to run its course before the change in the State Department could be carried out.

My memorandum to Byrnes not only clarified the Secretary's position, but it was the point of departure of our policy. "I'm tired of babying the Soviets," I had said to Byrnes, and I meant it.

I had hoped that the Russians would return favor for favor, but almost from the time I became President I found them acting without regard for their neighboring nations and in direct violation of the obligations they had assumed at Yalta. The first Russian leader I had had an opportunity to talk to was Molotov, and it had been necessary, even then, for me to speak bluntly and plainly. I was sure that Russia would understand firm, decisive language and action much better than diplomatic pleasantries.

In all subsequent relations, until he finally left office, Secretary Byrnes took great pains to keep me posted on what was going on. He would call daily if telephone connections were available, and his dispatches to the State Department would be placed before me regularly. It was therefore with a clear conscience that I could parry questions at press conferences during the year concerning rumors that he was about to resign or had resigned.

When General Eisenhower, whom I had appointed Chief of Staff of the Army to succeed General Marshall, went on an inspection trip to the Far East later that year, I told him that I had a message I wanted him to give to Marshall when he saw him in China. I said that I wanted him to tell Marshall that my Secretary of State had stomach trouble and wanted to retire from office and that I wanted to know if Marshall would take the job when it became vacant.

When Eisenhower returned, he reported that he had delivered the message and that Marshall's answer had been "Yes." When Marshall's mission to China came to an end, I announced his appointment without asking him again. Byrnes and I exchanged a number of friendly and personal letters after he left Washington. It was not until the civil-rights issue made him bitter and distant that our contacts diminished.

My second problem in the Cabinet arose when I named Ed Pauley to be Under Secretary of the Navy in January 1946—an appointment which President Roosevelt had intended to make. Indeed, Roosevelt and Forrestal had agreed that Pauley would be named Under Secretary and that he would then succeed Forrestal as head of the department.

I wanted Pauley in my official family. His record in the reparations program had only confirmed my high opinion of his administrative abilities. Forrestal thought very highly of him, urged him strongly on me as his choice of a successor, and had planned to travel with him to the Far East when Pauley went there on reparations business in the fall of 1945. This close association, Forrestal thought, would make the transition easier.

Forrestal had been trying to resign ever since the fighting had ended, and he would repeat the request at frequent intervals. I thought too highly of him as a public servant to allow him to resign and therefore told him that it was my plan to make Pauley Under Secretary. But Forrestal thought of Pauley as his own relief man.

When Pauley's appointment to the job of Under Secretary was announced in January, some Republicans in the Senate indicated they might want to look "closely" into the nomination. This was not unusual, and, since the Democratic majority was ample, there was nothing to worry about. Then on February 1, after the Cabinet meeting, Harold Ickes, the Secretary of the Interior, told me he had been asked to appear before the Senate Naval Affairs Committee in connection with the Pauley appointment. I did not ask Ickes why he had been called or what he intended to say. I merely said, "Tell 'em the truth and be gentle to Ed."

When Ickes went before the committee he testified under oath that Pauley had once told him that it might be possible to raise several hundred thousand dollars for the campaign fund of the Democratic party in California if the Justice Department would drop the plan to bring suit to have the tidelands oil deposits declared in the federal domain. Ickes made it sound as if Pauley had asked him to exert his influence with President Roosevelt to have the suit dropped in order that he might raise these funds. Pauley, on the other hand—and also under oath—said that Ickes was mistaken when he put it that way.

I had known Pauley for a number of years, and it did not sound like him to have made what Ickes called, a few days later and before the same committee, the "rawest proposition ever made to me." I knew Ickes had a reputation for picking fights. He was not given to tact and was not likely to admit that he might be wrong, or even mistaken.

I told my press conference on February 7 that I was behind Pauley and that Ickes might be mistaken. A few days later—on February 13—I received a lengthy letter from Ickes. It was his resignation as Secretary of the Interior. It was not a courteous letter. It was the kind of letter sent by a man who is sure that he can have his way if he threatens to quit. But I was not going to be threatened. Ickes had written at great length that he felt I should have known—though he never had told me—what he was going to say about Pauley, and that my remark at the press conference was, in effect, a declaration of no confidence. Of course Ickes suggested that there were so many things that only he would know how to attend to that he was willing to delay his departure from the government for another six weeks.

I wrote a brief note in reply. His resignation, I said, was accepted as of the following day. I assumed, I added, that he had intended to resign not only as Secretary of the Interior but from his other government positions as well. He retorted with an arrogant note and went on the air that night to defend his conduct. Pauley, however, although I backed him to the end, finally asked me to withdraw his nomination.

Ickes, in later years, began to write to me again, at first about race discrimination and tidelands oil, but later quite generally and in a friendly vein. I still think he was mistaken.

Ickes had been an able administrator in the Interior Department, and as Secretary of the Interior he was a protector of the public interest for the benefit of all the people. When I was chairman of the special Senate committee, Ickes complained to me that President Roosevelt had not asked him to the White House for six months because of a quarrel. Ickes said he thought Roosevelt would be better off taking his advice rather than that of some other members of the Cabinet, Hopkins in particular. I realized then he was a troublemaker and difficult to get along with. In a sense I was fond of him, especially because he was not a special-interests man. Although he was a scold and a gossip and everything that implies, I never had a personal clash with him, but when he got too big for his breeches and opposed me openly on my appointment of Pauley, I could not, as President, tolerate that.

My third Cabinet problem of the year involved Henry Wallace. Wallace had served eight years as President Roosevelt's Secretary of Agriculture. He had been Vice-President of the United States in Roosevelt's third term and had made a strong bid for renomination in 1944, which failed because it did not have the support of President Roosevelt. In January 1945, however, Roosevelt had appointed him Secretary of Commerce, although it had taken my own tie-breaking vote as Vice-President to make his confirmation come through.

Wallace had a vision of the "Century of the Common Man" about which he was eloquent and persistent. He was certain that the "Century of the Common Man" would start just as soon as the war ended and believed that good will would bring peace. He began to devote much of his energy to the problem of our relations with Russia and to spend much time away from his duties as Secretary of Commerce.

When I named General Walter Bedell Smith to be our Ambassador to Moscow in March 1946, Wallace spoke to me about what he called a "new approach" to Russia and followed this up with the following memorandum:

March 14, 1946

Dear Mr. President:
As you may recall, in the course of our talk on Tuesday I suggested that we would have a better chance to improve our relations with the Soviets if, in addition to our new diplomatic effort, we also made a new approach along economic and trade lines. I am hopeful, as I know you are, that General Bedell Smith will succeed in breaking the present diplomatic deadlock in U.S.-Soviet relations and that he will find a way of persuading the Soviet Government of the advantages of cooperating with the U.S.A. and with the U.N.O. in settling outstanding international issues.
I am deeply convinced that General Bedell Smith's task would be made easier and his success more lasting if we could also at the same time discuss with the Russians in a friendly way their long range economic problems and the future of our cooperation in matters of trade. We know that much of the recent Soviet behavior which has caused us concern has been the result of their dire economic needs and of their disturbed sense of security. The events of the past few months have thrown the Soviets back to their pre-1939 fears of "capitalist encirclement" and to their erroneous belief that the Western World, including the U.S.A., is invariably and unanimously hostile.
I think we can disabuse the Soviet mind and strengthen the faith of the

Soviets in our sincere devotion to the cause of peace by proving to them that we want to trade with them and to cement our economic relations with them. To do this, it is necessarry to talk with them in an understanding way, with full realization of their difficulties and yet with emphasis on the lack of realism in many of their assumptions and conclusions which stand in the way of peaceful world cooperation. What I have in mind is an extended discussion of the background needed for future economic collaboration rather than negotiation related to immediate proposals such as a loan. On our part, participants in such a discussion would have to be capable of speaking in terms of the general problems involved, as well as specific economic and commercial matters, and of relating the Russian approach to these problems to current U.S. Government and business policies and practices.

I know that we have good foreign service men in Moscow and that they are doing their best. But the task before us now is so big and so complex that it calls for a new start by a new group. My suggestion is that you authorize a group to visit Moscow for the talks which I suggested above. If you concur in this proposal, I am ready to make suggestions regarding the composition of this mission.

Sincerely yours,
Henry A. Wallace
Secretary of Commerce

With this letter, Wallace sent a memorandum in which he said that he had discussed the matter with General Bedell Smith. But General Smith had asked that he be given the original, with my initials on it to indicate that I had approved.

I ignored this letter of Wallace's. I had expressed my policy to Bedell Smith and had suggested the approach he should take to the Kremlin. I could see little to be gained from the Wallace proposal.

On July 23 Wallace wrote another letter on our relations with Russia —a letter which later burst into the headlines. In twelve pages of single-spaced typing he analyzed the problem as he saw it and listed a number of things that he believed we should do. He contrasted what he said our actions were with what he thought should be our ideas in the field of international relations. He recited the size of our defense budget, the testing of atomic bombs in the Pacific, the production of long-range bombers, the proposed co-ordination of armaments with the Latin-American countries, and our efforts to obtain air bases abroad. These actions, he wrote, "must make it look to the rest of the world as if we were only paying lip service to peace at the conference table. These facts rather make it appear either (1) that we are preparing ourselves to win the war which we regard as inevitable or (2) that we are trying hard to build up a preponderance of force to intimidate the rest of mankind."

He then addressed himself to the arguments of those who, he said, would put their faith in force and argued that the atomic age had made dependence on military solutions outdated. Our attempt to bring international control to atomic energy he thought defective because, in his eyes, "we are telling the Russians that if they are 'good boys' we may eventually turn over our knowledge of atomic energy to them and to the other nations."

Altogether, Wallace could see every reason why the Soviets would or should distrust us and no reason why our policy might bear fruit. His conclusion, therefore, was that we should change our policy in order to "allay any reasonable Russian grounds for fear, suspicion and distrust." But he had no specific proposals how this might be accomplished without surrendering to them on every count.

I read this letter and, although I could not agree with his approach, I let him know that I appreciated the time he had taken to put himself on record. I also sent a copy of the letter to Secretary Byrnes.

No Cabinet meetings were held between August 2 and September 6, and because Wallace was away from Washington for several weeks, he did not come to the September 6 session. On September 10 he had a fifteen-minute appointment with me, most of which was taken up with discussions of problems of his department and matters relating to the world food board. Just before he left, however, Wallace mentioned that he would deliver a speech in New York on the twelfth. He said that he intended to say that we ought to look at the world through American eyes rather than through the eyes of a pro-British or rabidly anti-Russian press. I told him that I was glad he was going to help the Democrats in New York by his appearance. There was, of course, no time for me to read the speech, even in part.

I had a press conference on the morning of the twelfth, and one of the reporters asked me if Mr. Wallace's speech that night had my approval. I said yes, it did. Of course I should have said, "He's told me he is going to make a speech," because everyone promptly took my answer to mean that I had read the speech and approved every part of its content.

To make things worse, when Wallace delivered the speech, which was an all-out attack on our foreign policy, he said at the most critical point in the speech that he had talked to me in this vein and that I had approved of what he was saying.

The White House correspondents queried me again. I told them that my earlier statement was never intended to convey such a meaning. I added that regardless of Wallace's speech there would be no change in the foreign policy of the United States. But when Wallace returned to Washington from New York on September 16 he made a public statement that he intended to go on fighting for what he conceived to be the right way toward peace. The following day he released to the press the text of his July 23 letter to me.

The release of this letter was never approved by me, but by the time I learned that Wallace had spoken to Charlie Ross about it and that the two had agreed on its release before its threatened publication by a columnist, it was too late to stop it. The reaction abroad, both to Wallace's speech and the release of the latter, was an even stronger echo of the furor in our own press. Our diplomats reported from the world's capitals that they were being besieged with questions: Was the United States about to change directions?

I called Wallace to the White House. The date was September 18, and it was three-thirty in the afternoon when Charlie Ross came in with Wallace and closed the doors behind him. Only the three of us were present during the nearly two-and-a-half-hour session that followed. I showed Wallace copies of the cables from our representatives abroad. I told him that he would always be free to speak his mind to me but that when he turned to the American public to criticize the American foreign policy he was hitting at the President.

Wallace proceeded to develop his ideas then at great length. He talked about the beauty of peace and how he knew that the people of all nations had no desire but to have peace. He said he felt sure that Russia wanted peace but was afraid of our intentions.

I have never doubted Henry Wallace's sincerity or honesty of purpose, but after this conversation I was afraid that, knowingly or not, he would lend himself to the more sinister ends of the Reds and those who served them.

Wallace had a following. I realized that his appeal had some effect. If I could keep him in the Cabinet I might be able to put some check on his activities. I explained to him the delicate nature of the negotiations Secretary Byrnes was just then carrying on in Paris. Wallace agreed that it would be better at such a time if public criticism of the State Department and the national foreign policy were withheld. He also agreed to make no further speeches or statements until after the adjournment of the Paris conference, and he wrote out a brief penciled statement which I authorized him to read to the press when he left the White House. It was agreed, too, that except for this announcement he would make no statement at all. But when he met representatives of the press on his way from my office he added to the statement, and when he returned to the Department of Commerce he called in a number of his assistants and told them in detail what had taken place in my office.

Meanwhile, at my direction, the Secretary of War and the Secretary of the Navy wrote me a joint letter proving how groundless one of Wallace's allegations was—a statement in his July 23 letter that there were some military men in the country who favored a "preventive war"—and this joint letter, on my order, was released for publication. Then Will Clayton, who was Acting Secretary of State while Byrnes was attending a meeting of the Council of Foreign Ministers in Paris, telephoned to say that a personal message for me had been received from Secretary Byrnes. He asked if he and Assistant Secretary Donald Russell might come over and see me early the following morning.

In the morning they brought with them a lengthy statement which Byrnes had given them over the teletype the preceding evening. In it Byrnes said that while it was naturally up to me to decide what course should be followed by members of my Cabinet it was very difficult for him to maintain his position as the representative of the United States at an international gathering if other Cabinet officers made speeches advocating a change in policy, especially if it was made to appear that such speeches were not only tolerated but were also approved.

Byrnes reminded me that he had submitted his resignation earlier in the year and had agreed to stay on only until the satellite peace treaties were completed.

"If it is not possible," he added, "for you, for any reason, to keep Mr. Wallace, as a member of your Cabinet, from speaking on foreign affairs, it would be a grave mistake from every point of view for me to continue in office, even temporarily."

Of course I understood Byrnes's irritation, and I had already reached my decision before hearing from him. I said I wanted to talk to Byrnes directly, and arrangements for a transatlantic conversation were made. Owing to some technical problems on the circuits, this connection could not be established, and in its stead we had a teletype conference.

Byrnes opened the conversation by saying that he understood from the news reports he had seen that there had been an agreement between Wallace and me about Wallace's future speaking activities. He added, however, that in his opinion this had not changed the situation but had merely postponed, and had not stopped, Wallace's criticism. If Wallace was motivated, he said, by ill will or personal rancor against him, then it would help my policy if he—Byrnes—were to resign.

I replied that I had made it abundantly clear to Wallace that I stood squarely behind Secretary Byrnes in carrying out our established foreign policy. I pointed out that I had made no commitment that Wallace would be free to resume his criticism after a given date. And I assured him that I would reaffirm my confidence in Byrnes when I met the press the following day. I said I wanted him and the delegation to stay on the job and finish it. I told Byrnes he was doing an excellent job and that I would continue to support him.

Shortly before ten o'clock in the morning on September 20 I called Wallace at his office and came directly to the point.

"Henry," I said, "I am sorry, but I have reached the conclusion that it will be best that I ask for your resignation." His reply was very calm.

"If that is the way you want it, Mr. President," he said, "I will be happy to comply."

I called the reporters in at ten-thirty and announced my decision.

Henry Wallace continued his speechmaking and eventually used foreign platforms in his attack on the foreign policy of his own country. It must have been difficult for him in later years to acknowledge the aggressive character of the Communists, but he had the good grace to express his full support of my policy when in 1950 I decided to support South Korea against the Red attack.

On September 20 I wrote to my mother and my sister:

Dear Mama and Mary:

Well I had to fire Henry today, and of course I hated to do it. Henry Wallace is the best Secretary of Agriculture this country ever had unless Clint Anderson turns out as I think he will. If Henry had stayed Sec. of Agri. in 1940 as he should have, there'd never have been all this controversy, and I would not be here, and wouldn't that be nice? Charlie Ross said I'd shown I'd rather be right than President, and I told him I'd rather be anything than President. My good counselor, Clark Clifford, who took Sam Rosenman's place, said *Please* don't say that." Of course Clark, Charlie and all the rest of my good friends are thinking in terms of 1948—and I'm not.

Henry is the most peculiar fellow I ever came in contact with. I spent two hours and a half with him Wednesday afternoon arguing with him to make no speeches on foreign policy—or to agree to the policy for which I am responsible—but he wouldn't. So I asked him to make no more speeches until Byrnes came home. He agreed to that, and he and Charlie Ross and I came to what we thought was a firm commitment that he'd say nothing beyond the one sentence statement we agreed he should make. Well, he answered questions and told his gang over at Commerce all that had taken place in our interview. It was all in the afternoon Washington News yesterday, and I never was so exasperated since Chicago. So—this morning I called Henry and told him he'd better get out, and he was so nice about it I almost backed out!

Well, now he's out, and the crackpots are having conniption fits. I'm glad they are. It convinces me I'm right. . . .

To fill the post of Secretary of Commerce, I decided on W. Averell Harriman, who had been Ambassador to Russia and was now Ambassador to Great Britain. I called him in London by transatlantic telephone and offered him the secretaryship. He accepted, and I was glad to have him in the Cabinet.

As I bring this, the first of two volumes of my memoirs, to a close and look back, the year 1945 stands out in my mind as a year of decisions—a year of many trying and fateful decisions.

I was sworn in as President by Chief Justice Stone at 7:09 P.M. on April 12, 1945. Much had happened in the months that followed. The world was undergoing great and historic changes. We had come into the atomic age. The wars in Europe and Asia had been brought to a victorious end. The United Nations had been launched. Churchill, Attlee, Stalin, and I had met at Potsdam in an effort to get Russian co-operation and help to assure the peace. The years ahead were to make great demands upon the wisdom, courage, and integrity of statesmen everywhere.

INDEX

A

Acheson, Dean, Under Secretary of State, 526, 548–49

Adams, John, as Vice-President, 196–97

Africa. *See* North Africa

Agricultural Adjustment Act of 1938, 155

Agricultural Adjustment Administration, 152

Agricultural production, 1945 demands on, 225

Agriculture, Department of, Clinton P. Anderson appointed Secretary, 326; in emergency food measures, 468–69; estimate of food shortages in Europe, 309

Air Force, attitude toward air-cooled engines, 181–82

Airports, appropriations bill for, 226

Alamogordo, N.M., first atomic explosion at, 415

Aleutian Islands, Soviet landing rights on, 443

Alexander, Field Marshal Sir Harold, 200–1, 239, 380; and Trieste situation, 244–46, 248–52

Allen, George, 192

Allied Control Commission, for Austria, 304; in Bulgaria, 15–16, 254, 385; in Rumania, 15–16, 253–54, 384–85

Allied Control Council for Germany, 62, 298, 300–6, 405

Allied Reparations Commission, 15, 307–8; Moscow meetings of, 310–11; Pauley and Lubin appointed to, 106, 111, 308; U.S. policy, 308–9

Aluminum, and strategic metals, 175–76

Aluminum Company of America, 175–76

American Magazine, Truman article in, 181

American Magnesium Corporation, 175

Anderson, Clinton P., as Congressman, 225; as Secretary of Agriculture, 326, 466, 468, 472, 526, 560

Anderson, Sir John, 230, 536, 539

Andresen, Rep. August H., 225

Anti-colonialism in North Africa, Middle East, and Asia, 237

Anti-trust laws, bill to restore to full force, 152

Antonov, Gen. Alexei, 306–7, 382–83, 443–44